From Spring Training to Screen Test
Baseball Players Turned Actors

Edited by Rob Edelman and Bill Nowlin

Associate Editors: Greg Erion, Len Levin, and Emmet R. Nowlin

Society for American Baseball Research, Inc.
Phoenix, AZ

From Spring Training to Screen Test: Baseball Players Turned Actors
Edited by Rob Edelman and Bill Nowlin
Associate Editors: Greg Erion, Len Levin, and Emmet R. Nowlin

Copyright © 2018 Society for American Baseball Research, Inc.
All rights reserved. Reproduction in whole or in part without permission is prohibited.

ISBN 978-1-943816-71-2
(Ebook ISBN 978-1-943816-70-5)

Book design: Gilly Rosenthol

Photo credits:
Cover images: *The Kid from Cleveland* poster courtesy of Rob Edelman. Photograph L to R: Mickey Mantle, Doris Day, Cary Grant, and Roger Maris in *That Touch of Mink*. Courtesy of the National Baseball Hall of Fame.

All photographs courtesy of the National Baseball Hall of Fame, except for the following:
Boston Public Library, Leslie Jones Collection - 182
Coca-Cola Archives – 381, 382
Rob Edelman – 55, 74, 165, 231, 369
Eddie Frierson – 170, 172
Harvard University – 354, 357
Bob Lemke - 385
Library of Congress – 53, 77, 110, 115, 176, 177, 234, 279, 281, 339, 369 (second photo)
Bill Nowlin – 97, 138, 274, 330, 398
Mark V. Perkins – 312, 313, 314, 316
Jacob Pomrenke – 372
Rochester Democrat & Chronicle – 344, 346 (latter photograph by Jamie Germano)
Greg Skidmore – 349
Andy Strasberg – 362, 364, 400
Tom Stringer – 268, 269

Society for American Baseball Research
Cronkite School at ASU
555 N. Central Ave. #416
Phoenix, AZ 85004
Phone: (602) 496-1460
Web: www.sabr.org
Facebook: Society for American Baseball Research
Twitter: @SABR

CONTENTS

1. INTRODUCTION 1
   By Rob Edelman

MAJOR LEAGUERS

2. BO BELINSKY 4
   By Gregory H. Wolf
3. JOHNNY BERARDINO 13
   By Alan Cohen
4. BOBBY BONILLA 20
   By Mark Souder
5. CHUCK CONNORS 27
   By Charlie Bevis
6. RON DARLING 37
   By Audrey Apfel
7. JOE DIMAGGIO 41
   By Lawrence Baldassaro
8. MIKE DONLIN 49
   By Rob Edelman and Michael Betzold
9. DON DRYSDALE 58
   By Joseph Wancho
10. MARK FIDRYCH 64
    By Richard J. Puerzer
11. PAT FLAHERTY 69
    By Bill Hickman
12. LEW FONSECA 75
    By John Gabcik
13. STEVE GARVEY 82
    By Maxwell Kates
14. AL GETTEL 91
    By Clayton Trutor
15. GREG GOOSSEN 95
    By Rob Edelman
16. WALLY HEBERT 101
    By Gregory H. Wolf
17. WALLY HOOD 108
    By Jay Hurd
18. BYRON HOUCK 113
    By Phil Williams
19. REGGIE JACKSON 119
    By Ted Leavengood
20. DEREK JETER 127
    By Alan Cohen
21. WALLY JOYNER 137
    by Paul Hofmann
22. FRANK KELLEHER 143
    By Adam Klinker
23. JOHN KRUK 149
    By Seamus Kearney
24. LEE LACY 154
    By Gregory H. Wolf
25. BILLY LOES 161
    By Gregory H. Wolf
26. CHRISTY MATHEWSON 169
    By Eddie Frierson
27. JOHN McGRAW 175
    By Don Jensen
28. GEORGE METKOVICH 180
    By Bill Nowlin
29. DON NEWCOMBE 188
    By Russell A. Bergtold

30. ERNIE ORSATTI 198
By Lawrence Baldassaro

31. ART PASSARELLA 203
By Rob Edelman

32. JERRY PRIDDY..................213
By Warren Corbett

33. BEANS REARDON..................218
By Bob LeMoine

34. BABE RUTH 229
By Allan Wood

35. BRET SABERHAGEN..................242
By Alan Cohen

36. ZIGGY SEARS (UMPIRE)..................250
By Bruce Bumbalough

37. SAMMY SOSA..................253
By Eric Hanauer

38. MONTY STRATTON..................260
By Gary Sarnoff

39. LOU STRINGER..................267
By Bill Nowlin

40. TONY TARASCO 272
By Will Osgood

41. JIM THORPE 278
By Don Jensen

42. BOB UECKER 283
by Eric Aron

43. PETE VUCKOVICH..................291
By Rory Costello

44. RUBE WADDELL 299
By Dan O'Brien

45. LEON WAGNER 304
By Jay Berman

46. EDGAR "BLUE" WASHINGTON 310
By Mark V. Perkins

47. BERNIE WILLIAMS..................320
By Rob Edelman

48. TODD ZEILE 328
By Jon Springer

FILMS, FANS, AND TELEVISION

49. GENE AUTRY 335
By Warren Corbett

50. RON SHELTON: ON *COBB*, *BULL DURHAM*, AND BASEBALL-ON-SCREEN..................342
By Rob Edelman

51. THOMAS TULL: ON DARK KNIGHTS, HANGOVERS, AND BASEBALL..................348
By Rob Edelman

52. DE WOLF HOPPER, DIGBY BELL, AND THE FIVE A'S 351
By Rob Edelman

53. HBO MOVIE *61**..................361
By Andy Strasberg

54. *BIG LEAGUER*: A SMALL-TIME FILM WITH BIG-TIME PERSONALITIES..................368
By Frederick C. Bush

55. *BALL FOUR*, THE TELEVISION SERIES: AHEAD OF ITS TIME?..................371
By Ron Briley

56. BASEBALL AND COCA-COLA: A MATCH MADE IN AMERICA 381
By Rob Edelman

57. BASEBALL AND CLASSIC TELEVISION: A BRIEF OVERVIEW..................384
By Rob Edelman

58. CONTRIBUTORS..................394

INTRODUCTION

BY ROB EDELMAN

Why would you want to squander a few hours taking up space in your behind-home-plate seat at a World Series game? For after all, you've been invited to a screening of a spanking new 35 mm print of Bela Lugosi Meets a Brooklyn Gorilla.

Why bother wasting time watching Bull Durham, Field of Dreams, Bang the Drum Slowly —*or Joe E. Brown cavorting in* Fireman, Save My Child, Elmer the Great, *and* Alibi Ike? *Instead, you could turn on the tube and take in a baseball game—ANY baseball game, even one between two second-division nines in the dog days of August.*

GRANTED, THESE QUERIES are exaggerations. But they only are slight ones. In truth, some baseball fan-atics see no purpose in savoring motion pictures with ballyard settings or references. Their argument is that baseball-on-screen has nothing whatsoever to do with *real baseball*. These detractors will emphasize only the factual errors in the screenplay, as if all baseball films are scripted by writers who neither understand nor care about the game. This simply is not so.

Conversely, some movie buffs become panic-stricken at the thought of appreciating sports in general, and baseball in particular. They contend that baseball is boring, is sleep-inducing. A film like *Bela Lugosi Meets a Brooklyn Gorilla* is far more intoxicating. But if you've ever stumbled upon a screening of *Bela Lugosi Meets a Brooklyn Gorilla*, you will see that this too simply is not so.

The book that you are about to peruse brings together these two separate yet inexorably connected domains: the sport of baseball and the art and creativity of film, television, and other forms of entertainment. Undeniably, for well over a century, acting onscreen and swatting horsehides have been interwoven—and innumerable real-life ballplayers have appeared in the movies, on Broadway, in vaudeville, and, eventually, on television.

Some baseball folk have had extensive careers in the performing arts. Such a list begins with Mike Donlin, Chuck Connors, Bob Uecker, Edgar "Blue" Washington, Jim Thorpe, Pat Flaherty, Greg Goossen, Art Passarella, John Beradino (whose surname while he played baseball was Berardino), and Bernie Williams. Show biz-luminaries who never played in the majors—they include Gene Autry, Ron Shelton, Thomas Tull, De Wolf Hopper, Digby Bell, Joe E. Brown, Buster Keaton, and Happy Felton—are among the celebs with major baseball connections. In the research for *Meet the Mertzes*, a double biography of *I Love Lucy*'s Vivian Vance and super-baseball-fan William Frawley, more of Frawley's baseball buddies were tracked down and interviewed than his Hollywood colleagues. In 2014, in a brief chat with Bill Murray at the Toronto International Film Festival, I queried this ardent Chicago Cubs aficionado as to when his team would cop the World Series. His ever-so-optimistic response was: two years. Wouldn't you know that Mr. Murray was spot-on in his prediction!

Other big-name players or managers occasionally have appeared onscreen, often as themselves, in starring or featured roles—or, in some cases, a single starring or featured role. Among them are John McGraw, Jackie Robinson, Lou Gehrig, Ty Cobb, and Babe Ruth. In particular, The Bambino's larger-than-life, overgrown teddy-bear personality registers well onscreen. If he had not been a ballplayer, he might have made an effective sidekick or foil for any number of screen comedians. One can imagine The Three Stooges being rechristened The Four Stooges, with Moe, Larry, and Curly being joined by The Babe as they gleefully hurl pies at one another, tweak each other's noses, and knock each other with mallets.

Occasionally, an unlikely personage even pops up onscreen and references the sport. Back in 2016, *My X-Girlfriend's Wedding Reception*, an obscure low-budget comedy from 1999, became a hot ticket. The reason: In its cast is none other than Bernie Sanders, presidential contender. He is billed as "Congressman Bernie Sanders," and he plays a rabbi by the name of "Manny Shevitz." (Now remember, this *is* a comedy.) At one point, Rabbi Manny is addressing the wedding guests. He begins by observing: "Today we celebrate life, a very sacred part of life." That's fair enough coming from a religious leader, but then Rabbi Manny, after declaring that he, like the man who plays him, was born and raised in Brooklyn, immediately goes on a riff about the tragedy of the Dodgers leaving the Borough of Churches. Then, as if he is addressing a convention of sports fans rather than a wedding party, he segues into a criticism of baseball free agency.

Clusters of big-league nines also have been featured in movies: the Cleveland Indians in *The Kid From Cleveland* (1949); the Los Angeles Dodgers in *The Geisha Boy* (1958); the New York Yankees in *Safe at Home!* (1962); the Dodgers and San Francisco Giants in *Experiment in Terror* (1962). Countless hitters and hurlers from Joe DiMaggio and Satchel Paige to the two Wallys—Hebert and Hood—have made token cameo appearances. Consequently, for researching this book and selecting its content, make no mistake: If we had set out to offer bios of every ballplayer

Baseball Meets Show Biz: Lou Gehrig, the Iron Horse, poses with, left to right, Groucho, Chico, and Harpo Marx.

who ever made even a single appearance in a single motion picture, the result would be a mini-encyclopedia. The purpose here is to offer a general survey of the connection between baseball and entertainment along with a range of select topics, from baseball on television shows and in Coca-Cola commercials to Jim Bouton's *Ball Four* TV series.

Anecdotes connecting ballplayers and movies are endless. Back in 2011, a piece on *The Jackie Robinson Story* (1950) and how it is a reflection of its era was published in *NINE: A Journal of Baseball History and Culture*.[1] While preparing the article, I scrutinized its credits on the Internet Movie Database and there, on this particular cast list, was a familiar name: Dick Williams, who is listed as "Jersey City Pitcher/Second Baseman (uncredited)." Was this *the* Dick Williams, who now is a Baseball Hall of Famer? Perhaps it might be because Williams started out in the Brooklyn Dodgers organization, which was involved in the film's production. Plus, upon a replay of *The Jackie Robinson Story* on DVD, that "uncredited" actor certainly resembled a young Dick Williams. But where was the proof? How did Williams become connected to the film? Well, it just so happened that the Hall of Fame Classic was momentarily being played in Cooperstown. Dick Williams was in attendance, and he was cornered and asked about the film. Even though *The Jackie Robinson Story* had been made over six decades earlier, Williams recalled it vividly and was quoted in the piece.

Additionally, beyond Williams's participation in *The Jackie Robinson Story*, and beyond the entertainment quotient in this or any film, motion pictures serve as reflections of history and the culture from which they emerged. And *The Jackie Robinson Story* is not the lone film that connects baseball and mid-twentieth-century America. Far from it. One of innumerable examples: Attitudes relating to US involvement in World War II at different moments in time are mirrored in the baseball sequences in *Woman of the Year* (1942), *The Best Years of Our Lives* (1946), and *Three Stripes in the Sun* (1955). Films can also serve as valuable educational tools: *A League of Their Own* (1992) almost singlehandedly revived interest in the long-extinct All-American Girls Professional Baseball League.

However, the essence of this book is the link between the real and the reel. And most tellingly, real-world baseball personalities occasionally offer knowing winks to savvy viewers. In *Big Leaguer* (1953), Carl Hubbell (playing "Carl Hubbell") arrives in spring training to evaluate New York Giants prospects. In the climactic game, with the Giants behind 7-4 in the ninth inning, King Carl perceptively notes: "The game's now getting interesting." In *Three Stripes in the Sun*, Chuck Connors appears as a GI stationed in postwar Japan who pitches in a game between the Americans and Japanese. Before the contest, as per custom, the Japanese players remove their caps and bow; they are followed by the umpires, and then the Americans. After the ritual, Connors's character comments: "What would Durocher say if he saw this?"

Some are intentionally funny: In a 1985 TV version of *Casey at the Bat*, Joe (Bob Uecker, he of the lifetime .200 batting average), an announcer, asks Casey (Elliott Gould) what it feels like to hit a baseball. Ernie (Howard Cosell), a fellow broadcaster, quips: "That's something Joe never experienced in his life." Others are unintentionally sad and ironic: In *Rawhide*, a 1938 sagebrush saga, Lou Gehrig stars as himself; at the outset, he catches a train at Grand Central Station and tells reporters: "I'm gonna wallow in peace and quiet for the rest of my life. I'm gonna hang up my spikes for a swell old pair of carpet slippers."

If you take pleasure in everything from privileged peeks at the post–World War II Cleveland Indians and newly-minted Los Angeles Dodgers to Don Drysdale cast as "Don Drysdale" on TV's *The Donna Reed Show, Leave It to Beaver,* and *The Brady Bunch,* you surely will savor watching and relishing baseball on the big and small screens. And you certainly will find much to enjoy, and much to discover, as you pore over this book.

NOTES

1   muse.jhu.edu/article/469498/pdf.

BO BELINSKY

BY GREGORY H. WOLF

"My only regret is that I can't sit in the stands and watch myself pitch."[1] No one ever accused southpaw Bo Belinsky of being modest. And probably no pitcher in baseball history ever got more mileage out of 28 wins (against 51 defeats) in parts of eight big-league seasons as Belinsky.

Belinsky took baseball by storm as a rookie with the Los Angeles Angels in 1962, and captured the hearts of the Hollywood jet set. Good-looking with a dark complexion and slicked-back black hair, the roughneck from the streets of Trenton, New Jersey, turned Tinseltown upside down when he tossed a no-hitter in his fourth big-league start, en route to winning six of his first seven starts. That gem changed his life, and cast him on an odyssey that few big-league players could ever imagine. Belinsky's ego was as big as his fastball was daunting. He flouted the conservative mores of baseball by praising himself and living by his own rules. Days after his no-hitter, he became a regular at Hollywood afterparties, where he met Walter Winchell, an aging influential gossip columnist, who introduced him to Hollywood A-listers, and plenty of B-listers, and a seemingly endless supply of actresses and wanna-be's who lined up to meet the most eligible bachelor in town not named Hugh Hefner. Belinsky was the country's best-known athlete-playboy, 3½ years before Joe Willie Namath took a bite out of the Big Apple. "Playing baseball seemed only incidental," said Belinsky in retirement. "I was just on a mad whirl day and night."[2]

Belinsky made as many headlines with women as for his occasional pitching victories. "For both variety and sheer volume of female companions," opined sportswriter Myron Cope, "Belinsky is an authentic lion of the boudoir."[3] He dated Ann-Margret, Tina Louise, and Connie Stevens, was briefly engaged to Mamie Van Doren in 1963, and married Jo Collins, *Playboy*'s 1965 Playmate of the Year, in 1968. "What I'm looking for is one with dough," said Belinsky as a rookie. "I need a poor one like Custer needed more Indians."[4] He got his wish more than a decade later when he married Jane Weyerhaeuser, the heiress to the Weyerhaeuser paper fortune, in 1975. Both the aforementioned marriages ended in divorce. "My philosophy of life?" said Belinsky in one of his most memorable quips. "That's easy. If music be the food of love, by all means let the band play on."[5]

Years before Nike ran an ad campaign focusing on two-sport star Bo Jackson, "Bo Knows" could have referred to Belinsky, as in "Bo Knows—No Rules." "I was serious when I pitched," he said after retiring, his memory of reality slightly distorted, "but off the mound I defined myself. I tried to live my life the way I wanted, with a little style, a little creativity."[6] He drove around Hollywood in a bright red Cadillac convertible, a gift from a local auto dealer after his no-hitter. Belinsky earned only $10,000 as a rookie, and $15,000 two years later, but enjoyed a supersized lifestyle. "I live like a man who makes $70,000," he once said. "The places I go and the people I bang into and the dinners that I don't pay for …"[7] Even Belinsky's mother seemed ill at ease with her son's predilection for glitz and glamour, but wasn't surprised. "Bo likes money," she said, "but he doesn't work hard to get it. He's always been that way. He was a kid with high ideas and low pockets."[8]

"My career?" said Belinsky in retirement. "It was no big thing."[9] Belinsky was correct about his pitching—it was dismal. But it was his life off the mound that made him one of the most colorful characters and most recognizable athletes of the early to mid-1960s. He captured the zeitgeist of the pre-Vietnam War swinging '60s, and marked the gradual dissolution of the button-down conservatism of the previous decade. "In the long run it wore me down physically and mentally," said Belinsky about his fast-paced living.[10] Writer Steve Oney described Belinsky as a cross between the debonair Dean Martin and the antiestablishment Jack Kerouac.[11] Belinsky's controversy-filled three-year stint with the Angels ended when he cold-cocked a 64-year-old reporter and was traded to the Philadelphia Phillies. Belinsky knocked around a few more years before retiring in 1970, the years of heavy drinking, smoking, and partying having taken a toll on his once svelte body.

Robert Belinsky was born on December 7, 1936, in New York City, to Edward and Anna (Polnoff) Belinsky. A few years later the family left its tenement house on the Lower East Side and moved to Trenton, New Jersey, where the elder Belinsky had been born. The Belinsky family, which grew to four with the birth of daughter Lorraine, had limited means; Edward had been a handyman at an apartment house, and later opened a TV repair shop; Anna was a stocking inspector at the Gold Stripe Hosiery Company. Though Belinsky is often identified as a Jewish ballplayer (his mother was Jewish and his father was Catholic), he was not raised in a religious household. Rather, Belinsky was proverbially baptized on the streets of Trenton, where he became a two-bit poolhall hustler and fighter, and was nicknamed Bo (he had been called Bob as a child) after boxer Bobo Olson. "When I think of Trenton," said Belinsky in a tell-all story about his life, *Bo: Pitching and Wooing*, by Maury Allen (published in 1973), "I can't imagine I lived there as long as I did. Things were tough."[12] Belinsky attended Trenton Central High School but didn't play sports. They were "too regimented," he claimed, plus he didn't like the rah-rah stuff.[13]

Belinsky's introduction to baseball was on Trenton sandlots and in semipro leagues which afforded him the freedom to come and go as he pleased. After graduating from school in 1955, Belinsky hung around Trenton, hustled in nearby cities with noted pool sharks, and took the mound occasionally. The Pittsburgh Pirates took a chance on the 6-foot-2 southpaw with a mean heater and signed Belinsky on May 15, 1956, to a contract on scout Rex Rowen's suggestion.[14] "I never liked baseball that much—at first, anyway," said Belinsky. "I only signed a contract to get out of Trenton."[15] Pittsburgh assigned him to Brunswick in the Class-D Georgia-Florida League where it was an unmitigated disaster. Feeling out of place and earning $185 per month, Belinsky quit the team in midseason with a 7.36 ERA in 33 innings.

The Pirates sold Belinsky to the Baltimore Orioles, for whom he spent the next five seasons moving up the ladder and flashing signs of greatness, but also establishing a reputation as a carouser who enjoyed the night life more than baseball and was in the doghouse of every manager he played for. In 1957 he went 13-6 with Pensacola and finished with 202 strikeouts, second most in the Alabama-Florida League. The next season he led the Class-C Northern League in ERA (2.24) and strikeouts (184) while posting a misleading 10-14 record with the Aberdeen (South Dakota) Pheasants. After splitting his time among four different teams in 1959, Belinsky was fed up, and threatened to quit. "My career wasn't going anywhere," he recalled. "The Orioles had two young left-handers (Steve Barber and Steve Dalkowski) ... that they liked a lot more than me."[16]

After a look-see at Baltimore's spring training in 1960, Belinsky was assigned to Vancouver in the Triple-A Pacific Coast League. His season was interrupted he was called to Army Reserve duties at Fort Knox. Discharged in July, he returned to the club, but injured his hand in a barroom fight and logged only 32 innings all season.

At spring training in 1961, Belinsky drove Orioles GM-manager Paul Richards crazy with his late-night drinking, partying, and womanizing. Assigned to Little Rock in the Double-A Southern Association, Belinsky enjoyed a breakthrough campaign. Expectations for the 24-year-old hurler were minimal—he had logged just 123 innings in the previous two seasons and relieved in more games than he had started. Belinsky unexpectedly blazed a trail, leading the circuit in punchouts (182 in 174 innings). He also kept his own counsel. After fanning 18 in an 11-inning no-decision on July 17, he announced he was quitting baseball to study electronics in Trenton.[17] He ultimately came to his senses, and returned to the club. "I hated minor-league baseball," said Belinsky later in his career. "[N]obody ever told me anything about pitching."[18]

Despite Belinsky's success, he was not added to Baltimore's 40-man roster, and was subsequently chosen by the Los Angeles Angels in the Rule 5 draft on November 27, 1961. Angels scout Sammy Moses had been tracking Belinsky in Little Rock, while scout Tufie Hashem was impressed with the lefty's recent pitching with Pampero in the Venezuelan Winter League.[19] Belinsky mowed down competition, setting a new league record with 156 strikeouts (in 156 innings), and posted a 13-5 record and 2.13 ERA for a 21-30 club.[20] He was transferred to Caracas for the postseason and won two more games, including the championship clincher.[21]

Belinsky was AWOL when the Angels camp opened in Palm Springs in late February 1962. He claimed he was "mentally tired" from winter ball in Venezuela.[22] "Sure I'm late," he said. "But it's not when you report that counts; it's how you pitch when they ask you to show your stuff."[23] Los Angeles sportswriters were soon to label the brash youngster as a kook, braggart, eccentric, and indifferent. Belinsky also objected to signing a $6,000 league-minimum contract. After pitching without a contract for two days, Belinsky faced his first ultimatum from GM Fred Haney, cut from the old school of top-down management: Either leave or sign. Belinsky acquiesced. He wouldn't take that posture many more times in an Angels uniform. The media was attracted to Belinsky for his good copy; *The Sporting News* even opined that "his brazen attitude was refreshing."[24] Belinsky spoke candidly, touted his own greatness, and broke the mold of a deferential company man. He wore fancy

Bo Belinsky, a lover of the Hollywood Fastlane, being mobbed by fans; at his side is an amused Leon Wagner.

clothes and dark sunglasses, and oozed a self-assurance rarely seen in unproven rookies. Braven Dyer, longtime sportswriter for the *Los Angeles Times* and Belinsky's future nemesis, referred to him as "Handsome Bo," a spitting image of Narcissus himself.[25] Pitching coach Marv Grissom immediately recognized Belinsky's potential in spring training, but also offered some of the first words of caution, suggesting the hurler's future rests upon "how hard he cares to work, how well he looks after himself."[26]

The circus ride began in earnest for Belinsky on April 18, 1962, when he scattered five hits and walked five, yielding two runs in six innings in front of a sparse crowd of 7,055 at Dodger Stadium to notch a victory in his big-league debut against the Kansas City A's, 3-2. In his second start, a week later, he tossed a complete-game four-hitter to defeat the Cleveland Indians, 6-2. Belinsky's life was forever altered in his fourth start, on May 5, against Baltimore. He overpowered the visiting Orioles with nine punchouts while walking four and not yielding a semblance of a hit to record the first major-league no-hitter on the West Coast. "Hollywood ... is gaga over Bo," gushed Dyer.[27] Belinsky was immediately catapulted into fame and was the toast of Hollywood. Living off an adrenaline high and just a few hours sleep a night, Belinsky followed up his no-hitter by fanning a career-high 11 in 7⅓ innings against the Chicago White Sox to win his fifth straight start. He rebounded from his first loss to blank the Boston Red Sox, 1-0, on two hits in the second game of a doubleheader on May 20. Behind the scenes Haney and skipper Bill Rigney were concerned for the hottest pitcher in baseball, and implored him to cut out his "activities."[28] Local sportswriter Melvin Durslag wrote that since Belinsky's no-hitter his "life that was once confused is now bedlam."[29]

Winless in his previous five starts, and suffering from a leg injury, Belinsky was involved in his first high-profile scandal on June 13 when he was stopped by police in Beverly Hills at 5 A.M. after a night on the town with his roommate, rookie pitcher Dean Chance. Passenger Gloria Eves claimed that Belinsky assaulted her and threw her out of the car.[30] (Eves's eventual $150,000 lawsuit against Belinsky was tossed out in court).[31] Belinsky was taken into police custody, but released. Belinsky's life seemed to be careening out of control. On July 6 he crossed a sacred boundary in a disastrous outing, resulting in his formal censure by Haney. After yielding four runs to Boston in one-third of an inning, Belinsky stormed off the mound before Rigney arrived and flipped off the L.A. crowd on his exit.[32] After just three months with the club, Belinsky had transformed from a budding superstar into a problem child with whom Haney vigorously sought to cut ties. The GM was worried about Belinsky's negative influence on the team and especially the effect he had on Chance, who was quietly developing into the club's best hurler.

Haney thought he found a golden parachute when he brokered a backroom deal with the Kansas City A's, agreeing to purchase prospect Dan Osinski for a player to be named later. The clubs had a gentlemen's agreement that Belinsky would be that player. With rumors circulating, the *Los Angeles Times* published a story about the deal on September 5.[33] Many pointed to Belinsky as the source of the rumors. No doubt the Casanova wanted to avoid Kansas City at all costs. Six days earlier, UPI ran a national story about Belinsky's guide to America after dark. He ranked Kansas City (with Baltimore) last in night life.[34] One day after Belinsky's trade was announced, Commissioner Ford Frick nullified the deal, stating that the transaction had been formally submitted as a cash deal.[35] Belinsky finished his tumultuous, tension-filled first big-league season with a 10-11 slate, 3.56 ERA in 187⅓ innings, and 145 strikeouts, and led the majors with 122 walks, while the Angels, in just their second season, finished in third place with an 86-76 record.

Always criticized for his work ethic and commitment to baseball, Belinsky seemed more interested in a movie career, models, and his postgame highballs. He hired an actor's agent and made some guest appearances in a few Hollywood productions, such as *77 Sunset Strip* (1963), the *Lloyd Bridges Show* (1963), and *That Regis Philbin* Show (1964). He also had a minor role in one feature film, *C'Mon, Let's Live a Little* (1967), a campy music drama starring popular pop singers Bobby Vee and Jackie DeShannon. According to Howard Thompson, writing in the *New York Times*, "Bo-Bo" is the "host of (an off-campus) twist nitery (and is played by), of all people, Bo Belinsky, right off the baseball diamond. Darkly handsome in a tux, the pitcher has a bit of acting to do and does it."[36]

Given an ultimatum by Haney in the offseason to tone down his excessive lifestyle or risk his career, Belinsky promised to reform. However, he arrived late to spring training, citing an unspecified illness, and resumed his playboy act in Palm Springs, punctuated by an announcement of his engagement to Mamie Van Doren on April 2.[37] Belinsky did not have another Cinderella story when the regular season began. He pitched terribly while rumors swirled that he'd be traded to the New York Yankees or Cleveland Indians. "[I]t's unconceivable," opined beat writer Al Wolf, "that Belinsky can stay under the same roof as Fred Haney."[38] In late May, a struggling Belinsky (1-7, 6.39) was optioned to the Angels' Triple-A club in Hawaii. The *Los Angeles Times* reported the story in one of its wittiest headlines, "Call Him a P(lei)boy Now: Belinsky's Off to Hawaii."[39] Belinsky laughed at the demotion ("Well at least Hawaii is a great place to be"[40]), then refused to report, setting off a seven-week soap opera. Suspended without pay, Belinsky finally reported to the Islanders on July 19. He pitched well and drew record crowds, leading the hurler to demand that the Angels reimburse him for his lost salary; an incredulous Haney laughed at the demand.[41] Recalled in September, Belinsky appeared contrite only after making headlines with comments that he had no desire or obligation to help the team.[42] Belinsky's second big-league season was a disaster (2-9, 5.75 ERA) as the Angels fell to ninth place. The pitcher-turned-performer's postseason began in late October when he began a seven-week gig as a lounge entertainer at the Silver Slipper club in Las Vegas.

Belinsky surprised everyone when he reported to the Angels' spring training on time in 1964. He seemed to take practice seriously; sportswriters even noted that he wore his cap and his hair was short. In his season debut, Belinsky held the Detroit Tigers to one run over eight innings, but also injured his back and was sidelined 10 days. After several ineffective starts, he tossed a complete-game seven-hitter to beat the hard-hitting Minnesota Twins, 4-1, in Los Angeles in the second game of a doubleheader on May 27, kicking off the best stretch of pitching in his career. From May 27 to July 9, Belinsky won six of eight decisions and carved out an impressive 1.82 ERA in 59⅓ innings, capped off with a two-hit shutout against the Chicago White Sox.

Five weeks later Belinsky's career with the Angels blew up. His downfall began with an interview with the AP's Charles Maher after a tough complete-game loss to the Cleveland Indians, 3-0, on August 11. "I've gotta make a move," said Belinsky. "This is my third year with the club and I'm going nowhere financially. You are never stable in this game."[43] Asked to comment on Belinsky's threat to quit the team, Haney replied, "That's up to Bo. He's got to run his own life."[44] By the time those words were published in a nationally syndicated story on August 14, Belinsky's fate had already been sealed. At about 1:30 A.M. the Angels and beat writers had arrived in Washington for a series with the Senators. Not long thereafter, sportswriter Braven Dyer, having caught wind of Maher's article, confronted Belinsky in his room at the Shoreham Hotel. Apparently fueled by alcohol, the episode turned personal with both men trading insults. Then Belinsky cold-cocked the 64-year-old scribe, knocking him out. Belinsky was sent back to Los Angeles that day and immediately suspended without pay. "Just what right do the Angels have to suspend me?" said the indignant pitcher, who claimed self-defense.[45] Days later, Belinsky, despite his 9-8 record and stellar 2.86 ERA, was optioned to Hawaii, but refused to report. "I didn't care anymore," said Belinsky. "I figured I was never going to play baseball anymore."[46] Haney's nightmare finally ended on December 4 when he shipped his problem child to the Philadelphia Phillies in exchange for pitcher Rudy May and first baseman Costen Shockley. "I never thought Bo was all bad," Rigney told Maury Allen. "I just think he was in the wrong business. He just wouldn't work."[47]

After his trade from the Angels, Belinsky won only seven more games (and lost 23) and logged just 266 more innings in his big-league career. Four of those victories came in a forgettable stint with the Phillies. "You want to be there when that arm comes back," said skipper Gene Mauch about Belinsky. "He could pitch. He just wouldn't work out. I wish I had a thousand guys with his arm and none with his head."[48] With Belinsky's firebrand personality, Mauch quickly clashed with him. After seven horrendous starts (6.58 ERA in 39⅓ innings), Belinsky was shuttled to the bullpen and used primarily in relief. Sidelined for much of September with a broken rib, Belinsky drew a line in the sand: "I won't be a relief pitcher next year. You can count on it." Retorted Mauch, "He might be a starting pitcher in Little Rock" [the Phillies Triple-A team].[49] Belinsky blamed Mauch for his pitching woes. "My arm just couldn't take it," he said of pitching long and short relief and starting. "I never really was a good pitcher after the 1965 season. ... Mauch had a lot to do with that."[50]

Belinsky's increased drug use also had profound effects on his career. Like many major leaguers before and since, Belinsky admitted to occasionally taking greenies (amphetamines) on days he started, but a change occurred with the Phillies. According to Steve Oney in his excellent profile on the pitcher, Belinsky began taking "red juice," a type of liquid amphetamine.[51] "[W]hen I got into the bullpen, I started getting loaded every day, because as a reliever, you never know when you might have to play," said Belinsky. "This chemical started coming into my life. I thought I could handle it."[52] Belinsky's drug habit progressively worsened over the next decade.

Confined to the end of the Phillies bench in 1966, Belinsky's tenure with the Phillies ended about two weeks after his "pitch me or trade me" ultimatum when he was optioned to the club's Triple-A affiliate, the San Diego Padres, in mid-June.[53]

The Houston Astros took a chance on Belinsky (despite his 4.83 ERA in 54 innings in the PCL), selecting him in the Rule 5 draft on November 28, 1966. Just weeks before spring training in 1967, the Astros must have wondered what they had gotten themselves into by acquiring the wacky hurler. "I want to play baseball," said Belinsky, "but I don't have the desire to be a great champion."[54] At 30 years old, Belinsky had become, according to sportswriter Pat Jordan, "a parody of himself."[55] When asked about his expectations for 1967, Belinsky replied matter-of-factly, "I'd say just hanging around the whole season would be a good year for me."[56] By that measure, his season was a grand success. He even flashed moments of brilliance, such as holding the New York Mets to just two hits and two runs over eight innings in a 3-2 victory in the Astrodome in July. Few could have imagined that it would be Belinsky's last win in the big leagues.

During spring training with Houston in 1968, Belinsky was more interested in his budding romance with *Playboy* model and still-married Jo Collins than baseball. Threatening to quit baseball, Belinsky was sold to his former team the Hawaii Islanders, which had become the Chicago White Sox' affiliate in the PCL. Belinsky was in his element living in Honolulu, surfing, swimming, and imbibing. He also pitched better than expected (9-14 and 2.97 ERA in 176 innings). On August 18, he tossed the first no-hitter in Islanders history, 1-0 against Tacoma, overcoming 10 walks and fanning 10.[57]

Belinsky returned to winter-league ball in Venezuela for the third and final time in the 1968-69 offseason. He carved out an impressive 1.94 ERA despite a 6-8 record for Navegantes del Magallanes; however, he quit the team in January and subsequently filed a lawsuit for unpaid wage and "moral damages."[58] Meanwhile he had been selected by the St. Louis Cardinals in the Rule 5 draft on December 2, 1968. An antithesis to the Cardinal Way, Belinsky clashed with the conservative, staid reigning World Series champions in spring training, where his now-centerfold wife was a bigger story than himself. "I think I'd have been better off in the Babe Ruth era when this wasn't such a fragile game," said Belinsky, miffed that the Cardinals would care what he did away from the park. "[M]aybe I haven't had the temperament to be a truly dedicated player."[59] At the end of camp the pitcher was sold to Hawaii, which coincidentally had just become an Angels affiliate again.

Playing for Chuck Tanner, a renowned players' skipper, Belinsky emerged as one of the PCL's best pitchers. "Bo was a fine person," said Tanner years later. "I didn't care about his reputation."[60] The Pittsburgh Pirates, seduced by Belinsky's 12-5 record and 2.82 ERA, purchased the flamboyant hurler, but it was a toxic match. Maury Allen wrote that Belinsky and Pirates skipper Larry Shepard were like "oil and water."[61] The last thing Shepard wanted was a distraction as the Pirates struggled to play .500 ball. Belinsky pitched sparingly, and poorly, losing all three of his decisions.

Traded to the Cincinnati Reds in the offseason, the 34-year-old Belinsky made his final three big-league appearances. In mid-May, he was optioned to Triple-A Indianapolis, where he was bothered by back pain and left the team in mid-August. Belinsky's 15-year professional career was over.

Maury Allen described Belinsky as "the reincarnation of Billy Loes."[62] Both were extremely gifted pitchers who critics felt should have won more games. However, that analogy might not be entirely fair to Loes, the eccentric right-hander for the Brooklyn Dodgers in the 1950s, who once claimed he'd rather not win 20 games or else management would expect such results every year. Loes (80-63 in parts of 11 seasons) won 50 games and lost just 25 over a four-year stretch (1952-55) with the Dodgers, pitched in three World Series, and was a member of Brooklyn's only World Series championship. Belinsky had a dismal 28-51 record and logged 665⅓ innings in parts of eight seasons, and was never on a first-place club. "I ended up devoting 15 years of my life to baseball," said Belinsky, looking back on his career. "Man, I loved it. I just didn't take it seriously. ... I don't take myself seriously."[63]

Already a heavy drinker and drug abuser, Belinsky's life was careening out of control by the time he was released by the Reds. "I didn't know what the hell I wanted to do," he said.[64] Steve Oney's account of Belinsky's life after his playing days, published in *Los Angeles Magazine*, is harrowing in its details.[65] It is a miracle that Belinsky survived the next six years, given his increasingly erratic, abusive, and dangerous behavior. Broke and living in Malibu, he and Jo divorced in 1971, exacerbating his depression and excessive tendencies. Belinsky ran with criminals and pimps, lived with a prostitute, and began using cocaine. There were numerous failed attempts to dry out. Former teammate and lifelong friend Dean Chance intervened and helped Belinsky enter a program at a hospital in Akron, Ohio, in 1972; he had a drink the day he was discharged. The next year Belinsky was once again cast into the national limelight following Maury Allen's candid best-seller *Bo: Pitching and Wooing* about the hurler's life, but the notoriety failed to effect change in his behavior. In 1974 Belinsky relocated to his former stomping grounds, Hawaii, where met Jane Weyerhaeuser. Their marriage in 1975 marked the beginning of Belinsky's darkest hours, filled with rage and depression fueled by cocaine and alcohol. After giving birth to six-week-premature twins in 1976, Jane returned home while the twins remained in the hospital. Oney described how a high Belinsky "snapped," brandishing a pistol, and threatened to kill his wife. He eventually shot her through the hip and pointed the gun to his head. Apparently only Jane's pleas stopped him from committing suicide. Despite her injuries, Jane did not call the police.

Oney points to 1976 as a turning point in Belinsky's life. He returned to Los Angeles, where he entered a rehab clinic in Santa Monica. Not only did Belinsky dry out, he became a born-again Christian. For the remainder of his life, Belinsky struggled to remain sober, occasionally falling off the wagon, and also battled other inner demons, like his temper. He and Jane divorced in 1981; another marriage, to a waitress in Hawaii, ended in divorce, too, in 1989. Through it all, Belinsky remained active in Alcoholics Anonymous and worked with a psychiatrist from California treating substance-abuse victims.

By 1990 Belinsky had settled in Las Vegas, where he remained until his death. He sold cars at a Toyota dealership, and even repaired his relationship with the Angels enough to be invited to an old-timers' game in 1997. Belinsky — billed as "Bo Bolinski" — appeared as a "Party Guest" in *Play It to the Bone*, a 1999 fight film written and directed by Ron Shelton, of *Bull*

Durham fame. Despite an outward appearance of having his life in order, Belinsky suffered from depression. Almost 30 years earlier, Belinsky broke a taboo for athletes by speaking publicly about his depression in a UPI article.[66] "I was out by the wolves by myself," Belinsky said about his anxieties after his initial success and precipitous failure with the Angels. "They were waiting for me to fall on my face."[67] Many sportswriters scoffed at Belinsky and chalked it up to yet another publicity stunt. But those feelings of fear stuck with Belinsky his entire life. He seemed to be on a perpetual search for something, someone, or himself, and was never satisfied. Instead he masked his depression with alcohol, drugs, and sex. According to Oney, Belinsky had a relapse on New Year's Eve 1997 and attempted suicide in a drunken stupor, slashing his wrists and plunging a knife into his stomach. He survived that ordeal, and with the help of friends became active in the Trinity Life church.

On November 23 2001, Bo Belinsky died at the age of 64 at his home in Las Vegas and was buried in Paradise Memorial Gardens. The cause of death was a heart attack. Belinsky had been in poor health for several years, and had been treated for bladder cancer, and had undergone hip-replacement surgery. "It's been a ball," Belinsky once said about his career in baseball. "There isn't one regret, not one. I've been there. I've done everything. I've heard the buglers. I've lived enough for two lives."[68] On that occasion, the good-looking southpaw with a mean heater and mesmerizing screwball was not exaggerating.

SOURCES

In addition to the sources noted in this biography, the author also accessed the *Encyclopedia of Minor League Baseball*, Retrosheet.org, Baseball-Reference.com, the SABR Minor Leagues Database, accessed online at Baseball-Reference.com, and *The Sporting News* archive via Paper of Record.

NOTES

1. Pat Jordan, "Once He Was an Angel," *Sports Illustrated*, March 28, 1994: 76. Reprinted article from March 1972.
2. Jonathan Mahler, "He Was no Koufax, But …," *New York Observer*, December 12, 2001.
3. Myron Cope, A Dialogue Between Baseball's Bigmouths," *True*. [Dated 1965; player's Hall of Fame file].
4. Melvin Durslag, "Hero Worship Tough on Bo, His Laundry and Landlady," *The Sporting News*, June 16, 1962:44.
5. Jordan: 76.
6. Jordan: 82.
7. Cope: 58.
8. Maury Allen, "Bo Belinsky Reveals: 'How I Won and Lost Hollywood's Stars,'" *Sport Today*, October, 1973: 83.
9. Jordan: 76.
10. Jordan: 82.
11. Steve Oney, Fallen Angel," *Los Angeles Magazine*, July 1, 2006. lamag.com/longform/fallen-angel-1/.
12. Maury Allen, with the Uncensored Cooperation of Bo Belinsky, *Bo: Pitching and Wooing* (New York: Dial Press, 1973), 18.
13. Braven Dyer, "Belinsky, Ex-Pool Shark, Pockets Win for Angels," *The Sporting News*, May 9, 1962: 20.
14. Allen, *Bo: Pitching and Wooing*, 32.
15. Jordan: 82.
16. Allen, *Bo: Pitching and Wooing*, 40.
17. "Litte Rock Southpaw Fans 18 Batters in 11 Innings," *The Sporting News*, August 9, 1961: 33.
18. Braven Dyer, "Belinsky, Ex-Pool Shark, Pockets Win for Angels."
19. Braven Dyer, "Bo's Success No Surprise to Scout Who 'Found' Him," *Los Angeles Times*, May 24, 1962: III, 4.
20. All statistics from the Venezuelan League are from Belinsky's page at Estadisticas Beisbol profesional Venezolano. purapelota.com/lvbp/mostrar.php?id=belib0001.
21. Frederico Rodolfo, "Lion Slab Stars Tame Indians in Playoff Triumph," *The Sporting News*, February 14, 1962: 31.
22. Braven Dyer, "Belinsky, Ex-Pool Shark, Pockets Win for Angels."
23. Braven Dyer, "Belinsky Concedes He's True 'Screwball,'" *Los Angeles Times*, March 2, 1962: III, 1.
24. "Word of Advice to Brash Bo," *The Sporting News*, June 2, 1962: 12.
25. Braven Dyer, "Soaring Seraphs Sing Bravos for Belinsky," *The Sporting News*, May 16, 1962: 21.
26. Braven Dyer, "Belinsky, Ex-Pool Shark, Pockets Win for Angels."
27. Braven Dyer, "Soaring Seraphs Sing Bravos for Belinsky."
28. "Rigney Tells Bo to Cut Out 'Activities,'" *Los Angeles Times*, June 8, 1962: III, 2.

FROM SPRING TRAINING TO SCREEN TEST

29 Melvin Durslag, "Hero Worship Tough on Bo, His Laundry and Landlady."

30 Belinsky, Chance Fined After 5 AM Ruckus," *Los Angeles Times*, June 14, 1962: III, 1.

31 'Woman Sues Bo Belinsky for $150,000," *Los Angeles Times*, August 16, 1962: I, 32.

32 Braven Dyer, "Bo Belinsky Censured by Haney," *Los Angeles Times*, July 8, 1962: D, 2.

33 Dan Hafner, "Angels Sell Belinsky to A's for Delivery in '63," *Los Angeles Times*, September 5, 1962: III, 1.

34 United Press International, "Bo Belinsky Reveals Playboy's Guide to American After Dark," *Los Angeles Times*, Augusts 31, 1962: III, 3.

35 UPI, "Angels Lose Pair—To Yanks, Frick," *Los Angeles Times*, September 7, 1962: III, 1.

36 Howard Thompson, "The Screen: 'Live a Little': Youngsters' Song Fest on Film Begins Run," *New York Times*, May 4, 1967: 34.

37 "Bo, Mamie Engaged; No Wedding Date Set," *Los Angeles Times*, April 2, 1963: III, 1.

38 Al Wolf, "If Alston Goes, Dressen Next, Not Durocher," *Los Angeles Times*, May 11, 1963: II, 2.

39 Braven Dyer, "Call Him a P(lei)boy Now: Belinsky's Off to Hawaii," *Los Angeles Times*, May 26, 1963: D1.

40 Ibid.

41 Sid Ziff, "Hickey on Spot," *Los Angeles Times*, September 4, 1963: III, 3.

42 Sid Ziff, "Big Train in Puddle," *Los Angeles Times*, September 11, 1963: III, 3.

43 Charles Maher, Associated Press, "Belinsky Wants Out," *San Bernardino CountySun* (San Bernardino, California). August 14, 1964: 46.

44 Ibid.

45 "Belinsky Punches Writer, Suspended," *Los Angeles Times*, August 15, 1964: II, 1.

46 Allen, *Bo: Pitching and Wooing*, 197.

47 Allen, *Bo: Pitching and Wooing*, 311.

48 Allen, "Bo Belinsky Reveals: 'How I Won and Lost Hollywood's Stars,'" 22.

49 Paul Zimmerman, "No One Gives Bo a 'Break,'" *Los Angeles Times*, August 27, 1963: III, 2.

50 Allen, *Bo: Pitching and Wooing*, 213.

51 Oney.

52 Ibid.

53 "Phils Ship Belinsky to Padres," *Los Angeles Times*, June 14, 1966: III, 4.

54 AP, "Bo Belinsky Plays Baseball for Fun," *Daily Mail* (Hagerstown, Maryland), February 9, 1967: 25.

55 Jordan: 78.

56 AP, "Bo Belinsky Plays Baseball for Fun."

57 AP, "Bo Belinsky Throws No-Hitter for Hawaii," *Fairbanks* (Alaska) *Daily News-Mirror*, August 19, 1968: 8.

58 AP, "Belinsky Suing Baseball Team," *Abilene* (Texas) *Register-News*, June 18, 1969: 9.

59 Bob Broeg, "Belinsky's Broke, Welcomes Chance With Redbirds," *St. Louis Post-Dispatch*, February 23, 1969: 23.

60 Allen, *Bo: Pitching and Wooing*, 317.

61 Allen, *Bo: Pitching and Wooing*, 278.

62 Allen, *Bo: Pitching and Wooing*, 235.

63 Jordan: 82.

64 Allen, *Bo: Pitching and Wooing*, 302.

65 Oney.

66 UPI, "Bo Belinsky Quiet Member of the Cardinals. Southpaw Talks About His Mental Depression," *Terre Haute* (Indiana) *Tribune*, March 30, 1967: 46.

67 Ibid.

68 Allen, "Bo Belinsky Reveals: 'How I Won and Lost Hollywood's Stars,'" 22.

JOHNNY BERARDINO

BY ALAN COHEN

"Berardino is one of those intense fellows who believe the greatest shame in the world is not doing your best every time. He hustles until the last out of every game, and he doesn't sit around crying about his hard luck."

—Bill Veeck, 1948.[1]

KNOWN TO GENERATIONS of television viewers as Dr. Steve Hardy on *General Hospital* (1963-1996), John Beradino, actor, had, during his early adult life, been Johnny Berardino, baseball player. And his first acting roles had come before television was invented.

John Berardino was born in Los Angeles on May 1, 1917. He was the third child born to Ignazio and Anna Musacco Berardino, both natives of Canneto, Rieti, Lazio, Italy, a town on the Adriatic Sea. Ignazio came to the United States in 1905. His mother immigrated in 1911. Ignazio was the foreman at a wholesale meat-packing company. John's older brother, Joseph, was born in 1914 and his sister, Mary, in 1916. His father died in 1965, and his mother died at 100, on April 5, 1989.

Berardino's movie career predated his first trip to the Los Angeles playgrounds to play baseball. At the age of 6, he appeared as an extra in three early Hal Roach "Our Gang" films, before sound came to film. His pay amounted to "box lunches that they handed out on the set." His mother felt he would be the next great child star and persuaded his dad to invest $10,000 in a movie starring the 10-year-old child. But the film was never finished.[2] "My dad gave me a bat and said, 'Go make like 'Push-em up Tony'." (Tony Lazzeri, like Berardino, an Italian from California, was his hero).'"[3] Young Johnny was off to the local playgrounds with a ball and bat. He attended Castelar Grade School and went on to Belmont High School, where he starred in football as well as baseball.

Berardino entered the University of Southern California in the fall of 1935, and served on the Sophomore Class Council during the 1936-37 school year. He was a member of Phi Kappa Tau fraternity. Fred Mosebach of the *San Antonio Express*, who spoke with Berardino during his minor-league days, wrote that Johnny's ambition was to become a sportswriter, but the youngster would find his career elsewhere.[4] He had also, during his time at USC, done some acting, but when asked about his acting during a 1939 interview, he was calm and modest, saying, "Just tell 'em I was a tree in the forest scene."[5] By then, his focus was on baseball.

In the spring of his sophomore year, Berardino made the varsity baseball squad as a second baseman, but when he suffered a broken finger fielding a ball, his coach temporarily switched him to the outfield to get him playing time without undue hazard to his finger. Despite the injury, Berardino led the Pacific Coast Collegiate League with a .424 batting average. He was scouted by Willie Butler and signed after that season by Jack Fournier of the St. Louis Browns, a signing protested by USC coach Justin M. "Sam" Barry.[6] The Browns sent Berardino to the Johnstown (Pennsylvania) Johnnies of the Class-C Middle Atlantic League. He so impressed the organization that Browns business manager Bill Dewitt said, "He's been hitting around .325, is exceptionally fast, has a strong arm, and is a good fielder. All our scouts agree that he's a sure major-league prospect. He'll probably serve with San Antonio next year."[7] At Johnstown Berardino batted .334 with 38 extra-base hits, 12 of which were home runs.

In spring training with the San Antonio Missions in 1938, Berardino went 5-for-5 with three homers on March 20 as the Missions defeated the Laredo Stars, 13-3.[8] During the season he batted .309 as the Missions finished second in the Class-A1 Texas League. He had 41 doubles, two triples, 13 home runs, and 20 stolen bases. Before the season Browns scout Ray Cahill had said, "The lad can't miss."[9]

In May of that season Berardino showed an ability to play while in pain. He played through a game with an injured finger. With his finger taped up, he fielded eight balls at second base and was involved in three double plays. The next day it was determined that the finger was broken.[10] When he was injured he was batting over .400. He missed 20 games, but still led the league in chances handled (810) and participated in a league-leading 107 double plays.

After excelling at San Antonio 1938, Berardino was praised by new Browns manager Fred Haney.[11] In spring training at San Antonio, Berardino and Sig Gryska, who had set a record for converting double plays the prior season at Mission Field, were pairing up to take their act to the major-league level.

Big leaguer John Berardino (on the ballfield) or Beradino (in movies and on TV) enjoyed a healthy big-and-small screen career; he is best-recalled as Dr. Steve Hardy on General Hospital.

Berardino was also showing off his basestealing skills, having stolen three bass in the early spring games.[12] Berardino and Gryska got more playing time in the spring as the regular Browns tandem of Don Heffner and Red Kress were holding out.[13] Heffner's holdout continued into April and Berardino took full advantage, getting the nod to start on Opening Day.[14]

On Opening Day, April 22, 1939, Berardino hit seventh in the batting order and went 1-for-4 against the White Sox at Comiskey Park. In the fourth inning, with the Browns leading 2-1 and runners on second and third, Berardino got his first major-league hit, a single off future Hall of Famer Ted Lyons, driving in the two runners. He hit safely in his first nine major-league games. As April ended, he was batting .333. However, a May slump shot Berardino's average down to .243. Nevertheless, his manager stuck with him and he was back on top in June, going 31-for-89 (.348) with eight extra-base hits, including his first big-league homer. The third-inning two-run blast on June 29 came off Thornton Lee and helped the Browns thump the White Sox, 9-3. However, Berardino's efforts were on most days lost in another year of frustration for the Browns. The team finished the season with a 43-111 record, worst in the major leagues. Berardino had a late-season slump and finished his first season with a .256 batting average. He hit five homers and drove in 58 runs in 126 games.

Hopes were high in St. Louis as the 1940 season begun, as their turn to youth was producing some early positive results, not the least of which was Berardino. The optimism was premature. Three games into the season, the record was above .500 (2-1). It was downhill from there. St. Louis quickly fell to eighth place. But from June 4 through July 2, the Browns went 19-12 and were in fifth place, four games below .500. On June 5, Berardino went 4-for-7 and scored the winning run as the Browns defeated the Red Sox 4-3 in 14 innings at Fenway Park. Four days later, at Philadelphia, Berardino homered in each game of a doubleheader, as the Browns swept the pair. The team, however, would revert to its losing ways and lose 14 in a row in July. Berardino had a role in stopping that streak with a game-winning homer on July 19. The team would up with a sixth-place finish (67-87), an improvement over the prior season's eighth-place result. Berardino improved on his 1939 numbers, raising his average to .258 with career highs in doubles (31) and homers (16). The Browns moved Berardino to shortstop during the season and the results were favorable. Dick Farrington remarked in *The Sporting News* that "some observers who have watched Berardino freely predict that he will be the best shortstop in the league in another year. He possesses what is known as 'ball sense' in tracking down grounders, has ample speed and a fine throwing arm."[15]

In the offseason between 1940 and 1941 Berardino was back performing as an actor, working at the Pasadena Playhouse in a performance of *A Slight Case of Murder*. In 1941, despite some injuries, Berardino played some of his best ball so far. As late as June 5, he was batting above .300, and for the season he would post his best average of his career, .271. Although the Browns (70-84) finished sixth, there was hope that improvement was on the horizon. When Berardino's name came up in trade rumors, the Browns were quick to stop such speculation. With only five home runs, he managed a career-high 89 RBIs, second best on the team.

And then things changed.

In January 1942, shortly after the United States entered World War II, Berardino enlisted in the US Army Air Corps and went off to Higley Field in Chandler, Arizona, for flight training. Unable to qualify as a flier, he was given a discharge and rejoined the Browns. He appeared in 29 games with the team in 1942, but had no set position. He registered only 74 at-bats and had an average of .284. Shortly after the season, he joined the Navy,[16] and was stationed at the Naval Air Station at Lambert Field, Missouri.[17] He moved on to the Physical Instructors' School at Bainbridge, Maryland, and then to the Naval Air Station in San Pedro, California, where he managed the facility's baseball team.[18] When the Browns won the 1944 pennant, Brown was stationed at Pearl Harbor. During his time there, he injured his back falling from a jeep.

Berardino returned from the Navy for the 1946 season and had a great start. At the time of the All-Star Game, he was batting over .300 and the Browns were miffed that he wasn't selected for the All-Star team. He fashioned a career-high 21-game hitting streak from May 30 through June 20. By season's end, his average had dropped to .265, but he had 39 extra-base hits and 68 RBIs. The Browns, after being as high as third place in early May, slipped back to their customary spot in the second division, finishing in seventh place, 38 games out of first. During the offseason, Berardino resumed acting, performing, and learning at the Pasadena Playhouse.

In 1947 with the Browns, Berardino got off to a terrible start at the plate, and on April 27 he had the dubious distinction of hitting into a triple play against the White Sox. He withstood persistent back pain from his Navy days, but was limited to 90 games by two serious injuries. The more severe injury was a broken arm on June 17 that caused him to miss 35 games. He sustained the injury when hit by a fastball thrown by Dave Ferriss of the Red Sox. At the time of his injury, he was batting only .180. After he returned, his hitting improved, but he was sent to the bench again on August 8 when he was hit on the hand by a pitch thrown by Cleveland's Allen Gettel. He missed all but one of his team's next 25 games, but returned to bat .362 in 24 September starts. For the season, he batted .261. His 22 doubles gave him more than 20 doubles in each of his first five full seasons in the major leagues. The Browns, however, were still the Browns, finishing again in last place.

After the 1947 season, the Browns sought to trade Berardino and worked out a trade with the Washington Senators for Jerry Priddy. Berardino saw no advantage in moving from an eighth-place team to a seventh-place team and announced his retirement to seek a full-time film career. His first role was as a horse trainer in the film *The Winner's Circle*, featuring jockey Johnny Longden. In announcing his retirement, Berardino said, "I'm getting a seven-year contract from Polimer Studios and it's a better deal than I could get in baseball. They like my future in the movies and so do I. Anyway, when they start moving you around like cattle without your consent, it's time to quit baseball. I was never approached on the trade and knew nothing about it until I read it in the papers."[19]

However, by the time the film was released on June 8, 1948, Berardino was back on the ball field, this time with a contender. After the deal between St. Louis and Washington fell through, Bill Veeck of the Cleveland Indians wanted to shore up his infield and to strike a pre-emptive blow against the Detroit Tigers, who were looking to acquire Berardino.[20] On December 9, 1947, he paid a handsome sum ($65,000) to the Browns for the handsome ballplayer and quickly, at the insistence of Berardino's film producer, insured John's face in the event the player suffered a baseball-related injury. Reports differ on the amount of the coverage. Contemporary reports had it at $100,000,[21] but more recent accounts showed the amount as $1 million.[22] Berardino also had an attendance clause written into his contract. For each 100,000 the Indians drew at home over 2 million spectators, the player would receive $1,000. To owner Veeck, the contract was little more than a publicity gag as the team had never drawn more than 1.6 million, its all-time high having been 1,521,978 in 1947.

Originally, George Metkovich was sent from Cleveland to St. Louis as part of the trade, but the Browns returned Metkovich to Cleveland, when it was determined that he had a broken finger, with the Browns getting $15,000 on top of the initial $50,000 for Berardino. Veeck's reasoning for the high price tag was, "He'll be worth the price and then some if one of our regulars goes into a slump or is injured. The way the Red Sox have loaded up for next year's pennant race, anyone who hopes to catch them will have to be as strong in reserves as on the front line."[23]

With Cleveland, Berardino backed up Joe Gordon at second base. He was used sparingly, appearing in 66 games and batting only .190. However, the average is deceiving. He started games at each of the four infield positions and, in spots, Berardino shined. He played in 10 straight games, mostly at second base, from May 25 through June 4, when Gordon was injured. During this time, he batted .344, as the Indians won six of the games. On 18 occasions, including 14 starts between June 27 and July 25, Berardino platooned with Eddie Robinson at first base and played errorless ball.

When shortstop-manager Lou Boudreau was injured in early August, Berardino stepped in for six starts. On August 8 he contributed to both wins in a doubleheader sweep of New York. In the 8-6 first-game win, in front of 73,484 at Cleveland Stadium, he homered off Spec Shea during a five-run sixth inning. He walked and scored ahead of Eddie Robinson's game-winning two-run homer in the eighth inning. In the nightcap, his seventh-inning sacrifice advanced the winning run to second base.

As September began, it was a three-team race in the American League for the pennant. The Athletics had fallen from contention. The Red Sox were in the lead, but the Yankees and Indians were in close pursuit. Unfortunately for Berardino, his bat went cold in the heat of the pennant race. From August 10 through September 18, he went 0-for-30 and saw his batting average plummet. As September turned into October, the Indians took the league lead and had a chance to clinch the pennant on the final day of the season. However, although Berardino broke his hitless streak with a pinch-hit single, the Indians lost to the Tigers and fell into a tie with the Red Sox. They defeated Boston in a one-game playoff to advance to the World Series, where they defeated the Boston Braves in six games. Berardino did not play in the World Series.

Berardino's foresight in insisting on the attendance clause in his contract paid off. The Indians drew a record 2,620,627 fans in 1948, and Berardino got a $6,000 bonus. That attendance record stood until 1995.

Berardino was still with the Indians in 1949 and used the season to play with the Indians and do a movie, *The Kid From Cleveland*, along with his teammates. In the film, starring George Brent, Berardino played a gangster character called Mac. Russ Tamblyn played a troubled youth who was helped by the members of the team. The film's premiere took place in Cleveland on September 2, 1949.[24]

Berardino spent his second season with the Tribe once again on the bench, getting into only 50 games. His .198 batting average once again did not show his value to the team. His voice was often heard from the bench by the opposing players and he became highly regarded as a bench jockey. Early Wynn told Berardino, "You got me so mad when I was with Washington (in 1948), that when you got on first base, I tried to throw the ball right at you." Al Simmons added, "That guy (Berardino) is a dandy. He used to get our (Athletics) players so bothered they'd come back to the bench cussing. Oh, is he rough!"[25]

During his time with Cleveland, Berardino was noted for his Captain Bligh speech, in which he imitated Charles Laughton's performance in *Mutiny on the Bounty*. In a reminiscence in 1998, teammate Bob Lemon said that Berardino was "one of the comrades on the team. He did it all," Al Rosen added, "He was a thespian. He would jump on a table in the clubhouse and sprinkle water on everybody while giving his Captain Bligh speech."[26]

In 1950, Berardino played in only four games with the Indians before being sent to their San Diego affiliate in the Pacific Coast League in May. In June, he was transferred to Sacramento in the same league, and on August 9, he was released by the Indians. He signed with the Pirates and was with them for the balance of 1950, playing in 40 games and batting .206.

After the season, the Pirates released Berardino and he signed with the Browns. A stellar performance during spring training earned him the nod at third base and he played in the first dozen games of 1951, batting .311. He played regularly through May, but his playing time diminished thereafter. His last game of the season was on July 4. When Bill Veeck took over the team on July 5, many players were shown the gate, and Berardino became a coach.[27] He was relieved of his coaching duties after the season.

Berardino returned to Cleveland at the beginning of the 1952 season, but not before making a return to movies, appearing as ballplayer Bill Sherdel in *The Winning Team*, which starred Ronald Reagan as Grover Cleveland Alexander. Prompting the invite to spring training from Cleveland general manager Hank Greenberg was the anticipated loss of players to the military draft during the Korean War. Berardino was clearly underperforming in 35 games with the Indians, going only 3-for-32 before being traded to the Pirates at the end of July. He finished his major-league career with the Pirates in September 1952. He went 8-for-56 with four doubles in 19 games with the Pirates, as the Bucs finished in the cellar with a 42-112 record, not much different from his first team, the 1939 Browns.

For his career, Berardino batted .249 with 167 doubles, 23 triples, and 36 home runs. He had 387 RBIs.

Berardino, who was an actor before, during, and after his baseball life, became a full-time actor after the 1952 season. He appeared in more than 25 movies, often in minor uncredited roles (including sitting at a bar in *Marty* and playing a police sergeant in *North by Northwest*), but his greatest success came in over 100 roles on the small screen. His early TV credits included *I Led Three Lives*, in which he appeared as Special Agent Steve Daniels. He appeared on *Superman*, in *The Cisco Kid*, and on *The Lone Ranger*, where he did four episodes (separate outlaw characters) in 1956.

Berardino turned to writing and co-authored scripts with Charissa Hughes for the television series *Shotgun Slade*, which aired from 1959 through 1961.

In 1960, Berardino returned to the big screen, appearing in *Seven Thieves*, which starred Edward G. Robinson and involved a caper that took Robinson and his comrades to a heist in Monte Carlo. This time Berardino was on the side of the law, playing a detective. The film received good reviews.

Still in detective garb, he joined the cast of *The New Breed* on television in 1961 as Sergeant Vince Cavelli, starring alongside Leslie Neilsen. The show was well received by critics but lasted only one season.

Berardino's big break came in 1963 when he took on the role of Dr. Steve Hardy on television's *General Hospital*. The program was the first foray into soap opera for ABC and John Beradino was with the show for 33 years, appearing for the final time one month before his death. In 1973, thinking that daytime performers were undervalued, he championed the cause of the Daytime Emmy Awards.[28] The first awards were presented on May 28, 1974. Although he was nominated for an Emmy in each of the first three years, he was not selected for the award.

In 1981, Beradino appeared in the made-for-television movie, *Don't Look Back*, the story of 1948 Cleveland Indians teammate Satchel Paige. In 1993, 45 years after receiving his World Series ring and 30 years after the debut of *General Hospital*, Berardino was awarded a place on Hollywood's Walk of Fame.

John married 18-year-old Jeanette Nadine Barritt on November 23, 1941, and they had two children, daughters Antoinette, born in 1942, and Celeste Ruth, born in 1945. They were divorced in March 1955.[29] Jeanette died in 1970. On January 20, 1961, he married actress Charissa Hughes, 17 years his junior, with whom he had collaborated as a writer. She died on June 14, 1963. He was married for the third time, to Marjorie Binder, on April 30, 1971. They had a daughter, Katherine (1973-2017), and a son, John Anthony (1974-). Berardino died from pancreatic cancer on May 19, 1996. Berardino's brother, Joseph, had died in 2002 and his sister, Mary, in 2011.

Actress Rachel Ames, who played Berardino's wife on *General Hospital*, talked lovingly of her co-star: "John was like a father confessor to everybody in the cast. He always had a cheery word and liked to tell funny stories. He was a great dancer and loved to ride horses. On breaks between acting, he would play catch."

SOURCES

In addition to the sources cited in the Notes, the author used Baseball-Reference.com, Ancestry.com, the Johnny Berardino player file at the National Baseball Hall of Fame, and the following:

Drohan, John. "It's Short Step From Field to Footlights," *The Sporting News*, April 4, 1956: 13-14.

Grimes, William. "John Beradino, 79, An Enduring Soap Opera Star," *New York Times*, May 22, 1996.

The following articles, although included in the notes, are singled out as being particularly helpful.

Dolgan, Bob. "Two Series Star: After Helping the Indians to the 1948 Title, Berardino Found Fame as Soap Opera Actor," *Cleveland Plain Dealer*, August 23, 1998: 1-C.

Farrington, Dick. "Dark and Handsome Berardino Started in Films — at Six," *The Sporting News*, July 13, 1939: 3.

NOTES

1. Gordon Cobbledick, "Veeck Applies Psychology in Reshuffling Roommates," *The Sporting News*, March 10, 1948: 4.

2. Eirik Knudsen, "Beradino, on 'Hospital' for 25 years, Operated in the Infield for '48 Tribe," *Cleveland Plain Dealer*, June 5, 1988: TV Week-2.

3. Jeanie Chung, "Player-Turned-Actor Is Just What Doctor Ordered," *Baseball Weekly*, May 23, 1991.

4. Fred Mosebach, "John Berardino of San Antonio Missions," *The Sporting News*, October 27, 1938: 10.

5. Dick Farrington, "Dark and Handsome Berardino Started in Films at Six: But with Eye on Lazzeri, Brown Rookie Landed on Diamond," *The Sporting News*, July 13, 1939: 3.

6. "Browns Signing of Collegian Brings Kick From Coast Coach," *The Sporting News*, June 17, 1937: 2.

7. Carl Felker, "Long Rookie String Lined Up by Browns," *The Sporting News*, September 9, 1937: 2.

8. "Missions Win Over Laredo Stars," *Dallas Morning News*, March 21, 1938: II-2.

9. "New Brownies Recruit: John Berardino," *The Sporting News*, January 19, 1939: 1.

10. Ibid.

11. "Mixing Old With New to Paint Brown Picture in Brighter Hue," *The Sporting News*, April 6, 1939: 1.

12. Brown Byrd, "Browns Taking on Rose-Colored Tint: Gryska, Berardino Develop into Nifty Keystone Combination," *The Sporting News*, March 30, 1939: 12.

13. Farrington, "Brownies May Fit Kids Into Keystone," *The Sporting News*, March 9, 1939: 2.

14. Byrd, "Berardino Scheduled to Open at Second Base for Brownies," *The Sporting News*, April 6, 1939: 2.

15. Farrington, "Berardino Browns' Tall Man at Short," *The Sporting News*, September 5, 1940: 2.

16. *St. Louis Post-Dispatch*, September 29, 1942: 4B.

17. *The Sporting News*, June 3, 1943: 11.

18. "In the Service," *The Sporting News*, May 11, 1944: 14.

19. Shirley Povich, "Swap for Berardino Turns Into Movie Shocker for Nats," *The Sporting News*, December 3, 1947: 10.

20. Bill Veeck (with Ed Linn), *Veeck as in Wreck* (Chicago: University of Chicago Press, 2001), 148.

21. Associated Press, "Berardino Gets Face Insured," *Sandusky (Ohio) Register*, January 5, 1948: 5.

22. Veeck, 134.

23. Ed McAuley, "Movie Actor Berardino Gets Into Cleveland Picture," *The Sporting News*, December 17, 1947: 11.

24 McAuley, "Indians' Reel Roles Marked by Realism: New Film Is Well Received at Cleveland Premiere; Diamond Sequences Good; Veeck in Prominent Part," *The Sporting News*, September 14, 1949: 19.

25 Hal Lebovitz, "Active-Sub Berardino Rates High as Jockey," *The Sporting News*, May 10, 1950: 16.

26 Bob Dolgan, "Two Series Star: After Helping Indians to the 1948 Title, Berardino Found Fame as a Soap Opera Actor," *Cleveland Plain Dealer*, August 23, 1998: 1C.

27 Ray Gillespie, "One Team Playing, One Coming, One Going," *The Sporting News*, August 8, 1951: 4.

28 Jerry Buck, Associated Press, "Daytime Opera Performers Want to Compete for Awards," *Cleveland Plain Dealer*, February 11, 1973: 22E.

29 Associated Press. "Berardino Is Sued for Divorce Third Time," *Sacramento* (California) *Bee*, March 2, 1955: 28.

BOBBY BONILLA

BY MARK SOUDER

"He's a quality player who's getting better all the time. A year ago, he played on talent alone. Now he's doing it on talent and know-how. His potential is unlimited."

– Pittsburgh Pirates manager Jim Leyland[1]

NO WORD BETTER DESCRIBES Bobby Bonilla's baseball career than "potential." He was selected as an All-Star six times. Bonilla won three Silver Slugger Awards while a Pirate. Toward the end of his career, he helped lead the Florida Marlins to an improbable World Series triumph. In spite of all this success, Bonilla seemed trapped inside a bubble of bigger expectations.

Standing 6-feet-3 and weighing 210 to 240 pounds, Roberto Martin Antonio "Bobby" Bonilla was always a big man from the time he began playing professional baseball. He was similar in build to two former Auburn University football players, Frank Thomas and Bo Jackson, who like Bonilla tantalized Chicago White Sox fans with their potential to put a big hurt on every baseball. Bonilla was not a finesse hitter, or even a traditional home-run hitter. "He simply muscled the ball with the brute strength of an offensive tackle, which he resembled in appearance," one writer explained.[2]

There is great irony in the pressure for Bonilla to achieve even more than he did. When Bobby was born on February 23, 1963, the area dominated by the Jackson Houses of the South Bronx was not a neighborhood full of high expectations. Puerto Rican families, mostly low income, were pouring into the Bronx in huge numbers. The Bronx has been the political bulwark of nationally ground-breaking Puerto Rican politicians including Herman Badillo, Fernando Ferrer, and Jose Serrano. The Bronx is the second largest population area of Puerto Ricans, behind only San Juan, Puerto Rico.

Bonilla is of Afro-Puerto Rican heritage, his parents having moved to the Bronx from Puerto Rico. Roberto Sr. was an electrician and Regina, his mother, was a psychologist. They divorced when Bobby was 8. He, his twin sisters, Socorro and Milagros, and his brother, Javier, grew up living with their mother. His father lived only five minutes away. Bonilla said that "he was always there if I needed him."[3] Both parents worked to instill values in him though actions and words. His father took Bobby on electrical jobs to demonstrate how hard he had to work as well as the dangers of his job, and then, according to Bonilla, would ask, "Is this what you want to do?" and Bobby would reply "No, Dad, I'll work at my baseball a little harder."[4]

His home area was the infamous 40th Police Precinct, known for its homicides and robberies and not many success stories. Bonilla said that he "had my sports." "It kept me away from the drugs, the gangs," he told Ross Newhan of the *Los Angeles Times*.[5] Amidst the chaos, Bobby focused on baseball. He told *People* magazine that he "played sports 24 hours a day. In a place like the South Bronx, you have to dream or else you'll get caught up in the mess."[6] His life in the Bronx led to one of his oft-repeated phrases when people asked him if criticism, booing fans or batting slumps were "pressure." He'd say: "This isn't pressure. Pressure is growing up in the South Bronx."[7]

Not only did Bobby have his family to keep him focused, but he had an extraordinary high-school baseball coach, Joe Levine. Beyond just helping develop Bonilla as a high-school player, Levine put him in the position to launch an improbable and extraordinary major-league career. The coach attended a seminar at which a high-school all-star team was being assembled to play in Scandinavia in the summer of 1980. High-school senior Bonilla was selected for the team, but did not have the money needed to go. His coach started a "Bobby Fund" to assist Roberto Sr. in paying for the summer trip. It is no wonder that Bonilla considered Coach Levine a second father.[8]

The coordinator and instructor for the trip was legendary baseball scout Syd Thrift. Thrift had spent nearly 20 years as the scouting coordinator of Pittsburgh Pirates, Kansas City Royals, and Oakland Athletics but had left baseball and was working during this nine-year stretch as a real estate agent. Here's how Thrift described the trip: "It was the season of the midnight sun. We all slept in one big room. There were no shades on the windows and the sun never set. It was the most bizarre thing you ever saw."[9] But it gave Thrift plenty of daylight to see Bobby Bonilla's potential.

Upon returning, Thrift called one of his old bosses, Pirates minor-league director Branch Rickey Jr., and within weeks of returning, Bonilla was at the Pirates' spring home in Bradenton, Florida for a tryout.[10] Bonilla was not an instant success story in minor-league baseball. He spent his first two years with the Pirates' rookie league team, hitting barely above the Mendoza line though occasionally flashing his potential power. At age 20, in 1983 at the Class-A level, Bonilla began to show improved skills so the Pirates advanced him to Nashua of the Double-A Eastern League in 1984. There he again slightly improved his power, average, and speed even though he had risen to a higher level in the minors.

In 1985 Bonilla was invited to spring training with the Pirates in Bradenton. He was getting his breakout chance, but Bonilla broke his leg in a collision with Bip Roberts while chasing a foul popup. He could have given up but did not. Bonilla credited his wife, Millie, his high-school sweetheart, with "keeping his head straight." "I was a big baby in a lot of ways," Bonilla said. "I had to learn to cope while wanting to be home. I earned $650 a month and spent $200 calling Millie. She picked up a lot of the slack. She kept my head straight."[11] The Pirates sent him back down to Class A with Prince William (Carolina League). There he met Barry Bonds, who was to become his closest friend in baseball.

In the winter of 1983-84, Bonilla had played his first baseball in his parents' native home of Puerto Rico. He was still a raw minor-league player when he joined the Senadores de San Juan. Mako Oliveras had taken over as manager and immediately liked the personable Bonilla. Since Bonilla had nowhere to stay, Oliveras asked his mother if Bobby could stay with them. He did so for two winters, where he loved the food and became part of their family.[12]

Bonilla played four additional seasons in the Puerto Rican Winter League. Before the 1984-85 season, the Indios de Mayaguez traded shortstop Adalberto Pena and pitcher Orlando Lind to San Juan for Bonilla. Assistant general manager Jorge Aranzamendi, based upon all the major-league scouting reports he had access to, supported going after prospect Bonilla because of his potential. While Pena helped lead San Juan to a championship, Bonilla was not a regular starter on Mayaguez until 1985-86.[13] Bonilla credited the Puerto Rican Winter League with advancing his skills. He had short high-school baseball seasons in New York City, so he entered minor-league ball without much game experience. After his spring-training injury in 1985, and his demotion back to Class A, the winter of 1985-86 was of great importance to his major-league career. His solid statistics during the last 39 games of the season at Prince William reflected improving skills that resulted in his starting for Mayaguez.

Based upon his broken leg and partial season in Class A, the Pirates had left Bonilla off their 40-man roster in the fall. They presumed that no team would select him in the Rule 5 draft because it would require placing an inexperienced, possibly damaged player on the 25-player roster for the season or potentially losing him. The Chicago White Sox had the advantage of being able to select the unprotected Bonilla after he had demonstrated recovery not only in a few months of minor-league baseball but also with the Indios in winter ball. For $50,000 the White Sox received a soon-to-be major-league star.

Bonilla astoundingly jumped from Class A to the majors without missing a beat. In 75 games for the White Sox, his .256 batting average slightly exceeded his best year in the minors and his on-base percentage and slugging average were roughly equal to his previous bests. No wonder Bonilla said that playing Puerto Rican Winter League baseball was particularly important to him because he skipped Triple A. Puerto Rico had been a critical training ground to maturing and developing his skills.

Bonilla had a friend who had never forgotten him: Syd Thrift. Thrift had been enticed back into baseball by the Pirates, who appointed him general manager. Thrift hired the White Sox third-base coach, Jim Leyland, to be the manager. In midseason the Pirates reacquired Bonilla for pitcher Jose DeLeon. In 2013 ESPN ranked each major-league team's best deadline trade. For the Pirates, it was receiving Bonilla for DeLeon.[14]

Bonilla returned to Indios de Mayaguez for the 1986-87 winter season. Post-season he was selected play for the Puerto Rican entry in the 1987 Caribbean Series held in Hermosillo, Mexico along with other major-league players Candy Maldonado and Juan Nieves, as were future stars Roberto Alomar and David Cone. Because of his Puerto Rican heritage, in the winter leagues and for the national team, Bobby Bonilla was classified as a Puerto Rican native player.[15] In retirement Bonilla has continued to support baseball efforts in Puerto Rico, including the Puerto Rico Baseball Academy that produced Houston Astros star Carlos Correa.[16]

In 1987 for the Pirates, Bonilla showed the first signs of a major breakout. He hit .300 (his previous high had been .269), topped 10 home runs for the first time, and slugged .481. He played his last year of winter ball for Mayaguez in 1987-88. In 1988 Bonilla hit 24 home runs and had 100 RBIs. The Pirates excelled as well, as Thrift built a powerhouse upon the ruins of the cocaine-devastated Pirates. From 1988 to 1991, Bonilla averaged 24 home runs, 38 doubles, 102 RBIs, and a 4.4 WAR. While Bonds was the top star with a Wins Above Replacement (WAR) average of 7.9, Bonilla was among the best players in the majors. In 1988, at the start of Bonilla's outburst, Philadelphia Phillies third baseman Mike Schmidt said, "He's the best all-around third baseman in the league."[17]

The Pirates had become the dominant team in the majors, winning three straight division titles in 1990, 1991, and 1992. Bonilla finished second in the National League's 1990 MVP voting (behind teammate Bonds) and third in 1991 (Bonds was second to Terry Pendleton of the NL Champion Atlanta Braves). The Spring 1991 issue of *Topps Baseball Card* magazine featured Bonilla and Bonds on the cover, calling them the "Killer B's."[18] Topps correctly realized that the double B's of Barry Bonds and Bobby Bonilla, combined with their first-second and second-third place MVP finishes, and the Pirates' natural bee-colored black and gold uniforms, made the duo the perfect "Killer B's" of all time.

Bonilla was not with the Pirates during the 1992 championship season. His life had started to take a bad turn during the 1991 season as his coming free agency began to raise dissatisfaction about money. Bonilla had always been known for having a "neon" smile. *People* magazine stated: "Perhaps not since Ernie ('It's a great day for a ballgame') Banks retired from the Chicago Cubs 17 years ago has baseball seen a man with a sunnier disposition swing a meaner bat." A teammate said it was nice to come to the ballpark and see his smiling face.[19]

Money had become a proxy for not only skill but respect. The Pirates had been a home to African American stars, and had fielded the first all-black lineup in 1971, anchored by Puerto Rican legend Roberto Clemente and Willie Stargell. However, Bonilla felt that teammate Andy Van Slyke and others were given large contract offers while the Pirates would not meet his request. The Yankees were interested in either Bonds or Bonilla but were rumored to prefer Bonilla because of his upbeat attitude.[20]

However, it was not the Yankees, but the New York Mets that brought Bobby Bonilla home to New York City. The Mets signed Bonilla to the highest dollar contract ever in the major leagues at the time, $5 million for five years. New York is considered a tough sports town, with many opinionated sports journalists competing for the attention of millions of opinionated and passionate sports fans. Bonilla, as the newly minted richest man in baseball, was going to have a bullseye on his head even if he performed well.

Barry Bonds accurately framed the difference between himself and his good friend. "I can handle New York because I don't get my feelings hurt the way Bobby does. I don't give a __ what people write about me or say. Bobby does. He's too sensitive. I told him before he went there that he wasn't going to be able to deal with it but he didn't believe me. Now, he believes me."[21]

Bonilla's return home started like the dream he hoped it would be. On February 3, 1992, he and his wife established the Millie and Bobby Bonilla Public School Fund. Bronx Borough President Fernando Ferrer proclaimed the day Bobby Bonilla Day, stating what a great pleasure it was "to welcome back the four-star slugger of the South Bronx." Surrounded by Mets officials and teacher union representatives, Bonilla pledged to donate $500 for each RBI he got for sports equipment and incentive programs to the Bronx schools he attended. It was expected to be around $50,000 because Bonilla had become a reliable 100 RBIs-a-year player. Lehman High School was not represented at the ceremony because the principal had fired Bonilla's beloved former coach Levine. Instead, Levine spoke at the ceremony and the *New York Times* noted that he would be the "unofficial administrator of the fund."[22]

From there, things went downhill. Bonilla sank back to the mediocre performance level of his first year—he was hitting only .130 in May—only now he was the highest paid player in baseball. He improved but still drove in only 70 runs, largely because the weak Mets lineup had 31 percent fewer runners for him to potentially drive in.[23] Regardless of the reasons, fans were focused upon his underperformance compared with his record-breaking salary. He was scalded in New York, where he took to wearing earplugs, and his baseball homecoming to Pittsburgh was a disaster, including having a bottle thrown at him. The Mets imploded. Then it got worse.

The days of fawning sports reporters was over. The adoring public was no longer so adoring but more sarcastic. The title of the book *The Worst Team Money Could Buy* suggests the views of the author about the 1992 Mets.[24] The generally ebullient Bonilla was already upset with the world and upset with himself. He said later that he perhaps should have handled the criticism better, but when he was called out for lying about his attempt to reverse an error call on what he thought was a hit, the festering wounds to his pride were picked open. The powerful Bonilla physically intimidated the less imposing author/*New York Daily News* baseball reporter Bob Klapisch by threatening to "show him the Bronx."[25] It was ironic since Bonilla had specifically separated himself from the more violent part of the Bronx his entire life, but the image of sunny Bobby never quite recovered.

After his poor performance in 1992, Bonilla recovered to have a solid season for the Mets in 1993, as well as in the strike-shortened seasons of 1994 and the first half of 1995. He was named to the NL All-Star team in 1993 and 1995. His statistics averaged over a full season were just shy of his annual performances in Pittsburgh. But now his personal image had been

Bobby Bonilla, one of the Three Big Whiffers (joining Barry Bonds and Pedro Guerrero) in Rookie of the Year.

damaged, and his contract had raised expectations to levels he could not achieve.

In late July of 1995 the Mets traded their All-Star slugger to the Baltimore Orioles for two minor-leaguers. Bonilla, clearly glad to escape, drove to Baltimore that night in order to be in the lineup against the White Sox.[26] He hit extremely well for the Orioles in 1995, batting .333 with a slugging average of .544 and an RBI rate of 123 in a 162-game season. He followed that with another solid season in 1996. Bonilla was one of the reasons the Orioles made the 1996 American League playoffs as the wild-card team. He hit a game-sealing grand slam in the first game against the Cleveland Indians, and then homered again in the decisive fourth game. Baltimore defeated the Indians three games to one but was easily subdued by the Yankees in the ALCS.

When his season concluded, Bonilla was again a free agent. He signed with the Florida Marlins, where he was reunited with his former Pirates manager Jim Leyland. In 1997 he batted .297 with 39 doubles, 96 RBIs, and 17 homers. The Marlins' owner, Wayne Huizenga, had decided to open his checkbook, not only for Bonilla but also for Moises Alou, Alex Fernandez, and Jim Eisenreich. The Marlins made the NL playoffs as the wild-card team. It was Bonilla's fourth trip to the playoffs. This time the Marlins won the World Series, against Cleveland.

After the World Series victory, Huizenga, a trash magnate, trashed his team. He sold, failed to re-sign, or traded most of the key players. The Marlins went from first to worst, finishing 1998 with a 54-108 record. In May 1998 Bonilla was traded, along with Gary Sheffield and three others, to the Los Angeles Dodgers for Mike Piazza and Todd Zeile, who were then flipped as well. Bonilla's glory days were gone. His hitting collapsed (.249 for the season) and he was bounced to the Mets for Mel Rojas after the season.

At this late stage of his career, Bonilla was not a hitting asset but was more like a good-luck charm. For the 2000 season, he signed with the Atlanta Braves. They won their ninth straight division title. He was not re-signed. For 2001, at age 38, he played in 93 games for the St. Louis Cardinals, who won the NL wild-card slot. They were eliminated by the eventual World Series champion Arizona Diamondbacks. Bonilla's stellar playing career ended much as it had begun. It was an arc, beginning in 1981 with the Pirates Rookie League team, for which he hit .217, and finishing with a .213 batting with the Cardinals 20 years later.

However, it did not end the baseball legend of Bobby Bonilla. In 1999, his last year with the Mets, Bonilla had agreed to have his contract bought out and accepted deferred payments that would begin in 2011 and continue until 2035. On July 1 of each year he receives a check for $1,193,248.20 from the Mets on what the media refers to as "Bobby Bonilla Day." Some refer to him as the "Patron Saint of Bad Contracts," and others refer to players who also are receiving deferred paychecks long after retirement as the "Bobby Bonilla All-Stars."

Since Bonilla has not played for the Mets since the last century, the fact that his annuity exceeds the salary, for example, of any of the 2016 Mets' top four pitching stars—Noah Syndergaard, Jacob DeGrom, Matt Harvey, and Steven Matz—causes lots of tsk-tsking by the media and fans. Of course, when Bonilla was slugging away as a youngster for the Pirates he was not earning the big money either. More importantly, even though the Mets will have paid Bonilla $29.8 million for the 2000 season in which he was not on the team, the deal was both logical at the time and worked out well for the Mets. The biggest problem was scam artist Bernie Madoff. Mets owner Fred Wilpon was one of the investors Madoff defrauded of $17 billion for which he was sentenced to 150 years in prison. Wilpon had been receiving 10-15 percent annual gains. Had he earned even 10 percent on the $5.9 million owed Bonilla in 2000, by 2035 Wilpon would have netted a $49 million profit. In attempts to recover losses, Wilpon was sued but found innocent of any crime. He was guilty only of a combination of misplaced trust and economic ignorance.[27]

The cash freed up by the Bonilla deferred deal resulted in the signing of Derek Bell, Todd Zeile, and Mike Hampton. They helped lead the Mets to the

National League title in 2000. Hampton earned the MVP of the NL Championship Series by pitching 16 shutout innings. When Hampton then signed with the Colorado Rockies, the Mets received as compensation a young ballplayer named David Wright, who developed into one of the 10 best Mets players ever.[28]

Bonilla had one other unique side of his personality: He had some minor success as an actor. Bonilla, Bonds, and Pedro Guerrero all had bit parts in the 1993 baseball movie *Rookie of the Year*. The movie is the story of a 12-year-old boy who, after hurting his arm, finds that the surgically repaired arm enables him to throw a baseball over 100 miles per hour. This results in his being signed by the Chicago Cubs and sparking them to a World Series victory. He reinjures his arm and returns to Little League baseball, only sporting a World Series ring.

The brief appearance of Bonilla is in one of the scenes that adds the patina of authenticity to the movie. The first is the day at Wrigley Field, filmed at the ballpark, when young Henry Rowengartner (Thomas Ian Nicholas) returns an opposing team's home run toward the field, only it goes to the catcher at home plate on the fly. Later, after his shaky early start, the "rookie" pitcher becomes a key part of the Cubs turnaround. Showing actual baseball players Bonilla, Guerrero, and Bonds swinging mightily, and late, on the alleged fastballs of the 12-year-old pitcher was a shortcut way to establish Henry's importance to the Cubs success. The ballplayers in the scene were billed as "The Big Whiffers."

The movie had mini-cult status among Cub fans desperate to win. Nicholas was invited to toss out the first pitch at a Cubs game in 2010, and to sing the National Anthem in 2015. After the Cubs won Game Seven of the 2016 World Series, he tweeted out the final shot from *Rookie of the Year*, when he held his World Series ring up to the camera.

The personable Bonilla was also interviewed on nontraditional baseball shows including *Late Night With David Letterman* and *Lauren Hutton and…* He also appeared in three television series. In 1994 Bobby was "Ronnie Holland" in the episode "The Friendly Neighborhood Dealer" on the Fox series *New York Undercover*. The series ran from 1994 to 1998, starring Michael DeLorenzo and Malik Yoba as NYPD detectives. DeLorenzo, like Bonilla, was of Puerto Rican descent and from the Bronx.

In 1995 Bonilla appeared on *Living Single* in an episode titled "Play Ball." The series was carried five years by Fox, ranking among the top five shows among African-Americans. Among its stars were Queen Latifah, Kim Fields, and Kim Coles. In 1998 Bonilla and Tony LaRussa appeared in the episode "The American Game" on the HBO television series *Arli$$*. While it was critically panned, *Time* magazine reported that so many viewers claimed *Arli$$* was the sole reason they subscribed to HBO that it remained on the year for seven seasons.

By any standard, young Roberto Martin Antonio "Bobby" Bonilla of the South Bronx achieved his potential.

SOURCES

In addition to the sources cited in the Notes, the author utilized Baseball-Reference.com for all baseball statistics and the website IMDb.com for information on Bonilla's movie and TV career.

NOTES

1. Ross Newhan, "An Act of Piracy: Getting Bonilla Back Was a Steal," *Los Angeles Times*, July 8, 1988.
2. Bob Klapisch and John Harper, *The Worst Team Money Could Buy* (Lincoln: University of Nebraska Press, Bison Books, 2005), 75.
3. Newhan.
4. Ibid.
5. Ibid.
6. Eric Levin and Mary Huzinec, "Save That Ball, Boys — The Way Bobby Bonilla's Going, It'll Be Valuable," *People* magazine, July 18, 1988.
7. Ken Rappoport, *Bobby Bonilla* (New York: Walker and Company, 1993), 91
8. Kenneth Shouler, "Swinging for the Fences," *Cigar Aficionado*, July/August 1998; Newman, "Act of Piracy."
9. Shouler.
10. Shouler.
11. Newhan.

12 Thomas E. Van Hyning, *Puerto Rico's Winter League: A History of Major League Baseball's Launching Pad* (Jefferson, North Carolina: McFarland, 1995), 29.

13 Ibid.

14 proxy.espn.com/blog/sweetspot/tag?name=bobby-bonilla.

15 Van Hyning, 111.

16 "MLB to Start Puerto Rico Summer League for 14-17-Year-Olds," Fox Sports, June 19, 2014.

17 Levin and Huzinec.

18 While some have included Sid Bream and Jay Bell among the Pirates' "Killer B's" and others later stretched the term to the powerful Houston "B's" (Jeff Bagwell, Craig Biggio, and Derek Bell), the term fit perfectly on Bonilla and Bonds.

19 Ibid.

20 Jon Heyman, "Yankees Are Targeting Bonds or Bonilla," *Newsday* (Long Island, New York), January 13, 1991.

21 John Feinstein, *Play Ball: The Life and Troubled Times of Major League Baseball* (New York: Villard Books, 1993), 26.

22 Bruce Weber, "Bobby Bonilla Puts His Bat to Work," *New York Times*, February 4, 1992.

23 Neil Paine, "Bobby Bonilla Was More Than the Patron Saint of Bad Contracts," FiveThirtyEight.com, September 30, 2016.

24 Klapisch and Harper.

25 Rappoport, 286.

26 Buster Olney, "All-Star Slugger Acquired From Mets for Minor-Leaguers Ochoa and Buford Orioles Get Their Cleanup Man: Bonilla," *Baltimore Sun*, July 29, 1995.

27 theundefeated.com/features/bobby-bonilla-was-more-than-just-that-mets-contracts-538/; Serge Kovaleski and David Waldstein, "Madoff Had Wide Role in Mets' Finances," *New York Times*, February 1, 2011; and Darren Royal, "Why the Mets Pay Bobby Bonilla $1.19 Million Every July 1," ESPN; July 1, 2016.

28 Mel Antonen, "Deferred Payment: Mets Owe Bobby Bonilla Nearly $30 Million From 2011-2035," *USA Today*, updated July 1, 2010; Ted Berg, "The Annual Deferred Payments to Bobby Bonilla Actually Worked Out Quite Well for the Mets," *USA Today*, July 1, 2015.

CHUCK CONNORS

BY CHARLIE BEVIS

CHUCK CONNORS WAS A career minor-league ballplayer who played portions of two seasons in the major leagues, with the Brooklyn Dodgers in 1949 and Chicago Cubs in 1951. Connors gained greater fame as one of the very few ballplayers who was a successful actor in his post-baseball career, best known for his role as Lucas McCain in the TV show *The Rifleman*. He also appeared in more than 50 movies during his lengthy acting career. Connors was also one of the few men who played both major-league baseball and basketball (with the Boston Celtics in 1946-47).

"I owe baseball all that I have and much of what I hope to have," Connors said in 1953 when he retired as a ballplayer. "Baseball made my entrance to the film industry immeasurably easier than I could have made it alone. To the greatest game in the world I shall be eternally in debt."[1] For Connors, the turning point in his life came during spring training in 1951 when the Chicago Cubs demoted him to their Los Angeles Angels farm club in the Pacific Coast League. "Greatest break I ever got," Connors said in 1954. "I'm out there right in the middle of the movie business where, if a guy has anything, he's got the chance to break in."[2]

Kevin Joseph Aloysius Connors was born on April 10, 1921, in Brooklyn, New York. He was the only son of Allan and Marcella Connors, Irish natives who came to the United States via Newfoundland. Connors had one sibling, his sister Gloria. Connors grew up in the Bay Ridge section of Brooklyn, where his parents struggled to eke out a living during the Great Depression of the 1930s. His father was unemployed for much of the decade, as his mother supported the family by scrubbing floors in office buildings; his father eventually found work as a night watchman. Connors said that growing up poor in his pre-adolescent years motivated him to work hard to achieve success as a ballplayer and later as an actor.

While he attended public schools as a youngster, Connors played on the sports teams sponsored by a local boys club, the Bay Ridge Celtics. John Flynn, who coached the teams, helped Connors gain a sports scholarship to Adelphi Academy, a private high school in Brooklyn, where he played football, basketball, and baseball. In his senior year at Adelphi, Connors was named the first baseman on the *Brooklyn Eagle* all-scholastic baseball team. "Because of baseball, I got a good education," Connors said later in life. "The coach [at Adelphi] was a former Southeastern Conference heavyweight boxing champion, Hollis Botts. He was a first baseman playing semi-pro ball on the weekends and coaching our team, so I was in good hands, both in sports and in school work."[3]

Following his graduation from Adelphi in June 1940, Connors pursued his dream to play for his hometown Brooklyn Dodgers when he signed a minor-league contract with the Dodgers. The *Brooklyn Eagle* gushed that it had "spotted a successor to Dolph Camilli," then the incumbent Dodgers first baseman, in the first of many rosy forecasts for Connors to achieve greatness with the Dodgers.[4] The Dodgers assigned Connors to their Newport, Arkansas, farm team at the bottom of the minor-league ladder, the Class-D Northeast Arkansas League. Connors played just four games for Newport, batting 1-for-11, before he changed his mind about professional baseball in favor of playing sports in college.

After he voluntarily retired from baseball following his short stint in the Dodgers organization, Connors attended Seton Hall College on a baseball scholarship. He played first base on the undefeated Seton Hall baseball team in the spring of 1942, which compiled an 11-0 record. A highlight for Connors that season was Seton Hall's 6–5 come-from-behind victory over Fordham on May 11, when Seton Hall scored three runs in the bottom of the ninth inning to win. As reported in the *New York Times* the next day, Seton Hall tied the score in that ninth inning when "Lacika scored on Connors' Texas Leaguer."

Although Connors often voiced an "aw shucks" attitude about his lack of formal training as an actor, his Seton Hall education provided the foundation for his oratory skills. After being goaded into participating in a declamatory contest, he chose to recite Vachel Lindsay's poem "The Congo," which was a complex verse concerning Mumbo-Jumbo the God of the Congo. When the judges declared Connors the winner, he was hooked on the performing arts.

Connors also played varsity basketball at Seton Hall during the winter of 1941-42. He was the backup center on the team led by Bob Davies, who went on to a stellar career as a pro player and enshrinement in the Basketball Hall of Fame. Seton Hall coach John "Honey" Russell inserted Connors into several games that winter to spell starting center Ken Pine. Connors scored a career-high six points on December 30, 1941, in Seton Hall's 59-15 rout of Maryland. "I wasn't a bad basketball player, but I was far from the world's greatest," Connors told biographer David Fury. "Good defense, no offense, that was me."[5] In 1942, the lanky Connors, who stood 6-foot-6, had more promise as a baseball player than as a basketball player, especially after he hit .360 for the Burlington, Vermont, ball club in the semi-pro Northern League during the summer of 1941.

During the summer of 1942, Connors wound up in the minor-league organization of the New York Yankees. The story goes that famed Yankees scout Paul Krichell signed Connors to a minor-league contract after he spotted his name on a list of unprotected minor-league players. Krichell may have seen Connors play for Seton Hall in nearby South Orange, New Jersey (other stories have Krichell scouting him at Adelphi and even arranging for his scholarship to Seton Hall.) However, the Yankees signed Connors in June of 1942 after he played for the Fraser Stars in Lynn, Massachusetts, a ball club in the semi-pro New England League. Connors, whose "work in college circles has been so outstanding that a number of big-league clubs are seeking his services," played only three weeks in Lynn before signing with the Yankees.[6] Why Connors did not return to his beloved Brooklyn Dodgers is unknown. The Yankees assigned Connors to their Norfolk, Virginia, farm club in the Class-B Piedmont League, where he batted .264 in 72 games.

In October 1942 Connors enlisted in the Army, where he spent the next three years state-side as a tank training instructor while the United States fought World War II. After his initial assignment to Camp Campbell in Kentucky, Connors was assigned to West Point, 50 miles north of his native Brooklyn. On weekends during the warm weather, Connors played semi-pro baseball in the New York City area, often with the Bushwick team in Brooklyn. During the colder months, he played pro basketball in the American Basketball League for the Brooklyn Indians (1943-44), Wilmington Bombers (1944-45), and Paterson Crescents (1945-46). Connors became more of a scorer during his wartime basketball years, averaging 6.1 points per game in 27 games for Wilmington and 8.8 points per game in 18 games for Paterson. During the war years, Connors concluded that he could make a decent living postwar as a year-round professional athlete, playing baseball from spring until fall and basketball during the winter. His plan was not all that unusual for the time period, because many athletes played multiple professional sports in the 1930s and 1940s.

In the war years, Connors also acquired the nickname "Chuck," which soon usurped his given name Kevin. The oft-told story that the nickname originated from his Seton Hall days, where first-baseman Connors was fond of saying to his infielders, "Chuck it to me, baby. Chuck it to me!" is likely apocryphal.[7] This story was told by his sister Gloria, in a 1997 biography of Connors. More probable is the explanation that Connors gave in the early 1980s: "They called me Chuck when I started playing baseball because they thought Kevin was effeminate."[8] Since its first published instance was in 1945, the nickname came from his days in semi-pro baseball.[9] In 1949 the *Brooklyn Eagle* reported that Connors was called Chuck "after the old Bowery character of the same name," which makes sense since Connors played semi-pro baseball mostly in the New York City area.[10] The original Chuck Connors, a talkative, shadowy character that was a political boss, was immortalized in the 1933 movie *The Bowery*, where Wallace Beery played tough-guy Connors in the rough-and-tumble world of the Lower East Side.[11] Chuck was the perfect nickname for a hard-nosed baseball player.

After Connors was discharged from the Army in February 1946, he immediately joined the Rochester Royals of the National Basketball League, which had greater stature than did the ABL. Connors played in 14 games for the Royals, scoring 28 points, before he left the club in early March to go to baseball spring training with the Yankees. Rochester went on to win the NBL title that spring, establishing a lengthy pattern of Connors playing on championship teams as a postwar athlete.

Connors found his way back to the Brooklyn Dodgers organization during spring training of 1946 after the Yankees asked waivers on him to move him down from their top minor-league farm club in Newark, New Jersey. Brooklyn picked up Connors off the waiver wire and assigned him to the Dodgers farm club in Newport News, Virginia, of the Class-B Piedmont League. Connors hit 17 home runs in 1946 to lead the Piedmont League and establish himself as a prime prospect to be the first baseman for the Brooklyn Dodgers. Newport News won the Piedmont League playoffs, the first of four consecutive championship minor-league baseball teams that Connors played on.

Returning to professional basketball in the fall of 1946, Connors played in the Basketball Association of America, a new league that competed with the established National Basketball League (the two leagues merged after the 1948-49 season to form today's National Basketball Association). With his former Seton Hall coach, Honey Russell, at the helm of the Boston Celtics club in the BAA, Connors signed to play with the Celtics for the inaugural 1946-47 season. Connors averaged 4.6 points per game in 49 games for the Celtics that season. He was no major offensive threat, as he sank less than one in four field-goal attempts (94-for-380) and less than half of his free throws (39-for-84). Connors later explained his primary role with the Celtics that season, which fortuitously led to the beginning of an acting career:

> I'm positive my greatest value to the Celtics was as an after-dinner speaker. It seems to me I did more public speaking for the team than playing that first season. They sent me all over New England on speaking engagements. I'd pick up $25 or $50 an appearance, whatever the traffic would bear. When I wasn't apologizing [for the few wins the team had], I was doing things like "Casey at the Bat" and "Face on the Bar Room Floor." I did "Casey" at the Boston Baseball Writers Dinner that first winter, and Ted Williams was there too after winning the 1946 American League MVP Award. Ted was very kind to me and laughed his head off at my rendition. Afterward, he said to me, "Kid, I don't know what kind of basketball player you are, but you ought to give it up and be an actor." So doing those after-dinner speeches was my raison d'etre.[12]

Where Connors did establish his renown with the Boston Celtics on the basketball court was in a pregame warm-up on November 5, 1946, when he became the first player in NBA history to shatter a glass backboard. Contrary to the legend that developed, Connors did not shatter the backboard while attempting to dunk the basketball. "During the warm-ups, I took a set shot, a harmless set shot, and crash, the glass backboard shattered," Connors recalled. The newfangled backboard was missing a key part, a piece of rubber between the glass and the rim, which caused the glass to shatter when the shot caromed off the rim. Because the Celtics game was being played at the Boston Arena, not at the Boston Garden, where Gene Autry's rodeo was playing to a large crowd, the Celtics management had to scramble to locate a replacement in order to play the game. Publicist Howie McHugh was dispatched to the Boston Garden to get a replacement backboard. "Howie tells how the Garden's backboards were stored behind the Brahma bull pens, and nobody was fool enough to challenge the bulls for them," Connors recalled. "Howie found two drunken cowboys and slipped them a couple of bucks to go into the pen, dodge the bulls, and get a glass backboard out. If he hadn't, we might still be waiting at the Arena."13

Connors is considered one of an elite group of fewer than a dozen athletes that played in both major-league baseball and the NBA, which includes Danny Ainge, Gene Conley, Dave DeBusschere, and Dick Groat. However, defining professional basketball as only teams in the NBA, or its forerunner the BAA, excludes many baseball players that played pro basketball in other leagues. According to Ted Brock's research in *Total Basketball*, another dozen major-league ballplayers logged minutes with NBL teams, including Lou Boudreau, George Crowe, Irv Noren, and Del Rice.14

Connors left the Celtics in late February 1947 to go to spring training with the Brooklyn Dodgers. For the 1947 baseball season, the Dodgers sent Connors to their farm club in Mobile, Alabama, in the Class-AA Southern Association. He compiled a .255 batting average, belted 15 home runs, and drove in 82 runs to help Mobile win the Southern Association playoffs. Connors continued his ascent up the Dodgers' minor-league chain, where the first base situation at the parent club was in a state of flux. For the 1947 season, Jackie Robinson played first base, which was not his natural position, just to get his bat into the lineup. Eddie Stevens, a regular first baseman for the Dodgers during the 1946 season, was shipped out to Montreal, Brooklyn's top farm team. Howie Schultz, who split time with Stevens at first base in 1946 (and was another dual baseball-basketball athlete), was sold to the Philadelphia Phillies. Stevens was sold to the Pittsburgh Pirates after the 1947 season, clearing the way for Connors to at least play for Montreal in 1948 if not make the Brooklyn squad.

Connors, now a shrewd negotiator, played hard-to-get with the Boston Celtics to sign for the 1947-48 BAA season by claiming he had a deal to be player-coach of a Birmingham team in the new Southern Basketball League. While the Celtics eventually caved in to his contract demands, Connors played only four games for the Celtics before the team put him on waivers in November 1947 to save money, when they had acquired another center, Ed Sadowski. Connors always claimed he left basketball to concentrate on baseball. "Well, baseball and basketball didn't mix. Definitely not," Connors said. "I had to leave the Celtics in late February for spring training and figured I was in great shape because I had been running on the boards all winter. But because of that I found my legs actually were much tougher to get

Chuck Connors, a marginal major leaguer, won success on the big and small screens; he is best-remembered as the star of television's The Rifleman.

into condition. I think my baseball legs were bothered very much by basketball."[15]

For the 1948 baseball season, the Dodgers assigned Connors to their top farm club in Montreal, where he hit a solid .307 with 17 home runs and 88 RBIs. Montreal won the International League playoffs and also the Little World Series, defeating St. Paul of the American Association. Back in Brooklyn, first base was still a merry-go-round until Gil Hodges became the regular first baseman midway through the 1948 season. Connors had a distinct shot at getting the first base job with Brooklyn in 1949, since Hodges hit just .249 in 1948. Connors did two things following the 1948 season to increase the odds of his promotion to Brooklyn. First, the 27-year-old bachelor settled down by marrying Elizabeth Riddell. Second, he finally abandoned his winter job as pro basketball player and played winter-league baseball with the Almendares ball club of the Cuban League.

Connors had a commanding presence, at 6-foot-6 and 200 pounds, with steely blue eyes and a loud voice. Yet he had a playful nature inside, although he wasn't a clown as many portrayed him. He had an inquisitive mind and a drive to succeed, a desire for achievement, whether in sports or the performing arts. Unfortunately, by 1949, Connors had acquired a bigger reputation as a comedian than as a ballplayer. He was the hit of the Dodgers Follies at the Vero Beach, Florida, spring training camp in March 1949.[16] He even got his picture in *The Sporting News* reciting "Casey at the Bat."[17] One writer remarked that "Kevin (Chuck) Connors, latest entry in Brooklyn's first base derby, is a ballplayer by occupation, a dramatic actor by instinct and a screwball by popular demand."[18] Connors even handed out calling cards that advertised his availability for "Recitations, After-Dinner Speaker, Home Recordings for any Occasion, Free Lance Writing."[19] In his book *Tales from the Dodger Dugout*, Carl Erskine tells a great story about how Connors entertained his Dodger teammates:

> Chuck Connors used to do card tricks in the big lobby. One trick he did required the help of an accomplice. Chuck would send Toby Atwell down the road to a phone booth. Toby would sit in the booth with a flashlight and read a paperback Western and wait. In the lobby, Connors would entice a few bets that he could have someone draw a card from the deck and then call the Swami, who would identify the card. The ten of hearts is drawn; everybody in the room sees it. Connors then dials the number of the phone booth. Toby answers on the first ring and immediately begins to name the suits, "spades, hearts ..." Connors interrupts when he hears "hearts" by saying "Hello, Swami." Toby then rapidly names the cards, "king, queen, jack, ten ..." Connors again interrupts on the "ten" and hands the phone to one of the bettors. In a monotone, Toby says, "This is the Swami. Your card is the ten of hearts," and hangs up. Connors picks up the money.[20]

After making a good impression with his bat rather than his mouth with the Dodgers' B squad during spring training in 1949, Connors got a shot at the Brooklyn first base job when he was elevated to the A squad for the April 7 exhibition game in Macon, Georgia. When Connors went 1-for-5 in that game, manager Burt Shotton penciled him into the lineup for the April 8 game in Atlanta. However, in a pregame fielding drill, Connors was hit in the mouth by a ball thrown by Bruce Edwards and was taken to a local hospital. He needed five stitches to close the wound, which swelled his upper lip to twice its size. That bad break cost Connors his major-league opportunity. After missing two exhibition games, he returned for the April 10 game, but went 0-for-3. His bad breaks continued when the next three games were rained out. In the April 14 game in Washington, D.C., Connors went 0-for-4. Worse, he had the crowd in stitches. "The fans laughed themselves silly over the performance of this bush league first baseman who seemed to be doing a takeoff on the old college try," one writer wrote. "Later Chuck said he hadn't tried to be funny, that he'd been hustling for keeps hoping to make an impression on Shotton."[21]

Shotton wasn't amused. For the three-game city series with the New York Yankees, he inserted Gil

Hodges back into the lineup at first base. Hodges proceeded to win the first base job and was in the opening day lineup at Ebbets Field on April 19. However, the day before, the Dodgers announced that they had acquired Connors from their Montreal farm club to back up Hodges. "The Mighty Kevin recited his version of 'Casey at the Bat' last night with new gusto at the Knothole Club dinner," the *Brooklyn Eagle* commented, "but he has no intention of playing Casey on the ball field." The *Eagle* added, though, that "Connors doubtless will wear out the seat of his breeches squirming around on the bench."[22]

Although Connors had made the Brooklyn team, Shotton kept him on the bench as Hodges played every day at first base. It wasn't until May 1 that Connors got an opportunity to play. With the Dodgers losing 4–2 to the Phillies in the bottom of the ninth inning, Shotton had Connors pinch-hit for Carl Furillo with one out and a runner on first base. Connors, the potential tying run, faced Russ Meyer, who was pitching for the Phillies. "I knew I was going to get a hit and win the game. I mean I was squeezing the bat so hard that sawdust started running down the handle," Connors recalled his big moment on the major-league stage. "On the next pitch Meyer threw me a belt-high fastball on the outside corner, I creamed it! I hit a one hop back to the mound and he turned it into a double play. I still see that pitch in my dreams. It's as big as a zeppelin. If I had waited on it a little longer, I might still be playing."[23] After the game when Shotton was asked why he used Connors as a pinch-hitter, he responded, with a sigh, "To reduce the possibilities of a double play."[24]

That was the extent of Connors' career with the Brooklyn Dodgers: two pitches, one swing, and 0-for-1 in the box score. Connors actually got one more opportunity in a Brooklyn uniform. On May 2, in an exhibition game at West Point against the Army varsity baseball team, Connors played first base and went 2-for-5 at the plate. However, his performance in the exhibition game didn't matter. He was soon ticketed back to Montreal for the remainder of the 1949 season, where he batted a hefty .319 with 20 home runs and 108 RBIs to lead Montreal to the International League pennant. Back in Brooklyn, Hodges had a 19-game hitting streak in May to solidify his hold on first base, as the Dodgers marched to the 1949 National League pennant.

He played one more year at Montreal in 1950, a solid but unspectacular season in which he compiled a .290 batting average but with just six homers and 68 RBIs. Connors knew he was going nowhere in the Brooklyn organization with Hodges now a fixture at first base, so he lobbied Dodgers president Branch Rickey to trade him. On October 10, 1950, Brooklyn announced that Connors had been traded to the Chicago Cubs along with Dee Fondy, another first baseman who had played with Fort Worth of the Texas League in 1950, for Hank Edwards and cash. When Chicago manager Frank Frisch installed Fondy as his first baseman during spring training in 1951, Connors was assigned to the Cubs top farm club, the Los Angeles Angels of the Pacific Coast League. Not making the Chicago Cubs turned out to be the best thing that ever happened to Connors. "Now who goes to the games in LA? Producers, directors, writers, casting directors," Connors recalled. "I became a kind of favorite of the show business people, unbeknownst to myself."[25]

In Los Angeles, Connors thrived playing for the Angels. During the first half of the 1951 season, he compiled a .321 batting average in 98 games, with 22 home runs and 77 RBIs. By early July, Connors got the call to join the Chicago Cubs, switching places with Fondy, who was farmed out to the Angels. Connors was unspectacular in his half-season with the Cubs, though, hitting a weak .239 in 66 games with just two homers and 18 RBIs. He played fairly well for Frisch. But when Frisch was fired and replaced by Phil Cavaretta, a player-manager who was also a first baseman, Connors's stock plummeted with the Cubs. Chicago finished in last place for the 1951 season and returned Connors to the Los Angeles Angels right after the season ended. Fondy became the Cubs' regular first baseman for the next five years.

In September 1951, Connors received a phone call that changed his life. Bill Grady, the casting director for Metro-Goldwyn-Mayer, was a passionate fan of the Los Angeles Angels and asked Connors to test for a small role in the movie *Pat and Mike*, a film starring Spencer Tracy and Katharine Hepburn. Connors got the five-minute part as the police captain and was paid $500 for just a few hours of work. Connors had found his post-baseball career. "I said right then, this is my racket," Connors remembered. "Playing with Tracy and Hepburn, I was in the big leagues much faster than I arrived there in baseball."[26]

Connors felt so strongly about his potential as an actor that in November 1951 he filed for an exemption to the major-league draft. "I'm more than satisfied to stay put in Los Angeles," Connors said at the time. "The Coast League is one of the best leagues in baseball and the living and playing conditions are superior."[27] While this was a legitimate move for Connors to secure his future, it all but sealed his fate as a minor-league baseball player who would never return to the major leagues.

He played the 1952 season with the Los Angeles Angels, where he is best remembered for his showboating than his playing ability. For example, after hitting one home run, he slid into second base, cartwheeled to third base, then crawled to home plate. These antics added to his "screwball" reputation, where at various times in his minor-league career he threw raw hamburger to rowdy fans at a road game and taunted umpires with Shakespearean quotes. Connors had his mind on his future in acting: "When you're playing professional sports, you're in show business, too. You're out there to please the crowd and a little showmanship doesn't hurt."[28]

After the 1952 baseball season concluded, Connors had roles in several more movies, including *Trouble Along the Way* and *South Sea Woman*. "I made $12,000 that offseason," Connors avidly remembered about being a budding movie actor and his baseball salary being less than half that amount, "so I never reported to the Chicago Cubs for 1953."[29] In February 1953, Connors retired from baseball to focus on acting, which he felt was the "proper step" for his family in light of his belief that his baseball career had "reached the twilight stage."[30]

For the next five years, Connors made regular guest appearances on television shows such as *Gunsmoke* and *Superman*, had supporting roles in a dozen movies, and starred in *Walk the Dark Street* and *Tomahawk Trail*. His big break came when he was cast in the role of Burn Sanderson, owner of the dog in the title role of the 1957 film *Old Yeller*. Connors portrayed a grizzled but sensitive man who gave the dog to the Coates family in the movie.

While he had a reputation as a "zany" ballplayer, Connors was no buffoon as an actor. He asked questions and picked people's brains to learn the show business. He took horseback riding lessons and learned to shoot a gun, to do his own stunts without need for a stuntman. He became renowned as a sharp businessman in the entertainment industry. "The day I left baseball, I became smart," Connors said. "When I was in baseball, I played for the love of the game. I'd sign any contract they gave me. But then I stopped playing and began doing interviews with the players at the ball park. I began to see the light."[31] Of course, Connors had observed one of the masters of baseball negotiation, Branch Rickey. Connors was famous for remarking: "It was easy to figure out Mr. Rickey's thinking about contracts. He had players and money—and just didn't like to see the two of them mix."[32]

His work blending external toughness with internal soft-heartedness in the movie *Old Yeller* led to his landing the role of Lucas McCain in the television series *The Rifleman*. The TV series ran for five years, from 1958 to 1963, and was very lucrative for Connors, who negotiated to receive a share of the show's profits. McCain was a single father who lived on a ranch in North Fork, New Mexico, in the late 1870s. He raised his son Mark (played by Johnny Crawford) with moral lessons, not brute force, while protecting the area from the dangers of the Wild West with his Winchester rifle. The tender relationship between father and son in a violent world was the successful formula of *The Rifleman*.

"Lucas was a righteous character, despite the violence," Connors explained. "We had the benefit of the father-son relationship, so I could have a little scene at the end of the show where I would explain to Mark, essentially, that sometimes violence is necessary, but it isn't good." When Mark would often say that Lucas had "won," Connors would disabuse him of that attitude. "Wait a minute, son," he would say. "You never win when you kill someone. It demeans you. It takes something away. People have got to learn to do away with violence and guns, and to love each other."[33] Connors had great admiration for that role: "I have a lot of pride in *The Rifleman*, because it was a great part, to play a good father, a strong man who believes in right and wrong."[34]

Westerns were hot in television in the late 1950s. In March 1959, eight of the top ten TV shows were westerns, including *The Rifleman* ranked at number six. Connors was associated with a group of elite star actors such as James Arness (*Gunsmoke*), Hugh O'Brian (*Wyatt Earp*), James Garner (*Maverick*), and Richard Boone (*Have Gun, Will Travel*). Baseball skills came in handy to get the part as Lucas McCain, as *Time* magazine noted: "When he walked in to try out for Rifleman, the director suddenly pitched a rifle at him. Chuck fielded it neatly, got the job."[35]

Ironically, as Connors became a star actor in Los Angeles during the late 1950s, the Dodgers relocated from Brooklyn to Los Angeles. Connors was often seen as a spectator at Dodger Stadium during the 1960s, talking to the likes of Sandy Koufax and Don Drysdale. Connors was even an intermediary in their contract talks following the 1965 baseball season, a negotiation that author Jeff Katz called a "significant convergence of baseball and show business" since the two pitchers staged a holdout using a movie contract as leverage.[36] Connors convinced Koufax and Drysdale to end their movie dreams and Dodgers management to offer each pitcher a contract worth more than $100,000 a season, then the benchmark salary for baseball's most exceptional ballplayers.

During the 1950s, Connors and his wife Elizabeth raised their four sons Michael, Jeffrey, Stephen, and Kevin in a house in Woodland Hills, California. He later moved to a ranch in Tehachapi, California, about two and a half hours north of Los Angeles. Following his divorce from Elizabeth, Connors married Kamala Devi in 1963, whom he met on the set of the movie *Geronimo*, where Connors portrayed the famous Apache warrior. After they later divorced, Connors married Faith Quabius in 1977, but this third marriage lasted just a few years. When asked about the possibility of marrying a fourth time, Connors often evoked an age-old baseball quip, "No, three strikes and you're out."[37]

The Rifleman lasted five seasons, but by the end of the 1962–63 season the TV western had run its course as popular shows among viewers. After starring in three more short-lived TV series (*Arrest and Trial*, *Branded*, and *Cowboy in Africa*), Connors returned to movies in the late 1960s with roles in spaghetti westerns, a genre made famous by Clint Eastwood with action-packed western thrillers. Connors appeared in several spaghetti westerns, including *The Proud and Damned* and *Kill Them All and Come Back Alone*.

After he turned age 50 in 1971, Connors was rarely cast as a leading man, so he gravitated to villain roles that he had successfully played back in the 1950s. "Chuck would be a tremendous villain the rest of his career," biographer Fury wrote, "because a man who was six and a half feet tall and capable of sheer menace in his eyes and demeanor, was truly a formidable and fearsome sight."[38] Christopher Sharrett, the author of the book *The Rifleman*, wrote: "Connors intended to parlay his threatening physique and face—with its ever-lengthening, lantern jaw—into recognition as the 'new Boris Karloff,' a status that never truly materialized."[39] Connors did attain modest acclaim as a screen villain in *The Mad Bomber*, *Soylent Green*, and *Tourist Trap*.

Connors was active in Republican politics in the 1960s and 1970s. He was a strong supporter of fellow Californian Richard Nixon, who was elected President in 1968, and fellow-actor Ronald Reagan, who was elected governor of California in 1966 and later was elected President in 1980. Connors had a celebrated meeting with Soviet leader Leonid Brezhnev in 1973, after meeting him at a party at Nixon's Western White House in San Clemente, California. "Spotting Mr. Connors in a denim shirt at the helicopter pad, Mr. Brezhnev rushed over and threw his arms around the tall rugged star, who hugged back and lifted the laughing Communist party leader off his feet," the *New York Times* reported.[40] The Connors/Brezhnev bear hug was captured by photographers and ran in many newspapers across the nation.

In 1977 Connors played slave-owner Tom Moore in *Roots*, a television mini-series that helped to raise the consciousness of America about the impact of slavery and racism. This villain role was the most challenging of his career, because the despicable Moore was so evil and racist. As biographer Fury wrote: "Connors was so convincing in his portrayal that he received hate mail for his fictional acts in the story, including Moore's rape of Kizzy, the young black woman portrayed by Leslie Uggams."[41] Following his critically acclaimed performance in *Roots*, Connors continued acting for another 15 years, with his most prominent films being *Airplane II* and *Salmonberries*.

In July 1984, he received a star on Hollywood Boulevard's celebrated Walk of Fame. Following the ceremony, the Los Angeles Dodgers hosted a party at Dodger Stadium to honor Connors, which Connors felt "was a bigger thrill than getting the star," given that he had just one lone at-bat during his brief baseball career with the Brooklyn Dodgers 35 years earlier.[42]

Connors died in Los Angeles, California, on November 10, 1992. He is buried in San Fernando Mission Cemetery in Mission Hills, California, where his gravestone is adorned by a photo of him as The Rifleman along with the logos of the Dodgers and Cubs baseball teams and the Celtics basketball team.

Despite his fame as an actor, Connors remembered his humble Brooklyn upbringing and remained grounded as a person. "I couldn't have all this as a ball player," he mused in a 1966 interview as he gazed at the view of the San Fernando Valley from his home. "But maybe baseball is a purer, healthier way for a guy to make a living."[43] He also maintained his sense of humor. While he always contended that he'd rather have been Gil Hodges than The Rifleman, Connors kept his feelings about that light-hearted. In the late 1950s when an interviewer said to him that "but for Gil Hodges, you might be playing for the Dodgers," Connors interrupted him by joking, "Shhhh! He'd be the Rifleman!"[44]

NOTES

1 "Chuck Connors Swaps Glove for Greasepaint, Acting Career," *Los Angeles Times*, February 13, 1953: C1.

2 Roscoe McGowen, "Connors, Disappointed Dodger, Proves He Can Play—In Films," *The Sporting News*, December 15, 1954: 22.

3 Cynthia Wilbur, "Chuck Connors," *For the Love of the Game: Baseball Memories from the Men Who Were There* (New York: William Morrow and Company, 1992), 48.

4 John Ross, "Kevin Connors Flock Farmhand," *Brooklyn Eagle*, June 18, 1940: 14.

5 David Fury, "*Chuck Connors: The Man Behind the Rifle*" (Minneapolis: Artist's Press, 1997), 36.

6 "Kevin Connors, College Star, Joins Fraser Club," *Lynn Evening Item*, June 6, 1942.

7 Fury, *Chuck Connors*, 20.

8 George Sullivan, "Kevin (Chuck) Connors," *The Picture History of the Boston Celtics* (Indianapolis: Bobbs-Merrill, 1982), 154–155.

9 "Lions, Bushwicks, Gamble Win Skeins in Game Tonight," *Brooklyn Eagle*, July 25, 1945: 15.

10 Harold Burr, "Revival of Vaudeville in Chuck Connors' Hands," *Brooklyn Eagle*, March 27, 1949: 31.

11 Mordaunt Hall, "Wallace Beery as Chuck Connors and George Raft as Steve Brodie in a New Film, 'The Bowery,'" *New York Times*, October 5, 1933: 24.

12 Sullivan, *History of the Boston Celtics*, 152–153.

13 Sullivan, *History of the Boston Celtics*, 153.

14 Ted Brock, "Multi-Sport Stars: Men for Two (or Three) Seasons," *Total Basketball: The Ultimate Basketball Encyclopedia* (Toronto: Sport Media Publishing, 2003), 339.

15 Sullivan, *History of the Boston Celtics*, 154.

16 "Dodgers Move from Diamond to Stage in Vero Beach Verities," *The Sporting News*, March 30, 1949: 22.

17 Tom Meany, "Connors Wins Laughs … Now Aims for Cheers," *The Sporting News*, May 4, 1949: 5.

18 United Press, "Bums' Rookie Connors Is Actor, Orator," *Hartford Courant*, April 12, 1949: 16.

19 Bill Roeder, "Mr. Connors a Funny Man—By His Own Admission," *The Sporting News*, October 25, 1950: 2.

20 Carl Erskine, *Tales from the Dodger Dugout* (New York: Sports Publishing, 2003), 209.

21 Roeder, "Mr. Connors a Funny Man."
22 Harold Burr, "Dodgers Take on Connors for First Base Insurance," *Brooklyn Eagle*, April 19, 1949: 17.
23 Fury, *Chuck Connors*, 48.
24 Tommy Holmes, "Dodgers, Below .500 Mark, Off to Disappointing Start in Race," *Brooklyn Eagle*, May 2, 1949: 13.
25 Wilbur, *For the Love of the Game*, 51.
26 Bob Hunter, "Connors Chucked Bat for TV Riches," *The Sporting News*, October 8, 1966: 32.
27 Associated Press, "Connors, Angels' First Baseman, First Player to Oppose Draft," *New York Times*, November 19, 1951: 41.
28 Sullivan, *History of the Boston Celtics*, 154.
29 Lynn Parrott, "The Chuck Connors Story—Ham to Star," *The Sporting News*, January 9, 1959: 3.
30 "Chuck Connors Swaps Glove for Greasepaint, Acting Career."
31 Murray Schumach, "Rifleman, Lawman," *New York Times*, September 15, 1963: 143.
32 Joe Garagiola, *Baseball Is a Funny Game* (Philadelphia: Lippincott, 1960), 148.
33 Fury, *Chuck Connors*, 136.
34 Fury, *Chuck Connors*, 294.
35 "The Six-Gun Galahad," *Time*, March 30, 1959: 60.
36 Jeff Katz, "Everybody's a Star: The Dodgers Go Hollywood," *The National Pastime*, 2011: 75.
37 Fury, *Chuck Connors*, 311.
38 Fury, *Chuck Connors*, 206.
39 Christopher Sharrett, *The Rifleman* (Detroit: Wayne State University Press, 2005), 99.
40 John Herbers, "Brezhnev Leaves West on a Note of Informality," *New York Times*, June 25, 1973: 1A.
41 Fury, *Chuck Connors*, 231.
42 Fury, *Chuck Connors*, 253.
43 Hunter, "Connors Chucked Bat for TV Riches."
44 Tony Salin, "Now Batting for Furillo, the Rifleman," *Baseball's Forgotten Heroes: One Fan's Search for the Game's Most Interesting Overlooked Players* (Chicago: Masters Press, 1999), 16.

RON DARLING

BY AUDREY APFEL

IF YOU WERE LUCKY ENOUGH TO bring Ron Darling to a party, how would you introduce him? Especially if the party was outside the New York City area, it's possible you would have to do just that. While he has numerous accomplishments on and off the baseball field, he hasn't grabbed the headlines (for all sorts of reasons good and bad) like other members of the 1986 Mets, Dwight Gooden, Darryl Strawberry, etc. So, what would you say? All-Star? Gold Glove recipient? World Series ring holder? Ivy League All American with the longest no-hitter in NCAA history? Emmy award winner? All would be true and might leave your friends wondering why they wouldn't have known all of this before.

At every point along the way, there seemed to be just a few things burning brighter in Ron Darling's vicinity, something that stole some of the spotlight. Perhaps in '86 (and after) it was all the attention paid to the other members of that famous (or sometimes infamous) team. Or that though he started the seventh game in the '86 World Series, more people remember the Bill Buckner blunder in Game Six. Or that the longest college no-hitter actually ended up in a loss for the Yale Bulldogs, Darling's team. Or perhaps it is just that there is little in the way of "negative press" that might have made even bigger headlines.

In total though, it all adds up to the solid, successful multifaceted career of someone who left a positive mark wherever he went. His life before and after baseball has had highs and lows but his achievement continued with a level of consistency most pitchers would love when standing on the mound. The best introduction might just be, "This is Ron Darling. Have a chat with him. He's smart, accomplished, and has some great stories to tell."

Ronald Maurice Darling Jr. was born on August 19, 1960, in Honolulu but grew up in Red Sox country—Millbury, Massachusetts. His mother was Hawaiian-Chinese, while his father was French Canadian, leading Darling to be fluent in Chinese and French as well as his native English.[1] When asked what the best 10 years of his life were, he said, "Right now I think from 10 to 20 were my favorite years. I had an idyllic family life, great parents, three younger brothers who adored me, thought I was the cat's meow. Went to an amazing high school. Went to Yale between those years. Played in the Cape Cod League, which was the last time I had fun. Now we use that term loosely. The last time I had fun playing the sport, you know, because it was before I was a professional. Yeah, 10 to 20 was amazing, because it got real serious after that."[2]

While Darling called his stretch in the Cape Cod League the last time he had fun in baseball, the league is serious business for major-league prospects. Part of the fun may have been due to the many roles he got to play. His major-league career as a starting pitcher overshadows the versatility he displayed throughout his years in the Cape Cod League. As an example, in the league's all-star game at Yankee Stadium, he played left field but jumped in to pitch and retire the final two batters in a one-run game. It is also worth mentioning that he came close to hitting for the cycle in this game, missing only a triple.[3] In 2002 Darling was inducted into the Cape Cod Baseball League Hall of Fame along with 11 others, including Nomar Garciaparra, Jason Varitek, and Buck Showalter. At the time, he was considered "one of the best-all around players in Cape league history." His league statistics include a .336 batting average, six home runs, and a 4-3 pitching record.[4]

Darling attended Yale University from 1979 to 1981, leaving after his junior year for professional baseball. He majored in French and Southeast Asian history. Upon entering Yale, his plan was to play both football and baseball. Once there, though, he focused on baseball, not for lack of love of the sport. A Yale sports department publication quoted him as saying, "If there were five or six regrets in my life, one is that I didn't continue to play football at Yale. I would've loved to play for Carm [referring to legendary Yale football coach Carmen Cozza]."[5]

At Yale Darling was a strong hitter (usually hitting second or third in the lineup) and a top pitcher. He was the Yale pitcher on the mound for an NCAA regional tournament game against St. John's in 1981, called by some the "greatest college baseball game ever played." Darling was up against opposing pitcher Frank Viola, who later became a fellow Met and a very good friend. For 12 innings the two teams fought until St. John's eked out a 1-0 victory. In a powerful display of pitching prowess, Darling pitched a no-hitter for 11 of those innings and struck out 16. The game ended on a double steal by St. John's.[6]

In 1981, after his junior year at Yale, Darling was drafted by the Texas Rangers in the first round of the amateur draft. That year he pitched for the Rangers' Double-A affiliate, the Tulsa Drillers of the Texas League, where he ended with a 4-2 record as a starting pitcher. Before the 1982 season he was traded to the Mets along with pitcher Walt Terrell for infielder-outfielder Lee Mazzilli, and pitched in 1982 and '83 for the Tidewater Tides. Called up to the Mets in September 1983, he made his major-league debut on September 6, starting and losing to the Philadelphia Phillies, 2-0. Darling gave up one run in 6⅓ innings with six strikeouts and one walk. He started five games for the Mets in September, ending up with a 1-3 record and a 2.80 ERA.

In 1984 Darling won a spot in the starting rotation, but had a mediocre start to the season. In April and May he had a 3-3 record and a 4.61 ERA. But in June and July he won seven straight and finished the season 12-9 and with a 3.81 ERA. He finished fifth in the voting for the Rookie of the Year Award; teammate Dwight Gooden was the winner.

In 1985 Darling shaved almost a run off his earned-run average (2.90) and had a 16-6 record despite giving up a league-leading 114 walks. He was the number-two starter behind Gooden and made the All-Star team that year. He made his first major-league relief appearance in a celebrated 19-inning game against the Atlanta Braves, which the Mets won 16-13. Although the Mets (98-64) did not make the postseason, the strong season and Darling's continuing improvement left them positioned well for the future.

The next year the Mets won the World Series over the Boston Red Sox with Darling as a key contributor. After posting a 15-6 record and a 2.81 ERA, he started World Series Games One, Four, and Seven, losing Game One, winning Game Four, and getting a no-decision in Game Seven. He posted a 1.53 ERA.

The years after the 1986 World Series were tough ones for the Mets and for Darling, described as "the dynasty that never happened." While the team remained competitive for a few more years, the decline was clear. Darling continued to pitch solidly in 1987 with a 12-8 record but a 4.29 ERA. His highest career win total came in 1988 when he recorded a 17-9 record with a 3.25 ERA in 240 innings, another career high. Darling followed up in 1989 with a .500 record (14-14) and 3.52 ERA.

The 1990 season saw the Mets in transition, coming off a lackluster 1989 and management uncertainty. Darling found himself split between starting and a new role as a relief pitcher. The bullpen did not serve him well, and 1990 went down as Darling's first losing season (7-9) with a bloated 4.50 ERA.

In 1991 Darling was again a starting pitcher; in fact, he started games for three teams. On July 15 he was traded along with pitcher Mike Thomas to the Montreal Expos for pitcher Tim Burke. Two weeks later, at the trading deadline, the Expos sent him to the Oakland Athletics for minor-league pitchers Matt Grott and Russ Cormier. With all the moving, Darling was 5-8 in the NL and 3-7 in the American league.

Darling had some success as a starter in Oakland, particularly in 1992, going 15-10. With his best stuff behind him, he made the adjustments that all major-league pitchers with long careers need to make. The A's led the AL West Division that season.

(Darling lost his only start in the ALCS as the Athletics fell to Toronto.)

Darling found the A's welcoming and family-friendly.[7] The good times in Oakland may have just added to the somewhat disheartening way that his playing career ended. On August 19, 1995, which also happened to be his 35th birthday, he was released; he chose to be released rather than be placed on the disabled list, which would have allowed him to remain with the team for the rest of the season. (He later admitted that he wasn't prepared for the ending when it finally came, still believing he could fight his way back to a semblance of his prior performance. However that was not to be.[8])

Darling won 136 major-league games and lost 116. His career ERA was 3.87. His performance on the mound could never be called flawless. There were times when he struggled with control (leading the National League in walks in 1985 was an example) but his "stuff" could be counted on to keep enough batters from putting together enough hits that runs would generally still be hard to come by. He also contributed through effective fielding, which earned him a Gold Glove in 1989. Darling was always a game-smart pitcher who was always ready to take the ball, and said he as proud of having a career that never included a trip to the disabled list.

For Darling, the 1986 Mets season and World Series win were important moments, but were just one stop in his multifaceted career of highs, lows, and reinvention. "I'm not always great at things, but I'm smart," he told the *New York Daily News*.[9]

His post-baseball life has been active and never too far from the sport. He moved into broadcasting and was involved with various sportscasts and shows for several years. In 2005 Darling was the color commentator for the first Washington Nationals season. In 2006 he joined Gary Cohen and Keith Hernandez in the broadcast booth for Mets games on the SNY network, and has won an Emmy award. As of 2017 he continued in the role of commentator/analyst.

In between the baseball, there was family, philanthropy, and writing a book. Darling and Antoinette Reilly, a model, were married in January 1986. They had two sons, Jordan and Tyler. They later divorced and in 2004 Darling married Joanna Last, a TV makeup artist.

In 2009 he founded the Ron Darling Foundation to help fund diabetes research (which his son Jordan contracted as an 11-year-old). The foundation later expanded its work to include collaborating with and donating to several organizations including Habitat for Humanity, the NYPD Foundation and Hurricane Sandy Relief.[10]

In 2009 Darling published a book, *The Complete Game: Reflections on Baseball and the Art of Pitching*, in which he gave a detailed view of what is going on inside the head of a major-league pitcher—inning by inning, pitch by pitch. He combined moments from his own games with the Mets and the Athletics as well as key innings he witnessed as a broadcaster.

*Ron Darling parlayed his charm into a post-big league career as a baseball broadcaster; he also occasionally has appeared onscreen (*Shallow Hal, The Day After Tomorrow, Mr 3000*).*

With his current days full as a New York Mets broadcaster, active philanthropist, father, and husband it seems his spectacular baseball career is certainly not Ron Darling's whole story, but just an important chapter among many.

SOURCES

In addition to the sources cited in the Notes, the author consulted the following:

Darling, Ron. *The Complete Game: Reflections on Baseball and the Art of Pitching* (New York: Random House, 2009).

newyork.mets.mlb.com/team/broadcasters.jsp?c_id=nym.

"The Web of the Game," *The New Yorker*, July 20, 1981.

All stats come from: baseball-reference.com.

NOTES

1. diabetesresearch.org/Ron-Darling-bio.
2. blogs.villagevoice.com/runninscared/2010/06/ron_darling_on.php?page=2.
3. capecodbaseball.org/about/welcome/#sthash.DPgtxjXY.dpuf.
4. capecodbaseball.org/news/league/?article_id=241.
5. yalebulldogs.com/sports/m-basebl/2014-15/releases/20150227l8rndr).
6. nytimes.com/2012/06/09/sports/baseball/darling-viola-pitchers-duel-lives-on-in-st-johns-baseball-lore.html?_r=1.
7. nytimes.com/1992/10/10/sports/sports-of-the-times-darling-s-chess-comeback.html).
8. deadspin.com/5912078/how-a-career-ends-ron-darling-celebrated-his-35th-birthday-by-getting-cut-and-being-left-alone-at-home.
9. nydailynews.com/blogs/bitterbill/ron-darling-talks-mets-sny-blog-entry-1.2168993.
10. rondarlingfoundation.org/.

JOE DIMAGGIO

BY LAWRENCE BALDASSARO

"Baseball isn't statistics; it's Joe DiMaggio rounding second."
— attributed to Jimmy Breslin by Herb Caen, *San Francisco Chronicle*, June 3, 1975.

JOE DIMAGGIO WAS ONE OF the most recognizable and popular men in mid-twentieth century America. He was celebrated in song and literature as an iconic hero, and he was married, briefly, to the nation's number one glamour girl. On March 16, 1999, the House of Representatives passed a resolution honoring him "for his storied baseball career; for his many contributions to the nation throughout his lifetime; and for transcending baseball and becoming a symbol for the ages of talent, commitment and achievement."[1]

But first and foremost Joe DiMaggio was a ballplayer. Known as the Yankee Clipper, he was the undisputed leader of New York Yankees teams that won nine World Series titles in his 13-year career that ran from 1936 to 1951, with three years lost to duty in World War II. He was three times the American League's Most Valuable Player and he holds what many consider to be the most remarkable baseball record of all, a 56-game hitting streak in 1941. As the son of immigrants, he was the embodiment of the American Dream, a rags-to-riches story played out in pinstripes.

Joseph Paul DiMaggio was born Giuseppe Paolo DiMaggio on November 25, 1914, in Martinez, California, 25 miles northeast of San Francisco. His parents, Giuseppe and Rosalia (Mercurio) DiMaggio, had settled there after emigrating from Sicily. After Joe was born they moved the family to San Francisco, where Giuseppe continued to work as a fisherman. Joe was the eighth of their nine children, one of five sons. Two of his brothers, Vince and Dominic, would also play in the major leagues.

Unlike two of his older brothers, Joe had no interest in joining his father on the fishing boat. Instead, he played for several amateur and semi-pro teams in baseball-rich San Francisco. It was 19-year-old Vince, who was then playing for the San Francisco Seals of the Pacific Coast League, who got Joe into professional ball. When the Seals found themselves in need of a shortstop near the end of the 1932 season, Vince convinced Seals manager Ike Caveney to give his 17-year-old brother a chance. Joe played in the final three games of the season, and then was signed to a contract in 1933 for $225 a month.

Moved to the outfield because of his erratic arm, DiMaggio hit .340 and set a PCL record by hitting in 61 straight games. In 1934, he hit .341, but a knee injury that sidelined him in August made major-league teams leery of signing him. The Yankees offered to buy his contract for $25,000 and five players, but with the contingency that he remain with the Seals in 1935 to prove he was healthy. DiMaggio made a convincing case by hitting .398, with 34 homers and 154 runs batted in.

In 1936, only two years after the departure of Babe Ruth, the heralded rookie came to spring training facing big expectations. Writing in *The Sporting News* on March 26, Dan Daniel noted, "Yankee fans regard him as the Moses who is to lead their club out of the second-place wilderness...."[2] It didn't take long for the rookie to make his mark. Halfway through the season, when he was hitting around .350 and had started in right field in the All-Star Game, his photo was on the cover of *Time* magazine. For the year he hit .323 with 29 homers and drove in 125 runs.

DiMaggio was the classic five-tool player; in addition to hitting for average and power, he could run, throw, and field. Joe McCarthy, the Yankees manager from 1931 to 1946, called him the best base runner he ever saw. His all-around play led the 1936 Yankees to the first of four straight World Series titles. The

21-year-old sensation had established himself as the successor to Babe Ruth. After the Series, he received a hero's welcome in his home town of San Francisco, where Mayor Angelo Rossi gave him the key to the city.

DiMaggio finished second in the MVP vote in 1937, despite leading the American League in home runs, slugging percentage, runs, and total bases. He won the first of his three MVP Awards in 1939, when he led the league with a career-best .381 average. Following that season, he married 21-year-old Dorothy Arnold, a singer, dancer, and actress he met while filming a bit part in the movie *Manhattan Merry-Go-Round*.

By then the 6-foot-2, 190-pound outfielder was acknowledged as the best player in baseball, but to some his ethnic background was still ripe for stereotypical portrayal. In a cover story in the May 1, 1939 issue of *Life* magazine, Noel Busch identified DiMaggio as a "tall, thin Italian youth equipped with slick black hair" and "squirrel teeth." But the young ballplayer apparently confounded Busch's general perception of Italian Americans. "Although he learned Italian first, Joe, now twenty-four, speaks English without an accent and is otherwise well adapted to most U.S. mores. Instead of olive oil or smelly bear grease he keeps his hair slick with water. He never reeks of garlic and prefers chicken chow mein to spaghetti."[3]

After winning a second consecutive batting title in 1940, DiMaggio reached a new level of fame in 1941. He set one of the most enduring records in sports by hitting in 56 consecutive games. On May 15, the day the streak began, the Yankees were in fourth place, and DiMaggio had batted a lowly .194 over the previous 20 games. On June 17, DiMaggio broke the Yankee hitting-streak record of 29 games, set by Roger Peckinpaugh in 1919 and equaled by Earle Combs in 1931.

As DiMaggio's streak continued to grow it gradually became a national obsession. Day after day, across the country, the question was: "Did he get one today?" In its July 14 issue, *Time* magazine wrote: "Ever since it became apparent that the big Italian from San Francisco's Fisherman's Wharf was approaching a record that had eluded Ty Cobb, Babe Ruth, Lou Gehrig and other great batsmen, Big Joe's hits have been the biggest news in U.S. sport. Radio programs were interrupted for DiMaggio bulletins."[4]

On June 29, in the seventh inning of the second game of a doubleheader in Washington, DiMaggio hit a single to pass George Sisler's 41-game streak set in 1922, commonly referred to as the "modern record" to distinguish it from Wee Willie Keeler's 44-game streak, the "all-time record" set in 1897. The *New York Times* reported on June 30 that the fans "roared thunderous acclaim" to "one of the greatest players baseball has ever known," while his teammates 'to a man,' were as excited as schoolboys over the feat."[5] On July 2, DiMaggio broke Keeler's record with a fifth-inning home run off Red Sox pitcher Dick Newsome.

Fifteen days later, on July 17, the streak ended in Cleveland's Municipal Stadium in front of 67,468 fans—at that time the largest crowd ever to see a night game—when Indians third baseman Ken Keltner robbed DiMaggio of hits with two spectacular plays. Over the course of the streak the Yankees moved from fourth place, 5 1/2 games back, to first, seven games ahead of Cleveland. DiMaggio went on to hit safely in his next 16 games, and the Yankees went on to win the pennant and then beat the Brooklyn Dodgers in the World Series.

One of the fascinating sidelights of the streak is that in his 223 times at bat, DiMaggio struck out only five times. In fact, he struck out only 13 times in the entire season. The late Harvard paleontologist and essayist Stephen Jay Gould, noting the streak, called it "the most extraordinary thing that ever happened in American sports."[6]

DiMaggio batted .357 for the 1941 season and led the league in runs batted in and total bases. He won his second MVP Award, receiving 15 first-place votes, while Ted Williams, who hit .406 and led the league in home runs, slugging percentage, on-base percentage, and runs, received eight.

DiMaggio batted just .305 in 1942, the lowest average of his seven years in the majors, and he also compiled the lowest number of home runs and runs batted in. The Yankees won the pennant, but they lost the World Series to the Cardinals, marking the team's only loss in 10 trips to the Series during DiMaggio's career.

On February 17, 1943, DiMaggio enlisted in the Army Air Force. Like many other major leaguers, he never saw combat, serving instead in a morale-boosting role by playing on service baseball squads. In June 1944 he was sent to Hawaii, where he continued to play ball but also spent several weeks in a Honolulu hospital suffering from stomach ulcers. After being sent back to the mainland, he was granted a medical discharge in September 1945. In the meantime, his wife had been granted a divorce and custody of their son, Joe, Jr.

DiMaggio's first season following the war was a disappointment for the thirty-one-year-old returning veteran, dubbed "America's No. 1 athletic hero" by the *New York Daily News*.[7] While his slugging percentage was fourth-best in the AL, his batting average (.290) and RBIs (95) were lower than in any previous season, and his home run total (25) the second lowest. As the 1947 season neared, the outlook for improvement was not good. The first news about DiMaggio that year was the announcement of his upcoming surgery to remove a bone spur from his left heel. On January 7, a three-inch spur was removed. Then, when skin-graft surgery was needed two months later to close the wound from the first operation, John Drebinger of the *New York Times* wrote that DiMaggio "seems to be giving more prominence to the human heel than it has received since the days of Achilles."[8]

Joe DiMaggio socializing, a long way from the ball field; here he is with Ethel Barrymore, legendary actress and celebrated baseball fan.

The injury kept him out of the lineup until April 19, when he appeared as a pinch-hitter. He made his first start the next day, hitting a three-run homer in a 6–2 win over the Athletics, but by the end of April he was hitting a paltry .143. A 4-for-5 performance against the Red Sox on May 25 put him over the .300 mark for the first time. On May 26, before 74,747 fans, the Yankees won their fourth straight over Boston, and fifth straight overall. In the 9–3 win, DiMaggio went 3-for-4 and raised his average to .323. On June 3, in a 3–0 win over the first-place Detroit Tigers, DiMaggio got four hits to raise his average to a league-leading .368. He had hit safely in 16 straight games since May 18, hitting .493 over that stretch.

The Yankees moved into first place on June 15 with a doubleheader sweep of the St. Louis Browns. A 19-game winning streak, between June 29 and July 17, put them 11 1/2 games ahead of Detroit, and they finished the season with a 12-game lead over the Tigers.

By the end of the season, DiMaggio's statistics were again below his pre-war levels. His average had fallen to .315, seventh best in the AL, with 20 home runs (his lowest total to date), and 97 RBIs, third in the league but his second lowest total. Although surpassed in virtually every offensive category by Ted Williams, who won his second Triple Crown, DiMaggio was awarded his third MVP Award on the basis of his all-around play in leading the Yankees to their first pennant since 1943. Receiving eight first-place votes compared to three for the Red Sox slugger, the Yankee Clipper edged his perennial rival by a single point, 202-201.

In the memorable World Series against the Dodgers, DiMaggio hit only .231, but he did hit two home runs, one of which gave the Yanks a 2–1 win in Game Five. In this Series, however, he is best remembered for his reaction to Al Gionfriddo's spectacular catch in Game Six. In the sixth inning, the Yankees, trailing 8–5, put two men on with two out, bringing DiMaggio to the plate as the tying run. Gionfriddo, a seldom-used outfielder, had entered the game that inning as a defensive replacement. The Yankee slugger launched a long drive toward the visitors' bullpen in deep left, but Gionfriddo was able to track it down and make a lunging catch just short of the bullpen before crashing into the waist-high gate near the 415-foot sign. No less memorable than the catch was DiMaggio's reaction. In a rare display of emotion, the famously stoic star kicked at the dirt near second base when he saw that Gionfriddo had caught the ball.

Nineteen forty-eight proved to be DiMaggio's last great season, at least in terms of statistics. Playing in 153 games, in spite of a bone spur in his right heel, he led the league in home runs, RBIs, and total bases, and finished second to Lou Boudreau in the MVP vote. The 1949 season proved to be one of the worst of his career; however, his heroic midseason return from injury helped cement his reputation as an inspirational team leader.

The lingering bone spur injury caused DiMaggio to miss the first 65 games of the '49 season. With the press speculating that the Yankee Clipper might be nearing the end of the road, a sullen DiMaggio isolated himself in his hotel room. Then, in mid-June, the pain suddenly disappeared. Two weeks later he made his debut in a crucial series against the Red Sox at Fenway. In the opener, on June 28, he drove in two runs and scored two in a 5–4 win. The next day he hit two homers and drove in four, then wrapped up his first regular-season series since the previous September with his fourth homer in three games and three RBIs. The sweep put the Yankees eight games ahead of the Red Sox.

Boston bounced back with a late-season surge that gave them a one-game lead over New York with two games at Yankee Stadium remaining. DiMaggio, meanwhile, had been hospitalized in September with pneumonia, but was in the starting lineup when the final series began.

The day of the opener, October 1, was also "Joe DiMaggio Day." Before 69,551 fans, the Yankee Clipper, with his mother and brother Dom by his side, was lauded in several speeches and received what the *New York Times* described as "a small mountain of gifts." At the conclusion of the hour-long ceremony, DiMaggio spoke to the crowd, ending his speech by saying, "I want to thank the good Lord for making me a Yankee."[9]

DiMaggio, described as looking "wan and weak after his recent siege," had told manager Casey Stengel that he hoped to play three innings.[10] Instead, he played the entire game. With the Yankees trailing, 4–0, he doubled in the fourth and scored their first run in the 5–4 win that brought the two teams to a tie with one game left.

In the finale, Vic Raschi held the Sox scoreless through eight innings, but in the ninth two runs scored when DiMaggio's tired legs weren't able to catch up to a drive by Bobby Doerr that went for a triple. Drained of energy and realizing that he was a detriment to his team, DiMaggio ran in from center field, taking himself out of the game. The Yankees held on to win the game, 5–3, and the pennant. Limited to 76 games, he hit .346 with 67 RBIs. The *Associated Press* gave him its award for sports' greatest comeback of 1949, with second place going to the Yankees, a team that had been plagued by injuries for much of the season.

DiMaggio was able to play in 139 games in 1950, hitting .301 with 32 home runs, 122 RBIs, and a league-leading .585 slugging percentage. But age and injury limited him to 116 games in 1951, when he hit only 12 homers and compiled the lowest average of his career at .263. On December 11, 1951, the 36-year-old veteran announced his retirement, saying, "If I can't do it right, I don't want to play any longer."[11]

In the six years he played after the war, DiMaggio remained the leader of a Yankees team that won the World Series in each of his final three seasons. But while he won the MVP Award in 1947, and 1948 was one of his best seasons, overall his postwar performance was not at the same level as it had been before the war. "Baseball wasn't much fun for Joe from 1949 until he quit," said teammate Phil Rizzuto. "He was getting older and he was hurt a lot."[12] His post-war batting average was .304, with an average of 24 home runs per year, compared to .339 and 31 homers per year between 1936 and 1942.

In his career, DiMaggio, hit .325 with 361 home runs, 1,537 RBIs, and for a .579 slugging average. He was an All-Star in each of his 13 seasons and, in addition to winning three MVP Awards, he finished in the top nine seven other times. Perhaps more impressive than any other statistic is the fact that in 6,821 times at bat, he struck out 369 times—only eight more than his total number of home runs—for an average of once every 18.5 times at bat.

Given the relative brevity of his career, DiMaggio's totals don't measure up to those of many other major stars. But he was admired not only for what he did on the field but for how he looked doing it. Columnist Jim Murray wrote: "Joe DiMaggio played the game at least at a couple of levels higher than the rest of baseball. A lot of guys, all you had to see to know they were great was a stat sheet. DiMaggio, you had to see. It wasn't only numbers on a page—although they were there too—it was a question of command, style, grace."[13]

In the eyes of his contemporaries, Joe DiMaggio was universally considered the best player they had ever seen. Even his arch-rival, Ted Williams, said, "I have always felt I was a better hitter than Joe, but I have to say that he was the greatest baseball player of our time. He could do it all."[14] Stan Musial, the often overlooked third member of the great triad of the 1940s and 1950s, said: "There was never a day when I was as good as Joe DiMaggio at his best. Joe was the best, the very best I ever saw."[15] Pulitzer Prize-winning columnist Red Smith called DiMaggio "indisputably the finest ballplayer of his time."[16]

Rico Petrocelli, a New York native who played for the Red Sox between 1965 and 1976, recalled going to Yankee Stadium as a youngster: "We were in the bleachers, and Joe DiMaggio was still playing. I looked around and noticed nobody was watching the pitcher throw the ball. Everyone was looking at DiMaggio. When he'd catch a ball, he'd lope after it. It was just beautiful to watch. I'll never forget it."[17]

An unsigned column in the *Washington Post* on July 2, 1941, the day after DiMaggio surpassed George Sisler's consecutive-game hit streak, placed the Yankee star alongside the other "Olympians" of baseball, such as Cobb, Ruth, and Speaker, and said of his style, "there is something about it, at bat and in the field, that suggests some of the great sculptures of the Italian Renaissance: Donatello's, for example."[18]

In the batter's box, DiMaggio was the picture of understated calm. He stood there motionless, hands and head still, feet wide apart. Only at the last moment, when he whipped the bat around in his trademark long swing, did he unleash the force that he had kept under tight control.

DiMaggio was no less adept at keeping his emotions under tight control, at least in public. DiMaggio embodied *sprezzatura*, the Italian term for the ability to make the difficult look easy. Teammate Jerry Coleman called him "the only professional athlete I've ever seen who had an imperial presence."[19] But DiMaggio's calm exterior masqueraded the inner turmoil that drove him to always be at his best. Whatever emotions he stuffed inside and hid from the paying customers manifest themselves in the ulcers that earned him a discharge from the service in 1945.

DiMaggio understood his role as a public figure and he did his best to live up to his image as the greatest player in the game and the leader of its best team. His grace and style on the field were matched by his appearance off of it. In his elegant tailored suits, he was the model of quiet elegance.

For all that, DiMaggio was an intensely private man who never felt completely comfortable in his role as hero. Before he became a national icon, he bore the additional, and unwanted, burden of being the great hero of Americans of Italian descent. Yankees pitcher Lefty Gomez, a close friend, said, "All the Italians in America adopted him. Just about every day at home and on the road there would be an invitation from some Italian-American club."[20]

For former New York Governor Mario Cuomo, DiMaggio's life "demonstrated to all the strivers and seekers—like me—that America would make a place for true excellence whatever its color or accent or origin."[21] *New York Daily News* columnist Mike Lupica acknowledged DiMaggio's significance for his father and grandfather: "There was only one ballplayer for them, an Italian American ballplayer of such talent and fierce pride it made them fiercely proud, fiercely biased toward their man even after he had left the playing field for good."[22] Hall of Fame manager Tommy Lasorda summed it up this way: "I knew every big leaguer when I was growing up, but Joe DiMaggio was my hero. He was our hero; he was everything we wanted to be."[23]

DiMaggio's appeal to the general public was due, in part, to the stylish way he displayed his all-around ability as a ballplayer. But beyond that his colorless but dependable performance was right for the times. This sober, serious young man who went about his work without bravado or flamboyance was the ideal hero for a nation that was struggling, first to survive the Great Depression and then to win a war. The refrain of "Joe, Joe DiMaggio, we want you on our side," from Les Brown's 1941 hit song was a timely reflection of how the public identified with the young star.

The 1941 hitting streak, followed by his military service in World War II, helped DiMaggio become a national hero whose ethnic background, often noted by the pre-war press, became increasingly irrelevant. His fame and popularity were celebrated in song and literature as he became a touchstone of popular

*Joe DiMaggio, the Yankee Clipper, appeared in one film near the start of his baseball career (*Manhattan Merry-Go-Round*) and one near its end (the original* Angels in the Outfield*).*

culture. In the 1949 Rodgers and Hammerstein musical *South Pacific*, sailors sing of the character named Bloody Mary that "her skin is tender as DiMaggio's glove." Santiago, the indomitable protagonist of Ernest Hemingway's 1952 novella, *The Old Man and the Sea*, says that he must be worthy of his idol, the great DiMaggio. Paul Simon's 1968 hit song, "Mrs. Robinson," expressed nostalgia for a simpler, more innocent time by asking, "Where have you gone, Joe DiMaggio, a nation turns its lonely eyes to you."

Unlike most professional athletes, Joe DiMaggio enjoyed a resurgence of fame and adulation in his post-baseball life. His legend was enhanced when, in January 1954, he once again made headlines by marrying Marilyn Monroe. But the ill-fated union of two of America's most celebrated personalities lasted only nine months. DiMaggio had naively expected the film star to become a devoted housewife. According to Joe's brother, Dom, "Her career was first. Joe could not condone the things that Marilyn had to do. Joe wanted a wife he could raise children with. She could not do that." But DiMaggio, who remained devoted to Monroe, held out hope that they would remarry. "Joe had wanted that relationship to work," said Dom. "He held on to it for the rest of his life."[24] When Monroe died in 1962, Joe took charge of her funeral and ordered that roses be placed at her crypt twice a week.

DiMaggio spent several years in relative obscurity before appearing, incongruously, in the green and white uniform of the Oakland A's, serving as a coach and vice president for Charlie Finley's newly-transplanted franchise in 1968-69. Then, in the 1970s, he re-emerged as a national celebrity when, overcoming the shyness that had inhibited him during his playing days, he became a television spokesman for New York's Bowery Savings Bank and the "Mr. Coffee" coffee maker. For much of his life thereafter, DiMaggio remained in the public eye by carefully orchestrating appearances at celebrity golf outings, card shows and Old-Timers' games, where he was introduced as "baseball's greatest living player," a title bestowed upon him in a 1969 poll. By limiting his personal appearances and rigidly protecting his privacy, he was able to sustain the mystique that made him one of the most admired men in America, even when his career was long over.

On October 12, 1998, DiMaggio was admitted to Regional Memorial Hospital in Hollywood, Florida, where he had been living for many years. (It was the same hospital where the Joe DiMaggio Children's Hospital had been established.) Two days later he underwent surgery for lung cancer and never fully recovered. He died at his home on March 8, 1999, at the age of 84.

One of those rare athletes—like Babe Ruth and Muhammad Ali—who transcended the world of sport, DiMaggio has been called by more than one writer the last American hero. Revisionist historians later offered a more nuanced view, portraying him as a flawed hero who became increasingly reclusive and suspicious of others. Nevertheless, when he died his enduring status as a cultural icon was confirmed by an outpouring of adulation which few public figures, in any walk of life, could evoke. His death was front-page news in every major newspaper, was covered extensively on television newscasts and specials, and was the cover story in *Newsweek* magazine. Referring to the frequent bulletins on DiMaggio's health that had been issued in the months prior to his death, Frank Deford wrote that it was "as if he were some great head of state."[25] As one Brooklyn native put it, DiMaggio "epitomized an era when, for a lot of us, baseball was the most important thing in life."[26]

The answer to Paul Simon's question—Where has Joe DiMaggio gone?—remains the same: Nowhere. He remains firmly lodged in the American consciousness as a stylish symbol of a time when baseball was the undisputed national pastime and America was enjoying unprecedented prosperity. On April 25, 1999, two months after his death, DiMaggio's monument was unveiled in Yankee Stadium's Monument Park, joining those honoring Miller Huggins, Lou Gehrig, Babe Ruth, and Mickey Mantle. The inscription reads, in part, "A Baseball Legend and An American Icon."

SOURCES

In addition to the sources cited in the Notes, the author also consulted:

Baldassaro, Lawrence. *Beyond DiMaggio: Italian Americans in Baseball* (Lincoln: University of Nebraska Press, 2011).

Cramer, Richard Ben. *Joe DiMaggio: The Hero's Life* (New York: Simon and Schuster, 2000).

DiMaggio, Dom, with Bill Gilbert. *Real Grass, Real Heroes: Baseball's Historic 1941 Season*. 1990 (New York: Zebra Books, 1991).

Johnson, Richard A., and Glenn Stout. *DiMaggio: An Illustrated Life* (New York: Walker, 1995).

Kahn, Roger. *The Era: 1947-1957, When the Yankees, the Giants and the Dodgers Ruled the World* (New York: Ticknor & Fields, 1993).

Moore, Jack B. *Joe DiMaggio: Baseball's Yankee Clipper* (New York: Praeger, 1987).

Seidel, Michael. *Streak: Joe DiMaggio and the Summer of '41* (New York: McGraw-Hill, 1988).

NOTES

1. H RES 105 EH, 106th Congress, March 16, 1999.13
2. Dan Daniel, *The Sporting News*, March 26, 1936: 3.
3. Noel Busch, *Life*, May 1, 1939: 62-69.
4. *Time*, July 14, 1941.
5. *New York Times*, June 30, 1941.
6. Stephen L. Gould, "Streak of Streaks," in Nicholas Dawidoff, *Baseball: A Literary Anthology* (New York: Library of America, 2002), 591.
7. *New York Daily News*, April 28, 1946.
8. *New York Times*, February 26, 1947.
9. *New York Times*, October 2, 1949.
10. Ibid.
11. *New York Daily News*, December 12, 1951.
12. Maury Allen, *Where Have You Gone, Joe DiMaggio? The Story of America's Last Hero* (New York: Dutton, 1975), 136.
13. Jim Murray, *Los Angeles Times*, July 7, 1994.
14. Ted Williams, *My Turn at Bat: The Story of My Life* (New York: Pocket Books, 1970), 209-10.
15. Stan Musial, quoted in .www.baseball-almanac.com.
16. *New York Herald Tribune*, August 13, 1950.
17. Rico Petrocelli, interview with author, February 12, 2004.
18. "The Great DiMagg'," *Washington Post*, July 2, 1941.
19. Jerry Coleman, interview with author, September 1, 2005.
20. Maury Allen, *Where Have You Gone, Joe DiMaggio?: The Story of America's Last Hero (*New York: Dutton, 1975). 25.
21. *New York Daily News*, March 9, 1999.
22. Ibid.
23. Tommy Lasorda, interview with author, January 19, 2001.
24. Ibid.
25. Michael Bamberger, "Dom DiMaggio," *Sports Illustrated*, July 2, 2001: 110.
26. cnnsi.com, March 8, 1999; *New York Daily News*, March 9, 1999.

MIKE DONLIN

BY ROB EDELMAN AND MICHAEL BETZOLD

A FLAMBOYANT PLAYBOY and partygoer who dressed impeccably and always had a quip and a handshake for everyone he met, Mike Donlin "may have been the most colorful character in the National League during his playing career.... Prone to late nights after afternoon games, he was a night crawler in the truest sense.... He was cocky and self-assured and, when he wanted to be, also a damn fine ballplayer who appreciated his own worth."[1] For indeed, Mike Donlin could hit as well as anyone in baseball during the Deadball Era. Though he rarely walked, the powerfully built 5-foot-9, 170-pound left-hander was a masterful curveball hitter with power to all fields. His career slugging percentage of .468 compares favorably to better-known contemporary hitters like Honus Wagner (.467) and Sam Crawford (.452), and his .333 lifetime batting average might have earned him a spot in the Hall of Fame had he sustained it over a full career. But Donlin's love of the bottle and frequent stints in vaudeville limited him to the equivalent of only seven full seasons.

Michael Joseph Donlin was born on May 30, 1878, in Peoria, Illinois, and grew up in Erie, Pennsylvania. When he was 8 his parents, railroad conductor John Donlin and his wife, Maggie, were killed in a bridge collapse. Forced to hustle for a living, young Mike worked as a machinist and was often in poor health, with a concave chest due to consumption. At 15 he got a job as a candy seller on a California-bound train. Mike stayed in California, where he ran foot races and played baseball, and the sun helped him grow stronger.

According to San Diego baseball historian Bill Swank, Donlin first played baseball with the newly formed San Diego Mercantiles, a semipro nine.[2] It was reported in his *New York Times* obituary that he later that year "entered professional baseball at Santa Cruz, Calif."[3] At this point, he was primarily a left-handed pitcher who also played some outfield. But his showy personality already was apparent, as was his understanding of the value of publicity. While playing for the Santa Cruz Sandcrabs, Donlin gave a photo of himself to *San Francisco Examiner* artist-sportswriter Hype Igoe, saying: "If you put a picture of me in the paper, I know I'll get a break. I know I'm going to be great."[4] Tom Kelly, later the University of Oregon baseball coach, recalled pitching against Donlin a month after Admiral Dewey's victory in the Battle of Manila Bay. His bat was painted red, white, and blue, and he called it "Dewey"—and Kelly thought the wannabe big leaguer had plenty of confidence and natural ability.

Halfway through the 1899 season, Donlin had appeared in 29 games for Santa Cruz and was batting .402. A correspondent for *The Sporting News* sent clippings about him to editor Joe Flanner in St. Louis, who passed them on to Patsy Tebeau, player-manager of the St. Louis Perfectos (who became the Cardinals the following season)—and the team acquired Donlin for "little more than train fare."[5] However, he learned he was going to the National League while locked up for drunkenness in a Santa Cruz jail. He reported to League Park in St. Louis wearing a medallion with a newspaper photo of himself on his lapel. When the gatekeeper refused him entry, he proclaimed "I am Mike Donlin," and pointed to the clipping.[6]

In his debut, on July 19, 1899, Donlin pitched in relief against Boston. Aware of Tebeau's need for a shortstop, the left-hander volunteered and handled several chances in his first game. "I was swelled on myself at shortstop that first day," he recalled.[7] The next day, in front of a big crowd, Donlin mishandled every chance and made several wild throws. He was moved to first base in the fifth inning and had trouble there, too. After a few days Tebeau put Donlin in the outfield, where he played most of his career despite a continuing reputation for subpar defense. But he batted .323 for St. Louis in 1899 and .326 in 1900, and he would bat over .300 in most of his 12 seasons.

In 1901 Donlin jumped to the American League with the Baltimore Orioles. He soon became friends with his new manager, John McGraw, who admired the young slugger's fiery temperament. One day in Detroit, Baltimore pitcher Harry Howell was ejected for arguing a call and Donlin responded by firing a ball at the umpire's back. Of course, Donlin's prowess at the plate also helped his standing with McGraw. On June 24, 1901, he got six hits in six at-bats: two singles, two doubles, and two triples. Donlin batted .340 in his first season as a full-time regular, and his future seemed unlimited. But in March 1902 he went on a drinking binge in Baltimore, urinated in public, and accosted two chorus girls.[8] He was sentenced to six months in prison and the Orioles released him. Paroled a month early for good behavior, Donlin joined the Cincinnati Reds in August, appearing in only 34 games and batting a career-low .287.

In 1903 Donlin managed to stay out of trouble—and he almost won the NL batting crown, hitting .351 to Honus Wagner's .355. He finished second in runs (110) and triples (18) and third in slugging (.516). The next summer Donlin was hitting .356 when he went on another bender in St. Louis. Cincinnati player-manager Joe Kelley suspended him for 30 days and then traded him to the New York Giants, reuniting him with McGraw.

Upon arriving in New York, Donlin promised to curb his behavior—at least off the baseball diamond. On the field he slashed pitches into the gaps, ran the bases with reckless abandon, argued incessantly with umpires—and became a fan favorite in New York. Because of his strutting walk and red neck, he was dubbed "Turkey." He hated the nickname but had such a following that kids imitated his strut. With his cap at a belligerent angle over one ear, a scar running down his left cheek from a knifing, and an ever-present plug of tobacco in his jaw, he looked the part of a rough, tough deadballer. When the Giants won their first pennant of the Deadball Era in 1904, Donlin was one of the team's offensive stars, with his .329 average (between Cincinnati and New York) second in the NL to Wagner. The following year he was named captain and enjoyed his greatest season, batting a career-high .356, third best in the NL. Donlin led the league with 124 runs and was second with 216 hits. The Giants won the pennant again and Donlin hit .263 in New York's World Series victory.

On April 11, 1906, Donlin married Mabel Hite, a pretty and talented comedian and top stage star. They first met in 1904 while she was on tour down south. "I didn't know anything about baseball and didn't care, and he was the same way about the stage," Hite recalled. "We didn't know we were interested in each other for two years after that, though I read the sporting pages of the newspapers for the first time and he began to scan the theatre notes."[9] The actress and the ballplayer reconnected in early 1906 and were wed two months later. The newspapers reported that marriage had tamed Donlin and loosened his attachment to the bottle. But Turkey Mike did not curb his quick temper. Upon his passing, it was recalled in his *Chicago Tribune* obituary that "In front of the old Knickerbocker hotel one night, as he was entering with his wife, an attorney named Edward N. Danforth brushed past and, Donlin told police, jostled and insulted Mrs. Donlin. The outcome was that Donlin and the attorney engaged in a fist fight

Ballplayer-actor Mike Donlin and Mabel Hite, his actress-wife.

until broken up by the arrival of police summoned by Mrs. Donlin."[10]

Meanwhile, early in the 1906 season, Turkey Mike broke an ankle sliding, finishing his campaign after just 37 games and depriving him forever of his blazing speed. In the spring of 1907 he demanded the same $3,300 he had been paid in 1906, plus a $600 bonus if he stayed sober all year. Owner John Brush declined—and so Donlin held out and eventually went on the vaudeville circuit with his wife, missing the entire season. "It is too bad for him to give up baseball," Hite admitted, "yet it's so pleasant for us to be together. We study our parts together and rehearse at home."[11] And with characteristic confidence, Donlin proclaimed: "I can act. I'll break the hearts of all the gals in the country."[12] Critics generally disagreed. Ward Morehouse, a theater reviewer, newspaper columnist, and playwright of note, pronounced that Turkey Mike "never was the actor he thought he was or wanted to be."[13]

Donlin, however, did return to the Giants for the 1908 season. Huge ovations greeted him at the home opener, with bleacherites yelling, "Oh, you Mabel's Mike!"—a chant that emanated from the stands even when he made a routine play.[14] In the ninth, the Giants were down by a run with two out and a man on second. Donlin worked the pitcher to a full count, then homered into the right-field bleachers to win the game. Thousands of fans mobbed the field, slapping him on his back as he rounded the bases, taking his cap, and ripping the buttons off his shirt—and it was the beginning of another great season for Donlin, who finished second in the NL in batting average (.334), hits (198), RBIs (106), total bases, and slugging percentage. After the season he was awarded the *New York Journal* trophy as New York's most popular player.[15] John Barrymore, one of Donlin's best friends and drinking buddies, performed Hamlet's soliloquy at a dinner in his honor.[16] (Indeed, according to Gene Fowler, Barrymore's biographer and close pal, the legendary actor was "at ease when among [his] friends," and they included everyone from a troupe of dwarfs to Jack Dempsey, Winston Churchill, Albert Einstein—and Mike Donlin. "It pleased him when any of these faces could be seen on his set or in his dressing-room," Fowler noted.)[17]

On October 26, 1908, Hite and Donlin's one-act play, *Stealing Home*, opened at the Hammerstein Theater in New York. "It is a great sketch," proclaimed one reviewer the following year, "and made a tremendous hit with the baseball fans." The scribe then described its plot: "Mike has a bad day on the diamond, he plays like a novice, and New York goes down to defeat before Pittsburg [*sic*]. Mike starts home, and had to steal in order to avoid the berating of his wife for poor playing, but he gets caught, however, and has an awful time trying to explain the reasons for his poor playing and the loss of the game." (Several paragraphs later, the reviewer notes: "As a juggler W.C. Fields has few if any equals. He is an artist in his especial line and provokes much mirth with some of his juggling stunts." So back in 1909, Donlin, Hite, and *Stealing Home* rated a more prominent notice than W.C. Fields.)[18]

While *Stealing Home* was acclaimed, however, reviews for the ballplayer-turned-actor were mixed. Some called him a delightful surprise, but another critic wrote: "Hite was so good she could carry him."[19] Yet Turkey Mike surely relished the praise he and his wife earned from one of the era's most beloved figures. "Mike Donlin (and) his wife, Mabel Hite, received the biggest reception I ever heard on a stage," observed Will Rogers two decades later.[20]

For the next couple of years the pair performed *Stealing Home* in front of sold-out houses from Boston to San Francisco. Initially, the ballplayer-turned-actor affirmed his allegiance to the game. "Baseball, boy, baseball," he told a writer from the *New York Review* in 1909. "Baseball first and show business second. Maybe we'll switch that order pretty soon, but right now your little playmate is mighty interested in the big game." Yet Donlin was not bothered by his transformation from big leaguer to stage actor. He later noted: "You see when a man's been playing baseball out in front of 30,000 people, and a lot of them of the critical sort, and mighty free with their remarks at that—well, it gives him a little assurance, enough, anyway, to let him get by when he faces an ordinary audience in a theater. So I'm not afraid on that score."[21]

Nevertheless, the bottom line was that at the time, Donlin had abandoned sports because he was making more money in show business. So one of the greatest players of his era missed two more seasons during his prime. By 1911, however, *Stealing Home* had run its course and on April 24, he and Hite opened at New York's Wallack's Theatre in *A Certain Party*, a musical that lasted 24 performances. Turkey Mike thus was forced to return to baseball—and the Giants—albeit not without a healthy dose of puffery. "Donlin has given up the stage, temporarily at least, and is again a baseball player," reported the *St. Louis Post-Dispatch*. "The lure of the diamond was too much for the once famous scrapper, and, after being two seasons out of baseball, and as many in vaudeville, he decided that his place was in the outfield of some big league team." The ballplayer declared: "I haven't taken a drink in four years. ... I feel as if I am as fast and can hit as well as ever."[22]

In reality, however, Donlin's lengthy hiatus had taken a toll. He had as many arguments as hits for the Giants, and on August 1, 1911, he was sold to the lowly Boston Rustlers (who became the Braves the following season). Donlin played center field and batted .315, but the Rustlers didn't need an aging star and his salary demands so they traded him to Pittsburgh. In 1912 Mike played 77 games, mainly in right field, for the Pirates and hit .316.

Donlin also supposedly had returned to baseball on the insistence of his wife. "Mickey's place is on the diamond in the summer time," Mabel Hite told the *Post-Dispatch*. "He can go back on the stage, if he wants to, but not until the 1912 season."[23] Tragically, it was just after that campaign that Hite died of intestinal cancer. The date was October 22. She was only 29 years old.

That same month, the Pirates put Turkey Mike on waivers. Philadelphia claimed him, but he announced his retirement. Late in the summer of 1913 Donlin attempted a comeback, playing 36 games with minor-league Jersey City. John McGraw then named him to a team that went on a postseason barnstorming tour through Europe, Asia, and Africa. Based on Donlin's hitting on the tour, McGraw decided to give his old friend another chance. "The Apollo of the whack-stick is back with the Giants," exclaimed the *New York World*.[24] But the erstwhile star was washed up at age 36, managing only five hits in 31 at-bats in 1914.

On October 20, 1914, Mike wed Rita Ross, the niece of Charles J. Ross and Mabel Fenton Ross, a famed vaudeville comedy duo of the era. It was around this time that Donlin also returned to vaudeville, pairing with major-league hurler/high baritone tenor Marty McHale. "Mike and I were together for five years," McHale told Lawrence S. Ritter, "doing a double-entendre act called 'Right Off the Bat'—not too much singing, Mike would only go through the motions—and we played the Keith-Orpheum circuit: twice in one year we were booked into the Palace in New York, and that was when it was the Palace. ... They had nothing but the big headliners. When Mike left for Hollywood, I went back to doing a single." Of their vaudeville success, McHale admitted: "Of course, Mike and I wouldn't have been such an attraction if it hadn't been for baseball."[25] Indeed, in McHale's *New York Times* obituary, it was noted that the pair also teamed up in an act titled "Donlin of the Giants and McHale of the Yankees."[26]

Prior to going Hollywood and commencing the second phase of his show-business career, Donlin appeared as himself in two 1914 releases: *The Giants-White Sox Tour*, a documentary featuring such luminaries as McGraw, Charles Comiskey, Christy Mathewson, Hans Lobert, and Jim Thorpe; and *Our Mutual Girl*, a weekly series of one-reel entertainments in which the title character (played by Norma Phillips) mixes with a host of celebrities. Donlin appears in Episode 10, along with McGraw, Comiskey, and Larry Doyle.

Then in 1915 Donlin began his screen acting career, starring in *Right Off the Bat*, a film that purportedly spotlighted his own life. *The Moving Picture World* promised that *Right Off the Bat* "ought to be a realistic baseball picture" as well as "a crime-free story presenting the career of Donlin from boyhood to manhood and a berth with the New York Giants."27 *Variety*, the show-business trade publication, reported that *Right Off the Bat* was "devoted to his experiences as a semiprofessional ballplayer and his subsequent entrance into the National League, where he stood as a prominent star for a number of years and from which he retired with an envious record and a reputation that should assist materially in making 'Right Off the Bat' a financial success." The paper labeled it "a cleverly constructed series of incidents that combine to make it an enjoyable feature throughout (its) five reels."28

However, as often is the case with celluloid biopics, the facts were altered for the sake of marketing and entertainment value. Donlin's *Right Off the Bat* hometown is Winsted, Connecticut, where the film was shot. His romantic interest is conjured up; as presented here, she is nothing like Mabel Hite, and neither his party boy personality, his troubles with the law, nor the trajectory of his baseball career are acknowledged. *Right Off the Bat* does chronicle Donlin's ascent to major-league stardom, albeit in a circuitous manner. He first is seen as a young southpaw hurler and is played by 13-year-old Roy Hauck. Upon growing into adulthood, Donlin takes over the role. Though devoted to baseball, he toils as a machinist because of his shaky financial situation. Even though he has saved his beloved, Viola Bradley (Claire Mersereau), from drowning, Donlin is considered a poor marital prospect by her mother. He becomes a bush-league star; refuses to take a bribe to throw the championship game; is assaulted and locked in a room; arrives (with the aid of Viola) at the ballpark in time to score the winning run; and signs a New York Giants contract. Finally, he has earned the right to wed Viola. Two major figures in Donlin's offscreen life appear in *Right Off the Bat*: John McGraw appears as himself, and Rita Ross Donlin plays Lucy, Viola's friend.29

Baseball Mixes With Broadway: New York Giant Mike Donlin hands a horsehide to theatrical producer Daniel Frohman.

Still, *Right Off the Bat* does hold a special place in the history of baseball-in-the-movies. Noted the *New York Times*: "For the first time baseball has been put on the screen in such a fashion that even an Englishman can understand it—and that, as (writer, playwright, and newspaper columnist) George Ade says, is Accomplishing the Impossible."[30] And Turkey Mike's on-camera appeal was cited by *Variety*, which reported: "Mike was a distinct surprise and, contrary to custom, could pass as a film lead on ability alone, despite the professional reputation which is his principal asset in this effort. Mike registered the various required points exceedingly, displaying emotion, joy and disappointment with a perfected ease that even suggests a sequel to his early life."[31]

There was, however, no *Right Off the Bat, Part II*—and the film was Donlin's lone starring feature. For the time being, he returned to baseball; he managed a semipro team in New Jersey in 1916 and the next winter ran a baseball clinic and boxing tournament in Cuba. In 1917 Donlin managed the Memphis Chicks of the Southern League. At first he was popular with the fans, but they booed him when he put himself in to pitch and made a farce of the game. He quit the Chicks—or by some accounts was fired—in midseason. Later that year the War Department appointed him to teach baseball to U.S. soldiers in France. In 1918 Donlin returned to California as a scout for the Boston Braves.

While occasionally reappearing on the stage (Donlin acted in *Smooth as Silk*, a melodrama that opened in New York's Lexington Theatre in February 1921 and lasted 50 performances) he now primarily was a screen performer. He was helped by his friend John Barrymore, and his next film role was with the great actor in 1917's *Raffles, the Amateur Cracksman*. Turkey Mike appears briefly as Crawshay, a stickup man, and he shares several minutes of screen time in the company of Barrymore and an astonishingly young Frank Morgan, 22 years before playing his most celebrated screen role: the title character in *The Wizard of Oz* (1939). In the film, Donlin's Crawshay points a gun at Barrymore's Raffles and Morgan's Bunny Manders. His intention is to pilfer some gems, which are referred to in the intertitles as "sparklers" and "dem jewels," but is easily manipulated by the crafty Raffles.

Donlin also played Flask opposite Barrymore in *The Sea Beast* (1926), a *Moby Dick* adaptation. Other notable roles included a movie studio gateman in the Colleen Moore romantic comedy *Ella Cinders* (1926); a Union general in Buster Keaton's *The General* (1927); Bill in *Beggars of Life* (1928), supporting Wallace Beery, Louise Brooks, and Richard Arlen; and Tout in Mae West's *She Done Him Wrong* (1933). He appeared in and was the technical adviser for the baseball melodrama *Slide, Kelly, Slide* (1927) and had roles in other baseball features, including *Hit and Run* (1924), *Warming Up* (1928), *Hot Curves* (1930), and *Swell-Head* (1935). In *Hot Curves*, an early talkie (*Raffles, the Amateur Cracksman*, *The Sea Beast*, and his initial credits are silent films), Donlin plays a gruff scout who signs frenetic, double-talking train concessionaire Benny Goldberg (Benny Rubin) to a contract. The scout utters a line that might have been ad-libbed by Donlin. It sounds like "I hope McGraw'll be sold," but the scout actually is referring to "McGrew," his team's skipper.

Donlin worked with such pantheon directors as John Ford, William A. Wellman, and Josef von Sternberg; he was employed by the A-list film studios; and he appeared in films starring a rainbow of screen legends. Yet just as often, his directors, costars, and films are long forgotten, and his studios were strictly Poverty Row. Increasingly, in many of his later films he even appears unbilled. In order to note his presence in a number of them, one has to stumble across him while watching the film. One such appearance is in *Picture Snatcher*, a 1933 James Cagney crime drama. *The American Film Institute Catalog, Feature Films, 1931-1940*, perhaps the definitive published reference on film credits for that decade, lists the bit players who appear in *Picture Snatcher*, cast in such roles as "fireman," "head keeper," "journalism student," and even "sick reporter" and "reporter outside prison." None is Mike Donlin. Yet there he is, unmistakable in one brief shot. He is seen in a pool hall, and he speaks the following words into a telephone: "No, Mr. McLean, he ain't been around here in over a week." After a brief pause, he adds: "Yeah, I'll tell him."[32]

What may be Donlin's most memorable screen appearance is equally fleeting. In one sequence in *Riley the Cop* (1928), a comedy-drama, a bunch of kids are playing baseball on an inner-city street. The title character (J. Farrell MacDonald) arrives on the scene to reprimand the lads and break up their game, yet the boyish Riley is quickly convinced to join the kids in their play. He picks up a bat and clumsily swings and misses at the first pitch tossed his way, in the process falling to the pavement. The cop does connect on his next swing, lifting a pop fly that crashes through a storefront window, necessitating the kids—and Riley—to scatter. After Riley's swing and miss, director John Ford includes an all-too-brief shot of Donlin looking up and smiling, with a cigarette dangling from his lips. While he is not billed onscreen, various film references list the actor-ballplayer's character as "Crook." Thus, the implication is that Donlin's character is amused because he is eluding the law while Riley is indulging in a child's game. Yet given his background, the sequence—intentional or not—serves as an homage to Donlin's past and a wink of the eye to anyone who recognizes him as an ex-major leaguer.[33]

Donlin's most revealing late-career screen role, however, is in *Madison Square Garden* (1932). The film is a sports buff's delight. A number of legendary scribes, among them Damon Runyon, Grantland Rice, Paul Gallico, and Westbrook Pegler, make cameo appearances, and Turkey Mike and other celebrated athletes of his era appear as themselves. They include jockey Tod Sloan, wrestler Stanislaus Zybyszko, and boxers Tom Sharkey, Billy Papke,

Mike Donlin thumbs out Wallace Ford in Swell-Head.

Tommy Ryan, and, most intriguingly, the controversial Jack "The Great White Hope" Johnson. All the ex-jocks portray low-level Garden employees; Johnson, who a decade earlier had appeared in *As the World Rolls On* (1921), in which he teaches baseball to a small but plucky lad who goes on to play for the Negro League Kansas City Monarchs, is reduced to impersonating a bug-eyed porter. Meanwhile, Donlin is cast as an usher. By then talking pictures were all the rage, and he has a pleasant speaking voice and an at-ease manner before the camera. With flagrant disregard of the Ruths, Cobbs, Speakers, Wagners, and other Hall of Famers of Donlin's day, he is introduced as "the greatest ballplayer of all time."[34]

Despite this accolade, Donlin at this point was experiencing chronic money troubles and was constantly scraping for jobs in baseball and acting. He also was dealing with health issues. The *New York Times* reported, "Athlete's heart brought (him) virtual retirement in 1927," at which time his "many friends among motion picture stars and stage actors" appeared in a minstrel show to raise money to send him to the Mayo Clinic for major surgery.[35]

While Donlin still managed to tackle roles on screen and stage, he was by this time viewed as a relic of an earlier era. In October 1930 he returned to Broadway, cast in a supporting role opposite Paul Muni in *This One Man*, a Sidney Buchman drama that lasted 39 performances. "Though it is faintly possible that there are adult men and women now living to whom the name Mike Donlin is the name of just another actor," one observer noted, "astute listeners who hear him speak his lines with some conviction these days … know very well where Mr. Donlin got his training. It was not in the theatre, but in the old-time ball parks. … In his time, however, (ballplayers) were all orators, and often very gifted ones, at that."[36]

At this time, Turkey Mike still wanted to get back into baseball, and in the spring of 1933 he asked a friend if he could get a coaching job with the Giants. But on September 24, 1933, he was felled by a heart attack in his sleep at his Hollywood home. Upon his death, *New York Times* sportswriter John Drebinger wrote: "A glamorous figure was Turkey Mike, the first of a long list of notables who came with the dawn of what might be called the modern era of baseball. … Turkey Mike was one of the first to grip and captivate the imagination of the public. The Mattys, Cobbs and Ruths came later. He was scrappy and witty, and for all his worldliness there was about him a certain naïveté which was not the least of his charming qualities."[37]

And then, two years later, Drebinger reported that the "committee conducting the baseball centennial celebration to be held in 1939 at Cooperstown, N.Y., commemorating the 100th anniversary of the origin of America's national pastime, has asked the scribes to assist in selecting the first group of names to be inscribed on tablets in the Hall of Fame." After citing such inner-circle superstars as Ty Cobb, Babe Ruth, and Tris Speaker and second-line talents Wee Willie Keeler, Ed Delahanty, Ross Youngs, Ed Roush, and Al Simmons, Drebinger quipped: "There are any number of others you might feel privileged to add to the general confusion." And one of them was "… the unforgettable Mike Donlin…"[38]

Note: A different version of this biography appeared in Tom Simon, ed., *Deadball Stars of the National League* (Washington, D.C.: Brassey's, Inc., 2004).

SOURCES

For this biography, a number of contemporary sources, especially those found in the subject's file at the National Baseball Hall of Fame Library, are cited.

NOTES

1. thedeadballera.com/BeerDrinkersMikeDonlin.html.
2. Bill Swank, *Baseball in San Diego: From the Plaza to the Padres* (Charleston, South Carolina: Arcadia Publishing, 2005), 31.
3. "Mike Donlin Dead; Once With Giants," *New York Times*, September 25, 1933: 15.
4. Hype Igoe, "Donlin Own Press Agent in Turkey Trot to Top," *The Sporting News*, January 25, 1945.
5. Quoted in an unidentified St. Louis paper, dated November 7, 1940, in Donlin's Baseball Hall of Fame player file.
6. Associated Press, "Donlin, Giant of 1905, Dead," unidentified newspaper clipping found in Donlin's Baseball Hall of Fame player file.

7   Quoted in an unidentified newspaper clipping found in the Hall of Fame file for Donlin.

8   Craig R. Wright, "Turkey Mike Donlin," baseballspast.com

9   Ada Patterson, "The 'Make-Up Half Hour With Mabel Hite," *The Theatre*, July 1911: 32.

10 "Mike Donlin, Star with Giants Early in Century, Dies at 56," *Chicago Tribune*, September 25, 1933: 19.

11 Ibid.

12 Wright.

13 Ward Morehouse, "Donlin a Colorful Figure," *New York Sun*, September 25, 1933.

14 David Quentin Voigt, *American Baseball, Volume II: From the Commissioners to Continental Expansion* (University Park and London: The Pennsylvania State University Press, 1983), 64.

15 Max Kase, "Suite to the Taste," *New York Journal-American*, May 18, 1964.

16 Ibid.

17 Gene Fowler, *Good Night, Sweet Prince* (New York, Viking Press, 1944), 190.

18 Rob Edelman, *Great Baseball Films* (New York, Citadel Press, 1994), 27.

19 Joe Williams, "Sports Stars Get the Beauties in Cupid's League," unknown publication found in Hall of Fame file stamped as January 23, 1954.

20 "Mr. Rogers Arises to Applaud Some Stars of Yesteryear," *New York Times*, March 25, 1932: 21.

21 Edelman, *Great Baseball Films*, 27.

22 "Mike Donlin Will Do No Stage Stint This Winter; His Wife Won't Let Him," *St. Louis Post-Dispatch*, August 6, 1911: 8.

23 Ibid.

24 "Mike Donlin, the 'Come-Back,'" *The World Magazine*, March 29, 1914.

25 John Thorn, ed., *The Complete Armchair Book of Baseball* (New York: Galahad Books, 1997), 254.

26 "Martin Joseph McHale, Former Yankee Pitcher," *New York Times*, May 10, 1979: D23.

27 "Donlin Plays in Bush League," *The Moving Picture World*, August 7, 1915, 1000.

28 Wynn, "Right Off the Bat," *Variety*, October 1, 1915: 18.

29 Rob Edelman, "The Baseball Film to 1920," *Base Ball: A Journal of the Early Game*, Spring 2007: 29.

30 "In the Movies," *New York Times*, October 10, 1915: 102.

31 Wynn.

32 Rob Edelman, "Turkey Mike Donlin in the Movies," *The Baseball Research Journal*, Number 30, 2001: 74.

33 Ibid.

34 Edelman, *Great Baseball Films*, 29.

35 "Mike Donlin Dead; Once With Giants."

36 "Lines for Scrapbooks: Mr. Donlin and Two Actresses, Who Seem to Be Helen Mehrmann and Armida," *New York Times*, November 2, 1930: X4.

37 John Drebinger, "Sports of the Times: Turkey Mike Passes On," *New York Times*, September 27, 1933: 26.

38 John Drebinger, "Sports of the Times: Only Standing Room Left," *New York Times*, December 26, 1935: 24.

DON DRYSDALE

BY JOSEPH WANCHO

"Hitters would dig a hole and really get anchored with their back foot. Willie Mays dug in sometimes with both feet and he looked up and realized it was Drysdale. I don't think he was even thinking at the time. He called time out and filled up the hole as if to say, 'I made a mistake. I didn't realize he was pitching.' VROOOOM, down he went."

Jeff Torborg, Los Angeles Dodgers catcher[1]

"He hit me more than anyone else. He kept me going like a rocking chair. That night, I always felt like I had been wrestling a bear. I was so tired when I left the ballpark. But I respected him for the way he went about his job.

Frank Robinson, Cincinnati Reds[2]

"I know Don Drysdale is trying to hit me. He'll even come to the batting cage and say, 'Where do you want it today, big boy?'"

Mickey Mantle, New York Yankees[3]

THE FIRST WORLD SERIES game at Dodger Stadium was played on October 5, 1963. The ballpark had opened its gates the previous season. Over the following six decades Dodger Stadium served as the backdrop for some of the greatest moments in major-league history. On October 5, the Dodgers' opponent was the New York Yankees. The Yankees were a particular thorn in the side of the Dodgers, going back to their days in Brooklyn when the Bronx Bombers won six of seven World Series from the neighboring borough.

But as Don Drysdale took the hill for Game Three, his teammates had to be feeling quite confident. Los Angeles had won the first two games of the Series at Yankee Stadium, in rather convincing manner. Sandy Koufax struck out 15 batters in the 5-2 Dodgers win in Game One. Johnny Podres was not as overpowering in Game Two, but still won, 4-1. In starting the two left-handers at Yankee Stadium, Dodgers manager Walt Alston pushed Drysdale, the winner of 19 games and the reigning NL Cy Young Award winner, back to Game Three.

The Dodgers reached the Yankees' Jim Bouton for a run in the bottom of the first inning. Jim Gilliam walked, went to second base on a wild pitch, and scored on a single by Tommy Davis. But that was all the offense the Dodgers could muster. Drysdale would have to be on top of his game to bring home the win. In the top of the third, Tony Kubek reached base on an error by Maury Wills. Not to worry; Drysdale picked Kubek off.

The final out caused the most angst for Drysdale and the Dodger fans. With two outs Joe Pepitone lifted a fly ball to left field. Left fielder Ron Fairly drifted back to the track, just short of the fence in front of the Yankees bullpen, to haul it in. "Pepitone hit it real good and I saw Fairly going back until he was almost touching the fence," Drysdale said. "Then he stopped and put his glove up and I knew I had won the game."[4] Drysdale struck out nine and scattered three hits while going the distance to stake the Dodgers to a 3-0 advantage in the series. "The extra rest helped me," Drysdale said. "I felt strong. I know I was pitching high, but the Yankees were apparently looking for low stuff, so I just stayed high."[5] Alston praised his right-handed hurler, saying, "He had the left-handers to contend with and he didn't make a mistake all through the game. His control was never better."[6]

Donald Scott Drysdale was born to Scott and Verna Drysdale on July 23, 1936, in Van Nuys, California. Scott Drysdale was a repair supervisor for the Pacific Telephone Company, which provided a comfortable middle-class upbringing. Scott had a brief career as a minor-league pitcher in 1935, the year before Don was born.

Drysdale credited his father with his early love of baseball. "We played catch in the afternoon," he said. "Often we'd go to the playground and Dad would hit me grounders and flies and I would take batting practice. He really taught me the game."7

It was not until his senior year at Van Nuys High School that Drysdale tried his hand at pitching. He posted a 10-1 record. Brooklyn signed the former second baseman to a $4,000 bonus contract. He was assigned to Bakersfield of the Class C California League. An astute observer, Branch Rickey, then with the Pittsburgh Pirates, scouted the 17-year-old pitcher and on June 15, 1954, wrote:

"A lot of artistry about this boy. Way above average fast ball. It is really good. Direction of the spin and the speed of rotation the same on all fast ball pitches. Angle of delivery is the same, stride is wide and his body is in all pitches. The pitching hand, and placement on fast and curve ball needs no coaching. He is good."8

Drysdale pitched well enough at Bakersfield (8-5, 3.46) to earn a promotion to Montreal of the International League in 1955. He started the season 10-2, but injured his right hand, and continued to pitch with the pain. It proved to be a broken bone and Drysdale lost nine games in the second half of the season to go 11-11. The next year he was promoted to Brooklyn, although Drysdale conceded that it took some good fortune to land him there. "I never would have made the majors the next season if luck wasn't with me," he wrote. "The Dodgers lost Johnny Podres to the Navy, and Billy Loes, Don Bessent, and Karl Spooner got hurt. Stuck for pitchers, the club took me, in desperation."9

It may have been luck that got Drysdale to Brooklyn, but it was skill that kept him there. He pitched in 25 games, mostly as a spot starter and reliever. But he showed enough (5-5, 2.64) to stay with the team all season. Trailing Milwaukee by one game, the Dodgers won the pennant by sweeping the Pirates as the Braves lost two of three at St. Louis.

In the World Series, they took a 2-0 lead against the Yankees. But their old nemesis took four of the next five games to win the world championship.

Drysdale was promoted to starter in 1957 and led the club with a 17-9 record. His 2.69 ERA was tied for second in the league with Warren Spahn, right behind his teammate Podres' 2.66. Drysdale's best effort was a two-hitter against Philadelphia. He struck out six and gave up an unearned run in the 5-1 Brooklyn victory.

The young side-armer was getting a reputation as a headhunter in only his second season. With his 6-foot-6, 190-pound frame, Drysdale was an intimidating sight to most batters. On June 13, 1957, against the Milwaukee Braves. "Big D," as he was often called, was not having one of his better days. Bill Bruton homered to begin the game. In the second inning Bobby Thomson doubled and came home on a double by Carl Sawatski. Bruton followed with his second round-tripper. The Braves were up 4-0. "Johnny Logan was up next," recalled Drysdale. "He

Don Drysdale exchanged Dodger Blue for western gear for his appearance on The Lawman *TV series.*

was strutting around up there and digging in and showing me his teeth and acting like he owned the place. A charge went right through me. I look at this guy and tell myself, 'Okay Buster, you asked for it.' And I aim one inside to let him know who's boss."[10] The baseball nearly took Logan's head off his shoulders as he spun out of the way and got hit at the base of his neck. Logan jogged to first base, all the time jawing at Drysdale and Don giving it right back. As Logan took his lead off first, Drysdale threw over in a pickoff attempt. First baseman Gil Hodges stuck out his glove, but missed the ball. Johnny was beaned yet again. Logan charged the mound and set off one of the biggest donnybrooks in years. There was a near-riot as both benches emptied. Drysdale was attacked from all sides, and when the dust cleared, he and Logan were ejected. The Braves had their own nickname for him, the Shooting Gallery Kid.

That 1957 season was a watershed year for major-league baseball. Although expansion had been a movement in recent years, no team moved west of St. Louis or the Mississippi River. Brooklyn Dodgers owner Walter O'Malley and New York Giants owner Horace Stoneham both saw the infinite possibilities for growth on the West Coast. Even though the Dodgers had drawn more than a million to Ebbets Field in 1955, O'Malley was not fond of the park, which was surrounded by a congested and deteriorating neighborhood. The Dodgers moved a handful of home games to Roosevelt Stadium in Jersey City in 1956 and 1957. With cities like Hoboken and Union City to draw from, it also had 10,000 parking spaces, compared with several hundred at Ebbets.

Although the move of games to Jersey was a ploy to strong-arm Brooklyn for a new ballpark, in September 1957 the Dodgers signed a deal to move to Los Angeles for the following season. They would build a new ballpark on 300 acres of land within Chavez Ravine. Similarly, Stoneham moved the Giants to San Francisco.

From 1958 through 1961 the Dodgers played their home games at the Los Angeles Memorial Coliseum. The Coliseum was one of the great football stadiums of all time, serving as the home field for the Los Angeles Rams and the University of Southern California Trojans. The seating capacity was 90,000 and it easily set baseball attendance records. Because it was built for football, and was in the shape of an oval, it lent itself to some strange dimensions. It was 250 feet to left field, 320 feet to left-center, 425 feet to center field, and 440 feet to right-center field. Hence, 260-foot home runs and 430-foot fly outs were a common sight for the fans.

The 1958 Dodgers finished under .500 for the first time since 1938 (not including the 1944 war year record of 69-85) with a record of 71-83. It was not all bad for Drysdale, though. He married Ginger Dubberly, a model and former Rose Bowl Parade Queen, in September 1958. They had one child, a daughter, Kelly.

In 1959 Drysdale led the team in wins with 17 and the league in strikeouts with 242. He also led the league in hit batsmen with 18. He made the first of nine All-Star Game appearances on July 7 at Pittsburgh's Forbes Field, as he got the starting assignment for the National League and pitched three hitless innings. (There were two All-Star Games that season. Drysdale also started the second one, on August 3, and took the loss, giving up three runs in three innings.)

The Dodgers finished strong in 1959, coming from third place on September 14 to overtake the Braves and the Giants for the pennant. They won 9 of 11 down the stretch. Their opponent in the World Series was the Chicago White Sox, a team built on pitching, defense, and speed. The White Sox drubbed LA in the opener, 11-0 behind Early Wynn. But the Dodgers came back to win the next four of five, with Drysdale picking up the 3-1 victory in Game Three.

Over the next three seasons the Dodgers fell short in their bid to return to the World Series. Drysdale led the league again in strikeouts in 1960 with 246 and hit batsmen with 10. The following year he hit 20 batters to pace the senior circuit.

Drysdale put it all together in 1962. He posted a 25-9 record with a 2.83 ERA. He led the league in wins, starts (41), innings pitched (314⅓), and strikeouts (232). His 41 starts were the most by a Dodgers hurler since Oscar Jones started 41 games in 1904. It was the first of four straight years in which Drysdale led the NL in starts. "Batting against him is the same as making a date with the dentist," said Pittsburgh's Dick Groat.[11] "Drysdale has simply got more stuff than ever before," said Alston.[12] Drysdale won the Cy Young Award and was named *The Sporting News* Player and Pitcher of the Year.

Sandy Koufax, who like Drysdale began his career back in Brooklyn, was mostly a .500 pitcher until the 1961 season, when he hurled his way to an 18-13 record. Beginning in 1962, he led the National League in ERA for five straight seasons. He gave the opposition a much-dreaded combination of power pitchers, one right-handed and Koufax left-handed. He didn't intimidate batters the way Drysdale did by plunking them. Koufax had 18 hit batsmen in his career. He intimidated them with his speed, as he was considered one of the fastest pitchers to ever toe the rubber in the major leagues.

Drysdale may have felt his 1962 awards bittersweet. The Dodgers had put together a seven-game winning streak to take a four-game lead over San Francisco on September 15. But they could muster only three more wins the rest of the season, which placed them in a tie with the Giants at the end of 154 games. The Giants won a best-of-three playoff in three games and advanced to the World Series.

After celebrating the world championship in 1963, the Dodgers slumped in 1964, finishing two games under .500. But they resurfaced to win the pennant in 1965. Drysdale (23 victories) and Koufax (26) accounted for more than half of the team's 97 victories. "When you've been pitching on the same staff for as long as we have, you know when the other one is doing something right or wrong," said Koufax. "We're quick to tell the other one about it, too."[13] Drysdale threw a one-hitter against Bob Gibson and St. Louis on May 25. He was no slouch at the plate that season, tying his career high with seven home runs, driving in a career-best 19 runs, and batting .300.

Going into September, the Dodgers sat atop the standings with a 1½-game lead over San Francisco and two games over Milwaukee and Cincinnati. But a 22-8 record, which included a 13-game winning streak (from September 16 to 30) helped LA distance itself from the others.

The World Series started off bleakly for the Dodgers. They dropped the first two games to Minnesota at Metropolitan Stadium, Drysdale and Koufax taking the losses. Both pitchers won the next games; Drysdale fanned 11 Twins in a 7-2 win in Game Four. Koufax won the seventh game, 2-0, to secure another world championship for Los Angeles. "I threw one bad pitch and Harmon Killebrew hit for a home run and I got a curve up high on Tony Oliva and he smacked it out," said Drysdale after his victory in Game Four. "When I saw my breaking stuff wasn't working too well early in the game, I went to my fastball. But the main thing was that I kept moving the ball around, inside and out, and I thought I was setting up the batters pretty well."[14]

After battling San Francisco again, the Dodgers won the pennant once more in 1966, but were swept by the Baltimore Orioles in the World Series. Drysdale (13-16) had his first losing season since 1958. He lost two World Series games. He pitched well in Game Four, but was outdueled, 1-0, by Dave McNally, on a home run by Frank Robinson.

An arthritic elbow forced Koufax to retire after the 1966 season, prematurely ending his great career at the age of 30. Even though the Dodgers were not an offensive power, the great pitching of Koufax, Drysdale, and Claude Osteen had always given the team a chance to win.

From May 14 to June 8, 1968, Drysdale set a record for consecutive scoreless innings pitched. His new mark was 58⅔ innings, breaking the record of 55⅔ innings set by Walter Johnson in 1913. In three of the games during the streak, the margin of error was slim. Drysdale beat the Cubs and the Astros by a 1-0 score. He topped the Cardinals in another, 2-0. The string ended when Philadelphia scored a run in the fifth inning of a 5-3 LA win at Dodger Stadium. "I have two things to say about Drysdale," said Phillies manager Gene Mauch. "He's a hell of a man and the most knowledgeable pitcher in the game. We didn't think much about the record but I know he was thinking about it, and has for a long time. He's been through a hell of an emotional strain."[15]

The Phillies' Roberto Pena grounded out to third baseman Ken Boyer to begin the third inning, which gave Drysdale the record. "I wanted the record so bad," said Drysdale, "but I'm relieved that it's over. I could feel myself go 'blah' when the run scored. I just let down completely. I'm sure it was the mental strain."[16]

Twenty years later, Drysdale was working in his first year as a broadcaster for the Dodgers. On September 28, 1988, Orel Hershiser was zeroing in on Drysdale's scoreless-innings record. When Hershiser tied the mark pitching against San Diego, he asked to be removed from the game, out of respect for Drysdale. But manager Tommy Lasorda and pitching coach Ron Perranoski persuaded him to go for the record, and he set a new record: 59 scoreless innings. (Hershiser pitched 10 scoreless innings in that game.) When Drysdale was told that Hershiser wanted to be taken out of the game, he said "I would have gone out there and kicked him in the rear."[17]

Recurring shoulder injuries slowed Drysdale down. He was an ironman as pitchers go, as he started 35 or more games for nine straight seasons. His injury, which was diagnosed as a torn rotator cuff, never got better. After making just 12 starts in 1969, Drysdale retired as a player. In 14 seasons, all with the Dodgers, he compiled a record of 209-166 with an ERA of 2.95. He struck out 2,486 batters, posted 49 shutouts and hit 154 batters. He struck out 200 or more batters six times. Drysdale hit 29 home runs, sixth all-time for pitchers. He was 3-3 in the World Series, with an ERA of 2.95. He pitched in eight All-Star Games.

Drysdale never left the game. He went right to the broadcast booth. Drysdale was a radio and TV color man for the Montreal Expos (1970-1971), Texas Rangers (1972), California Angels (1973-1979, 1981), Chicago White Sox (1982-1987), and the Dodgers (1988-1993). He broadcast regional and national telecasts for both NBC and ABC. For ABC he contributed to *Wide World of Sports* and *Superstars*. His good looks made him a natural for television shows. He made cameo appearances on *The Brady Bunch, Beverly Hillbillies, Leave It to Beaver* and the *Donna Reed Show*, among others.

Don and Ginger divorced in 1982. In 1986 Drysdale married Ann Myers, a college basketball player who was an All-American at UCLA and is a member of the National Basketball Hall of Fame. She was the only woman to be signed to a professional contract in the NBA, with the Indiana Pacers in 1979. They had three children—two boys, Don Jr. and Darren, and a daughter, Drew. "I won't play against her, she's too tough one-on-one," said Drysdale.[18]

On August 12, 1984, Drysdale was elected to the National Baseball Hall of Fame with Harmon Killebrew, Pee Wee Reese, Rick Ferrell, and Luis Aparicio. Drysdale was in his 10th year of eligibility and received 78 percent of the vote.

In 1990 Drysdale published his autobiography, *Once a Bum, Always a Dodger*, written with Bob Verdi.

Upon the Brooklyn Dodgers abandoning the Borough of Churches for the orange groves of Southern California, Don Drysdale regularly guested on countless TV series.

Drysdale gave readers a candid look into his baseball career and his personal life.

Drysdale died on July 3, 1993 of a heart attack in Montreal, where he was with the Dodgers to broadcast a Dodgers-Expos series. A week earlier, the Dodger family had lost Roy Campanella, also to a heart attack. "I think God need a battery, because he got one of the best that heaven could have ever accepted," said Dodgers manager Tommy Lasorda.[19]

On July 9, 1961, the Cincinnati Reds were playing the Dodgers at the LA Coliseum. The Reds were atop the National League standings, and the Dodgers were four games behind them in second place. Drysdale came into the game in the fifth inning as a reliever. When the Dodgers came to bat, they were down 7-2. Reds second baseman Don Blasingame was knocked down on a pitch that whizzed by his head, courtesy of Drysdale, to lead off the sixth inning. Big D received a warning from home-plate umpire Dusty Boggess. Blasingame popped out and the next batter was Vada Pinson, who doubled. Frank Robinson stepped to the plate.

Drysdale's offering was an inside pitch that sent Robinson sprawling. Boggess again came out to warn Drysdale. "Shit, Dusty," said Drysdale. "What do you want me to do? Lay the ball right down the middle so he can beat my brains in?"[20] Drysdale came inside with the next pitch, and hit Robinson on the right forearm. Boggess immediately ejected Drysdale.

The next day, Drysdale was given a five-game suspension and fined $100 by National League President Warren Giles. Drysdale decided to pay his debt in person. The next time the Dodgers were in Cincinnati, where Giles had his office, Drysdale stopped at a bank and got $100 worth of pennies. He emptied all of the pennies into a sack, walked to Giles' office, and placed them on the desk of Giles' secretary. He walked back to his hotel room, feeling proud of himself, when the phone rang and he was summoned back to Giles' office. The conversation was amiable and it ended with Giles saying, "And by the way, I want you to take those pennies of yours and roll them back up for me."[21] Drysdale spent the next few hours cursing and rolling pennies.

Don Drysdale may have been rolling pennies, but to Dodger fans, he was a million-dollar pitcher.

NOTES

1. *When It Was a Game III*, HBO Sports, 2000.
2. Ibid.
3. "Suddenly, Don's Gone Too," *New York Daily News*, July 5, 1993: 48.
4. "Drive by Pepitone Produced One of Big Thrills of Game," *The Sporting News*, October 19, 1963: 27.
5. "Drysdale Sparkles, Blanks Bombers With 3-Hit Gem," *The Sporting News*, October 19, 1963: 27.
6. Bill Becker, "Drysdale Had Visions of Pepitone's Last-Out Drive Going Into the Seats", *New York Times*, October 6, 1963: S-3.
7. Melvin Durslag, "L.A.'s Fiery Strike-Out Artist," *Saturday Evening Post*, July 1, 1961: 56.
8. Branch Rickey Papers at the Library of Congress; Don Drysdale player file at the National Baseball Hall of Fame.
9. Drysdale player file.
10. Al Stump, "Headhunter With a Horsehide," *True Magazine*, May, 1980: 102.
11. Bob Hunter, "Drysdale Crowned Slab King of Year," *The Sporting News*, November 17, 1962: 1.
12. Huston Horn, "Ex-Bad Boy's Big Year," *Sports Illustrated*, August 20, 1962.
13. Bob Hunter, "Sandy and Big D Super Stoppers," *The Sporting News*, July 17, 1965: 4.
14. "Speed-Boy Dodgers Force Twins Into Key Blunders," *The Sporting News*, October 23, 1965: 27.
15. Al Goldfarb, "Don Drysdale: What Does He Do for an Encore?" *Complete Sports*, May 1969.
16. Ibid.
17. Steve Wulf, "Deep Roots," *Sports Illustrated*, December 19, 1988: 69.
18. Ross Forman, "Don Drysdale Reflects on HOF Career," *Sports Collectors Digest*, June 28, 1991: 111.
19. Associated Press, July 13, 1993, in Drysdale player file.
20. Don Drysdale with Bob Verdi, *Once a Bum, Always a Dodger* (New York: St. Martin's Press, 1990), 181.
21. Drysdale and Verdi, 182.

MARK FIDRYCH

BY RICHARD J. PUERZER

ALTHOUGH HE PITCHED IN only 58 major-league games in his tragically brief career, Mark Fidrych made an enduring impression on the history and culture of professional baseball. Fidrych had one stellar season, in 1976. That season, he first made an impression on baseball fans with his pitching prowess when he came out of nowhere to become one of the best pitchers in baseball. But it was Fidrych's antics on the mound, his genuine exuberance in playing the game, and his "just folks" persona that made a permanent impact on the American public and brought Fidrych his lasting fame, making him one of the most inspirational players in the history of the game.

Mark Steven Fidrych was born August 14, 1954, in Worcester, Massachusetts, to Paul and Virginia Fidrych. He grew up in the town of Northboro, Massachusetts, where his father was a public-school teacher. Fidrych went to Algonquin High School in Northboro, where he played baseball as well as basketball and football. Because Mark was held back two years while in elementary school, in his senior year he attended a private school, Worcester Academy; age restrictions would have prevented him from playing sports in public school. While he was not a star pitcher in high school and was not offered any collegiate athletic scholarships, Mark caught the attention of both the Boston Red Sox and the Detroit Tigers on the strength of his hard fastball. On the recommendation of Joe Cusick, the New England scout for the Detroit Tigers, Fidrych was selected in the 10th round of the 1974 free-agent draft.

Fidrych began his professional career in 1974, pitching as a reliever in the Appalachian League for the Bristol Tigers. He was tall, at 6-feet-3, and lanky, weighing only 175 pounds, and had a moptop of curly blond hair. At Bristol Fidrych was given his nickname, "Bird," by coach Jeff Hogan.[1] Hogan thought Fidrych looked like Big Bird from the television show *Sesame Street*, and the name stuck.

After the 1974 season, Fidrych played winter ball in the Florida Instructional League to prep for the 1975 season. In that season he progressed rapidly through three levels of the Tigers' minor-league system. He began the year in the Class-A Florida State League as a starting pitcher for the Lakeland Tigers. Although he pitched well, recording 73 strikeouts in 117 innings, he had a losing record, 5-9.[2] Fidrych was promoted in midseason to the Montgomery Rebels of the Double-A Southern League. He pitched for Montgomery for only about two weeks and was used exclusively as a reliever. Fidrych was then sent to the Evansville Triplets of the Triple-A American Association, where he once again pitched as a starter. While in Double A and Triple A, Fidrych developed a changeup to go along with his fastball. He also markedly improved his control, walking relatively few batters. In Evansville Fidrych hit his stride, posting an ERA of 1.58 and striking out 29 while walking only 9 in 40 innings. To finish off the season, he started the American Association championship game, going 12 innings for the win. After the season Fidrych again pitched instructional league ball to prepare for the year ahead.

To begin the 1976 season, the 21-year-old Fidrych was promoted to Detroit's major-league roster. The Tigers had traded their best pitcher, Mickey Lolich, after the 1975 season, and sold Joe Coleman to the Chicago Cubs when the season was two months old, creating openings in the starting rotation. Fidrych began the season in the bullpen and made only two appearances, both in relief, on April 20 and May 5, during the first five weeks of the season. When Coleman came down with the flu and could not make his scheduled start on May 15, Fidrych was given a chance to start at home against the Cleveland Indians. In what may have been his best outing in what proved to be a spectacular pitching season, Fidrych did not allow a hit for the first six innings and pitched a complete game, giving up one run on only two hits and one walk, for his first major-league win. Catching that game was the Tigers' backup catcher, Bruce Kimm. Because of their success in this game, Kimm became Fidrych's personal catcher and caught all 29 of his starts that season.

Fidrych had developed into a control pitcher with a good fastball. Ralph Houk, his manager with the Tigers, described him as having "unbelievable control with a fastball that moved."[3] One prominent feature of Fidrych's pitching was that he worked very fast. Bill James calculated the game time for all starting pitchers in 1976, and found Fidrych to be the fastest-working pitcher in the American League, with an average game time of 2 hours and 11 minutes, 17 minutes quicker than the league average.[4]

Despite his performance, Fidrych was not yet made a regular starter for the Tigers. Ten days after defeating Cleveland, he started again, versus the Red Sox at Fenway Park. Though he pitched another complete game, Fidrych and the Tigers lost, 2-0, on a two-run home run by Carl Yastrzemski. But based on his strong performance, Fidrych became a regular starter for the Tigers, and won his next eight starts.

Soon after he became a regular starter, sportswriters covering the Tigers began to write about Fidrych's antics on the playing field. A June 5 article in *The Sporting News* described him on the mound: "He talks to the ball. ... He talks to himself. ... He gestures toward the plate, pointing out the path he wants the pitch to take. ... He struts in a circle around the mound after each out, applauding his teammates and asking for the ball. ... And he's forever chewing gum and patting the dirt on the mound with his bare hand." The article quoted Fidrych as saying, "I really don't know what I do out there. That's just my way of concentrating and keeping my head in the game."[5]

The game that firmly established the legend of Mark Fidrych was one on June 28 against the New York Yankees. The national media had picked up on both Fidrych's success — he was now 7-1 — and his antics on the field. In turn, baseball fans and the American public were taking notice of the Bird. The game, pitting Fidrych against the first-place Yankees, was televised nationally on ABC's *Monday Night Baseball* and received a great deal of attention. Fans came in droves to attend the game at Tiger Stadium; 47,855 people got in, and it was reported that another 10,000 were turned away more than an hour before the game was scheduled to start.[6] Fidrych shut down the Yankees, allowing seven hits, no walks, and just a solo homer by Elrod Hendricks as the Tigers won 5-1. Chants of "Go Bird Go!" echoed through the crowd during the game. The Yankees, however, were unimpressed with Fidrych and his nonpitching actions on the field. In particular, Thurman Munson, who did not play in the game because of a bruised knee, was angry and felt that Fidrych was showing up the Yankees. He was quoted as saying, "Tell that guy if he pulls that stuff in New York, we'll blow his ------ out of town." Willie Randolph, who admitted that he was distracted during his first at-bat against Fidrych, simply said, "You want to send a line drive right through his head."[7]

Tigers fans, however, were ecstatic. When the game, ended, Fidrych ran around the infield, shaking the hands of his teammates before going into the dugout and clubhouse to the ovation of the fans. After the game, as a light rain fell on the crowd, the fans did not leave. They chanted "We want the Bird! We want the Bird!" Fidrych finally returned the field, laughing and smiling at the crowd as he tipped his cap to them. Bob Prince, who was announcing the game on ABC, said that in his 35 years in baseball, he had never seen anything like this, and that it gave him goose bumps. Ernie Harwell later wrote that he thought Fidrych to be "the first big-leaguer to take curtain calls on a regular basis."[8]

After the game Tigers right fielder Rusty Staub said of Fidrych: "It's no act. There's nothing contrived about him and that's what makes him a beautiful person."[9] Staub continued, "There's an electricity that he brings out in everyone, the players and the fans. He's different. He's a 21-year-old kid with a great enthusiasm that everyone loves. He has an inner youth, an exuberance."[10]

His defeat of the Yankees made Fidrych a huge star. Having amassed a record of 9-2 and an ERA of 1.78, he was named the starter for the American League for the 1976 All-Star Game. Fidrych gave up two runs in the first inning of the game and was charged with the loss as the American League lost, 7-1.[11] Fidrych bounced back from the All-Star Game loss to finish the season with a record of 19-9 while posting an American League-best ERA of 2.34. He also led the league in complete games, with 24 complete games, including five in extra innings, among his 29 starts. He won the American League Rookie of the Year Award and came in second, behind Jim Palmer, for the AL Cy Young Award. The Tigers finished with a record of 74-87, 24 games behind the American League East-winning Yankees.

When Fidrych started his first game against the Indians, there was a crowd of 14,583 at Tiger Stadium. Against the Yankees that June 28, the crowd was 47,855. For the remainder of the season, whether the team was on the road or in Detroit, huge crowds came to see Fidrych pitch. Three of his starts attracted more than 50,000. Attendance at Tigers games went from 1,058,836 in 1975 to 1,467,020 in 1976, an increase of almost 39 percent.

Despite his stardom, Fidrych still demonstrated his innocence in the world of big-time sports, as evidenced by the contract he signed after the 1976 season. Although agents flocked to him, Fidrych resisted signing with one as he and his father negotiated directly with the Tigers. In the end he accepted a retroactive raise to his major-league minimum contract for 1976, hiking it from $19,000 to $30,000, and received a three-year contact starting at $50,000 for 1977. While the contract put his mind at ease—"Now I can concentrate on playing baseball," Fidrych declared—many felt he could have demanded far more money.[12] Early in the 1977 season, Fidrych appeared on the cover of *Rolling Stone* magazine. He was among the first athletes to appear on the cover of the magazine (after Muhammad Ali and Mark Spitz), which was then a countercultural and rock-and-roll institution. The article in the magazine described him as having a style that is "singular in baseball, a game which, in any case, doesn't place great value on singular style." The article also describes Fidrych as "the embodiment of rock & roll" in baseball.[13]

During spring training to start the 1977 season, Fidrych injured his knee while shagging flies. He had surgery on the knee and was able to return to the mound on May 27. When he did return, there was great fanfare, including a cover story in *Sports Illustrated* and a crowd of 44,027 on hand for his first start of the season at Tiger Stadium.[14] Although he lost his first two starts of the season, he was as dominant as he had been in 1976, winning six straight games from June 6 to June 29. He pitched complete games in seven of his eight starts. Then, in a game against the Baltimore Orioles on July 4, he felt his arm go dead as he gave up six runs in 5⅔ innings. His arm, and his pitching, would never be the same. He made two more starts, but did not finish the first inning of his final start of the season, on July 12.

In 1978 Fidrych came back to start the season and pitched an Opening Day complete-game win. He

During his oh-so-brief big-league career, Mark Fidrych (along with Al Hrabosky) had a bit role in The Slugger's Wife.

followed that with another complete-game win. But by the time he appeared again on the April 24 cover of *Sports Illustrated*, he had made his third and last start of the season. Still he persisted, making four starts in 1979, but posting an ERA of 10.43. He was limited to nine starts in 1980. He did win his final major-league start, the last game of the 1980 season.

Fidrych even returned to the minors for portions of the 1980 season and all of 1981. After the 1981 campaign he was released by the Tigers but was signed by the Red Sox. He continued to try to return to the majors, pitching in the minors for the Pawtucket Red Sox in 1982 and 1983. But his pinpoint control was gone and he walked far more batters than he struck out. He finally retired from baseball on June 29, 1983, at the age of 28. An article in *The Sporting News* said Fidrych tried everything short of surgery in an attempt to find a solution to the recurring tightness in his shoulder.[15] In 1985 Fidrych went to see Dr. James Andrews, who diagnosed him with a torn rotator cuff and successfully operated to repair his shoulder. However, it was too late for a comeback.

It is easy to speculate what brought about Fidrych's career-ending injury. The knee injury before the 1977 season may have precipitated a change in his pitching motion which in turn may have caused the tear in his rotator cuff. There is certainly no question that he threw a high percentage of complete games in his starts. In the period 1976-1978, Fidrych threw complete games in 77 percent (33 of 43) of his starts. Although pitch counts for his starts were not recorded, the number of batters he faced can be calculated. In 1976 Fidrych faced 34 or more batters in 17 of his starts. Given an approximate average of 3.5 pitches per batter faced, Fidrych, at age 21 with one full season in the minors behind him, was likely throwing more than 120 pitches in most of the games he pitched. In one game he faced 47 batters, which meant that he threw approximately 165 pitches. Regardless of the cause, Fidrych's career was cut severely short by his injury.

Fidrych went back home to Northboro, Massachusetts, where he became a licensed commercial truck driver and later purchased a farm. He married his wife, Ann, in 1986, and they had a daughter, Jessica.[16] He made appearances for charity groups and nonprofit organizations over the years, making himself rather accessible to fans who fondly remembered the career of the Bird. Tragically, Fidrych died on April 13, 2009, at age 54, in an accident as he worked underneath a truck.

Both before and after his death, Fidrych remained in the consciousness of America. He was the inspiration behind, among other things, a coloring book on his career;[17] a unique autobiography, titled *No Big Deal*, that he co-authored after the 1976 season;[18] a poem by his biographer, Tom Clark;[19] an independent film, *Dear Mr. Fidrych*, written and directed by Mike Cramer, a lawyer from Chicago;[20] and the song "1976" by the band the Baseball Project.[21] Each of these works reflects the exuberance, idealism, innocence, humility, and greatness found in the career and life of Mark Fidrych.

Fidrych and fellow pitcher Al Hrabosky played bit parts in the 1985 movie *The Slugger's Wife*, which—although written by the acclaimed playwright Neil Simon—was panned critically.[22] Fidrych played a much greater role in the movie from 2009, *Dear Mr. Fidrych*. As one might assume from the title, this film was greatly inspired by Fidrych and features him primarily as an unseen character, but also includes him playing himself for a brief but significant segment. The storyline follows a boy, Marty Jones, from the Detroit suburbs who comes to love Fidrych in 1976 and mails him a poem. Fidrych writes back, inspiring the youthful baseball career of the boy. The movie then moves forward 30 years, with Marty now going through something of a midlife crisis and embarking on a road trip with his son. At the suggestion of his son they decide to travel to Massachusetts and try to meet Fidrych. They arrive at Fidrych's farm, meet the father's boyhood hero, who is generous with his time and wisdom, and even play catch with him. While the movie was a low-budget ($30,000) dream project of its creator, with himself and his family playing the leading roles, it has a big heart, much like Fidrych himself.[23] Fidrych died weeks before the movie was first screened.

After his playing career ended, Fidrych was never bitter about his shortened career. He always referred to himself as "lucky," saying, "I got a family, I got a house, I got a dog. I would have liked my career to have been longer, but you can't look back."[24]

NOTES

1. Mark Fidrych and Tom Clark, *No Big Deal* (New York: J.B. Lippincott Company, 1977), 82-83.
2. All playing statistics were accessed at baseball-reference.com.
3. Bill James and Rob Neyer, *The Neyer/James Guide to Pitchers* (New York: Simon and Schuster, 2004), 203.
4. Bill James, *1977 Baseball Abstract* (self-published, 1977), 37.
5. Jim Hawkins, "The Bird Amuses Tigers, Befuddles Enemy Swingers," *The Sporting News*, June 5, 1976: 8.
6. Jim Benagh and Jim Hawkins, *Go Bird Go!* (New York: Dell Publishing, 1976), 142.
7. Pat Calabria, "Yanks Object to a Presentation," *Newsday*, June 29, 1976: np.
8. Ernie Harwell, "Mark Fidrych," in Danny Peary, ed., *Cult Baseball Players* (New York: Simon and Schuster, 1990), 323-327.
9. Calabria.
10. Thomas Rogers, "Rookie Hurls 7-Hitter for 8-1 Record," *New York Times*, June 29, 1976: 37-38.
11. Lowell Reidenbaugh, "Insult Added to Injury: AL's Sad All-Star Fate," *The Sporting News*, July 31, 1976: 5.
12. Jim Hawkins, "Bird a Tabby Cat at Contract Table," *The Sporting News*, October 30, 1977: 20.
13. Dave Marsh, "The Tale of the Bird," *Rolling Stone*, May 5, 1977: 42-47.
14. Peter Gammons, "The Bird Flaps Again and Doesn't Flop," *Sports Illustrated*, June 6, 1977: 20-21.
15. "Fidrych, Facing Cut, Chooses Retirement," *The Sporting News*, July 11, 1983: 45.
16. Bryan Marquard, "Mark 'The Bird' Fidrych, 54; Pitcher Enthralled Fans," *Boston Globe*, April 14, 2009: B14.
17. Rosemary Lonborg and Diane Houghton, *The Bird of Baseball: The Story of Mark Fidrych, A Coloring Book* (Northboro, Massachusetts: Fidco Distributors, 1996).
18. Fidrych and Clark.
19. The poem can be found in Richard Grossinger and Lisa Conrad, eds., *Baseball I Gave You All the Best Years of My Life, Fifth Edition* (Berkeley, California: North Atlantic Books, 1992), 90.
20. *Dear Mr. Fidrych*, An Independent Film by Mike Cramer, Monkeydog Media LLC, 2009.
21. The Baseball Project, "1976," (written by Steve Wynn), Volume 2: High and Inside, Yep Roc Records, 2011.
22. One such critical review can be found at: rogerebert.com/reviews/the-sluggers-wife-1985, accessed January 2, 2017.
23. Phone interview with Mike Cramer by Richard J. Puerzer, January 25, 2012.
24. Marquard.

PAT FLAHERTY

BY BILL HICKMAN

HIS NAME WAS EDMUND Joseph Flaherty. People called him Ed, Eddie, and Pat. He was a pitcher who became a spring training prospect with the Washington Senators and Boston Red Sox, but he never played in a major-league regular season game. He received a World Series medal with the New York Giants, though he spent the entire Series in the bullpen. His name isn't in any baseball encyclopedia, but his life is indeed worth remembering. Ironically, through his career outside of baseball Flaherty was seen by more people than were most of his contemporaries who weren't named Cobb or Ruth.

Born March 8, 1897, in Washington, D.C., Flaherty attended Eastern High School for a couple of years, and finished that academic level by prepping at the Dean Academy in Franklin, Massachusetts. He played baseball and football, boxed, and wrestled. He was gaining attention from the Washington sports reporters before he graduated from high school.

He made connections all his life. While in high school, he became a page to House Speaker James Beauchamp "Champ" Clark. Through that contact, he was assured an appointment to West Point. But he never went to college. He was too busy taking on jobs in sports and in the military.

Pat's uncle was Patrick Henry Flaherty, a major-league third baseman with the 1894 Louisville team in the National League. Pat's father Mike was a friend of Clark Griffith, who signed the lad in 1916 while he was still a teenager. Pat's best pitch was reputed to be a spitball, which was legal at that time.

Pat first arrived at the Senators spring training camp in Augusta, Georgia, on February 28, 1917, at the age of 19. It had already been decided that he would be farmed out to the Des Moines Boosters in the Class-A Western League as final payment in a swap for Nats hurler Claude Thomas. But Griffith wanted Pat to get a workout with the big leaguers while awaiting final instructions from Des Moines. On March 12, Pat made his first appearance in an inter-squad game. He gave up only one run in four innings and hit a long single that turned into an out as he tried to stretch it into a double. He hurled again on March 14, yielding four runs in one inning and holding the opposition scoreless in the following three frames. Pat continued to pitch in Senators inter-squad games until March 30, when he was shipped out.

In 1918, Pat was missing from spring training because he was a World War I pilot with the U.S. Army Aviation Corps in Memphis, Tennessee. In the latter half of 1917, he had attended the School of Military Aeronautics at Princeton University. He graduated from there on January 26, 1918.

Flaherty reappeared at a Nats training camp in Augusta, Georgia, on March 16, 1919. He changed his motion from overhead to sidearm. His control began to improve, but he was inconsistent. In a game on March 30, he was rocked by opposing batters and gave up a home run to Walter Johnson. He asked his manager for permission to pitch again two days later and came back with four scoreless innings. Returning to the mound on April 3, he yielded only one run in four innings, despite his fielders' committing six errors behind him. The (Washington DC) *Evening Star* reporter opined that no runners would have reached second base if it had not been for the sloppy fielding of Flaherty's teammates. On April 5, Flaherty pitched four scoreless innings, but evinced some control problems again. On April 7, he started complaining about a sore arm. On the morning of April 10, he participated in his final workout with the Senators. He rejected their offer to go to a minor-league team, and headed home.

Flaherty spent the rest of 1919 with the Baltimore Dry Docks semipro team, where he chalked up a

31-7 record. The Dry Docks played in the Delaware Shipyard League and won the championship that year. The Dry Docks had high-caliber talent, with future Hall-of-Famer Waite Hoyt being their other main starter for the first part of the season. Hoyt had performed so well in an exhibition game against the Cincinnati Reds that he had been subsequently signed to a Boston Red Sox contract. Former big-leaguers Dave Danforth, Hugh Canavan, Eddie Zimmerman, and Johnny Bates were also on the Dry Docks' staff.

During the 1919 season, the Dry Docks played exhibition games against the Red Sox, Braves, and Reds, and encountered a rainout for a game scheduled with the Phillies. In the September 7 game against the Red Sox, 10,000 Baltimore fans filled Orioles Park to witness the return of Babe Ruth to his hometown. The Babe did not disappoint, as he slugged two homers off Pat Flaherty and also pitched for the final two innings. Although Flaherty and the Dry Docks lost 10-6, Pat pitched a complete game. The *Baltimore Sun* reported that he only suffered two bad innings and was not roughed up during the rest of the game.

After the 1919 season ended, the International League champion Baltimore Orioles entered into a seven-game series with the Dry Docks for the honor of being Baltimore's best team. The Dry Docks won the series, four games to three. Flaherty won one game and lost one. His most memorable game during this series came on September 21. He threw a pitch close to the head of Oriole (and former major leaguer) Merwin Jacobson. The two then rushed towards each other and threw a few punches. Other players and some members of the crowd came into the fracas. It ended with the police seizing both players, and hauling them to the Northern Police Station, where they were charged with "acting in a disorderly manner in a public resort." The two players were back playing ball against each other the next day.

Flaherty spent the 1920 spring training season with the Boston Red Sox. On March 18, he earned a win over the Pittsburgh Pirates, despite giving up two runs in three innings. On March 29, he pitched against the New York Giants and yielded six hits and six runs in five innings. The Red Sox kept him on into the beginning of the season, mostly as a batting practice pitcher. On April 17, they traded him to the San Francisco Seals for former major-leaguer Herb Hunter, who would get another crack at the big leagues for a few games with the Red Sox. Flaherty subsequently moved on from San Francisco to Akron.

In 1920, Flaherty pitched for the Akron Buckeyes in the International League. Jim Thorpe was one of his teammates and made a lasting impression on him. Flaherty had a 12-5 record with a 3.35 ERA for the Buckeyes. Thorpe hit .360 in 128 games. This was the season after Thorpe's major-league career had ended, but he still had his batting skills.

Flaherty began 1921 pitching for the San Francisco Seals of the Pacific Coast League. This stint brought him his only baseball card, a 1921 Zeenuts issue. He moved on to the Shreveport Gassers in the Texas League before the New York Giants announced on September 12 that Pat Flaherty was being promoted to their team. In 1921, the World Series had the potential to run nine games, so it appears that the Giants were stocking additional pitching help for an emergency. The Giants beat the Yankees in eight games, and Flaherty got to watch the proceedings from the bullpen.

Flaherty did rise to the major league level in football. He was an end and halfback, and a fine punter. He played at the opposite end of the line from George Halas with the 1923 Chicago Bears. The *Washington Post* of December 24, 1923, carried an article entitled "Flaherty Back Home After Great Season." The article said: "Patsy Flaherty, last year's star end for the Washington professional football team, has just returned to town after a successful season with the Chicago Bears, runners-up in the national pro race and winners of the 1923 Western professional title. Flaherty participated in twelve of the thirteen games, which the Bears played and made quite a name for himself in the Windy City as a punter. He started the season at end but, because of his passing and booting ability, was shifted to the back field where he starred." He also played for the Bears in 1924.

Flaherty played in one game in 1926 with the Brooklyn Horsemen of the old American Football League. Red Grange had been blocked from starting an NFL team in the New York area, so he formed the AFL instead. Quarterback Harry Stuhldreher, one of the Four Horsemen of Notre Dame, led the Horsemen. On November 7, in a game against Red Grange's team, Flaherty played and scored a touchdown by grabbing a deflected pass and scampering 35 yards down the field. The Horsemen franchise only played four games before they were merged into the Brooklyn Lions. Boxing promoter Humbert Fugazy was the owner of the Horsemen. In 1929, Pat Flaherty would marry Fugazy's daughter, Dorothea. She too was an athlete, having qualified for the Olympics in swimming.

Flaherty also played pro football with the New York Giants. A Charlottesville, Virginia, newspaper article places him with the football Giants in the era of Bruce Caldwell, Jack McBride and Hinkey Haines, the latter a fellow who also played briefly in the majors with the Yankees. Since Caldwell's first year with the Giants and Haines' last year were the same, 1928, the Flaherty who appeared with the Giants at left end in a September 30 game that year was Pat.

Along with the above experience in pro football, Flaherty also played for several Washington, D.C., independent teams for a number of seasons.

He was in the military service during the Mexican border war, World War I, World War II, and the Korean War, having attained the rank of major by the time of his final discharge. After his professional athletic career ended, he went into the music publishing business with the DeSylva-Brown firm of New York. And after that, he became a Hollywood actor, with around 250 films to his credit. He was in many of the baseball classics and other recognizable movies.

He was first drawn to California because his brother, Vincent X. Flaherty, had preceded him there. Through his brother's connections, he landed a job working as a producer for Joseph Kennedy in 1930. As the Great Depression took hold, he lost the job as a producer and turned to acting.

Pat Flaherty may never have made the major leagues, but he worked for years in the movie industry and had roles in scores of baseball and non-baseball films.

He played Red Sox manager Bill Carrigan in *The Babe Ruth Story*. He was umpire Bill Klem in *The Winning Team*. He taught Gary Cooper to pitch and appeared with him in *Meet John Doe*. Pat and his good friend Lefty O'Doul worked on Cooper's baseball skills for the latter's role as Lou Gehrig in *Pride of the Yankees*. Pat had a small acting part in that movie as well. He was in *The Jackie Robinson Story*. He was the Braves manager in *Angels in the Outfield*. He played in *The Stratton Story*, *Death on the Diamond*, *It Happened in Flatbush*, and *Take Me Out to the Ball Game*.

Flaherty had first befriended Jim Thorpe when the two were playing baseball. He campaigned to have Thorpe's Olympic medals restored and developed the initial writing for what later became a movie, *Jim Thorpe-All-American*. Pat turned his work over to his brother, Vincent X. Flaherty, who became a screenwriter for the movie. Vince was also a screenwriter for the movie *PT 109*, about John F. Kennedy. Earlier in his career, Vince was a sportswriter for the *Washington Times-Herald*.

Flaherty was in some of the top all-time films. The following three of his movies won Academy Awards for Best Picture of the Year: *Mutiny on the Bounty* (he was the lead mutineer), *You Can't Take It With You*, and *The Best Years of Our Lives*. The following films in which he appeared won nominations for Best Picture or Outstanding Motion Picture: *Sergeant York*, *The Grapes of Wrath*, *The Treasure of The Sierra Madre*, *Yankee Doodle Dandy*, and *Naughty Marietta*. *My Man Godfrey* was the first movie to receive Oscar nominations in all four acting categories (Best Actor, Best Actress, Best Supporting Actor, Best Supporting Actress). He became friends with Ronald Reagan when the two worked together on *Knute Rockne All American*, the movie remembered for the "Win One for the Gipper" speech. Flaherty appeared in other classic films: *A Day at the Races*, *Boom Town*, *Dodge City*, *Key Largo*, *The Lemon Drop Kid*, *Gentleman Jim* [Corbett], and *The Asphalt Jungle*. He was also in popular film series like Blondie, the Bowery Boys, the Thin Man, and Charlie Chan.

Moreover, he appeared with the Marx Brothers, Charlie Chaplin, Bob Hope, Red Skelton, Joe E. Brown, and the adorable young Shirley Temple. He was with heartthrobs Errol Flynn, Clark Gable, Cary Grant, and Frank Sinatra. There were the famous pairs Humphrey Bogart and Lauren Bacall, Spencer Tracy and Katharine Hepburn, Nelson Eddy and Jeannette MacDonald, William Powell and Myrna Loy, not to mention Bud Abbott and Lou Costello. Finally, there were beauties like Esther Williams, Doris Day, Marilyn Monroe, Betty Grable, Jean

Pat Flaherty, center standing, in It Happened in Flatbush; *Lloyd Nolan, playing a Brooklyn skipper not named Leo Durocher, is on the right.*

Harlow, Janet Leigh, Debbie Reynolds, and Jane Powell.

Starring roles weren't in the cards for him. One of his highlights was having 10 or so lines in *Meet John Doe* with Gary Cooper and Barbara Stanwyck. He appeared without credit in many movies, and even his credited roles tended to be relatively brief. He accepted it all with good humor. An article by Bob Ray in the September 8, 1940, issue of the *Los Angeles Times* quoted him as follows: "Strangely, in about nine out of ten parts that come my way, the script always calls for me to be knocked down. And I've compiled a pretty good list of screen celebrities who've either won decisions over me or kayoed me. Among them are Clark Gable, Spencer Tracy, Jimmy Cagney, Melvyn Douglas, Brian Aherne, Dick Arlen, Andy Devine, Jack Holt, Big Boy Williams, Wayne Morris and—don't laugh—Jane Withers." Having been a competitive boxer and wrestler in his youth, it must have been difficult for Flaherty to become a fall guy, but he was very adaptable as a Hollywood actor.

As Hollywood moved into the 1950s, television began to take hold in American households. It became more difficult to make a living as a film actor, so Flaherty moved on to become a public relations specialist with Sperry-Piedmont, an affiliate of the Sperry Rand Corporation. He did make a few television appearances, but his acting career was essentially completed.

Flaherty was married twice. His first wife was the former Dorothy Fiske. From census data, it is estimated that the marriage took place around 1919. The couple had one child: Edmund Flaherty Jr. was born in 1919 and died in 1995, by which time his name had been changed to Edmund Graham. The first marriage ended in divorce during the 1920's. At the time of the 1930 census, Dorothy Fiske had re-married and was living as Dorothy Graham in the Bronx, New York, with her son Edmund Jr. and some additional children. Pat had married Dorothea Fugazy, the daughter of New York boxing promoter Humbert Fugazy, on January 19, 1929. Fugazy had grand visions of using outdoor venues to draw larger fight crowds. He was the first promoter to gain the exclusive right to use the Polo Grounds and Ebbets Field for boxing matches. Indeed, Fugazy promoted two of Jim Braddock's fights—against Norman "Doc" Conrad in Jersey City on December 26, 1926, and against Joe Sekyra in Ebbets Field on August 8, 1928. Considering some of the people who decked Pat in the movies, it's clear that the script didn't allow Pat to follow his father-in-law's advice! Dorothea and Pat had two children—Patrick Joseph Flaherty and Frances X. Flaherty Knox.

He died on December 4, 1970, in New York City. He was a man of many talents who knew how to live life to the fullest by making many friends. The list of celebrities who considered him a friend is enormous. As just one example, when it came time for his daughter Frances to learn to play golf, it was his friend Smoky Joe Wood who taught her. His Washington Senators teammates enjoyed having him around in spring training, and they missed him when he was shipped out. It was the Senators fans' loss that they were never able to see him pitch for the team during the regular season.

SOURCES

Edmond "Pat" Flaherty's daughter, Frances Flaherty Knox, generously provided a great deal of information for this article. Other sources not already cited above include many issues of the *Washington Star*, *Washington Post*, *Baltimore Sun*, and *New York Times*. During the week of November 5, 1951, Dan Parker wrote a column about the athletic Flaherty family for the *New York Daily Mirror*. On January 9, 1957, Bob Addie published a column about the Flaherty men in the *Washington Post and Times Herald*.

The Encyclopedia of Minor League Baseball, by Lloyd Johnson; *The International League*, by Marshall Wright; and *Baseball: The Biographical Encyclopedia*, by the editors of *Total Baseball*, were used as references. Two other helpful sources were the Internet Movie Data Base (IMDb) website, and email correspondence with Bob Carroll of the Professional Football Researchers Association. Rob Edelman, a SABR expert on baseball's connection to the movies, also kindly corresponded with me on this subject. SABR member Tom McElroy contributed the research on the Baltimore Dry Docks exhibition game against the Boston Red Sox.

FROM SPRING TRAINING TO SCREEN TEST

Additional Information

Pat Flaherty was in films with almost every Hollywood legend of his day: Jimmy Stewart, Loretta Young, Elsa Lanchester, Kirk Douglas, John Wayne, Judy Garland, Burt Lancaster, Ginger Rogers, Henry Fonda, Rosalind Russell, Lionel Barrymore, John Barrymore, Claire Trevor, Edward G. Robinson, Jane Wyman, Rita Hayworth, Olivia de Havilland, Carole Lombard, Barbara Stanwyck, Ann Sheridan, Jean Arthur, Charles Laughton, Irene Dunne, Douglas Fairbanks Jr., William Holden, and many others. Jazz fans found him in *New Orleans*, along with Louis Armstrong, Billie Holiday, and Woody Herman.

LEW FONSECA

BY JOHN GABCIK

LEW FONSECA WAS A BATTING champion, a versatile fielder who played multiple positions, a manager, and a batting instructor. Off the field, he was an accomplished singer, radio announcer, and a film director and producer. But most of all, he was a promoter of and educator for the game of baseball, taking the technical resources at hand to help others better understand the sport he loved. Today, when Little Leaguers watch DVDs so they can learn how to hit, when a college coach spends hours in the film room discovering how to make his team better, when an umpire's inaccurate call is overturned thanks to a slow-motion replay, even when a designated hitter comes to bat — all of those modern instances got their start, in part, over 80 years ago when Lew Fonseca purchased his first motion-picture camera

Lewis Albert Fonseca was born in Oakland, California, on January 21, 1899, the son of European immigrants. Lew's father, Joseph, a barber, was from Lisbon, Portugal; his mother, Anna, a baker, was from Switzerland. The parents set up their respective businesses in San Francisco, where they raised Lew and his two siblings, Ava and Joseph II. Lew would always remember a night in his childhood when it began raining in his bedroom. The date was April 18, 1906, and the "rain" was actually plaster, falling from the ceiling, as the devastating San Francisco Earthquake began; the Fonsecas ended up sleeping in Golden Gate Park with many others.

As Lew grew into manhood, it became apparent that he was gifted both in athletics and as a singer, with a beautiful baritone voice. Lew gave both talents their due, playing ball on the sandlots during the day with Lefty O'Doul and the San Francisco "Park Bums,"[1] then singing in local music halls at night. He enrolled at St. Mary's College of California, attending classes for dentistry and playing ball for the St. Mary's Phoenix during 1918-1919. St. Mary's baseball, under the direction of Brother Agnon McCann, had become a pipeline for a number of major-league baseball players, including Harry Hooper.[2] Fonseca's skills were noted by the San Francisco Seals, who signed him for the 1920 season. But after spring training and only two at-bats, Fonseca moved on. The Seals wanted Fonseca to gain experience with an affiliate in Vancouver, but instead the self-assured young man got himself hired as the player-manager of Smithfield in the outlaw Northern Utah League. There, Fonseca not only won the league batting title, hitting .469, but also made himself a favorite at the local vaudeville house with his singing performances.

In 1921 Fonseca signed with the Cincinnati Reds as a "bonus baby" of sorts. The contract called for him to be paid $1,500 by the Reds, but only if he made the team out of spring training. Fonseca did, starting at second base in the team's first game of the season; batting against Babe Adams of the Pirates, he hit a single and triple in four at-bats. But Fonseca was soon sidelined with injury. He seemed to have a penchant for running into immovable objects, especially on the basepaths where collisions loomed. Although Fonseca was a good-sized man at 5-feet-11 and 185 pounds, he often got the short end of confrontations.[3] In the 1924 season, as an example, he played in only 20 games, hitting .228; his season was wrecked when he ran into second baseman Rogers Hornsby of St. Louis and broke his left arm. After four years with the Reds, he had averaged .301 at the plate, but had appeared in only about 40 percent of the Reds' games. His Cincinnati career ended on March 30, 1925, when the Philadelphia Phillies selected him off waivers.

Fonseca had continued his singing career while in Cincinnati, appearing in local theaters with the billing "A Better Ballplayer than any Singer — A Better Singer than any Ballplayer."[4] But during his recuperation from injury in 1924, he married Ruth Burr Doolittle, a nurse from San Francisco; this seemed to bring an end to his stage career. The couple had a son, Lewis Jr., in 1925 and a daughter, Carolyn, in 1930.

When Fonseca came to the Phillies in 1925 it seemed that he had finally found a home and a jump-start to his career; in Philadelphia; he was healthy—and hitting. Playing in 126 games, he hit .319 with a .802 OPS.

Despite Fonseca's efforts, the Phillies were not a good team, and getting worse; they would be a losing team with or without him. The Phillies solution was to offer Fonseca less money—and he balked. So when he stayed home with his $6,000 contract ($500 less than 1925), the Phillies chose a practical solution, sending Fonseca's rights to the Newark Bears of the International League. Fonseca reluctantly reported to the Bears and soon became the darling of their fans, hitting .381 with 40 doubles and 21 home runs. Newark finished third in the standings but first in attendance. The Bears capitalized on their hot commodity, selling Fonseca to the Cleveland Indians for $50,000 and three players. In 1927 he justified the Indians' investment, hitting .311 and playing both second base and first base in 112 games.

That winter, back in his home state of California, Fonseca had the opportunity to be an extra in Hollywood movies, including the baseball movie *Slide, Kelly, Slide*.[5] Throughout Fonseca's lifetime, articles were written about his developing a passion for various avocations; he threw himself into a new interest the same way he threw his body into an obstacle on the field—singing, public speaking, golf, ping-pong, magic tricks, mountain climbing, it didn't matter.[6]

Raised on the West Coast with Hollywood in its infancy, and singing in venues where film was part of the undercard, it's not surprising that Fonseca developed an interest in movies. So when the Stewart-Warner Company decided to stop producing movie cameras, Lew decided to purchase a 16-millimeter version at the $50 sellout price. The new hobby was to change the direction of his life.

Fonseca returned to Cleveland for the 1928 season, but again incurred injuries; while hitting a spiffy .327, he played in only half the Indians' games. Then in 1929, Fonseca showed what he was capable of when healthy. Playing 148 games, all at first base, Fonseca led the American League in hitting with a .369 batting average; he had 44 doubles and 103 RBIs. Fonseca even stole a career-best 19 bases that year, a heady number for a notoriously slow runner. After the season he was named as the Most Valuable Player of the American League by the Baseball Writers Association of America.[7]

The following January, Fonseca became ill with scarlet fever and was ordered to bed-rest for several weeks. He missed much of 1930 spring training, entered the season weakened and out of shape, and then injured his wrist. Fonseca had only 129 at-bats that year with a .279 batting average; his inability to stay healthy was again being noticed. When Fonseca started 1931 with a hot .370 average in his first 26 games, the Indians wasted no time in trading him to the Chicago White Sox for dependable third baseman Willie Kamm. The White Sox moved Fonseca to the outfield; there, in 121 games, he hit .299, accumulating a .312 batting average in 573 at-bats for the season. His efforts, however, did little to help the Sox, who finished eighth.

After the season White Sox manager Donie Bush resigned, and on October 12, 1931, owner Charles Comiskey named Fonseca to succeed Bush; the deal was for two years.[8] Fonseca continued to be listed on the active roster, but his playing time diminished greatly.[9]

The congratulatory messages on Fonseca's promotion were muted. The White Sox were a franchise in crisis. They weren't a young team, and their ho-hum pitching staff was the oldest in the league.[10] They had 31-year-old Ted Lyons and rookie Luke Appling, both future Hall of Famers, but not much else. They had not had a winning season in five years or a first-division finish in 11 years—and Fonseca was unable to change the trend. His 1932 White Sox were 49-102, setting franchise records for the fewest wins, lowest winning percentage, and lowest attendance. Amazingly, the Sox moved up a notch from the year before to finish seventh. J. Louis Comiskey gave Fonseca the go-ahead to deal for better talent that winter. Fonseca made a slew of trades that winter, and with Philadelphia's Connie Mack holding one of his periodic fire sales, Fonseca picked up future Hall of Famer Al Simmons, third baseman Jimmy Dykes, and outfielder Mule Haas for $150,000. The reinforcements, along with Appling's development, allowed the White Sox to improve by 18 wins and a rise to sixth place in 1933.

But Fonseca's movie camera, to that point only a hobby, became an important element in the manager's thoughts in 1933. Fonseca was intrigued by aspects of the game that the human eye couldn't process—but that perhaps the camera could. Simmons, for instance, appeared to put his left foot in the bucket (move it away from the ball as he swung), but the camera showed the foot striding into the ball at contact. Fonseca began taking slow-motion and stop-action film of the stars of the game, dissecting swings and throws, how the body coordinated its parts into successful action. He began filming his players in the spring, using the results to tutor them out of their various ineffective tendencies. At the start of league play, the effect of this practice seemed positive, as the White Sox were 19-14 and in third place near the end of May. However, the team's record began to erode by midsummer; they slipped below .500 in late July with a nine-game losing streak, finishing the season sixth with a 67-83 record. Perhaps Fonseca and his camera's candid eye had become too demanding for his players and their modest aspirations.[11] Nonetheless, Fonseca had become a zealot; that winter, in San Francisco, he was showing schoolboy audiences the film he shot, demonstrating the right and wrong way to do things on the field.[12]

The following season, on May 8, the White Sox had a 4-11 record, and were in a five-game losing streak. Lou Comiskey woke up the following morning and decided that Fonseca was no longer his man.[13] He called Jimmy Dykes to his room and immediately appointed him as his new player-manager. Dykes went to the ballpark, where it became apparent that Fonseca had not been informed of the change; Dykes didn't have the heart to break the news. So Fonseca, in his unofficial final game as manager, led the team to an 8-1 win over the Senators.[14]

Fonseca put his freedom and the money he had saved to good use. He filmed a variety of action throughout the American League, creating images of the game's top players and the techniques that made them successful. He wrote to all of the American League owners, explaining how film could be used as both a promotional and educational tool. He showed up at the American League office in August with the 45-minute film he had shot and edited, and asked AL President Will Harridge to hire him as a promoter for the league. Harridge gave Fonseca three months and $500 to prove himself; Fonseca became a one-man show, lugging camera and screen to more than 100 venues so that 40,000 attendees had seen his presentation by December. He also managed to get to the World Series during that time span, shooting

Multi-talented Lew Fonseca: major leaguer; film director-producer; "baseball educator."

footage to add to another film for the following year. His work was rewarded by Harridge, who signed Fonseca to a one-year contract for 1935.

That December Fonseca presented the film *Play Ball*; his career was established. Harridge created the position of American League promotional director for Fonseca, and installed him in his own office on Michigan Avenue in Chicago.[15] Fonseca was to shoot a film or two every year, see that it was made available to the public, and to also act as an ambassador of the AL, often accompanying the film with personal appearances to schools and civic clubs, offering anecdotes along with hitting and fielding tips for the youngsters in his audience. The films were premiered each winter at a dinner attended by the game's dignitaries. Fonseca was the producer, director, scriptwriter, and sometimes narrator. Film titles included *The First Century of Baseball* (1938), *Touching All Bases* (1940), *Batting Around the American League* (1940), and *The Ninth Inning* (1941). The films often concentrated on specific skills like pitching, baserunning, even umpiring. Fonseca had produced 12 films for the American League by the end of 1946.[16]

The films and their presentations were not Fonseca's only educational activities. He made appearances as an instructor at offseason amateur baseball camps, wrote the book *How to Pitch Baseball* for youngsters, and produced baseball instructional material for General Mills to use in marketing Wheaties. His audiovisual résumé expanded as he broadcast Chicago Cubs games in 1939 and 1940 for WJJD in Chicago with Charlie Grimm as his sidekick.[17] Always thinking of ways to use his camera, Fonseca devised an experiment to gauge the speed of Bob Feller's fastball.[18]

When the United States entered World War II, another opportunity developed for Fonseca to expand his career. President Roosevelt had insisted that major-league baseball continue operations as a means of sustaining American spirit and giving hard-working citizens both entertainment and a degree of normalcy. Weren't the American military entitled to the same support? Fonseca approached Commissioner Kenesaw M. Landis with the concept of producing a World Series film to be distributed to armed-forces bases throughout the world. Landis agreed; equipment manufacturers Hillerich & Bradsby and A.G. Spalding & Bros. agreed to sponsor the film's production and distribution.

The 1943 World Series was a good opportunity for Fonseca to get some experience as a producer without embarrassing himself. The Yankees won the Series in five games; there were no unusual plays or controversial calls that the camera might have missed or caught. And *The 1943 Baseball Classic: The World Series* was geared toward the patriotism of the war effort, so a substantial amount of footage dealt with nongame subject matter. The 23-minute film began with such elements as the singing of "Take Me Out to the Ball Game" (complete with lyrics and bouncing ball), Babe Ruth reading a script extolling the virtue of baseball as a bedrock of American culture, and shots of various baseball dignitaries in the stands. Announcer Bob Elson did not have any game action to describe until the seventh minute of presentation. Much of the action showed batters swinging and baserunners circling the bases; the ball was rarely in view once it left the infield. But other than brief snippets of film from movie-house newsreels, it was the only view that the soldiers—and many fans—had; it was wonderful.

Both in New York and St. Louis, Fonseca was limited to cameras on the first-base side. A lower camera shot the infield play, much of it focused on the baserunners between home and first or second. A higher camera would try to catch plays at the plate or the outfield. Hard-hit balls were difficult to view once beyond the infield, and had only Elson's reporting to make them exciting. But in the following years, more cameras were added, the sight lines became more refined, and the live ball was kept in view. The shadows in the late afternoon played havoc with the visibility, but the image was on camera. Fonseca was able to capture more of the spectacular, unusual, or important plays.[19] The fans not only knew what happened by reading about it; they really knew what happened by seeing it themselves. When a ball eluded Hank Greenberg in the 1945 World Series, he was charged with an error. The official scorer later reversed the call, and Fonseca's film confirmed to the viewer that the ball had taken a strange hop, high over Greenberg's shoulder.

World War II had ended by the following season and, with the troops back home, it seemed pointless to some to keep up the Series films. Why would fans have much interest in watching games that had been decided two months earlier? Fonseca lobbied Commissioner Happy Chandler and the major leagues for continuation, and won. The National League threw in its support and the Major Leagues Motion Picture Division was formed with Fonseca in charge. Fonseca would continue to produce and direct the World Series film each year, and would also produce a film of the annual All-Star Game. He would also continue to produce films on the history of the game along with educational films about baseball technique.

But the fans soon became jaded, expecting the cameras to capture every nuance on the field. In the 1948 World Series between the Indians and Braves, when Fonseca missed filming a pickoff tag by Lou Boudreau on the Braves' Phil Masi—who then went on to score the game's only run—skeptics opined that Fonseca "lost" the evidence that would prove that umpire Bill Stewart had made a bad call, that the National League had pressured him to do so. Regardless of what the camera showed, it was not prudent for the narrator to comment on the umpiring.[20] In the 1955 World Series, there were two attempted steals of home during the first game. Billy Martin was called out, while Jackie Robinson was safe; the cameras distinctly showed the opposite. Fonseca, who was the narrator, never uttered a peep despite the stop-action evidence.

In 1958 Fonseca made a proposal to American League President Will Harridge that caused a stir throughout baseball. Fonseca thought the game would be improved if the substitution rule was relaxed: that a player could exit a game—due to temporary injury or strategy—then re-enter the game at another time. Fonseca had nothing to gain; his affiliation with the game was nonpartisan. But he could see that older players—especially sluggers like Ted Williams—could be more than once-a-game pinch-hitters. The idea presaged today's designated-hitter rule, but in 1958 there were few backers. Baseball leaders like Casey Stengel and Frank Lane ridiculed the idea.[21]

In August of 1959, Fonseca's motion picture dynasty began to change. For 15 years he had been the baseball movie czar, taking the support of Spalding and Hillerich & Bradsby to use as he saw fit. But now the giant Coca-Cola Company was to be the sole sponsor and producer of the films. The supervision of the films remained with Fonseca, but the control was starting to slip. That fall Vin Scully narrated the first World Series film in color, with the Coca-Cola distribution network delivering the film to the public, worldwide.

Other factors were making inroads into Fonseca's domain. By 1960 a high percentage of American households now had a television set to watch the nationally aired World Series. Videotape made the programs immediately available to those who had missed the live airing. Primitive instant replay made controversial or unusual plays immediately available for review during the games, eliminating the need to wait two months for Fonseca's editing process to be completed. Fonseca's work had gone from marquee status to rain-delay fodder. Fonseca remained true to himself through 1968, working hard to create revealing films without disrespecting the efforts of players, managers, and umpires, but taking more and more flak from critics who remarked on his reluctance to avoid film commentary on debatable umpire calls. In 1969 Dick Winik became the producer of the World Series films. Fonseca was given credit as a technical adviser for two years, and then his involvement completely ended. Fonseca had retired from filmmaking with 60 movies in the can, but he hadn't retired from baseball.

The Chicago Cubs admired Fonseca's eagle-eyed ability to dissect what was happening on the field, and hired him as a batting instructor for their major-league players at the beginning of the 1970 season; the Cincinnati Reds soon followed suit, giving Fonseca the distinction of working for rival teams simultaneously. For the next nine years, Fonseca instructed hitting stars like Johnny Bench, Rick Monday, Billy Williams, Bill Madlock, and any hitter on any team who asked for advice.[22] He was straightforward and succinct. More than anything, he advised his students to have patience, to wait until the last possible instant before attacking the ball.

Lew Fonseca finally retired from his beloved game at age 80, after 60 years of service to the major leagues. He died on November 27, 1989, at 90, in Ely, Iowa. He was survived by his son, Lewis Jr.; his daughter, Carolyn Rusoff; and three grandchildren.

SOURCES AND ACKNOWLEDGMENT

In addition to the sources cited in the Notes, I also used the Baseball-Reference.com and Retrosheet.org websites for player, team, box-score, and season pages, pitching and batting game logs, and other material pertinent to this biography. I obtained information from *The Sporting News* through PaperofRecord.com and also used the archives.chicagotribune.com, GenealogyBank.com, and NewspaperArchive.com websites. I consulted *The Official Major League Baseball World Series Film Collection* (MLB Publishing/A&E Home Entertainment, 2009). Finally, I greatly appreciate the assistance of Jenifer Fonseca of Beaverton, Oregon, Lew's granddaughter, who provided me with family and background information.

NOTES

1. The Park Bums were a San Francisco semipro tradition with many famous alumni including Fonseca, O'Doul, Willie Kamm, Harry Heilmann, Jimmy Caveny, and George Kelly. *The Sporting News,* January 19, 1933: 7.

2. St. Mary's had the reputation as a place where "they raise ball players in the oven." Paul J. Zingg, *Journal of Sports History Vol. 17,* Spring 1990. (Hooper, a Deadball Era outfielder with the Boston Red Sox and then the White Sox, was inducted into the Hall of Fame in 1971.)

3. Fonseca's injuries over his playing career include the following: four broken shoulders, a fractured wrist, a chipped ankle bone, a dislocated hip, a concussion, a broken arm, and a severed artery in his leg. Russell Schneider, *The Cleveland Indians Encyclopedia* (Champaign, Illinois: Sports Publishing LLC., 2004), 168.

4. This billing appeared as an advertisement for the Palace Theater in Cincinnati. *Cincinnati Post,* February 24, 1922. A Fonseca profile printed a decade later noted that Fonseca was holding out in 1923 in Cincinnati, and that Reds owner Garry Herrmann, upon hearing him sing at Keith's Vaudeville Theater, gave him a $1,000 raise. "Leaves From a Fan's Scrapbook," *The Sporting News,* January 19, 1933: 7.

5. *Slide, Kelly, Slide* was a baseball comedy produced by Metro-Goldwyn-Mayer starring William Haines and Sally O'Neil, directed by Edward Sedgwick. New York Yankees Bob Meusel and Tony Lazzeri were part of the cast, along with umpire Beans Reardon. TCM.com.

6. Fonseca spent his winters at his home in California focusing on whatever interest captivated him at the time; his activities were always good for a line or two in the hot-stove editions of *The Sporting News.*

7. Fonseca overcame very formidable competition in the American League of 1929. Sixteen batters in the league that year batted at least the 450 times necessary to qualify for the batting title, and were to become Hall of Famers; that year, Fonseca outperformed them all.

8. Charles Comiskey died two weeks later, on October 26, to be succeeded by his son, J. Louis Comiskey; J. Louis was referred to amicably as Lou or J. Lou by the press. Throughout his life, Fonseca took pride in the trust the senior Comiskey had showed in hiring him. *The Sporting News,* January 3, 1962: 19.

9. Fonseca had intended to return to his regular outfield post for 1932, but his injured ankle kept bothering him; over 1932 and 1933, he managed 17 hits in 105 plate appearances, then took himself off the roster.

10. Donie Bush explained his resignation: "I don't mind losing ball games if there is a prospect of better days ahead, but I feel that whatever reputation I possess as a manager would be jeopardized by remaining another year." John Snyder, *White Sox Journal* (Cincinnati: Cleresy Press, 2009), 187.

11. With all of the trades the White Sox had made in 1932-1933, the team's average age became two years older (29.7), only five years younger than Fonseca and unfamiliar with his ways. It's difficult to imagine a group of grizzled veterans taking lessons from an exuberant but inexperienced manager. Fonseca, with his personality and style, would more likely have succeeded at the college level.

12. *The Sporting News,* December 21, 1933: 2, refers to Fonseca as "the ambassador of the American League, spreading the gospel of the game throughout the country."

13. J. Louis Comiskey: "I had no intention of letting him go two days ago. I made up my mind on that while watching yesterday's ballgame." International News Service, *Hammond (Indiana) Times,* May 9, 1934: 9.

14. Dykes: "Hell, I wasn't going to tell him. All I know is that on my first day as manager of the White Sox, Lew Fonseca managed the team." Fred Stein, *And the Skipper Bats Cleanup* (Jefferson, North Carolina: McFarland, 2002), 205.

15. Fonseca had a counterpart in the National League, another former ballplayer, Ethan Allen. Over time, Fonseca did most of his teaching through film, whereas Allen was more a writer

16 *The Sporting News*, December 25, 1946: 10.

17 A hilarious combination, Fonseca and Grimm would get the official attendance one-half inning before it was announced. They would then "predict" the number to the radio audience, just a few off from the announcement that was about to come. Tiring of the ruse, they decided to "predict" the exact number one day, then told their fans they were no longer going to do it because it had become "too easy." John C. Skipper, *The Cubs Win the Pennant!: Charlie Grimm, the Billy Goat Curse and the 1945 World Series* (Jefferson, North Carolina: McFarland, 2004), 22.

18 Bob Feller: "Radar guns were a generation away, but Lew Fonseca came up with a way not only of testing my speed, but illustrating it in a dramatic exhibition. He wanted it to be man against machine, me against a guy on a motorcycle. I was to throw against a standard shooting target with a bull's eye, on a hot day in Chicago's Lincoln Park. The cycle was going 86 mph when the driver blew past me, but the baseball won by three feet. The pitch was calculated at 104 mph." See Bob Feller and Bill Gilbert, *Now Pitching, Bob Feller* (Charleston, South Carolina: The Citadel Press, 2002), 111.

19 Observations and descriptions of Fonseca's World Series films are based on the author's own viewing of *The Official Major League Baseball World Series Film Collection*.

20 Fonseca is credited as the "Baseball Supervisor" on the 1949 feature *The Kid from Cleveland*. For more info, check: "*The Kid from Cleveland*: A Celebration of the Postwar Cleveland Indians," by Rob Edelman, in *Batting Four Thousand: Baseball in the Western Reserve*, ed. Brad Sullivan, a 2008 SABR publication.

21 *The Sporting News*, August 13, 1958: 1, 4, 10, 12, and August 27, 1958: 14, 43.

22 After 45 years of studying major-league hitters, Fonseca made this comment in 1965: "The only players who ever inquired about what I had learned have been the top stars like Ted Williams, Joe DiMaggio, Ernie Banks, Hank Greenberg and Stan Musial. Never has a .250 hitter consulted me." *The Sporting News,* March, 6, 1965: 7.

(continued from previous: of books. Bernard Crowley, "Ethan Allen," SABR Biography Project, sabr.org.)

STEVE GARVEY

BY MAXWELL KATES

STEVE GARVEY WAS THE EPITome of the Southern California cultural icon in baseball spikes. Photogenic, fan-friendly, and media accessible, he projected the image of an All-American success story and devoted family man. As a Los Angeles Dodger in 1974, he won the National League Most Valuable Player Award after starting the All-Star Game at first base as a write-in candidate. In 1984, then a member of the San Diego Padres, he delivered a clutch home run at a critical moment in the National League Championship Series. During the intervening decade, Garvey rapped 1,995 base hits and drove in 1,025 runs for a sterling .303 batting average. By the end of the 1980s, however, his baseball career was a fading memory and his image became that of a human being who erred like any other.

In a Tampa hospital on December 22, 1948, Joseph and Mildred Garvey welcomed the birth of their only child, a son they christened Steven Patrick. Both Joe and Millie were transplanted Long Islanders and Joe passed on his love of baseball, and specifically the Brooklyn Dodgers, to young Steve:

"I always had balls available for me because we had 11 grapefruit trees in the backyard. In the spring I'd take the little hard grapefruits that had fallen off and I'd hit them with a broomstick. I'd be the whole Dodgers lineup … Neal, Gilliam, Campanella, Snider, Hodges."[1]

Fate smiled on Joe Garvey, a bus driver for Greyhound, when in March 1956, he was assigned to drive the defending world champion Brooklyn Dodgers to spring training in Vero Beach. Joe asked permission for his 7-year-old son to be the Dodgers' batboy. It was a position young Steve held for the following six springs whenever the Dodgers came to Tampa.

One particular player impressed Steve both on and off the field. As Mort Zachter chronicled in his biography of Gil Hodges, Steve was amazed at how the taciturn first baseman "always seemed to have time for autograph requests … asking how he was doing in school and Little League, and even taking a few minutes to play catch with him." Zachter identified Hodges as the player Steve intended to emulate.[2] Millie Garvey remembered the ambitions of her young son:

"Steve was about nine or ten when we asked what he would like for Christmas. He said a new baseball glove … but when I asked him where he'd seen the glove [he wanted] and how much it cost, he told me $25. I was shocked. That was a lot of money and I told him so. He said, "Mom, look at it this way: $25 now will bring $25,000 later on.""[3]

Though Garvey was small for a high school athlete at 5-feet-7 and 165 pounds, that did not prevent him from excelling at Chamberlain High, both on the diamond and the gridiron. Batting .472 in his junior year and .465 as a senior attracted the attention of scouts throughout Organized Baseball, as well as Danny Litwhiler, head coach at Michigan State University.[4] Garvey rejected an offer from the Minnesota Twins in 1966 to play for Litwhiler in East Lansing.

The Dodgers' selections in the 1968 amateur drafts are considered to be the greatest in the history of the sport. Then based in Los Angeles, the Dodgers drafted Davey Lopes in January before selecting Bill Buckner, Ron Cey, Tom Paciorek, Joe Ferguson, Bobby Valentine, Geoff Zahn, and Doyle Alexander in June.[5] The Dodgers' shopping spree continued when, in the first round of the secondary phase, they drafted Steve Garvey. Litwhiler gave a glowing report of his young third baseman:

"Steve was an awesome hitter in college. He hit towering home runs. But it was his mental toughness that was so impressive. He could accept the defeat of striking out. … My only question about his making it was his defense. He didn't have the arm for left field. He was acceptable at third, but no more than that."[6] After Garvey spent parts of two seasons at Ogden and Albuquerque, the Dodgers deemed his skills ready for the major leagues. At Albuquerque in 1969 Garvey batted a robust .373 with 18 doubles, 14 home runs, and 85 RBIs in the thin New Mexico air, and the Dodgers called him up. In his major-league debut, on September 1, Garvey struck out against Jack DiLauro of the New York Mets as the Dodgers defeated the eventual world champions, 10-6.[7]

The dawning of a new decade brought challenges to Garvey's burgeoning baseball career. A college football injury limited his fielding range as a third baseman. When he began the 1970 season 2-for-23, he was optioned to Spokane at the end of April.[8] Recalled after the rosters expanded in September, Garvey managed to improve his average to .269, but his fielding remained a problem. With 14 errors at the hot corner in 1971, hecklers began to chant, "When Steve Garvey plays third base, it's Ball Night at Dodger Stadium."[9] To make matters worse, a Mike Marshall screwball fractured his wrist in June, sidelining him for five weeks.[10] In only 85 games in 1972, Garvey made a league-leading 28 errors.[11] Rumors began to circulate that his days in the Dodgers' organization were numbered.

It was the benevolence and ingenuity of a Dodgers teammate that led to Garvey's break at stardom. Steve began the 1973 season on the bench and remained there through the end of June. As the team suited up for a June 23 contest against the Cincinnati Reds, manager Walter Alston was faced with lineup issues. With Von Joshua and Manny Mota both injured, who was going to play left field? Bill Buckner remembered:

"The Dodgers tried Steve Garvey at third base and at left field. Except for pinch-hitting, his career was not looking too well. He could play some first base at Albuquerque [in 1969] and he played well. I suggested this to Alston and rest assured, I never played first base again. Alston moved me to left field."[12] The experiment worked. Although Buckner continued to see action at first base, Garvey batted .304 while improving his fielding percentage to .993 after the transition to first base.[13] Meanwhile, Garvey's personal life was changing. He graduated from Michigan State with a Bachelor of Science degree in 1971; on October 29 that year, he married Cynthia Ann Truhan.[14]

After eight years in the wilderness, the Dodgers were ready to contend again in 1974. They traded for Jimmy Wynn from Houston, Mike Marshall from Montreal, and by June commanded a torrid eight-game lead over Cincinnati.[15] As for Steve Garvey, expectations were modest to the point that his name was not even included on the All-Star Game ballot. That's where the new first baseman defied all odds. By June Garvey was batting .338 with 11 home runs and 46 RBIs.[16] Fans began to notice, and in the weeks leading to the All-Star Game on July 23, Garvey was receiving nearly as many votes as Tony Perez. In the end, Garvey beat Perez by nearly 20,000 votes. It was only the second time in baseball history (Rico Carty in 1970 was the first) that a player was voted to start an All-Star Game without appearing on the ballot.[17]

At the game in Pittsburgh, Garvey went 2-for-4 with a single against Gaylord Perry and a double against Luis Tiant. Augmented by some fancy fielding in the 7-2 victory for the National League, he was named the All-Star Game's Most Valuable Player.[18] Even more impressive, Garvey was ill and remembered "my mouth was full of cotton, all dry from the antibiotics," when Commissioner Bowie Kuhn presented the Arch Ward Trophy to him.[19]

For the regular season, Garvey led the Dodgers to a division title with 200 hits, 21 home runs, and 111 RBIs, scoring 95 runs, batting .312, and making only eight errors at first base.[20] The Dodgers dispatched the Pirates three games to one in the National League Championship Series, highlighted by a 12-1 barrage in the deciding Game Four. Garvey hit a pair of two-run home runs and captured the NLCS MVP.[21] Although the Dodgers lost the World Series to the Oakland A's, Garvey capped his 1974 campaign by winning the National League MVP as well. Perhaps most noteworthy given the obstacles earlier in his career, Garvey won the first of four consecutive Gold Glove Awards at first base.

Not everybody agreed with Garvey's selection. Finishing second with 233 votes to Garvey's 270 was Lou Brock of the St. Louis Cardinals.[22] Although he set a new single-season record with 118 stolen bases, the achievement was underplayed by many of the writers. As Brock remarked in 1975, "a good deal of it had to do with ... the old prejudice ... about base stealers ... that they do it for personal gain, not for the welfare of the team."[23] He continued, "It's true I didn't win it, but it's not true I lost it. I earned it."[24] The MVP fracas was Garvey's first introduction to controversy. It would not be his last.

At 25, Garvey had developed into one of the most consistent players in the National League. Yankees scout Clyde Kluttz even compared him to "a right-handed Lou Gehrig."[25] Batting .319 in 1975 and .317 in 1976, Garvey recorded only three errors in over 1,500 chances in the Bicentennial year.[26] On September 3, 1975, after sitting out the day before, Garvey played the first of 1,207 consecutive games. Garvey was Lou Gehrig. Along with Davey Lopes, Ron Cey, and Bill Russell, he formed part of a Dodgers infield that remained ironclad until 1981. Garvey was selected to the All-Star Game each of those years. In 1977 the Dodgers rewarded their superstar, now the father of two young daughters, with a six-year, $1.971 million contract that expired in 1982.[27] Garvey hit 33 home runs in 1977, one of four teammates to reach the 30 plateau in a season the Dodgers returned to the World Series under new manager Tommy Lasorda. Off the field, Garvey took his star to Hollywood in 1975 when he was featured in the television movie *Hey Coach*. Appearances on *The Mike Douglas Show*, *Fantasy Island*, and the *Mickey's 50* documentary about the Disney character soon followed.

Garvey's rise to stardom could not have been better timed. As the decade of the 1970s evolved, millions of young Americans grew weary of the constant images of explicit violence, illicit drug use, and gratuitous sexuality, not to mention higher taxes on stagnant wages. Paradoxically and in spite of the permissiveness of the times, they began to gravitate toward more traditional values and ideals. William C. Berman chronicled this political phenomenon in his book *America's Right Turn*. Berman described the young Americans as "militants" and observed this conservative revival among Democrats as well as Republicans, transpiring in all 50 states, "…not just in the sunbelt."[28] Berman continues:

"Those militants … were engaged in a cultural civil war … over such matters as the definition of the family, the content of public education, the role of the media … and the various court definitions affecting personal values." These debates "touched on longstanding national conflicts, which were rooted in the profoundly different belief systems and operating codes separating moral traditionalists from social liberals of a secular persuasion."[29]

Not surprisingly, Berman's "moral traditionalists" were dissatisfied with acceptance of the rebel and the scofflaw as protagonists in sports and entertainment, while authority figures including police officers were now considered to be antagonists. They sought heroes who reflected their values. In an era when outspoken

Steve Garvey and his movie star looks made him a natural for appearances in theatrical films, television movies, and television series.

iconoclasts like Reggie Jackson, Dave Kingman, and Dave Parker dominated the headlines, the populist right became more comfortable with the wholesome images of Nolan Ryan, Gary Carter, and George Foster. In football, Roger Staubach raised eyebrows when he proclaimed that "I like sex as much as Joe Namath does; I just have it with one woman."[30]

In was amid this political climate that as "the Gipper" ran for president, "Steve Garvey, All American" became a star both at Chavez Ravine and on Madison Avenue. Garvey was well dressed and clean shaven with every hair in place and did not chew tobacco, swear, or wear jeans. Garvey attended church frequently, was always available to the media for a quotation, helped elderly women across the street, and signed thousands of autographs until every kid had one. A school in the San Joaquin Valley even rededicated itself as the Steve Garvey Junior High School. Tommy Lasorda remarked that "if [Garvey] ever came to date my daughter, I'd lock the door and not let him out."[31] Even in Cincinnati, young Petey Rose came to dinner one night wearing a Steve Garvey T-shirt until his father made him change into a Pete Rose T-shirt.[32]

Although Los Angeles fans and media loved him, Garvey had hordes of adversaries in other National League cities and those in the Dodgers clubhouse who were watching his every move. Joe Garvey conveyed that his son's image was nothing new—even in high school during the turbulent 1960s he wore slacks and monogrammed sweaters.[33] The observations of the elder Garvey, however, did nothing to convince his son's Dodgers teammates of his authenticity.

As early as 1975, Betty Cuniberti of the *San Bernardino Sun* wrote that Garvey "doesn't have a friend on this team.[34] As someone who did not smoke or drink, the perception was that Garvey was judgmental of teammates who did. Several teammates were resolute that Garvey's photographs and autographs were not initiated on his own volition, but rather as a means to gain popularity in order to generate endorsements."[35] Cynthia even pleaded with him, "[C]ouldn't you drink a beer or two? They'll like you better."[36] As a member of the Chicago Cubs in 1986, Davey Lopes expressed where he and his teammates were coming from:

"The problem was that he was presented as better than we were. The press did that. The organization did that. Nobody can question that Garv came to play. . . . It was all the other stuff. It created a tension that never went away, that never eased."[37]

In 1977, Garvey underwent a colossal slump, batting only .205 in 45 games from July 4 through August 24.[38] Although his batting average recovered, it was the only season between 1974 and 1980 in which he failed to hit .300. There was more than enough perverse pleasure in the Dodgers clubhouse when Garvey hit into a double play or was thrown out at home plate. He hit .316 with 202 hits and 113 RBIs in 1978, but again found himself at the center of controversy when teammate Don Sutton agreed to an interview with Thomas Boswell of the *Washington Post* at Veterans Stadium in Philadelphia.

A mercurial personality from rural Alabama, Sutton was not convinced that the media image of his first baseman was the genuine article. As Sutton told Boswell on August 15, "[A]ll you hear about on our team is Steve Garvey, the All-American boy. Well, the best player on this team for the last two years—and we all know it—is Reggie Smith. As Reggie goes, so [go] us. . . . Reggie doesn't go out and publicize himself. He doesn't smile at the right people or say the right things. He tells the truth, even if it sometimes alienates people."[39] Five days passed without controversy but on August 20, as the Dodgers prepared to play the Mets at Shea Stadium, Garvey expressed displeasure to Sutton over his published remarks:

"We are a team," he reminded the pitcher, adding, "If you have something to say to me, say it to my face."[40] There are different interpretations of the events that followed but all parties agree that within moments, Steve Garvey and Don Sutton fell to the floor in a battle royal, "clawing and scratching each other."[41] The press dubbed the incident "the Grapple in the Apple." Milton Richman, who covered the incident for United Press International, recalled seeing that Sutton "leaped at Garvey and shoved him into the lockers."[42] As four of the larger players on the team separated the two, Joe Ferguson remarked that if the fight continued, "maybe they'll kill each other."[43]

A bruised eye did not prevent Garvey from completing a sterling season for the Dodgers:

"Afterwards I went out and got a couple of hits against the Mets, and hit something like .430 [actually .369] for the rest of the season."[44] Much like the 1974 season, Garvey won the MVP Award in both the All-Star Game and the NLCS. At the All-Star Game in San Diego, he rapped a two-run single in the third inning before igniting an eighth-inning rally with a triple to win the game, 7-3.[45] In the NLCS, Garvey hit four home runs and a triple in a 3-games-to-1 win over the Phillies.[46] For the third time in five years, however, the Dodgers lost the World Series. After losing a one-game playoff to the Astros in 1980, the Dodgers behind rookie ace Fernando Valenzuela were once again poised for greatness in 1981.

The new decade brought more opportunities for Steve Garvey, both on Elysian Park Avenue and Hollywood Boulevard. In 1980, he played a cameo role in *The Gong Show Movie*. The following year, he hosted *The Steve Garvey Celebrity Sports Classic* for the Multiple Sclerosis Society, his favorite charity. Notwithstanding a midseason strike that eliminated two months of the season, Garvey batted only .283 with 10 home runs and 64 RBIs. With the Dodgers having clinched the first half before the strike, Garvey saved his heroics for the postseason. Entering Game Four of the NLCS, he hit safely in every playoff contest.[47] Everyone remembers the Rick Monday home run, but in Game Four Garvey put the Dodgers ahead, 3-1, with a two-run homer off Montreal's Bill Gullickson. After losing to the Yankees in 1977 and 1978, the Dodgers finally defeated the Bronx Bombers to win the World Series in 1981.

Expectations were high on the Dodgers to repeat as world champions in 1982. Uncharacteristically for an impending free agent, meanwhile, Garvey suffered an off-year, failing to reach .300, 200 hits, 20 home runs, or 100 RBIs.[48] Under general manager Al Campanis, signing the team's own free agents did not comply with the Dodger Way. Since players earned the right to free agency, the only Dodgers free agent to re-sign with Los Angeles had been Bill Russell in 1980. The team had traded Davey Lopes to the Oakland A's in spring training and would trade Ron Cey to the Chicago Cubs in 1982. Meanwhile, first-base prospect Greg Brock was tearing up the Pacific Coast League, batting .310 with 44 home runs for Albuquerque.[49] Garvey remembered the negotiations with the Dodgers:

"Final offers had to be made. [Peter O'Malley] said his final offer was $5 million for four years, no incentives. We drew the line at $6 million for four years."[50] The erstwhile Brooklyn batboy would not be a Dodger for life, instead on December 21 signing a five-year, $6.6 million contract with the San Diego Padres.[51] Ever conscious of his image, Garvey chuckled that he "looked like a taco" when he first adorned the yellow and brown colors of his new team.[52] By now, Garvey was also beginning a new chapter on his personal life, as his marriage to Cynthia had ended.

On April 15, 1983, Garvey returned to Dodger Stadium as a member of the Padres to a chorus of 53,392 cheering fans.[53] Though he was hitless in four at-bats, the contest was significant as it was Steve's 1,117th consecutive game, tying Billy Williams for the National League record. Garvey extended the streak an additional 90 games, to 1,207.[54] He was batting .294 with 14 home runs and 59 RBIs on July 29, the night the streak ended painfully:

"I was at third. One run was in and we had two men out. The second pitch to Garry Templeton was a fastball, way up. Bruce Benedict, the [Atlanta] catcher, never touched it, and I headed for home." Ninety feet later, pitcher Pascual Perez tagged him at the plate, "I put my hand back for support and felt my thumb—something happened."[55] Garvey broke his thumb in the collision and was out for the remainder of the season.

Manager Dick Williams observed that "Steve did help us" in his truncated 1983 campaign. "He worked hard, influenced the kids, and made it easier for us to get rid of more veterans who weren't producing."[56] Two new veterans who did produce in 1984 were

Yankee imports Graig Nettles and Goose Gossage. Together with a core of young players centered on Tony Gwynn, the Padres were about to shed their reputation as divisional doormats, reaching the postseason for the first time in their history.

Garvey recovered from his thumb injury to play the entire 1984 season without committing an error.[57] Though he was named to start the All-Star Game, his offensive numbers continued to decline; he batted .284 with only eight home runs. Williams wondered if Garvey "left his best days at Dodger Stadium."[58]

That question would be answered in the NLCS against the favored Chicago Cubs, winners of the first two contests. Facing elimination, the Padres won Game Three, 7-1, to set the stage for a monumental Game Four on October 6. In the words of his manager, Garvey "controlled nine innings of baseball like few other hitters in the history of the game."[59]

The game was scoreless until the third inning; after Tony Gwynn broke the stalemate with a sacrifice fly, Garvey drove in the second run with a two-out double. The Cubs scored three but the Padres forced a tie in the fifth when Steve singled in Tim Flannery. San Diego extended its lead to 5-3 in the seventh but the Cubs scored two in the eighth off Gossage to tie once again. Lee Smith was brought in to pitch the ninth for the Cubs. If the Padres lost, they would go home. With one out, Tony Gwynn was on first with Garvey at the plate and Williams in the dugout:

"There was no way Garvey could pull us out of the fire once more and—BOOM!—my thoughts were interrupted by the loudest crack I ever heard. Then I saw the white ball heading towards the right center field fence. ... It really was going out of the ballpark, wasn't it? It was! After what felt like forever, the ball dropped into the stands and Garvey had his homer."[60] The Padres won, 7-5, on Garvey's home run and after winning the following night, they were going to the World Series. Garvey took home his third NLCS Most Valuable Player Award. More than three decades later, Padres fans consider the home run to be the greatest moment in franchise history. Legend had it that on an inbound flight to San Diego not long after, the in-flight service showed *The Natural*; during the famous home-run scene, passengers actually began to chant "GAR-VEY! GAR-VEY!"

The cultural divide between Garvey and his teammates remained pronounced in San Diego, but the players were able to resolve it in a more pleasant way. Goose Gossage remembered a swimming pool party at his home:

"On this particular evening ... Steve looked a little too suave for his own good. As he walked past the swimming pool, several guys tossed him into the shallow end. Head first. When Garvey came up for air, every hair was still in place. 'Perfect,' I muttered. 'Steve Garvey has to be the only guy in the world who could get tossed in a swimming pool and come out looking the same way he did going in.'"[61]

Although Garvey batted an even .300 during the 1984 World Series, the Padres lost in five games to the Detroit Tigers. By 1987, a damaged tendon in his left shoulder limited him to a .200 average with one home run and 9 RBIs in 78 official at-bats.[62] In late May, Garvey learned that his shoulder would require surgery if he wished to prolong his career. Larry Bowa was managing the Padres at the time:

"On May 23 in San Diego," as Bowa remembered, "Garvey took his last major league [at-bat], a ninth inning pinch-hit appearance against Montreal's Neal Heaton. He flew out lazily to center field. A day later, Garvey began to prepare for surgery. There was not enough power left in the shoulder for him to make a comeback in 1988."[63] Steve's final numbers consisted of 2,599 base hits with 440 doubles, 272 home runs, 1,308 RBIs, and a near-perfect .996 fielding percentage.[64]

On April 16, 1988, the Padres retired Garvey's uniform number 6, the first San Diego player to be so honored. After his retirement, Steve founded Garvey Communications, a television production company, while lending his name to corporate products including *Sport* magazine and Fleer Skybox. He continued to serve the Multiple Sclerosis Foundation as its honorary chairman, and he also founded a counseling firm for retired athletes. Appearances in television, film, and documentaries continued in the 1990s and beyond. A gentleman of leisure, Garvey enjoyed golf and skiing. He has also worked in alumni relations for the Dodgers.

In January 1989, Garvey met the former Candace Thomas, a divorced mother of two, at a benefit for the Special Olympics. After a whirlwind courtship with stops at the presidential Inauguration for George H.W. Bush and the Super Bowl, Candace became the new Mrs. Steve Garvey on February 18. Before the ink on their marriage license had even dried, their nuptials would soon be tested.

The spring of 1989 was an inopportune time to be a baseball superstar. After the sport was jolted by scandals involving Pete Rose and Wade Boggs, two women filed paternity suits against Garvey.[65] For a player who went to great lengths to preserve a family-friendly image in Ronald Reagan's America, the suits represented a precipitous fall from grace.

Although never a Steve Garvey fan, Dick Williams rushed to his defense. In the three years that he managed Garvey, Williams affirmed, "I never saw any of that. ... I never saw him in bars" and "he seemed as clean as his image."[66] To his credit, Garvey never denied the charges, as evidenced by the candor of this 2003 interview:

"Could I have been more careful? Yes. Are they my responsibility? Yes. They were two personal choices, and if I had them to do over again, obviously I would do them differently. I made two poor choices, but it happened. I didn't commit a felony, and I stood there and answered every question. I took responsibility. But what I did was out of character."[67]

Like Gil Hodges before him, Garvey was a mainstay as a Dodgers first baseman for over a decade, but like his idol, Garvey continued to be bypassed for induction into the Baseball Hall of Fame. In 1986 he was considered one of the 10 active players most likely to be enshrined in the Hall.[68] During his 15 years on the ballot, Garvey's high-water mark was 43 percent of the vote, in 1995.[69] Bruce Markusen, author of the "Cooperstown Confidential" column, offered the following explanation:

"Garvey's Hall of Fame case has been hurt by SABRmetrics, which show him to be a weaker offensive player than originally thought. He never drew a lot of walks—and that worked against him. He was ... more of a line drive hitter who hit a decent but not overwhelming number of home runs per season." Markusen continued, "On the other hand, he spent a large majority of his career playing at Dodger Stadium, a ballpark that has suppressed offensive numbers for years.[70]

The call from Cooperstown notwithstanding, Garvey has been honored by the Michigan State University Athletics Hall of Fame in East Lansing and the Irish American Baseball Hall of Fame in New York. After many years in Utah, Steve and Candace returned to Southern California with their three children.

For a time, it seemed that if any player was destined to be a Los Angeles Dodger it was Steve Garvey. The former batboy broke in with his favorite team in 1969 and after switching positions from third base to first, became a model of consistency at the plate and on and off the field. The rise of his career was timed with an increasingly conservative undertone in America, and Garvey's image made him an appropriate spokesman for the movement. No longer a "Dodger for life," Garvey hung his star in San Diego in 1982 and brought instant credibility to the Padres franchise. The indiscretions that were revealed after his retirement did not negate the positives. Rather, they made him human. Whether Cooperstown finds him worthy of membership or not, Steve Garvey remains an important link in Dodgers lore between Koufax and Drysdale on one end and Fernandomania on the other.

SOURCES

The author would like to express his appreciation for assistance to Roland Andreassi (1933-2007), William Berman, Barry Bloom, Bill Buckner, Fred Claire, Chris Dean, Bill Deane, Dan Epstein, Michael Fallon, Colin Gunderson, Mrs. P.L. Hirsch, Mark Langill, Bruce Markusen, Wayne McBrayer, Dan Schlossberg, Bill Swank, and Alain Usereau.

NOTES

1   Roy Blount Jr., "Born to Be a Dodger," *Sports Illustrated*, April 7, 1975.

2. Mort Zachter, *Gil Hodges: A Hall of Fame Life* (Lincoln: University of Nebraska Press, 2015), 157.

3. Steve Garvey and Skip Rozin, *Garvey* (New York: Times Books, 1986), 27.

4. Garvey, 34-35.

5. David Manuel, "The History and Future of the Amateur Draft," *Baseball Research Journal*, Volume 39, Number 1 (Cleveland: Society for American Baseball Research, 2010), 66.

6. Garvey, 40.

7. retrosheet.org.

8. Garvey, 56.

9. Rob Neyer, *Rob Neyer's Big Book of Baseball Lineups* (New York: Simon & Schuster, 2003), 119.

10. Garvey 56-57. (Marshall had been a guest lecturer in one of Garvey's courses at Michigan State University.)

11. Neyer, 115.

12. Author interview with Bill Buckner, May 7, 2016.

13. retrosheet.org.

14. David Porter, ed., "Steve Garvey," *Biographical Dictionary of American Sports* (Westport, Connecticut: Greenwood Press, 2000), 540.

15. Garvey, 73-74.

16. Garvey, 74.

17. Michael Fallon, *Dodgerland: Decadent Los Angeles and the 1977-78 Dodgers* (Lincoln: University of Nebraska Press, 2016), 26. (Rico Carty was the first, in 1970.)

18. baseball-reference.com.

19. Garvey, 77.

20. Dan Epstein, *Big Hair and Plastic Grass: A Funky Ride Through Baseball and America in the Swinging 1970s* (New York: St. Martin's Press, 2010), 141.

21. Garvey, 81.

22. baseball-reference.com.

23. Lou Brock and Franz Schulze, *Stealing Is My Game* (Englewood Cliffs, New Jersey: Prentice-Hall, Inc., 1976), 192.

24. Ibid.

25. Fallon, 145.

26. Porter, 541.

27. Garvey, 108.

28. William C. Berman, *America's Right Turn: From Nixon to Clinton*, second edition (Baltimore: The Johns Hopkins University Press, 1998), 60-61.

29. Berman, 61.

30. Dominic Sandbrook, *Mad As Hell: The Crisis of the 1970s and the Rise of the Populist Right* (New York: Alfred A. Knopf, 2011), 323.

31. Rick Reilly, "America's Sweetheart," *Sports Illustrated*, November 8, 1989.

32. Zander Hollander, "Pete Rose," *The Complete Handbook of Baseball: 1978 Edition* (Chicago: Signet Press, 1978), 177.

33. Fallon 149.

34. Betty Cuniberti, "Garvey: The Exception More Than the Rule," *San Bernardino County Sun*, June 15, 1975: 54.

35. Garvey, 91.

36. Cynthia Garvey and Andy Meisler, *The Secret Life of Cyndy Garvey* (New York: St. Martin's, 1989), 136.

37. Garvey, 100.

38. Fallon, 154-155.

39. Tom Boswell, "As Smith Goes, So Go Dodgers, 5-4 Win Over Phils," *Washington Post*, August 16, 1978.

40. Milton Richman, "LA's Garvey, Sutton Explode in Fist Fight," *Salina* (Kansas) *Journal*, August 21, 1978: 9.

41. Epstein, 269.

42. Richman, 9.

43. Fallon, 331.

44. Garvey, 119.

45. Fallon, 321.

46. retrosheet.org.

47. Alain Usereau, *The Expos in Their Prime: The Short-Lived Glory of Montreal's Team, 1977-1984*, English edition (Jefferson, North Carolina: McFarland & Company Inc., 2013), 144.

48. baseball-reference.com.

49. Neyer, 121.

50. Garvey, 176.

51. Garvey, 183.

52. Bill Swank, *Baseball in San Diego: From the Padres to Petco* (Charleston, South Carolina: Arcadia Publishing Inc., 2004), 84.

53. Garvey, 187.

54. Douglas B. Lyons, *100 Years of Who's Who in Baseball* (Guilford, Connecticut: Rowman & Littlefield, 2015), 121.

55. Garvey, 5.

56. Dick Williams and Bill Plaschke, *No More Mr. Nice Guy: A Life of Hardball* (Orlando: Harcourt Brace Jovanovich, 1990), 243.

57. Porter, 541.

58. Williams, 241.

59. Williams, 265.

60 Williams, 266.

61 Richard Gossage and Russ Pate, *The Goose Is Loose* (New York: Ballantine Books, 2000), 199.

62 Larry Bowa and Barry M. Bloom, *I Still Hate to Lose* (Champaign, Illinois: Sports Publishing Inc., 2004), 90.

63 Bowa, 92.

64 Porter, 540-541.

65 Charles F. Faber and Zachariah Webb, *The Hunt for Red October: Cincinnati in 1990* (Jefferson, North Carolina: McFarland, 2015), 75.

66 Williams, 243.

67 Bruce Schoenfeld, "Steve Garvey's Public Exile" on *Street & Smith's Sports Business Daily Global Journal* (March 3, 2003), sportsbusinessdaily.com, accessed December 7, 2016.

68 Zev Chafets, *Cooperstown Confidential* (New York: Bloomsbury Publishing, 2010), 69.

69 baseball-reference.com.

70 Author interview with Bruce Markusen, May 26, 2016.

AL GETTEL

BY CLAYTON TRUTOR

AL "TWO GUN" GETTEL pitched in 184 major-league games over the course of seven seasons between 1945 and 1955. The 6-foot-3 right-hander was frequently traded or sold during his career, pitching for six franchises: the New York Yankees (1945-1946), the Cleveland Indians (1947-1948), the Chicago White Sox (1948-1949), the Washington Senators (1949), the New York Giants (1951), and the St Louis Cardinals (1955). Nicknamed "Two Gun" late in his career for his appearances in several television and movie Westerns, Gettel was a standout in the Pacific Coast League during a long tenure with the Oakland Oaks (1949-1955) and a brief stint with the San Diego Padres (1956). He also excelled during his one offseason pitching in the Cuban Winter League for the pennant-winning Habana Baseball Club (1952-1953). Altogether Gettel pitched in professional baseball for 22 seasons, beginning in 1936 for his hometown Norfolk Tars of the Piedmont League and finishing his career at the age of 41 with the Asheville Tourists of the Sally League in 1959, after a two-year absence from Organized Baseball.

In recent years Gettel gained notoriety from a quote he gave to Joshua Prager of the *Wall Street Journal* in 2001 for a 50th-anniversary retrospective on the 1951 New York Giants and their remarkable turnaround in the second half of the season that culminated with Bobby Thomson's "Shot Heard 'Round The World," a walk-off three-run home run off the Brooklyn Dodgers' Ralph Branca that clinched the pennant for the Giants.[1] Gettel spent the majority of the 1951 season with the Giants before being sold back to the Oakland Oaks in August. He appeared in 30 games for the Giants, primarily as a relief pitcher, and posted a 1-2 record with a lackluster 4.87 ERA. In his 2001 interview with Prager, Gettel said that the Giants had been stealing signs from opposing catchers since the middle of the 1951 season, employing an elaborate system that included a telescope, a buzzer system, and hand signs relayed from the bullpen to alert Giants batters about what to expect on an impending pitch. "Every hitter knew what was coming," the then 83-year-old Gettel told Prager, and that knowledge "made a big difference." Gettel's quote on the 1951 Giants' sign-stealing was corroborated by teammates Sal Yvars and Hall of Famer Monte Irvin, both of whom were on the Giants' roster throughout the season. In the *Wall Street Journal* piece, Prager asserted that Bobby Thomson's pennant-winning home run was in part the product of the Giants' sign-stealing and capped off a half-season's worth of spying on opposing pitchers organized by manager Leo Durocher.[2] The *Wall Street Journal*'s article on the 1951 Giants was the first time that a journalist was able to get anyone from the team to affirm on the record that the Giants had stolen signs during the season. In 1962 a member of the 1951 Giants had been quoted anonymously in an Associated Press story as saying that the Giants had stolen signs from the Dodgers during their pennant-deciding three-game playoff series, including on the fateful pitch from Ralph Branca to Thomson.[3]

Allen Jones Gettel was born in Norfolk, Virginia, on September 17, 1917, to Edward A. and Sarah F. (Jones) Gettel. He was raised on the farm of his maternal grandfather, Nathaniel Jones, in Kempsville, Virginia, in rural Princess Anne County just outside the city of Virginia Beach. Gettel attended Kempsville High School and was signed as an 18-year-old by the New York Yankees in 1936. The Yankees assigned the young right-hander to their Class-B Piedmont League affiliate in Norfolk. Over the next nine seasons, Gettel pitched successfully for seven different Yankees minor-league affiliates, garnering at least a .500 winning percentage in every season except his 1936 rookie year, when he was 0-1.

*Al Gettel, who acted on television (*Steve Donovan: Western Marshal*) and in film (*Tin Star*).*

A pitcher with as accomplished a minor-league pitching record as Gettel's 93-64 (101-70 from 1936 through 1944) would have almost certainly gotten an opportunity at the major-league level in any other organization, but cracking the big-league roster of the Yankees during their late 1930s and early 1940s dynasty was an almost uniquely difficult task. The Joe McCarthy-era dynamic Yankees lineup of hitters was complemented by a pitching staff that included the likes of Red Ruffing, Lefty Gomez, Johnny Murphy, Monte Pearson, Spud Chandler, Atley Donald, and Tiny Bonham.

The Yankees and their manager, Joe McCarthy, finally gave Gettel an opportunity to pitch in the major leagues in 1945. The pitching staff had been severely depleted during the 1944-1945 offseason by the draft call-ups of several pitchers.[4] McCarthy employed the 27-year-old rookie as a starter and middle reliever on a fourth-place Yankees team that finished 6½ games behind Detroit. Gettel had a solid rookie year, compiling a 9-8 record with a 3.90 ERA. He displayed his characteristic control on the mound in 1945, walking a mere 53 hitters in 154⅔ innings.[5] In 1946 Gettel continued to take advantage of his opportunity at the major-league level, posting a strong 2.90 ERA with a tough-luck 6-7 record in 11 starts and 26 total appearances on a Yankees team in transition.

Gettel's ascension to the Yankees came at a time of regime change for the organization. In January 1945 the estate of Jacob Ruppert sold the club to Dan Topping, Del Webb, and Larry MacPhail. Sixteen months later, in May 1946, manager Joe McCarthy resigned because of poor health and pressure from the new owners to return the Yankees to the top of the American League standings.

The Yankees traded Gettel to the Cleveland Indians in December 1946 as part of a five-player deal that brought rookie catcher Sherm Lollar, later an All-Star with the Chicago White Sox, and former All-Star and longtime Tribe second baseman Ray Mack to New York. In addition to Gettel, the Bill Veeck-owned Indians also acquired right fielder and frequent pinch-hitter Hal Peck and left-handed pitcher Gene Bearden, who went on to become a 20-game winner for the Tribe in their 1948 world championship season. Gettel put together what was arguably his best major-league season for the much-improved 1947 Indians, who earned a fourth-place 80-74 finish one season after finishing 68-86, in sixth place, 36 games behind the 1946 pennant winners, the Boston Red Sox. Gettel became the Indians' number-four starter during the 1947 season, garnering an 11-10 record with a 3.20 ERA. He rolled off five consecutive wins in August 1947, which drew the notice of *The Sporting News*, which asserted that Gettel had earned a spot in the 1948 rotation with his impressive performance. Never a power pitcher, Gettel excelled during the 1947 season with his excellent control of several off-speed and breaking pitches.[6]

The 1948 season proved to be a much different one for Gettel. The 30-year-old pitcher got off to a rough start for the upstart 1948 Indians, who found themselves one game out of first place on Memorial Day. In five appearances, he had a 0-1 record with a 17.61 ERA. He started two games and lasted a combined total of four innings, surrendering eight earned runs. On June 2 the Indians dealt Gettel and outfielder Pat Seerey to the White Sox for outfielder Bob Kennedy. Gettel continued to slump in June and July 1948 for the soon-to-be 101-loss White Sox, who used him primarily as a starter. On August 1 Gettel's record stood at 2-7 with a much improved, though hardly impressive, 6.13 ERA. In the final months of the season, Gettel turned things around considerably, winning six of his last 10 decisions and finishing with an 8-11 mark and a 4.01 ERA.[7] Gettel got his only career opportunity to field a position other than pitcher on July 22, 1948, filling in at second base for four innings following the ejection of Cass Michaels in the second game of a doubleheader against the Red Sox. Gettel handled all three of his fielding opportunities cleanly and earned three assists in a 5-3 defeat.[8] Gettel's baseball talents off the mound also included unusual skill at the plate for a pitcher. He compiled a .228 career batting average.

During the 1949 season, Gettel struggled as both a starter and a middle reliever for the White Sox before being sold to the Washington Senators on July 12. His difficulties on the mound continued and Washington sold him to the Oakland Oaks of the Pacific Coast League on August 15. At that time he had a 2-7 record and an unhealthy 6.08 ERA.

In Oakland Gettel found his longest and most successful home as a player. He excelled against the Triple-A competition, going 4-0 with a 3.62 ERA in 12 appearances for the Oaks in the waning days of the 1949 season. He re-signed with the Oaks for the 1950 season and enjoyed his most successful season as a professional pitcher. Gettel went 23-7 with a 3.62 ERA for the PCL champion Oaks, earning him the first of his three spots on the PCL All-Star Team.

Gettel's success in the Pacific Coast League drew the attention of the New York Giants, who acquired him from the Oaks in a six-player deal in October 1950. Though an ace in the PCL, Gettel proved unable to match that success in his return to the major leagues. He appeared in 30 games for the Giants, all but one as a reliever, and posted an ERA close to 5.00 with a record of 1-2. In late July 1951, the Giants sold Gettel back to the Oaks, where he resumed his successful career in the PCL. Gettel led the Oaks in wins in 1952 and 1953, tying the franchise record with 24 the latter season.[9] Between 1949 and 1955, Gettel won 101 games for the Oaks and became one of their most popular players. The Oaks won two league championships during Gettel's tenure with the team (1950, 1954).[10]

Gettel pursued a career as an actor during his years in the Pacific Coast League, appearing in several television and movie Westerns. He received the nickname "Two Gun" from his teammates in Oakland during the 1953 season when he earned a screen test with Paramount Pictures.[11] Gettel was a skilled horseman who fostered the public persona of a cowboy by several times riding out to the mound on his palomino for the first inning.[12] His best known work as an actor included an appearance as a villainous cowboy on the television show *Steve Donovan, Western Marshal* (1955), and a brief role in the Henry Fonda-Anthony Perkins Western *Tin Star* (1957).[13]

In 1955, at the age of 37, Gettel had his final major-league stint, with the St. Louis Cardinals, who had purchased him from the Oaks. He went 1-0 with an ERA of 9.00 in eight appearances in August and September. Gettel finished his major-league career with a 38-45 record and a 4.28 ERA. He played his last season in the Pacific Coast League in 1956 with the San Diego Padres. Gettel then worked briefly as a coach for Oakland and continued to pursue an acting career. He returned to professional baseball briefly in 1959, pitching in five games for the Asheville Tourists of the Sally League. After his baseball career he returned to his family farm in Kempsville, Virginia. In addition to farming, he operated a machine shop and worked in construction.[14] Gettel died on April 8, 2005, in Norfolk, Virginia, at the age of 87. He is buried in the Emmanuel Episcopal Church Cemetery in Kempsville (now incorporated into the city of Virginia Beach).

NOTES

1. Joshua Harris Prager, "Was the '51 Giants Comeback a Miracle, Or Did They Simply Steal the Pennant?" *Wall Street Journal* January 31, 2001.

2. Prager; "Evidence Supports Belief that Giants Stole Pennant," *Los Angeles Times,* February 1, 2001.

3. Prager; "Evidence Supports."

4. Dan Daniel, "Yankees Lineup Looks Formidable, but Draft Calls Make It Vulnerable," *The Sporting News*, March 29, 1945: 4.

5. "Official A.L. Pitching Records," *The Sporting News*, December 27, 1945: 11; Ken Smith, "Lippy Waves Hand and Produces New Gateway Guardian," *The Sporting News*, January 31, 1951: 7.

6. Ed McAuley, "Gettel Clinches '48 Tribe Post," *The Sporting News*, August 20, 1947: 20; Ken Smith, "Lippy Waves Hand."

7. Bob Burnes, "Tough Luck Story of the Year: Al Gettel," *The Sporting News*, October 13, 1948: 12.

8. "Pitcher Gettel at Second," *The Sporting News* August 4, 1948: 30.

9. "Pacific Coast League," *The Sporting News*, August 5, 1953: 24.

10. The Oaks won the PCL playoffs.

11. "Gettel Switches Starts, Stopped on 8 Game Streak," *The Sporting News*, August 5, 1953: 23; "Pacific Coast League," *The Sporting News*, August 11, 1954: 26.

12. "Pacific Coast League," September 22, 1954, *The Sporting News*: 34.

13. "Tuning In," *The Sporting News*, August 17, 1955: 15.

14. Stephen Miller, "Al Gettel, 87, Pitcher for Yankees and Giants," *New York Sun*, April 27, 2005.

GREG GOOSSEN

BY ROB EDELMAN

ACROSS THE DECADES, VARious New York Yankee, New York Giant, and Brooklyn Dodger baseball names have acted on-screen. Babe Ruth, for one, appeared in silent-era features; played himself in *The Pride of the Yankees* (1942), the Lou Gehrig biopic; and starred in various short subjects. Gehrig was toplined in *Rawhide* (1938), a B-Western. Jackie Robinson played himself in *The Jackie Robinson Story* (1950), as did John McGraw in *Right Off the Bat* (1915), *One Touch of Nature* (1917), and several short subjects; Muggsy even was cast as the title character in *Detective Swift* (1914), a crime tale. The list goes on and on ...

But if you want to cite a New York Met in the movies, the first name that pops into mind is neither Seaver nor Strawberry nor Gooden. It is Greg Goossen, the 1960s catcher-first sacker, he of the .202 batting average in his four Mets seasons. Granted, Goossen did not only play in the Big Apple: He was an original Seattle Pilot, remaining with the franchise when it became the Milwaukee Brewers, and briefly was a Washington Senator. But it was as a New York Metropolitan that he is best recalled.

Gregory Bryant Goossen was born on December 14, 1945, in Los Angeles. His father, Elliott "Al" Goossen, was a Los Angeles Police Department detective-turned-private investigator; he and his wife, Anna Mae, had eight sons and two daughters. Greg starred in baseball and football at Notre Dame High School in Sherman Oaks, from which he graduated in 1964. The 6-foot-1, 210-pounder lettered for four years in baseball, hitting an even .500 during his junior year and .447 as a senior. On the gridiron, he played linebacker and center and, on six occasions, he earned All-Catholic League and All-CIF (California Interscholastic Federation) honors in both sports. A host of major colleges recruited him, including UCLA, USC, Stanford, Colorado, Utah, and Arizona State; reportedly, he even earned a football scholarship from USC. But Goossen, who was scouted by Ben Wade of the Dodgers, chose to sign with the Los Angeles nine for "a 'sizable' bonus in five figures."[1]

Goossen, who batted and threw right-handed, caught that summer for the 1964 rookie Pioneer League Pocatello Chiefs, compiling solid numbers (29 games; 121 at-bats; 40 hits; 8 home runs, 34 RBIs, a .331 batting average). His statistics fell after he was promoted to the Class-A St. Petersburg Saints in the Florida State League (35 games; 114 at-bats; 23 hits; 2 home runs; 18 RBIs, a .202 batting average); he also played for the Arizona Instructional League Dodgers, hitting .182 in 31 games with 16 hits, two of which were homers, and 10 RBIs in 88 at-bats.

Then in 1965, the Dodgers invited Goossen to spring training. "It was amazing," he recalled in 1991. "My first major-league locker room and I look around and who's standing next to me? Sandy Koufax and Don Drysdale and Tommy Davis and all those guys. It was pretty spectacular."[2] One reason for his sharing space with the stars was that Goossen was so highly touted. "Big fellow, likes to play. Hits well and with power. Major League potential," was how he was described in the March 1965 issue of *Baseball Digest*.[3] But his Dodgers career was short-lived. A foreshadowing of Goossen's future came on February 15, when the *Los Angeles Times* announced that a "prominent cast of Los Angeles major and minor league players will face the USC baseball team today at 2:30 on Bovard Field." Goossen was listed as the team's backstop, and the item concluded with the following: "Scheduled to pitch for the Trojans are lefthanders Larry Fisher and John Herbst and righthander Tom Seaver."[4]

On April 9 Tom Terrific's future employer acquired Goossen for $8,000 in the waiver draft, which allowed the more ineffectual franchises—a term that certainly applied to the New York Mets—to purchase players after their initial bush-league seasons. The youngster showed promise during the 1965 campaign, playing for the Auburn Mets in the Class-A New York-Penn League. Appearing in 109 games, Goossen hit a solid .305 (115 hits in 377 at-bats) with 24 home runs and 84 RBIs. The 19-year-old capped off the season by making his major-league debut. The date was September 3, the Mets were battling the St. Louis Cardinals, and Goossen had two hits in four at-bats; his first, a single, came in his initial plate appearance. Then, on September 25, his first major-league homer helped the Mets beat the Philadelphia Phillies, 4-1, in the second game of a twin bill.[5] All told, he appeared in 11 games, going 9-for-31 with 2 RBIs. His batting average was .290.

As the 1965 season came to a close, the Mets announced that a slew of young players would comprise the team's nucleus during the coming campaign. "Perhaps the brightest prospect aside from (Tug) McGraw and (Dick) Selma is Goossen," reported the *Washington Post*. "…'I would say that Goossen is the most advanced of our young players who served in the minors this year,' said Eddie Stanky, in charge of player procurement. 'He could conceivably catch 125 games for the Mets next year.'"[6]

Stanky's prognostication was wishful thinking as Goossen's primary team in 1966 was the Triple-A International League Jacksonville Suns. In 128 games, he hit .243 (97 hits in 400 at-bats) with 25 home runs and 64 RBIs. But he also made it into 13 Mets games, hitting .188 (6 hits in 32 at-bats) with one home run and five RBIs. (Various sources list Goossen as having been behind the plate for the major-league debut on September 11 of 19-year-old Nolan Ryan. One example: In his *New York Times* obituary, it is reported that, "As a Met, he caught Nolan Ryan's first big-league game in 1966."[7] But this is incorrect. On that date the Braves beat the Mets, 8-3. Dennis Ribant started for the New York nine and was relieved by Selma, Ryan, and Bill Hepler. Jerry Grote was the starting backstop; John Stephenson pinch-hit and took over for Grote behind the plate. Goossen is not to be found in the box score.[8]) Then in 1967, Goossen split the season between the Mets (37 games, 69 at-bats, 11 hits, no home runs, 3 RBIs, a .159 batting average) and the Suns (70 games, 235 at-bats, 55 hits, 11 home runs, 37 RBIs, a .234 batting average).

Despite these numbers, the Mets still regarded Goossen for his hitting prowess. But they were questioning his ability behind the plate. The story goes that a scout once remarked, "Goossen's a hell of a hitter." "Yeah," chimed in another talent evaluator. "But what kind of catcher is he?" The response: "He's a hell of a hitter."[9] So the team's hierarchy decided to expand his fielding repertoire and mentor him at first base, and he was dispatched to the Florida Instructional League to learn the position. That May manager Gil Hodges declared, "Greg has been swinging the bat real good. So we're going to use him at first for the next few days. He certainly has been adequate as a fielding first baseman."[10] Yet the 1968 campaign for Goossen was a virtual repeat of the previous season, only with a bit of a demotion. He made two minor-league stops: Jacksonville (32 games, 116 at-bats, 25 hits, 9 home runs, 30 RBIs, a .216 batting average); and the Double-A Texas League Memphis Blues (10 games, 38 at-bats, 8 hits, 1 home run, 4 RBIs, a .211 batting average). In 38 games with the big club, he hit .208 (22 hits in 106 at-bats) with no homers and six RBIs. His one highlight came on May 31, when St. Louis Cardinals pitcher Larry Jaster was on his way to a perfect game. But with two outs in the bottom of the eighth, Goossen broke up the no-no with a line single to left.[11]

Hodges' praise aside, the 1968 campaign would be the last for Goossen as a Met. On February 5, 1969, he was traded (along with an unspecified amount of cash) to the newly christened Seattle Pilots for a player to be named later. (On July 14 the Pilots completed the deal by sending outfielder Jim Gosger to the Mets.) Had Goossen remained in New York, he might have been a part of the "Miracle Mets" nine that copped the World Series. But this was not to be. Observed Rich Tosches in a 1991 *Los Angeles Times* profile, "Goossen was always on the fringe, always one break away from becoming a permanent fixture in the (Mets) lineup."[12]

By this time, Goossen's catching days were behind him; he was strictly a first baseman, but added left field to his résumé for the remainder of his career. And he still was unable to remain on a big-league roster for an entire season. In 1969 he yet again split time between the majors and minors. He began the season with the Triple-A Pacific Coast League Vancouver Mounties (104 games, 363 at-bats, 108 hits, 18 home runs, 57 RBIs, a .298 batting average) and was called up by the Pilots on July 25 to replace Mike Hegan, who was off to complete his military service. Platooning at first base with Don Mincher, Goossen put up impressive numbers in 52 games: 43 hits in 139 at-bats with a whopping 10 home runs—by far the most he belted in any one big-league campaign—24 RBIs, and a .309 batting average. Additionally, he put in time with the Pilots' Arizona Instructional League affiliate.

Goossen embraced his one season in Seattle. In 2009, he appeared at a 40-year reunion for the Pilots, telling his fellow celebrants, "I was happy to be with the Seattle Pilots. I was happy to play in the major leagues. I would've played here my whole career." To which Tommy Davis, another ex-Pilot (who also played for the Dodgers and Mets) quipped, "You did!"[13] Even more significantly, Goossen was a featured character in *Ball Four*, Jim Bouton's iconic memoir-diary. Much of *Ball Four* deals with the Pilots' lone major-league season before the franchise was purchased by a Milwaukee car dealer named Bud Selig, who abandoned the Pacific Northwest and re-christened the franchise the Milwaukee Brewers. Bouton reported that, in a spring-training game against the Cleveland Indians, Goossen was "the designated pinch-hitter under the experimental rule that allows one player to come to bat all the time during the game without playing the field. 'Are they trying to tell me something about my hands?' Goossen went around saying. 'Are they trying to tell me something about my glove?' And after that he became the first Seattle Pilot to say, 'Play me or trade me.'"[14]

In mid-March Goossen was one of a half-dozen or so ballplayers dispatched to the minor-league camp. Bouton observed, "The only one I was really interested in was Greg Goossen, whom I'd come to like, mainly because he had the ability to laugh at himself." Upon his return to the majors, Bouton described Goossen as "a burly guy with kinky blond hair and looks like a bouncer in an English pub. He is also a flake." Referring to his liquor intake, Bouton wrote that Goossen told catcher Jim Pagliaroni, "I found I can't play if I feel good. I've got to have a little bit of a hangover to get the best out of me." Then in August, according to Bouton, the team was riding a bus "from the airport to the Shoreham Hotel in Washington (and) we passed a huge government building that had a bronze plaque on the front announcing it had been 'erected in 1929.' And Greg Goossen said, 'That's quite an erection.'" But in the most celebrated (and oft-quoted) Goossen reference, Bouton cited the ballplayer's first big-league skipper. "Greg Goossen was doing his Casey Stengel imitation," he recalled, "and he remembered the best thing the old man ever said about him. 'We got a kid here named Goossen, 20 years old, and in 10 years, he's got a chance to be 30.'"[15]

Greg Goossen, whose post-baseball career included working as both Hollywood bit player and stand-in for Gene Hackman.

Despite his 1969 stats, Goossen yet again spent the following campaign as a big leaguer and busher. He started the 1970 season as the Brewers' starting first sacker, but after appearing in 21 games (12 hits in 47 at-bats, with one home run, three RBIs, and a .255 batting average), he was sent down to the Pacific Coast League Portland Beavers (77 games, 281 at-bats, 84 hits, 20 home runs, 69 RBIs, and a .299 batting average). Then on July 14, Goossen was purchased by the Washington Senators. He made it into another 21 games in DC, with eight hits, no home runs, a single RBI, and a .222 batting average in 36 at-bats. And on November 3 the Senators traded him along with left fielder Gene Martin and pitcher Jeff Terpko to the Philadelphia Phillies for Curt Flood (whose landmark lawsuit against MLB involving players' bargaining rights with management was pending) and a player to be named later; the following April the Phillies returned Terpko to Washington to complete the transaction. But Goossen had seen his last days as a big leaguer. He spent the 1971 campaign playing with three Pacific Coast League nines: the Eugene Emeralds (affiliated with the Phillies); Tacoma Cubs (Chicago Cubs); and Salt Lake City Angels (California Angels). The following season, he played for the Union Laguna Algodoneros in the Mexican League. And then he was out of professional baseball.

During his career, Goossen appeared in 705 minor-league games. In 2,376 at-bats, he had 653 hits, 130 of which were home runs; he drove in 454 runs and compiled a .275 batting average. (If only these were his big-league stats!) In his four seasons with the Mets, Goossen never played in more than 38 games during any one campaign. He made 99 appearances total, with 48 hits in 238 at bats for the aforementioned .202 average, hitting but two dingers and driving in all of 16 runs. Add on his totals with Seattle-Milwaukee (73 games, 186 at-bats, 55 hits, 11 home runs, 27 RBIs, a .296 batting average) and Washington, and his major-league numbers are undistinguished: six seasons, 193 games, 460 at-bats, 111 hits, 13 homers, 44 RBIs, and a .241 batting average.

Goossen's final major-league game came on October 1, 1970. The Senators took on the Baltimore Orioles that day, and he was hitless in one at-bat. He was just 24 years old: an age when innumerable ballplayers are first breaking into the big time. Despite his relative youth, Goossen by then had played on around two dozen separate major, minor, and Mexican League nines. "Either everyone wanted me or everyone wanted to get rid of me," he recalled in 1996. "I could never figure out which." Perhaps he provided his own answer when he observed, "I can't play if I feel good. I've got to have a little bit of a hangover to get the best out of me."[16] Rich Tosches, writing in the *Los Angeles Times*, noted that Goossen "brought an attitude that placed more importance on having fun than on playing baseball. Common among the players of that era was a desire to play some baseball and visit some bars. 'There were so many good times, I can't remember many of them,' (Goossen) said."[17]

So how was Greg Goossen going to spend his life post-baseball? He was employed by his father's detective agency and worked at a number of other jobs, from telephone marketing to selling office supplies to hawking ladies' footwear. "I had been playing ball in Shea Stadium and Dodger Stadium, the dream of my entire life," he recalled years later. "And suddenly I'm in Van Nuys selling women's shoes. It was more than a shock."[18] Eventually, however, Goossen found his calling first as a boxing trainer and then in the film industry. He linked up with brothers Dan and Joe Goossen, who operated Ten Goose Professional Boxing, a Southern California-based gym. Then in 1988, Joe Goossen suggested that Greg take a meeting with Academy Award-winning actor Gene Hackman, who was researching *Split Decisions* (1988), a boxing tale. The pair became fast friends, and Hackman hired Goossen to work as his stand-in; the actor insisted that it be stipulated in all his contracts that Goossen be well compensated. Of his stand-in work, the ex-ballplayer observed, "I've had to stay on the same spot for three straight hours. But it never gets boring. Every day I think how lucky I am to be with Gene Hackman."[19]

Goossen also began appearing in bit parts in a variety of films. In *The Package, Loose Cannons,*

Class Action, Unforgiven, The Firm, Geronimo: An American Legend, Wyatt Earp, The Quick and the Dead, Waterworld, Get Shorty, Midnight in the Garden of Good and Evil, The Replacements, Heist, The Royal Tenenbaums, and *Behind Enemy Lines,* all released between 1989 and 2001, Goossen's characters respectively were: "Soldier in Provost Marshal's Office"; "Marsh Policeman"; "Bartender at Rosatti's"; "Fighter"; "Vietnam Veteran"; "Schoonover Gang"; "Friend of Bullwacker"; "Young Herod's Man"; "Sawzall Smoker"; "Duke, Man at the Ivy"; "Prison Cell Lunatic"; "Drunk #2"; "Officer #1"; "Gypsy Cab Driver"; and "CIA Spook."[20]

Any bit of dialogue assigned to Goossen never could be confused with a Shakespearean soliloquy. In *The Chamber*, Hackman's character, a jailed white supremacist, is about to be executed. Goossen plays a fellow inmate. "See you soon, Sam," is his one line, as Hackman heads for the gas chamber. (Bo Jackson—another ballplayer, albeit one with a higher profile than Greg Goossen—appears in a supporting role as a prison guard.) And in 2009, Goossen was an interviewee in the documentary *Seattle Pilots: Short Flight Into History*, which charts the team's all-too-brief existence.

Of his post-major-league career, Goossen observed, "It was tough, but I made the transition from baseball. There were some bad years, but I always had a great family to help me, to encourage me. And now, with acting, I find the same feeling I had as a baseball player, the same heart-pounding feeling of nervousness, the same adrenaline rush. I'm not sure why, but I just didn't get that feeling selling ladies' shoes."[21]

Baseball was not completely absent from Goossen's life. He frequently was found cheering on his nephews at their ballgames; in 2014, one of them, Josh Goossen-Brown, was selected by the Chicago White Sox in the 31st round of the free-agent draft. However, three years earlier—on February 26, 2011—Goossen was slated to be inducted into the Notre Dame High School Hall of Fame. After failing to show up for a photo shoot, his daughter Erin Hyder was dispatched to his Sherman Oaks home and discovered that he had died. Goossen was 65 years old; the cause of his death remained unspecified, but he reportedly was felled by a heart attack. He was divorced, and was survived by three daughters (Tracey Woodside and Kimberly Goossen in addition to Erin) and four grandchildren.

A memorial service was held in St. Francis de Sales Church in Sherman Oaks, and his body was donated to the UCLA medical school. However, upon his death, Pete Rose, who also was a Goossen pal, declared, "He was a fun guy to be around, so upbeat. I told Dan (Goossen), with the following Greg's got, we might have to hold the service at the Rose Bowl."[22]

NOTES

1. Frank Finch, "'FEED YOU GOOD': Dodgers' Bonus Baby Goossen Likes Life as Varsity Member," *Los Angeles Times*, March 7, 1965: H4.
2. Rich Tosches, "Finding Ring He Could Not Win as a Met," *Los Angeles Times*, July 20, 1991: VYC 16.
3. metsmerizedonline.com/2012/05/old-time-mets-greg-goossen.html/.
4. "Trojans Face Dodger Stars," *Los Angeles Times*, February 15, 1965: B6.
5. "Goossen Paces Mets to Split," *New York Times*, September 26, 1965: C4.
6. "Mets to Go With Youth Next Year," *Washington Post*, September 14, 1965: B2.
7. Douglas Martin, "Greg Goossen, 65, a Ballplayer Who Was in on the Joke," *New York Times*, March 6, 2011: 26.
8. baseball-reference.com/boxes/NYN/NYN196609110.shtml.
9. Franz Lidz, "Double Duty Former Mets Catcher Greg Goossen Has a Second Career as Gene Hackman's Stand-In," *Sports Illustrated*, October 28, 1996.
10. "Hodges Gives Goossen 1st Chance," *Chicago Tribune*, May 15, 1968: D5.
11. "Jaster Perfect to 8th, Wins 2-0," *Boston Globe*, June 1, 1968: 18.
12. Tosches.
13. Larry Stone, "Former Seattle Pilot, 'Ball Four' Character Greg Goossen Dies," *Seattle Times*, February 28, 2011.
14. Jim Bouton, *Ball Four: My Life and Hard Times Throwing the Knuckleball in the Big Leagues* (New York, Cleveland: World Publishing Company, 1970), 36.
15. Bouton, 57, 274, 284, 290.
16. Lidz.
17. Tosches.

18 Ibid.

19 Lidz.

20 imdb.com/name/nm0329659/?ref_=fn_al_nm_1.

21 Tosches.

22 Anthony McCarron, "Greg Goossen, Former Mets Catcher, Boxing Trainer, Private Detective and Actor, Dead at Age 65," *New York Daily News,* March 1, 2011.

WALLY HEBERT

BY GREGORY H. WOLF

BASEBALL HAS ALWAYS loved an underdog. Rugged southpaw Wally Hebert gave fans across the nation during the Great Depression what they craved, at least for a short while: a story about David defeating Goliath. Hebert went from the sandlots of Louisiana in 1929 to the St. Louis Browns and the big leagues in 1931. In his first start, he tossed a complete-game victory to beat Connie Mack's two-time-reigning World Series champion Philadelphia A's. Three more distance-going victories followed in rapid succession, including another against the A's, and one against the New York Yankees in the Big Apple, thrusting the hurler into the national spotlight. Despite his auspicious start, Hebert won only seven more games in three seasons with the Browns before being sold to the Hollywood Stars in the Pacific Coast League. At the age of 35, Hebert was back in the majors, as a wartime player with the Pittsburgh Pirates in 1943, winning 10 games.

Save for 14 springs and summers playing professional baseball, Wallace Andrew Hebert spent his entire life living on the bayous in the extreme southwest corner of Louisiana. On August 21, 1907, he was born in a small rural community in Cameron Parish near Sweetlake, on the outskirts of the swampy marshes that defined the landscape.[1] His parents were John Aurelian and Matilda (née Smith) Hebert, hardworking country folk who welcomed eight children (three boys and five girls) into the world over a period of almost two decades. When Wally was still a toddler the Heberts moved to nearby Big Lake, and finally settled in Lake Charles, then a city of about 10,000. Around the time Wally was in first grade at Fourth Ward School, his classmates began calling him "Preacher" for the hat he wore; locals said it looked like a hat a preacher would wear. That peculiar moniker stuck, and forever thereafter, Hebert was known to friends and family as Preacher.

"My father was from a poor Cajun family," said Hillene Hebert Deaton. "They'd go out into the swamps and hunt and fish."[2] In a time when money was scarce, the Heberts were independent and self-reliant. What they lacked in formal education, they made up for in an acute understanding of nature. Hebert's other daughter, Linda Todd Hebert, told the author a story that seemed to capture her father's determination, courage, and spirit, but also served as a snapshot of an era that might be hard to imagine today.[3] At about the age of 13, Hebert went with his father into the swamps to hunt alligators, then considered a nuisance because they preyed on muskrat, mink, and other lucrative fur-bearing animals that could be sold. A nearby wealthy landowner paid the Heberts a premium for all the alligators they could kill and skin. After a few days his father returned home and left his son to fend for himself. Living in an old dilapidated houseboat, the teenager spent the nights in a thin hand-carved canoe tracking down the dangerous beasts and then blasting them with his shotgun. When the youngster returned home a few months later, continued Linda, he had grown about six inches and his mother barely recognized him.

Hebert's interest in baseball began around 1920 when Connie Mack's A's conducted spring training in Lake Charles for two seasons. The teenage Hebert was often at the park, hustling balls from the players. After getting his start in baseball on local sandlots, Hebert emerged as a four-sport star at Lake Charles High School, moving between baseball, football, basketball, and track as the seasons progressed. "I never dreamed of playing pro baseball," Hebert once said. "I just played for fun."[4] Hebert left school after the 11th grade and soon thereafter began working for a gas company, Gulf State Utility, which sponsored a team in a local semipro league. Hebert, who had grown to a stout 6-feet-1 and almost 200 pounds, distinguished himself on the mound with his strong left arm. In a tournament in Houston against other Gulf State teams in 1929, Hebert caught the attention of Ray Cahill, a scout for the St. Louis Browns. By the end of the summer, Cahill had signed Hebert to a contract.

Hebert's career in Organized Baseball got off to a thunderous start with the Springfield (Illinois) Midgets in the six-team Class-C Western Association in 1930. In his first professional game, and the Midgets' season opener on April 24, Hebert tossed a resounding 15-inning complete game to defeat the Joplin Miners, 5-2.[5] Described as "nigh unbeatable in the first half," Hebert came down with arm fatigue in the second half of the season, finishing with a 15-16 record and logging 241 innings.[6]

Hebert got the surprise of his life when the St. Louis Browns invited him to spring training in West Palm Beach in 1931. The Browns had enjoyed their best decade in the 1920s, posting winning records in five campaigns and finishing in the first division seven times; however, skipper Bill Killefer's squad fell to 64-90 in 1930 and had the worst pitching staff in the AL. Ordinarily an untried green recruit from the low minors like Hebert would not get a look-see in camp; however, with only one other southpaw on the staff, 20-game winner Lefty Stewart, Killefer thought Hebert might serve as a good batting-practice pitcher. Hebert quickly made an impression. "[I] have lots of confidence in the young man," said Killefer.[7] "The kid has a deceptive delivery and a good knowledge of pitching."[8] Notwithstanding his success, Hebert had no inkling that he'd make the club. "I was supposed to be moved up to Wichita Falls in the Class A leagues," said Hebert, "but at the last moment in spring training … Killefer told me that I was going to stay."[9]

Hebert didn't mind spending the first six weeks of the regular season primarily tossing BP. "[I]t's good to be in the big leagues," he said enthusiastically. "Take Springfield. We played night baseball, then climbed into a bus and drove darn near all night to the next stop." The first night game in the history of professional baseball took place on April 28, 1930, when the Independence (Kansas) Producers hosted the Muskogee (Oklahoma) Chiefs at Riverside Park in the Class-C Western Association in 1930.[10] The only time Hebert took the mound in a game during that stretch was on May 1 in the "Baseball Palace of the World," Comiskey Park in Chicago. "I was so nervous that my teeth rattled," said Hebert. "I walked Lu Blue, the first man up."[11] After catcher Rick Ferrell picked Blue off first, Hebert retired the next two batters.

Hebert began to see more action when the Browns kicked off a grueling three-week, season-longest 20-game Eastern road swing on May 26. After hurling 2⅔ innings of scoreless relief against the New York Yankees in two outings and another scoreless frame against the Boston Red Sox, Hebert had what sportswriter George Mackay called his "baptism of fire" by making his maiden big-league start against the reigning two-time World Series champion Philadelphia A's on June 11.[12] He held the slugging A's to seven hits and two runs (one earned) in a complete-game victory, 8-2, and also collected his first hit. His name suddenly graced the front pages of sports sections across the nation. In the grand baseball tradition of obfuscating age, Hebert was hailed as a teenage wonder even though he was 23 years old. St. Louis sportswriter L.C. Davis was moved to write a poem about Hebert's unlikely feat:

> Fans, Meet Mr. Hebert.
> Young Wallace Hebert, Brown recruit,
> Put on his junior baseball suit,
> And neatly trimmed the A's.
> When Wallace gave the Browns a leg,
> And moved his playmates up a peg,
> The fans were in a daze.
> The world-renowned White Elephants
> Could do but little with his slants,
> And proved an easy mark.
> Though Wally was still in his teens,
> He spilled the scrapple and the beans,
> All over Connie's park.
> The A's were eating from his mitt,
> And as the pill they couldn't hit,

> He had them on the run.
> Not only that, the useful ace,
> Struck Simmons out with three on base,
> A thing that's seldom done.[13]

After a rough outing against the Senators in the nation's capital (seven runs in 6⅔ innings), Hebert became the talk of the baseball world by tossing three consecutive complete-game victories in eight days at Sportsman's Park in St. Louis. He downed the Yankees, 8-2, the A's, 6-5, and the Boston Red Sox, 5-4. Sportswriter John Nolan described him as a "cool, accomplished chucker,"[14] while John Wray of the *St. Louis Post-Dispatch* opined that "Hebert's 'arrival' at this time may be the turning point for the Browns."[15]

A level-headed Hebert took his new-found notoriety in stride. "I ain't got much speed," he said in a Southern drawl with a twinge of the Cajun-French accent that remained with him his entire life. "I just try to fool 'em. I got a good hook, though, then I try to give 'em the change of pace."[16] Never a hard thrower despite his robust stature, Hebert had a deceptive sidewinding delivery that was hard for batters to time. He also hid the ball easily in his big left hand. Killefer once described Hebert's hands as the biggest he'd ever seen, which punctuated long, "gangling" arms.[17]

Sportswriters had a field day with Hebert's name and heritage. The *Post-Dispatch*, playing on the stereotype of flaky left-handers, noted that Hebert "has but one eccentricity," namely the pronunciation of his name.[18] His name was pronounced "Ay-Bare," the paper often reminded readers, and not "Hee-burt" as everyone called him, and was widely reported as the first Cajun big leaguer.

Hebert's three-week fairytale began to unravel in July. He lost five of his next six starts. According to Killefer, "a lump almost as large as an egg" formed under "Hebert's shoulder blade" during a rainy game in Washington on July 23, and the pitcher was never the same thereafter.[19] Confined mainly to the bullpen and little used in the last two months of the campaign, Hebert tossed a darkness-shortened eight-inning complete-game 8-3 victory against the Chicago White Sox to finish his rookie season with a 6-7 record and a 5.07 ERA in 103 innings.

Coming off a dismal 63-91 record and fifth-place finish in 1931, Killefer expected Hebert to join Sam Gray (11-24), Lefty Stewart (14-17) and George Blaeholder (11-15) to form a durable quartet of starters in 1932. "I am banking a great deal on Wallace Hebert," said Killefer. "He seemed to find himself all of a sudden last year."[20] Stewart, Hebert's road roommate, also predicted success; "[H]e's got what most southpaws lack — control."[21] In his first appearance of the season, Hebert tossed 11⅓ innings and yielded only one earned run in heartbreaking walk-off 3-2 loss to the Detroit Tigers on April 16 at Navin Field. After retiring just one batter and surrendering four runs in his next start, Hebert was moved back to the bullpen, and occasionally made a spot start. He struggled with shoulder pain the entire season; terrible swelling made it difficult for him to raise his arm into a windup. In a trying season, Hebert lost his first eight decisions, and finished the campaign with an unsightly 1-12 record. In his lone victory, he was whacked for 13 hits and seven runs (three earned) in 7⅔ innings against Detroit on July 24, but made up for it by clubbing four hits and scoring three times. His 6.48 ERA (in 108⅓ innings) was easily the highest in the majors among pitchers with at least 100 innings. Despite the Browns' identical record from the previous season and his own personal hurling struggles, Hebert kept a positive attitude, and was typically described as a popular player with fans and teammates alike. "I probably should have had a couple more years in the minors before going up," he said, looking back on his career in retirement.[22] Though some baseball players have had success after just one year in the minors, few, if any, made the monumental jump from one season in Class C to find success in the majors.

When the Browns' cash-strapped owner, Phil Ball, sold the club's three best players, Lefty Stewart, future Hall of Fame outfielder Goose Goslin, and outfielder Fred Schulte, to the Senators for three players and cash in the offseason, Brownie fans knew it would be another long summer in 1933, and it was. The Great

Wally Hebert, one of a dozen-plus professional ballplayers cast in Joe E. Brown's Alibi Ike.

Depression had hit the Gateway City hard, with unemployment running at over 30 percent, and the Browns acutely felt its effect. They had averaged a major-league low 1,501 spectators per game in 1932; in 1933 that number dipped to 1,144, marking the eighth of 18 consecutive seasons that the Browns ranked last in the AL in attendance. The departure of Hebert's roommate seemed to open the door for the 25-year-old hurler, but he struggled in spring training and was confined to the far end of the bullpen when the season opened. He made his first start on May 20 against the left-handed-heavy Yankees in the Bronx. With "great perspicacity and redoubtable effect," wrote St. Louis scribe Allen Gould, Hebert set down the reigning World Series champions on six hits in a distance-going outing, 4-2.[23] Two starts later, he tossed a complete-game eight-hitter to beat the Tigers, 3-1, in the Motor City. Soon thereafter he came down with a sore shoulder again. After he yielded 25 earned runs over a stretch of 18⅓ innings (June 19-July 11), Killefer lost confidence in him; by that time the Browns were firmly entrenched in the AL cellar. Ball tried to make a splash by signing an aging Rogers Hornsby as player-manager on July 26, the day he was released by the Cardinals. "If you'd talk baseball, you'd get along with him good," said Hebert about the Rajah, whose contempt for pitchers was well known. "If you'd change the subject, he'd move on."[24] With only three appearances in the final month of an abysmal season, Hebert could see the writing on the wall. On December 14 he was shipped to the Hollywood Stars of the Double-A Pacific Coast League along with flychaser Smead Jolley and middle infielder Jim Levey for shortstop Alan Strange. "I hadn't been pitching regular with the Browns," said Hebert (4-6, 5.30 ERA in 88⅓ innings). "I didn't feel bad at all about going to Hollywood, ... I always liked pitching in warm weather."[25]

With the balmy climate and six-month baseball seasons with as many as 180 games, the PCL afforded Hebert the chance to pitch regularly. His combined record of 21-28 in his first two seasons with the Stars did not portend his subsequent success and his emergence as a future three-time 20-game winner. One of Hebert's biggest highlights during his years in Tinseltown was a cameo appearance in the film *Alibi Ike* (1935), a romantic comedy based on a Ring Lardner story. Actor Joe E. Brown starred as Frank Farrell, a rookie pitcher for the Chicago Cubs, who aggravates both his manager and fiancée with his crazy alibis and excuses en route to trying to lead his team to the pennant. Director Ray Enright filmed game action at Wrigley Field, located about 10 miles from Hollywood in south Los Angeles; the stadium, owned by the Wrigley family who also owned the real-life Chicago Cubs, was a popular place to film baseball movies. About 18 professional baseball players made cameos in *Alibi Ike*, but none had speaking roles, nor were they listed in the credits. "My father put his foot on the running board of a car," said Linda Todd Hebert with a chuckle. "He was in the film for a nanosecond."

Hebert's career took off when Stars owner Bill Lane relocated the team to San Diego and rechristened them the Padres for the 1936 season. For years, the Stars had played second fiddle to the city's other, more successful PCL club, the Wrigley-owned Los Angeles Angels, and had played in the Angels' home park, Wrigley Field. Player-manager Frank Shellenback, one of the most successful minor-league pitchers in history with 316 victories, including 296 in the PCL, took Hebert under his wing. The arrival of 18-year-old Ted Williams on the team in 1937 marked a magical season for the Padres. Hebert tossed his first and only no-hitter, against the Valley All-Stars in an exhibition game at the Padres' home stadium, Lane Field, a former Navy athletic field that had been renovated as part of a Works Progress Administration project. The Padres went on to win the PCL championship, sweeping the Portland Beavers in four games. As of 2016, it was the only championship in the history of professional baseball for a team in San Diego. Hebert went on to win 20 games in 1939, 22 in 1941, and 22 in 1942 while also hurling 33 complete games and logging 319 innings. After enduring rumors in previous seasons that he'd be sold to a major-league club, Hebert finally got another chance on the big stage when the Pittsburgh Pirates acquired him in the Rule 5 draft on November 2, 1942. The Pirates, who had conducted spring training in San Bernardino, had regularly faced the hurler in exhibition games.

At the Pirates camp, which had been relocated to Muncie, Indiana, because of wartime travel restrictions, Hebert quickly showed that he was not the same pitcher he had been during his first stint in the big leagues. Possessing the confidence inspired by 147 wins in the PCL, Hebert was a crafty, now 35-year-old southpaw, but still relied on his curves, changeups, and good control, kept the ball low, and pitched to contact. Pirates skipper Frankie Frisch, coming off a lackluster 66-81 season, looked to Hebert to replace the club's only southpaw, Ken Heintzelman, who was now in the Army. In his second start of the season, Hebert blanked the Chicago Cubs on six hits to record his first and only big-league shutout, 3-0, in the first game of a doubleheader at Forbes Field on May 2. He concluded the month with a 10-inning complete-game victory over the Phillies, 2-1, in the Smoky City. Hebert finished the season with a misleading 10-11 record; his 2.98 ERA (in 184 innings) was much better than the 3.42 league average. He also completed 12 of 23 starts, and relieved in 11 others for the fourth-place Bucs (80-74). Despite his success, he clashed with Frisch, renowned for his hothead demeanor. He objected to the Fordham Flash's penchant to juggle his pitchers to play for matchups, and thought it disrupted his continuity.

Hebert returned to Lake Charles in the offseason, as he had done every year since 1930, but this time it was different. He knew his career was over even though he had signed a contract for the 1944 season. Hebert had married Nannie Locke Bostick on November 25, 1932, and had two daughters, Linda and Hillene. Preacher was tired of dragging his family around the country, and Linda was about to start school. "I turned down the best contract I was ever offered," Hebert recalled, and decided to stay in Louisiana. He also admitted that the situation with the Pirates made it easier for him to hang up his spikes. "I guess if Frisch had not been the Pirates manager," he said years later, "I would have kept pitching."[26] His final slate read 21 wins, 36 losses, and a 4.63 ERA in 483⅔ innings; of his 125 appearances, 61 were starts, including 22 complete games. He also batted .270 on 43 hits.

Hebert exchanged the long train rides and road trips of baseball for the bayous and swamps that never left his heart. He and his wife welcomed three more children into the family, Wally Jr., David, and Steve. The family resided in Westlake, adjacent to Lake Charles, and for 29 years Preacher worked as an operator in a Firestone plant in the city.

"Once my father got out of baseball, that was sort of the end of it," said Linda. "He never coached or was active in it." He didn't talk much about his career, never bragged, or called attention to himself. Linda recalled sleeping as a kid in her father's San Diego Padres jersey and attending games in Forbes Field, but simply took it for granted that he had been a player. Hillene recounted a story about the time she "discovered" that her father had been a ballplayer. "My brothers and I were playing in the attic and came across an old suitcase full of clippings," she said. "We bombarded [my father] with questions and he began to tell us some of his baseball stories. One of the clippings was about a game against the Yankees. Well, when sharing time came in my third-grade class, I stood up and said, 'My daddy struck out Babe Ruth,' and the boys in the room laughed and told me I was making it up. It spilled out onto the playground where I got into a fight and had a black eye for my efforts. The next day I brought the clipping and read the whole thing to the class. Now the boys wanted his autograph."

Linda described her father as "the most easygoing person you'd ever meet. I can't remember him being mad about anything, and he never lost his temper." Nature was Hebert's playground, just as it was when he was a teenager. He hunted, fished, and skinned gators, kept a garden until he was in his late 80s, and enjoyed cooking family Cajun recipes. "He could have lived two or three centuries ago, and been fine," said Linda with a laugh.

Wally "Preacher" Hebert died on December 8, 1999, at the age of 92 in Westlake. He was buried in Westlake Memorial Gardens. "He was a Renaissance Man," said Hillene sincerely when the author asked her to sum up her father's life. "He could do anything he put his mind to."

SOURCES

In addition to the sources noted in this biography, the author also accessed Hebert's player file and player questionnaire from the National Baseball Hall of Fame, the *Encyclopedia of Minor League Baseball*, Retrosheet.org, Baseball-Reference.com, the SABR Minor Leagues Database, accessed online at Baseball-Reference.com, and *The Sporting News* archive via Paper of Record.

The author also expresses gratitude to Linda Hebert Todd and Hillene Hebert Deaton for their interview on August 12, 2016, and many subsequent email exchanges thereafter.

NOTES

1 According to Hebert's daughter, Linda Hebert Todd, the baseball player was born on August 21, 1907. Wally Hebert's mother, Matilda Hebert, celebrated her son's birthday on August 21; as did the baseball player and his family his entire life. The Lake Charles, Louisiana, courthouse burned down when Wally was a youth, and all birth certificates were destroyed, including Wally's. Mrs. Todd explained that another reason for the confusion about her father's birth date was his baptismal certificate, which gave August 22 as the birth date.

2 Author's interview with Hillene Hebert Deaton on August 12, 2016. All quotations from her are from this interview.

3 Author's interview with Linda Hebert Todd on August 12, 2016. All quotations from her are from this interview. A more detailed version of the story about the teenage Hebert's exciting summer hunting alligators can be found in Peter and Barbara Jenkins, "A Walk Across America 2," *Louisiana Life*, January/February 1982: 54-60.

4 Yancey Roy, "Preacher Hebert Played Baseball Games for Fun," *Lake Charles* (Louisiana) *American Press*, December 14, 1986.

5 John Snow, "Hebert Battles Miners, Midgets Win Opener," *Springfield* (Illinois) *Ledger*, April 25, 1930: 19.

6 "Hebert, Southpaw, and Right-hander Terhune Have Made Fine Records With Kid Elberfeld's Club," *St. Louis Post-Dispatch*, August 21, 1930: 2B.

7 "Waddey Appears to Be Browns' Best Bet for Right-Field Position," *St. Louis Post-Dispatch*, March 27, 1931: 2E.

8 Browns' Contest With Atlanta Is Called Off; Play Birmingham Next," *St. Louis Post-Dispatch*, March 31, 1931: 2C.

9 Bill Dixon, "From Bog Lake to the Big Leagues: The Story of Preacher Hebert," *Sports World*, September 12, 1984.

10 Oscar Eddleton, "Under the Lights," *SABR Research Journal Archives*. research.sabr.org/journals/under-the-lights.

11 George Mackay, "Preacher Hebert Is Interviewed After Trouncing World's Champs." [Dated June 1931; unknown source. Player's Hall of Fame file].

12 Mackay.

13 L.C. Davis, "Fans, Meet Mr. Hebert," *St. Louis Post-Dispatch*, July 13, 1931: 10.

14 John Nolan, "Hebert, St. Louis Rookie Chucker, Crippled A's in His First Start." [Dated June 1931; unknown source. Player's Hall of Fame file].

15 John Wray, "Wray's Column. Flash in the Pan," *St. Louis Post-Dispatch*, June 12, 1931: 2N.

16 Mackay.

17 "Oh! Those Hands," *Cincinnati Enquirer*, April 10, 1932: 34.

18 L.C. Davis, "Sport Salad," *St. Louis Post-Dispatch*, July 1, 1931: 2B.

19 William Braucher, "Killefer Grooms Hebert to Lift Brownies Out of Second Division," *Jefferson City* (Missouri) *Post-Tribune*, March 24, 1932: 5.

20 Ibid.

21 James M. Gould, " 'Preacher' Hebert's Got What Most Southpaws Lack—Control; The Brownies Sure Like Him, Too," *St. Louis Post-Dispatch*, June 28, 1931: 3E.

22 Dixon.

23 Allen Gould (Associated Press), "Hebert to Get Starting Job With Browns." [Dated June 1932; unknown source. Player's Hall of Fame file].

24 Tony Salin, "Wally Hebert," *Baseball's Forgotten Heroes* (New York: McGraw Hill, 1999), 156.

25 Salin, 149.

26 Dixon.

WALLY HOOD

BY JAY HURD

FRED C. NEWMEYER HAD "WON another" game for his Bay City, Texas, baseball team in July of 1911.[1] Through circumstance and personal motivation, Newmeyer would, after four years in professional baseball, begin and maintain a career in the motion-picture industry, rising from film extra to film director. In 1928, having worked with numerous silent film stars, including Harold Lloyd, he directed Paramount Studios' "first feature with synchronized core and sound effects."[2] The film, titled *Warming Up*, reflected Newmeyer's attachment to baseball and starred Richard Dix and Jean Arthur. To give credence to the film's premise, plot, and action, he employed—in uncredited roles—professional baseball players from the Pacific Coast League. One of these players was Wally Hood.

Wallace James "Wally" Hood was born in Whittier, California, on February 9, 1895. His parents, James Gideon Hood, a butcher, and Catharine Ann (Moreland) Hood, both Canadian born, had settled in Whittier, where they married in 1892.[3] Wally had three sisters, Catharine H., Vera I., and Minnie M. It appears that James and Catharine divorced between 1912 and 1914 and that each remarried.[4] Catharine died, at age 64, in 1937. Identified as Catharine A. Pruitt, "A Pioneer of [the] City [Whittier], she had been struck by a motorcycle in Whittier. Police deemed the accident unavoidable."[5] James died in 1959 at age 80.

Wally attended public schools in Whittier, an early Quaker settlement named for poet and abolitionist John Greenleaf Whittier.[6] Academically sound and athletically inclined, he served as vice president of the Whittier High School student body in 1912, his junior year, and president in 1913, his senior year. His yearbook notes that he participated in debate and oratorical contests.[7] He captained the baseball and basketball teams, and participated in football and track and field. High-school baseball garnered attention in Whittier as a February 22, 1913, article in the *Whittier News* attests, referring to players and their positions, including "Ernie Chandler … backstop … [who] will attempt to hold Captain Wally Hood's curves."[8] One of Wally's nicknames in high school, "Jimmie," appeared in a high-school annual publication praising his baseball abilities:

> "Jimmie" Hood captained the team and started the season in the box "but threw his arm out" and was transferred to second base where he played a spectacular game, causing the failure of many attempts to steal second, and robbing batters of good hits. He batted .375 for the season.[9]

After high school, Wally ventured to Fullerton College. At Fullerton, about 12 miles southwest of Whittier, the right-handed pitcher-hitter earned the following praise, and a contract signing with the Pacific Coast League's Vernon Tigers, in 1915:

> Wally Hood, Fullerton's pet pitcher, with the chrome vanadium steel arm and machine control, signed up with Vernon this afternoon.… Since Hood first pitched for the team July 11, he has won nine games and lost one at San Diego, average .900. His batting average to date is .350.[10]

Hood's stint with the Tigers was brief. As early as March of 1916 the *Salt Lake Telegram* noted that Vernon "has only 10 pitchers to cut down to six and Fairbanks, Hood and McElroy are pretty certain to be among the also rans."[11] The Vernon club did release Hood, but he was soon picked up by the Vancouver Beavers: Quoting a Western League writer, the *Los Angeles Times* wrote, "Wallace Hood, released by Vernon last spring and signed by Vancouver, seems to have the making of a star."[12] By May of 1916, Hood appears on the roster of the Beavers. However, and perhaps ironically, his name appears in a column stating, "The Tigers hit Hood all over the lot."[13] From late 1915 into early 1916, and when not playing baseball, Hood remained active on the roster of the Whittier Crescents, a basketball team in a new AAU league. As a forward, he became known as one of the "demon shot[s]" in the league.[14]

In 1917 the United States became embroiled in World War I. Driven by a sense of duty and responsibility, Hood applied, at the age of 22, for military service in the United States Aero Corps. His draft registration card, dated May 31, 1917, noted an exemption for him because his mother was dependent upon him. He was not called to duty immediately, which allowed him to rejoin the Vancouver Beavers.

For 1916 and 1917, Hood compiled a 12-win, 23-loss pitching record and a .243 batting average. (Between pitching record and batting average, he had begun a shift to playing in the field.) In 1918 he was called to military service. In 1919, now primarily used as an outfielder, he returned to baseball, playing with two teams in two leagues. He joined the Moose Jaw Robin Hoods of the Western Canada League, appeared in 67 games, and hit .316. Although actual playing time with the Vancouver Beavers of the Northwest International League was limited, he did receive attention in the form of an on-the-field exposition. The president of the Beavers, Bob Brown, and "officials of the Aerial Club of Canada" devised a plan "whereby one of the aeroplanes of the league will fly over Atlantic Park ... and will drop several baseballs ... which Wally Hood ... a commissioned flyer himself ... will attempt to catch."[15] Whether or not Hood actually caught any of the dropped baseballs is unclear.

By 1920, Hood's talent brought him to the major leagues. The 5-foot-11, 160-pound Hood, who threw and batted right-handed, made his major-league debut on April 15, 1920; his career would span three seasons, 1920-1922, with appearances on the rosters of two National League teams, the Brooklyn Robins and the Pittsburgh Pirates. Brooklyn placed him on waivers in late May, and the Pirates quickly claimed him to replace injured outfielder Carson Bigbee. However, when Bigbee returned to the field sooner than expected, the Pirates released him, and "Charley Ebbets instantly reclaimed the young outfielder."[16] Eventually he was sent to the Salt Lake City Bees of the Pacific Coast League. Before being shipped from Brooklyn to Pittsburgh, Hood played in a historic game — the 26-inning contest between the Robins and Boston Braves on May 1, the longest game by innings in major-league history. Hood went into the lineup after Hi Myers was injured. He got a single, a walk and a sacrifice hit in eight plate appearances and stole a base.

Hood performed very well with the Bees, appearing in 111 games, hitting .307 and maintaining a fielding (outfield) percentage of .962; he also pitched in one game with the Bees. After the 1920 season he and other players, including Sammy Bohne, Billy Cunningham, Eddie Ainsmith, and Les Nunamaker, traveled to Japan with a troupe assembled by Los Angeles sports promoter Gene Doyle. Hood's passport application, dated September 30, 1920, had him leaving San Francisco on October 30, 1920, and his name appears on the passenger list of the ship *Tenyo Maru*, returning to San Francisco from Yokohama, Japan on February 21, 1921.[17] He played two more seasons in the majors with the Robins, appearing in 56 games in 1921 and two games in 1922. Although a reliable outfielder, his .238 average would not be enough to keep him on the roster; he played his final major-league game on April 22, 1922. He finished the season with the Seattle Indians of the Pacific Coast League. On October 24, 1922, in Olympia, Washington, he married Edna Bernadine Rooks of Pullman, Washington. They had one child, Wallace James Jr. (The son pitched at the University of Southern California and was the first USC pitcher "to earn All-American first team acclaim. He was also a two time All-Conference first teamer."[18] Young Hood spent seven seasons in the minor leagues, mostly at the Triple-A level, and he pitched in two games with the New York Yankees in 1949. He was elected into the USC Athletic Hall of Fame in 2005.)

In 1923 the elder Hood joined the PCL's Los Angeles Angels; that season, he was named the Angels' Most Valuable Player, having batted a team high .340.[19] He played with the Angels through the 1928 season. The final two years of his professional career, 1929 and 1930, saw him on the rosters of four teams: the Reading Keystones of the International League; the Seattle Indians of the PCL; the Memphis Chickasaws of the Southern Association; and finally, in 1930, the Sacramento Senators, of the PCL.

While with the Angels in 1928, Hood was one of several players (including Truck Hannah and Mike Ready) called upon to appear (in uncredited roles, appearing as themselves) in the Paramount Studios film *Warming Up*. Director Fred C. Newmeyer, a baseball player himself, knew that his film needed professional ballplayers to give a realistic vision of baseball. Released on July 25, 1928, the film starred Richard Dix and Jean Arthur. The film was Paramount's first sound production. A reviewer declared: "You actually hear the crack of the bat, the call of the umpire, the roar of the crowd. ..."[20] Richard Dix studied the players and even emulated the superstitious behaviors of some. Hood was acknowledged for one of his superstitions: " 'Sure Fire' is the laconic explanation of Wally Hood, formerly with the Brooklyn club and a member of the cast of 'Warming Up,' for his peculiar custom when two strikes are called against him of taking his chewing gum from his mouth and sticking it on the button on the top of his cap."[21]

Hood appeared in three other films: *Alibi Ike* in 1935, *The Stratton Story* in 1949, and *Rhubarb* in 1951.

In *Alibi Ike*, a Warner Bros. film adapted from a Ring Lardner story, Joe E. Brown and Olivia de Havilland (in her first role) led a cast that included 26 ballplayers, among them Jim Thorpe. Whether

Wally Hood, a big leaguer for three seasons, can be found in four feature films: Warming Up; Alibi Ike; The Stratton Story; *and* Rhubarb.

or not any of these players had lines to speak, Joe E. Brown, an athlete with baseball experience, insisted that the film represent baseball faithfully.[22] The *New York Times* reviewer wrote of the film: "Warners have fashioned a merry little film that will appeal first to the Brown enthusiasts, second to the Lardner disciples, third to the followers of the national sport and fourth to the rank and file of film-goers who think there is nothing like a harmless comedy to brighten the dull moments of a hot summer's day."[23]

In 1935 Hood began a career as a PCL umpire. In his first month of umpiring, he earned praise: "Wally Hood, who used to be known as the 'Whittier Walloper' during his outfielding days, is coming along surprisingly well in his new role as umpire."[24] He quickly acquired a reputation which would serve him well at times. During an argument with a baserunner in a September 1935 game, the runner (Gene Desautels) shoved him. However, Mr. Hood refuses to be shoved around by a common ball player, so he called Desautels out again — this time out of the ball game."[25] His career, though, led him into numerous disagreements and confrontations, and not always pleasant critiques. For example, in 1939 a columnist wrote that Hood said, "If I were pitcher Larry Powell of the Seals, I'd give up throwing the screwball." In response the columnist wrote: "If I were umpire Wally Good, I'd give up umpiring.— Almost any Pacific Coast League ball player."[26] By 1944 the PCL had seen enough and, after nine years as an umpire, league President Clarence Rowland included Hood among four umpires whose contracts were not renewed.

After losing his job, Hood worked as an electrician and was still called by filmmakers to appear in baseball-themed films. In 1949 he appeared in the MGM production of *The Stratton Story*, starring James Stewart and June Allyson. While some of the 72 ballplayers who worked in this film did have speaking roles — including Jimmy Dykes as team manager — Hood appeared as himself in an uncredited role.[27] Among the ballplayers were Bill Dickey and Roy Partee. The film earned good reviews.

Hood's final film role came in the 1951 Paramount film *Rhubarb*, starring Ray Milland and Jan Sterling. His film career ended as his professional career in baseball did– as an umpire. The film earned the following headline: "*Rhubarb* Rollicking Fun; All Runs, Hits, No Errors."[28] It was further noted that "most of *Rhubarb* was shot on the Paramount lot, with the baseball sequences lensed at Wrigley Field, home of the Los Angeles Angels in the Pacific Coast League."[29]

Hood lived out the remainder of his life in the Los Angeles area. Records are not clear, but it appears that he had married twice. He was found by his ex-wife, Irene Cooke, collapsed in his apartment on May 2, 1965. A newspaper report read: "Wally Hood, Sr., a utility outfielder with the Brooklyn Dodgers [reports often refer to the Dodgers, not the Robins] in the early 1920s, was found dead in his apartment yesterday, his ex-wife reported."[30]

Hood was 70. He is buried in Rose Hills Memorial Park in Whittier. In 2014 Hood was inducted into the PCL Hall of Fame.

NOTES

1. "Newmeyer Won Another," *Houston Post*, July 8, 1911: 4.
2. "Richard Dix." *The Internet Movie Database*. IMDB.com, Inc, n.d. Web. imdb.com/name/nm0228715/bio?ref_=nm_ov_bio_sm.
3. Catharine Hood's name appears as both Catherine and Catharine.
4. "Town Is Dry. Charge Man Is Drunk," *Los Angeles Times*, July 15, 1914: Part II, 12. After their divorce, Catharine later found work as a dressmaker, and James became an oil-field worker.
5. "A Pioneer of City Passes," *Whittier News*, July 23, 1937: 2. Whittier Public Library Digital Archives. digi.cityofwhittier.org/awweb/main.jsp?flag=browse&smd=1&awdid=2g.
6. "About Us — A Short History," City of Whittier, California. cityofwhittier.org/about/default.asp.
7. "Whittier High School Yearbook, 1913," Whittier Historical Society, email communication.
8. *Whittier News*. February 22, 1913: 2.
9. "Baseball," *Cardinal and White*, Whittier High School, 1913, 3. Whittier Historical Society, email communication.
10. "Pitcher Hood Has Signed Up With Vernon Team," *Santa Ana* (California) *Daily Register*, December 27, 1915: 2.
11. "BEST CLUB," *Salt Lake Telegram*, March 12, 1916: 13.
12. "Quite a Change," *Los Angeles Times*, June 16, 1916: 23.

13 "At Vancouver Yesterday," *Tacoma Times*, May 12, 1916: 6.

14 "Basket Teams After Blood," *Los Angeles Times*, January 28, 1916: 22.

15 "Aeroplane at Athletic Park." *Vancouver* (British Columbia) *Daily News*, May 16, 1919: 12.

16 "May Repurchase," *Pittsburgh Daily Post*, December 17, 1921: 10.

17 "Wallace J. Hood, in the Passenger and Crew Lists, 1882-1959," Ancestry.com.

18 "Memoriam Page," USC Baseball Alumni. baseball.usclegacy.com/members/in-memorium, September 29, 2017.

19 "Wally" Hood: Pacific Coast League Content—Minor League Baseball." milb.com/content/page.jsp?ymd=20140430&content_id=73836990&fext=.jsp&sid=l112&vkey=.

20 "'Warming Up' Great Picture," *Shreveport Times*, September 23, 1928: 31.

21 "Ball Players Fear The Jinx," *Arizona Daily Star* (Tucson), September 23, 1928: 16.

22 "26 Big Leaguers in Joe E. Brown's 'Alibi Ike' Film," *Greenwood* (Mississippi) *Commonwealth*, July 13, 1935: 6.

23 "The Screen; Joe E. Brown Returns in a Merry Film Version of Ring Lardner's 'Alibi Ike,' at the Cameo," *New York Times*, July 17, 1935. nytimes.com/movie/review?res=9407E2DB1E39E-33ABC4F52DFB166838E629EDE. September 29, 2017.

24 "Wally Hood Making Good in Umpiring Role," *Los Angeles Times,* April 3, 1935: 31.

25 "Desautels Chased," *Los Angeles Times*, September 10, 1935: 28.

26 "Short, Short Story," *Oakland Tribune*, July 6, 1939: 24.

27 "It's a True Life Story," *The Sporting News*, May 11, 1949: 13.

28 "'Rhubarb' Rollicking Fun; All Runs, Hits, No Errors," *Tampa Bay Times,* October 8, 1951: 10.

29 "Ray Milland Co-Stars With a Cat in 'Rhubarb,'" *Brooklyn Daily Eagle,* August 19, 1951: 30.

30 "Ex-Dodger Player Found Dead by Wife," *Louisville Courier-Journal,* May 3, 1965: 28.

BYRON HOUCK

BY PHIL WILLIAMS

RARE IS THE PLAYER IN MAjor-league history who, after being part of a World Series winner, joins an equally great team in another profession in his post-baseball life. Pitcher Byron Houck provides such an example. He was part of the Philadelphia Athletics' championship staff in 1913, but his major-league career soon faded away. A decade later, he was in the movies—but behind the camera rather than in front of it. As a member of Buster Keaton's production unit, Houck helped to film some of the finest moments in the silent movie era.

Byron Simon Houck was born on August 28, 1891, in Prosper, Minnesota. He was the fifth of Arthur and Ida Houck's six children. Arthur farmed in the small community just north of the state line with Iowa. Sometime after the turn of the century, the family moved west to Portland, Oregon. Arthur found work as a plasterer.

Byron attended Portland's Washington High School, and emerged as a pitching ace. The undefeated squad claimed the state championship in 1909. "It is predicted," reported a local scribe, "that Houck will some day be a twirler in one of the big leagues."[1] After graduating from high school in 1910, Houck enrolled at the University of Oregon. He made the Oregon baseball team as a freshman and caught the attention of Joe Cohn, the owner of the Northwestern League's Spokane Indians. Cohn signed him on July 26, 1911.[2] Houck went 4-4 over 14 games with the Indians. Per Cohn's advice to Connie Mack, the Philadelphia Athletics drafted the youngster that September.[3]

The Athletics were two-time defending world champions, with five veteran starters returning for the 1912 campaign: Jack Coombs, Eddie Plank, Cy Morgan, Chief Bender, and Harry Krause. Houck was a raw project. "How different young players look on the field from the glowing recommendations that a manager receives about them," Mack sighed as spring training began.[4] With his senior catcher, Ira Thomas, he started the hopeful process of molding the youngster into big-league material. "Houck may need a little seasoning," observed Philadelphia sportswriter William Weart.[5]

Somewhat bowlegged, Houck stood 6-feet and weighed 175 pounds.[6] A right-hander, he possessed "a peculiar cross-fire delivery."[7] His "sharp-breaking curve ball" drew more praise than his fastball.[8] Houck's most noteworthy characteristic on the mound was the speed—or lack of it—with which he worked. He would eventually be called "the slowest boxman in baseball."[9]

As the 1912 season progressed, Krause and Morgan proved mostly ineffective, while Coombs lost time to injury. Houck made his major-league debut on May 15, starting against the visiting White Sox. In 6⅓ innings, he yielded five hits and six walks. Houck contributed strong relief efforts against the Browns on May 21, and the Red Sox three days later. Mack gave him another start in Boston on May 28. Houck didn't survive the first inning. Over the next five weeks, he sporadically appeared in relief.

On July 2 Houck entered the starting rotation. From this point forward, his performance improved, and Philadelphia won 10 of his 15 starts. But Boston ran away with the AL flag. The Athletics finished in third place with a 90-62 record. Houck finished with an 8-8 mark and a 2.94 ERA (and a retrospectively calculated ERA+ of 106, with anything over 100 being considered better than average).

It was a credible rookie campaign. That August Houck initially was mentioned as one of several Athletics to be dealt to the International League's Baltimore Orioles for outfielders Eddie Murphy and Jimmy Walsh. Mack re-engineered the trade so as to retain the young pitcher.[10] During the offseason,

Houck re-signed with Philadelphia for $2,100, a $600 raise from his rookie salary.[11]

Houck was not the only young arm Mack had stockpiled. The Athletics' 1913 staff also featured 24-year-old Carroll Brown, 20-year-old Joe Bush, 19-year-old Herb Pennock, 22-year-old Bob Shawkey, and 22-year-old Weldon Wyckoff. In the season's opening series, Coombs was lost to illness, which kept him shelved all year. Not wanting to overwork Plank and Bender, Mack told the team he would pull pitchers with regularity.[12] For the first time in baseball history, three pitchers—Bender, Bush, and Houck—on the same staff compiled at least 20 relief appearances. Mack's strategy helped the Athletics cruise to the pennant.

But Houck regressed in his sophomore season. In his first start, on April 21 vs. Boston, "there was scarcely a minute during the entire fuss that Byron wasn't planted on the brink of a yawning abyss."[13] Somehow, despite yielding eight hits and nine walks over 8⅔ innings, Houck escaped with the victory. Sometimes he lost composure. On June 11 at St. Louis, he took a 1-0 lead into the eighth inning. After walking the leadoff hitter, Houck cleanly fielded a bunt "but for some unknown reason failed to chuck to [Eddie] Collins, who covered first, for which oversight he was soundly berated by the aforesaid Mr. Collins."[14] Frank Baker then had the ball knocked out of his glove at the front end of a double steal. With the next batter Houck missed a high return from catcher Wally Schang, and the tying run crossed the plate. After Houck almost launched a wild pitch to the next batter, Mack sent in Bender. Philadelphia went on to lose the affair, 5-2.[15] Other times, such as a July 10 relief stint in Cleveland in which he surrendered two hits and four walks in one inning, "Houck rendered a decidedly unchampion-like display of hurling."[16]

For a two-month stretch starting in late July, Houck pitched with greater control and confidence, and won six straight decisions. A strong showing in his final appearances might have earned him pitching opportunities in the coming World Series against the Giants. But he was shelled in a relief appearance in Boston on September 26, yielded 12 hits in a complete-game loss to the Red Sox the next day, and "was as wild as a March hare" in three innings against the Yankees in the regular-season finale.[17]

By comparison, Bush finished strong and earned a World Series start. Houck saw no game action, and Philadelphia dispatched New York in five games. He finished the 1913 season with a 14-6 mark. In addition to his 4.14 ERA (an ERA+ of 67), Houck issued an alarming 122 walks in 176 innings.[18]

Houck began the 1914 season with three abbreviated, unimpressive starts. With the other youthful pitchers progressing, he was expendable, and Mack released him to Baltimore. Houck refused to report, and instead signed with the Federal League's Brooklyn Tip-Tops. His new three-year contract was for $3,500 per season.[19]

Tip-Tops manager Bill Bradley immediately fit his new recruit into the starting rotation. Houck lost his first four starts, then Brooklyn lost each of his next four appearances. "Byron Houck just can't lose the wild habits he contracted while a member of the Athletics," groused a Brooklyn sportswriter.[20] Houck pitched better as the summer progressed. But after an outing in Kansas City on August 20, Bradley ignored him for the remainder of the season. With the Tip-Tops in 1914, Houck amassed a 2-6 mark and a 3.13 ERA (an ERA+ of 102) in 92 innings.

Lee Magee replaced Bradley for the 1915 season and had no interest in retaining Houck. The pitcher, fearing the club might not honor his contract, reported for spring training. Brooklyn sent him down to the Colonial League, a circuit the Federal League had recently financed. Houck began with New Haven, which soon dealt him to Pawtucket. He finished 14-8 in Colonial League action. After the season, Brooklyn settled the remaining year of his contract by paying him half of it, then released him.[21]

As Houck had never signed with Baltimore, he was still Philadelphia's property as the 1916 season approached. But Mack had no interest and, after no contract came his way by March 1, Houck became a free agent.[22] He signed with Portland of the Pacific Coast League. With the Beavers in 1916, Houck went 17-19 with a 3.36 ERA.

In 1917 he struggled out of the gate. Houck had occasionally used a spitball since high school.[23] With his career in jeopardy, he doctored the ball with determination. "Houck shines the ball on one side and applies saliva to the other side," explained a local sportswriter.[24] He was soon "pitching the best ball of his career" in Portland.[25] Capping an improbable comeback, the St. Louis Browns drafted Houck that September. He finished his 1917 season with a 23-15 record and a 2.21 ERA.

Yet Houck's return to the majors in 1918 was unimpressive. He mostly pitched out of the bullpen and by July "had notions of quitting the team but was talked out of it."[26] He finished the campaign with a 2-4 record and a 2.39 ERA (an ERA+ of 114) in 71⅔ innings. Houck worked, and pitched, for the Tacoma Foundation Shipyards that fall.

The PCL's Vernon Tigers purchased Houck from St. Louis in February 1919.[27] Several months later, movie comedian Roscoe "Fatty" Arbuckle purchased the team and became its president. His business manager, Lou Anger, was installed as the team's general manager. Neither possessed any particular baseball experience, but no matter. Arbuckle and his fellow screen clowns—including his protégé Buster Keaton—kept crowds in stitches with in-game routines.[28] The Tigers cruised to the pennant. Houck finished with a 19-16 record and a 3.88 ERA. He added another two victories in the Junior World Series against the American Association's St. Paul Saints.

After the 1919 season, Houck began working as a cameraman. His entrée into this new profession seems to have been based on family connections. In 1913 he had married Kittye Isaacs. His wife's sister,

Byron Houck may have compiled an undistinguished 26-24 major league pitching record, but he worked as a cameraman on a number of classic Buster Keaton silent films.

Sophye Barnard, a noted vaudeville entertainer, was married to Anger.[29] Contemporary reporting, or later scholarship, does not identify what studio Houck initially worked with.[30] It may have been at Paramount with Arbuckle. It may also have been at Keaton's independent production unit.

Houck put aside moviemaking to return to Vernon for the 1920 season. That summer scandal engulfed the team. Tigers first baseman Babe Borton was accused of offering bribes to Salt Lake City players to throw games in the previous season's PCL pennant race.[31] Borton implicated many of his teammates. Houck, he claimed, was present at a meeting at Anger's home when the bribes were planned.[32] Borton was expelled. Houck, and most of his teammates, avoided any punishment. Vernon again won the pennant. Houck finished with a 10-17 record and a 2.62 ERA.

Houck's baseball career wound down. He pitched some semipro ball in 1921, then came back unimpressively to PCL action for a few weeks in 1922. Mention of Houck's participation in a movie crew over this span is rare.[33] Kittye was afflicted with chronic encephalitis, and died in March 1923.[34]

Soon after, Houck was a regular on Keaton's film crew. He was photographed on the set of *The Balloonatic*, and was mentioned as working on *Our Hospitality*.[35] "But you had to play baseball to work with Keaton," a documentarian notes; "he'd pick up a bat at the slightest excuse, and in the most unlikely places." Stills exist of batter and pitcher on top of a train car during the making of *The General*.[36] In the fall of 1923, Houck "threw a wicked and deceptive ball" for the Keaton nine.[37]

Houck earned photography credits, alongside Keaton's first cameraman, Elgin Lessley, for two 1924 classics: *Sherlock Jr.* and *The Navigator*. He also was credited alongside Lessley for *Seven Chances* (1925). For Keaton's masterpiece, *The General* (1926), Houck was an uncredited camera operator and still photographer.

In the silent era, in addition to managing photography, a first cameraman was often also responsible for lighting and developing film. A second cameraman such as Houck worked alongside a first cameraman such as Lessley in shooting scenes. The first camera created the domestic negative, the second camera the foreign negative. Both usually worked with comparatively slow orthochromatic film. "Consequently," film historian Kevin Brownlow wrote, "accuracy with focus and exposure was imperative." The cranking of the camera required great skill. Undercranking resulted in a speeded-up action, comparatively rare in Keaton's movies but an added value to chase scenes. Finally, Brownlow noted, special effects such as fades, dissolves, and superimpositions "were the responsibility of the cameraman."[38]

Camerawork on a Keaton set went beyond this norm. Film scholar David Thomson noted: "It has been argued, with justice, that his films are 'beautiful,' which means that their comedy is expressed in photography that is creative, witty, and excited by the appearance of things. That sounds obvious, but most comedy films of the silent era did little more than film the comedian's 'act.'"[39] Lessley lit a stage scene in *Sherlock Jr.* to appear as a movie screen, then used surveyor's tools to create a surreal sequence of cuts as Keaton (whose character is a movie-theater projectionist) leapt into the movies. *The Navigator*'s underwater scenes were shot in the clear, chilly depths of Lake Tahoe. Lessley and Houck filmed from a specially designed box lowered into the lake. Lest it mist up from their body warmth, ice was packed around them. The scenes of Keaton on *The General*'s moving trains required the camera crew to shoot from another train running on parallel track.[40]

Scandal destroyed Arbuckle's career in the early 1920s. By mid-decade, with the assistance of friends like Keaton, he attempted a return. Houck may have also felt loyalty toward Arbuckle, or wished to take on the duties of a primary cameraman. Whatever the case, for a handful of the shorts Arbuckle directed as "William Goodrich" for Educational Pictures in 1925 and 1926, Houck served as his cameraman. They were cheaply produced and unremarkable.

Arbuckle's comeback with Educational fizzled out. After *The General*, Keaton began to lose creative control of his work. Houck was remarried in 1927, to Rose

Carr. His career as a cameraman apparently ended. He disappeared from movie credits, and references to his involvement in production units ceased as well. Houck remained in Los Angeles. City directories and census records indicate he sold paper boxes. In his free time, Houck played golf and was actively involved with the Association of Professional Ball Players of America.

Byron and Rose eventually relocated to Eugene, Oregon. Then, in 1956, they moved to Santa Cruz, California. He remained active with the local Grange and assisting cancer patients. On June 17, 1969, Byron Houck died from septicemia after years of suffering from kidney disease.[41] He was buried in Rosedale Cemetery in Los Angeles. Rose survived him. Neither of his marriages produced any children.

SOURCES

In addition to the sources noted in this biography, the author also accessed Houck's file from the National Baseball Hall of Fame, and a number of sites such as ancestry.com,

baseball-reference.com, cdnc.ucr.edu, chroniclingamerica.loc.gov/newspapers, genealogybank.com, imdb.com, newspapers.com, oregonnews.uoregon.edu, and retrosheet.org.

NOTES

1 "Champs Win Again," *Oregonian*, June 3, 1909.

2 "Byron Houck Will Toss for Spokane," *Oregon Daily Journal* (Portland), July 26, 1911.

3 "Houck Makes Hit with Connie Mack," *Oregonian* (Portland), April 9, 1912.

4 William G. Weart, "Quaker Fans Quit," *The Sporting News*, September 26, 1912: 1.

5 William G. Weart, "Jinx Rests on Phils," *The Sporting News*, April 11, 1912: 1.

6 Back home in Oregon, he was sometimes called "Bandy Legs." See "Byron Houck with Philadelphia Team," *Eugene* (Oregon) *Guard*, February 15, 1913.

7 J. Ed Grillo, "Nationals Should Improve Position From Now On," *Washington Evening Star*, July 3, 1912.

8 William Peet, "Batting Rally in Eighth Defeats Athletics," *Washington Herald*, July 3, 1912.

9 "Bob Dunbar's Sporting Comment," *Boston Herald*, November 6, 1917.

10 William G. Weart, "Mack Not Done Yet," *The Sporting News*, August 29, 1912: 1.

11 Per the salary card in Houck's Hall of Fame file.

12 Norman Macht, *Connie Mack and the Early Years of Baseball* (Lincoln: University of Nebraska, 2007), 580-581.

13 Jim Nasium [Edgar Wolfe], "Byron Houck Would Have Scored Shutout Over Red Sox with Perfect Support by the Fielders," *Philadelphia Inquirer*, April 22, 1913.

14 Jim Nasium [Edgar Wolfe], "Agnew's Homer With Two On in the Ninth Was Cause of it All," *Philadelphia Inquirer*, June 12, 1913.

15 Ibid.

16 "Macks Unable to Tame Lanky Cy," *Philadelphia Inquirer*, July 11, 1913.

17 "Yankees Quit Cellar by Grace of Mack," *New York Tribune*, October 5, 1913.

18 Or 6.24 walks per 9 innings. No other pitcher hurling at least 150 innings in a season in the Deadball Era averaged over 6 walks per 9 innings.

19 "Brooklyn Feds Get Houck," *Brooklyn Daily Eagle*, May 21, 1914; Francis C. Richter, "The World Champions," *Sporting Life*, May 30, 1914: 10. On his salary, see "Houck, Out in Cold, Despairs of Game," *Oregonian*, November 5, 1915.

20 "Brooklyn Feds Lose a Close Game," *Brooklyn Daily Eagle*, June 10, 1914.

21 Chandler D. Richter, "Athletic Affairs," *Sporting Life*, April 3, 1915: 6; "Federal League Facts," *Sporting Life*, April 24, 1915: 10; Robert Peyton Wiggins, *The Federal League of Base Ball Clubs* (Jefferson, North Carolina: McFarland, 2009), 228-231; "Adams Football Player as Well," *Pawtucket Times*, June 2, 1915; *Pawtucket Times*, October 4, 1915; Wm. J. Granger, "Brooklyn's Finish," *Sporting Life*, October 9, 1915: 9; "Houck Sells Contract," *St. Louis Star and Times*, November 1, 1915.

22 "Many Fed Players Made Free Agents," *Oregonian*, January 20, 1916; Roscoe Fawcett, "Byron Houck Now on Portland Roll," *Oregonian*, March 2, 1916.

23 For an early mention of his spitter, see "Columbia Boys Crack Players," *Oregon Daily Journal*, March 22, 1908. But at no juncture before 1917 was Houck referred to as a spitballer per se.

24 "Spit Ball Is Big Aid," *Oregonian*, September 9, 1917.

25 "Portland Manager Has Mind on Next Season," *The Sporting News*, October 11, 1917: 5.

26 "Cards' Spurt Fails to Stir Community," *The Sporting News*, July 18, 1918: 2.

27 "Byron Houck to Pitch Balls on Vernon Payroll," *Oregon Daily Journal*, February 3, 1919.

28 For an overview of Arbuckle's time leading the Tigers, see Greg Merritt, *Room 219: The Life of Fatty Arbuckle, The Mysterious Death of Virginia Rappe, and the Scandal That Changed Hollywood* (Chicago: Chicago Review Press, 2013), 186-188.

29 For this background, see Reed Heustis, "Madman Runs Fat Arbuckle's Studio—Sure, It's Lou Anger," *Los Angeles Herald*, November 3, 1919.

30 A valuable synopsis of Houck's movie career may be found in Lisle Foote, *Buster Keaton's Crew: The Team Behind His Silent Films* (Jefferson, North Carolina: McFarland, 2014), 21-25.

31 For an overview of the scandal, see Dennis Snelling, *The Greatest Minor League: A History of the Pacific Coast League, 1903-1957* (Jefferson, North Carolina: McFarland, 2012), 83-94.

32 "Borton's Tale Is Related to Jury," *Oregonian*, October 19, 1920.

33 The only such mention the author found was for the John Gilbert drama *Calvert's Valley*. See "Rim of the World," *San Bernardino Daily Sun*, September 4, 1921.

34 Foote, *Buster Keaton's Crew*, 23.

35 Foote, *Buster Keaton's Crew*, 199; "Sport-O-Graphs," *Oxnard Press-Courier*, August 30, 1923.

36 Kevin Brownlow and David Gill, "Buster Keaton: A Hard Act to Follow, Part 2." This acclaimed three-part television documentary from 1987 is as of 2017 available on YouTube. For more on Keaton and baseball, see Rob Edelman, "Buster Keaton: Baseball Player," as published in the 2011 *The National Pastime*, sabr.org/research/buster-keaton-baseball-player, accessed December 1, 2016.

37 "Oxnard Defeats Keaton Team in Airtight Pitcher's Battle," *Oxnard Press-Courier*, October 22, 1923.

38 Kevin Brownlow, *The Parade's Gone By* (New York: Alfred A. Knopf, 1968), 211-221.

39 David Thomson, *The New Biographical Dictionary of Film* (New York: Alfred A. Knopf, 2004), 471.

40 Brownlow and Gill, "Buster Keaton: A Hard Act to Follow."

41 Foote, *Buster Keaton's Crew*, 24.

REGGIE JACKSON

BY TED LEAVENGOOD

REGINALD MARTINEZ Jackson was born on May 18, 1946, in Wyncote, Pennsylvania, a largely white suburb north of Philadelphia's central city. His father, Martinez Jackson, ran a dry-cleaning and tailoring business. As a grown man, Reggie claimed he still knew how to cuff a pair of slacks.[1] His father was a veteran of World War II who flew a P-51 Mustang fighter during the North Africa campaign and used his Army Air Corps savings to start his business in a modest two-story structure, home to both family and business.

Reggie's father was a significant presence in his early life who provided a working-class environment amid somewhat more affluent surroundings. His mother, Clara, left with three of the children when he was 6 years old. His father raised Reggie, older brother James, and an older half-brother, Joe. Martinez continued to provide important stability until Reggie's senior year in high school.

Jackson was often one of the few black students attending his school. His background differed greatly from that of other black major leaguers of his generation who came of age in segregated communities and learned early the importance of a low profile. His comfortable demeanor among whites of relative affluence was at times a source of problems with other players, the press, and ownership.

Jackson starred in high-school sports including football, basketball, baseball, and track, and his games attracted many scouts. Martinez father wanted his son to get a college education and urged him to eschew a professional contract. When Reggie graduated from high school and made his way to Arizona State University on a football scholarship, the most important figure in his life was not present. Martinez Jackson had been arrested and jailed near the end of Reggie's senior year in high school for making moonshine in his basement.

Later, when he played for the Baltimore Orioles, Jackson reconnected with his mother and sisters Tina, Beverly, and Delores, who lived in Baltimore. He maintained a relatively close relationship with both sides of his family during his adult years.

With his father imprisoned, Jackson found important new mentors at Arizona State. The football coach was Frank Kush, who later was inducted into the College Football Hall of Fame. Jackson said Kush taught him toughness in relentless, physically demanding drills for the football team. An excellent football player, he could run the 60-yard dash in sprinter speed, 6.3 seconds.[2] By the beginning of his sophomore year he was a starting defensive back and the defensive captain in a Top 20 program.

Jackson found baseball more by accident than by intent. He had asked permission to play baseball as part of his scholarship agreement, but had to maintain a B average to do so. In the spring of his freshman year, he arranged a tryout. He displayed the tape-measure power he had even as a young man and was asked to join the freshman team. His skills were still rough and coach Bobby Winkles suggested that he play baseball in the summer with a Baltimore amateur team to sharpen them. It was an all-white team run by a Baltimore Orioles scout, Walter Youse.

Neither Youse nor anyone else on the team understood Reggie to be black until he showed up for the tryout. Youse watched the tryout and told Reggie years later, "The more I saw you that day, the whiter you got."[3] After a summer playing competitive baseball almost every day, Jackson returned for his sophomore year at Arizona State and claimed the starting job in center field.

The position had been manned the prior year by Rick Monday, who Jackson said "was a big league ballplayer when he was 19."[4] Monday was the best college player in the country when he left Arizona State and signed a $100,000 bonus contract with the

Kansas City Athletics at the end of Jackson's freshman year. Reggie opined that replacing Monday in center field was like "replacing the sun and moon."⁵

Jackson had a remarkable sophomore baseball season and was drafted by the A's, the second player chosen in the June 1966 draft. What followed was the first of many protracted negotiations between Jackson and Athletics owner Charles O. Finley. Jackosn and his father (now out of jail), traveled to Finley's Indiana farm, where they agreed to a contract with an $85,000 bonus.

Jackson began at Lewiston (Idaho) of the low Class A Northwest League, but was quickly moved to Modesto of the high-A California League, where he met many of players with whom he would share some of the greatest moments of his early years in the majors. Rollie Fingers, Joe Rudi, and Dave Duncan played for Modesto and were a cut above the rest even then. When the team traveled to Bakersfield for a series, the local paper's headlines read, "Call Out the National Guard, the Modesto Reds Are in Town."⁶

The next season the foursome continued as the backbone of Birmingham in the Southern League. It was Jackson's introduction to the unique cultural institutions of the South as they existed in 1967. Segregation was enforced unofficially in many aspects of life in Alabama and Jackson said that he felt the "uncomfortableness, the awkwardness, the fear … in the heart of Dixie."⁷ He played well enough for the Birmingham A's to earn a midseason promotion to Kansas City.

In his first exposure to the majors, Jackson hit only .178 and was sent back down. The demotion was difficult for him emotionally, but Birmingham manager John McNamara provided important support. McNamara managed Jackson again in Oakland and Anaheim, and Jackson said his help was essential for a 21-year-old trying to grow up and handle both success and failure in a Deep South environment.

Jackson started the 1968 season with Oakland, where Finley had relocated the Athletics. He shrugged off the tentative emotions from his prior "cup of coffee" and started the season strong. At the end of April he was hitting .309 with four home runs. He cooled off and saw his average drop to .231 in early June. In May he hit only one "dinger," as he liked to call his home runs.

Then in June Jackson found his power stroke again. He ended the season with 29 home runs and batted .250. His ability to hit the long ball established him as a permanent feature in a lineup anchored by Sal Bando, also from Arizona State, Joe Rudi, and Bert Campaneris, the dynamic basestealer who hit at the top of the lineup. Rick Monday was in center field, but it was Bando, Jackson, Campaneris, and Rudi who became the backbone of the Oakland Athletics teams that dominated the American League in the 1970s.

The '68 Athletics finished sixth, winning 82 games. They were on a slow ascent and the next year Jackson

Reggie Jackson, "Mr. October"; he memorably plays an assassin intent on killing the Queen of England in The Naked Gun: From the Files of Police Squad!

was at the center of it all. He became a national celebrity during the 1969 season as he put up home run numbers that compared to those of Roger Maris and Babe Ruth. By July 5 he had 34 home runs; Frank Howard and Harmon Killebrew had 30 and 22 respectively.

"Microphones were shoved in my face for the first time. ... Fans grabbed and screeched for autographs," Reggie said, acknowledging that he was not ready for the pressure his success had created.[8] He was only 23 years old and described himself as "tired and beat up" by the end of the season. Managing only a single home run in September, he ended the season with 47 home runs, third behind Killebrew with 49 and Howard (48). Jackson led the league in slugging, at .608, and the 47 home runs were his career best.

The next season was one of the worst in Jackson's early life. He hit .237 with only 23 home runs. He and his wife, Jennie, whom he had met at Arizona State and married in 1968, divorced. Very little went right during the year and Reggie decided to play winter ball in Puerto Rico in hopes of finding his swing. At Santurce he played for future Hall of Famer and inveterate tough guy Frank Robinson, who was a positive influence and helped Jackson put his life back on track.

In 1971 the Athletics began to establish their dominance in the American League. They won 101 games and won the West Division. Sal Bando most often was the dominant force in the clubhouse and just as important in the lineup. Jackson said of him, "When Sal talked, people listened."[9] The atmosphere in the clubhouse was pugnacious at times and it took a strong personality to keep order. According to Reggie that decorum led to execution on the field. "Just do it," was Bando's motto. No whining, no excuses, just get the job done.[10]

With Bando, Jackson, and Mike Epstein at its heart, the A's offense was potent, but the pitching was even better. The 1971 season saw the emergence of Vida Blue (24-8, 1.82 ERA), who won both the Most Valuable Player Award and the Cy Young Award. Catfish Hunter won 21 games and had an ERA of 2.96.

The Athletics were swept in the 1971 American League Championship Series to the Baltimore Orioles. From that near-miss, the Athletics and Jackson began a historic run, winning three straight World Series, 1972-1974. No franchise other than the New York Yankees has achieved a similar level of dominance. For a team that defined the term "small-market franchise," it was a remarkable feat.

In 1972 Jackson set a goal of winning the MVP, but failed, hitting only .265 with 25 home runs. First baseman Epstein led the team with 26 home runs and Joe Rudi (.305) was the only Athletic to hit over .300. The A's won the pennant because they featured the best combination of hitting and pitching, finishing second-best in the American League in both runs scored and fewest runs allowed.

In the ALCS the A's beat the Tigers in the playoffs in a tight five-game series where pitching dominated. Jackson was not a deciding factor in any of the games, but played well. In the fifth and final game, Oakland manager Dick Williams called for a double steal with Jackson on third base, Epstein on first, and one out. On the pitch Gene Tenace swung and missed for the second out, and Bill Freehan fired for second base. As soon as the ball went past the pitcher, Jackson bolted from third. Epstein beat the throw and shortstop Woody Fryman threw back to home. Jackson felt his hamstring give 20 feet from home.[11] Despite doing serious damage in the process, Jackson continued down the baseline and executed a perfect slide around Freehan to score what proved to be the winning run. His determination gave Oakland its first American League championship, but he had to be carried from the field with a torn hamstring.

His foot in a cast, Jackson missed the World Series between Oakland and Cincinnati's Big Red Machine. With Reggie watching on crutches from the dugout, the A's defeated the Reds in seven games. The Series MVP was Gene Tenace who had four home runs and hit .348. Though Jackson missed the World Series, he was still in the spotlight and he wanted more. In 1973 he would grab it in earnest.

Early in 1972 Jackson said in an interview, "I want to make me $100,000." He believed he could become an MVP-caliber player and told the interviewer, "I want to be hitting .300 and some change, hitting 35-40 homers, and driving in 100-110 runs."[12] He did not have that kind of year in '72, but it was coming.

In 1973 Mike Epstein was gone and Gene Tenace took over at first base with Ray Fosse catching most games. Tenace had a fine season, hitting 24 home runs with a .259 average. Bando had one of his best years with 29 homers and a .287 average. But this was the first season that Reggie Jackson's name was written into the heart of the lineup without fail every day. Manager Williams also moved him from center field to right, where he would face fewer defensive pressures.

With their strong pitching and Brooks Robinson a third, the Orioles had the best regular-season record in 1973. But in the ALCS Oakland had too much firepower and pitching. Catfish Hunter threw a shutout in the fifth game to win the pennant for the Athletics. Jackson batted only .143 against the Orioles. His fame as the postseason player who became known as Mr. October was still to come.

In the 1973 World Series, Oakland drew the New York Mets, who had surprised Cincinnati for the NL crown. Oakland got the best of it and won in seven games, giving the A's back-to-back titles. Jackson hit his first World Series home run in Game Seven. He hit .310 for the Series, drove in six runs, and was named Series MVP.

It was the first of many honors Jackson won for his 1973 season. He led the league with 32 home runs and 117 RBIs. He batted .293 and stole 22 bases. The collective numbers gave him the MVP season he had sought the year before. He was a unanimous selection, joining an elite group of five other players who had been elected unanimously: Hank Greenberg, Al Rosen, Mickey Mantle, Frank Robinson, and Denny McLain. In January, *The Sporting News* made Jackson its Player of the Year.[13]

Joining such select company was precursor to an almost certain contract war with Charlie Finley. Jackson credited Finley with putting the team together and keeping the squad playing at a high level. But Finley was a one-man operation, filling the jobs of general manager and others to cut his administrative budget to the bone. Jackson said that Finley was a sharp businessman who taught him many things about the world of business, but said above all else, "he was cheap."[14]

Finley issued each player two Oakland A's hats and 24 bats to last the season. During the postseason, when other teams provided a separate plane for press and families, Finley paid for one plane and anyone who could fit. When the trainer taped his ankles, Jackson said, he used tape sparingly and saved whatever was left of each roll, never throwing anything away because there might not be a replacement.[15]

The tight-fisted Finley made contract negotiations high drama. After his MVP season in 1971, Vida Blue held out in April 1972, saying he would retire before taking the $50,000 contract Finley offered. For Jackson the negotiations were just as contentious. Finley drew the line at $100,000, saying he could not pay Jackson more than he paid Catfish Hunter. Jackson was sensitive to the needs of others on the team, saying, "I suppose I could shoot for $175,000 or $200,000, but that would lower the take for the other guys."[16] He maintained that he would not play for less than $125,000. The impasse was resolved in baseball's newest institution, salary arbitration, where the arbitrator bridged the difference at $135,000.

Jackson described the 1974 Athletics as a team that could "win at will."[17] The comment papered over clubhouse angst that began to surface around him that season. A serious physical confrontation with center fielder Bill North stung Jackson because of North's allegations that Jackson spent too much time with whites, especially white women. Jackson's mood soured over the course of the season and during a game he angrily threw a bat into the stands, where it narrowly avoided injuring manager Alvin Dark's wife and two young boys.[18]

Despite the tensions, the deeply talented Athletics team won the Western Division handily and faced the Orioles again for the pennant. As in the previous year, the talented pitching of Jim Palmer, Mike Cuellar, and Dave McNally provided problems, but Oakland won in four games. The A's won the World

Series against the Los Angeles Dodgers in five games. Jack had a good Series with the bat, though nothing to rival the previous year. This time it was a great defensive play that defined his contributions to Oakland's third consecutive World Series win.

In Game Five, with the A's leading 3-2 in the eighth inning, Bill Buckner hit a single that North misplayed in center field. Buckner took second and was headed to third with the tying run. Jackson had backed up North and, corralling the ball, he threw a bullet to cutoff man Dick Green who fired to third baseman Bando. Bando applied a sweep tag and Buckner was out, erasing the Dodgers' last threat.

During the offseason, Finley's dynasty began to crumble. Catfish Hunter was awarded free agency by arbitrator Peter Seitz because Finley had failed to make a payment to an annuity as required under Hunter's contract. Hunter signed with the Yankees for $2.85 million over five years. Finley then traded reliever Darold Knowles to the Chicago Cubs for Billy Williams, and Blue Moon Odom to Cleveland. Oakland's diminished potency was underscored when Hunter faced his former teammates for the first time and shut them out, 3-0. Jackson went 0-for-3 and began to question whether he too should be looking for greener pastures and bigger paydays.

As if to make a case, Jackson began an assault on American League pitching that carried him to another home-run title and the Athletics to another West Division title. He was aided by a newcomer, Claudell Washington, Finley's rookie sensation, whose natural position was the same as Jackson's: right field. Neither Washington nor Jackson could get the A's past the Boston Red Sox in the ALCS. Jackson and Sal Bando tore up the Red Sox pitching staff, but Oakland missed Catfish Hunter and was swept by Boston in three games. There was no World Series in Oakland for the first time in three years and there would be more bad news in the months to come.

In December 1975 arbitrator Peter Seitz expanded his prior year's finding for Catfish Hunter by declaring Andy Messersmith and Dave McNally free agents, thus nullifying the reserve clause. Finley, who had been shopping Jackson in 1975, began a more serious attempt to trade Jackson and other players who would be hitting the free market at season's end.

Seven days before Opening Day of 1976, Finley traded Jackson and pitcher Ken Holtzman to the Orioles. Despite wanting to test the free agent market and often asking Finley to trade him, Jackson was devastated by the news. He had made his life in Oakland and considered it home. Despite fights with teammates and Finley's tight-fisted oversight, he said of his time there, "The eight years I spent in Oakland were the best baseball years of my life."[19]

Jackson took his frustrations out on the Orioles, laboring to reach a suitable deal with GM Hank Peters and owner Edward Bennett Williams over the first few weeks of the season. His holdout impressed neither the Baltimore fans nor the players and when he finally signed at the end of April, he was out of shape. He started the season slowly and on June 13 his batting average was .208 with a paltry four home runs. He started to hit for power late in the month and wound up with 27 homers. The Orioles were never able to close the gap on the Yankees, finishing second in the AL East, 10½ games back. Jackson put a positive spin on his time playing for Earl Weaver and the Orioles in 1976. "Weaver is a great manager," he said. "He made you get more out of yourself."[20]

Still, Jackson resolved to taste free agency and the riches it promised. After the season he listened to offers from the Orioles and the Montreal Expos, but signed with the Yankees—not only were they the best team with the most money, but they were the Yankees, home to baseball's Pinstripe tradition. Owner George Steinbrenner paid him $2.96 million to play five years for New York. It was more than Catfish Hunter got, and more than any of the veteran Yankee players were making at the time.

Players like Graig Nettles and Thurman Munson had carried New York to the World Series in 1976 and like manager Billy Martin they believed they could do it again without Jackson. Many in the Yankee organization had argued against signing him, saying that the team had Nettles and Chris Chambliss and didn't need another left-handed bat. But the idea of bringing Jackson's huge personality to the Big Apple appealed to owner Steinbrenner. Tension with his teammates began almost immediately. Jackson described the Oakland clubhouse as being "like a college frat house," yet was never part of the club with the '77 Yankees.[21] Billy Martin was particularly problematic. The volatile Martin had once knocked out one of his pitchers at Minnestoa, Dave Boswell. A similar confrontation was narrowly averted between Jackson and Martin in 1977.

On June 18 the Yankees were in Boston playing the Red Sox at Fenway Park in a nationally televised game. Late in the game Jackson misjudged a pop fly off the bat of Jim Rice that fell for a hit. Martin believed Jackson was loafing and the simmering feud that had started with Jackson's signing reached a critical mass.

Martin was angry enough to pull Jackson from the game in mid-inning. When his right fielder entered the dugout, Martin confronted him with pugnacious obscenities. Jackson responded that he wasn't loafing, but escalated the rhetoric when he told Martin, "You never wanted me on this team," and followed it up by calling Martin an "old man."[22] The two came dangerously close to blows and a fistfight was avoided only when Yankee coaches Yogi Berra and Elston Howard strained to keep the two men apart. Much of the scrum was captured on national television, and media attention boiled over in the following days. Despite numerous rumors that Martin would be fired because of the fracas, Steinbrenner and Yankees general manager Gabe Paul and brought the two men together to make peace.

According to Jackson, New York City hosted an ongoing media circus that was a major factor in the difficulty he experienced over his five-year tenure with the Yankees. Jackson said off-handed and off-the-record comments that would not have been printed in other cities regularly became public in New York.

Despite the lack of comity among the star players on the team, the Yankees won the AL East in 1977. Jackson's season was typical: 32 home runs, 110 RBIs, and third in the league in slugging. But Steinbrenner had brought him aboard to win the World Series, to revisit the glories that Yankees teams had not experienced since 1962.

Jackson went 1-for-14 in the first four games of the Championship Series against the Kansas City Royals and Billy Martin benched him for the final game. Insulted and incensed, Jackson still drove in a key run with a pinch-hit single late in the game. New York beat the Royals to earn a match against the Dodgers in the World Series.

Jackson started the Series slowly, going 1-for-6. But in Games Four and Five he hit home runs, helping give the Yankees a three-games-to-two lead as the Series moved to New York. With the Dodgers ahead 3-2 in the fourth inning of Game Six, Jackson faced Burt Hooton, who had handcuffed the Yankees in Game Two. With Thurman Munson on base, he hit a fly ball that just made the right-field stands to give the Yankees the lead. He hit two more homers, in the fifth and eighth innings, drove in five of the victorious Yankees' eight runs — and listened gleefully to deafening chants from the crowd of "Reggie, Reggie" as New York City found itself a new hero.

The press made much of Jackson's World Series, comparing him with Babe Ruth, even calling him the "black Babe Ruth."[23] Jackson made good on Steinbrenner's investment, winning the Series MVP award for the second time in his career. The nickname "Mr. October" stuck to him.

In 1978 the Yankees defeated the Dodgers in the World Series again with Jackson and Graig Nettles leading the way for the powerful New York lineup. The following season was very different. Team captain Munson died in a crash of his airplane on August 2. The loss devastated the team and Jackson as well. Jackson had smoothed over the tempests of 1977 with Munson and had flown with Munson just days before the crash.

The Yankees never regained their form without Munson, finishing fourth in 1979. Billy Martin was fired after the season. Martin's fall from grace buoyed Jackson, who had his best season in 1980, batting .300 for the first time and hitting 41 home runs. It was good enough to help the team to a first-place finish in the AL East, but the Yankees were swept by the Royals in the ALCS.

In the strike-shortened 1981 season, Jackson played less of a role, but he and the Yankees made it to the World Series one last time. He continued to earn his reputation as a clutch player in October, but he did not lead his team to the championship; the Dodgers beat the Yankees in six games. Jackson missed the first three games with a calf injury.

With that Series loss, Jackson's five years as a player with the Yankees were over. Looking back, he told a biographer that signing with New York and playing in the city had been a huge mistake. Asked if he would do it again, he said, "I would not have signed with them in a million years. Not a chance."[24] Aching to get out of New York and return to his home in California, he signed a five-year deal with the California Angels starting in 1982. Playing that year for Gene Mauch, he had a fine season, hitting 39 home runs and driving in 101 runs. The veteran Angels lineup won the American League West title but did not advance in the postseason.

In his second year with the Angels, 1983, Jackson was pleased to be reunited with former manager John McNamara, but had the worst year in his career. He was 37 years old and hit only .194 for the season with 14 homers. He was more productive the remaining three years of his Angels contract, but the team failed to make the postseason.

His time with the Angels done, Jackson chose to close out his career in Oakland. He was 41 for his final season and numerous teams marked his last appearance with special Reggie Jackson days. It was one final time for fans to chant, "Reggie, Reggie," and a victory lap for one of the most talented and colorful players of his era. After 21 seasons in the majors, Jackson hung up his spikes at the end of the 1987 season with 563 home runs, good enough at the time for sixth on the career list.

Jackson prided himself in his investments and his business acumen. He had wealth from endorsements, real estate, and other investments. But he was not ready to dedicate himself to life in business. He wanted to try his luck as a manager, but was unwilling to work his way up the ladder from the minors. He served in Oakland as a broadcaster and hitting coach, but it wasn't enough. He wanted to call the shots, to own a team, but that remained beyond his reach.

On January 5, 1993, Jackson was voted into the Baseball Hall of Fame on the first ballot. His plaque in Cooperstown has him in the uniform of his first team, the Athletics. His father, Martinez, who had been so important to the young Reggie, lived long enough to see his son inducted, but died the next spring. (Part of Jackson's dream of owning a baseball team had been making his father a scout for the team.)

Having his own family and closing the gap with his mother, father, and siblings were the most elusive thing Jackson ever set his sights upon. He remained unmarried, but a woman friend gave birth to his child, a daughter named Kimberly. She became an important and enduring presence in his life, his most meaningful ownership stake to date.

Jackson has additionally acted on a number of TV series (*The Love Boat, Diff'rent Strokes, MacGyver*) and in films (*Richie Rich, BASEketball, Summer of Sam*, and, most famously, *The Naked Gun: From the Files of Police Squad!*, playing a comically crazed assassin intent on killing the Queen of England). In 2007, actor Daniel Sunjata played him in *The Bronx Is Burning*, an ESPN mini-series charting the 1977 Bronx Bombers. And finally, in addition to his Hall of Fame induction, the Yankees retired Jackson's uniform (also in 1993); the Athletics did the same 11 years later. For many years, Mr. October also has been a special advisor to the Yankees.

SOURCES

Jackson, Reggie, and Kevin Baker, *Reggie Jackson, Becoming Mr. October*, (New York: Random House, 2013).

Jackson, Reggie, and Mike Lupica, *Reggie: The Autobiography* (New York: Villard, 1984).

Perry, Dayn, *Reggie Jackson* (New York: Harper Collins, 2010).

Bergman, Ron, "A Bunt or a Home Run, A's Jackson Can Deliver," *The Sporting News*, May 6, 1972, 9.

Bergman, Ron, "Reggie Jackson Named Player of the Year," *The Sporting News*, January 12, 1974, 29.

Pepe, Phil, "Peace Pipe or Exit Sign for Yanks' Martin," *The Sporting News*, July 2, 1977, 19.

Spander, Art, "Reggie Is a Man for His Times," *The Sporting News*, November 5, 1977, 14.

NOTES

1. Reggie Jackson and Mike Lupica, *Reggie, the Autobiography*, 16.
2. Jackson and Lupica, 44.
3. Jackson and Lupica, 45; Dayn Perry, *Reggie Jackson*, 21.
4. Jackson and Lupica, 41.
5. Jackson and Lupica, 47.
6. Jackson and Lupica, 54.
7. Jackson and Lupica, 58.
8. Jackson and Lupica, 73.
9. Jackson and Lupica, 82.
10. Jackson and Lupica, 82.
11. Jackson and Lupica, 89; Perry.
12. Ron Bergman, "A Bunt or a Home Run, A's Jackson Can Deliver," *The Sporting News*, May 6, 1972, 9.
13. Ron Bergman, "Reggie Jackson Named Player of the Year," *The Sporting News*, January 12, 1974, 29.
14. Jackson and Lupica, 72.
15. Jackson and Lupica, 71; Perry, 103.
16. Jackson and Lupica, 71.
17. Jackson and Lupica, 100.
18. Perry, 125.
19. Jackson and Lupica, 86.
20. Jackson and Lupica, 123.
21. Jackson and Lupica, 148.
22. Jackson and Lupica, 169-173; Perry, 190-191; Phil Pepe, "Peace Pipe or Exit Sign for Yanks' Martin," *The Sporting News*, July 2, 1977, 19.
23. Art Spander, "Reggie Is a Man for His Times," *The Sporting News*, November 5, 1977, 14.
24. Jackson and Lupica, 151.

DEREK JETER

BY ALAN COHEN

Seems to Move in Perpetual Sunshine.[1]

"Baseball is a lot about attitude—not getting too up or down, enjoy each game, then forget it and go on. Review the game, learn from your mistakes, but don't let it burden you. A lot of things matter more than talent: work, education, never being satisfied. These intangibles have made Derek what he is."—S. Charles Jeter, 2002[2]

THE YOUNG BOY WENT WITH his parents and sister to Tiger Stadium in Detroit on a Sunday afternoon in 1985, three days before his 11th birthday. He was a Yankees fan at the time. Although he had grown up in Michigan, he spent summers with his maternal grandparents in New Jersey and had been going to games at Yankee Stadium from an early age. His favorite player was Dave Winfield, and he was able to obtain Winfield's autograph after the game. That evening he told his parents, "One day, you're gonna go to Tiger Stadium and see me play." Two decades later, Jeter recalled, "I went to sleep that night knowing what I wanted to do with my life. I had great dreams about it. And I'm not sure if I've woken up since."[3]

On June 7, 1996, Derek Jeter, in his 68th big-league game, made his first appearance at Tiger Stadium. His parents were there, as they would be for many great moments over his career.

In 1996 Jeter was unanimously selected the American League Rookie of the Year and was on a world championship team as the Yankees won the World Series for the first time since 1978. In the decisive Game Six, Jeter was in the middle of a three-run third-inning rally that put the Yankees ahead of the Atlanta Braves. His single to left field scored Joe Girardi with the Yankees' second run. Jeter stole second base and scored on a single by Bernie Williams. The Yankees won, 3-2, and it was time for the players to parade through New York's Canyon of Heroes. After the parade Jeter said, "I've never in my life seen that many people. It was unbelievable. It was overwhelming. I'd never seen anything like it before. I didn't realize there were that many Yankee fans. I didn't realize that there were that many people in New York, period. It was absolutely packed. Unless you're there, you really can't describe it."[4]

Derek Sanderson Jeter was born in Pequannock Township, New Jersey, on June 26, 1974, to a mixed-race couple, Dorothy Connors Jeter, an accountant, and Sanderson Charles Jeter, a substance-abuse counselor. His parents met while serving in Germany with the US Army. His father had played shortstop at Fisk University in Tennessee. When Derek was a child, his parents made him sign a contract each year that defined acceptable and unacceptable forms of behavior. Charles Jeter outlined the terms of the contract: "First of all, we want (Derek and sister Sharlee, five years younger) to do well academically. And we want them to be involved in things (outside of the classroom). The contract outlines study hours, and participation in school activities."[5] Sharlee, like Derek, took an interest in athletics and was a star softball player in high school.

The Jeters moved from New Jersey to Kalamazoo, Michigan, when Derek was 4 years old. There, Derek's father completed his graduate studies at Western Michigan University. Derek and Sharlee lived in Kalamazoo with their parents during the school year and spent their summers with their maternal grandparents in New Jersey. It was during these summers that Jeter became a fan of the Yankees. He also had more values instilled in him by his grandparents, Sonny and Dot Connors.

Derek starred at Kalamazoo Central High School and in his junior season batted .557 with seven home runs and 34 RBIs. When not on the diamond, he participated in cross-country and basketball. He was named honorable mention to the all-conference basketball team in his junior year. Before his senior year, he won a full scholarship to the University of Michigan to play for coach Bill Freehan, who, in his 15 years as a catcher with the Detroit Tigers, had been named to 11 All-Star teams and been awarded five Gold Gloves. As he began his final year of high-school play, Jeter, who had been named a "Super-25 Player" by *USA Today*, was attracting scouts from most major-league teams. As April turned into May, he was batting .643 and was the top prospect in the country. Playing on an icy, muddy infield, he suffered a severe ankle sprain rounding first base in an early-season game and played in pain for the bulk of the season.[6] Nevertheless, he finished the season with a .508 average and four home runs in his team's 24 games. (Three of the four homers came before the ankle injury.) Playing for coach Don Zomer, Jeter was named the top high-school player in the country by *Baseball America*. Zomer said, "He's got a gun for an arm. He was timed at 91 miles per hour from shortstop to first. One of the problems was getting a first baseman who could handle his throws. He's got it all, and I still say he's a better person than a baseball player."[7]

On the eve of the June 1, 1992, draft, it was clear that Jeter would be selected early in the first round. The only question was where. Each team had its own needs, and Jeter's name was not called by the first five selecting teams, each of which selected a college player. The Yankees, after their third consecutive losing season (71-91) in 1991, had the sixth pick. It was a no-brainer. On the recommendation of scout Dick Groch, the Yankees offered Jeter $800,000 to sign and take a road that would see him playing at Yankee Stadium during the 1995 season.

Jeter, after signing on June 28, 1992, did not get off to the best of starts in the minor leagues. He began with the Yankees' entry in the Gulf Coast League. Errors in the field and frustrations at the plate led him to question whether he had made the right decision in forgoing the scholarship at Michigan. The Rookie League season was two weeks old when he first saw action, on July 2.[8] He was hitless in his first 14 at-bats. As the summer wore on, Jeter, under the tutelage of manager Gary Denbo, began to find his stroke at the plate and finished with a .202 batting average. Playing in 47 games, he led his team in doubles (10), homers (3), and RBIs (25). The Yankees were encouraged and sent him to Greensboro in the Class-A Sally League, where he played in 11 games and began his long association with Greensboro teammates Andy Pettitte and Jorge Posada.

After the season, Jeter attended the University of Michigan for the fall semester. It was his goal to get a college education but he would not return to school after that first semester.

Jeter played the full season at Greensboro in 1993 and it appeared that the Yankees' investment would harvest the anticipated dividend. He batted a team-leading .295 and his 30 extra-base hits were punctuated by a team-best 11 triples. Mariano Rivera was a teammate for the first time. Jeter got a taste of postseason play as the Greensboro Hornets advanced to the best-of-five league championship round, losing to Savannah in five games. During the season, Jeter's fielding was not on a par with his hitting. He made 56 errors, and there were those in the organization who felt his future was not at the shortstop position. In *The Life You Imagine*, Jeter said, "I was the king of robbing a player of a potential hit and whipping it past first so the hitter wound up on second."[9] Despite his fielding lapses, he was named to the All-League team at shortstop.

The 1994 season was all the dreams of youth wrapped up in a miracle ride that took Jeter from Single-A Tampa to Double-A Albany-Colonie to Triple-A Columbus on a whirlwind tour. With each team, he batted well over .300—his combined average was .344 with 43 extra-base hits and 50 stolen bases. By the time the dust had settled, Jeter was named minor-league player of the year.

Jeter's road to the big leagues appeared to be without impediment, However, the Yankees acquired shortstop Tony Fernandez from Toronto before the 1995 season and after being out of post-season play since 1981 were on a path to return to the playoffs. In

1995, the postseason had been expanded to include a wild-card team in each league. How would all this affect Jeter's dream?

Injuries to middle infielders Fernandez and Pat Kelly forced the Yankees to make a move and they called up Jeter from Triple-A Columbus. He played in his first game on May 29, 1995, at Seattle. Batting ninth, he went 0-for-5, but he found the range a day later, going 2-for-3. In the fifth inning, with the Yankees trailing 2-0, he led off with a single against Tim Belcher and scored on a double by Jim Leyritz double. Leading off the seventh inning, Jeter singled again and scored on a single by Paul O'Neill. Seattle won, 7-3, but Jeter had his first taste of contributing to the team. On June 2, 1995, for the first time, he stepped to the plate at Yankee Stadium and received the ever-familiar introduction, "Batting for the Yankees, Number 2, Derek Jeter, Number 2." The sound was that of the legendary Bob Sheppard, but on that day, in that first at-bat, Jerry Seinfeld, doing an impression of Shepard, did the honors. Henceforth, it would be Shepard at the microphone. Once the injured players returned, Jeter and his .234 batting average (11-for-47 with 11 strikeouts) returned to Columbus. With the Clippers, he posted a .317 batting average with 38 extra-base hits in 123 games. He rejoined the Yankees for the stretch run but played in only two games, getting a double in his only at-bat. He was not named to the postseason roster.

Just before the start of the 1996 season, despite his being a top prospect, Jeter's status with the Yankees was uncertain. That is until Gene Michael, one of owner George Steinbrenner's most trusted aides, came out in support of Jeter. Jeter was the Opening Day shortstop in 1996 and would be the Opening Day and everyday shortstop for the next 17 seasons.

On April 2, 1996, the Yankees not only had a new shortstop, they had a new manager as well. Joe Torre had taken over from Buck Showalter. Yankee Stadium had seen great players over the three-quarters of a century before Jeter took to the field and many uniform numbers had been retired. The only single-digit uniform numbers left were Jeter's number 2 and Torre's 6. A little more than two decades later,

Derek Jeter; a list of his myriad show biz appearances only begins with Seinfeld *and* Saturday Night Live.

those numbers were also affixed to the wall in New York's Monument Park.

Opening Day at Cleveland proved to be a harbinger of things to come. Batting against Dennis Martinez, Jeter led off the fifth inning with a home run to left field to extend the Yankees' lead to 2-0. The score was still 2-0 when Cleveland batted in the bottom of the seventh inning. With a runner on second and two outs, Omar Vizquel lifted a short fly ball over the infield and Jeter chased after it into short center field, making the grab to keep Cleveland off the scoreboard. With his bat and his glove and his flair for the dramatic Derek Jeter was well on his way to becoming the Yankees' marquee player.

Teammate Paul O'Neill said, "I remember saying—actually a lot of us saying—Derek was the best all-around player we ever played with. From day one, that day in Cleveland, you knew that Derek was to become this great player. The confidence he had. There's just so many ways he helps you win a game."[10]

Although the Yankees won their division in 1996, there were some tense moments. With George Steinbrenner as the owner, there seemed to always be anxious moments. The Yankees went into first place to stay on April 28 and three months later had a commanding 12-game lead in the American League East. As August came to a close, the lead had shrunk to four games. Jeter took a batting average of .306 into September and fashioned a 17-game hitting streak from September 7 through 25 during which he batted .412 with 22 runs scored and 13 RBIs. Jeter sat out the second game of a doubleheader on September 25 after the Yankees clinched the division crown in the opener with Jeter's second-inning double plating two runners in the midst of a 10-run uprising that led to a 19-2 win over Milwaukee. Four days earlier, in one of the iconic moments that would dot his career, Jeter had, with the bases loaded, delivered a 10th-inning game-winning single, his third hit of the game, against the Red Sox, prompting him to say, "When the games mean more, it's a lot easier to play."[11]

That month the Yankees swept a three-game series in Detroit, with Jeter going 6-for-13 with a triple and three RBIs. Before the series, he shared a pizza with his dad and talked about life. Derek told his father that he wanted to start a foundation to give something back to the community, much as his hero, Dave Winfield, had done. On February 7, 1997, the Turn-2 Foundation was born and was dedicated to fighting drug abuse through working with at-risk teens. It has flourished in the years since, raising upwards of $11 million.[12]

In the Division Series against Texas, Jeter, after going hitless in Game One, posted a .412 average for the series (7-for-17) with key hits in each of the Yankees' three wins. It was then on to the League Championship Series against Baltimore where Jeter and a young boy, with one out in the eighth inning of the first game, would become part of baseball lore. The Yankees were trailing 4-3 and Jeter came to the plate against Armando Benitez. Facing the hard-throwing Benitez, Jeter used the inside-out swing that he had perfected and hit a fly ball to the opposite field and the familiar short porch. Baltimore right fielder Tony Tarasco went back to the wall and reached up to corral Jeter's fly ball, but the flight of the ball was interrupted by a young spectator. Reaching over the wall with his gloved hand was 12-year-old Jeffrey Maier. The ball bounced off Maier's glove and went into the seats. First-base umpire Rich Garcia ruled that Jeter had his first postseason home run, and was besieged by protesting Orioles. The game was tied and went into extra innings. Bernie Williams's 11th-inning homer gave the Yankees a one-game lead in the series. Maier was an instant celebrity.

Jeter batted .417 in the LCS and fielded Cal Ripken Jr.'s grounder for the final out of the five-game series as the Yankees advanced to the World Series against the National League champion Atlanta Braves, who were looking to win their second straight World Series. Jeter would play most of the Series in pain after he was hit in Game Two by a Greg Maddux pitch as the Braves took a 2-0 lead. In Game Three, won by the Yankees, Jeter didn't get the ball out of the infield safely, but made his presence felt nonetheless. A first-inning sacrifice set up the Yankees' first run and a seventh-inning infield single ignited a three-run rally that gave the Yankees a 5-1 lead. In Game Four, after the Braves had taken a 6-0 lead, the Yankees fought back. Jeter's leadoff single to short right field in the seventh inning ignited a rally that cut the lead to 6-3. The game went into extra innings and, in the 10th inning a walk, an infield hit by Jeter, and another walk filled the bases with two out. The Yanks scored twice in the inning, won the game and evened the Series. New York won Game Five in Atlanta and returned to the Bronx to wrap up the Series. In Game Six, Jeter's single plated Joe Girardi with the first of three third-inning runs and the Yankees went on to clinch the Series with a 3-2 win.

After his rookie season, there were questions as to whether Jeter could repeat his 1996 performance and go on to the great career that some thought was a guarantee. Jeter kept things in perspective when he was presented with the Rookie of the Year Award: "Baseball is a real humbling sport. You are on top one day and the bottom the next. I'll enjoy this (rookie award) now, but you don't have to worry about me getting a big head."[13]

Over the next 18 seasons, Jeter's career would be marked by iconic performances on iconic teams on the biggest of stages. Five times his team won the World Series. His face would become as recognizable as that of any Yankee legend, any United States president, any Oscar-winning movie star, any other star athlete in any sport. His off-the-field endorsements and appearances on television (his first *Seinfeld* appearance came shortly after the 1996 season) and in movies made him wealthy beyond the dreams that marked his youth in Michigan. A unique accolade for Jeter came shortly after the World Series when he appeared on *The Late Show with David Letterman* and was called "Dr. Hardball" by the host.

In 1997, the Yankees returned to postseason play for the third consecutive year, this time as a wild card, but were eliminated by Cleveland in the Division Series. The season was filled with frustration as Jeter's average dropped to .291, its lowest in any season between 1996 and 2009.

Second place was never good enough for either Derek Jeter or owner George Steinbrenner and there was a new determination in 1998. There were also new faces as second baseman Chuck Knoblauch and third baseman Scott Brosius flanked Jeter in the Yankee infield. And after the team lost four of its first five games, the ever-volatile Steinbrenner was ready to pounce. However, the team quickly turned things around and surged to a 114-48 record, the best in the history of the franchise. Jeter rebounded to bat .324 with 19 home runs and 84 RBIs. He was named to his first All-Star team and finished third in the MVP balloting.

And the young Jeter, only 24 years old, became the acknowledged team leader. Pitcher David Cone said, "He was more of a leader than anyone knew. We had a relentless nature where nobody gave away an at-bat no matter what the score was, and that's who Derek was."[14] Jeter's life off the field was guarded, but when he began dating superstar singer Mariah Carey, four years his senior, on whom he had had a crush since high school, it was hard for Jeter to avoid the 24-hour-a-day limelight. Their relationship ended during the course of the 1998 season.

The Yankees raced through the postseason in 1998, sweeping the Texas Rangers and eliminating the Cleveland Indians in six games before sweeping the San Diego Padres in the World Series, in which Jeter batted .353.

The Yankees continued their winning ways in 1999 and 2000. In 1999 they faced several challenges, not the least of which was an early-season bout with cancer by manager Joe Torre. But they prevailed, winning the AL East by four games. Jeter had 219 hits to lead the American League and posted a career-high .349 batting average. He also had career highs in homers (24) and RBIs (102). Once again. the postseason went by in a blur. The Yankees swept the Rangers for the second consecutive season and went on to face the Red Sox in the LCS. They thwarted Boston's hopes of returning to the World Series for the first time since 1986 by eliminating the Red Sox in five games. Jeter was the picture of consistency, batting .455 against the Rangers and .350 against Boston. Against the Braves in the World Series, the Yankees had their second sweep in as many years as Jeter batted .353 in the four games.

The 2000 season saw the Yankees win their fourth World Series in five seasons. Jeter was elected to start the All-Star Game at shortstop for the first time in a league that seemed to have more premier shortstops than Santa had reindeer. He was named the game's MVP, going 3-for-3 with a double and two RBIs. He eclipsed the 200-hit mark (with 201) for the third time in as many seasons. The Yankees won their third of nine consecutive division titles. In the postseason, they bested Oakland in five games and Seattle in six games to advance to the World Series against their crosstown rivals. The New York Mets were in the World Series for the first time since 1986. Jeter batted .409 in the Series. The Yankees won the first two games, marking 14 consecutive World Series games won by manager Torre. After the Mets won Game Three, Jeter took care of matters in Game Four. His leadoff homer gave the Yankees a 1-0 lead and he tripled and scored in his second at-bat to make it 3-0. The Yankees won the game, 3-2. In the fifth and final game, Jeter tied the contest with his second homer of the Series as the Yankees went on to win 4-2 and clinch the championship. Jeter was selected the MVP of the Series, becoming the first player to be named All-Star Game and World Series MVP in the same season.

In 2001 Jeter was once again named to the All-Star team and, after entering the game as a defensive replacement in the top of the sixth inning, led off the home half of the inning with a homer that gave the American League a 3-1 lead in a game they went on to win 4-1. The Yankees once again won the AL East with Jeter batting .311. He also joined the 20/20 club for the first time, stealing 27 bases and hitting 21 home runs. But the early 2001 season was one of challenge for the Jeter family as his sister Sharlee was diagnosed with Hodgkin's Disease. She had been diagnosed in late 2000 and underwent six months of chemotherapy. In May 2001, she was free of the cancer.

The postseason iconic moments for Jeter resumed in 2001. He batted .444 in the LCS against Oakland, but it is not for his bat that he will be remembered. The A's had won the first two games at Yankee Stadium and the third game was a nail-biter. The Yankees took a 1-0 lead in the fifth inning on a Jorge Posada home run, and the score had not changed when the A's came up in the seventh inning. With Jeremy Giambi on first base with two out, Terrence Long hit a ball down the right-field line for a double. Yankees right fielder Shane Spencer's throw-in was way off-line. Jeter, backing up on the play, raced across the infield, grabbed the errant throw and backhanded the ball to catcher Posada, who tagged Giambi as he tried to score from first base standing up. The Yankees held on to win the game and stay alive. Game Four went to the Yankees, 9-2, and, in the decisive Game Five, the Yankees took a 5-3 lead into the eighth inning. Long came up with a runner on base and hit a foul fly ball in the direction of the third-base stands. Jeter grabbed the ball and went over the short wall into the stands. Four outs later, the Yankees were on their way to the World Series.

Still another iconic moment came in 2001. The Yankees were looking for their fourth consecutive World Series win. They were playing the upstart Arizona Diamondbacks and the mound staff of Randy Johnson, Curt Schilling, and little else. Arizona won the first two games easily and Jeter went 0-for-7 over the course of the two games. The Yankees came back to win Game Three by the barest of margins, 2-1, and Jeter contributed a single. Schilling was back on the mound for Game Four, on Halloween night, October 31. Arizona scored two eighth-inning runs to take a 3-1 lead and Byung-Hyun Kim took over on the mound for Schilling. He struck out the side and the game went to the ninth inning. The Yankees were down to their last out when a two-run homer off the bat of Tino Martinez tied the score. Extra innings dawned, as did the beginning of a new day and month. After Mariano Rivera retired Arizona in order in the top of the 10th inning, Kim recorded two quick outs in the bottom half. Jeter came to the plate. He was 0-for-4 in the game and 1-for-15 in the Series. After falling behind 0-and-2, Jeter worked the count to 3-and-2 and found a pitch he liked. Early in the at-bat, the scoreboard flashed "Welcome to November Baseball," and eight pitches into the at-bat, a fan stood up and showed a homemade "Mr. November" sign. As if by design, the ninth pitch was intercepted by Jeter's inside-out swing and sailed into the right-field seats. The homer, the first walk-off of Jeter's career, came after midnight and earned him the title Mr. November. The Yankees lost the World Series in seven games, and Jeter batted only .148. Nevertheless, he had carved another notch on the baseball memory tree. On December 1, he hosted *Saturday Night Live*. At the beginning of the show, Jeter was interrupted by applause on several occasions, and completed the opening monologue by apparently hitting balls into the audience, injuring the spectators. Of course, it was a staged gag, and the home audience was in on the joke. In a sketch, involving "Yankee Wives," Jeter, dressed in drag, became a Yankee wife. He made quite a good-looking lady.

In 2002 Jeter and the Yankees once again won their division, this time with a 103-58 record. Jeter's batting average slipped to .297. In the Division Series against the Angels, although Jeter went 8-for-16 with a pair of homers, the Yankees lost in four games.

The next season, on June 3, 2003, Jeter was officially named the team captain. But his season almost didn't happen. On Opening Day, he dislocated his shoulder sliding headfirst into third base in the third inning, and missed the next 36 games, returning to the lineup on May 13. Jeter's batting average was once again above .300 and the shortstop's career hit total went above 1,500. The Yankees were in their familiar postseason spot, having once again won the AL East. In the playoffs, they ousted the Twins and Red Sox. The Twins had won the opener of the Division Series, but the Yankees came back to win three straight, with Jeter's ninth-inning homer completing the scoring in the final game. In the LCS, the teams went to extra innings in the seventh game. Although Jeter did not have a productive series, his bat came alive at the right moment. With one out in the bottom of the eighth inning and the Red Sox in front, 5-2, Jeter stroked a double that ignited a three-run rally and tied the game. Aaron Boone's leadoff homer in the 11th inning propelled the Yankees to the World Series. The Yankees lost to the Marlins in the World Series, as Jeter's .346 batting average went for naught. During the season, he appeared on the big screen, playing himself in a brief scene in the film *Anger Management*.

After the 2003 season, a series of circumstances took place that changed the face of the Yankees. An offseason injury to Aaron Boone created a void at third base and by the time the dust settled, Alex Rodriguez, who had been coveted by the Red Sox to replace Nomar Garciaparra (who was not expected to re-sign with Boston), was with the Yankees. Rodriguez was, along with Jeter, one of the premier shortstops in the league. They had been friendly rivals over the years, as Rodriguez put up power numbers that put him on a collision course with the all-time greats. Over the prior three seasons with the Texas Rangers, he had hit 156 homers and batted .305. He had also won a Gold Glove in 2002 and 2003, an honor that had eluded Jeter. But Jeter was the Yankees shortstop, and Rodriguez moved to third base after joining the Yankees.

If there was a defect in Jeter's approach to the game, it was in his tendency to swing at pitches early in each at-bat. By not being selective, he was chasing bad pitches and the pitchers were cognizant of this weakness. Cognizant or not, it had not been a big problem for Jeter, who through 2003 had a career batting average of .317 with 1,546 hits. However, in 2004 Jeter got off to a terrible start. At one point, from April 20 through April 28, he went 0-for-32 before homering on April 29. At the end of April, his batting average stood at .168. But he turned things around. He put together a 17-game hitting streak that extended from July 30 through August 17, batted .379 during the stretch drive, and by the end of his season had brought his average to .292.

Once again, it was the Yankees and Red Sox competing for the AL East Championship and, during the season, it was time again for a Jeter iconic moment in perhaps the most thrilling game of the season. The date was July 1, and the Red Sox were visiting Yankee Stadium. The Yankees had won four in a row and were seeking to extend their lead on the second-place Red Sox. Matchups between the teams seldom ended in less than four hours. Before a packed house of 55,265, the Yankees took a 3-0 lead, but the Red Sox came back to tie things up in the seventh. The game went into extra innings and, in the 12th inning, the Red Sox mounted a rally. They had runners on second and third with two out and pinch-hitter Trot Nixon at the plate. The left-hander hit a Tanyon Sturtze pitch in the air down the left-field line. Jeter made a mad dash for the ball which, had it landed safely, would have given the Red Sox a two-run lead. He grabbed the ball crossing the line into foul territory, plunged into the stands and emerged with a bloody nose and the third out of the inning. In the next inning, the Red Sox took the lead on a Manny Ramirez homer, but the Yankees scored two runs in their half of the inning to win the game and extend their first-place lead to 8½ games.

The Yankees finished first in the AL East and advanced to the postseason for Jeter's ninth consecutive appearance in the playoffs. Jeter led the Yankees past the Twins in the Divisional Series with a .316 batting average. In the League Championship Series, the Yankees won the first three games against the Red Sox, but their leadoff hitter was slumping with only two hits and a stolen base to show for his first 11 at-bats. The Red Sox came off the floor to win the final four games (two in their last at-bat) and Jeter could not muster more than one hit in any of those games. For the series, he batted .200 (6-for-30). At season's end, there was some consolation for Jeter. His fielding, which had never been perceived by critics as a strong point, was rewarded with the first of five Gold Gloves.

New York's media put Jeter under a searing spotlight but he held up to the pressure of not only the media but playing for owner George Steinbrenner. The euphoria of four world championships in his first five years with the team had evaporated into frustration in succeeding years. Most of the cast from those early years was gone, and the new players were unable to blend as a cohesive unit. The frustration continued from 2005 through 2008. Although the Yankees reached the playoffs in each year from 2005 through 2007, they were unable to advance to the World Series.

In 2008, for the first time in his career, Jeter did not play in the postseason. In a city impatient with defeat, the headlines were negative. The New York tabloids were quick to stir the pot by focusing on an uneasy peace between Jeter and Rodriguez stemming from negative remarks attributed to A-Rod. In 2009 things turned around. By then, Joe Girardi was in his second season as Yankees manager and Derek Jeter came into the season sitting on 2,535 hits and a career batting average of .316. Not known as a slugger, he had managed to go over the 200 mark in home runs for his career. For most mortals, these were borderline Hall of Fame numbers but that was all secondary. With the Yankees and Jeter, it was all about winning the World Series, and the failure to win since 2000 was gnawing at the Yankee captain.

The unfinished business of one more championship was resolved in 2009. Jeter batted .334, and was selected to start at shortstop in the All-Star Game. He batted .407 (including 3-for-5 with a double in Game Six) in the World Series, as the Yankees defeated Philadelphia in six games for their 27th championship. He was named *Sports Illustrated*'s Sportsman of the Year. He also appeared in the forgettable action adventure film *A Trivial Exclusion*.

In 2010 Jeter set the all-time Yankees hit mark, passing Lou Gehrig with hit number 2,722. He returned to the silver screen, appearing as himself in the police comedy *The Other Guys*, where he was inadvertently shot in an early scene by actor Mark Wahlberg, who co-starred in the film with Will Ferrell. A scene toward the end of the film with Jeter appearing destitute after his shooting was deleted from the theatrical release. However, the picture of Jeter appearing as a bum made its way to the New York tabloids. Baseball fans were quick to observe that the Police Captain in the film, portrayed by Michael Keaton, was named Gene Mauch. Baseball's Gene Mauch had managed the Angels and Ferrell was an Angels fan.

July 9, 2011, was a very special day for Jeter. He had been chasing the 3,000-hit mark and suffered an injury in mid-June, missing 18 games stuck on hit number 2,994. He returned to action on July 4 at Cleveland. Going into the game against the Tampa Bay Rays on July 9 at Yankee Stadium, he still needed two hits to become the first Yankee to get 3,000 hits. He went 5-for-5 and his 3,000th hit was a homer on a 3-and-2 count to tie the game. Later in the game, hit number 3,003 was an RBI single that gave the Yanks a 5-4 win. During the weeks leading up to this milestone, HBO cameras followed Jeter from injury to rehab to his glorious day in a documentary, *Jeter—3K*. Cameras were rolling as he returned to Tampa to train at the Yankee facility and they followed him through a two-game rehab stint with the Double-A Trenton Thunder. He revealed more of himself in the documentary than he had in thousands of newspaper and magazine interviews over the years.

There was one more great season left for Jeter. In 2012, he batted a team-leading .316 with a league-leading 216 hits as the Yankees advanced to the postseason for the 17th time in Jeter's 18 years with the team. But this time the iconic moment would not be accompanied by cheers, but with an eerie silence. In the Division Series against Baltimore, Jeter batted .364 and had a team-leading eight hits as the Yankees eliminated the Orioles in five games. The first game of the League Championship Series against Detroit saw its share of thrills. The Yankees, down 4-0, had tied the game in the bottom of the ninth thanks to homers by Ichiro Suzuki and Raul Ibanez. In the top of the 12th inning, Detroit had pushed a run across and had a runner on second base. Jhonny Peralta sent a groundball to the left side. A diving Jeter gloved the ball but could do nothing with it. That Detroit now had runners at the corners was irrelevant as Jeter lay motionless on the ground.[15] He had suffered a broken ankle that would effectively end his productive career.

The Yankees failed to make the playoffs in each of Jeter's last two seasons. He missed much of the 2013 season, playing in only 17 games and batting .190. Before the 2014 campaign he announced that he would retire at the end of the season, and he filled seats around the major leagues in his final trip into each city. The accolades were well beyond Jeter's productivity; he batted only .256. But Jeter's last game at Yankee Stadium was something special. On September 25, it came down to the ninth inning. Against the Orioles, the score was tied 5-5 and there was a runner on second base. Before Bob Sheppard had passed away in 2010, he had recorded the introduction which was used at each of Jeter's at-bats through 2014. So, one last time, the crowd heard the intonation of Sheppard, the Voice of God since 1951, saying, "Now Batting for the Yankees, Number Two: Derek Jeter, Number Two." And one last time, Jeter brought the crowd to its feet, singling home the winning run in his last at-bat at Yankee Stadium.

Two games later, it was all over. Twenty seasons, 3,465 hits, 260 home runs, 1,311 RBIs, five world championships, and 14 All-Star Games. Although he never was named league MVP, he finished in the top 10 eight times, and every part of his early-childhood dream was fulfilled.

Although often seen in the company of starlets, Jeter managed to keep his life away from baseball quite private. Fewer than 100 people were in attendance when he married model Hannah Davis, a native of the US Virgin Islands, on July 9, 2016 (the fifth anniversary of his 3,000th hit) in California's Napa Valley. Their courtship had begun in 2012.

In early 2016 Jeter appeared in the baseball documentary *Fastball*, in which he discussed what it was like to go up against the hardest throwers in the game. Many hard throwers were featured in the film, including Sandy Koufax, Bob Gibson, and Nolan Ryan. In September 2016 Jeter was inducted into the Michigan Sports Hall of Fame. The Yankees retired his number 2 on May 14, 2017. It was Mother's Day, a fitting time for Derek to be with the four most important women in his life—his grandmother, his mom, hi sister, and his wife. The tributes were many, from contemporaries to former teammates. Perhaps the most fitting came from Bryce Harper who saw Jeter as not only the captain of the Yankees, but a captain for all baseball. Four months later, on August 17, Derek and Jeter welcomed their first child, Bella Raine Jeter.

On October 2, 2017, a group including Jeter and principal owner Bruce Sherman purchased the Miami Marlins from Jeffrey Loria. Jeter was named to oversee baseball operations as CEO.

SOURCES

In addition to the sources cited in the Notes, the author used the Derek Jeter file at the National Baseball Hall of Fame and Museum, Baseball-Reference.com, and the following:

Appel, Marty. *Pinstripe Empire* (New York: Bloomsbury, 2012).

Thornley, Stew. *Derek Jeter; Daring to Dream* (Berkeley Heights, New Jersey: Enslow Publishers, 2004).

NOTES

1   Ira Berkow, *Summers in the Bronx* (Chicago: Triumph Books, 2009), 23.

2   Curt Smith, *What Baseball Means to Me: A Celebration of Our National Pastime* (New York: Warner Books, 2002), 123-124.

3   Alan Schwartz, *Once Upon a Game: Baseball's Greatest Memories* (New York: Houghton Mifflin, 2007), 77.

4   Bob McCullough, *My Greatest Days in Baseball: 1946-1997* (Dallas: Taylor Publishing Company, 1998), 116.

5. Mike McCabe, "Kalamazoo's Jeter a Lock for Round 1," *Detroit Free Press*, May 27, 1992: 6D.
6. Kimberley Gatto, *Derek Jeter: A Baseball Star Who Cares* (Berkeley Heights, New Jersey: Enslow Publishers, 2014), 17.
7. McCabe.
8. Ian O'Connor. *The Captain: The Journey of Derek Jeter* (New York: Houghton-Mifflin, 2011), 45. Baseball-Reference.com reports that Jeter signed on June 27.
9. Derek Jeter with Jack Curry, *The Life You Imagine* (New York: Crown Publishers, 2000), 35.
10. Bill Madden, *Pride of October: What It Was to Be Young and a Yankee* (New York: Warner Books, 2003), 415-416.
11. O'Connor, 96.
12. Jeter with Curry, 198, 203.
13. Joel Sherman, *New York Post*, November 5, 1996.
14. O'Connor, 136.
15. David Waldstein, "For Yankees, Thrilling Rally Ends Badly," *New York Times*, October 14, 2012.

WALLY JOYNER

BY PAUL HOFMANN

THE 1983 FILM *NATIONAL Lampoon's Vacation* introduced moviegoers around the world to Walley World, a fictitious Southern California amusement park billed as "America's favorite family fun place." The film depicts Clark Griswold, played by Chevy Chase, leading his family on a cross-country journey from the suburbs of Chicago to Walley World. Following an everything-that-can-go wrong-does-go-wrong plot, the quest to take his family to Walley World becomes an obsession for Clark. Three years later "Wally World" came to Anaheim in the form of a 23-year-old rookie first baseman named Wally Joyner.

Wallace Keith Joyner was born on June 16, 1962, in Atlanta. He was the youngest of five children born to Cliff and Karma (Fickes) Joyner. Cliff served in the Air Force for four years, then began his career as an air traffic controller for the Federal Aviation Administration. He worked for the Southern Regional Air Traffic Control Center in Hampton, Georgia, for 30 years.[1] Karma was a faithful member of the Church of Jesus Christ of Latter-day Saints (LDS) who was an early-morning seminary and music teacher for youth in Atlanta..[2]

The fact that Wally survived childhood was somewhat miraculous in itself. He was born with orange skin, the result of an Rh factor that forced him to have two complete blood transfusions during his first 24 hours of life.[3] At the age of 9 he contracted a kidney disease that caused a dangerous backup of fluids and bacteria that resulted in his gaining 15 pounds overnight. Had his parents waited a day longer to seek medical attention, doctors said, he would have died of heart failure.[4]

After overcoming these early-childhood health challenges, Wally attended and graduated from Redan High School in Stone Mountain, Georgia, the same school that produced major-league infielder Brandon Phillips. During his senior year, 1980, Joyner was honored as the Georgia High School Player of the Year. He went 5-0 with a 1.40 ERA as a pitcher and when he wasn't on the mound he drove in a Georgia high-school record 44 runs.[5]

A devout Mormon, Joyner chose to attend Brigham Young University in Provo, Utah. He majored in business administration and was a mainstay on the Cougars baseball teams from 1981 to 1983. As an 18-year-old freshman in 1981, Joyner hit .333 with 10 home runs and 48 RBIs. The left-handed-hitting first baseman followed that with an even better sophomore season, when he hit .445 with 10 home runs and 63 RBIs. As he entered his junior year in 1983, great things were expected of Joyner and the Cougars, and neither disappointed.

In addition to Joyner the 1983 BYU baseball team featured five other future major-league players: Rick Aguilera, Cory Snyder, Scott Nielsen, Gary Cooper, and Colby Ward.[6] The team compiled a 54-11 record and entered the NCAA Regionals as the nation's top-ranked team. Joyner hit his 23rd home run of the year in an opening-round game against Arizona State, but the Cougars lost to the Sun Devils, who rode freshman Barry Bonds' seventh home run of the season to victory. The next day the Cougars were eliminated from the tournament when they lost to Fresno State. In 64 games that season, Joyner hit .462, scored 89 runs, belted 23 home runs and drove in 95 runs on his way to earning second team All-American honors.[7] On June 6 the California Angels selected him in the third round of the 1983 draft.

After signing on June 16, the first baseman began his professional baseball career with the Peoria (Illinois) Suns of the Class-A Midwest League. Joining the Suns at midseason, Joyner appeared in 54 games and batted .328 with 3 home runs and 33 RBIs. Despite having a roster that included future major leaguers Mark McLemore, Devon White,

Wally Joyner, a "good, all-American kid," has appeared in Little Big League, *among other films.*

Bob Kipper, Pat Clements, and Urbano Lugo, the Suns finished 54-85, last place in the circuit's South Division.

The next spring Joyner was promoted and spent the entire 1984 season the Waterbury (Connecticut) Angels of the Eastern League. Appearing in 134 games, he led the Double-A Angels in batting average, home runs, and RBIs (.317/12/72) as the team finished in second place with a 76-64 record. His performance at Waterbury earned him a promotion to the Triple-A Pacific Coast League's Edmonton Trappers for the 1985 season. With Edmonton he hit .283 with 12 homers and 73 RBIs.

With the retirement of Angels first baseman Rod Carew after the 1985 season, Joyner appeared to have the inside track on the job for 1986. During the winter he dedicated himself to getting stronger while he played winter ball in Puerto Rico. He added 10 pounds of muscle to a physique that in college had drawn comparisons to a bowling pin, and won the Puerto Rican League triple crown with a .356 average, 14 homers, and 48 RBIs in 54 games.[8] This solidified Joyner as Carew's heir-apparent.

Joyner enjoyed a solid spring and was rewarded with the everyday first-base job out of spring training. He made his major-league debut on April 8, 1986, against the Seattle Mariners at the Kingdome in Seattle and went 1-for-5. He recorded his first major-league hit in the top of the seventh inning when he doubled to deep center off right-hander Mike Moore. The next night he hit his first major-league home run, a two-run shot in the third inning off Mark Langston. By the end of April Joyner was batting .333 with 6 home runs and 16 RBIs.

When the Angels returned to Anaheim Stadium in early May, Wally World had officially come to Anaheim. *Sports Illustrated* reporter Craig Neff recorded the event. "One fan draped a WALLY WORLD sign over the terrace-level railing in right field, another started a Walleee! cheer, and that was it. An age of good, clean fun had begun."[9]

Wally World continued to grow in popularity not only in Anaheim but also nationwide. On July 15, 1986, Joyner was the American League's starting first baseman in the All-Star Game, played at the Houston Astrodome. It was the first time fans had voted a rookie into the starting lineup for the midsummer classic. Batting fifth, Joyner faced Dwight Gooden to lead off the top of the second inning. The sweet-swinging left-handed first baseman sent a short pop fly to shallow left field that was gloved by Ozzie Smith. This was Joyner's only plate appearance of the game and, surprisingly, he never played in another All-Star Game.

Joyner's early success at the major-league level was complemented by his reputation as modest, polite, and unassuming rookie. That season, Angels broadcaster Ron Fairly commented, "He's such a good, all-American kid. You'd want to stand next to him in a rainstorm because you know lightning won't hit him."[10] Divine intervention may explain how Joyner was not seriously injured in a knife-throwing incident at Yankee Stadium later that season.

The incident occurred on August 26. The Angels had just wrapped up a two-game series against the

Yankees in New York and Joyner was walking off the field with winning pitcher Mike Witt, who had shut out the Yankees on four hits. As the two approached the dugout, Joyner was hit on the left forearm by a knife that was thrown from the stands. "I thought it was a comb or something somebody threw from the second row. Then I looked down, and it was this big knife. The thing had about a 5-inch blade on it."[11] Fortunately for Joyner, the knife only grazed his forearm.

By the end of the 1986 season Wally World was a fixture in the Angels lineup and a fan favorite. He played in 154 games that season and finished with a .290 average, 22 home runs, and 100 RBIs in leading the Angels to the AL West division title. In many years these numbers would have been good enough to easily win the Rookie of the Year award, but not this year. He was edged out by the Oakland A's Jose Canseco for AL Rookie of the Year honors. Interestingly, Joyner finished eighth in the AL MVP balloting, while Canseco finished a distant 20th.

Joyner and the Angels met the Boston Red Sox in the 1986 ALCS. The series started on a high note for both Joyner and the Angels. The first baseman batted .455 with a home run, two doubles, and two RBIs in the series' first three games as the Angels jumped out to a two-games-to-one series lead. However, the 24-year-old rookie was hospitalized before Game Four with an inflamed right leg.[12] The Angels won the game, and it was hoped Joyner would return for Game Five. As it turned out, Joyner spent the remainder of the series in the hospital and the Angels, despite being only one strike away from the World Series, failed to close out the Red Sox in Game Five. The Red Sox rallied to the take the series in seven games and Joyner would not wear an Angels uniform in another postseason game.

There was no sophomore jinx for Joyner. In fact, 1987 was the best offensive season of his career. In 149 games he hit .285 and amassed career highs in runs scored (100), home runs (34), and RBIs (117). The effort garnered him enough votes to place 13th in the MVP balloting. The individual highlight of his season came on October 3 when he belted three solo round-trippers against the Cleveland Indians in a 12-5 victory in Anaheim. The first baseman took Ken Schrom deep in the first and third innings and added his third of the day off Sammy Stewart in the sixth inning.

While Joyner was able to replicate his personal success of 1986, the Angels were unable to recover from the disappointment of the previous fall. The team fell to 75-87 and finished tied for last in the AL West. Nonetheless, reflecting back on his career, Joyner said, "Those first two years were my favorite two years I ever had."[13]

Although his first two seasons belied Joyner's claim that he was not a power hitter, from 1988 to 1991 he settled back into being a productive gap hitter who entertained Angels fans with his elegant play at first base.[14] While he hit only 13 home runs in 1988, he still managed to hit .295 and drive in 85 runs. In 1989 he played in a career-high 159 games and hit .282 with 16 home runs and 79 RBIs. Joyner suffered the first major injury of his career in 1990. An injured knee ended his season after just 83 games and resulted in an uncharacteristic .268 batting average. The next season he demonstrated that he was once again healthy and rebounded to his old form. His .301 average, 21 home runs, and 96 RBIs positioned him well to test free agency.

Joyner's departure from the Angels after the 1991 season was somewhat unexpected, particularly in light of the fact that he rejected a four-year contract worth nearly $16 million and signed a one-year, $4.2 million agreement with the Kansas City Royals.[15] It was common knowledge that he and Jackie Autry, the club's executive vice president and the wife of owner Gene Autry, had a strained relationship during the first baseman's tenure with the Angels. Ultimately, Joyner put his principles above his market value and Wally World left Southern California for Kansas City.

Joyner spent four relatively productive years in Kansas City. Despite hitting .269 in his first season with the Royals, from 1992 to 1995 he hit .293 and averaged 30 doubles per season. In 1994 he led the team in batting with a .311 average despite being limited to

97 games by a nagging shoulder injury and the players strike that ended the season on August 12, 1994.[16] He followed that with a .310 average the following year. He also had his best year defensively in 1995, leading all American League first basemen with a career-high .998 fielding percentage.

During his time with the Royals, Joyner made his first foray into film when he made a cameo appearance in the 1994 baseball film *Little Big League*. The plot featured a 12-year-old kid from a wealthy family who inherits the Minnesota Twins from his grandfather. The boy, with all the credentials of a 12-year-old baseball-crazed boy, goes on a power trip, installing himself as general manager, field manager, and first-base coach. Joyner was one of about a dozen ballplayers who appeared in the movie, including Carlos Baerga, Dave Magadan, Rafael Palmeiro, Randy Johnson, and Ken Griffey Jr.[17] Joyner even had a line in the movie. After a base hit by Twins first baseman Lou Collins (played by Timothy Busfield), Joyner turns to him and asks, "Man, do we ever get you out?"

On December 21, 1995, Joyner was traded to the San Diego Padres for utilityman Bip Roberts and right-handed pitching prospect Bryan Wolff. Although his most productive offensive years were behind him, Joyner was a prominent member of two of the best teams in Padres history. He contributed both clutch offense and steady defensive play at first. Padres infielders, including third baseman Ken Caminiti and shortstop Chris Gomez, who often threw from difficult positions across the infield, knew Joyner would corral any wild throws.[18]

In his four seasons with the Padres (1996-1999), Joyner hit a combined .291. In 1996 he appeared in 121 games and hit .277 with 8 home runs and 65 RBIs. He also had a NL-leading .997 fielding percentage in helping the Padres to the West division title, the team's first since 1984. The Padres were swept in three games by the St. Louis Cardinals in the 1996 NLDS. Joyner went 1-for-9 in the series, managing only an infield single in Game One.

In 1997 Joyner hit a career high .327 while again leading NL first sackers in fielding percentage (.996) as the Padres fell to fourth place in the NL West with a 76-86 record. Joyner continued his steady hitting in 1998 and finished with a .298 average with 12 homers and 80 RBIs as the Padres won a franchise-record 98 games and their second NL West title in three years.

The Padres dispatched the Houston Astros in the NLDS three games to one. Joyner shared time at first with Jim Leyritz and went 1-for-6 with a two-run, eighth-inning home run that added to the final margin of victory in the Padres' 6-1 series-clinching Game Four win. The Padres then faced the Atlanta Braves in the NLCS. Joyner went 5-for-16 with a pair of RBIs to help the Friars advance in six games. After 13 major-league seasons, Joyner was headed to the World Series.

The 1998 World Series was an anticlimactic end to the Padres' season. The American League champion New York Yankees swept the Padres in four games. Joyner, like many of his teammates, struggled throughout the Series and went 0-for-8.

In a November 2005 interview with *ESPN The Magazine*, Joyner revealed that he had briefly used steroids during 1998. At age 36, as his career was beginning to decline, Joyner admitted that he asked Caminiti to help him obtain steroids. Caminiti, who was just two years removed from his 1996 MVP season, supplied Joyner with pills. Joyner claimed he took only three pills before he threw the rest away.[19] He later said his admission of steroid use was to set the record straight for the sake of his family.

Joyner played one final season with the Padres in 1999. With his skills clearly diminishing, he managed to hit only .248 with 5 home runs and 43 RBIs. On December 22 that year the Padres traded Joyner, Reggie Sanders, and Quilvio Veras to the Atlanta Braves in return for Bret Boone, Ryan Klesko, and Jason Shiell. The trade allowed Joyner to play for the hometown team he rooted for as a child.

In 1999 Joyner appeared in his second film, *The Darwin Conspiracy*. The made for TV sci-fi film depicted a self-serving government scientist who discovers a superior form of DNA in an ancient Ice Man and injects it into the mentally impaired brother of a colleague, with the hopes of selling the product to a drug manufacturer. Those close to the research team up to stop the government from using the untested scientific advancement on others.²⁰ Joyner played himself in the film.

Joyner hit .281 with 5 home runs and 32 RBIs for the Braves and once again found himself back in the playoffs when Atlanta won its ninth consecutive NL West title. Coming off the bench as a pinch-hitter in all three games of the 2000 NLDS against the St. Louis Cardinals, Joyner went 1-for-3, a single in Game One, as the Braves were swept. After the season, Joyner filed for free agency and on January 25, 2001, he signed a one-year deal with the Anaheim Angels.

In 2001 Wally World returned to where it all had begun 15 years earlier. Joyner started the 2001 season slowly and was hitting under .200 through the end of April. On June 14 he appeared in his final major-league game when he pinch-hit for Mark Lukasiewicz in the top of the fifth inning at Pac Bell Park in San Francisco. Joyner delivered a RBI single off the Giants' Ryan Vogelsong, bringing his season totals to .243 with 3 home runs and 14 RBIs. Two days later he was released, ending his 16-year major-league career. He finished with a .289 average, 204 home runs, and 1,106 RBIs. Despite his .994 career fielding percentage and leading the league in fielding percentage four times, Joyner never won a Gold Glove.

After retiring as a player, Joyner became more active in films and filmmaking, investing and appearing in films marketed to members of the LDS community. His most critically acclaimed work was the 2002 romantic comedy *The Singles Ward*. The screenplay, written by himself and John Moyer, is about a congregation of college-age Latter-day Saints in a typical singles ward — an institution sometimes thought of as a "marriage mill."²¹ Joyner also starred in the film and played the role of Brother Angel (a reference to his time with the California and Anaheim Angels). In the film, Brother Angel (Joyner) performs a stand-up comedy routine lampooning the Mormon lifestyle.

In 2003, Joyner played Brother Jensen in the movie *R.M.*²² The film is a comedy that portrays the life of Jared Phelps, a returning LDS missionary who believes he has everything all worked out before going on his mission. His mission president promised him that he would be blessed for his service. His girlfriend promised to wait for him. His boss promised that he could have his old job back, and he had already submitted his application to BYU. Upon his return from missionary service, nothing is as he thought. His girlfriend dumps him. He loses his job, and he isn't accepted to BYU.

In 2004, Joyner also appeared in *The Home Teacher*, another comedy film geared toward LDS audiences. The film is about LDS home teacher Stocky Greg. Greg is a passionate football fan who rounds up his family from their respective church meetings and rushes home just in time to make the kickoff of the Sunday afternoon Vikings game. He has just planted himself in front of his massive television screen when Nelson, his home-teaching companion, calls to inform him that he has set an appointment to visit the Mori family in 15 minutes. Mormon males serving as home teachers are admonished to visit with their assigned families once a month to bring them a spiritual message and provide help as necessary. Nelson, a nerdy "letter of the law" kind of Mormon who will not even purchase gas on a Sunday, is intent on making this visit on the final day of the month despite Greg's efforts to get back to his football game.²³ Joyner played the character of Donald Terry.

Joyner made his last appearance in a motion picture in 2007. He again played the role of Brother Angel in *The Singles 2nd Ward*, the sequel to *The Singles Ward*. The movie is a continuation of the dating highs and lows and prenuptial misadventures of LDS singles.²⁴

Joyner also remained active in baseball as a coach and instructor. From 2003 to 2007 he was a roving minor-league hitting instructor for the Padres. On July 31, 2007, he was hired by Padres to replace Merv Rettenmund as the team's hitting coach. He held that position until September 2008 when due to a number of factors, including the team's low rankings in batting categories and a difference in philosophy in regard to hitting, he stepped down. From 2008 to 2012 Joyner worked as the lead hitting instructor for

MLB International's Elite-level development programs in Italy and Brazil.[25] On October 15, 2012, he was hired by the Philadelphia Phillies as assistant hitting coach. After manager Charlie Manuel was fired in 2013, Joyner became the first-base coach under interim manager Ryne Sandberg. In November 2013, he joined Brad Ausmus's staff as hitting coach for the Detroit Tigers, a position he held until he resigned at the end of the 2016 season.

As of 2017 Joyner resided in Mapleton, Utah, with his wife, Lesly, a former BYU gymnast whom he married on March 12, 1983, and their four children. He was the vice president of strategic development for Onset Financial. He was also actively involved in Padre Associates, an environmental-services company in Southern California, and Xocai Chocolate.

NOTES

1 Clifford Mervyn Joyner. Retrieved from findagrave.com/cgi-bin/fg.cgi?page=gr&GSln=Joyner&GSiman=1&GScid=109343&GRid=8516077&.

2 Karma Leona Joyner. Retrieved from walkersanderson.com/obituaries/Karma-Leoan-Joyner/Payson-UT/1396471.

3 Craig Neff, "The Wonderful World of Wally," *Sports Illustrated*, May 26, 1986: 31.

4 Ibid.

5 "Wally Joyner." Retrieved from byucougars.com/athlete/m-baseball/wally-joyner.

6 Ralph R. Zobell, *Reunion of 1983 Cougars Ranked #1*, retrieved from byucougars.com/m-baseball/reunion-1983-cougars-ranked-no-1.

7 Ibid.

8 Craig Neff, 29.

9 Neff, 28.

10 Neff, 31.

11 "Knife-Throwing Incident Puzzling," *New York Times*, August 28, 1986. Retrieved from nytimes.com/1986/08/28/sports/knife-throwing-incident-puzzling.html.

12 "The Best and Tightest: Revisit the 1986 ALCS," retrieved from espn.com/page2/s/1986/revisit/alcs.html.

13 Wally Joyner Video. Retrieved from video.search.yahoo.com/search/video?fr=yfp-t&p=Wally+Joyner#id=4&vid=4e-5bee6596e9e61a297389d09a55db86&action=click.

14 "The 100 Greatest Angels: #20 Wally Joyner," Retrieved from halosheaven.com/2006/2/8/32353/36909.

15 Helene Elliot, "Popular Wally Joyner Is an Angel No More: Baseball: He Rejects a 4-Year, Nearly $16-million offer in favor of 1-year, $4.2-Million Pact With Kansas City," *Los Angeles Times*, December 10, 1991. Retrieved from articles.latimes.com/1991-12-10/news/mn-200_1_baseman-wally-joyner.

16 "Joyner on DL." *Deseret News* (Salt Lake City), July 3, 1994. Retrieved from deseretnews.com/article/362371/JOYNER-ON-DL.html.

17 Max Rieper, "Best Performance in a Motion Picture by a Kansas City Royals Player: February 26, 2016," Retrieved from royalsreview.com/2016/2/26/10963876/best-performance-in-a-motion-picture-by-a-kansas-city-royals-player.

18 Bill Center, "Wally Joyner, Andy Green Join My Padres' Top 100: Veteran 1B, Rookie Manager With Club at Key Times," January 16, 2017. Retrieved from padres.mlblogs.com/wally-joyner-andy-green-join-my-padres-top-100-cdb8b24eed6e.

19 "Steroid Investigation: Who Knew and When?" Retrieved from espn.com/mlb/news/story?id=2217361.

20 "The Darwin Conspiracy." Retrieved from hollywood.com/tv/the-darwin-conspiracy-59453379/.

21 "The Singles Ward." Retrieved from hollywood.com/movies/singles-ward-59281718/.

22 R.M. is an LDS abbreviation for returned missionary.

23 "The Home Teachers." Retrieved from imdb.com/title/tt0377071/fullcredits?ref_=tt_cl_sm#cast.

24 "The Singles 2nd Ward." Retrieved from imdb.com/title/tt1109520/?ref_=nm_flmg_act_1.

25 Ryan Lawrence, "Wally Joyner Joins Phillies Coaching Staff," *Philadelphia Inquirer*. October 15, 2012. Retrieved from philly.com/philly/blogs/phillies/174254131.html.

FRANK KELLEHER

BY ADAM KLINKER

THOUGH A RENOWNED POWER hitter in 12 seasons in the Pacific Coast League and a bit player in a handful of films at midcentury, Frankie Kelleher's top billing as a slugger and a star is perhaps dubiously enshrined in a one-night performance he sparked on a hot Los Angeles Sunday afternoon in 1953, a scene seemingly ripped out of a James Ellroy novel or inspiring the brawl in the first film of *The Naked Gun* franchise.

On August 2 of that year, Kelleher's Hollywood Stars found themselves pitted against the crosstown PCL rivals Los Angeles Angels at Gilmore Field, the Stars' home ballpark, in the closing doubleheader of an eight-game series that had already featured several close games and flared tempers. Kelleher's heroics in the previous two games—a ninth-inning single to win the Friday contest and an eighth-inning home run to seal a Saturday night victory—may have marked him for retribution.

Kelleher was a quiet, dignified man, by all accounts, a fan favorite and a paragon among his teammates. He didn't argue with umpires, didn't quarrel with opponents, and had never been ejected from a game to that point in an 18-year professional career. His sheer size (6-feet-1, 200 pounds) and the heft in his bat—eight seasons with 20-plus home runs, including a 40-homer season in 1950—was enough to ward off most challengers.

Having tripled and scored on a close squeeze play earlier in the first Sunday game, Kelleher was still giving the Angels fits, especially the LA starting pitcher Joe Hatten. The three-bagger was Kelleher's sixth consecutive hit off Hatten, formerly of the Brooklyn Dodgers and Chicago Cubs, and the lefthander's patience had reached an end. When the Stars outfielder came to the plate in the sixth, Hatten chucked his first two pitches high and tight, brushing Kelleher back. The southpaw's third offering finally found Kelleher's back, and something inside the slugger snapped.

The umpire behind the plate that day, Cece Carlucci, a longtime PCL official, said it shocked him to see the mild-mannered Kelleher take the hit, drop his bat and go after Hatten. "He'd never been in trouble, never disputed a call," Carlucci remembered in a 2007 interview with the *Los Angeles Times*. "So I went over to pick up the ball and I see him running toward Hatten. And, I'll tell you, he threw a haymaker. He knocked Hatten right off the god-darn mound."

Bob Usher, an Angels outfielder, recalled the moment a tad differently. Kelleher didn't rush at Hatten, Usher said in an interview at the 2010 PCL reunion. "Frank walked to the mound," Usher said. "Normally they charge today, but he walked to the mound and started beating up on Joe Hatten and that emptied the [benches]."[2] Usher's version of the story is repeated in the August 12, 1953, edition of *The Sporting News*, which reported "(Kelleher) laid down his bat and calmly walked to the mound, where he started swinging on Hatten," under the terse subheadline "A Hit Batsman, a 60-foot Stroll and BANG!"[3]

Hatten, himself a 6-foot, 180-pounder who also typically didn't throw in for fistfights, managed to return a few blows and there was some pushing and shoving among the rest of the assembled players. When the row broke up, Carlucci thumbed Kelleher but not—to the chagrin of Stars manager Bobby Bragan—the offending Hatten. Ted Beard, a onetime Pittsburgh Pirate and journeyman farmhand, came in to run for Kelleher and it appeared the fracas had been brought to a cooling simmer, even as Beard promptly stole second base. But when Beard decided to swipe third on the next pitch, all hell broke loose. Out by a considerable length, Beard leapt, spikes first, at Angels third baseman Moe Franklin, planting his feet into the infielder's chest and arms. Before the dust in that tiff settled, both benches had sailed out of the dugouts and fights had broken out all over the turf at Gilmore Field.

Kelleher returned to the diamond to aid his teammates in what had suddenly become a riot. In two photos taking up a half-page in the *Times* sports section the next morning, Kelleher is shown with his back to the camera and his left arm sweeping forward to maul an Angels player. The headline over the caption reads, "Kayo Kelleher."[4] For the better part of half an hour, the Stars and Angels waged a pitched battle in front of 10,000 fans (the *Times* wryly added a thankful note that "audience participation" was avoided in the meltdown) as the outmanned umpiring crew vainly tried to put a lid on the fisticuffs. "It was probably the biggest fight in baseball history—the biggest I remember, anyway," Carlucci said, "I've never seen that many guys fighting. *Everybody* was flinging."[5] Finally, legendary Los Angeles Police Chief William H. Parker, watching the game on TV, mobilized more than 50 officers to converge on Gilmore Field to restore order. After 90 minutes, officers finally managed to separate the factions. All those players not involved with the game on the field were ordered from it and somehow, play continued under armed guard until the Stars won out, 4-1. Amazingly, the second game of the twin bill also took place and the Angels saved some face with a 5-3 triumph. The Stars, meanwhile, went on to win their second straight PCL championship.

Kelleher, who finished the 1953 season with a .329 average, 15 homers, and 65 RBIs, was fined $100 for his role in the melee, the sentence aggravated by his returning to the field after his ejection. PCL President Clarence "Pants" Rowland, who had a box-seat view to the carnage, said, "Fights don't belong in baseball."[6] The brawl was an outlier in the otherwise sterling and steady PCL career of Kelleher, a man whom teammates nicknamed "Mousey," given his diffidence and general good nature.[7]

Kelleher retired after the 1954 season at the age of 38, a career .284 hitter in the PCL, with 234 homers and 876 RBIs. He was inducted into the PCL Hall of Fame in 2004, a quarter-century after his death in 1979 at age 62.[8] His two brief stints in the majors—38 games with the Cincinnati Reds in 1942 and another nine games in mid-1943—saw him hit .167 with 3 homers, 3 doubles, a triple, and 12 runs driven in.

The grandson of German, Austrian, and Irish immigrants, Francis Eugene Kelleher was born on August 22, 1916, in San Francisco to William Francis and Mary C. (Kleinhans) Kelleher. In 1920, the Kellehers were living with Mary's parents, Jacob J. and Mary C. Kleinhans, and her six sisters in Crockett, California, just northeast of San Francisco. William Kelleher was working as a clerk in a warehouse and Mary Kelleher was a bookkeeper in a bank. William eventually ended up in the sheet-metal shop of the California and Hawaiian Sugar Co., headquartered in Crockett, where his father-in-law was employed as an engineer.

Frankie Kelleher attended John Swett High School in Crockett, and St. Mary's College in Moraga, California, alma mater of Hall of Famers Hank O'Day and Harry Hooper, and, with Hooper, another of the Red Sox' "Million-Dollar Outfield," Duffy Lewis. During his sophomore season at St. Mary's, in 1936, Kelleher abruptly left the school, a find of New York Yankees scout Joe Devine, reportedly a distant cousin.[9] The Yankees sent Kelleher to Akron of the Class-C Middle Atlantic League. But Devine's efforts in securing the services of what *Akron Beacon-Journal* sportswriter Lincoln Hackim called "one of the most highly publicized recruits of the year" were marred by a dispute with St. Mary's athletic director and Knute Rockne disciple, Edward "Slip" Madigan, who complained to Commissioner Kenesaw Mountain Landis that the Yankees should have allowed Kelleher to complete the term.[10]

Madigan's protest met with unsympathetic ears in the commissioner's office and Kelleher joined the Akron team with Hackim noting Devine as saying Kelleher was one of the best prospects he'd signed, and one who could play any position in the infield. Akron manager Nick Allen slotted Kelleher at short and in the youngster's May 27, 1936, debut, he singled and homered, en route to marks of .348, 17 homers, and 61 RBIs in 56 games.

But in the panoply of emerging Yankee deities, Kelleher, though turning in strong numbers, became lost in the shuffle. Still, he had earned a promotion to the Yankees' top farm club, the Newark Bears of the International League, where he played parts of six seasons. In 1937, Kelleher was a regular backup and sometime starter at third base on an Oscar Vitt-managed team that finished 109-43—one of the best minor-league seasons in history.

Playing in Newark alongside Joe Gordon, Tommy Henrich, Charlie Keller, Spud Chandler, Babe Dahlgren, and Willard Hershberger, Kelleher hit .306 with 11 home runs and 48 RBIs in 92 games.

In 1938, after a brief stint with the Kansas City Blues in the American Association, Kelleher had his first brush with the PCL, playing 18 games with the Oakland Oaks before returning to Newark to play 77 games, hitting .282 with 12 homers while playing the outfield, third base, and first.

In the middle of the 1938 season, on July 12, Kelleher married Frances Amy Woodward. The couple would have two daughters and a son.

Kelleher spent all of 1939 with Newark, but played in just over half of the team's games, batting .278 with 12 homers, mostly at third base while Tommy Holmes, Wally Judnich, and Buster Mills patrolled the outfield.

With so much talent on his Newark teams, Kelleher found himself in a constant state of flux. With the exceptions of pitching, catching, and playing first, Kelleher had stints at every position on the field for the Bears.[11]

Returning to the PCL in 1940, Kelleher played 68 games with Jack Lelivelt's Seattle Rainiers, hitting .281 with seven home runs.

Back east with Newark in 1941, the 24-year-old Kelleher had a breakout season, finally settling into a job as the Bears' everyday left fielder, playing in 151 games and hitting .274 with an International League-leading 37 homers, 125 RBIs, and 106 runs scored. The Bears continued to be a formidable force, winning 100 games for manager Johnny Neun.

On July 16, 1942, Kelleher's Newark contract was purchased by the Cincinnati Reds, who also received Joe Abreu and Jim Turner as consideration from the Yankees. George Weiss, vice president for the Yankees and general manager of the Newark Bears, said that in consultation with Yankees manager Joe McCarthy, McCarthy was wary of the right-handed Kelleher's potential in the Bronx, relative to the short porch at Newark. "He didn't like the prospect of Kelleher's long outs in Yankee Stadium," Weiss told Shirley Povich in 1943.[12]

The Sporting News of July 23, 1942, was fairly teeming with the news of Kelleher's sale to Cincinnati. Michael F. Gaven wrote of Kelleher's significant impact on New Jersey fans: "Kelleher doesn't have that sparkling personality that breeds hero worship, yet the dyed-in-the-wool fans admired him as a hard and loyal worker, and he had become somewhat of an institution."[13]

Kelleher debuted for the Reds on July 18, 1942, the 25-year-old rookie hitting cleanup and patrolling left at Crosley Field against the visiting New York

Frank Kelleher, stalwart minor leaguer who appeared in a trio of films: The Stratton Story; Kill the Umpire; *and* Three Little Words.

Giants. One of just 76 players (as of 2017) who batted cleanup in their major-league debuts, Kelleher went 0-for-4 in the 3-1 Giants win.[14] The next afternoon, backing Johnny Vander Meer in the second game of a doubleheader against the Giants, Kelleher notched his first big-league hit, an RBI single to left off Ace Adams to score Frank McCormick and tie the game at 3-3 in the bottom of the eighth. New York won the game in the ninth, but the rookie's clutch drive earned him a starting spot in the next two games as the Reds traveled to Brooklyn.

Tom Swope, writing under the headline "Reds Bring Up More Reinforcements in Third-Place Battle," in the July 23, 1942, issue of *The Sporting News*, noted that Cincinnati manager Bill McKechnie called a team meeting on a train the night of the July 19 loss to the Giants, formally introducing Kelleher and Eric Tipton, who had also been purchased from the Yankees by way of the Kansas City Blues. The Reds were on their way to Brooklyn and McKechnie and the Cincinnati brass were concerned that the team, just two seasons removed from a World Series championship, seemed to be adrift as World War II raged.

The investment in Kelleher and Tipton, Swope noted, intended to belay some of the anxiety over wartime baseball: "In obtaining Kelleher and Tipton, the Redleg bosses bought the men they and their scouts believe to be the best hitting outfield prospects in the AA leagues, and in obtaining them they made a big gamble that there will be a National League season in 1943. If they had reason to believe the majors will shut up shop next year, as often is prophesied, for the duration of the war, they would not be laying out the heavy dough they did for men of military age in getting Kelleher and Tipton." Swope's piece is also accompanied by a jump headline reading: "Reds Feel They Landed Killer in Kelleher."[15]

But after McKechnie's train pep talk en route to the East Coast, though the Reds livened up a bit, Kelleher scudded along against Brooklyn, New York, Philadelphia, and Boston, turning in an 0-for-15 road trip. He next picked up a hit against the St. Louis Cardinals at home on August 4. Kelleher proved the hero of a marathon contest on August 8, lashing a pinch-hit walk-off RBI single to beat Lon Warneke and the Cubs at Crosley Field, 2-1 in the bottom of the 12th inning.

As the summer waned, Kelleher's average hovered around the .150 mark until September 6, when he went 2-for-4 against Mort Cooper and the Cardinals, hitting his first big-league home run in the bottom of the second—the only Reds runs in a 10-2 defeat. Including the performance against the Cardinals ace, Kelleher went 8-for-24 for the rest of the season, hitting two more home runs, a double, and a triple, and driving in six runs to bring his season average to .182.

Kelleher spent most of the 1943 season with the Syracuse Chiefs of the International League, hitting .245 with 11 home runs and 57 RBIs. He had a brief call-up to Cincinnati, appearing in nine games between May 2 and June 14, mostly as a pinch-hitter. He failed to collect a hit in any of the games, walked twice, and scored a run. As a player, he would not see the majors again, completing his big-league career with an average of .167, 3 home runs, and 12 RBIs.

On May 10, 1944, Kelleher was optioned to the Hollywood Stars, where he regained some of the early promise he had shown. In 130 games, Kelleher led the PCL with 29 homers and 121 RBIs and missed out on the league's Triple Crown by thousandths of a percentage point in batting average, hitting .32854 to .32886 for Les Scarsella of Oakland. Kelleher was hitting .339 and had a 14-point lead on Scarsella as late as August 20.[16]

Appearing poised for a return to Cincinnati, Kelleher was recalled by the Reds in September 1944, but finished out the season in Hollywood, earning the Helms Athletic Foundation's recognition as the Stars' most valuable player in a ceremony on September 10.[17]

In February 1945, Kelleher was inducted into the US Army and reported to Hamilton Field, near San Francisco, as part of the Army Medical Corps.[18] He missed the entire 1945 season and the beginning of 1946 before returning to the Stars, picking up where he left off in the power department with 18 homers and 54 RBIs and a .286 average in 91 games.

Kelleher's years between 1947 and 1951 were among the most productive for a minor-league hitter in history. In 750 games in those five seasons, he notched 143 homers, and 519 RBIs. He also scored 463 runs and hit .281. His .333 average in 1948 marked his highest average since his first season as a pro with Akron in 1936, and 1950 was his 40-homer season for the Stars.

Those 40 homers Kelleher hit in 1950 marked the second and final time a Hollywood Star's home-run total had shined so bright. Gus Zernial hit 40 in 1948 and given the rather cavernous expanses of Gilmore Field — 335 feet down the left-field line and 385 to the gap — 40 was a prize number.

In a 1993 piece for Sports Illustrated, John Schulian, who grew up watching PCL baseball at its apex in LA, said the ballyard Kelleher called home for 10 seasons could seem quaint in its old-school ambiance, but daunting in proportion: "At Gilmore the long ball was a much tougher proposition. In the park's 19-year history, Kelleher and Zernial were the only Stars with 40-homer seasons, and just three players — Luke Easter and two singles-hitting surprises, Lou Stringer and Bill Gray — were able to clear its towering centerfield wall, 400 feet away. But talk of those wide-open spaces ... shouldn't fool you; Gilmore was really as cozy and intimate as a ballpark could be. It was built entirely of wood — no concrete, no girders — and when CBS's TV City went up next door in the early '50s, the ballpark's anachronistic charm was magnified."[19]

At about the same time he was hitting his longest power stretch, Kelleher launched a new venture in his Hollywood career: that of an extra in a trio of films that came out between 1949 and 1950. Two of the films, The Stratton Story (1949) and Kill the Umpire (1950), featured baseball as central themes.

The Stratton Story, starring James Stewart and June Allyson, is a biopic taking Chicago White Sox pitcher Monty Stratton, whose career was cut short when his leg was amputated following a hunting accident, as its subject. In the film, Kelleher, uncredited, takes the role of a Stratton teammate on the White Sox. He is clearly visible onscreen during two dugout scenes, the first when he's framed on the bench behind Stratton (played by Stewart) and pitching coach Barney Wile (played by Frank Morgan of The Wizard of Oz fame) at the 31-minute, 54-second mark, just after Joe DiMaggio, in archive footage, is seen slamming a home run. A few moments later, at 33:30, after Stratton comes into the game and surrenders a hit to Bill Dickey (playing himself), Kelleher is seen sitting beside Wile as the latter mutters, "Omaha" — where Stratton will be designated after a rough outing against the Yankees.[20]

In a case of art portending life, Kelleher appears briefly in the slapstick comedy Kill the Umpire as a shortstop for a Texas League team. The climactic scene features William Bendix, playing the lead role of Bill "Two Call" Johnson; Kelleher's character makes a throw home to nab an opponent whom Johnson calls out. The call, though correct, leads to a riot. Kelleher is visible between Bendix and Jeff York (playing the role of Panhandle Jones, a gambler attempting to fix the game) at about 60:45. He's visible again a few moments later when Panhandle Jones takes a bat to Johnson's head.[21]

The third film in Kelleher's acting credits, Three Little Words (1950), is a Fred Astaire/Red Skelton vehicle that tells the story of the songwriting duo Bert Kalmar (played by Astaire) and Harry Ruby (Skelton). Kelleher has two short speaking bits, both saying the same thing. At the 59:03 mark, Harry — hoping to draw inspiration for a new song from big-league baseball at the Washington Senators' spring-training camp — is upended while taking a throw at second base. Kelleher is the first man entering screen right to Ruby's aid, asking, "Are you all right, Harry?" and helping Ruby to his feet. Two scenes and about 30 seconds later, Kelleher and three other Senators, along with Ruby, are catching fly balls. Kelleher makes a catch behind his back and Ruby says he wants to give the trick a try, with the fly promptly smacking him in the head. Once again, Kelleher helps Skelton to his feet, asking, "Are you all right?"[22]

With the exception of 1953, Kelleher's last three years in professional baseball were a marked downturn from his earlier career, marred by age and injury. In 1952 and 1954, he hit a combined .242 with 21 homers. But he had one last surge of offensive power in 1953, the year of the Stars-Angels brawl, when he played 109 games and hit .329 with 15 home runs, 22 doubles, and 65 RBIs.

After retiring in 1954 at the age of 37, Kelleher made his home in Culver City, California, and took a position as sports director with the 7-Up Youth Foundation, sponsoring and fostering sports teams for children in the greater Los Angeles area.[23] His number 7 was ultimately retired by the Stars.[24]

Kelleher died in Stockton, California, on April 13, 1979, of a heart attack. In his last years, he worked as a self-employed tool distributor.[25]

SOURCES

In addition to the sources cited in the Notes, the author also consulted:

baseball-reference.com.

O'Neal, Bill. *The Pacific Coast League: 1903-1988* (Austin, Texas: Eakin Press, 1990).

NOTES

1 Jerry Crowe, "Umpire Needed Help to Break Up Pitched Battle," *Los Angeles Times*, June 11, 2007. articles.latimes.com/2007/jun/11/sports/sp-crowe11.

2 "Remembering a Good Brawl." *Baseball Past and Present*. August 30, 2010. baseballpastandpresent.com/2010/08/30/remembering-a-good-brawl/.

3 John B. Old, "Casualties and Fines Heavy in Free-For-All at Hollywood," *The Sporting News*, August 12, 1953.

4 Paul J. Zingg and Mark D. Medeiros, *Runs, Hits, and an Era: The Pacific Coast League, 1903-1958* (Urbana, Illinois: University of Illinois Press, 1994), 134-136.

5 Crowe.

6 Old.

7 John Schulian, "Of stars and Angels," *Sports Illustrated*. June 21, 1993. si.com/vault/1993/06/21/128782/of-stars-and-angels-once-upon-a-time-tinseltown-was-a-heavenly-place-to-watch-minor-league-baseball.

8 Pacific Coast League Hall of Fame website. milb.com/content/page.jsp?sid=l112&ymd=20110610&content_id=20287736&vkey=league3.

9 J.G. Preston, "They Batted Cleanup in Their First Major League Game," *The J.G. Preston Experience*. April 17, 2015. prestonjg.wordpress.com/page/7/.

10 Lincoln Hackim, "Akron Lands Francis Kelleher," *Akron Beacon Journal*. June 4, 1936.

11 Bill Dougherty, "Bears' Star Joins Cincinnati Today," *Newark Evening News*, July 17, 1942.

12 "Why Yankees Sold Kelleher," in Kelleher's Hall of Fame player file, dated February 4, 1943.

13 Michael F. Gaven, "Newark Loses a Bear With Bat in Kelleher, Sold to Cincinnati," *The Sporting News*, July 23, 1942: 3.

14 Preston.

15 Tom Swope, "Reds Bring Up More Reinforcements in Third-Place Battle," *The Sporting News*, July 23, 1942: 1, 2.

16 Unidentified newspaper clippings dated August 31, 1944, and January 15, 1945, from Kelleher's player file at the National Baseball Hall of Fame.

17 Unidentified newspaper clipping dated September 14, 1944, from Kelleher's player file at the National Baseball Hall of Fame.

18 Unidentified newspaper clipping dated February 22, 1945, from Kelleher's player file at the National Baseball Hall of Fame.

19 Schulian.

20 *The Stratton Story*. Dir. Sam Wood. Metro-Goldwyn-Mayer, 1949.

21 *Kill the Umpire*. Dir. Lloyd Bacon. Columbia, 1950.

22 *Three Little Words*. Dir. Richard Thorpe. Metro-Goldwyn-Mayer, 1950.

23 Unidentified newspaper clipping dated July 31, 1957, from Kelleher's player file at the National Baseball Hall of Fame.

24 Schulian.

25 Bill Lee, *The Baseball Necrology* (Jefferson, North Carolina: McFarland & Company, Inc., 2009), 211.

JOHN KRUK

BY SEAMUS KEARNEY

A quick, short tale of a man named Kruk
Who ran the bases for 30 years
When he finished up, we shed no tears
'Cause on TV he became our Puck [1]

YES, IT IS KRUK-AS-PUCK THAT keeps extending his career in baseball. Ten years as a player, where his bat spoke for him, but as a baseball commentator his wit is the voice that keeps us listening. In fact, when ESPN let him go in October 2016, his comment to inquiring media about his future proved it. He said he was thinking of becoming a fitness expert. He is, uh … hefty, and, uh … doesn't fit the bill, so to speak.[2]

John Martin Kruk first breathed the air of West Virginia in Charleston on February 9, 1961, but his family moved to New Jersey one year later, settling near the Jersey Pinelands. In Jersey, his father worked two shifts in a bottling company so his kids could play ball. Kruk said his parents, Moe and Lena Kruk, did everything to ensure that their children played baseball. When he was 11, his father moved the family back to West Virginia, settling in Keyser and reducing his workload to one job.[3]

Kruk played baseball at Keyser High School, then went on to Potomac State College and thence to Allegheny Community College in Maryland. In January 1981 the Pittsburgh Pirates drafted him but John didn't sign. However, while playing for New Market in the Shenandoah Valley League, an NCAA-sanctioned league operating under NCAA rules, he was drafted in the third round of the June 1981 Draft Secondary Phase by the San Diego Padres. This time he signed.

Kruk spent five full seasons in the minors, steadily progressing through each classification and excelling each year. He started in the minors in 1981 with the Walla Walla Padres of the Class-A Northwest League as a left-handed batter and thrower. He did not perform well, batting a middling .242. He improved notably in 1982 for the Reno Padres of the Class-A California League with a .311 batting average, and finished second on the team with 92 RBIs. Promoted in 1983 to the Beaumont Golden Gators of the Double-A Texas League, Kruk led the team in average [.341, sixth in the league] and placed third with 88 RBIs. San Diego moved him to Triple A, the Las Vegas Stars of the Pacific Coast League, in 1984. His batting average of .326 led his team and placed him 12th in the league. In 1985 Kruk finished fourth in the league with a batting average of .351, again the best on the Stars. Impressed, the Padres brought him to the major leagues at the start of 1986.

Kruk played in the majors for the Padres, the Philadelphia Phillies, and the Chicago White Sox, finishing up with Chicago in 1995. With the Phillies he made the All-Star team three times. Like his own oft-said Round Figure, he had four career round-figure statistics: 10 years in the majors, 1,200 games played, 100 HRs, and a .300 BA—and just missed two more round figures: 199 doubles and 701 strikeouts. Incredibly, the hefty Kruk also stole 58 bases! In his only postseason, with the 1993 Phillies, he hit a combined .298 with one homer and nine RBIs in the NLCS and World Series. In the all-important 1993 World Series against the Blue Jays, he sported a .348 batting average with four runs scored and four RBIs.

Kruk fielded excellently, suffering only 42 errors over 10 years (4.2 errors annually) and only 3.1 a year at first base. His .9946 fielding average at first is tied for 36th all-time—not bad for a person noted for his bulk.

(References to Kruk's build have led to any number of humorous asides. At the 1999 All-Star Game, the height- and weight-challenged Tom Lasorda wanted to walk off a practice field with Kruk. He called out to Kruk, "Wait up, I want to walk with you so I can look real thin." Kruk's response: "You're still gonna be real short."[4])

Kruk's physical appearance was the subject of frequent comment but he is officially listed at 5-feet-10 and 170 pounds. It may strike some as surprising that the portly Kruk's major-league debut came as a pinch-runner on April 7, 1986. He was caught stealing. He made outs in his first three pinch-hitting appearances, but finally singled and drove in a key run on April 14. The Dodgers were visiting at Jack Murphy Stadium and took a 3-2 lead in the top of the 10th; Kruk singled off Bob Welch to tie the game, one that Bruce Bochy won with a walkoff homer in the bottom of the 11th.

Kruk appeared in 122 games in 1986 with the Padres, most of them in left field, starting in 65 of them. He hit well—.309/.403/.424 with 4 homers and 38 RBIs. In his 122 appearances he made only three errors.

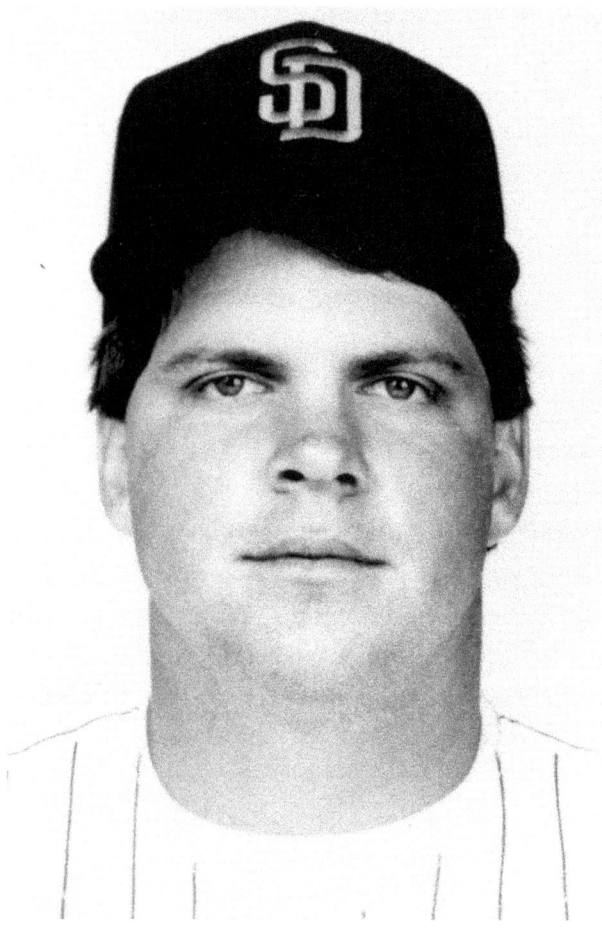

John Kruk segued from the major leagues to a career as a television commentator and occasional screen actor.

The Baseball Writers Association of America voted Kruk seventh in the 1986 Rookie of the Year polling for the National League. He placed just above Barry Larkin and just below Barry Bonds but with a batting average and on-base percentage better than any of the other nine candidates.

In 1987 Kruk had a career year, hitting .313 with 20 homers and 91 RBIs while playing in 138 games. He led the team in home runs and RBIs. But in 1988 his numbers plummeted. He finished at .241 with 9 homers and 44 RBIs. That was also the year that his West Virginia roots bit him in the butt.

The year before, two West Virginia buddies, one of them a hard-nose, inveigled Kruk into a living situation during his second year with the Padres. The hard-nose flashed a lot of money, which puzzled Kruk because he wasn't working. It turned out the two housemates were robbing banks. When the FBI put them on the wanted list, Kruk heard they suspected he turned them in. (He didn't.) He feared for his life during his third season and he did not perform well on the field, significantly affecting his productivity with San Diego. Fortunately for Kruk, later that season, the FBI nabbed the bank robber—who forgave Kruk for the rumored snitching transgression.[5]

Kruk started slowly in 1989 with the Padres. After 31 games he was batting .184, had notched as many strikeouts as hits (14) and plated only six RBIs. The Padres responded in June by trading him to the Phillies, along with Randy Ready, for Chris James. With the Phillies, he responded by batting .331 with 5 HRs and 38 RBIs.

The Phillies proved a good fit for Kruk as he settled into being a first baseman for the Phils, a natural infield position for the stocky left-hander. He didn't hit as well in 1990 (.291) for the Phillies but upped his home runs and RBIs (7 and 67). In 1991 he had an exceptional year. He played his most games in the big leagues (152), and batted .294 with 21 homers and 92 RBIs. He led the Phils in all three stats. He fell off a bit in 1992, playing in eight fewer games, hitting 11 fewer home runs, and knocking in only 70 runs but hitting at a .323 clip. The Phillies in those years did not match Kruk's productivity as they finished fourth, third, and sixth respectively in the NL East.

He bounced back in 1993 with 14 home runs, 84 RBIs, and a .316 batting average. From 1991 through 1993, Kruk made the National League All-Star team three years in succession. He did not appear in the 1991 game, but was 2-for-2 in 1992. In the 1993 game, he was 0-for-3. One of those outs was a strikeout by Randy Johnson. Kruk struck out, demonstrating hilarity, on four pitches with the first being a 98-mph heater above and behind him. In the locker-room afterward, he opined, "When I stepped in the box, I said all I wanted to do was make contact. And, after the first pitch all I wanted to do was live. And I lived, so I had a good at-bat."[6]

That All-Star Game produced a lot of humorous commentary from his contemporaries. Reggie Jackson said, "John Kruk's hitting .350, man. I don't care, don't matter what you look like, that boy can hit." Barry Bonds said, "I think he's a good role model. He gets to bring the hillbillies back into the game. ... He's a stud." Andy Van Slyke added, "John Kruk'd be the one guy I'd pay for of any player in the big leagues to see, 'cause he'd be like the truck driver, delivery beer guy who somehow slipped past security and put a uniform on." Kruk making the All-Star squad in the first place prompted Mark Grace to quip, "Society's really coming to a standstill when something like this can happen."[7]

The 1993 season was magical for the success-starved Phillies fans. Not picked to win the National League East, the team went wire-to-wire to cop the division crown. They were dubbed the Wild Bunch while the sluggers earned the nickname Macho Row—all because of their scruffy appearance and demeanor. They were the Philly version of the 1934 St. Louis Cardinals Gas House Gang. Team leaders included Darren Daulton, Lenny Dykstra, and John Kruk. Philadelphians loved them and still do.

They beat the Braves to nab the National League title and make the World Series. In Game One of the NLCS, Kruk doubled in the bottom of the 10th and scored the winning run when Kim Batiste doubled behind him. He homered and drove in three runs in a losing effort in Game Three. He drove in the first run in the deciding Game Six, which the Phillies won, 4-3.

In the World Series, the Phillies won two games against the Toronto Blue Jays. Unfortunately, for the Phils, the Jays beat them in the Series—but only on a dramatic walkoff homer in the final Game Six. Kruk contributed four more RBIs in the Series, his double in Game Two providing the first Phillies run and his first-inning grounder in Game Five driving in the winning run in a 2-0 Phils victory.

For Kruk, 1994 did not pan out. Though he hit .302, he played in only 75 games as the Phils failed to repeat their prior year's success—in part because of failure on the field but mostly by events occurring off the diamond. Acting Commissioner Bud Selig suspended play in September due to the protracted players strike that began in August.

Things happen to guys like Kruk that don't happen to regular folk, such as the bank robbers saga. But for 1994? During the 1993 season, pitcher Mitch Williams plunked Kruk with an errant pickoff throw that hit him in the groin and broke his protective cup. A medical examination during spring training in 1994 revealed the presence of testicular cancer. He underwent surgery to remove the affected testicle and missed the opening part of the season, but the strike finished it.[8]

After the strike-shortened 1994 season, Kruk was granted free agency and signed with the Chicago White Sox for 1995, but his physical condition hindered him. His retirement also reflected his sense of theater. He singled against the Orioles in Camden Yards on July 30, 1995, advanced to third and at inning's end stepped off third base into retirement in a prearranged plan with the White Sox.[9]

But even before he retired, John Kruk's wit surfaced in his autobiography, coauthored with Paul Hagen. *I Ain't an Athlete, Lady* (1994) is filled with his insights, goofs, and humor. He based it on his self-deprecating rejoinder to a woman in a restaurant who questioned his unhealthy depiction of an athlete as he gorged on his food, beer, and cigarettes in public. "I'm a ballplayer," he said.[10]

That kind of remark plus his funny asides, let alone his hilarious appearances on *Late Night With David Letterman*, led Kruk to a post-baseball career in movies and sports-talk-TV-theater.[11] He became a baseball commentator in retirement, although he briefly worked in the minors as hitting coach for the Reading Phillies. He worked for Fox Sports, among others, and in 2004 settled in with ESPN. He and the channel had a mutual parting with ESPN in 2016, in part, he said, because their phone calls interrupted his golf games. "The phone calls weren't that bad," he later clarified, adding a joke for good measure: "It was having to listen to them that was painful."[12] Comcast made him part of its Phillies broadcast crew in December 2016 and through the 2017 season he regaled his audience with his unique inside take on the national pastime.[13]

As with other baseballers of his ilk (Casey Stengel, Yogi Berra, Bill Lee, etc.) who were playful, goofy, and clever, there are lots of stories about him and his character. But unlike Berra and Stengel, Kruk's stories can be corroborated. Many of them are on the web but some still reside in print.

His wit is noted for its self-deprecation, while his humor is usually of the "aw, shucks" variety, but both are delivered deadpan and are most effective in interviews. Many know of his comment to the lady in the restaurant but in 1988, as an emerging star in San Diego, he said during an interview, "You know what I like? I like walking with Tony Gwynn across the street from the hotel to the stadium. All the kids with pens grab at Gwynn. They look at me and ask if I'm a ballplayer. I tell them, 'No, I'm his bodyguard and if you touch him, I'm killing you.'"[14] It's not known if the kids recoiled but coming from a burly guy who once left a hot tub during deer season in his West Virginia home, grabbed a rifle and, wearing only boots and a swim suit, dropped a buck in his back yard, one can only imagine.[15]

Asked one time if fans mistook him for a ballplayer, Kruk said, "Me, no! John Goodman, maybe."[16] After he retired from baseball in dramatic fashion, right after a single for the White Sox in 1995, he commented on criticism at his action. "People say I quit on the Sox. But I wasn't going to play anymore. I wasn't physically able to compete. I would have been stealing from the White Sox if I had stayed."[17]

After his playing career, John Kruk found occasional employment in motion pictures. As of 2017 he had five screen credits to his name:

The Fan (1996), in which Kruk plays a player who is slain at the ending by a deranged fan played by Robert De Niro.

American Pastime (2007). Kruk plays a broadcaster during a game between a Japanese internment camp team and a local nine.

The Sandlot: Heading Home (2007), in which he plays the coach of an opposing team during this time-travel movie on rediscovering team spirit.

Aqua Teen Hunger Force (2008). In this animated film, Kruk is a siren who is tortured by two other sirens that some viewers describe as a "twisted sex act."

Ring the Bell (2013). Kruk plays himself in a cameo appearance in this film about spiritual values and ego.[18]

Kruk's appearances on *Letterman* highlighted more of his wit. On a 1992 show, Letterman asked him about the dreadful Phils: "Are you optimistic for the rest of the season for your team's chances?" Kruk deadpanned, "To finish the season?"[19] In a 1993 appearance, Kruk commented on trading his number to new teammate Mitch Williams. "I saw where Rickey Henderson gave a guy $25,000. … I got two cases of beer." Williams wanted Kruk's 28 because his wife had lots of jewelry with Williams's former number on them. "The best part of it is, now, he got divorced, now he wears 99 and the two cases of beer are gone! It's a sad story."[20] The 1995 show featured a newly retired Kruk. During a conversation about a movie offer, Kruk opined, "What the hell kind of movie can it be where I never acted? He wants me to be a lead? I'm pretty certain it's gonna be very low-budget."[21]

Kruk has been married twice. His first wife was Jamie Heeter. They divorced in 1998. His second wife is Melissa (McLaughlin) Kruk, a former Miss New Jersey (1999), whom he met at a "setup" dinner by former teammate Mitch Williams. As of 2017 they lived in Naples, Florida, with their two children, Kyle and Keira. John credited Melissa with a life-changing epiphany: "I was a mess. She saved my life."[22]

He is candid about the problem he credits his wife for saving him from—alcoholism. A steady drinker during his career, he became a heavy drinker in retirement. "I was no angel when I played the game. … When I went out, I drank to get drunk because I wanted to be drunk—not because I couldn't go without it. And you don't stop doing something like that by taking a pill or getting some medicine. You stop when you realize that you're an idiot. I've heard all the talk about chemical imbalances and the other crap about some people being predisposed to addiction. Let me tell you all something: It still comes down to a choice. I never chose to have cancer, but I did choose to have a drink."[23]

As a ballplayer, Kruk is estimated to have earned more than $11 million. He must have held on to a lot of it and invested it wisely because some estimates of his net worth have topped $25 million. One of his financial actions was to use his wealth for the benefit of his parents. He talked them into retiring so he could provide for them as they had provided for him. "It was only right," he said.[24]

SOURCES

In addition to the sources cited in the Notes, the author also consulted baseball-almanac.com, Baseball-Reference.com, and Retrosheet.org.

NOTES

1. Seamus Kearney, copyright 2017.
2. Rob Tornoe, "Former Phillies Great John Kruk and ESPN Have Parted Ways," October 4, 2016. philly.com/philly/blogs/real-time/Former-Phillies-great-John-Kruk-and-ESPN-have-parted-ways.html.
3. John Kruk and Paul Hagen, *I Ain't an Athlete, Lady* (New York: Simon & Shuster, 1994), 62.
4. "Vintage John Kruk," YouTube, uploaded August 15, 2011, Bryan Sargent. See youtube.com/watch?v=58i725rhklo.
5. Kruk and Hagen, 141-143.
6. YouTube, Midsummer Classics [1993], uploaded June 12, 2011, MLB Baseball. See youtube.com/watch?v=9SH715tr6ek.
7. youtube.com/watch?v=58i725rhklo.
8. See banishedtothepen.com/the-1994-strike-what-was-the-deal/, community.seattletimes.nwsource.com/archive/?date=19940310&slug=1899466,
9. articles.baltimoresun.com/1995-07-31/sports/1995212095_1_kruk-white-sox-designated-hitter.
10. Kruk and Hagen, 57.
11. From 1986-1993, the show was titled *Late Show With David Letterman*; from 1993-2015, it was *Late Night With David Letterman*.
12. nypost.com/2017/02/07/john-kruk-the-worst-part-about-working-for-espn/.
13. m.phillies.mlb.com/news/article/214728408/phillies-broadcasters-prep-for-spring-training/.
14. Bill Plaschke, "Country Kruk: Padre First Baseman Came From the Sticks Carrying a Big Stick," *Los Angeles Times*, April 14, 1988.
15. Patrick Reusse, "Kruk's W. Virginia Roots Still Run Deep," *Minneapolis Star Tribune*, October 24, 1993.
16. "John Kruk, White Sox Designated Kidder, er, Hitter," *Chicago Tribune*, June 27, 1995.
17. Fred Mitchell, "Sure, Jordan's Rich, but He's No Bill Gates," "Odds and Ins," *Chicago Tribune*, August 9, 1996. articles.chicagotribune.com/1996-08-09/sports/9608090155_1_sox-success-bill-gates-john-kruk.
18. Kruk's full list of credits can be found at imdb.com/name/nm0472658/?ref_=nv_sr_1.
19. youtube.com/watch?v=wkLV5xV5ezc.
20. youtube/watch?v-00-MPOMvnZl.
21. youtube.com/watch?v=MCtdTIJ4x6s.
22. Martin Kaufman, "ESPN Duo Makes Perfect Double Play," *Golf Week*, April 6, 2009. golfweek.com/2009/04/06/espn-duo-makes-perfect-double-play/.
23. John Kruk, "The Hypocrisy of Sports," ESPN.com, espn.com/espn/page 2/story?page=kruk041008.
24. Kruk and Hagen, 62.

LEE LACY

BY GREGORY H. WOLF

"I CAN PLAY THIS GAME," SAID Lee Lacy confidently. "For hustle and determination, I won't take a back seat to anyone."[1] An All-Star at three different infield positions in the minors, the right-handed-hitting Lacy broke in with the Los Angeles Dodgers in 1972 and fashioned a 16-year big-league career spent primarily as a versatile utilityman and platoon player whose calling card was consistent line-drive hitting with an occasional pop, and plenty of speed. "I've always been able to hit all kinds of pitchers," said Lacy, whose most productive seasons were in his early 30s with the Pittsburgh Pirates. "Basically, I'm a bad-ball hitter, so it doesn't matter where you throw it. I don't pay a lot of attention to fundamentals. I just attack the ball."[2]

Leondaus "Lee" Lacy was born on April 10, 1948, in Longview, Texas, but grew up in Oakland, California, where his Lone Star State-born parents, Berry and Johnny Lee Lacy, had relocated by the early 1950s. The elder Lacy was a former semipro ballplayer in Texas and one-time teammate with future Dodgers All-Star infielder Charlie Neal. By all accounts, Lee was raised with a baseball in his hand and learned his trade as a youth on the sandlots of Oakland's west side. "They told me I was too skinny to play ball," recalled Lacy about trying out for a Babe Ruth league.[3] But the youngster was undeterred. With the encouragement from his father and neighbor Charlie Beamon, a former right-handed pitcher who had a cup of coffee with the Baltimore Orioles in 1958, Lacy stuck with baseball as a way to escape the poverty and social unrest of Oakland of the 1960s. He was a standout infielder at McClymonds High School, whose contributions of players to the ranks of professional sports are among the most impressive in the country. The list includes Frank Robinson, Ernie Lombardi, Vada Pinson, and Curt Flood in baseball, Bill Russell and Paul Silas in basketball, and many others since. After graduating from high school, Lacy played baseball for Laney College, a local community college, earning second-team all-Golden Gate Conference honors as a third baseman in 1969.[4] He also polished his skills in the semipro ranks with the Alameda Braves. Based on the recommendation of longtime team scout Bill Brenzel, the Dodgers selected Lacy in the second round with the 29th overall pick in the January 1969 amateur draft.

Lacy joined an organization whose farm system was the best in baseball and stacked with major-league talent. In his first season he batted .293 for the Ogden (Utah) Dodgers, earning a berth on the All-Star team of the short-season Rookie-class Pioneer League. "I was surprised that most of the players weren't superhuman at all, they were just like me, normal," said Lacy.[5] With sluggers Steve Garvey and Ron Cey tabbed as the heirs apparent to the hot corner on the big-league club, Lacy was moved to shortstop in the Arizona Instructional League. He struggled in the field (63 errors in 111 games) at his new position for Bakersfield in the Class A California League in 1970, but was once again named an All-Star owing to his .301 batting average. While the Dodgers had at least four major-league shortstop prospects (Lacy, Bobby Valentine, Ivan De Jesus, and Tim Johnson), Bakersfield manager Don LeJohn praised Lacy for his "aggressiveness," noting that the 22-year-old "hustles so we like to think that his chances are good at making it."[6] The only question was at what position.

In 1971 Lacy got a taste of what the big leagues might be like by participating in spring training with Los Angeles at Dodgertown in Vero Beach, Florida. Lauded by skipper Walter Alston and praised by sportswriter Bill Fleishman as the "top rookie" in camp, Lacy was assigned to Albuquerque in the Double-A Dixie Association.[7] At 6-feet-1 and about 170 pounds, Lacy was quick and agile, characteristics the Dodgers thought could land him a spot in the big leagues as a second baseman. Moved to the keystone sack, Lacy seemed to find his home. More at ease in the field (.967 fielding percentage), Lacy continued his steady hitting (.307 average), but with little power (.371 slugging percentage) to earn his third consecutive league All-Star berth, all at different infield positions. He was also named the second baseman on the Topps-National Association Double-A All-Star team.[8]

Lacy honed his craft at second base with Hermosillo in the Mexican Winter League in the offseason in preparation for Dodgers spring training in 1972. (In characteristic fashion, he also bashed pitchers south of the border, setting a league record with 11 straight hits.[9]) But the Dodgers had the luxury of depth. Lacy began the season back in Double A, with El Paso in the Texas League, while their top second-base prospect, the speedy Davey Lopes (a converted outfielder), remained in Triple A for the third straight season.

Lacy finally had some chips fall his way when he got off to a torrid start with El Paso in 1972, earning the Topps Double-A Player of the Month award in June, when he batted .389, lined 20 doubles and knocked in 26 runs.[10] Dodgers GM Al Campanis turned to the hot-hitting Lacy, and not Lopes, for a look-see to shore up a suddenly depleted infield. Garvey was bothered by nagging injuries, infielder Billy Grabarkewitz was out with a broken finger, and shortstop Bill Russell was called to complete a two-week stint in the Army Reserve. Lacy debuted on June 30, batting leadoff and playing second base, going 1-for-5 in an 8-4 loss to the San Francisco Giants at Candlestick Park. After a successful pinch hit on July 2, Lacy went on a roll, batting .407 (11-for-27, all singles) with six runs and four RBIs to share NL Player of the Week honors with Pittsburgh's Manny Sanguillen. Lacy went from a short-term fix to the starting second baseman, supplanting Valentine, who moved into a super-utility role. Described as "an excellent fielder, with good hands, arm and range," Lacy fielded just a few percentage points under the league average and batted a respectable .259 in an era where middle infielders weren't expected to contribute much offensively. His season abruptly ended in the second game of a doubleheader on September 4 when Cincinnati's Hal McRae took him out on an aggressive slide, resulting in a strained tendon in his knee. Lacy was still hobbling two months later when he was sent to the Arizona Instructional League to work with Russell, his double-play partner, who had been converted from an outfielder in light of shortstop Maury Wills's age.

Lacy began the 1973 season as the Dodgers' regular second baseman, but not for long. Batting a paltry .226 with just one double after 16 games, he was benched in favor of Lopes. The slap-hitting Lacy, who critics claimed lacked a natural position, found himself on a team with what emerged as the most stable infield in baseball history. The quartet of Garvey, Lopes, Russell, and Cey remained together through the 1981 season, by which time each had earned a combined 21 All-Star selections. Not just good, the quartet was also remarkably resilient and

Lee Lacy, who is one of a load of big leaguers (from Todd Cruz to Derrel Thomas and Bobby Tolan) to appear in Talent for the Game.

healthy. Occasionally spelling Lopes and pinch-hitting, Lacy hit a disappointing .207 and slugged an anemic .222 in his sophomore season. A rusty Lacy played winter ball in Puerto Rico for San Juan, skippered by former Dodgers great Jim Gilliam.

For the remainder of his tenure with the Dodgers, through 1978 (interrupted by a brief interlude with the Atlanta Braves), Lacy bided his time as a role player, making occasional starts at second base, all three outfield positions, and a few times at third base. In 1974 the Dodgers captured their first NL pennant since 1966, in the heyday of Sandy Koufax and Don Drysdale. Lacy played only 35 games in the field, including 17 starts at second base, and batted a respectable .282 in just 78 at-bats. In the postseason he had only one plate appearance, striking out in the fifth inning as a pinch-hitter against Catfish Hunter in Game Three of the Dodgers' eventual World Series loss to the Oakland A's in five games.

While manager Walter Alston lauded his bench players like Lacy, Tom Paciorek, and Rick Auerbach as one of the strengths of the club, Lacy made it known that he would play anywhere, including the outfield. "I'm not yelling about wanting to be traded or anything," said Lacy. "I just know I can play. I can always hit."[11] He got his chance when early-season injuries moved Lopes to the outfield and later in the season when left fielder Bill Buckner was sidelined with a badly sprained left ankle that eventually required season-ending surgery. On May 17 Lacy finally launched his first career home run, after 535 at-bats, a three-run shot off Pittsburgh's Jim Rooker. Three days later, he connected for his second one. He made history with his first career pinch-hit round-tripper, on July 23 against St. Louis, when he followed Willie Crawford's blast to become with Crawford just the sixth set of teammates to have pinch-hit homers in the same inning.[12] Lacy proved that he was a bona-fide hitter (.314 average and impressive .451 slugging percentage), but it was his fielding that turned heads. "[M]ost spectacular has been his throwing from the outfield," gushed sportswriter Gordon Verrell, noting that Lacy threw out seven runners in just 43 games in the outfield."[13] Widely seen as the center fielder of the future, replacing the achy-kneed Jim Wynn, Lacy impressed the Dodgers' brass in the Arizona Instructional League. "He gets rid of the ball very well, like an infielder does," opined Alston.[14] But just when Lacy had a starting position in his sights with the Dodger blue, he was traded, along with Wynn, Paciorek, and Jerry Royster, to the Atlanta Braves for left fielder Dusty Baker and utiltyman Ed Goodson on November 17.

Atlanta moved Lacy back to second base, but as fate would have it, the 28-year-old's stint as a starter for the Braves lasted only about 2½ months. On June 23 he was shipped back to the Dodgers, along with pitcher Elias Sosa for outspoken and disgruntled reliever Mike Marshall. "I'm a smarter hitter now from just playing," said Lacy, whose center-field spot had been taken by offseason acquisition Rick Monday. Making starts in all three outfield positions and pinch-hitting, Lacy finished with a .269 batting average.

With the advent of free agency in 1976 contributing to the rise of salaries across baseball, Lacy's frustration as a utility player mounted. "There's not much chance of getting the (financial) security I want the way I'm being used," said Lacy as the Dodgers marched toward another NL pennant in 1977. "I can't overly enjoy this season, although it's a winning situation."[15] The lack of playing time affected Lacy's hitting (.266 in just 169 at-bats). In Game One of the World Series against the New York Yankees, Lacy connected for the biggest hit of his career, lining a one-out pinch-hit single off reliever Sparky Lyle and driving in Dusty Baker to tie the game 3-3 in the top of the ninth during an eventual 12-inning New York victory, 4-3, at Yankee Stadium. With the Dodgers later down two games to one, first-year skipper Tommy Lasorda shuffled his outfield, moving Reggie Smith to center and installing Lacy in right field for Games Four and Five. In the latter game Lacy went 2-for-3 with a run and an RBI single in the Dodgers' 10-4 victory in Los Angeles. New York captured the title the next game, 8-4, when starting hurler Mike Torrez caught Lacy's pinch-hit bunt popup to record the final out, setting off a melee at Yankee Stadium in a game most remembered for Reggie Jackson's three home runs on three consecutive pitches.

In what seemed like an annual tradition, trade rumors swirled around Lacy in the offseason. This time sportswriters had him in a package deal to the San Diego Padres in exchange for Dave Winfield, but Lacy was still with the team when the season opened. Making starts at five positions and pinch-hitting regularly, the valuable utility player had his best season at the most opportune time. On May 17 he connected for a home run off Pittsburgh's Will McEnaney to set a major-league record with his third pinch-hit home run in as many at-bats. (In 1979 Del Unser tied the record.) Lacy batted only .261, but for the first time in his career, he showed power, clouting 13 home runs and 16 doubles in just 245 at-bats, good for a career-best .518 slugging percentage. Lacy's late-season slump continued into the postseason for the pennant winners. He managed only two hits in 14 at-bats with no runs and one RBI in four starts as DH in the World Series as the Dodgers once again fell to the Yankees in six games. Declared a free agent in the offseason, he signed a lucrative six-year deal with Pittsburgh for a reported $1.05 million.

Lacy's contradiction-filled tenure with the Pirates marked both the zenith and nadir of his career. He proved he could be a consistent .300 hitter while also revealing a flawed side as he was involved in the Pittsburgh drug trials that rocked baseball in 1985 and 1986. He achieved personal and team success, yet could not shed a new label as platoon player.

"I can play five different positions, all the outfield plus second and third," responded Lacy when asked why the Pirates signed him. "I can give them a pinch-hitter, I can hit with power and I know how to win."[16] The signing seemed odd, given that all three Pirates outfield positions were occupied by well established veterans: perennial All-Star and former MVP Dave Parker in right, Omar Moreno in center, and the dependable Bill Robinson in left. Nonetheless the signing was lauded by pundits. "He'll help (the Pirates) win a lot of games that won't show up in his personal stats," suggested Dick Young in *The Sporting News*.[17] At Pirates spring training in Bradenton, Florida, the 31-year-old Lacy explained his approach to a new chapter in his career. "I am the Pirates' utility player," he said. "I've got to work harder because of my versatility. I have to concentrate more, and I've got to keep myself in good physical shape."[18]

Manager Chuck Tanner expected Lacy to have a big role on the team; however, Lacy "rusted on the bench," wrote Pittsburgh sportswriter Charley Feeney.[19] Suffering from a sore heel early in the season and slowed by a bad back and viral infection at the end of one of the most exciting campaigns in Pirates history, Lacy made only 41 starts (38 in left field) and hit a disappointing .247 in 182 at-bats. For the third consecutive season, Lacy was on a pennant-winning club. After not playing in the Pirates' three-game sweep of the Cincinnati Reds in the best-of-five NLCS, Lacy made four pinch-hitting appearances in the World Series against the favored Baltimore Orioles, connecting for a single in Game Five of the "We Are Family" Pirates' eventual title after being down three games to one.

"I wouldn't say that it was a wasted year," responded Lacy when asked about his first season in the Steel City. "A lot of positive things happened. It was a year where I didn't have too many alternatives. I was labeled an outfielder, but there was little room to play in the outfield."[20] Lacy spent most of the 1980 season platooning in left field with left-handed slugger Mike Easler while Robinson moved to first with reigning NL co-MVP Willie Stargell hobbled by bad knees. Lacy got off to a hot start, keeping his batting average north of .400 through June 21 (42-for-103, .408), including three three-hit games and one four-hit game. On July 20 Lacy punctuated a successful late-game at-bat in the first game of a doubleheader against Los Angeles by going 5-for-5 in the second game, giving him seven consecutive hits (over three games), scoring three times and driving in two runs on "Willie Stargell Day" in front of a raucous crowd of 41,932 at Three Rivers Stadium. Before the celebrations honoring the Pirates' captain between games took place, an ugly incident marred the first game when Dave Parker was almost hit in the head by a battery thrown from the right-field stands, and was removed for his safety. While the Pirates finished a disappointing third (83-79) in the NL East, Lacy batted a career-best .335 and slugged .511 to form with Easler (.338/.583) a potent one-two punch in left field. That success didn't assuage Lacy's frustrations, though. "A good ballplayer is never satisfied. I'm a platoon ballplayer because they think of me as a platoon player," he said. "I've never considered myself a platoon ballplayer."[21]

The fifth work stoppage since Marvin Miller became head of the Major League Players Association in 1966 led to the cancellation of 713 games of the 1981 season from June 12 through August 10. The Pirates (46-56) had their first losing season since 1973, as injuries and growing dissent among players marred the forgettable campaign. On May 22 Lacy was almost hit by a bottle while playing left field at Three Rivers Stadium, but refused to press charges. "A person is going to have to do a lot more than that for me to file a complaint," he said. "I did some things when I was young that I shouldn't have."[22] While Lacy's batting average slipped to .268, he emerged as a threat on the basepaths, crediting pinch-runner Matt Alexander for teaching him how to take big leads.[23] After stealing 18 bases in the previous season, he swiped 24 in 27 attempts in 1981.

Lacy took some heat in the offseason when he referred to Dave Parker "as a bad person to have on this team."[24] Since signing the largest contract in Pirates history during the 1979 season, the enigmatic Parker had become a target for fans' frustrations with the team and with what many perceived as exorbitant player salaries while Pittsburgh was gripped by economic woes after the collapse of the steel industry. Seemingly discontent, Lacy also added a jab about Three Rivers Stadium: "I like the guys on the Pirates, but I wouldn't mind being traded. The field is very hard, the worst in the league."[25] The Pirates had no intention of moving Lacy, widely regarded as one of the best-hitting platoon and bench players in baseball.

While Lacy and Parker avoided one another in the clubhouse in spring training, the Pirates got off to a slow start in 1982 and finished in fourth place in the division despite leading the league in hitting (.273) and slugging (.408) and placing second in runs. Lacy, making 53 starts for the injured Parker in right field, batted .312 while setting new personal bests for hits (112), runs (66), and stolen bases (40). On May 14 it appeared as though Lacy had finally hit his first career grand slam. With the Bucs trailing Cincinnati, 7-5, at Three Rivers, Lacy launched an offering from Reds reliever Tom Hume over the right-field wall with the bases loaded. In his excitement, Lacy passed Moreno about halfway to second base, and the result was an automatic out. "I grabbed my head and stopped, but I was already past Omar, and it was too late," said Lacy, whom teammates razzed mercilessly for his baserunning blunder and three-run single. "It goes to show you what happens when you don't know your own power," he joked.[26] Lacy never hit a grand slam in the big leagues.

Making starts in all three outfield positions in 1983, Lacy batted over .300 for the third time in four seasons and stole 31 bases, but was criticized for his lack of production. He started out with a "real bang" batting leadoff in the season opener in St. Louis as he hit the first pitch of the game, thrown by Bob Forsch, for a home run, but he drove in only 13 runs in 288 at-bats while the Pirates duplicated their 84-78 record from the previous season, although finishing two positions higher, in second place.

The next three years were trying ones for Lacy. His name seemed to regularly grace the front pages of Pittsburgh's sports pages in the 1983-84 offseason. After rumors of Lacy's trade to San Francisco proved to be false, he figured prominently in a mini-scandal when team coach Joe Lonnett castigated his defense in a widely reported interview. "Lacy can't play center field. Man, he'd kill you in center," said the longtime coach, explaining why rookie Marvell Wynn took over for Moreno, who had departed via free agency. "Wherever you put [Lacy], he's going to hurt you."[27] Lonnett also criticized the play of outfielder Lee Mazzilli, infielder Jim Morrison, and first baseman Jason Thompson, but somehow weathered the storm by issuing a feeble public apology, and was with the team when the club opened spring training.

The first salvo in the eventual drug scandals that rocked baseball in 1985 and 1986 occurred during spring training in 1984. Sportswriter Dan Donovan of the *Pittsburgh Press* reported on March 21 that Lacy was involved in a contentious child-custody suit in Oakland.[28] According to that report, Cecelia Trainor Chapman had filed an affidavit claiming that Lacy was "dependent on cocaine" and was unsuited to have custody of their daughter, Jennifer. Lacy was raising the child with his wife, Suzanne (née Mitchell), whom he had married in San Diego in July 1979. Lacy emphatically denied the charge, claiming, "How could I play baseball at age 34 if I did that?"

Despite the off-field distraction that forced Lacy to occasionally miss games to tend to personal matters in California, he entered his contract season with a vengeance while the Pirates plunged to last place in the NL East for the first time since division play began in 1969. He started a career-high 116 games, including 86 in right field, where he platooned with weak-hitting Doug Frobel (.203), and led the team with a .321 batting average (second highest in the league, but well behind Tony Gwynn's .351) on a career-best 151 hits. Declaring free agency after the season, Lacy signed a three-year deal with the Baltimore Orioles in January 1985.

"I hit the ball all over and have occasional power down the lines," said the 37-year-old Lacy, whose 70 RBIs in 1984 were easily the best total of his career. "I'll chink it over the infield or beat out chops. I love to bunt. If I see crumbs in the third baseman's eyes, like he's been out too late the night before, I'll lay one down for a hit."[29] But before Lacy could showcase his hitting in the AL, he severely injured his thumb diving for a fly ball in an exhibition game on March 12. He required surgery and missed five weeks.

Lacy's spring training went from bad to worse when Dan Donovan published a bombshell article in the *Pittsburgh Press* on March 31, 1985.[30] He reported that no fewer than eight major-league players, among them Lacy, Keith Hernandez, Tim Raines, and Enos Cabell, had testified before a federal grand jury in Pittsburgh before spring training about the sale of cocaine, as part of an investigation targeting dealers and not players. The ensuing trial, which began in September 1985, made national headlines with testimony from seven players, including former Pirates Dave Parker and Dale Berra, about widespread cocaine use among major-league players in the previous five years, and even inside the clubhouse at Three Rivers Stadium. Lacy was sworn in to testify, but did not. The trial eventually resulted in the conviction of seven drug dealers. Commissioner Peter Ueberroth considered the episode closed on February 28, 1986, when he suspended 11 players (seven for one year, Parker and Berra among them; and four for 60 days, including Lacy);[31] however, players were permitted to play if they agreed to donate 10 and 5 percent, respectively, of their salary to antidrug programs; all players agreed to the stipulation.

The drug trials notwithstanding, Lacy was steady offensively, though far from spectacular in his first two seasons in Baltimore, but proved to be a liability in right field. In 1985 he walloped his first and only walk-off home run, connecting off the California Angels' Donnie Moore with one on and one out in ninth to give the Orioles a 7-5 win on June 3. At the end of the same month he commenced a personal-best 20-game hitting streak (38-for-84, .452) en route to 144 hits and a .293 average as the oldest starting outfielder in the league; only the Angels 39-year-old first baseman Rod Carew was an older starting position player in the AL. Lacy inherited that mantle the following season, scored a career-high 77 runs and batted .287. Among his 91 big-league home runs, three came on June 8, 1986, at Yankee Stadium when he went 4-for-6 and set personal bests with four runs scored and six RBIs in the Orioles 18-9 thrashing of New York. With his playing time reduced in 1987, Lacy was released by the Orioles near the end of spring training in 1988, and subsequently retired.

In 16 big-league seasons, Lacy batted .286 and collected 1,303 hits. In parts of four seasons in the minors, he hit .314. Lacy enjoyed great success against pitchers Rick Reuschel (14-for-29, .483), Jerry Koosman (16-for-41, .390) and Steve Carlton (33-for-88, .372), while having difficulty against Gene Garber (1-for-20, .050), Joe Niekro (5-for-38, .132), and Bob

Shirley (6-for-37, .162). And Lacy always seemed to take his game to another level when playing the Dodgers, against whom he batted .348 (49-for-141), his highest average versus any team. In 1989 and 1990 Lacy played in the short-lived Senior Professional Baseball Association.

As of 2016 Lacy resided in metropolitan Los Angeles, where he has long been active in various community outreach and charity programs sponsored by the Los Angeles Dodgers Foundation. He has regularly served as a guest instructor at youth baseball campuses and participated in events focusing on education and baseball opportunities for inner-city youth, such as Dodgers RBI (Reviving Baseball in Inner Cities). "I just want to play," Lacy once said.[32] That remark aptly serves as an epitaph for his baseball career and reflects his passion for the sport that he has worked diligently to advocate and teach to youngsters.

SOURCES

In addition to the sources noted in this biography, the author also accessed the *Encyclopedia of Minor League Baseball*, Retrosheet.org, Baseball-Reference.com, the SABR Minor Leagues Database, accessed online at Baseball-Reference.com, and *The Sporting News* archive via Paper of Record. Special thanks to Bill Mortell for his assistance with genealogical research.

NOTES

1. *The Sporting News*, June 27, 1981: 28.
2. *The Sporting News*, March 11, 1985: 6.
3. Fred Lewis, "Lee Lacy 'Too Skinny to Play Ball' Fattens Average on Caloop Hurlers," *Bakersfield Californian*, August 1, 1970: 11.
4. "All Conference Trio Honored," *The Times* (San Mateo, California), May 20, 1969: 30.
5. Lewis.
6. Ibid.
7. *The Sporting News*, April 17, 1971: 39.
8. *The Sporting News*, December 4, 1971: 39.
9. *The Sporting News*, January 29, 1972: 42.
10. *The Sporting News*, August 5, 1972: 26.
11. *The Sporting News*, June 21, 1975: 3.
12. Crawford and Lacy's feat also marked just the fifth time in big-league history that teammates hit back-to-back pinch-hit home runs.
13. *The Sporting News*, October 11, 1975: 8.
14. Ibid.
15. *The Sporting News*, June 25, 1977: 24.
16. Marino Parascenzo, "Versatile Lacy Joins Bucs," *Pittsburgh Post-Gazette*, January 20, 1979: 10.
17. *The Sporting News*, February 3, 1979: 2.
18. Dan Donovan, "Motto of New Pirate Lacy: Be Prepared," *Pittsburgh Press*, March 2, 1979: 24.
19. *The Sporting News*, December 22, 1979: 6.
20. Dan Donovan, "Lacy'll Be Hanged If He Doesn't Help," *Pittsburgh Press*, March 5, 1980: 64.
21. Dan Donovan, He's Platooned but Lacy's a Good Soldier," *Pittsburgh Press*, August 3, 1980: 3.
22. *The Sporting News*, June 20, 1981: 30.
23. *The Sporting News*, June 27, 1981: 28.
24. "Lacy Labels Parker 'Bad,'" *Pittsburgh Press*, October 26, 1981: 3.
25. Ibid.
26. Russ Frank, "Lacy's Slam That Wasn't Still Grand," *Pittsburgh Press*, May 15, 1982: 8.
27. *The Sporting News*, February 13, 1984: 46.
28. Dan Donovan, "Lacy Used Cocaine, Witnesses Say," *Pittsburgh Press*, March 21, 1984: 51.
29. *The Sporting News*, March 11, 1985: 8.
30. Dan Donovan, "Ex-Pirate Lacy Called as Witness in Drug Probe," *Pittsburgh Press*, March 31, 1985: B10.
31. Charley Feeney, "Commissioner Penalizes 11," *Pittsburgh Post-Gazette*, March 1, 1986: 19.
32. *The Sporting News*, June 21, 1975: 3.

BILLY LOES

BY GREGORY H. WOLF

IN A WIDELY CIRCULATED NAtional profile of the Brooklyn Dodgers' Billy Loes in the *Saturday Evening Post* in 1953, journalist Jimmy Breslin described the young hurler as a "Dizzy Dean from the sidewalks of New York."[1] That reference would not have been lost on readers at the time. The former 30-game winner Dean parlayed his down-home, country-boy personality into one of the most recognizable baseball broadcasters of the 1950s. The youthful Loes, on the other hand, made headlines for his wacky statements and bizarre, typically candid pronouncements that left many wondering whether he was cocky, stupid, or a combination of both.

On the eve of the 1952 World Series, Loes found himself in a mini-controversy when reporters asked him to clarify his prediction that the New York Yankees would beat his Dodgers in six games. Claiming that he was misquoted, Loes responded, "I never told that guy the Yanks would win it in six. I said they'd win it in seven."[2] Loes almost had the chance to foil his own prophecy by holding the Yankees scoreless through six innings in Game Six, with Brooklyn leading three games to two. A sequence of peculiar events led to his unraveling in the bottom of the seventh and an eventual Yankees victory. Loes was charged with a balk when he dropped the ball in his windup and then misplayed a grounder back to the mound leading to a run. Afterward, Loes calmly explained his miscues in his strong New York City accent and gruff, profanity-ridden language (which sportswriters liberally edited): "I might have had the deleted thing if it wasn't for the low sun shining in my face"[3]

Loes cultivated his zany persona, which many sportswriters and fans considered part of Brooklyn's screwball tradition dating back to the "Daffiness Boys" of managers Wilbert Robinson and Casey Stengel more than a generation earlier. The team's "right-handed weirdie" was a typical epithet for Loes.[4] Prior to the 1952 season, Loes told reporters that no Dodgers pitcher would win at least 15 games, and then made an early-season amendment. "Better make it seventeen," he said after his hot start. "I looked pretty good out there today."[5] Loes once claimed he never wanted to win 20 games because then the Dodgers would expect him to win that many every year, and would cut his salary if he didn't. Twelve or 13 wins would be plenty, he suggested.[6] Oddball comments like those might have made him a quirky favorite of fans, but they exasperated his managers and the front office. "How can the public be so gullible?" said Loes in 1956, after he had been traded from the Dodgers to the Baltimore Orioles. "Don't the people know that most of the stories are phony?"[7]

Loes was a complicated and unpredictable player, filled with contradictions and myriad superstitions. Behind what Brooklyn beat writer Tommy Holmes called a "brusque exterior," Loes was a brooding type away from the game, yet a practical joker and clown with teammates.[8] However, he never seemed at home with reporters, despite his penchant for good copy; rather, he often brushed them off with "I don't know nothing about anything."[9] Nervous and fidgety in the dugout on game days, Loes was more at ease on the mound, where he was typically undemonstrative. Later in his career he developed a reputation for arguing with umpires and even his catcher. "I used to think Durocher was a nut on superstitions," said Dodgers skipper Chuck Dressen, "but this kid is even worse."[10] According to Dressen, Loes dropped his glove in a certain spot in the dugout after arriving from the mound each inning, and it had to land in a specific way; and he could go to the mound only after the opposing base coaches got into position. Whereas many pitchers like to be left alone between innings, Loes sat in a same spot in the dugout and

Billy Loes, who (along with fellow Brooklyn Dodgers Roy Campanella, Carl Erskine, and Russ Meyer) plays himself in Roogie's Bump.

chatted with the same teammates every time, and required a few words of encouragement from Dressen each inning on his way back to the mound. He also went through periods when he refused to talk on the mound, including to his manager. Despite his eccentricities, Loes was generally well liked by his teammates. Many of them no doubt laughed when Loes once demanded that the Dodgers pay for a stray dog he took home to his mother as a legitimate business expense.[11]

Loes was praised as having unlimited natural talent, while his work ethic and attitude were publicly questioned by his managers, and he was dismissed as a flake. "Loes wears an aggravated look constantly, as if Lady Luck mistreats him with steady rudeness," wrote sportswriter Arthur Daley in the *New York Times* in 1956. "He also seems to carry a chip on his shoulder … and thinks that he has received bad press without justification."[12] Loes' volatile personality and blowups contributed to that impression. "The only thing I like about baseball is the salary," he told Jack Orr in a *Sport* profile in 1958. "I never get a kick out it. I haven't got one of these feelings that it's the greatest thing in the world. It's just a job." Plagued by chronic shoulder pain throughout his career, Loes never reached the potential many predicted, finishing with an 80-63 record in parts of 11 big-league seasons, including a stellar 50-25 slate with Brooklyn from 1952 to 1955.

William Loes was born on December 13, 1929, in Long Island City, New York, and was raised in Astoria, about a half-hour from Ebbets Field. (Both Long Island City and Astoria are sections of the New York City borough of Queens.) He was the only child of James and Filo Loes, Greek immigrants who, according to Loes, had shortened their surname. The younger Loes lived in a small apartment and grew up with limited means. The elder Loes suffered a debilitating injury while serving in the Maritime Service in World War I, and did not work; Billy's mother provided for the family by working in a furniture store. By the time Billy was a teenager, he was obsessed with baseball. He worked to save some money to attend occasionally a big-league game. Like many other kids, he played on local sandlots and in the street, pretending to pitch to the likes of Joe DiMaggio and Bill Dickey, and began playing for a local YMCA youth team.

Loes emerged as one of New York City's best pitchers during his last two years at William Cullen Bryant High School in Long Island City. After his junior year he led the Astoria Cubs to the Kiwanis League state title in the summer 1947, and was selected as the most valuable player.[13] At 6-feet-1 and just 150 pounds, Loes possessed a wicked curveball that helped him fashion five no-hitters (four as a senior), the last of which was in the semifinal game of the 1948 Public School Athletic League championship with a flock of big-league scouts in attendance.[14] The overly confident teenager often tooted his own horn, angering friends and foes alike. "I was misunderstood in high school," he once said. "There's a difference between cockiness and confidence."[15] Loes finished his prep career by tossing a one-hitter and knocking in the winning run to lead coach Vince Starace's squad to the title.[16] For his MVP performance, he won a weeklong tour with the New York Giants. Upon returning home, the legend of Loes' head-scratching comments was cemented when he compared himself to the Giants' star righty Larry Jansen and boldly announced, "I forgot more [about pitching] than he ever knew."[17]

In baseball's postwar big-bonus era, Loes was angling for a hefty payday from teams lining up to sign him. Tom Yawkey, owner of the Boston Red Sox, had been fined by Commissioner Happy Chandler for attempting to ink the teenager while he was still in high school, a serious transgression at the time.[18] As a member of the Brooklyn Eagle All-Stars after graduating from school, the 18-year-old Loes dominated competition on a traveling tour against other all-star squads in Washington, D.C., and Canada.[19] At the tour's conclusion, Loes played semipro ball in Queens.[20] He became one of the most sought-after pitchers in New York after an excellent outing in a showcase game with scouts from supposedly all 16 big-league clubs except the Yankees and Dodgers.[21] The Cleveland Indians offered the precocious youth an $18,000 signing bonus, yet Loes hesitated. The Dodgers, sensing an opportunity, had one last chance. After working out in front of Dodgers brass at Ebbets Field, Loes accepted GM Branch Rickey's offer of a $21,000 bonus, the largest in club history at the time, and signed with Brooklyn. "I knew I wasn't worth no big dough," said Loes in typical fashion in the *Saturday Evening Post* piece, "but I figured those kids weren't worth it either."[22] Rickey seemed to agree, but knew that it would be public-relations nightmare had the New York City native signed elsewhere. "He's just about a $10,000 player," said the Mahatma, "but Loes is a local boy and I just can't let another club sign him."[23]

During the Dodgers minor-league spring training in Vero Beach, Florida, in 1949, Loes' "every move was followed closely" reported Brooklyn sportswriter Ben Gould.[24] Loes began his professional career with Nashua in the Class-B New England League, where he blazed a trail, going 11-3, including a no-hitter, before he was promoted to Fort Worth in the Double-A Texas League. With a combined 16-5 record and 2.69 ERA in 194 innings, Loes was added to the Dodgers' big-league roster in mid-October.[25] Under the bonus rules then in effect, Loes would have otherwise been eligible for the amateur draft slated in November, and was required to remain on the Dodgers' roster for the entire 1950 season.

Obviously not yet prepared to face major-league hitters, Loes' rookie campaign in 1950 was a washout. The 20-year-old hurler languished on the far end of skipper Burt Shotton's bench, primarily confined to the role of BP pitcher, logging just 12⅔ innings and yielding 11 earned runs. He debuted in mop-up duty against the St. Louis Cardinals on May 18, walking five, balking once, and surrendering one hit (a two-run homer to Johnny Lindell) in two innings.

While Loes' skills rusted on the bench, his career encountered another setback when he was drafted into the Army and inducted in early February 1951.[26] Stationed primarily at Fort Devens in Massachusetts, Loes served with the 314th Quartermaster Subsistence Company. He pitched for the base team in the semipro Blackstone Valley League and against other military base squads.[27] In mid-October he received his discharge as a hardship case, citing his financial support of his parents. Two years later, he purchased them a house with his 1952 World Series earnings.[28]

Loes was itching to play baseball, but only on the big stage in 1952. He supposedly told second-year pilot Chuck Dressen that he'd quit baseball if he were demoted. "I've learned all any minor-league manager can teach me," said Loes. "I'd be wasting my time down there."[29] Described already as "insufferably conceited" by beat writer Roscoe McGowen, Loes had a surprisingly productive spring, and then shocked his team in the Dodgers' home opener on April 18 by hurling five scoreless innings of two-hit ball to pick up the victory over the New York Giants in 12 innings. After yielding just two earned runs in 19 innings of relief, Loes tossed a six-hit shutout against the Pittsburgh Pirates on May 15 at Ebbets Field in his first big-league start. Two starts later, he blanked Philadelphia on five hits at Shibe Park. Hurling consistently all season long as a starter and reliever, Loes emerged as one of the Dodgers' most effective hurlers. While the Bums captured their second consecutive pennant, Loes posted a 13-8 record, including four shutouts, and a 2.69 ERA (fourth lowest in the NL) in 187⅓ innings.

Facing the Yankees in the World Series for the third time in five seasons, the Dodgers had a chance to capture their first, elusive championship in Game Six at Ebbets Field. Dressen called upon Loes despite the right-hander's shaky relief outing in Game Two (two hits and two runs in two innings). Loes mowed the Yankees down through six before Yogi Berra led off the seventh with a home run to tie the game, 1-1. Loes committed a balk two batters later, then misplayed Vic Raschi's two-out grounder, which bounced off his knee and caromed into right field, enabling Gene Woodling to score. In the bottom of the frame, Loes singled and then added to his growing legend for zaniness by stealing second. Whether it was a failed attempt at a hit-and-run by Billy Cox or Loes' own idea will forever be a mystery. Loes himself, however, took credit for the adventure: "I just saw nobody was watchin' me, so I ran to second."[30] In the eighth, Loes yielded a towering home run to Mickey Mantle, and was ultimately charged with the loss (nine hits and five walks in 8⅓ innings). The Yankees broke Brooklyn's collective heart the next day by capturing the title with a 4-2 victory.

While his comments about being blinded by the sun looking down to field a grounder added to his eccentric reputation, Loes found himself embroiled in a less savory episode just weeks after the World Series when a warrant for his arrest was issued in New Jersey as part of a paternity suit. The Dodgers front office brushed off the case as yet another example of "blackmail"[31]; and indeed the case was eventually thrown out four years later.

Loes was often described as a good-looking player, with a dark complexion and dark eyes situated on a thin baby-face. He bulked up to about 175 pounds, but never put on the weight that his managers thought was necessary to be a durable ace, and always appeared thin. According to Breslin, Loes was "popular with the bobby-soxers"; however, the eligible bachelor initially preferred spending his nights at home, where he resided with his parents during his tenure with the Dodgers.[32]

Loes' success rested on four pitches: curve, fastball, changeup, and, beginning in 1952, a slider. In Loes' rookie campaign, the Dodgers felt that he lacked a serious heater, though Dressen later claimed that was a mistake, and that "he was faster than the average pitcher."[33] Brooklyn's MVP catcher Roy Campanella was more direct in his assessment: "He's got the best fastball in the National League."[34] Loes had a fluid, graceful pitching motion, as can be seen in the video of Game Six of the 1952 World Series.[35]

Highly touted as a possible 20-game winner in 1953, Loes emerged as Brooklyn's only reliable starter in the early part of the season. By the end of June he had won 10 games, but had also been hit hard in some contests, resulting in a bloated 4.49 ERA. After that Loes was a "complete loss for two months," opined Brooklyn sportswriter Dave Anderson, plagued by shoulder pain that would accompany the hurler for the remainder of his career.[36] It was during that stretch (on August 23) that Breslin's piece in the *Saturday Evening Post* appeared, causing quite a stir. A sensitive Loes threatened to sue (though he didn't refute the portrayal) while Tommy Holmes of the *Brooklyn Eagle* thought it made the pitcher look like a "Simple Simon."[37] On September 7 Loes tossed a complete-game four-hitter against Philadelphia to win his first start in two months, and suddenly his name was bandied about as a possible World Series starter for Brooklyn, which was then cruising to a franchise-record 105 wins.

With the Dodgers trailing the Yankees two games to one, Loes (14-8, with a 4.54 ERA in 162⅔ innings) battled his friend and fellow Astoria resident, Whitey Ford, in Game Four, at Ebbets Field. While Ford was knocked out after one inning, Loes scattered eight hits and gave up three runs over eight frames to earn his only World Series victory, 7-3. The Bronx Bombers, led by Billy Martin's heroics, took the next two games to capture their record-setting fifth consecutive championship.

Chided as a "crazy, mixed-up kid—even unpredictable in the Spring,"[38] Loes embroiled himself in yet another brouhaha in spring training 1954, with the statement, "I hate baseball," claiming to prefer a 9-to-5 job.[39] Those comments drew the ire of local sportswriters who had berated him as too sensitive since the Breslin episode. Loes suffered a severe elbow injury in late April and pitched sporadically and poorly afterward, leading new Dodgers skipper Walter Alston to chastise him publicly as a "mystery" whose pitches were "half-dead."[40] Just when it appeared that Loes had lost it, he tossed an overpowering complete-game victory against the Pittsburgh Pirates, whiffing a career-best 11, on July 5. Defying expectations, he won his next eight decisions, including five straight starts in August, keeping Brooklyn in a tight pennant race with the Giants. But Loes slumped in September, re-aggravating his elbow and shoulder injuries, and was ultimately exiled to the pen. A seemingly exasperated Alston, who rarely complained about players in the press, openly questioned Loes' mental preparation and commitment as the Dodgers finished in second place, five games behind their crosstown rival Giants.[41]

Shortly after the 1954 season, Loes made his first and only appearance in a film, *Roogie's Bump*.[42] The comedy was about a young Flatbush boy, Remington Rigsby; his nickname is Roogie. The actor who plays him is Robert Marriott. Roogie develops a bump on his arm that enables him to throw with great speed. He eventually lands a spot on the Dodgers.[43] Four of his teammates are real-life Dodgers—Roy Campanella, Carl Erskine, Russ Meyer, and Loes, all of whom play themselves. Film critic Jane Corby of the *Brooklyn Eagle* was excited by some action shots of the team and Ebbets Field in the film, but added, "the story is weak."[44]

Despite a 13-5 record and 4.14 ERA in 147⅔ innings in 1954, there was a "feeling that Loes could have been much better," wrote Roscoe McGowen.[45] It was the typical refrain heard about the hurler who drew charges of indifference. In the offseason, GM Buzzie Bavasi expressed his frustration by remarking that "Loes is old enough now to realize he's got to settle down."[46] The United Press opined that "nobody takes baseball less seriously and gets more results than Brooklyn's unorthodox Billy Loes."[47] Bothered by shoulder pain most of the 1955 season, Loes pitched well when he could (19 starts), including matching his career high with 11 strikeouts in a complete-game win against Chicago on June 11. On September 7, after being sidelined for a month, Loes tossed a stellar complete-game six-hitter to defeat the Milwaukee Braves at County Stadium and give the Dodgers at least a tie for the pennant. Few could have guessed that it would be Loes' last victory as a Dodger. While "Dem Bums" finally beat the Yankees in the World

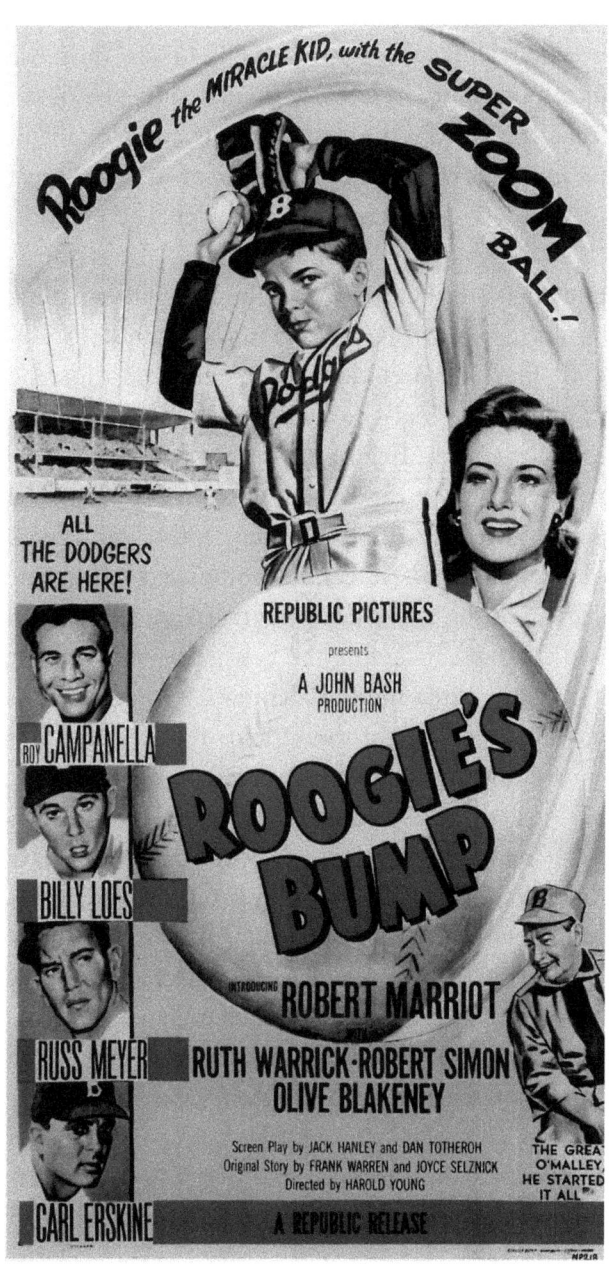

Series in seven games, Loes' start in Game Three was deemed a "complete failure."[48] After hurling just 18 innings in September, Loes shook off the rust to toss three scoreless frames before imploding in the fourth. He was charged with the loss (seven hits and four earned runs in 3⅔ innings) and tied a World Series record by hitting two batters.

Loes endured so much shoulder pain during spring training in 1956 that he threatened to quit baseball altogether. He didn't, but the Dodgers cut their ties with the oft-injured hurler on May 14 by selling him in a waiver transaction to the Baltimore Orioles. "For four years we've been waiting for him to produce," said Bavasi. "I'm beginning to wonder how long it'll take. His trouble is he has no sense of responsibility."[49] Loes, who made just one disastrous start before the deal (five hits and six runs in 1⅓ innings), welcomed the change of scenery. "I just couldn't get comfortable in Brooklyn," he claimed. "I was always under too much strain."[50] Loes transitioned into the bullpen with Baltimore with middling results (2-7, 4.76 ERA in 56⅔ innings).

With few expectations for success, Loes emerged as one of the feel-good stories of the first half of the 1957 season. Beginning with a complete-game 11-2 victory over the Kansas City A's on May 8, he won eight consecutive decisions in the best stretch of pitching in his career. He completed six of nine starts, posting a 1.89 ERA in 71⅓ innings, and spun two shutouts, including the best game of his career, a sparkling three-hitter with no walks against the A's on June 25 as part of the Orioles' record-tying four consecutive shutouts. "I know his arm has been sore, but he's still young enough to recover," said Orioles GM-manager, Paul Richards, who appeared to have fleeced the Dodgers.[51] When asked to explain his sudden success, Loes responded in usual curt fashion: "Luck and a bigger ballpark."[52] Selected by Casey Stengel to his first and only All-Star Game, Loes followed starter Jim Bunning's three hitless innings with three scoreless innings of his own, yielding just three hits, which probably made Walter Alston, skipper of the NL squad, squirm on the dugout bench. Loes improved his record to 12-5 with his third shutout of the season, on August 4, but it proved costly. He reinjured his elbow and was confined to the bullpen, save for one start, for the rest of the season.

There was no fairy-tale return for Loes in 1958, as he lost his first seven decisions (all as a starter). His career may have reached its nadir in an ugly incident on June 1 in Baltimore. Trailing 1-0 in the fifth, Loes caught Bob Aspromonte of the Washington Senators in a rundown between third base and home after retiring Camilo Pascual on a grounder to the mound. Loes took matters in his own hands and attempted to chase down Aspromonte himself. When Aspromonte eluded his tag and was called safe by home-plate umpire Larry Napp, Loes went ballistic. He threw the ball in disgust against home plate and shoved Napp. Julio Becquer, on first via a single, rounded the bases to score. Loes was immediately ejected, and subsequently earned a fine and suspension from the AL, and also by the Orioles for "deliberately throwing away a game."[53] Loes took his frustrations out on the autocratic Richards. "He doesn't care whether you win or lose, just so that you don't make him look bad," said the volatile hurler. "He's got all the pitchers on this club scared to death of him."[54] Despite rumors that he'd be traded, Loes remained with the club, spending the final three months of the season in the bullpen.

An exasperated Richards was desperate to rid the club of the sore-armed Loes in 1959. "Know anyone who wants him?" he asked rhetorically in mid-March.[55] Richards found a taker, sending Loes to the Washington Senators on April 1; however, the trade was voided by Commissioner Ford Frick eight days later when Loes was incapable of pitching. Back with Baltimore, Loes found yet another of his nine lives, pitching effectively much of the season as a reliever, recording 14 saves, before his aching wing limited his effectiveness in the final two months of the season.

Loes spent his final two big-league seasons with the San Francisco Giants when Baltimore traded him along with pitcher Billy O'Dell for infielder Jackie Brandt, pitcher Gordon Jones, and catching prospect Roger McCardell on November 30, 1959. Confined to mop-up duty in 1960, Loes had a surprisingly productive spring in 1961 and earned a spot in skipper Al Dark's rotation. Given ample time between outings, Loes enjoyed some early-season success, tossing the last of his nine career shutouts on May 7, blanking the Philadelphia Phillies on seven hits. Inconsistent and injury-plagued, Loes (6-5, 4.24 ERA) logged 114⅔ innings, his most in three years, but wasn't in the Giants' long-term plans.

In the offseason Loes was sold conditionally to the expansion New York Mets, but quit in a bizarre tirade before spring training began. "It was a matter of pride and decency," said Loes contemptuously.[56] Loes was insulted that Mets president George Weiss did not publicly acknowledge the hurler's sore shoulder and welcome him with open arms. "I'm no animal," said Loes. "I've got feelings, too."[57] The Mets returned Loes to the Giants, who released him on March 2.

So ended Loes' tumultuous 11-year big-league career. He expressed a desire to coach and even volunteered to return to baseball in 1963, but the player who spent the previous decade antagonizing his managers and front office had no takers. His final slate included an 80-63 record and 3.89 ERA in 1,190⅓ innings. He batted .110 on 38 hits.

Loes' transition away from baseball was not easy. He returned to Long Island, where he remained for most of the rest of his life, and drifted away from baseball. "I was floating from job to job," said Loes about 10 years after he left the game.[58] He drove a cab, worked a lunch counter, and served as a youth counselor in a Greek organization "I never liked stayin' in one place too long," he declared.[59] In 1990 he was inducted into the Brooklyn Dodgers Hall of Fame at the Brooklyn Museum, and momentarily soaked up the media's attention. If those in attendance hoped that Loes would offer sentimental words about Brooklyn and the Dodgers of the 1950s, they were sorely disappointed. "I think Brooklyn was dying at the time," said Loes with the frankness that defined his career. "[Team owner Walter] O'Malley had foresight and [the Dodgers' move] was a great thing for baseball." And then he offered a morsel of romantic dreaming by adding, "Brooklyn needs a baseball team."[60]

On July 15, 2010, Billy Loes died in Tucson, Arizona at the age of 80. According to his *New York Times* obituary, he had been suffering from diabetes for many years, and had not been in good health.[61] He was survived by his wife, Irene; the two had been separated.

SOURCES

In addition to the sources noted in this biography, the author also accessed Loes' player file and player questionnaire from the National Baseball Hall of Fame, the Encyclopedia of Minor League Baseball, Retrosheet.org, Baseball-Reference.com, the SABR Minor Leagues Database, accessed online at Baseball-Reference.com, and *The Sporting News* archive via Paper of Record. Special thanks to Bill Mortell for his assistance with genealogical research.

NOTES

1   Jimmy Breslin, "The Dodgers' New Daffiness Boy," *Saturday Evening Post*, August 23, 1953: 115.

2   Breslin, 116.

3   Tommy Holmes, High Homers, Low Sun Foil Pale Face Kid," *Brooklyn Eagle*, October 7, 1952: 13.

4   "Flock Wants Heavier Loes," *Brooklyn Eagle*, February 1, 1954: 14.

5   Breslin, 116.

6   *The Sporting News*, January 19, 1955: 13.

7   Jack Orr, "Has Success Spoiled Billy Loes," *Sport*, June 1958: 85.

8   Tommy Holmes, "The Sudden Rise of Billy Loes," *Brooklyn Eagle*, May 27, 1952: 19.

9   Dave Anderson, "Loes to Miss Next Start," *Brooklyn Eagle*, April 29, 1954: 18.

10   *The Sporting News*, August 27, 1952: 3.

11   "Dodgers Won't Pay for Loes' Gift Dog," *Brooklyn Eagle*, July 3, 1953: 11.

12   Arthur Daley, "Sports of the Times," *New York Times*, March 4, 1956: S2.

13   Zander Hollander, "It's Look but Don't Touch for Scouts Tailing Loes," *New York World-Telegram and Sun*, June 15, 1948.

14   "Bryant in Final on Loes No-Hitter," *Brooklyn Eagle*, June 15, 1948: 15.

15   Zander Hollander, "Pro Ball Modifies Loes, But He's Still Hot Stuff," *New York World-Telegram and Sun*, July 12, 1996.

16   "Bryant Gains City P.S.A.L. Title on Brilliant One-Hitter by Loes," *Brooklyn Eagle*, June 26, 1948: 7.

17   Breslin, 116.

18 Zander Hollander, "It's Look but Don't Touch for Scouts Tailing Loes."

19 James Murphy, "All-Stars Leave for Washington," *Brooklyn Eagle*, July 26, 1948: 13.

20 'Loes Stars in Debut as Semi-Pro Hurler,' *Brooklyn Eagle*, August 16, 1948.

21 Breslin, 116.

22 Ibid.

23 *The Sporting News*, February 4, 1953: 6.

24 Ben Gould, "Bonus Player Loes Faces Jump to Flock in Only One Season," *Brooklyn Eagle*, April 27, 1949: 23.

25 "Dodgers Call Up Bankhead, 4 Others," *Brooklyn Eagle*, October 10, 1949: 24.

26 Joe Lee, "Dodgers Lose Billy Loes to Uncle Sam," *Brooklyn Eagle*, February 7, 1951: 20.

27 "Billy Loes of Dodgers Get Out of Army," *Brooklyn Eagle*, October 20, 1951: 6.

28 "Loes Due for Discharge," *Brooklyn Eagle*, October 16, 1951: 12.

29 *The Sporting News*, August 27, 1952: 3.

30 Breslin, 116.

31 "Dodger Chief Brands Loes Paternity Case 'Blackmail,'" *Brooklyn Eagle*, October 20, 1952: 1.

32 Breslin, 117.

33 *The Sporting News*, August 27, 1952: 3.

34 Breslin, 118.

35 Game Six of the 1952 World Series, You Tube, youtube.com/watch?v=ry-qwiXt82w.

36 Dave Anderson, "Erskine Rates as Only Brooks Sold?? Starter," *Brooklyn Eagle*, September 9, 1953: 19.

37 Tommy Holmes, "Scatter Shot at the Sports Scene," *Brooklyn Eagle*," August 24, 1953: 13.

38 "Loes to Know No Behavior Pattern," *Brooklyn Eagle*, March 26, 1954: 14.

39 Harold C. Burr, "Billy Loes Is Not Alone in Indifference to Game," *Brooklyn Eagle*, April 2, 1954: 2.

40 "Loes Termed 'A Mystery' by Flock Manager," *Brooklyn Eagle*, June 21, 1954: 13.

41 Dave Anderson, "Absence of Dodgers Spirit Annoys Alston in Drive for Second Place," *Brooklyn Eagle*, September 20, 1954: 19.

42 Watch the entire movie on YouTube. youtube.com/watch?v=Z-PaIYL-Neoc.

43 "Flatbush Boy, Gaining Fame on TV, Is Still Kid at Home,' *Brooklyn Eagle*, March 4, 1954: 7. In the film, the ghost of Red O'Malley, a deceased Dodgers star hurler, appears before Roogie and provides him with the bump that transforms him into the "miracle kid with the super zoom ball." Rob Edelman adds: In the film, Red O'Malley is nothing less than saintly, and even is patronizingly referred to as the "Great O'Malley." One has to ask: Is there any connection here to the name of the real Dodgers owner?

44 Jane Corby, "'Duel in the Sun,' 'Roogie Bump' Share Boro Paramount Bill," *Brooklyn Eagle*, October 13, 1954: 12.

45 *The Sporting News*, January 19, 1955: 13.

46 Dave Anderson, "Weirdie Loes May Mellow With Age," *Brooklyn Eagle*, December 29, 1954: 17.

47 United Press, "Billy Loes Is Baseball Gem, Dodgers Say," *Logansport* (Indiana) *Pharos-Tribune*, January 12, 1955: 18.

48 *The Sporting News*, October 12, 1955: 7.

49 Orr, 94.

50 Ibid.

51 United Press International, "'Orioles' Loes Seeks 'Comeback' Honors," *Austin* (Minnesota) *Herald*, June 26, 1957: 12.

52 *The Sporting News*, July 17, 1957: 15.

53 *The Sporting News*, June 11, 1958: 11.

54 UPI, "Loes, Orioles Parting," *New York World Telegram and Sun*, June 2, 1958.

55 "Orioles Give Up, Loes Headed for Minors," *New York World Telegram and Sun*, March 13, 1959.

56 Milton Richman, UPI, "Loes Quits Due to Conditions," *Tyrone* (Pennsylvania) *Daily Herald*, February 10, 1962: 8.

57 Ibid.

58 Bill Madden, UPI, "Ex-Dodger Pitcher Billy Loes, Who Once 'Lost' Ground Ball in the Sun, Has Found Himself." [Article dated October 10, 1973. Player's Hall of Fame file].

59 Ibid.

60 Michael George, "Ex-Bum Loes Says Baseball Shouldn't Dodge Brooklyn," *New York Post*, June 11, 1990.

61 Richard Goldstein, "Billy Loes, Quirky Pitcher for Dodgers, Dies at 80," *New York Times*, July 27, 2010.

CHRISTY MATHEWSON

BY EDDIE FRIERSON

IN THE TIME WHEN GIANTS walked the earth and roamed the Polo Grounds, none was more honored than Christy Mathewson. Delivering all four of his pitches, including his famous "fadeaway" (now called a screwball), with impeccable control and an easy motion, the right-handed Mathewson was the greatest pitcher of the Deadball Era's first decade, compiling a 2.13 ERA over 17 seasons and setting modern National League records for wins in a season (37), wins in a career (373), and consecutive 20-win seasons (12). Aside from his pitching achievements, he was the greatest all-around hero of the Deadball Era, a handsome, college-educated man who lifted the rowdy world of baseball to gentlemanliness. Matty was the basis, many say, for the idealized athlete Frank Merriwell, an inspiration to many authors over the years, and the motivation for an Off-Broadway play based on his life and writings. "He gripped the imagination of a country that held a hundred million people and held this grip with a firmer hold than any man of his day or time," wrote sportswriter Grantland Rice.[1]

The oldest of six children of Minerva (Capwell) and Gilbert Mathewson, a Civil War veteran who became a post-office worker and farmer, Christopher Mathewson was born on August 12, 1880, in Factoryville, Pennsylvania, a small town in the northeastern part of the state, not far from the New York border. His forebears, original followers of Roger Williams in Rhode Island, had settled in the region as the nation began to expand westward after the Revolutionary War. The blond-haired, blue-eyed Christy was always big for his age—he eventually grew to 6-feet-1 1/2 and 195 pounds—and his playmates called him "Husk." At age 14 he pitched for the Factoryville town team. Christy continued pitching for semipro teams in the area while attending Keystone Academy, a Factoryville prep school founded by his grandmother. The summer after his graduation from Keystone, Christy was pitching for the team from Honesdale, Pennsylvania, when a left-handed teammate named Dave Williams, who later pitched three games for the Boston Americans in 1902, taught him the fadeaway.

In September 1898 Mathewson enrolled at Bucknell University in Lewisburg, 75 miles west of Factoryville. He pitched for the baseball team and played center on the basketball team, but football was his chief claim to fame at Bucknell, which played a rugged schedule that included powerhouses such as Penn State, Army, and Navy. For three years Christy was the varsity's first-string fullback, punter, and drop kicker; no less an authority than Walter Camp, the originator of the All-America team, called him "the greatest drop-kicker in intercollegiate competition."[2] Majoring in forestry, Mathewson also was a top-flight student who excelled in extracurricular activities, serving as class president and joining the band, glee club, two literary societies, and two fraternities. It was also at Bucknell that he met his future bride, Jane Stoughton.

During the summer after his freshman year, Mathewson signed his first professional contract with Taunton, Massachusetts, of the New England League. He pitched in 17 games and went 2-13. To make a bad season worse, Taunton folded and the players had to arrange a Labor Day exhibition just to raise funds for their transportation home. Before the start of the Bucknell-Penn football game that fall (in which Matty kicked two long-range field goals, then worth five points apiece, the same as touchdowns), an old major-league pitcher named Phenomenal Smith signed him to a contract with Norfolk of the Virginia League for the following summer. Reporting right after final exams, Mathewson became an immediate sensation in the Virginia League, amassing a 20-2 record by mid-July. After the last of those victories,

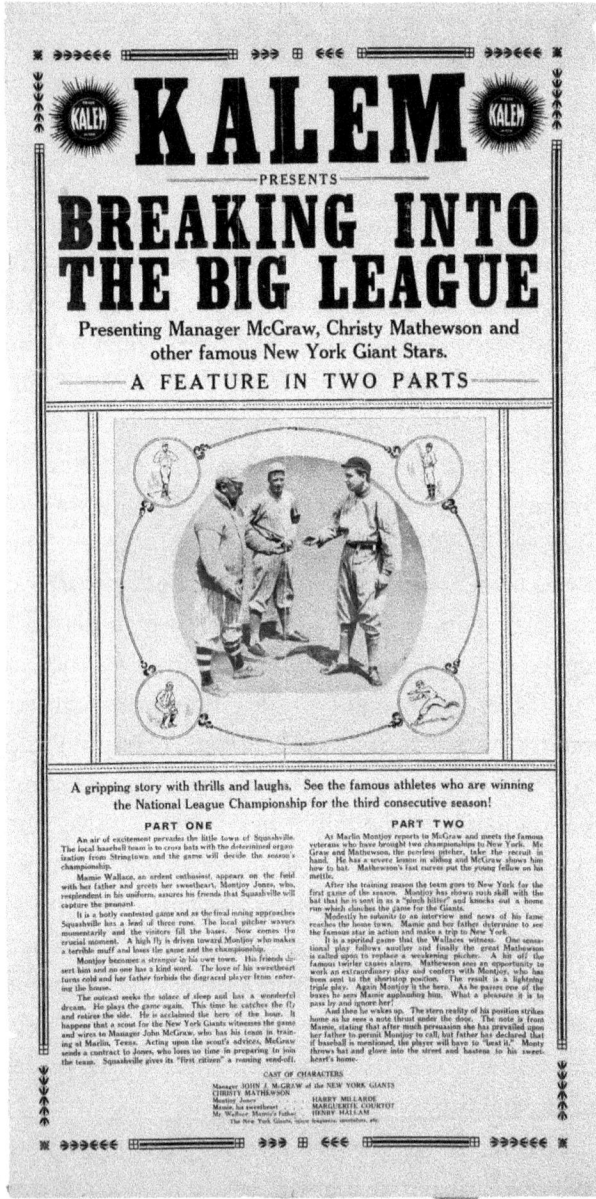

Smith took Matty aside in the clubhouse and offered him a choice between being sold to Philadelphia or New York of the National League. Christy chose New York, thinking the Giants needed pitching more than the Phillies, and made his major-league debut on July 17, 1900, one month shy of his 20th birthday.

Mathewson did little more than pitch batting practice for the Giants, becoming so frustrated that he wrote a friend, "I don't give a rap whether they sign me or not."[3] Towards the end of the season he received two starting assignments and lost both, ending the year winless in three decisions with a 5.08 ERA. The Giants returned him to Norfolk. That offseason the Cincinnati Reds drafted him for $100, then promptly traded him back to the Giants for a washed-up Amos Rusie. It was part of a collusive master plan to save $900; the Giants would have had to pay $1,000 to Norfolk if they'd kept Mathewson after the season, and Reds owner John T. Brush was negotiating to purchase the Giants from Andrew Freedman. In 1901, his first full season in the majors, Mathewson pitched a no-hitter against the St. Louis Cardinals on July 15 and went 20-17 with a 2.41 ERA for the seventh-place Giants. New York fans started calling their ace "The Big Six." Matty thought it was because of his height, but the nickname probably originated when sportswriter Sam Crane compared him to New York City's Big Six Fire Company, the fastest to put out the fire.[4]

The Giants floundered again at the start of 1902, prompting new manager Horace Fogel to play Mathewson in three games at first base and four in the outfield in addition to his pitching duties. Many have implied that this was a sign of Fogel's ineptitude, but years later Matty defended Fogel, explaining that the manager knew he was a good hitter and fielder and was willing to try anything to turn around his team. The experiment ended, however, when John McGraw took over as manager on July 19. To that point Mathewson had won only one game, but over the rest of the season he won 13, eight of them shutouts, winding up at 14-17 with a 2.12 ERA as the Giants finished last. That winter Matty married Jane Stoughton while McGraw rebuilt his team through trades and free-agent acquisitions. The Mathewsons honeymooned in Savannah, where the Giants held spring training. Blanche McGraw took the young pitcher's wife under her wing, while the McGraws treated Christy like the son they never had.

Christy Mathewson enjoyed a breakout year in 1903, the first of three consecutive 30-win seasons. That year he went 30-13 with a 2.26 ERA and a career-high 267 strikeouts, which stood as the NL record until Sandy Koufax struck out 269 in 1961. Matty was just as good in 1904, leading the Giants to the NL pennant with a 33-12 record and 2.03 ERA, but the following year he was even better. Mathewson was 31-9 with a miniscule 1.28 ERA, capping off his banner 1905 season with the best World Series any pitcher ever had. Opposing him in the opener on October 9 was Philadelphia's Eddie Plank, a fellow Pennsylvanian who'd pitched against him several times while attending Gettysburg College. Mathewson got the victory, as he had in each of their college match-ups, shutting out the Athletics on four hits. After Chief Bender shut out the Giants in Game Two, Matty was ready to pitch again in Game Three but received an extra day's rest when the game was rained out. On October 12 he shut out the Athletics, 9-0, on another four-hitter. The next day Joe McGinnity defeated Plank, 1-0, and Mathewson returned on just one day's rest to clinch the Series with a 2-0 victory over Bender. Within a span of six days, he'd pitched 27 innings, allowing 14 hits, one walk, and no runs while striking out 18. The next week Matty and his catcher Frank Bowerman went hunting in Bowerman's hometown of Romeo, Michigan. Coaxed to pitch for Romeo in its final game of the season against archrival Lake Orion, Christy lost, 5-0, to an obscure group of semipros.

Mathewson was the toast of New York. Endorsement offers poured in, with Matty "pitching" Arrow shirt collars, leg garters (for socks), undergarments, sweaters, athletic equipment, and numerous other products. He received an offer to put his name on a pool hall/saloon but turned it down when his mother asked, "Do you really want your name associated with a place like that?"[5] But in a pattern that haunted him for the rest of his life, disappointment and tragedy followed his greatest triumph. In 1906 Matty caught a dose of diphtheria and nearly died, struggling to a 22-12 record and an uncharacteristic 2.97 ERA. Late that season the Giants called up his brother Henry, who was only 19 years old. In his first start Henry walked 14 Chicago Cubs. Disappointing though the '06 season was, Matty experienced his greatest joy on October 6 when Jane gave birth to the couple's first and only child, a son they named Christopher Jr.

Mathewson's biggest year came in 1908, when he set career highs in wins (37), games (56), innings (390 2/3), and shutouts (11). His control was never better, averaging less than one walk per nine innings. Matty's season ended in disappointment, however, when he took a no-decision in the "Merkle Game" and lost to Mordecai Brown, 4-2, in the one-game playoff. By his own admission he had "nothing on the ball" in that contest, and he also felt responsible that four people had lost their lives in falling accidents at the Polo Grounds that day (according to Christy's second cousin, Harold "Alvie" Reynolds, if Mathewson had only said the word, the Giants would've refused to play and those tragedies would've been averted).[6] Compounding his guilt, in January 1909 Christy found the body of his youngest brother, Nicholas, dead in his parents' barn of a self-inflicted gunshot wound. Two years earlier, Detroit Tigers manager Hughie Jennings had wanted to sign the 17-year-old Nicholas and bring him directly to the majors, but Christy had advised against it.[7]

Mathewson nonetheless bounced back to go 25-6 with a career-best 1.14 ERA in 1909. He helped the

The legendary Christy Mathewson, whose screen credits include Matty's Decision, Love and Baseball, *and* Breaking Into the Big League.

Giants win three consecutive NL pennants from 1911 to 1913, leading the NL in ERA in both 1911 (1.99) and 1913 (2.06). In 1914, however, the 34-year-old Mathewson started experiencing a constant pain in his left side towards the end of the season. Doctors found nothing wrong and told him he was just getting old. It affected his performance, however; his ERA increased to 3.00 in 1914 even though he still managed to win 24 games, and the following year he was just 8-14 with a 3.58 ERA. By the midpoint of the 1916 season Matty had won just three games. Knowing that his days as an effective pitcher were behind him, he decided that he wanted to manage. On July 20 McGraw came through for his friend, trading him for Cincinnati Reds player-manager Buck Herzog on condition that he replace Herzog as manager.

Mathewson was a good manager who might have become a great one, but he could do little with Herzog's leftovers and finished tied for last in 1916. At least he added some interest to an otherwise dismal season, pitching one last game against his old rival on "Mordecai Brown Day" in Chicago. In the only major-league game he ever pitched in a uniform other than New York's, the 36-year-old Matty yielded 15 hits but defeated a nearly 40-year-old Brown, 10-8, giving him the 373rd and final victory of his 17-year career. In 1917 Mathewson guided Cincinnati to a 78-76 record, its first winning season since 1909, but tragedy struck on July 1 when his brother Henry died of tuberculosis at age 30, leaving behind four young daughters. Matty's Reds continued their improvement in 1918, but on August 9 he suspended his notorious first baseman, Hal Chase, after confronting him about some suspicious-looking misplays and a $50 payment to pitcher Jimmy Ring. Cincinnati went on to finish third but by that point Mathewson was in France, having been commissioned a captain in the Army's Chemical Warfare Division. While Mathewson was overseas, Chase's case came before the National Commission; without the star witness against him, Chase was exonerated.

While in France Mathewson endured a bad bout of influenza and was exposed to mustard gas during

a training exercise. He was hospitalized and apparently had recovered by the time he returned to the United States in the spring. On his arrival, however, he discovered that Pat Moran was managing the Reds. When owner Garry Herrmann didn't hear from Mathewson that he'd be back in time for spring training (both had written to each other but neither had received the other's message), he did what he felt he needed to and hired a new manager. Mathewson resigned from the Reds and accepted a position from McGraw as assistant manager of the Giants. In 1919 New York finished second to the Matty-built Reds, and Mathewson covered the World Series for the *New York Times*. Before the first game he saw several Chicago White Sox conversing with Chase in the lobby of Cincinnati's Hotel Sinton. It has been rumored that, doubting the legitimacy of the Series before a single pitch was thrown, Mathewson discussed the possibility of a fix with sportswriter Hugh Fullerton and agreed to circle suspicious-looking plays on his scorecard.[8] Angry at what he witnessed, believing that "his" team would have won the Series on its own merit, Matty forwarded his findings to the National Commission and walked away from the Black Sox Scandal.

Returning to the Giants in 1920-21, Mathewson was unable to shake the cough that had plagued him since joining the club in 1919, and the pain in his left side was back and worse than ever. The physicians who examined him in 1921 immediately diagnosed the condition as tuberculosis. It's possible that he'd contracted the disease from his brother Henry and had it since 1914, but the physicians who'd examined him then were looking for muscle strain, not lesions irritating his lung and rubbing the inside of his ribs. Along with his wife, Jane, Christy set off for the tuberculosis sanitarium in Saranac Lake, New York, where he initially received a prognosis of six weeks to live. For the next two years he fought as hard as he ever had on the diamond to recover from the deadly disease. By the winter of 1922-23 Matty thought he was strong enough to return to baseball.

That winter McGraw urged Judge Emil Fuchs of New York to purchase the Boston Braves. "And if you buy them," McGraw said, "I've got the man who can run the club for you."[9] On February 11, 1923, Fuchs announced that he'd bought the Braves and Christy Mathewson would run the club as president. His physicians warned him that he couldn't undertake too much, but Matty nonetheless threw himself into the task of rebuilding the pitiful Braves. Some reports say that his cough returned in 1925 after he was soaked in a spring-training rain shower. Whether it was stress, the rain, or a disease that wouldn't give in, Mathewson's body began to fail and he was forced to return to Saranac Lake where he died on October 7, 1925. On that day McGraw was in Pittsburgh, covering the World Series for a newspaper syndicate. When he received the news, he immediately left for New York to meet his wife, Blanche. Together they went to Saranac Lake to be with Jane Mathewson and Christy Jr.

Three days later, with his manager, wife, and son standing graveside, Christy Mathewson was laid to rest in Lewisburg, Pennsylvania, in view of the Bucknell campus. Today there is a memorial gate at the entrance to the campus, built in 1927 with donations from every big-league team, and in 1989 the Bison football stadium was renovated and re-dedicated as Christy Mathewson Memorial Stadium.

Note: This biography originally appeared in Tom Simon, ed., *Deadball Stars of the National League* (Washington, D.C.: Brassey's, Inc., 2004).

SOURCES

For this biography, the author used a number of contemporary sources, especially those found in the subject's file at the National Baseball Hall of Fame Library.

NOTES

1. Grantland Rice, "Christy Mathewson," obituary, *New York Herald-Tribune*, October 9, 1925.
2. *A Loomis Field Hero* (Christy Mathewson Stadium Re-Dedication Program), Bucknell University Athletics, September 30, 1989, 3.
3. Personal letter written to Earl Manchester by Christy Mathewson, dated July 26, 1900. Facsimile copy in author's possession.

4   The Big Six Fire Company in New York won several contests among New York fire departments in the early part of the twentieth century and was regarded as the quickest able to respond to an emergency. The nickname for Mathewson ("The Big Six") is noted in Frank Graham, *The New York Giants: An Informal History of A Great Baseball Club* (New York: G P Putnam and Sons, 1952), 30.

5   Author interview with Alvie Reynolds, August 1984, Factoryville, Pennsylvania.

6   Ibid.

7   Author interview with Grace Mathewson Van Lengen (niece of Christy Mathewson, daughter of Henry Mathewson) Taped Interview, August 15, 1985, Liverpool, New York.

8   Hugh Fullerton, "Is Big League Baseball Being Run for Gamblers, with Players in the Deal?" *New York Evening World*, December 15, 1919. Fullerton went into a lot more detail about his World Series conversations with Mathewson in Hugh Fullerton, "I Recall," *The Sporting News*, October 17, 1935. Thanks to Jacob Pomrenke for these citations.

9   *Baseball's Immortals* No. 7 (Cooperstown, New York: Home Plate Press, 1961), 27.

JOHN MCGRAW

BY DON JENSEN

JOHN MCGRAW WAS PERHAPS the National League's most influential figure in the Deadball Era. From 1902 to 1932 he led the New York Giants to 10 National League pennants, three World Series championships, and 21 first- or second-place finishes in 29 full seasons at their helm. His 2,784 managerial victories are second only to Connie Mack's 3,731, but in 1927 Mack himself proclaimed, "There has been only one manager—and his name is McGraw."[1]

The pugnacious McGraw's impact on the game, moreover, was even greater than his record suggests. As a player he helped develop "inside baseball," which put a premium on strategy and guile, and later managed the way he'd played, seeking out every advantage for his Giants. Known as Mugsy (a nickname he detested) and Little Napoleon (for his dictatorial methods), McGraw administered harsh tongue-lashings to his players and frequently fought with umpires; he was ejected from 118 contests during his career, far more than any other manager. "McGraw eats gunpowder every morning for breakfast and washes it down with warm blood," said Giants coach Arlie Latham.[2]

The oldest of eight children of Ellen (Comerfert) and John McGraw, an Irish immigrant who fought in the Civil War and later worked in railroad maintenance, John Joseph McGraw was born in working-class poverty on April 7, 1873, in the village of Truxton, New York, about 25 miles south of Syracuse. During the winter of 1884-85 a diphtheria epidemic claimed Ellen and three of her children, leaving John Sr., a heavy drinker, alone to raise Johnny and the other four survivors. One night in the fall of 1885, 12-year-old Johnny received such a severe beating from his father that he moved across the street to the Truxton House Inn, where a kindly widow named Mary Goddard took him in and raised him along with her own two sons. Besides attending school, Johnny performed chores around the hotel, delivered newspapers, and peddled candy, fruit, and magazines out of a basket on the train from Cortland to Elmira. He used the money to buy new baseballs and the annual Spalding guide, parts of which he memorized.[3]

At 16 years old, Johnny McGraw stood barely 5-feet-7 and weighed little more than 100 pounds, but that didn't stop him from becoming the star pitcher for the local Truxton Grays. When Truxton's manager, Bert Kenney, became part owner and player-manager of the Olean franchise in the New York-Penn League in 1890, Johnny begged for and received a place on the team. In his first game on May 18, McGraw played third base and made eight errors in 10 chances. He was released after six games but caught on with Wellsville of the Western New York League, batting .364 in 24 games.[4]

One of his teammates was a former National Leaguer named Al Lawson, who was organizing a winter tour of Cuba. McGraw went along and played shortstop for the "American All-Stars." On the way home, Lawson's team stopped in Gainesville, Florida, to play a spring-training exhibition against the NL's Cleveland Spiders. McGraw collected three doubles in five at-bats, receiving national publicity when the game story appeared in *The Sporting News*. From among the resulting offers he received for the coming season, he chose Cedar Rapids of the Illinois-Iowa League and batted .276 in 85 games as the club's regular shortstop.[5]

That August McGraw made his major-league debut with the Baltimore Orioles of the American Association, filling in at various positions and hitting .270 in 33 games. In 1892 the AA disbanded and Baltimore was absorbed into the 12-team National League. McGraw started the season as utilityman but took over as the regular third baseman after Ned Hanlon was appointed manager in midseason. Under

Hanlon's tutelage, McGraw became the NL's best leadoff hitter, batting over .320 for nine straight years, twice leading the league in runs and walks, and stealing 436 bases; his career on-base percentage of .466 ranks behind only those of Ted Williams and Babe Ruth. McGraw choked up on the bat and swung with a short, chopping motion that diminished his power, but he could place the ball virtually anywhere he wanted. He also wasn't above cheating. "McGraw uses every low and contemptible method that his erratic brain can conceive to win a play by a dirty trick," wrote one reporter.[6]

With players like Willie Keeler, Joe Kelley, Hughie Jennings, Wilbert Robinson, Steve Brodie, Sadie McMahon, and Dan Brouthers, most of whom remained associated with and often employed by McGraw in later years, Hanlon's Orioles won three consecutive pennants in 1894-96 and finished second in 1897-98. Concerned about slumping attendance in Baltimore, Orioles owner Henry Von der Horst tried to transfer most of his key personnel to Brooklyn in 1899, but McGraw and his friend Robinson refused to report, claiming business interests that demanded their attention in Baltimore. Von der Horst reluctantly let them stay, and the 26-year-old McGraw managed the Orioles to an 86-62 record and a surprising fourth-place finish, 15 games behind Hanlon's first-place Brooklyn Superbas.[7]

*John McGraw, the famed New York Giants skipper, who appeared in vaudeville and in the movies (*Fighting Mad, Detective Swift, Breaking Into the Big League, One Touch of Nature...*) during the second decade of the 20th century.*

Baltimore might have done even better had not another tragedy befallen its manager. In late August McGraw's wife, Mary (Minnie), died from a ruptured appendix; a grieving John missed much of September. The Orioles disbanded when the NL contracted to eight teams in 1900 and, after again refusing to report to Brooklyn, McGraw was sold to the St. Louis Cardinals along with Robinson. Agreeing to go only when the reserve clause was removed from his contract, he signed for a salary of $10,000—the highest in baseball history—and hit .344 in 99 games.[8]

In 1901 McGraw returned to Baltimore as manager and part owner of that city's franchise in Ban Johnson's new American League. Throughout that season and the next, he and Johnson quarreled constantly—the latter habitually supported his umpires in their frequent disputes with McGraw, and tension also existed over McGraw's interest in the team's ownership. Johnson finally suspended McGraw indefinitely in July 1902, and at that point the temperamental manager jumped back to the NL as player-manager of the New York Giants, even though he'd recently married a Baltimore woman, Blanche Sindall. One of his first acts New York was to release nine players, despite the protests of Giants owner Andrew Freedman. McGraw also brought six key players with him, including pitcher Joe McGinnity, catcher Roger Bresnahan, and first baseman Dan McGann. The Giants finished last that season but rose to second in 1903, even though McGraw's much-injured knee finally gave out for good during spring training that year, effectively ending his career as a player.[9]

In 1904 the Giants became NL champions, finishing with a won-lost record of 106-47, 13 games ahead of the Chicago Cubs. McGraw and new Giants owner John T. Brush so detested Ban Johnson and his league that they refused to play the Boston Americans in what would've been the second World Series. After winning again in 1905, however, they agreed to play the AL-champion Philadelphia Athletics. New York triumphed in four out of the five games, three of them shutouts by Christy Mathewson. McGraw led the Giants to pennants again in 1911, 1912, 1913, and

1917, but lost the World Series each year. His regular-season success was due to his knack for evaluating and acquiring players who fit into his system, which stressed good pitching, sound defense, and aggressive baserunning. McGraw bought, sold, and traded players more than his counterparts, grooming prospects for years before letting them play regularly. He also was an innovator, using pinch-runners, pinch-hitters and relief pitchers more than other managers.[10]

Many commentators believed that McGraw's lack of World Series success was due to his strong preference for players who fit his system. The Giants were generally considered less talented than other top teams—they were a second-class team with a first-class manager, claimed the Cubs' Johnny Evers. Until left fielder Ross Youngs entered the league in 1917, catcher Roger Bresnahan was McGraw's only Deadball Era position player who eventually made the Hall of Fame. McGraw's teams also had trouble reacting to events on the field. They sometimes made mental errors in big games, as though they didn't know what to do or were paralyzed at the thought of how the Old Man might react if they lost. After New York's 1913 World Series defeat by the Athletics, even the usually loyal Mathewson blamed McGraw for the team's setbacks in an article ghostwritten under his name in *Everybody's Magazine*. The Giants, said the article, were a "team of puppets being manipulated from the bench on a string."[11]

McGraw's fiery personality made him fascinating to contemporaries outside sports. Gamblers, show-business people, and politicians were drawn to him. As his celebrity grew, McGraw became increasingly involved in various, sometimes questionable off-field activities. He ventured into vaudeville for 15 weeks in 1912, appearing with such acts as "Odiva the Goldfish Lady." For a while McGraw owned a poolroom in Manhattan with gambler Arnold Rothstein, who later became the principal financial backer of the 1919 World Series fix, and he sometimes spent winters in Cuba, where he and Giants owner Charles Stoneham owned a share of a racetrack and casino. When Stoneham bought the Giants in 1919, McGraw became vice president of the

Babe Ruth and John McGraw; in their day, both baseball legends made their way onto movie screens.

club and minority owner. Between 1912 and 1923 he helped resolve various ownership crises of the Boston Braves—which usually paid off in trades that helped New York more than Boston. Fatefully, McGraw also was instrumental in Col. Jacob Ruppert's purchase of the Yankees and the decision to allow that team to share the Polo Grounds when the Giants were on the road.[12]

In 1920 Babe Ruth arrived to play for the lowly Yankees. The team's attendance soared as Ruth began hitting home runs out of the Polo Grounds, prompting an enraged McGraw to instruct Stoneham to evict their upstart tenants. In what was widely viewed as a battle between Inside Baseball and the new Power Game, McGraw had the consolation of beating the Yankees in the World Series of 1921-22 ("I signaled for every ball that was pitched to Ruth during the last World's Series," he gloated). The tide turned for good in 1923, however, when the Yankees crushed the Giants, four games to two, for their first world championship, with Ruth clouting three home runs. In 1924 the Giants won a record fourth consecutive NL pennant but lost another World Series, this time to the Washington Nationals. As the years passed, McGraw evolved with the game. Early in his career his teams emphasized the stolen base, but as the long ball began to dominate baseball, McGraw—despite his personal dislike of the home run—adapted to the change. For the rest of the decade and the early 1930s, the Giants fielded some fine teams but were never good enough to win. Plagued by health problems, McGraw resigned on June 3, 1932.[13]

McGraw made his last major public appearance at Comiskey Park in July 1933, managing the National League against Connie Mack's American Leaguers in baseball's first All-Star Game. He was 60 years old when he died at his home in New Rochelle, New York, on February 25, 1934, of prostate cancer and uremia—but mostly, according to one reporter, because he was no longer top dog. He was buried in New Cathedral Cemetery in Baltimore, near several of his old Orioles teammates, as well as his first wife, Mary. McGraw was inducted into the National Baseball Hall of Fame in 1937. Blanche McGraw inherited her husband's stock in the Giants and carried on his memory, frequently attending games with Mathewson's widow. Her most tragic time, at least according to the New York newspapers, was on that September day in 1957 when the Giants played their final game at the Polo Grounds before departing for San Francisco. She said the move would've broken John's heart. Nonetheless, she was present at Seals Stadium in April 1958 at the team's first game on the West Coast, and again when Candlestick Park opened two years later. Blanche McGraw died on November 5, 1962, only a few weeks after attending the New York games of the Giants-Yankees World Series.[14]

SOURCES

Articles

Lamb, Bill. "A History of the New York Giants Franchise," *Outside the Lines*, Vol. 22 No. 2, Fall 2016, Society for American Baseball Research Business of Baseball Committee, sabr.box.com/shared/static/jkkos9d0isz30ardpcw648zoxdwydrcz.pdf.

Lamb, Bill. "Manhattan Field," sabr.org/bioproj/park/8a2a9a1f.

Mathewson, Christy. "Why We Lost Three World's Championships," *Everybody's Magazine*, vol. XXXI, July-December 1914: 537-547.

Books

Graham, Frank. *The New York Giants: An Informal History of a Great Baseball Club* (Carbondale: Southern Illinois Press, 2002).

Glueckstein, Fred. *The '27 Yankees* (Xlibris Corporation, July 26, 2005). Greenberg, Eric Rolfe. *The Celebrant* (Lincoln and London: University of Nebraska Press, 1983).

Hynd, Noel. *The Giants of the Polo Grounds: The Glorious Times of Baseball's New York Giants* (Dallas: Taylor Publishing, 1995).

Klein, Maury. *Stealing Games: How John McGraw Transformed baseball With the 1911 New York Giants* (New York: Bloomsbury Press, 2016).

Mansch, Larry D. *Rube Marquard: The Life and Times of a Baseball Hall of Famer* (Jefferson, North Carolina: McFarland & Co., 1998).

Mathewson, Christy. (Introduction by Eric Rolfe Greenberg). *Pitching in a Pinch or Baseball From the Inside* (Lincoln: University of Nebraska Press 1994).

McGraw, John J. *My Thirty Years in Baseball* (Lincoln and London: University of Nebraska Press (reprint of book published in 1923).

Robinson, Ray. *Matty: An American Hero* (New York: Oxford University Press, 1993).

Seymour, Harold. *Baseball: The Golden Age* (New York: Oxford University Press, 1971).

Smith, Robert. *Baseball: The Game, the Men Who Have Played It, and its Place in American Life* (New York: Simon and Schuster, 1947).

Stark, Benton. *The Year They Called Off the World Series: A True Story* (Garden City, New York: Avery Publishing Group, 1991).

Newspapers and Magazines

Baseball Magazine, New York Herald, New York Times, Sporting Life, The Sporting News.

NOTES

1. baseballhall.org/hof/mcgraw-john.
2. thejeopardyfan.com/2016/06/june-1-1932-john-mcgraws-final-mlb-game-as-new-york-giants-manager.html.
3. John McGraw file, Giamatti Research Library, National Baseball Hall of Fame. Accessed September 3, 2017.
4. Ibid.
5. Ibid.
6. espn.go.com/page2/s/list/cheaters/ballplayers.html.
7. John McGraw file.
8. Ibid.
9. Ibid.
10. Ibid.
11. leaptoad.com/raindelay/matty/whywelost.shtml. Christy Mathewson, "Why We Lost Three World's Championships," *Everybody's Magazine*, vol XXXI, July-December 1914: 537-547.
12. John McGraw file.
13. Ibid.
14. Ibid.

GEORGE "CATFISH" METKOVICH

BY BILL NOWLIN

AMERICA AS A LAND OF IMmigrants sometimes produces a number of unexpected surprises. One of them was a Croatian nicknamed Catfish. The outfielder/first baseman George Michael Metkovich played in over 1,000 major-league games from 1943 to 1954, with a career batting average of .261 working for six different big-league teams. He was dubbed "a meteor—never a star."[1]

Metkovich was born in Angel's Camp, Calaveras County, California on October 8, 1920. His father John worked as a gold miner, a grinderman in a gold mill. John and his wife Kate (Klaich) were both immigrants from Croatia, John arriving in America in 1901 and Kate in 1907. Both became naturalized U. S. citizens in 1908. They had children—Kris, Helen, Louis, Martin, George, and John.[2]

John Metkovich died in Fresno in the late 1920s, sometime between 1927 and 1929. At the time of the 1930 census, the family was in Los Angeles. At least as late as 1943, Kate Klaich still spoke her native Croatian.[3] She died in 1984.

George attended Brad Hart (or Bret Harte) School for grades one through nine, and then graduated from Fremont High School in Los Angeles. He'd planned to go on to college and become a physical education coach, but his talents on the ballfield opened up opportunities in baseball. Metkovich also played basketball in high school. He was first-team All-City in 1938-39.[4] At Fremont High, he played for Leo Haserot, the same coach who had helped develop Bobby Doerr, Mickey Owen, Steve Mesner, Jerry Priddy, and Hal Spindel.

All the Metkovich boys played baseball in high school. Chris signed professionally and played center field with Macon in 1937.[5] He reportedly got as far in professional ball at Houston in the Texas League.[6] In early 1947, younger brother John Metkovich signed to play pro ball. In 1952, he was still seen in pro ranks, playing for Ottawa, and in 1953 for Sacramento.

George played semipro baseball in 1938. He was just 17 when he was spotted and signed by scout Marty Krug of the Detroit Tigers, who signed him to a Beaumont, Texas contract. George graduated during the winter of 1938-39. He went to spring training with Beaumont, and was assigned to play for the Fulton (Kentucky) Tigers in the Class-D Kitty (Kentucky-Illinois-Tennessee League). He put in a full 1939 season for Fulton, playing every one of the team's 126 games as their first baseman while batting for a .310 average, with 12 homers, 10 triples, and 40 doubles. Fulton finished seventh in the eight-team league. At the very end of the season, he got into three games at Class C, with Henderson Oilers of the East Texas League. He was 0-for-6.

Then he was emancipated—set free by the January 14, 1940 "emancipation proclamation" issued by Commissioner Kenesaw Mountain Landis, which made him a free agent. Metkovich and 92 other players in the Detroit system were all declared free agents at once, a harsh penalty promulgated by the commissioner to punish the Tigers after a nine-month investigation that characterized the Tigers as having "mis-handled" the players. Five major leaguers and 88 minor leaguers were all "set free" at once. The team was said to have acted to "cover up" its players in "wholesale violation" of the rules.[7] The commissioner also fined the Cubs and Browns for meddling, in contacting some of the Tigers players before they were truly free agents. He warned other clubs of stronger action if they didn't handle player transactions more properly in the future. The action hadn't come out of the blue; two years earlier, he had similarly freed 100 players in the Cardinals system.

George played semipro winter baseball in Los Angeles, and Boston Bees (the Braves were the Bees from 1936 through 1940) manager Casey Stengel signed the new free agent on February 13.[8] In making the announcement, Secretary John Quinn said, "Casey saw a lot of him in winter baseball circles out on the coast this season, and it was at the manager's instigation that we acquired him. Casey is crazy about this lad."[9] There had been some competition for his services and the team had had to pay him a bonus for signing.

He was 6-feet-1 and weighed 165 pounds, batting and throwing left-handed. By 1941, he'd filled out and put on another 20 pounds.

Metkovich picked up his nickname at Bradenton, Florida during spring training in 1940 with the Boston Bees. Manager Casey Stengel told sportswriter Frederick Lieb, "You've heard of a lot of injuries to ball players, but you can't tie this one. I've got a young first baseman by the name of Metkovich, who's in the hospital. Do you know how? He was attacked by a catfish…That catfish almost took his leg off."[10]

Metkovich himself told Lieb the story in some detail:

"One day after practice, Wilbur McElroy, a young Brave pitcher, and I were fishing off a bridge over the Manatee River. Wilbur pulled up a three-foot catfish, one of the biggest you ever saw, but the 'cat' swallowed the hook, and McElroy couldn't get it out. 'Give it a yank, will you?' he said.

"So I yanked, but nothing happened: I couldn't get the hook out. So I put the catfish on the bridge, put my foot on its back and tugged. In its dying gasp, that catfish raised a sharp fin out of its back — a sort of extra fin, I guess, and stuck it right through the bottom of my crepe sole shoe! It penetrated the bottom of the foot and almost came out at the instep.

"McElroy and I worked with it, but we couldn't get that fin out of my foot. It was a saw-tooth fin, and broke off. They took me to the Bradenton hospital, where they had to give me a local anesthetic. I couldn't play ball for a week, and for some time afterwards I had to play with a sponge on my foot."[11]

Stengel quipped, "It couldn't have been a catfish. It must have been filet of sole."[12]

During his playing career, he was often as not simply called "Cat," a nickname of a nickname.

It was another injury that robbed him of much of the 1940 season. He was optioned to Boston's Evansville Bees, in the Class-B Three-I League where he tore a ligament in his knee when sliding into second base during the June 7 game in Springfield. He was carried off the field and spent a good part of the season unable to play, coming back in time for 50 more games in the final couple of months; he managed only a .227 batting average. The knee still bothered him the following spring, and Boston had so many outfielders that they worked him out at first base. The Evansville Bees used him to an outfielder. He hit .287, with nearly a third of his hits extra-base hits (including 30 doubles). Evansville (with a lot of help from pitcher Warren Spahn) won the 1941 pennant.

In 1941, he married Peggy Morrison.

Advancing to the Single-A Eastern League, with the 1942 Hartford Bees, may have been a little too much for the still-young Metkovich. He started the season well, but after the first month he "failed to live up to advance notices" and tailed off sharply.[13] He hit .238 in 90 games. On July 31, he was returned to Evansville, where he played in 35 more games, batting .308.

With the country at war, Metkovich was classified 1-A and expected to be called to service at any time. He asked the Braves if they would let him play closer to home. The San Francisco Seals offered $500 to buy his contract, and the Braves accepted the offer on March 17, a conditional deal that allowed them to bring him back any time until June.[14] Working under Seals skipper Lefty O'Doul helped him, and he was a standout for San Francisco, drawing numerous comparisons to Ted Williams — though with a stronger outfield arm.[15] The Braves, though, never pulled the trigger to exercise their option and bring him back. It may be that they lost their rights to him, once again thanks to Commissioner Landis. The *Boston Globe* reported that Landis had "stepped in and declared Metkovich the full property of the Seals."[16]

Metkovich fully credited O'Doul, "Until I got to Lefty, nobody had spent any time coaching me at the plate, I'd had to go along, picking up what I could by myself…But O'Doul really went to work on me and he has a swell way of teaching you."[17]

In his first 71 Pacific Coast League games, he was hitting .325 and the Boston Red Sox, themselves decimated by players leaving for the service, purchased his contract for a reported $25,000 (and Dee Miles) on July 6, 1943.[18] Despite the Seals being in second place and Metkovich being considered "the backbone" of the team, Seals owner Charley Graham was under heavy financial pressure to pay off a large mortgage by September, or lose his ballclub. Scout Ernie Johnson had recommended Metkovich to the Sox, and Boston manager had actively pursued the possibility.[19]

At age 22, George Metkovich made his major-league debut for the Boston Red Sox on July 16 in Washington. He was 0-for-4 with two strikeouts. (In an exhibition game against the Washington Senators at Camp Meade on July 14, he had homered and singled.) It took until his third game to collect his first hit in the big leagues, but in the July 18 doubleheader he was 1-for-4 in the first game and 2-for-5 with a double in the second game. His first RBI was in the first game on the 21st, at Fenway Park against the visiting White Sox. He drove in the first run of a three-run rally in the bottom of the eighth that propelled the Red Sox from a 2-0 deficit to a 3-2 win.

Three days later, facing the St. Louis Browns, he hit his first home run, a three-run homer that was part of a four-RBI 3-for-5 day, the winning hit in the 5-3 game.

By season's end, he had played in every game since he'd joined the team (78 games), all but two in either

L to R: Tom McBride, Leon Culberson, and George "Catfish" Metkovich, who reported that he had roles in "11 movies altogether…."

right field or center. He'd batted .246 (.294 on-base percentage), driven in 27 runs and scored 34. He had five home runs, and recorded a .955 fielding percentage. His career fielding percentage in the majors was .976.

He played some ball in Los Angeles after the season, including a memorable exhibition game against Satchel Paige and the Baltimore Colored Giants. Playing in the Southern California Winter League was brought to a halt when Commissioner Landis announced he would fine him and 13 other major leagues for violating the rules against playing postseason exhibition games.[20]

At some point, Metkovich was declared 4-F, and thus not at likely to be drafted.

In April 1944, the Sox sold Tony Lupien and handed Metkovich the first-base job—though in the end, Lou Finney played more games at first with Metkovich in the outfield. He appeared in 134 games, scoring 94 runs (and driving in 59), with a .277 batting average. Fifty of the games were at first base. Probably his most satisfying game came on June 1 in Cleveland where his three-run homer with two outs in the ninth inning boosted Boston to a 7-6 win over the Indians—though he ranked the June 15 game (his son George Jr.'s date of birth), when he hit safely twice. The Red Sox put up a good fight for the pennant, in second place much of the year until very late August when they finally lost too many key players to the military. As late as September 16, they were only three games out of first, but then tumbled over the final two weeks to finish 12 games behind.

Opening Day 1945 saw Metkovich set a new major-league record for a first baseman, committing three errors in the same inning. He played 97 games at first base in 1945, only committing 12 other errors all season (for a .985 fielding percentage.) He drove in 62 runs (batting .260). For whatever reason, Metkovich's batting average in night games was a league-leading .421.[21] The Red Sox finished seventh.

With the war over, all the Red Sox stars came back in 1946. The team shot off to a start that saw them 21-3 as of May 10. They never looked back and finished 104-50, coasting to the pennant with a 12-game pad. The lack of competition in the final weeks may have hurt them when it came to the World Series against the Cardinals.

Rudy York had played first base most of the year, Metkovich working exclusively in the outfield, mostly in right field. He appeared in 86 games and hit .246 (though his .333 on-base percentage was the best of his career until the 1951 season), driving in 25 runs and scoring 42. One of the most exciting plays of his year came courtesy of his steal of home plate, with Ted Williams at bat, on June 23 against the Indians.

In the World Series, Cronin only put him in twice. He pinch hit for Jim Bagby in Game Four and flied out to left field. And in the final Game Seven, in the top of the eighth inning with Boston losing the game, 3-1, Metkovich pinch hit for Joe Dobson with one on and nobody out. Facing Murry Dickson, he doubled to left field and all of a sudden the Sox had the two runs they needed on second and third. Harry Brecheen came in and got the next two men out but then Dom DiMaggio tied the game up with a double. DiMaggio tried to stretch the double to a triple and came up lame. Thus he wasn't in center field when Harry Walker hit the ball to center in the bottom of the eighth, and Enos Slaughter scored all the way from first on his famous "Mad Dash." The Cardinals won the game, and the Series, 4-3.

Playing the Cardinals in 1947 spring training, Metkovich hit a homer to win the game on March 25, but he didn't make the team.

On April 1, 1947, the Cleveland Indians purchased Metkovich's contract from the Red Sox, though the announcement was held until the following day. George's younger brother John signed earlier in the year with the Minneapolis Millers.[22] Arthur Sampson of the *Boston Herald* wrote that George had seemed to have everything, but fell into prolonged slumps which were difficult to shake.[23] As the "meteor, never a star" comment from Harold Kaese had indicated, he had proved "a beautiful, but unsubstantial dream."[24]

Not much was made of his acquisition in the *Cleveland Plain Dealer;* he was characterized as "one of Boston's spare outfielders."[25] He saw a lot of duty, though, almost all in center field. Metkovich appeared in 126 games, hit for a .254 average, and drove in 40 runs.

He did a roundtrip during the offseason, traded by Bill Veeck on December 9 to the St. Louis Browns (along with $50,000) for Johnny Berardino. He never played for the Browns, however, other than in spring training. His arm, which had bothered him in the latter part of the 1947 season, had still not come around. The December trade had been conditioned on his arm improving. He was returned to Cleveland on April 20, 1948, with the Indians paying the Browns $15,000. Three weeks later, he was traded to the Oakland Oaks of the Pacific Coast League on May 5; Les Webber joined him. The Indians had traded for minor-leaguer Will Hafey.

He had a very good year with Oakland (reunited with manager Casey Stengel), batting .336 and hitting 23 home runs, driving in 88 runs, and scoring 116. He was named to the Northern All-Stars at midseason. The Oaks won the PCL pennant and the playoffs.

And he started off 1949 at more or less the same pace, batting .337 with 14 homers through his first 77 games. When Gus Zernial broke his collarbone, the Chicago White Sox made a move, offering cash and a player to be named later (Earl Rapp) to bring in Metkovich as a replacement. Back in the big leagues, Metkovich appeared in 93 games. He hit .243, and drove in 45. The White Sox finished sixth; Oakland might have repeated, had it not lost Metkovich. They finished second, just five games behind the Hollywood Stars. And then they won the pennant again, with him, in 1950.

Oakland had reacquired him outright from the White Sox in February, and he'd blasted the Chisox in spring training, charging that GM Frank Lane had told him to swing for the fences, while manager Jack Onslow had told him to just go for base hits. Lane said it was sour grapes, that no one else had been willing to bring him to the majors and that the only time he'd talked with Metkovich was the time the outfielder had complained to him that Onslow wouldn't let him play because he was chewing bubble gum. "I suggested that Onslow's reluctance might have been due to the fact that Metkovich had gone to bat 51 times for one base hit."[26]

Metkovich drove in 141 runs for the Oaks, scoring 150. The PCL played a much longer season; he appeared in 184 games, which helped bump up the numbers. He hit .315. George Metkovich was voted the Pacific Coast League MVP in 1950.

The Pittsburgh Pirates took him in the November 1950 major-league draft. He spent the next 2 ½ seasons playing for the Pirates. Needless to say, Oakland owner Clarence "Brick" Laws was less than pleased. "That's out-and-out robbery!" he declared. "I paid $25,000 for Metkovich last winter when no major league club apparently wanted him, at least for that kind of money. So he has a big year…and now they're hot to have him back—for [the prescribed draft price of] $10,000."[27]

Pittsburgh finished seventh in 1951 and last in 1952, but Metkovich was reasonably productive for them each year, playing in 120 and 125 games respectively. He hit .293 and .271, driving in 40 runs and then 41.

Metkovich played April and May 1953 for the Pirates, too, but Pirates GM Branch Rickey saw it a good time to market Ralph Kiner, the National League's reigning home run champion (for all seven years he'd been in the majors), and finally put together a package attractive enough for the Chicago Cubs to acquire him. On June 4, the Pirates sent Kiner, Metrovich (batting only .146 in 41 at-bats), Joe Garagiola, and Howie Pollet to the Cubs, receiving in exchange Bob Addis, Toby Atwell, George Freese, Gene Hermanski, Bob Schultz, Preston Ward, and $150,000 in cash. Metkovich hit .234 in 61 games for the Cubs in the remainder of 1953.

On December 7, the Milwaukee Braves bought Metkovich's contract from the Cubs in a straight cash transaction, for an amount thought to be around $10,000, purchased for "reserve protection."[28] It was thought he could offer "valuable left-handed pinch hitting strength."[29] He gave them the protection they likely sought. In 1954, Milwaukee used him in 68 games and batted .276, with 15 RBIs. They were his last games in the majors. On March 4, 1955, he was released.

He still had two more solid years of playing in him. In 1955, he played for Oakland again and returned to glory, with a league-leading .335 batting average over 151 games, with 17 homers and 79 RBIs. He was one of the three outfielders on the league All-Star team. The Oaks finished in seventh place, though.

In 1956, he played for last-place Vancouver (under manager Lefty O'Doul again), appearing in 132 games and batting .294. It was his last full season of play. His contract was sold to Charleston in February 1957. He indicated he might retire instead. Charleston sold his contract to Louisville, which in turn sold his contract to the closer-to-home San Diego Padres. He began the season playing first base and appeared in 24 games, batting .267. They were his last games in the field. In mid-May, GM Ralph Kiner (his former roommate with the Pirates) asked him to take over for manager Bob Elliott and Metkovich managed San Diego for four seasons.

The 1957 Padres finished fourth, moving up to second-place and just 4 ½ games behind Phoenix in 1958. He was a bit of a fiery manager; in 1957 alone, "I got kicked out of so many games last year it costs the club $1,150 in fines."[30] The 1959 Padres finished fourth, though only 6 ½ games off the pace. He didn't complete the 1960 season; the team finished fifth.

In late July 1960, he resigned as manager of the Padres, "after being criticized by members of the team."[31] There had been a deterioration of morale, the same problem that saw Bob Elliott lose his job back in 1957. He could have remained but felt the team was going nowhere and neither was he, and he was displeased by the way San Diego fans heaped abuse on his wife during games. *San Diego Union* sports editor Jack Murphy wrote, "He's never been able to overcome the resentment of following Bob Elliott, perhaps the most popular figure in the history of San Diego baseball."[32] Jimmy Reese replaced him.

In January 1961 he was hired to scout for the Washington Senators, and did that work from 1961 through 1963. His territory included Southern California, Utah, and Arizona. In his first year, he signed Ron Stilwell out of USC.

Metkovich, described at times during his baseball career as a "fashion plate," had long been a member of the Screen Actors Guild, since he was a high school student in 1938 when an MGM official had been seeking a basketball player for a movie. "I remember Spencer Tracy was in the movie but can't recall the name of the picture," he said.[33] He received $350 pay for a few days. "I liked the word and tried to follow it every winter since. I've been in 11 movies altogether and worked with some of the most beautiful women in the world." He went on to name Elizabeth Taylor, Rita Hayworth, Doris Day, Kathryn Grayson, Janet Leigh, Esther Williams, and Zsa Zsa Gabor, and the films *The Jackie Robinson Story, The Stratton Story, Angels in the Outfield, Gilda,* and *Big Leaguer.*

Shortly after becoming President of the United States, Ronald Reagan told an anecdote about working with Metkovich in *The Winning Team*, in which he starred as Grover Cleveland Alexander. Metkovich had a bit part. "Metkovich memorized everybody's lines. Then on the bus back from location, he'd imitate us and give everybody a hard time. One day, he finally got his speaking line. He was supposed to chew out an umpire. We told Metkovich just to yell anything he usually would at an ump. As the camera started rolling, you could tell something was wrong. His bat was shaking. I throw the pitch, the umpire bellows, 'Strike one.' George steps out, goes nose to nose with the ump and in this meek voice says, 'Gee sir, that was no strike.'" After his audience laughed, Reagan added, "The picture wasn't a comedy, so we couldn't leave it in."[34]

Though he said he hoped to get into the movie business fulltime after baseball, his regular work in the offseasons was as an airplane inspector. He also owned a restaurant in the Los Angeles area, Metkovich's Crown Room, located next to Los Angeles International Airport and run by the three brothers Chris, George, and John Metkovich.

George enjoyed hunting and fishing, presumably now warier about catfish. In 1969 both he and Jerry Priddy were working as "executives for a Los Angeles paper company," making the news when George's

55-foot cabin cruiser "ran into rocks in San Diego harbor."[35] No one was injured.

In his latter years, Metkovich suffered from Alzheimer's disease and in 1991 a *Los Angeles Times* story raised the alarm that he had taken a car and driven off from his home, saying, "I have to go home." That, even though his wife had assured him they both were at home. The next day's newspaper reassured readers that he had been found at 4:40 AM the next morning—"wandering near an El Segundo park asking for directions to a baseball game." A police lieutenant explained, "He was coherent and incoherent. He said he had been at a ballgame and then said he was looking for a ballgame to go to."[36]

George Metkovich died from complications of Alzheimer's (acute respiratory arrest) at age 74, on May 17, 1995 at a hospital in Costa Mesa, California. He was survived by his wife Peggy and their sons George and David. He is interred at El Toro Memorial Park in Lake Forest, California.

Nearly 20 years after his passing, in 2013, he was inducted into the Pacific Coast League Hall of Fame.

SOURCES

In addition to the sources noted in this biography, the author also accessed Metkovich's player file and player questionnaire from the National Baseball Hall of Fame, the *Encyclopedia of Minor League Baseball*, Retrosheet.org, Baseball-Reference.com, and the SABR Minor Leagues Database, accessed online at Baseball-Reference.com. Thanks to Rod Nelson of SABR's Scouts Committee.

NOTES

1 Harold Kaese, "Metkovich Either Very Good—or Vice Versa," *Boston Globe*, April 3, 1947: 12.

2 Information comes from the 1920 and 1930 United States census. There may have been a sixth son as well. Kate's surname was perhaps originally spelled Klaic. Their first-born Kris seems to have become the more Americanized Chris by 1930. There is a possibility that George was born on October 8, 1921 as self-reported on his Social Security application and by Find-A-Grave.com.

3 Bob Stevens, "Metkovich is Sold! Red Sox Buy Seal Star," *San Francisco Chronicle*, July 7, 1943: 13.

4 Carl Blume, "Five Schools Place Men On All-City Quintet," *Los Angeles Times*, February 10, 1939: A17.

5 See, for instance Associated Press, "Houston Ships Players to Jacksonville Club," *Dallas Morning News*, March 28, 1936: II, 5, and "Sam Butz, "Stock and Bolling Ejected and Peaches Divide Pair with Jacksonville," *Macon Telegraph*, May 27, 1937: 8.

6 Frederick G. Lieb, "Catfish 'Attack' Delayed Metkovich," *The Sporting News*, June 21, 1945: 5.

7 Associated Press, "Landis Wields Big Stick in Declaring 93 Detroit-Owned Players Free Agents," *Hartford Courant*, January 15, 1940: 10.

8 Ibid.

9 Burt Whitman, "Baseball Trails," *Boston Herald*, February 14, 1940: 26.

10 Ibid.

11 Ibid.

12 "Young Bee First Sacker is Just A Sucker for Catfish," *Evansville Courier and Press,* April 14, 1940: 21.

13 "Bissonette Places Self On Active List, Sends George Metkovich To Evansville." *Hartford Courant*, August 1, 1942: 9.

14 INS, "Seals Tentatively Get Fielder From Boston," *Sacramento Bee*, March 11, 1943: 10.

15 See, for instance, Bob Stevens, "Gorgeous Georges—Seals' Wonderman of Throw," *San Francisco Chronicle*, June 11, 1943: 18. "There have been stronger arms," O'Doul said, "but I've never seen one to equal it for accuracy. Never a foot off his target."

16 Roger Birtwell, "Red Sox Buy Metkovich from San Francisco Seals," *Boston Globe*, July 7, 1943: 19.

17 Ed Rumill, "Lefty O'Doul Aided Rookie Red Sox Star," *Christian Science Monitor*, July 26, 1943: 13. Rumill quoted Metkovich at length on the work O'Doul had done with him.

18 United Press, July 6, 1943.

19 Bob Stevens, "Metkovich is Sold! Red Sox Buy Seal Star," *San Francisco Chronicle*, July 7, 1943: 13. By September 1, Metkovich could have been snapped up for $7,500 in the major-league draft. Boston owner Tom Yawkey knew Metkovich was 1-A and could be taken into the Army at any time, but he approved the transaction nonetheless.

20 Associated Press, "Landis To Fine Big Leaguers Playing Winter Ball on Coast," *Boston Globe*, November 17, 1943: 18.

21 Wilbur Adams, "Between the Sport Lines," *Sacramento Bee*, March 23, 1946: 10.

22 Daniel W. Scism, "Sew It Seams," *Evansville Courier and Press*, January 21, 1947: 10

23 Arthur Sampson, "Metkovich 'Natural' Who Didn't Develop," *Boston Herald*, April 3, 1947: 11.

24 Kaese.

25 Alex Zirin, "Indians Are Picked to Wind Up Fourth," *Cleveland Plain Dealer*, April 13, 1947: 20.

26 Associated Press, "Bubble Gum Caused Metkovich Trouble with Sox, Lane Reports," *Washington Evening Star*, March 13, 1940: 15.

27 Al Wolf, "Loss of Metkovich Irks Acorn Owner," *Los Angeles Times*, November 17, 1950: C1.

28 United Press, "Braves Obtain Metkovich for 'Reserve Protection," *Boston Globe*, December 8, 1953: 22.

29 Bob Wolf, "Braves Get George Metkovich of Cubs in Straight Cash Deal," *Milwaukee Journal*, December 7, 1953. A July 1954 column by Sam Levy offered Metkovich the opportunity to present his thoughts on what it takes to be a good pinch-hitter. "Job of Pinch Hitter No Position for Laggard; Catfish Metkovich of Braves Explains Why," *Milwaukee Journal*, July 11, 1954.

30 Phil Collier, "Metkovich Banished, Padres Beat Mobile," *San Diego Union*, March 24, 1958: 17.

31 "Metkovich Resigns," *Cincinnati Post and Times*, July 25, 1960.

32 Jack Murphy, "Wife, Future in Baseball, Keys to Metkovich Decision," *San Diego Union*, July 25, 1960: 24.

33 Les Biederman, "Scoreboard," *Pittsburgh Press*, March 14, 1952.

34 Thomas Boswell, "Cooperstown Comes to the White House," *Washington Post*, March 28, 1981: A1.

35 "Notes…off the cuff," *Plain Dealer* (Cleveland), February 1, 1969: 31.

36 "Ailing Ex-Ballplayer, 70, Found Safe in El Segundo," *Los Angeles Times*, July 25, 1991: OCB12. The prior day's story had been headlined "Man, 70, With Alzheimer's Is Feared Lost."

DON NEWCOMBE

BY RUSSELL A. BERGTOLD

"What I have done after my baseball career and being able to help people with their lives — means more to me than all the things I did in baseball."

Don Newcombe[1]

DON NEWCOMBE WAS THE third black pitcher to appear in a major-league game after Dan Bankhead and Satchel Paige. Playing at a height of 6-feet-4 and listed at 220 pounds, the right-hander earned the nickname "Newk" or "Big Newk" as a derivative of his last name and his imposing physical presence on the field. He exploded onto the baseball scene when he was selected to appear in the 1949 All-Star Game during his rookie campaign, becoming the first African-American pitcher to do so. Newcombe would go on to win the Rookie of the Year Award as well as becoming the first recipient of the Cy Young Award in 1956, when he was also named the NL Most Valuable Player. As of 2017, Newcombe was the only player to win all three major awards in addition to a World Series ring. Despite his tremendous ability, however, Newcombe's temper and attitude got him into trouble from his earliest days in Organized Baseball. He could be headstrong, belligerent, and impulsive. His behavior would cost him dearly through his career and his life.[2]

Newcombe was born in Madison, New Jersey, on June 14, 1926, to Roland and Sadie Newcombe. The Newcombes had three other sons, Harold, Norman, and Roland Jr., as well as a daughter, Dolly, who died at the age of 8. Newcombe's father was employed by a wealthy family as a chauffeur for 28 years. He also became adept at making home-brewed beer, which he shared with his boys around the time Don was 8 years old. Growing up, young Don witnessed several arguments between his parents.[3] By the age of 13, he would leave the house to buy his own beer and hang out with his friends.[4]

During the 1930s Roland Newcombe would often take Don and his three brothers to Ruppert Stadium in Newark, where they would pay 25 cents apiece to sit in the left-field bleachers and watch either the Newark Eagles of the Negro National League or the Newark Bears, the Yankees' Triple-A team, since both teams shared the park. Young Don's favorite player was Bears outfielder Bob Seeds, a well-traveled veteran who played for five major-league teams in a nine-year span. However, as Newcombe later recalled, one player stood out from the rest, "If you were black and a baseball fan, then you knew about Satchel Paige. He was a legend."[5]

Eventually the Newcombes moved to Elizabeth, New Jersey, where 14-year-old Don excelled at baseball for Lafayette Junior High School, although his coach, Hermie Kaufman, was hesitant to let him pitch, citing a lack of talent. Later on, when Don entered Jefferson High School in Elizabeth, he began playing semipro baseball for the Roselle Stars because his high school did not have a baseball team.

One man who had a tremendous influence on young Don was his next-door neighbor, Johnny Grier. Grier was probably 12 years older than Don, and mentored him during his adolescence. "Johnny kept me out of a lot of trouble ... [and] taught me the big wind-mill windup and high kick I would use my entire career," Newcombe said.[6]

By the age of 15, Newcombe was an even 6 feet and 200 pounds. He was sitting in a barroom having a beer when he heard about the attack on Pearl Harbor.[7] Already grown up, but underage, Newcombe falsified his date of birth to enlist in the US Army in 1942. When military personnel realized that he was still a minor, they notified his father to come pick him up.[8]

Because of the segregation that existed in major-league baseball, Roland Newcombe had envisioned his son as possibly being the next Joe Louis, not the next Dizzy Dean. But "Don told me he didn't want to fight because he didn't want to get his face punched," recalled his father.[9] On a December afternoon in 1943, while playing checkers at Pryor's Barbershop, the 17-year-old Newcombe met Buddy Holler, an acquaintance of Abe Manley, owner of the Newark Eagles of the Negro National League. Two months later, Holler drove Newcombe to the Manley residence, where he was introduced to Abe's wife, Effa Manley. Effa, who co-owned the team with her husband, was the team's business manager. Impressed by his physical size alone, Abe took Newcombe with him the next morning to the Eagles training camp in Richmond, Virginia.[10] Newcombe dropped out of high school during his junior year to pursue baseball as a full-time job, earning $170 per month.[11] He made his professional debut on May 14, 1944, at Ruppert Stadium, working in relief.[12] In one game Newcombe faced the Baltimore Elite Giants. When Roy Campanella stepped into the batter's box, the fledgling pitcher was ordered by his manager, "Mule" Suttles, to knock him down.[13] "So I threw the ball high, but I didn't get it in enough, and Roy hit the ball into the seats," recalled Newcombe.[14] It would serve as a dubious beginning to a lifelong friendship.

In October of 1945 Newcombe and Campanella crossed paths again at Ebbets Field, this time as teammates. During an exhibition series that featured white major leaguers versus Negro League players, Newcombe and Campanella were impressive enough to be considered in Branch Rickey's second wave of integration, although they were scouted long before the actual series took place. Campanella was already deemed major-league material, while Newcombe was still seen as a raw talent. "He wasn't by any means the best pitcher in Negro baseball," wrote Wendell Smith, "but Rickey signed him because he's young, big, and has all the natural ability necessary to get him into the big leagues."[15] Newcombe's signing embittered Effa Manley, who never received compensation for her young hurler. "(The Dodgers) don't deserve to win for what they did to Negro baseball," Manley retorted years later."[16]

With the 1946 season months away, the Dodgers were looking for a team within the organization willing to accept Newcombe and Campanella on their all-white roster. The batterymates were slated to report to the Danville Dodgers of the Three-I League but league President Tom Fairweather reportedly stated that he would rather close the league down than to integrate it.[17] In a desperate move, Rickey contacted Buzzie Bavasi, the general manager of the Nashua Dodgers in the New England League, who replied, "If they can play ball better than what we have, then we don't care what color they are."[18]

While Rickey took great measures in bracing Jackie Robinson for the racism he would face, he did not prepare Newcombe and Campanella as stringently for those same challenges. Instead, Robinson met privately with Newcombe and Campanella in New York, where they talked about the trials they would face. Throughout the season, according to Newcombe,

Don Newcombe, who (along with Duke Snider, Ernie Banks, Bill Mazeroski, Harmon Killebrew, and Bob Feller) pops up onscreen in Pastime.

he and Campanella kept in contact with Robinson.[19] "We're being depended on by black people all over this world," Newcombe remembered Robinson saying. "We can't afford to fail."[20]

After Newcombe married "Freddie" Cross in 1945, the newlyweds joined Campanella and his wife in Nashua, where they reportedly were the only black people in the New Hampshire town. Rickey failed to inform the newly appointed manager, Walter Alston, of their arrival. Alston took it in stride: "I didn't think too much about it. ... When I saw them play a few games I was glad I had them on my club."[21]

Campanella, a veteran of nine seasons in the Negro leagues, had a calming effect on the young, temperamental, and somewhat insecure Newcombe,[22] as he pitched a shutout in his Nashua debut and won his first four starts. In addition to pitching and driving the team bus,[23] Newcombe showed enough proficiency with the bat that many wondered if he would switch positions to play every day. Swinging from the left side, he became Alston's most reliable pinch-hitter. Nashua started out slowly. By mid-June the team was 13 games behind the league-leading Lynn Red Sox. By early August Newcombe's pitching record stood at 8-3 and his batting average was an impressive .349.[24] With Newcombe and Campanella paving the way down the stretch, they made the playoffs. Newcombe threw a shutout in Game Three to give the Dodgers a sweep over the Pawtucket Slaters. They went on to beat Lynn in six games for the New England League championship, with Newcombe nailing down the Game Five win.[25]

In preparation for Robinson's major-league debut in 1947, Rickey moved the Dodgers' spring training site to Havana to avoid the Jim Crow laws in Florida. It proved to be a disaster in regard to the travel expenses, hotel accommodations, and costs of flying in other major-league teams from the mainland. However, those were just the monetary expenses. When Rickey made reservations for the Brooklyn Dodgers to stay at the luxurious Hotel Nacional and housed the Triple-A Montreal Royals at the new Havana Military Academy, he segregated Robinson, Newcombe, Campanella, and Roy Partlow to a "musty, third rate hotel" to avoid any racial tension. Robinson was furious. To make matters worse, the four black ballplayers were given meal tickets to use in Havana's less-than-sanitary restaurants. "One night I sat in the restaurant next to the hotel eating a bowl of soup," recalled Newcombe, "and I stirred the soup and a cockroach came up out of it. I threw up everything I had in me all over the counter."[26]

Weakened by the deplorable living conditions, a dejected Newcombe lost 35 pounds and was sent back to Nashua for another year to work on his control.[27] Meanwhile Robinson went on to debut for the Brooklyn Dodgers while Campanella moved up to the Montreal Royals.

In 1948, Campanella accompanied Robinson to Brooklyn, while Newcombe earned a promotion to Montreal. Poised with an explosive fastball, a slow, looping curve, and a slider, Newcombe improved considerably at the Triple-A level. He tossed his only no-hitter as a professional, en route to posting a 17-6 record. Manager Clay Hopper would often refer to him as the next Dizzy Dean.

In the postseason, Newcombe eked out a win in the first game of the opening round against the Rochester Red Wings. After he was staked to a 4-0 lead with two outs in the top of the ninth, he gave up a three-run triple to Rocky Nelson before getting the final out. In the fourth game, Newcombe took the loss, 1-0. The only run scored on a fielder's choice by first baseman Chuck Connors in the first inning.

In the seventh game, Newcombe continued his dominance. Locked up in a 0-0 pitchers' duel in the bottom of the ninth, the Royals got a three-run homer from league MVP Jimmy Bloodworth to advance them to the Governor's Cup against the Syracuse Chiefs, as fans carried both Bloodworth and Newcombe off the field. The Royals went on to win the Governor's Cup in five games as Newcombe notched a 2-1 win in Game Three.

When the St. Paul Saints defeated the Columbus Red Birds, the stage was set for a Junior World Series that would feature two Triple-A clubs within the Dodgers organization. Saints manager Walter Alston was quite familiar with Newcombe, having managed him the previous two seasons at Nashua. More importantly, Alston and Hopper were vying for the vacancy created by the firing of Brooklyn's manager, Leo Durocher, as both Rickey and Dodgers co-owner Walter O'Malley were in attendance.

Newcombe was unimpressive in his Game One start, which the Saints won 4-0. The Royals came back to win Games Two and Three. In Game Four, Newcombe delivered a no-hit performance through six innings before settling on an 8-3 win in his last start at Montreal's Delorimier Downs. The Royals won Game Five, 7-2, which secured their second Junior World Series title in three years.[28]

When the 1949 season arrived, Newcombe was certain that he would be heading north with the Brooklyn Dodgers. Although he pitched well during spring training, the Dodgers returned Newcombe to the minors at the beginning of the year, claiming he had not matured enough. Newcombe, upset with his demotion, went home instead and had to be persuaded by his wife to return to Montreal.[29] Provisional manager Burt Shotton branded the pitcher as a fire-eater who "couldn't keep his mouth shut." Shotton patronizingly added that he didn't want Newcombe "spoiling it for the other two [black] fellows." By May the Dodgers were floundering, and Shotton had no choice but to accept Newcombe's promotion.[30]

Newcombe made his big-league debut on May 20, 1949, against the St. Louis Cardinals, as a reliever. He struck out the first batter he faced, Chuck Diering, on three straight pitches, but then got knocked around. Two days later against the Cincinnati Reds he threw a shutout in his first start. By July he was selected to play in the only All-Star Game held at Ebbets Field. He went on to finish the season with 17 wins while leading the league in shutouts. He nearly led the league in strikeouts, but finished two behind the league leader, Warren Spahn, who pitched 58 more innings. He was named the National League Rookie of the Year, becoming the second African-American in three years to capture the award after Jackie Robinson was initially honored in 1947.

Newcombe was encouraged by having Robinson and Campanella there to support him during his rookie campaign. "Jackie always knew that getting inside Newk's head and rattling his cage a bit made him pitch better," explained Carl Erskine. "But Campy was just the opposite. He would soothe Don in his own way. Cool and easy, Campy soothed Newk every time and emotionally stroked his confidence, like a balm on a wound."[31] Conversely, both Robinson and Campanella benefited greatly from Newcombe's presence as word got around that he would retaliate if their pitchers continued to take aim at the Dodgers' two black hitting stars.[32] Coincidently, Robinson had his best season and was named the National League MVP that year.

With the 1949 season coming down the stretch, the Dodgers and Cardinals were locked in a tight race. During August and September, Newcombe went 8-5. Four of those eight wins were shutouts, while two of his losses were by 2-1 and 1-0 scores.[33] From August 16 through September 6, Newcombe threw six complete games in six starts, including three consecutive shutouts, and had a 31-inning scoreless streak. On October 2, the final day of the regular season, the Dodgers needed to defeat the Phillies at Shibe Park to secure the pennant, so they turned to Newcombe, who was given a 5-0 lead heading into the bottom of the fourth, when he surrendered a three-run home run to Puddin' Head Jones. A single and a double later, Newcombe was removed in favor of Rex Barney. Although the Phillies eventually tied it up, the Dodgers went on to win the game in 10 innings, 9-7, to secure the National League pennant. When the New York Yankees eliminated the Boston Red Sox that afternoon by a score of 5-3 to capture the American League championship, it marked the first time in major-league history that both pennant races were decided on the final day of the regular season.

Game One featured Allie Reynolds of the Yankees against Newcombe, on two days' rest, who became the first African-American to start a World Series game. They were locked in a 0-0 pitchers' duel heading into the bottom of the ninth at Yankee Stadium when leadoff hitter Tommy Henrich delivered a game-winning home run off Newcombe over the right-field wall. After the game, it was discovered that Newcombe had pitched with an ingrown toenail.[34] He recovered well enough to start Game Four but was ineffective, allowing three runs in the fourth inning before he departed. Even though the Dodgers went on to lose the Series in five games, Newcombe found enough comfort in his World Series earnings ($4,272.74) to put a down payment on a house in Colonia, New Jersey. He also joined the local volunteer fire department and took to refereeing wrestling matches during the offseason.[35]

The 1950 season marked the second year in a row that Newcombe was selected for the All-Star team as the Dodgers continually chased the Phillies throughout the campaign. Once again Newcombe carried quite a workload. He threw five consecutive complete-game victories beginning on August 21 through the first game of a September 6 doubleheader against the Phillies. He also started the second game of that doubleheader before he left in the seventh inning with a 2-0 deficit. Nevertheless, the Dodgers came back with three runs in the top of the ninth to take both ends of the twin bill. On September 18, 1950, the Phillies held a nine-game lead over the Dodgers with less than two weeks left in the season. When the Phillies came into Ebbets Field on September 30, the Dodgers had closed the gap to two games. If they could win those final two games, they would finish even and force a playoff.[36] The Dodgers won that Saturday, 7-3. On Sunday, October 1, the Phillies held a one-game lead as Robin Roberts took the mound for the Phillies to face Newcombe. Not only were both pitching for the National League pennant, but they were each looking to become a 20-game winner for the first time.

The Dodgers had their chance to win it in the bottom of the ninth, when Cal Abrams led off with a walk, followed by single from Pee Wee Reese. With nobody out, Duke Snider singled sharply to center field as the slow-footed Abrams was waved on home but was thrown out at the plate. Reese advanced to third while Snider took second on the throw to home.

With first base open, Robinson was walked intentionally to load the bases. With only one out, Carl Furillo fouled out to first for the second out before Gil Hodges flied out to right to strand the runners and end the inning. With the game knotted at one run apiece heading into the top of the 10th inning, Newcombe was still on the mound. He gave up back-to-back singles to Robin Roberts and Eddie Waitkus to start the inning, before Dick Sisler hit a three-run homer that would hold up to give the Phillies the pennant while making Roberts a 20-game winner.

Once again Newcombe pitched brilliantly in a crucial, must-win game only to surrender a walk-off home run in the late innings. After the game, Newcombe was especially hard on himself. Ralph Branca tried to cheer him by reminding him that they came this far because of his pitching down the stretch. Branca, for one, questioned Shotton's managerial decisions for leaving Newcombe in there for the 10th.[37] Walter O'Malley, who had recently become the majority owner of the Dodgers, may have also questioned Shotton's decision-making process. When O'Malley refused to renew Rickey's contract for the 1951 season, Shotton was relieved of his managerial duties as well. O'Malley took over as team president and hired Charlie Dressen as his new manager for the 1951 season. Meanwhile, in an effort to earn some extra cash, Newcombe spent his offseason working at a men's clothing store in New York.[38]

Dressen was a former coach under Leo Durocher and his one goal for the 1951 season was to beat his former mentor, now managing the New York Giants, in their head-to-head games and in the standings.[39] Beginning in the middle of May, the Dodgers began to distance themselves from the rest of the league. By Sunday, August 12, when Newcombe defeated Johnny Sain and the Boston Braves, the Dodgers were up by 12½ games over the second-place Giants.

Heading down the stretch, the Giants miraculously pulled into a first-place tie with the Dodgers on September 28. For the third straight year, the pennant would be decided in a season-ending series between the Dodgers and the Phillies. On September

29, Newcombe outdueled Robin Roberts with a 5-0 shutout, making him a 20-game winner for the first time in his major-league career. However, the Giants also won, defeating the Boston Braves, 3-0, to keep pace with Brooklyn. Once again, the season came down to the final game.

On September 30, the Dodgers were trailing the Phillies, 8-5, heading into the top of the eighth inning when they tied it up. Dressen brought in Newcombe to relieve the bottom of the frame. He held the Phillies scoreless for 5⅔ innings before he was removed in the bottom of the 13th. With the score still tied, 8-8, in the top of the 14th, Jackie Robinson lifted a solo homer into the left-field seats that proved to be the difference as the Dodgers held on to win, 9-8. However the Giants kept pace by beating the Braves in Boston to force a three-game playoff series against Brooklyn.

After the Dodgers lost Game One at Ebbets Field on October 1, the series shifted to the Polo Grounds, where they won a 10-0 blowout. Newcombe was the starter for the decisive Game Three, pitching six more shutout innings before allowing a run in the bottom of the seventh. When Willie Mays grounded into a 6-4-3 double play to end the inning, Newcombe returned to the dugout and told Dressen "that his arm was dead."[40] Nevertheless Newcombe went out to pitch the bottom of the eighth and retired the Giants in order. Because of Newcombe's propensity to make contact, Dressen allowed him to bat rather than waste a pinch-hitter for him. He grounded out second to first. In the bottom of the ninth, with a 4-2 lead, Newcombe departed after allowing an RBI double to Whitey Lockman. Ralph Branca came in to relieve Newcombe with runners on second and third when he surrendered a pennant-winning home run to Bobby Thomson. Magnified by the fact that it was the first sporting event that was televised coast to coast,[41] the *Daily News* headlined it "The Shot Heard 'Round the World,"[42] and the moment has been forever etched in baseball lore.

That game would be Newcombe's last major-league appearance for the next two years as he was inducted into the military on February 26, 1952.[43]

When he returned to the rotation in 1954 he showed some rust with a 9-8 record. Under rookie manager Walter Alston, the Dodgers finished 30 games above .500, but were still five games behind the World Series-winning Giants.

When the 1955 season got underway, Alston became more reliant on Carl Erskine, Billy Loes, Russ Meyer, and Johnny Podres. Newcombe was in the rotation, but he wasn't the dominant pitcher that Alston remembered from their days at Nashua. Out of frustration, Newcombe went to Alston with an ultimatum: Pitch me or trade me. Alston reached in his pocket to pull out a schedule and told Newcombe he would start on Friday, May 6, against the Phillies. However, on May 5, coach Joe Becker told Newcombe to throw batting practice. Infuriated, Newcombe stormed into Alston's office, where he was told to take off his uniform and go home if he didn't like it. Against the advice of Campanella and Robinson, that's exactly what he did. When Newcombe got home he received a telegram from GM Buzzie Bavasi informing him that he was suspended and fined. Newcombe called Bavasi and the two agreed to lift the suspension, but Newcombe was still fined $350 for leaving the team. Newcombe did not start that May 6 game in Philadelphia, but pitched two innings in relief to pick up his third win of the season.[44]

All was forgiven in his next start, on May 10 at Wrigley Field, when Newcombe faced the minimum 27 batters as he threw a one-hit shutout against the Cubs. That seemed to jump-start his season, as he reclaimed his role as the team ace, leading the staff in virtually every category by season's end. He also led the team with a .359 batting average and a .632 slugging percentage by collecting 42 hits in 117 at-bats. Nine of those hits were doubles, one was a triple, but more significantly seven were home runs, which set the National League record for pitchers.

On the Fourth of July Newcombe pitched a complete game to push his record to 14-1, which earned him a spot on the All-Star team. After the break he threw back-to-back complete games to push his record to 16-1, and another one on July 31 to move his record to 18-1. It would be a month before he won another game as he lost three complete games by one run. On September 5 Newcombe pitched his last complete game of the season to notch his 20th win. He contracted a virus that limited him to two innings of work over the next two weeks.

The Dodgers won the pennant by 13½ games, taking over first place on April 16 and never relinquishing it. In his only World Series appearance that year, Newcombe was the Game One starter against Whitey Ford at Yankee Stadium. After the Dodgers staked Newcombe to a 2-0 lead, he gave up a two-run homer to Elston Howard in the second inning. Duke Snider led off the third with a solo home run to put the Dodgers back in front, 3-2, before the Yanks tied it again in their half of the inning. Newcombe eventually gave up two more home runs to Joe Collins and left the game after 5⅔ innings pitched, trailing 6-3. The Yanks held on to win the game, but the Dodgers came back to win the Series in seven games. It marked the first and only time that the Dodgers won the World Series while in Brooklyn.

Newcombe claimed that he did something to damage his arm when he came back in September, "The whole night before the opening game of that World Series my wife sat up putting hot compresses to my arm," he said. "Alston knew it, although nobody else did, and that's why he didn't use me again after I got beat in the first game."[45]

Coming off that World Series championship, the Newcombes adopted two children, Gregory and Evit, during the offseason. Newcombe enjoyed his finest year as a professional in 1956, leading the majors in victories and winning percentage by posting a 27-7 record. So dominant was Newk's presence on the mound that year that beginning on September 19, he was pitching regularly on two days' rest to keep pace with the Milwaukee Braves. On September 26, in a loss to the Phillies, Dodgers left fielder Sandy Amoros dropped a fly ball that started a three-run rally. When Newcombe got back to the dugout, tension was running high when he yelled at Alston to "get somebody out there who can catch a fly ball."[46] Right fielder Carl Furillo took exception and stood up for the diminutive outfielder. The following day,

Robinson corralled Newcombe into apologizing to Amoros. The Dodgers won the pennant on the final day of the season when Newcombe threw 7⅓ innings in a win over the Pittsburgh Pirates, but it was Amoros's two home runs that made the difference.[47]

For the second year in a row, the Dodgers faced the Yankees in the World Series. In Game Two, a Yogi Berra grand slam drove Newcombe from the game in the top of the second inning. Newcombe left the ballpark while the game was still underway and assaulted Michael Brown, a parking-lot attendant outside Ebbets Field.[48] After Don Larsen threw a perfect game in the fifth game, the Dodgers won Game Six, 1-0, to force a Game Seven. Newcombe got the start and gave up a two-run homer to Yogi Berra in the top of the first inning. He gave up another two-run homer to Berra in the top of the third, and a solo home run to Elston Howard to lead off the fourth inning before he was mercifully removed. As he did in Game Two, Newcombe left the ballpark before the game was over. The Yankees went on to win by a score of 9-0 to capture their 17th World Series title.

Immediately after the World Series, the Dodgers departed on a 19-game barnstorming tour through Japan. When they returned, Newcombe was named the Most Valuable Player in the National League. A week later he was recognized as the first recipient of the Cy Young Award for his brilliance during the regular season. In other news, an aging Jackie Robinson announced his retirement from baseball and took a position with Chock Full O'Nuts as the vice president and director of personnel.

The 1957 season marked the end of an era for the Dodgers as it was their last year in Brooklyn. At 84-70, they finished in third place, 14 games behind the Milwaukee Braves. Newcombe finished with an 11-12 record, and was making more headlines off the field than on it. On August 21, after pitching a five-hit shutout over the Cincinnati Reds, Newcombe was driving his father home to Colonia when he struck 4-year-old John Chase Jr. with his car.[49] In December, Newcombe and two of his brothers were accused of assaulting Ulysses Ross, a former East Orange (New Jersey) policeman, at Newcombe's Newark tavern.[50]

However, the most shocking news affecting the Dodgers during the offseason was a car accident that left Roy Campanella paralyzed. With the legal matters surrounding the parking-lot attendant, the 4-year-old boy, and the former policeman, Newcombe's marriage was starting to crumble.[51] In 1957 he left his wife and two adopted children.[52] Without Robinson and Campanella as chaperones, Newcombe began the 1958 season with a 0-6 record. He also began dating Billie Roberts, a statuesque, well-educated (UCLA) woman, when the team moved to Los Angeles.[53]

With the Dodgers now calling Los Angeles their home, air travel became the new standard for road trips back east. That presented another problem for Newcombe, who developed a fear of flying in the early 1950s when he witnessed an airplane crash in Elizabeth, New Jersey.[54] Through hypnotherapy he eventually overcame his fears to earn a pilot's license,[55] although some reports indicate that he relied more on whiskey and vodka to quiet his nerves.[56] By now Bavasi and the Dodgers were running out of patience with Newcombe's behavior. On June 15, 1958, he was traded to the Cincinnati Reds in exchange for right-handed pitcher Johnny Klippstein and first baseman Steve Bilko, along with two players to be named later. "When you're a winner, they don't give a damn. When you're a loser, they release you," Newcombe lamented years later.[57] In 18 starts for the Reds that year, Newcombe went 7-7 with a 3.85 ERA.

Newcombe had a resurgent year in 1959 while pitching for the Reds. Posting a 13-8 record for a team that finished in fifth place, six games below .500, Newcombe led the team in wins, strikeouts, ERA, innings pitched, and complete games.

During spring training of 1960, the Newcombes were granted a divorce in Juarez, Mexico.[58] Freddie was given custody of their two children as part of the settlement.[59] A week later, Newcombe married Billie Roberts.[60]

Around this time, the 240-pound Newcombe pulled a muscle in his right thigh.[61] As a precautionary measure, manager Fred Hutchinson ordered him to stay off his feet for a couple of days. While he was recovering from his leg injury, Newcombe began taking diet pills in an effort to take some weight off the injured leg.[62]

By Opening Day of 1960 Newcombe was well enough to pinch-hit for pitcher Jim O'Toole as the Reds won 9-4 over the Phillies. He made his first start on April 17, shutting out the Pirates through four innings when he was struck in the right wrist by a Bill Virdon line drive that forced him from the game.[63] The rest of season was dismal as Newcombe failed to live up to the expectations he had shown in the previous year. He won only four games in 15 starts.

The frustration reached a climax on July 17 at Forbes Field while Newcombe was preparing for game two of a Sunday doubleheader. Prior to his warm-up tosses, the Pirates protested that Newcombe's sweatshirt had one sleeve longer than the other. When umpire Dusty Boggess ordered him to change his sweatshirt, Newcombe sarcastically replied, "Supposing Pete Gray came out on the mound? What would you do then?" After a few words were exchanged, Newcombe was ejected.[64]

On July 29, Newcombe was sold to the Cleveland Indians, for whom he was used almost exclusively out of the bullpen. He played his last major-league game on October 1, 1960.

When the Indians released Newcombe prior to the 1961 season, Bavasi signed him to a minor-league contract to play in the Pacific Coast League for the Dodgers' affiliate in Spokane. In 1962, he joined Larry Doby to play for the Chunichi Dragons in Japan, where he was used primarily as a first baseman for his hitting prowess.

Throughout his career Newcombe was known to have a few drinks, but it wasn't until after his playing days were over that he revealed the true nature of his alcoholism. Some of his former teammates were astonished by his admission, but those who were closest to him took the brunt of it. Newcombe "confessed publicly that, for many years, he was a stupefied, wife-abusing, child-frightening, falling-down drunk."[65] It may also help to explain the lack of prudence that seems to have plagued him throughout his career.

By 1965 Newcombe was forced to declare bankruptcy.[66] At one time, he became so desperate to pay for his drinking habit that he pawned his 1955 World Series ring and an expensive watch. The jewelry was later bought and returned to him by Peter O'Malley, who was then Dodgers vice president.[67] It wasn't until his second wife threatened to take their 4-year-old son, Don Jr., and leave him in 1966, that he quit drinking. The Newcombes went on to have two more children, Kelley and Tony, as Newcombe continued to straighten out his life.[68]

Newcombe became a staunch advocate of recognizing alcohol abuse, and began Don Newcombe Enterprises, a personal-services company, in 1976. He was named director of community relations for the Los Angeles Dodgers in 1970 and still held the post in 2017. As a recovering alcoholic, he created the Dodger Drug and Alcoholic Awareness Program in 1980 and became a consultant for the National Institute on Alcohol Abuse and Alcoholism, as well as director for special projects for the New Beginning Alcohol and Drug Treatment Program.[69]

After 30 years of marriage, Billie and Don divorced.[70] In 1990, a very recognizable Don Newcombe appeared as himself onscreen in *Pastime*, which resembles the more celebrated *Bull Durham* as a depiction of life in the minors and a portrait of a veteran minor leaguer. The year is 1957 and the central character is a 40-year-old hurler (played by William Russ) who pitched in one major-league game (in which he surrendered a grand slam to Stan Musial) and who mentors a shy, well-mannered 17-year-old black kid (Glenn Plummer). *Pastime* is of note for the ever-so-brief cameo appearances of Newcombe, as well as Duke Snider, Ernie Banks, Bill Mazeroski, Harmon Killebrew, and Bob Feller.[71]

All these ex-ballplayers but Newcombe became Hall of Famers. In retrospect, Newcombe shared his thoughts on what may have been a Hall of Fame career cut short by his own transgressions: "I was only 34, but the alcohol had taken its toll. I think it shortened my major-league career by about six or seven years. I regret that I didn't take better care of myself in the latter part of my career because I would like to have made the Hall of Fame, where I think I belong."[72]

NOTES

1. Don Newcombe website: donnewcombe.com/.
2. Rick Swaine, *The Black Stars Who Made Baseball Whole* (Jefferson, North Carolina: McFarland & Company, Inc., 2006), 54.
3. A.S. Doc Young, "Don Newcombe, Baseball Great Wins Fight Against Alcoholism," *Ebony*, April 1976: 55.
4. Dan Coughlin, "Second Chance Saves Newcombe," *Cleveland Plain Dealer*, January 30, 1976: 6.
5. Danny Peary, *We Played the Game* (New York: Tess Press, 1994), 8.
6. Peary, 150, 151.
7. Young, 56.
8. Tom Cohane, "Newcombe Meets All the Demands," *Look magazine*, April 11, 1950: 100.
9. Bard Lindeman, "Don's Fight Hits Top of League," November 21, 1956. Unidentified newspaper clipping in the Don Newcombe player file, National Baseball Hall of Fame Library.
10. Bob Luke, *The Most Famous Woman in Baseball: Effa Manley and the Negro Leagues* (Dulles, Virginia: Potomac Books Inc., 2011), 103.
11. Luke, 109.
12. Luke, 104, 105.
13. Neil Lanctot, *Campy, the Two Lives of Roy Campanella* (New York: Simon and Schuster, 2011), 101.
14. Peter Golenbock, *Bums: An Oral History of the Brooklyn Dodgers* (New York: Putnam's, 1984), 235.
15. Jules Tygiel, *Baseball's Great Experiment: Jackie Robinson and His Legacy* (New York: Oxford University Press, 2008), 68.
16. Tygiel, 147.
17. Peary, 9.
18. William C. Kashatus, *Jackie & Campy: The Untold Story of Their Rocky Relationship and the Breaking of Baseball's Color Line* (Lincoln: University of Nebraska Press, 2014), 85.
19. Ibid.
20. "A Task That Was Too Important to Fail," *Kansas City Star*, January 25, 2007.
21. Tygiel, 148.
22. Kashatus, 87.
23. Tygiel. 150.

24 Tygiel, 149.

25 Tygiel, 151, 152.

26 Tygiel, 165, 166.

27 Don Newcombe as told to Milton Gross, "I'm No Quitter," *Saturday Evening Post*, March 9, 1957: 91.

28 William Brown, *Baseball's Fabulous Montreal Royals* (Montreal: Robert Davies Publishing, 1996), 118-126.

29 William Marshall, *Baseball's Pivotal Era, 1945-1951* (Lexington: The University Press of Kentucky, 1999), 284.

30 Carl E. Prince, *Brooklyn's Dodgers: The Bums, The Borough, and The Best of Baseball* (New York: Oxford University Press, 1996), 71. Both quotations come from the same source.

31 Kashatus, 130.

32 Swaine, 54.

33 Prince, 72.

34 Golenbock, 247.

35 *Look magazine*, April 11, 1950: 98.

36 Ralph Branca with David Ritz, *A Moment in Time* (New York: Scribner Publishing, 2011), 113, 114.

37 Branca, 115, 116.

38 Marshall, 301.

39 Branca, 118.

40 Joshua Prager, *The Echoing Green, the Untold Story of Bobby Thomson, Ralph Branca, and the Shot Heard Round the World* (New York: Pantheon Books, 2006), 202.

41 Marshall, 423.

42 Prager, 251.

43 "Newcombe Reassigned to Camp in Texas," *Brooklyn Daily Eagle*, February 17, 1953.

44 *Saturday Evening Post*, March 9, 1957: 92.

45 *Saturday Evening Post*, March 9, 1957: 91.

46 *Saturday Evening Post*, March 9, 1957: 92.

47 Ibid.

48 *The Sporting News*, October 7, 1956: 8.

49 "Newcombe to Settle, *New York Times*, September 24, 1959. The suit claimed that the boy suffered a fractured skull and shoulder and multiple abrasions. A settlement of $5,000 was approved by Union County Judge Carrol W. Hopkins.

50 "Three Newcombes Freed," *New York Times*, February 3, 1959. A year later the three brothers were acquitted by an Essex County jury.

51 "Marriage on Rocks, Newcombe Reveals," *New York Journal American*, January 27, 1960.

52 *Ebony:* April 1976: 58.

53 Ibid.

54 Associated Press, "Newcombe Conquers Fear of Flying," December 15, 1957.

55 Associated Press, "Now Newk's Flying His Own," February 23, 1959.

56 Dan Coughlin.

57 Ibid.

58 *Ebony,* April 1976: 54.

59 "Mexico Divorce to Newk; Wife Awarded Two Children," March 27, 1960, unidentified newspaper clipping in the Newcombe player file, National Baseball Hall of Fame Library.

60 "Newcombe Takes Bride," *Cincinnati Enquirer*, March 22, 1960.

61 "'Newk' Set Back Month by Injury," *Cincinnati Enquirer*, April 9, 1960.

62 *Cincinnati Post,* April 6, 1960.

63 *The Sporting News*, April 27, 1960: 25.

64 *The Sporting News*, July 27, 1960: 7.

65 *Ebony:* 54.

66 *Ebony:* 60.

67 Sean Waters, "Former Ace Delivers a Timely Pitch: Ex-Dodger Don Newcombe Fought Alcoholism to Build a Career After Baseball. He Warns Students Not to Repeat His Mistakes," *Los Angeles Times*, February 6, 1994.

68 *Ebony:* 55.

69 William J. Serow, *Biographical Dictionary of American Sports, Baseball Revised and Expanded Edition: G-P*, edited by David L. Porter (Westport, Connecticut: Greenwood Publishing, 2000), 1118.

70 *Los Angeles Times*, February 6, 1994.

71 Across the years, Newcombe has appeared as himself in a number of TV series and made-for-TV movies and documentaries, from *Simon & Simon* (1988) and *Hank Aaron: Chasing the Dream* (1995) to *Rome Is Burning* (2007) and *Pride Against Prejudice: The Larry Doby Story* (2007). He and umpire Art Passarella had cameo roles in "Peanuts and Crackerjacks," an episode of *Nichols*, James Garner's short-lived NBC-TV series. "Peanuts and Crackerjacks" was broadcast on November 4, 1971.

72 Peary, 480, 481.

ERNIE ORSATTI

BY LAWRENCE BALDASSARO

FEW PEOPLE HAVE THE TALENT and good fortune to have successful careers in two such diverse fields as professional sports and the film industry. Ernie Orsatti was one of those lucky few.

In his nine-year career with the Cardinals (1927-1935), Orsatti hit .300 or better in six seasons, twice hit over .330, and finished with a lifetime average of .306. The Los Angeles native's colorful wardrobe also lent a touch of Hollywood glamor to the notoriously unkempt Gas House Gang. As successful as it was, Orsatti's baseball career was really an interlude in a more extensive career in Hollywood. Before he became a professional ballplayer, he was a movie stuntman, prop man and bit player. Then, when his major-league career ended, he and his brothers ran one of the most influential talent agencies in Los Angeles.

Ernest Ralph Orsatti was born in Los Angeles on September 8, 1902. He was the sixth of seven children born to Maurizio and Maria (Manze) Orsatti, Italian immigrants whose names were anglicized to Morris and Mary in the US. Employed as a tailor when the couple were living in Philadelphia, after moving to Los Angeles Morris became the owner of the International Steamship and Railroad Ticket Agency.

Orsatti's path to professional baseball was anything but typical. In fact, he had no childhood aspirations of playing baseball. Growing up in Los Angeles, he dreamed of a career in the movies and spent his spare time hanging around the studios and doing odd jobs. "My interest, as a boy, was in motion pictures and not in baseball," he told *The Sporting News*. "I wanted to be an actor, a director, a cameraman, anything that would identify me with motion pictures. In 1920, I decided to quit school and devote all my time to the picture business."[1] He went to work full-time at the studios, first as a "gofer," then as a stunt man. He walked on the wings of airplanes, dived off cliffs, and did automobile and boat stunts.

In 1922 Orsatti went to work as a prop man and bit player at the studio of the great silent film comedian Buster Keaton. Though he never doubled as a stuntman for Keaton (who did his own stunts), he did double for the actor in a scene in the 1924 film *Sherlock, Jr*. At 5-foot-7 and 150 pounds, Orsatti was a good physical match for the 5-foot-6, 140-pound Keaton.

A lifelong baseball fan and a decent player, Keaton had an indoor baseball team and was also part-owner of the Vernon (California) Tigers in the Pacific Coast League. Orsatti played first base and caught for Keaton's team from 1922 to 1925. When Turkey Mike Donlin, a former major leaguer turned Hollywood supporting actor, saw Orsatti play, he told Keaton that the young man could make more money playing baseball than by working in the studio. In the spring of 1925, Keaton walked onto the movie set where Orsatti was working and handed him a contract to play for Vernon.

After appearing in six games for Vernon, Orsatti was sent to Cedar Rapids (Iowa) in the Class-D Mississippi Valley League, where he hit .347. It was while Orsatti was at Cedar Rapids that Branch Rickey saw him play and made him part of the Cardinals organization by purchasing his contract.[2] Orsatti moved up the Cardinals' minor-league ranks quickly, hitting .386 at Omaha of the Class-A Western League in 1926 and .330 with Houston of the Double-A Texas League in 1927. The 24-year-old, left-handed-hitting outfielder made his major-league debut on September 4, 1927.

Though he showed he could hit major-league pitching (.315 in 92 at-bats), Orsatti was less adept at playing the outfield (five errors in 26 games) and was sent to the Minneapolis Millers of the Double-A American Association in 1928. After hitting .381

with a career-high 15 homers, he was recalled by the Cardinals on August 18.

On August 24 Orsatti's first-inning home run gave the Cardinals a 1-0 win over the Philadelphia Phillies, keeping the team in first place, where it remained for the rest of the season. In his first six games, Orsatti hit three home runs, the only homers he would hit in 69 times at bat that season. (That brief power surge notwithstanding, in 2,165 career at-bats with the Cardinals, Orsatti hit only 10 home runs.)

In 1929, appearing in more than 100 games for the first time, Orsatti hit .332 while playing all three outfield positions. He did not play in 100 games again until 1932, when he had his best season, hitting .336 (sixth best in the NL) and driving in a career-high 44 runs.

After the 1932 season Orsatti was sent a contract offering the same $4,500 he received in 1932. He met with Branch Rickey, hoping to convince him that his performance merited a raise. No sooner did Orsatti raise the issue than Rickey received a phone call he said was from the general manager of one of the Cardinals' minor-league clubs. Rickey purportedly said, "You need an outfielder? I'll call you back in a few minutes. I think I'll have one available for you."[3]

When Orsatti again tried to discuss the contract after Rickey hung up, the phone rang again. This time it was the GM of another farm team asking Rickey for an outfielder. To this request Rickey replied, "I'm sure I've got the guy for you." When Rickey hung up and asked Orsatti what it was he wanted, Orsatti replied, "I just wanted to ask you for a pen, Mr. Rickey, so I can sign my contract." According to William Veeck, Sr., the Chicago Cubs executive (and father of the more famous Bill Veeck), the phone calls were fake. Rickey could set off the telephone bell by stepping on a foot pedal under his desk.[4]

After hitting under .300 (.298) for the first time in 1933, Orsatti hit an even .300 in 1934, then slumped to .240 in 1935. Before the 1936 season the Cardinals planned to send him to Rochester, but Orsatti refused and left baseball.

Orsatti's first four seasons with the Cardinals (1927-1930) came at a time when batting averages were among the highest in history. In fact, three of the top 10 National League averages were recorded in those four years. Still, Orsatti hit well above the league average in every one but the last of his nine seasons. In 1930, when the NL batting average of .303 was the second highest in history, Orsatti beat it by 18 points. And in 1932, his career-high average of .336 was 60 points above the league average.

Orsatti played in four World Series (1928, 1930, 1931, and 1934). In the 1934 win over the Tigers, he appeared in all seven games and hit .318 with a .423 on-base percentage. According to player-manager Frankie Frisch, Detroit fans were so bitter about losing the 1934 Series to St. Louis that when Orsatti was in Detroit on a business trip 25 years later and tried to check into the Sheraton-Cadillac Hotel, where the Cardinals stayed during the '34 Series, the desk clerk refused to give Orsatti a room. "Ernie had to go over the clerk's head to get a room at the hotel," said Frisch.[5]

For a consistent .300 hitter, Orsatti had a hard time cracking the starting lineup. In only four of his nine seasons did he play in more than 100 games. (An ankle injury limited him to 48 games in 1930.) A 1931 preseason article in *The Sporting News* speculating on who might start in left field concluded that Orsatti "seems to be the outstanding candidate for the job" since he was "an athlete with plenty of color and a fine competitive spirit. He is fast and able to cover a large outfield, and with a better-than-average throwing arm."[6]

However, Orsatti played in only 70 games that season, 32 as a starting outfielder. Chick Hafey replaced him in left field (even though "Orsatti was pounding the ball hard") because left field was the only position Hafey could play. As for a possible trade, "the little Italian probably would not object to a transfer, if it meant he could play regularly. No ball player hates the bench more than Ernie."[7]

Orsatti himself attributed his limited playing time to the abundance of good outfielders in the Cardinals organization. "In one way, I came along at the wrong time," he said. "The Cardinals were loaded with outfielders. Every year I'd go to camp thinking I finally had a regular job locked up when some phenom would come along. In 1934, I finally thought I had a regular job in right field. But Branch Rickey drafted an American League retread, Jack Rothrock, who had the best year of his career."[8] Rothrock started nearly every game in right field, while Orsatti started 90 in center.

It was during that 1934 season that Orsatti made a brief return as an actor. On June 26, before a game against the Giants, a scene from a murder mystery, *Death on the Diamond,* was filmed at Sportsman's Park. In the movie a number of Cardinals players are murdered as part of a plot to keep the team from making it to the World Series. The scene takes place late in the season, when the fictional Cardinals are fighting for the pennant. Orsatti played the role of a player who was shot to death while running the bases.[9] A *New York Times* movie critic wrote that in the film the "hitherto unsuspected hazards of ball playing are described with an entertaining combination of humor and grim melancholy."[10]

Having risked his life as a Hollywood stuntman, Orsatti brought that same daredevil mentality to the baseball diamond. Leo Durocher, who joined the Cardinals in 1933, described baseball in that era as "a rough-and-tumble no-holds-barred game played predominantly by farm boys. Generally unschooled, generally unspoiled, generally unsophisticated. Right off the farm or down from the hills."[11]

According to Durocher, Orsatti fit right in with the scrappy Gas House Gang. Along with Pepper Martin and Frisch, who were called the "diving seals" because of their penchant for sliding head-first, Orsatti, a speedy baserunner, also liked to slide head-first. "The uniforms were so filthy that we could have thrown them in the corner and they'd have stood up by themselves," said Durocher. "The bills of our caps were all bent and creased and twisted. We looked horrible, we knew it and we gloried in it."[12]

Teammate Jim Mooney noted that Orsatti was also a regular part of the famous pepper game the Cardinals put on to amuse the fans during warmups. "Orsatti was a great little ol' outfielder," recalled Mooney. "One time we were playing in Chicago, and someone hit a line drive out into center field, and he went out there and caught it and turned two or three somersaults. He was a great little fellow. Orsatti was a showman."[13]

But if Orsatti's aggressive style and soiled uniform made him a bona fide member of the Gas House Gang on the field, he did not glory in looking horrible off the field. Once the uniform came off and he put on his civilian clothes, he stood apart from his teammates. In addition to his impressively consistent hitting, Orsatti brought a splash of Hollywood style to the happily disheveled Cardinals. A photo above a 1932 *Sporting News* story shows him wearing fashionable golf knickers and looking for all the world like golf legend Bobby Jones. In the accompanying story, Harry T. Brundidge described Orsatti's look: "He never wears a hat, and his thick growth of well-oiled black hair is pushed back from his forehead. His flashy sweaters, golf hose, knickers and sports suits

Ernie Orsatti, a nine-year major leaguer, enjoyed success as a movie industry stuntman, prop man, and bit actor.

are Hollywood importations, and his wardrobe is the envy of most of the younger players."[14] In its obituary of Orsatti *The Sporting News* wrote that "Ernie's ensembles made him stand out like a peacock in the ranks of the Gashouse Gang."[15]

At a time when ethnic terminology now considered offensive was commonplace, in the same 1932 *Sporting News* story Brundidge referred to Orsatti as the Dashing Dago, and added that the player, "affectionately known as The Wop in the Cardinals baseball clubhouse, is one of the most popular players on the team."[16]

When Orsatti's major-league career ended in 1935, he returned to Los Angeles and joined his brothers, Frank, Vic, and Al, in the Orsatti Talent Agency.[17] According to Orsatti's son, Ernest F. Orsatti, it was the largest agency in Hollywood.[18] Among its clients were such stars as Sonja Henie, Margaret O'Brien, Betty Grable, Judy Garland, and Edward G. Robinson.

In 1939 Orsatti returned to the minor leagues for one season, appearing in 37 games for Hollywood in the Pacific Coast League and in 31 games for Columbus in the American Association. At the time of his signing with the Hollywood Stars, the *New York Times* reported that Orsatti, "now an actors' agent, is expected to prove a strong drawing card in the film colony."[19]

While still working with his brothers in the talent agency, at some point in the mid-1940s he opened Ernie Orsatti's Oddity Shop and Florist on Sunset Boulevard in Hollywood. His business cards were decorated with a replica of the Cardinals redbirds perched on a bat. According to *The Sporting News*, at that time Orsatti also held a patent on a candy-vending machine and "collects the royalties on the candy bars found in the lobbies of most theaters throughout southern California."[20]

For Orsatti, who spent most of his career in the film industry, the Hollywood lifestyle carried over into his nonprofessional life. In January 1929 he married Martha Von Estey, a San Antonio newspaper writer he met while playing for Houston. In February 1934 Orsatti sued for divorce from Von Estey, charging her with "impairing his baseball efficiency by her 'constant nagging and quarrelsome nature.'"[21]

Orsatti wed for a second time in September 1934, marrying opera singer Inez Gorman in Beverly Hills. The couple had two sons, Ernest F. and Frank. While Orsatti's own career as a stunt performer was short-lived, his two sons continued a tradition that as of 2013 included four generations of Orsattis.

Both sons had long and distinguished careers, each appearing in dozens of films and TV series. In *The Poseidon Adventure* (1972), Ernie, known as "The Legend," performed the death-defying stunt of falling from an upside-down table through what had been the ballroom's ornate glass ceiling. Frank, who died in 2004, worked as Arnold Schwarzenegger's stunt double in *The Terminator* and doubled for Burt Reynolds for nine years.[22] Young Ernie's son, Noon, has also appeared in dozens of films and TV series since beginning his career in 1983. Noon's son, Rowbie, and his daughter, Allie, continue to maintain the Orsatti legacy as stunt performers.

Orsatti's marriage to Gorman ended in 1952. His son, Ernie, who was 12 years old when his parents divorced, described his father as a great athlete and a talented chef. "One of the biggest parties was held on Christmas Eve," he recalled, "when he cooked for dozens of people from show business and the opera world."[23]

In 1960 Orsatti married Canadian native Alice Joyce Ritchie. He and Ritchie operated Orsatti Bail Bonds in Van Nuys, California, until his death at the age of 65 of a heart attack on September 4, 1968. He is buried in San Fernando Mission Cemetery, Mission Hills, California.

SOURCES

In addition to the sources cited in the Notes, and consulting Baseball-Reference.com and Retrosheet.org, the author also conducted a telephone interview with Scott Orsatti on May 31, 2013.

NOTES

1 *The Sporting News*, February 4, 1932: 5.

2 Ibid.

3   *Toledo Blade*, April 1, 1972: 16.

4   Ibid.

5   Frank Frisch, as told to J. Roy Stockton, *Frisch: The Fordham Flash* (Garden City, New York: Doubleday, 1962), 177.

6   *The Sporting News*, April 9, 1931: 1.

7   *The Sporting News*, November 5, 1931: 1.

8   *The Sporting News*, September 21, 1968: x.

9   John Snyder, *Cardinals Journal: Year by Year & Day by Day with the St. Louis Cardinals Since 1882* (Cincinnati: Clerisy Press, 2010), 264.

10 *New York Times*, September 24, 1934.

11 Leo Durocher and Ed Linn, "That Old Gang Of Mine," *Sports Illustrated*, April 7, 1975: 84.

12 Ibid.

13 Peter Golenbock, *The Spirit of St. Louis: A History of the Cardinals and Browns* (New York: Avon Books, 2000), 186.

14 *The Sporting News*, February 4, 1932: 5.

15 *The Sporting News*, September 21, 1968: 36.

16 *The Sporting News*, February 4, 1932: 5.

17 Vic, who starred in football and baseball in high school, was honored as the best all-around athlete in Los Angeles in 1923 and went on to play quarterback at the University of Southern California. As the prize for winning a home run-hitting contest while in high school, he received the bat used by Babe Ruth to hit the first homer in Yankee Stadium, on April 18, 1923. Ruth had donated the bat to the *Los Angeles Evening Herald*.

18 Ernest F. Orsatti, telephone interview, March 7, 2013.

19 *New York Times*, March 29, 1939.

20 *The Sporting News*, February 5, 1947: 7.

21 *San Antonio Light*, February 8, 1934: 17.

22 Frank, who aspired to follow in his father's footsteps as a ballplayer, appeared in 12 games with the Cardinals' affiliate Brunswick in the Georgia-Florida League in 1963, but his career was cut short by an

23 Ernest F. Orsatti, telephone interview, March 7, 2013.

ART PASSARELLA

BY ROB EDELMAN

ACROSS THE DECADES, BASEball players from the celebrated to the obscure have traded in their spikes for movie or TV scripts. Some — Chuck Connors, Bob Uecker, and Greg Goossen come to mind — enjoyed careers in the entertainment industry as, respectively, the star of TV's *The Rifleman*, a sometime film and TV actor and full-time raconteur, and the longtime stand-in for Gene Hackman.

Such also was the case with Art Passarella, a big-league umpire from 1941-42 and 1945-53. After leaving the majors, Passarella regularly worked in front of the camera — and it is not surprising that a Google search for him results in as many showbiz as baseball-related hits. But Passarella did enjoy a healthy career in the majors, and he once offered a spot-on definition of an umpire: "…(W)hen the game starts there has to be a boss, a guy who has the say-so. History has shown that the umpire should have this authority. So I know where I stand and I call 'em as I see 'em regardless of what anybody else thinks."[1]

Arthur Matthew Passarella was born on December 23, 1909, in Rochester, New York. He was the eldest of four children — he had two brothers and a sister — and around his tenth birthday his family moved to Los Angeles.[2] Although many parents are averse to their offspring's desire for a career in the arts, Passarella's situation was the opposite. In his youth, he studied the violin for a decade and his father hoped that he would become a professional musician. But young Arthur had other ideas, wishing instead to be a major-league ballplayer. (A similar child-parental conflict was dramatized in the 1930s in playwright Clifford Odets' *Golden Boy*. Here, the father of Joe Bonaparte, the title character, pressures his son to be a classical violinist, but Joe yearns to take up prizefighting rather than ballplaying.)

In the early 1930s Passarella began playing semipro ball in the Los Angeles area and was proficient enough to sign a couple of professional contracts. Eventually, he rose to the Class B Decatur Commodores (Three-I League) but his baseball skills — not to mention a busted knee — prevented him from moving any higher. So he switched to umpiring and, by 1937, was working semipro diamonds throughout Los Angeles. He also umpired a few games at a tryout at Wrigley Field, where he caught the attention of Russ Hall, a two-year big leaguer (1898, 1901) and secretary of the Association of Professional Ball Players of America. This led to Passarella's being hired to ump in the Class D Evangeline League for $80 per month; ten days later, his paycheck increased to $100 when he switched to the Class C Cotton States League. The Pine Bluff Judges were one of the league teams; while umping in the Arkansas town, Passarella met and began dating Elvina Laurich, whom *The Sporting News* described as "a woman fan [who] stood out as about the only one who didn't razz the umpire."[3] The two wed on March 14, 1938, in Garland, Arkansas, and purchased a home in Pine Bluff.[4]

Next, Passarella moved on to the Class A-1 Texas League, where he umped from 1938 to 1940. League President Alvin Gardner was impressed with Passarella, telling *The Sporting News* that he "learned faster than any umpire … in the league in years."[5] Connie Mack and Joe McCarthy observed him in exhibition games and liked what they saw. American League President Will Harridge sent Tommy Connolly, his supervisor of umpires, to check out Passarella, and Connolly also was impressed. So on November 10, 1940, Harridge announced the purchase of two new AL umpires, Ernie Stewart and Passarella. It was noted in *The Sporting News* that both would be "assigned to service for spring exhibition games, where their work will determine whether they will be retained or farmed out for seasoning."[6] Passarella's efforts were deemed sufficient and he made his AL debut on April 16, 1941. Two years later, he candidly recalled, "My first major-league game behind the plate is easy to remember. I walked out of the dugout and saw Bob Feller warming up. Boy, was I scared. I was my own worst enemy that day, nervous and unsure of myself. But I got by all right. Feller beat John Niggeling of the Browns and I didn't get into any trouble!"[7]

A couple of weeks after Passarella's hire, *The Sporting News* ran a feature article spotlighting his career—and his personality. "He will take a lot of color into major company," wrote reporter Flint Dupre. "Passarella once was credited in the box score with a run kicked in, which he doesn't consider exactly a high point in his short career. He explains that a man was on third base, when the pitcher threw the ball. 'The catcher dropped the throw and in trying to get out of the way, I kicked the ball into the dugout, with the runner from third scoring,' says Passarella. 'I was credited with a run kicked in and the players had considerable fun at my expense.'" The article also foreshadowed his future work as a mentor to wannabe umpires. "He aided a lot of kids in Dallas last winter," wrote Dupre, "and now is doing the same in San Antonio, where he is working in the capacity of a public relations man in a large hotel." Dupre also commented on his stature: "He looks like a small man, because of his build, but actually weighs 182 pounds and stands five feet 11."[8]

Passarella umped in the AL for the following two seasons. While quickly developing a reputation as a top-flight arbiter, he was prone to the kind of freak on-field mishaps that characterized his career. For example, during the 1942 season, a foul tip off the bat of the Red Sox' Bobby Doerr left him with a broken mask, a cut lip and nose, and a pair of chipped teeth.

At the start of the 1943 season, Passarella's AL career was halted temporarily—but not because of injury. On April 18 he became the first major-league arbiter to enter the US Army during World War II. After his induction in Chicago, he was dispatched to Camp Grant, Illinois, where he took his basic training in the Medical Corps. Almost immediately, he began umpiring games between competing camp teams. "After all," he noted, regarding his leave from the majors, "I'm the same as other American boys and I want to get this thing over and get back to baseball." Of military baseball, he observed that the "difference between our games and games in the fine big league parks is great—but it's still the National Pastime—make no mistake about that. The boys won't do without it."[9]

While in the service, Passarella held a range of jobs including work as an MP and guard in a POW camp. Most significantly, during the spring of 1944, he began directing an umpire school at Camp Grant. As reported in the *Toledo Blade*, the school was "believed to be the first of its kind in the country." Its purpose was to "train soldiers planning umpiring careers after the war. A boom in baseball and softball in the postwar period, camp officials said, would create many umpiring jobs."[10]

Passarella was discharged from the Army on December 11, 1944, and he resumed his big-league

Art Passarella, major-league umpire, appeared in films and on TV series—often playing umpires.

career at the start of the 1945 season. His return to the AL was not stress-free. On June 20 he was umpire-in-chief in a game between the Chicago White Sox and St. Louis Browns at Sportsman's Park in St. Louis. Karl Scheel, a 23-year-old former semi-pro hurler and ex-marine who was Chicago's batting practice pitcher, began goading the Browns' bench. In the eighth inning several St. Louis players charged the White Sox dugout and began badgering Scheel in what manager Jimmy Dykes called "the most brutal" attack he had ever witnessed on a ball field. During the melee, fans entered the field; Passarella and his fellow umps needed police assistance to restore order. He submitted a report of the incident to the American League office, which resulted in fines imposed on Browns manager Luke Sewell and several players. Outraged, Browns president Don Barnes declared that Dykes also should have been censured because he "egged on Scheel." Sewell agreed. "It seems to me there was guilt on both sides," he declared.[11]

When Passarella was separated from the military, the AL already had the required 12 arbiters. But he was rehired; at the start of the 1945 campaign, the league employed 13 umps, but this changed on August 15 when Ernie Stewart was fired. The reason given was "disloyalty," with Harridge claiming that he was causing dissension among his fellow arbiters. For Stewart's part, he noted that he merely was attempting to win higher salaries for himself and his colleagues. Stewart reported that on July 20 Passarella and fellow ump Hal Weafer were discussing the low pay of umpires with Commissioner Happy Chandler. At this time, Stewart was brought into the conversation and was asked by the commissioner to sound out other arbiters on the subject. After reporting to Chandler, Stewart noted, Harridge "found out about this, it made him mad, and he fired me."[12] Harridge, however, did not fault Passarella, and that year he umpired in his first World Series; he went on to work two others, in 1949 and 1952, and umped in the 1947 and 1951 All-Star Games.

As time passed, Passarella developed his own on-field style—and it was anything but low-key. Lou Adamie, the scoreboard operator at Sportsman's Park, was famed for his ability to accurately call balls and strikes and post them on the board before the home-plate ump signaled his decision. "I merely study the mannerisms of the umpires," Adamie explained. "I usually can tell whether it's a ball or a strike, but I can't call 'em on my own, so I look for some telltale mannerism which tips me off." Adamie described Passarella as the "most jittery" of the big-league arbiters: an ump who "jumps when about to shout 'Steeeriiike.'"[13] Not surprisingly then, Passarella occasionally was excessively theatrical. On May 22, 1949, he inspected the glove of White Sox hurler Clyde Shoun and determined that the location of its light-tinted manufacturer's label was in violation of baseball's equipment code. Shoun disagreed. The problem was solved when the label was removed from the glove with a pair of shears, but only after Passarella, as reported in *The Sporting News*, "put on a noisy, gesturing performance."[14] Leonard Koppett described Passarella as "talkative and friendly ... [and] one of the best umpires to be stuck in a club car with." But Koppett added that "players would accuse him of showboating, of putting on an act."[15]

Like any person whose workplace is a ball field, Passarella experienced his share of on-field close calls and injuries. On July 8, 1945, James P. Dawson, writing about a Yankees-Tigers contest in the *New York Times*, reported, "In the Tigers' half of the inning a line single by [Hal] Newhouser almost decapitated Art Passarella, working back of second. He ducked just in time."[16] Then on May 12, 1946, in a game pitting the Senators and Athletics, he suffered a broken jaw when he was hit by a foul ball off the bat of Washington's Mickey Vernon. Ten days later, he returned to the field as home-plate ump in an Indians-Red Sox game and, as reported in *The Sporting News*, his "mask was nipped by Johnny Lazor's seventh-inning foul, but he suffered no ill effects."[17] Four days after that, on May 26, Passarella left the field after colliding with the Senators' Buddy Lewis in the first inning of a Washington-Philadelphia game. He did so again on August 30 after suffering a second jaw injury. This time, he was hit by a foul tip at Fenway Park.

Passarella's calls occasionally were not the most popular — and he sometimes felt the brunt of fan frustration. Wrote Louis Effrat in the August 6, 1946 *New York Times*, "While the majority of 25,067 fans booed, Mayor William O'Dwyer presented the Mayor's Trophy to Manager Bill Dickey of the Yankees, immediately after the American League club had beaten the Giants 3-2... The disapproval ... was not against Dickey or the mayor, but in protest against the decision of plate umpire Art Passarella, who called Joe DiMaggio safe at home with the tie-breaking run." As reported in *The Sporting News* on July 9, 1947, "Although umpire Art Passarella was standing right behind the play, 36,752 Cleveland cash customers and manager Lou Boudreau protested his decision calling George Dickey of the White Sox safe on a steal of second, from which he scored the winning run [on] June 29. Boudreau contended Dickey slid into the ball, held by Lou, but the umpire didn't see it that way." If any umpire is around long enough, he likely will find himself at ground zero of a high-profile play. On August 19, 1951, Passarella was the first-base umpire when Eddie Gaedel came to the plate to pinch-hit for the Browns. Gaedel was of course only 3-feet-7-inches tall and weighed 65 pounds — and Passarella and home-plate ump Ed Hurley immediately halted the game. Zach Taylor, the St. Louis skipper, produced the player's contract that Gaedel had signed with Browns owner Bill Veeck, and so the umps allowed him to bat.

Even more significantly, Passarella was at the center of a controversial play that occurred in the fifth game of the 1952 World Series. The Yankees were playing the Dodgers, and Passarella was the first-base ump. The series was tied at two games apiece and the game — in which Brooklyn starter Carl Erskine retired 19 straight Yankees — was tied, 5-5, in the bottom of the 10th inning. Yankee hurler Johnny Sain led off against Erskine and grounded to Jackie Robinson at second. Robby fielded the ball and threw it to Gil Hodges, Brooklyn's first sacker. It seemed that Sain was safe, but Passarella called him out. Sain and first-base coach Bill Dickey vehemently protested, but to no avail. The Dodgers won the game in the next inning, with Duke Snider doubling home the winning run.

Afterward, photos of the play clearly indicated that Passarella had blown the call. For one thing, Sain's foot touched the bag before the ball reached Hodges. For another, before catching the ball, Hodges took his foot off the bag. Red Patterson, the Yankees PR director, admonished Passarella for making "two lousy calls on a single play."[18] The *St. Louis Post-Dispatch*'s J. Roy Stockton labeled the call the "worst decision" of the Series. Passarella responded by declaring that "pictures don't always tell the true story. I was on top of the play and called it as I saw it. That's the way I called it, and I'll stick to it."[19]

Commissioner Ford Frick added some much-needed insight into the hullabaloo, declaring:

> It looks like Passarella called a wrong play, but if he did he's only human. I assure you it's not the first wrong call ever made by an umpire, if it was that. What's all the shouting about? Players make mistakes, too. So do officials. So does the commissioner. A player makes an error, another forgets to cover a base, a pitcher makes a wild pitch, a catcher lets the ball get away from him. Very little is said. But once an umpire makes a wrong call, he is crucified. Why? An umpire is only human. He can make mistakes, too. All I'm interested in is whether he was in the right position to make a call. The picture shows he was.[20]

As the years passed, it seemed that Passarella was increasingly victimized by controversy and physical injury. In 1951 an ankle injury he incurred was originally believed to be a sprain; in August it was diagnosed as a fracture, thus ending Passarella's season. Then in an April 23, 1952, Yankees-Red Sox game, he angered Boston catcher Sammy White after being hit by a foul tip off the bat of Gene Woodling. A momentarily stunned and staggering Passarella instinctively grabbed White's shoulder, which displeased the rookie backstop. Later in the game, a second foul tip, this one off the bat of Hank Bauer, crushed Passarella's mask, and the ump had to be treated with icepacks. The following day, when he was umping at third base, a screaming line drive forced him to sprawl over backward to avoid being hit. Then on July 2 he was hospitalized in New York after pulling a muscle in the previous day's Yankees-Red Sox contest. In a May 15, 1953, Browns-Senators game, Passarella tossed Browns manager Marty Marion and coach Bob Scheffing in the eighth inning after thinking that they were protesting a called strike on Bob Elliott, their third sacker. Marion immediately declared that he was playing the game under protest. The following day, Passarella acknowledged that upon further review Marion and Scheffing were not disputing his call, but the protest was voided because the Browns had won by a 4-0 score. Then on July 5, the ump was right in the middle of a bench-clearing ruckus that resulted when the Tigers' Johnny Bucha, attempting to score from third base on a fly ball, barreled into the Browns' Clint Courtney.

Passarella's plight was summed up in a promotion sponsored by the Simmons mattress company, whose ad campaign awarded Beautyrest mattresses to deserving consumers. One of the "winners" was Passarella. Under a photo of him jawing with a ballplayer and published in the April 13, 1953, *Life* magazine was a caption that read: "Who needs rest more than an umpire? Every day during the season, nine innings of baseball and ten innings of headaches! To Art Passarella of the American League, the Simmons Company presents a Beautyrest mattress."

Still, it was a bit of a shock when, on November 4, 1953, just over a month before his 45th birthday, Passarella announced that he had submitted his resignation to Harridge. He declined to comment on the reason why he quit, and it remained a mystery if he had done so on his own volition or if he was forced out by Harridge. Perhaps Passarella's resignation was linked to backlash relating to the Sain call. "Discussion of the game and the call persisted past the Series," wrote Roger Kahn, "and the umpire, Art Passarella, announced at length that he was 'resigning' from the American League staff. 'It turns out,' Dick Young said through a nasty smile, 'that Erskine didn't really retire 19 straight Yankees. He retired 18 Yankees and one umpire.'"[21]

Nonetheless, Passarella explained that he wished to remain connected to the sport. On the day his retirement was revealed, Eddie Joost was named skipper of the Philadelphia Athletics. A couple of months earlier, rumor had it that Joost was up for the appointment. *The Sporting News* reported that Passarella — perhaps with tongue implanted in cheek — told Joost, "If you ever get to be manager of this club, and don't hire me as a coach, I'll certainly be disappointed in you, Eddie."[22]

Passarella's final big-league appearance was on September 27, 1953. All told, he umpired in 1,668 major-league contests. (Some sources list the number as 1,670.) During his career he ejected players on 21 separate occasions. One whom he tossed twice — both times for bench jockeying — was Johnny Berardino, who eventually altered his name to John Beradino and also opted for a showbiz career, playing Dr. Steve Hardy on the long-running TV soap *General Hospital*.

One of the ejections was reported in *The Sporting News* on June 13, 1951:

> Umpire Art Passarella chased Johnny Berardino, Browns veteran utility infielder, from the bench during the June 5 game with the Athletics, though Berardino claims he "didn't say a word." However, here's what happened: After Passarella had made two trips to the Browns' dugout, warning the players to stop "riding" him, he pointed his finger menacingly at catcher Matt Batts and Berardino, and told them: "One more word out of either of you, and out you go!" All was silence for a few moments. Then suddenly, players in both the Browns' and A's dugouts broke out in loud guffaws. Members of the Athletics pointed to the Browns' bench and Passarella, glancing around, nearly blew a gasket when he saw what was going on. Berardino had slipped back to the trainer's room, obtained a piece of adhesive tape and there he was sitting in the front row of the dugout with the wide piece of white tape

pasted across his mouth. It was only a "gag," but it was more than Passarella had asked for when he demanded silence from his tormentors.

After he exited the majors, the question facing Passarella was: How would he earn a living? (Certainly he was not meant to coach for Eddie Joost.) During the 1947-48 and 1948-49 offseasons, long before his retirement, he worked as an instructor at Bill McGowan's School for Umpires in Florida. In 1949-50 he opened his own arbiter academy. An advertisement in *The Sporting News* on December 7 featured a photo of the smiling ump and some inviting ad copy: "Art Passarella Says: Write me about my Umpire Training School. You will be amazed and interested in my proposition."

The instruction was held in Bartow, Florida, in conjunction with the Bartow Baseball School and the Gus Mauch Trainer's School. During the following offseason, the school was expanded to include a "Players' Division" for young baseball hopefuls, with instruction by pitcher Ed Lopat. After his retirement from the major leagues, Passarella continued his involvement with the school. Some of the advertising highlighted his participation, while others centered on Lopat and Mauch. The school's locations and affiliations also changed. For the 1952-53 offseason, the trio was connected to the St. Augustine Baseball School in St. Augustine, Florida, where Passarella now resided. But in 1953-54, only he and Lopat were involved. The ump's work was featured in a 1955 *Sports Illustrated* article on the proliferation of baseball academies. "[Passarella] trains them and if they show promise, he tries to get them jobs umpiring in Class D leagues," wrote James T. Farrell. "This year he took only four young umpires, all of whom admitted that they had once dreamed of becoming ballplayers before they realized they would never succeed. They took up umpiring to stay in baseball."[23]

Meanwhile, Passarella attempted to find other baseball-related work. He briefly considered a public-relations job but failed to secure a spot with the West Texas-New Mexico League. So he had no choice but to return to the Texas League, where was named umpire-in-chief for the 1954 campaign. But injuries still dogged him. Early in the season he was forced out of action after reinjuring his knee while ducking to avoid a line drive. In June he entered a Fort Worth hospital for a knee operation and was on the shelf for the rest of the season. That August he was removed from the league payroll.

Passarella then hired on as an agent at the St. Augustine branch of the Prudential Life Insurance Company and began hosting *Sports and Scores,* a television show, on WJHP-TV in St. Augustine. The 1955 season found him umping in the Pacific Coast League, where he yet again was felled by injuries. On June 8, in just his second week in the PCL, he suffered a mild concussion when Pete Milne of the Sacramento Solons crashed into him while running out a grounder. Meanwhile, Passarella's knee still bothered him; that August, he consulted with Dr. Bobby Brown, the former New York Yankee, who then was practicing in San Francisco. He underwent knee surgery early in the 1956 season and returned to action on June 16, only to suffer another season-ending leg injury on July 22.

Most significantly, Passarella at this juncture decided to try show business. Johnny Berardino, his old on-field nemesis, reportedly suggested this career change, telling him, "You've been acting all your life—as an umpire."[24] So in 1958, Berardino helped him find an agent and he began securing acting roles in films and on television series; this led to Passarella's entrance into the Screen Actors Guild. (Passarella's movie industry connection dates from the mid-1940s. On December 16, 1945, he, along with Red McDonald, Dewey Widner, and Spike Jordan, three PCL umps, officiated in a contest pitting two teams comprised of major-league players in a benefit for a hospital Christmas fund. Jeanette MacDonald, Frances Langford, Carole Landis, Martha Raye, Kay Francis, and other "film celebrities" also participated in the event.)[25]

Early on, Passarella was the umpire on *Home Run Derby* (1960), a half-hour syndicated TV show that was the brainchild of Mark Scott, a part-time actor and play-by-play announcer for the PCL's

Hollywood Stars. The program, filmed at Wrigley Field in Los Angeles, featured the era's top sluggers in one-on-one competitions that were the precursors of contemporary home-run hitting contests. The "derby" was divided into nine "innings," with three outs to an inning. The batter was not obliged to swing at every pitch; Passarella's job as "umpire-in-chief" was to determine if any pitches not swung at were strikes — and a strike (or any ball not hit over the fence) was the equivalent of an out.

In some of his acting assignments, Passarella was appropriately cast as an arbiter. He and Emmett Ashford were respectively the "1st Umpire" and "2nd Umpire" in a 1969 episode of the TV series *Ironside*, and he was behind the plate on several other shows, including *Guestward Ho!* (1961), a brief summer-replacement series titled *Summer Fun* (1966), *Nichols* (1971, in an episode titled "Peanuts and Crackerjacks"), and, most impressively, the John Ford-directed "Flashing Spikes," a 1962 *Alcoa Premiere* episode featuring James Stewart as an ex-major leaguer banned from baseball for accepting a bribe.

In the *Guestward Ho!* episode, Passarella played a Little League ump who tosses a female manager, played by Joanne Dru. In a UPI piece that appeared around the time the episode was aired, Passarella claimed that he was "type-cast as a hood ... a gangster. I'm always somebody's henchman. It's like when I went into the service, they made me an MP right away."[26] He observed that he had played thugs on *The Untouchables* and *Malibu Run* — but also a "hayseed" on *The Andy Griffith Show*. Other nonbaseball roles included "Prison Guard #2" on an episode of *Sea Hunt* (1959) and "Officer Sekulovich" on various mid-1970s episodes of *The Streets of San Francisco*. Passarella's character was named for series star Karl Malden, whose birth name was Mladen Sekulovich, and he earned a steady paycheck as Malden's longtime stand-in. But perhaps his most intriguing small-screen appearance came in a 1963 installment of *General Hospital*. Passarella played a patient; this particular episode also featured Yogi Berra as Dr. Aloysius Sweeney, a brain surgeon.

Passarella umpired on the big screen in *Critics Choice* (1963), a Bob Hope-Lucille Ball comedy. He is not credited as having appeared in the film version of *Damn Yankees* (1958); however, according to the *American Film Institute Catalog of Feature Films*, "Modern sources add Nesdon Booth, Joseph Mell, Leo Theodore, and Art Passarella to the cast" — although Passarella cannot be spotted anywhere in the film. Easily his most memorable movie appearance was in *That Touch of Mink* (1962), a romantic comedy in which he worked the plate at Yankee Stadium and mixed with a quintet in the Bronx Bombers dugout. Two were "civilians": Cathy Timberlake (Doris Day), an unemployed "computer machine" operator; and Philip Shayne (Cary Grant), a wealthy mover and shaker. The remaining three were Roger Maris, Mickey Mantle, and Yogi Berra.

Passarella's film and television career was noted by industry types who were baseball buffs. A letter penned by longtime entertainment industry publicist Cliff Dektar and headlined "SHOW BIZ UMP," was published in the April 18, 1977, *Sports Illustrated*. "When Danny Kaye's show-biz types play Roy Clark's Tulsa Drillers ... they will need an umpire. I nominate Art Passarella, the retired American League ump who has been working off and on in show business for the last 20 years." Dektar added that Passarella was well-suited to acting because he "admits to being a ham as an umpire. ..."

Passarella was 71 when he died of a heart attack on October 12, 1981, in Hemet, California, where he and his wife, Elvina, had settled. So little was known about him that his brief *New York Times* obituary was filled with errors. For instance, it was stated that he was an AL arbiter from 1945-1953; not cited were the two seasons he spent in the majors prior to his military service. Also mentioned was that "for ten years, he appeared on television as Sergeant Sekulovich, alongside Karl Malden and Michael Douglas, in *The Streets of San Francisco*." Not only was Passarella in just a handful of episodes, but the series itself lasted not quite six seasons, from September 1972 to June 1977.

Passarella was buried in Graceland Cemetery in Pine Bluff, Arkansas; Elvina died four years later, in 1985. Interestingly, Art's gravestone references his military service—it is noted that he was a "Sgt US Army"—but not his baseball or show-business careers.

SOURCES

Edelman, Rob, *Great Baseball Films* (New York: Citadel Press, 1994).

Kahn, Roger, *Memories of a Summer: When Baseball Was an Art, and Writing*

About It a Game (New York: Diversion Books, 2012).

Koppett, Leonard, *All About Baseball* (New York: Quadrangle Books, 1974).

Birtwell, Roger, "Open season on Passarella in Red Sox-Yankee Games," *The Sporting News*, May 7, 1950.

Dawson, James P., "Yanks Lose, 3-2, in Tenth Inning," *New York Times*, July 8, 1945.

Dupre, Flint, "Passarella, New A.L. Umpire, Uses Color in Getting Up Ladder,"

The Sporting News, November 28, 1940.

Edelman, Rob, "Damn Yankees: A Washington Fan's Fantasy," *The National Pastime*, 2009.

Effrat, Louis, "Yanks Top Giants, 3-2, on Run in Ninth, *New York Times*, August 6, 1946.

Farrell, James T., "Get Your Mitt, Johnny—It's Time for Class!" *Sports Illustrated*, February 28, 1955.

Felker, Carl T., "Barnes Calls Browns' Brawl Fines 'Unfair.'" *The Sporting News*, June 28, 1945.

Ferdenzi, Til, "Ben Casey Beware! Yogi Winning Raves as Surgeon on Video," *The Sporting News*, August 24, 1963.

Gillespie, Ray, "Battler Clint Gets a New $1,000 Hint to Mind Manners," *The Sporting News*, July 15, 1953.

------, "Short Career of Midget in Brownie Uniform," *The Sporting News*, August 29, 1951.

Ruhl, Oscar, "From the Ruhl Book," *The Sporting News*, July 25, 1951.

------, "From the Ruhl Book," *The Sporting News*, April 30, 1958.

------, "Scoreboard Magician Beats Umps to Punch," *The Sporting News*, March 3, 1948.

Schumach, Murray, "Yankee Sluggers Make Film Debuts," *New York Times*, August 24, 1961.

Siler, Pfc. Tom, "Passarella Still Calling 'Em as He Sees 'Em, Views of

Colonels, Captains Notwithstanding," *The Sporting News*, June 10, 1943.

St. Amant, Joe, "Ex-Ump Passarella Now an Actor," *Hammond (Indiana) Times*, May 1, 1961.

Stockton, J. Roy, "Highs and Lows of Yank-Dodger Slam-Bang," *The Sporting News*, October 15, 1952.

Zminda, Don, "Home Run Derby: A Tale of Baseball and Hollywood," *The National Pastime*, 2011.

"19th Hole: The Readers Take Over," *Sports Illustrated*, April 18, 1977.

Advertisement. *The Sporting News*, September 10, 1947

------. *The Sporting News*, December 10, 1947.

------. *The Sporting News*, October 27, 1948.

------. *The Sporting News*, December 7, 1949.

------. *The Sporting News*, December 28, 1949.

------. *The Sporting News*, September 13, 1950.

------. *The Sporting News*, October 3, 1951.

------. *The Sporting News*, October 29, 1952.

------. *The Sporting News*, November 26, 1952.

------. *The Sporting News*, September 9, 1953.

------. *The Sporting News*, September 30, 1953.

"A.L. Ump Assignments," *The Sporting News*, March 15, 1945.

"All Umpires Dissatisfied With Wages, Claims Ernie Stewart, Fired by A.L.,"

The Sporting News, August 23, 1945.

"American League," *The Sporting News*, July 9, 1947.

"Art Passarella, Ex-Umpire, Later Acted in Films and TV," *New York Times*, October 16, 1981.

"Art's Start in Army," *The Sporting News*, April 15, 1943.

"Berardino Puts on 'Gag'—Gets Thumb From Umpire," *The Sporting News*, June 13, 1951

"Big League Stars to Play in Coast Benefit Game," *The Sporting News*, December 13, 1945.

"Buffs' Radio Night Draws 11,483," *The Sporting News*, September 8, 1954.

"Camp Grant Starts School to Train Baseball Umpires," *Toledo Blade*, April 5, 1944.

"Caught on the Fly," *The Sporting News*, December 3, 1942.

------, *The Sporting News*, August 8, 1956.

"Decision on 'Battle of Dugout' In St. Louis Now Up to Harridge," *New York Times*, June 22, 1945.

"Firing of Umpire Creates Big Stir," *New York Times*, August 16, 1945.

"Frick Indicates Umpire Made Bad Call on Sain," *New York Times*, October 6, 1952.

"From Blue to Khaki," *The Sporting News*, April 29, 1943.

"Jaw Dislocated," *The Sporting News*, May 16, 1946.

"Major Flashes," *The Sporting News*, June 5, 1946.

"Major League Flashes," *The Sporting News*, July 9, 1952.

------. *The Sporting News*, May 27, 1953.

"Minor Meetings," *The Sporting News*, January 27, 1954.

"Obituaries," *The Sporting News*, October 31, 1981.

"Passarella an Insurance Agent," *The Sporting News*, November 24, 1954.

"Passarella Decides to Quit; On A.L. Ump Staff Since '41," *The Sporting News*, November 11, 1953.

"Passarella Gets His Umpiring Job Back," *Toronto Daily Star*. January 11, 1945.

"Passarella Joshed Joost: 'Hire Me as Coach, Eddie,'" *The Sporting News*, November 25, 1953.

"Passarella on Ump Faculty," *The Sporting News*, May 7, 1947.

"Passarella Out for Season," *New York Times*, August 29, 1951.

"Passarella Promoted," *Pittsburgh Press*, December 21, 1943.

"Russ Hall, Charity Leader, Dies; Served as Player, Pilot, Umpire," *The Sporting News*, July 8, 1937.

"Senators Defeat Athletics, 3 to 2," *New York Times*, May 27, 1946.

"Shoun in Stormy Debut, Loses Trademark on Glove," *The Sporting News*, June 1, 1949.

"Texas League," *The Sporting News*, May 5, 1954.

------, *The Sporting News*, May 12, 1954.

------, *The Sporting News*, May 26, 1954.

"Texas Releases 2 Umpires in League Economy Move," *The Sporting News*, June 16, 1954.

"To Celebrate National Beautyrest Month Simmons Announces: 1953 Beautyrest Award," *Life*, April 13, 1953.

"Tuning In," *The Sporting News*, May 26, 1955.

"Two New A.L. Umpires," *The Sporting News*, November 14, 1940.

"Ump Art Passarella Back With Army Sergeant Lingo," *The Sporting News*, December 21, 1944.

"Ump Passarella Suffers Mild Concussion in Field Mishap," *The Sporting News*, June 22, 1955.

"Umpires Only Human, Too, Says Frick, Defending Passarella on Disputed Call," *The Sporting News*, October 15, 1952.

"Woe for the Umpire," *Newsweek*, May 27, 1946.

afi.com/members/catalog/DetailView.aspx?s=&Movie=52519

arkbaseball.com/tiki-index.php?page=Art+Passarella

baseball-reference.com/bullpen/Art_Passarella

baseball-reference.com/bullpen/Evangeline_League

familysearch.org/pal:/MM9.1.1/XC8Z-DV8

imdb.com/name/nm0664819/

retrosheet.org/boxesetc/P/Ppassa901.htm

search.ancestry.com/cgi-bin/sse.dll?gl=allgs&gsln=Laurich&gspl=6&gss=seo&ghc=20

NOTES

1 Pfc. Tom Siler, "Passarella Still Calling 'Em as He Sees 'Em, Views of Colonels, Captains Notwithstanding," *The Sporting News*, June 10, 1943.

2 The 1910 United States Census lists "Arthur Passarella" with a 1910 birth year. His parents are "Robert Passarella" and "Lullu Passarella" and his residence is "Rochester, Ward 8, Monroe, New York." The 1930 United States Census lists "Arthur Passarella" and his three siblings (Matthew, Pauline, and John) as Los Angeles residents. Only here, his parents are "Rocco Passarella" and "Lulu Passarella." In the 1940 census, "Lulu Passarella" is listed as the "head of household." She died on December 21, 1953, and a brief obituary was published in *The Sporting News* on January 6, 1954.

3 Flint Dupre, "Passarella, New A.L. Umpire, Uses Color in Getting Up Ladder," *The Sporting News*, November 28, 1940.

4 Passarella's marriage to Elvina Laurich is duly noted in various sources. However, under "California, County Marriages 1850-1952," "Arthur Matthew Passarella" (birth year: 1909; father: "Rocco Passarella"; mother: "Lulu Matlie") is listed as having married Anna Mary Manguso in Los Angeles on January 25, 1931. "Arthur Matthew Passarella" (birth year: 1910; father: "Rocco Passarella"; mother: "Lulu Matalie") also is listed as having married Lucille Afton Cheshire in Los Angeles on October 28, 1934.

5 Dupre, "Passarella, New A.L. Umpire."

6 "Two New A.L. Umpires," *The Sporting News*, November 14, 1940.

7 Siler, "Passarella Still Calling 'Em."

8 Dupre, "Passarella, New A.L. Umpire."

9 Siler, "Passarella Still Calling 'Em."

10 "Camp Grant Starts School To Train Baseball Umpires," *Toledo Blade*, April 5, 1944.

11 Carl T. Felker, "Barnes Calls Browns' Brawl Fines 'Unfair'." *The Sporting News*, June 28, 1945.

12 "Firing of Umpire Creates Big Stir," *New York Times*, August 16, 1945.

13 Oscar Ruhl. "Scoreboard Magician Beats Umps to Punch," *The Sporting News*, March 3, 1948.

14 "Shoun in Stormy Debut, Loses Trademark on Glove," *The Sporting News*, June 1, 1949.

15 Leonard Koppett, *All About Baseball* (New York: Quadrangle Books, 1974).

16 James P. Dawson, "Yanks Lose, 3-2, in Tenth Inning," *New York Times*, July 8, 1945.

17 "Major Flashes," *The Sporting News*, June 5, 1946.

18 Roger Kahn, *Memories of a Summer: When Baseball Was an Art, and Writing About It a Game* (New York: Diversion Books, 2012).

19 "Umpires Only Human, Too, Says Frick, Defending Passarella on Disputed Call," *The Sporting News*, October 15, 1952.

20 Ibid.

21 Kahn, *Memories of a Summer*.

22 "Passarella Joshed Joost: 'Hire Me as Coach, Eddie,'" *The Sporting News*, November 25, 1953.

23 James T. Farrell, "Get Your Mitt, Johnny—It's Time For Class!" *Sports Illustrated*, February 28, 1955.

24 "Obituaries," *The Sporting News*, October 31, 1981.

25 "Big League Stars to Play in Coast Benefit Game," *The Sporting News*, December 13, 1945.

26 Joe St. Amant, "Ex-Ump Passarella Now an Actor," *Hammond (Indiana) Times*, May 1, 1961.

JERRY PRIDDY

BY WARREN CORBETT

JERRY PRIDDY'S LIFE WENT from pinstripes to prison stripes.

When second baseman Priddy and shortstop Phil Rizzuto came up to the Yankees together in 1941, Priddy "was the hotshot of the pair," sportswriter Milton Richman wrote. "He was smart in the sense that the chances were good he would succeed in anything he undertook."[1] But Priddy failed in New York and Hollywood. He failed on the PGA tour. His failure at extortion put him behind bars.

After the Yankees traded him, manager Joe McCarthy said, "Priddy is the best ballplayer I ever let go."[2] Priddy did turn into a productive player with a slick glove, high on-base percentage, and decent bat, but he never lived up to the stardom that was predicted for him.

Priddy was tarred as a clubhouse lawyer, a term that meant "troublemaker." To sportswriters of the day, a clubhouse lawyer was any player who said anything besides "I'm just so happy to be here." But Priddy had an unfortunate knack for rubbing people the wrong way, especially people in authority.

Gerald Edward Priddy was born in Los Angeles on November 9, 1919, to Gerald Howard Priddy and the former Beatrice Briggs. Although the son was usually called Gerald or Gerry in newspaper stories, he preferred "Jerry."

His father worked as a shipping clerk for a hardware company until he was accused of theft and fired. "After a year and a half, after we'd been living on beans and rice, the company discovered the real culprit and asked my father to come back to work," Jerry said. "They gave him a raise and tried to make amends for their error."[3] Decades later Jerry would claim that he, too, was wrongly accused.

Young Jerry preferred tennis to baseball because he didn't like the ball stinging his hand. A reluctant convert, he became a star second baseman and pitcher at Washington High and in Junior American Legion ball. When Yankee scout Bill Essick offered him a contract, he signed because his family needed money. He left school at 17 to go to Class-D ball in Rogers, Arkansas, in 1937.

Priddy was an immediate success. A right-handed batter, he hit .336 with 25 doubles, 10 triples, and 10 home runs, then went home to finish high school. He met Rizzuto the next year at Class-B Norfolk, and they were the prodigies of the Piedmont League. Rizzuto, two years older at 20, hit .336 to Priddy's .323. (Rizzuto was believed to be 19; like many players, he lopped a year off his age.)

They rose together in 1939 from Class B to the highest minor-league level, Double-A Kansas City. Even in the loaded Yankees farm system, the heavenly twins were surefire stars in the making. They were roommates on the road and practically inseparable on and off the field. One writer quipped that Priddy's high-school girlfriend, Evelyn Herberger, agreed to marry him only if he promised that Rizzuto would not come along on the honeymoon.

Priddy was just under 6 feet tall, weighing 170 to 180 pounds, blond and self-assured. Rizzuto, 5-feet-6, was a timid Brooklyn boy who became the butt of jokes. If an older teammate told him to order a soup sandwich, he'd do it. Priddy was his protector and mentor. "He was a natural-born leader," Rizzuto said. "He felt he was as good as anybody on the ball field. Even better."[4]

The 1939 Kansas City Blues were one of the strongest minor-league teams in history. Managed by Billy Meyer, they won 107 games, the most by any American Association team in a 154-game schedule. The Blues had their own DiMaggio, Vince, who hit 46 home runs. Priddy led the team with a .333 batting average and led the league in total bases with 44 doubles, 15 triples, and 24 homers. Rizzuto's .316

average came with less power, but 33 stolen bases.⁵ Their sparkling defense dazzled the league. Both led their positions in double plays, and Priddy topped all second basemen in putouts and assists.

But these were the Yankees, winners of four straight World Series. There was no room for the phenoms on the major-league roster, so they went back to Kansas City in 1940 and did it all again. The team set a league record for double plays. Priddy batted .306/.383/.493 with 38 doubles, 10 triples, and 16 homers. Rizzuto was even better: .347/.397/.482 and 35 stolen bases. He was named American Association MVP and *The Sporting News* Minor League Player of the Year.

The Yankees slipped to third place in 1940, a humiliation that called for radical change. Even before spring training the club handed the shortstop job to Rizzuto, replacing Frank Crosetti and his .194 batting average. But what to do with Priddy? Yankee second baseman Joe Gordon was coming off a 30-homer season at age 25 and was considered the AL's best on defense.

Manager McCarthy made his opinion of Priddy clear when he traded first baseman Babe Dahlgren during spring training. McCarthy shifted his All-Star second baseman to first, opening a spot for the prize prospect. "I have no doubts about Priddy," the manager said. "Mark my words, New York fans will go nuts over Gerry and Phil."⁶

From the moment Priddy put on pinstripes, his cocky attitude got him into trouble. "That first day he walked into the Yankee camp," Rizzuto recalled, "he went over to Joe Gordon and told him, right to his face, that he was a better second baseman than him."⁷ The two rookies were threatening the jobs of popular, proven Yankees, so the other players shunned or hazed them. When they were shoved aside in batting practice, Rizzuto took it and said nothing, but Priddy talked back. Before long Joe DiMaggio stood up for Rizzuto, leaving Priddy to bear his teammates' resentment.

The 1941 season opened with Gordon at first, Priddy at second, and Rizzuto at short, but both newcomers showed early jitters. Priddy was uncharacteristically shaky in the field and was hitting .204 after his first 27 games. Rizzuto stood at .246 the same day. Gordon was uncertain and unhappy in his new position. With the Yankees one game under .500 on May 15, McCarthy gave up on his experiment and benched both rookies.

Rizzuto went back into the lineup when Crosetti was spiked a few days later and stayed there, except for military service, for 11 years. Priddy stayed on the bench. He thought he deserved a shot at the first-base job when another rookie, Johnny Sturm, failed to hit, but McCarthy gave him only a handful of games there. Priddy did get some playing time at third when Red Rolfe got sick, but he batted only .213 in 56 games. McCarthy thought the great expectations might have overwhelmed him.

Rolfe, who had chronic colitis, was not ready for Opening Day in 1942. Priddy took his place for the first 17 games, but batted just .229 with three extra-base hits. Back on the bench, he grew frustrated and sulky. By the end of the season he had raised his average to .280 in 59 games and was begging McCarthy to trade him. The manager, who had no use for malcontents, obliged, though he acknowledged he might be making a mistake.

In January 1943 the Yankees swapped Priddy to Washington. The deal raised questions because, with World War II underway, a player's military draft status was more important than his batting average. At 23, Priddy was prime draft bait since he and Evelyn had no children. (Evelyn was pregnant with the first of three.) Washington manager Ossie Bluege, with fingers crossed for luck, described Priddy as "the man who'll be the making of our infield. And he'll give us that long ball we've needed for years."⁸

The Senators had been hit harder by the draft than any other team in 1942. With their two best players, Cecil Travis and Buddy Lewis, in the Army, the team finished seventh. When other clubs began feeling the pinch as draft calls grew in 1943, owner Clark Griffith said, "The rest of the league is coming back to us."⁹ Washington climbed to second place, albeit 13½ games behind the Yankees.

Given a regular job, Priddy batted .271 with a .709 OPS, better than average, and played his usual sterling defense. He also brought the pinstripe mystique to Washington. "Having Jerry Priddy at second base made the difference," outfielder Bob Johnson said. "You know, Priddy isn't a great ballplayer. But the son-of-a-goat's a Yankee."[10]

After the season Priddy's draft number came up. Even in the Army Air Force he couldn't get away from Joe Gordon; they wound up on the same team at Hickam Field in Hawaii. Playing ball was Priddy's primary occupation during his two years in the service.

Returning in 1946, Priddy gave the Senators about average offensive production, then fell off a cliff in 1947. His batting average dropped to .214 as the club sank to seventh place. He won praise as a smart, hypercompetitive player, but some teammates resented his take-charge personality. He and first baseman Mickey Vernon had a fistfight in the clubhouse. "Get this straight," Priddy told a reporter. "I play to win. If I'm dogging it I expect to get told off; if the other guy's loafing he's going to hear from me and I don't give a hoot whether he likes it or not."[11]

Priddy also had differences with manager Bluege. At one point during the losing season, he refused to sign a public statement of support for the manager—the only player to say no—and told Bluege, "I don't like you and you don't like me. I know it and you know it."[12]

It was no surprise when the Senators traded Priddy to the St. Louis Browns for infielder Johnny Berardino, but the deal was canceled because Berardino announced his retirement to concentrate on his acting career. So the Browns paid $35,000 for Priddy. That *was* a surprise; nobody suspected that the cash-poor Browns had $35,000. Owner Bill DeWitt recouped the money when he sold Berardino to Cleveland for a reported $50,000, and Indians owner Bill Veeck talked the Hollywood wannabe into playing another year.

Priddy's career turned around in the winter of 1947-48. On a barnstorming tour with Bob Feller, he took batting tips from the National League home-

Jerry Priddy, who hoped for a post-baseball Hollywood career—which failed to materialize.

run champion, Ralph Kiner. He also had surgery for a sinus ailment that had affected his eyesight. In 1948 he hit .296 with 40 doubles, 9 triples, and 8 homers, adding 86 walks for a .391 on-base percentage. Batting third in the order, he drove in a career-high 79 runs while leading all major-league second basemen in putouts, assists, double plays, chances per game, and errors. At 28 he looked like the player the Yankees had expected him to be. He put up similar numbers in 1949, but the Browns were still losers and still broke.

Somehow Priddy had squeezed a $24,000 salary out of owner DeWitt, making him the club's highest paid player since Hall of Famer George Sisler two decades earlier. DeWitt remarked later, "He was a fast liver and a big spender."[13] After the 1949 season DeWitt unloaded that salary, sending Priddy to Detroit for pitcher Lou Kretlow and a reported $100,000.

Detroit manager Red Rolfe, Priddy's former Yankees teammate, slotted him second in a strong lineup, ahead of the 1949 batting champion, George Kell, and outfielders Vic Wertz, Hoot Evers, and Johnny Groth. The Tigers spent much of the summer in first place, but the Yankees caught them in September and finished three games in front. Priddy set major-league records by starting five double plays in one game and turning 150 for the season. He hit .277 with a career-best 13 homers, 104 runs scored, and 95 walks.

Priddy's offensive production slipped a bit in 1951 while he still played every game and led the league's second basemen in putouts, assists, and double plays. He had played 386 consecutive games by July 6, 1952, when his season ended with a gruesome injury. Sliding home, he caught his spikes on the plate and broke his right leg and dislocated his ankle. He returned in 1953 to appear in 65 games before the Tigers released him in October.

At 34, Priddy managed for a year at Seattle in the Pacific Coast League, then played in the PCL for two more seasons. He finished his career with the San Francisco Seals under his nemesis Joe Gordon in 1956.

Priddy had long been looking forward to a career in the Hollywood film industry after baseball. As early as 1942 he took an offseason job at the Paramount studio, working on the technical crew for the Bing Crosby movie *Dixie*. He served as a technical adviser for the 1952 film biography of Grover Cleveland Alexander, *The Winning Team*, starring Ronald Reagan as the Hall of Fame pitcher.

The finale of *The Winning Team* is set during the 1926 World Series between Alexander's St. Louis Cardinals and the New York Yankees. Stock footage of Babe Ruth is seen throughout; he is shown in the Yankee dugout (along with Joe McCarthy, even though Miller Huggins managed the Yankees that season) as well as swinging at a pitch, circling the bases after belting a homer, and trotting down to first after being walked. However, in a newly filmed sequence, #3 is shown coming to the plate and swinging at a pitch. Bob Lemon, who served as Reagan's pitching coach, said Priddy put a pillow under his shirt and appeared here as The Bambino.

According to the Internet Movie Database, Priddy had unbilled bit parts in three other movies with baseball scenes: *The Stratton Story* (1949), *Kill the Umpire* (1950), and *Three Little Words* (1950). He had hoped to work his way into an executive position, but that opportunity never materialized.

Instead, he tried to make it as a professional golfer. A Los Angeles car dealer sponsored his unsuccessful run on the PGA Tour in 1960 and 1961, but his winnings in his first year totaled only $1,105.54.

In the 1960s he was president of Priddy Paper Products Co., a wholesale distributor, with former outfielder George Metkovich as vice president. By 1973 Priddy was running an advertising and public-relations agency in Los Angeles when the sky fell.

On the morning of June 5, 1973, a man called the Princess cruise line in Los Angeles and warned that there were bombs aboard one of the company's ships, the *Island Princess*, which had just left Long Beach for Mexico carrying 850 passengers and crew. The caller said he would reveal the location of the bombs if the company paid him $250,000.

The cruise line called the FBI and ordered a search of the ship. Two mysterious small packages were found, each about the size of a pack of cigarettes. The captain threw them into the sea without looking inside.

The anonymous caller set up a money drop in a garbage can. When Priddy came to pick up the cash (actually a bundle of newspapers), agents arrested him. The drop turned out to be near his office in Burbank. The episode, a model of criminal ineptitude, was over in about eight hours.

"That wasn't the Jerry I knew," Rizzuto said. "He was outspoken and hotheaded … but outside of baseball he was a regular guy. He knew a lot of prominent businesspeople. It just didn't make sense."[14]

At trial the prosecutor said Priddy needed money because his business was failing. Testifying in his own defense, Priddy admitted making the phone calls, but said he did it because he feared for his life. He said an unknown man with a Mexican accent had threatened to kill him and his family unless he agreed to serve as front man for the extortion scheme.

The jurors didn't buy it. They took less than five hours to convict him.

The judge sentenced Priddy to nine months in prison, a remarkably lenient penalty. He could have gotten 20 years. The judge said he took into account Priddy's spotless record and more than 40 letters, from entertainers Bob Hope and Gene Autry and many former ballplayers, attesting to the defendant's good character.[15]

Priddy served 4½ months at Terminal Island federal penitentiary in Los Angeles County. "He called me when he got out of prison," Rizzuto said, "and he told me if he'd had to spend one more day in there he would have been a hardened criminal."[16]

When he was released, Priddy was dead broke. It's not known how he supported his family for the next six years. On March 3, 1980, he got up from the breakfast table and fell dead of a heart attack. He was 60.

His obituary in *The Sporting News* began, "Gerald E. (Jerry) Priddy, who spent much of his 11-year major league career denying he was a clubhouse lawyer…"[17] Such was his reputation. The reality is that he put up better numbers than Rizzuto—at bat and in the field—in a shorter career, but Rizzuto is the one with a plaque in the Hall of Fame.

SOURCES

In addition to the sources cited in the Notes, the author also consulted:

Baseball-reference.com.

Crissey, Harrison. "Baseball and the Armed Services," in *Total Baseball*, Second Edition (New York: Warner, 1991).

James, Bill. *The Politics of Glory* (New York: Macmillan, 1994).

Thackrey, Ted Jr. "Big Potential Eventually Led to Big Problems for Athlete," *Los Angeles Times*, March 10, 1980: 32.

NOTES

1. Milton Richman, United Press International, "Recalled Priddy as Confident, Shrewd Player," *Independent* (Long Beach, California), June 7, 1973: 47.
2. "Marse Joe Rated Priddy 'Best Player I Ever Let Go,'" *The Sporting News*, October 29, 1947: 5.
3. Bob Broeg, "Public Microscope Again Focused on Jerry Priddy," *St. Louis Post-Dispatch*, June 7, 1973: 3C.
4. Richman.
5. Bill Weiss and Marshall Wright. "Top 100 Teams." Minor League Baseball website, milb.com/milb/history/top100.jsp?idx=12, accessed April 17, 2016.
6. Dan Daniel, "McCarthy Sees Priddy Tops," *New York World-Telegram*, April 9, 1941, in Priddy's file at the National Baseball Hall of Fame Library, Cooperstown, New York.
7. Richman.
8. Shirley Povich, "This Morning," *Washington Post*, April 2, 1943: 13.
9. Bill Gilbert, *They Also Served* (New York: Crown, 1992), 83.
10. Red Smith, "Sport Cameos," syndicated column in the *St. Louis Post-Dispatch*, December 11, 1949: 57.
11. Frank Finch, "Roller-Coaster Priddy Rolls High Again," *The Sporting News*, February 8, 1950: 3.
12. Al Costello, "Priddy Offsets Light Hitting With Fast Thinking," *The Sporting News*, October 29, 1947: 5.
13. Broeg.
14. Carlo DeVito, *Scooter: The Biography of Phil Rizzuto* (New York: Triumph, 2010), 261.
15. Accounts of the case from the *Los Angeles Times*: John Kendall, "Ex-Major Leaguer Priddy Faces Arraignment in Ship Bomb Plot," June 6, 1973: 3; "Priddy Convicted of Extortion in Threats to Blow Up Cruise Ship," December 10, 1973: 3; and United Press International, "Former Yankee Star Held in Extortion Plot," *Progress Bulletin* (Van Nuys, California), June 6, 1973: 2.
16. DeVito.
17. "Obituaries," *The Sporting News*, July 19, 1980: 47.

BEANS REARDON

BY BOB LEMOINE

"When Mr. Reardon speaks you are under the impression that he has just spit out a hand grenade."

Harry A. Williams, *Los Angeles Times*[1]

BEANS REARDON LEARNED A lot about umpiring at the age of 16 when he worked as a riveter's assistant. "Riveting was good education for umpiring," he recalled. "If I didn't make the rivet hot enough the riveter would cuff me over the face with his leather glove and cuss me out. As a result, I was pretty good with those cuss words and rough work when I decided to try umpiring."[2]

The self-proclaimed "last of the cussin' umpires," Beans Reardon led a remarkable life both inside and outside of the baseball diamond. He was a small but scrappy Irish kid from the Boston area who learned never to back down from a fight. His grittiness carried him through the tough neighborhoods of Los Angeles and his days constructing boilers and swinging a pickaxe. He found his place in the sandlots around Los Angeles, where his tough but fair demeanor was discovered as the stuff umpires were made of. Reardon had a right arm that would call players out, or throw a fist when needed in the days when donnybrooks were common. With his distinctive polka-dot bow tie, he became one of the most visible and respected umpires over his 24-year National League career. Reardon also had cameo appearances in the early years of Hollywood, befriended celebrities, and was featured in a Norman Rockwell painting that placed him on the cover of the *Saturday Evening Post*. He left umpiring at an early age because he could make more money selling beer, but treasured his surplus of umpiring stories, which he was delighted to share for the rest of his life. He followed his own advice: "Hustle, be on top of plays, know the rules, and be honest with yourself."[3]

John Edward Reardon was born on November 23, 1897, in Taunton, Massachusetts, the son of William F. and Margaret (Ennis) Reardon. Both paternal and maternal grandparents had emigrated from Ireland. William Reardon was a dyer and foreman in a cotton mill, and the part-owner of a saloon. William was injured as a catcher in a 1910 semipro game when, not wearing a chest protector, was hit by a foul ball above his heart. His injuries led to his death from a "tumor of mediastinum" in 1913 when John was a child.[4] John's older brother, Bill, attended college, but John did not. "I never graduated from any place but grammar school. … I wasn't the best scholar who ever lived," Reardon said.[5]

Reardon learned his brute honesty from his mother, who impressed upon him not to tell a lie. "I've always been a little thickheaded and quick to tell somebody to go to hell. I got sent home from school one time for calling a nun an SOB. I don't know why I'm like that. Maybe I'm just honest," Reardon said.[6] At 14 he worked at the Reed & Barton silversmith shop in Taunton.[7] He loved baseball, but was undersized. "I had to stand twice in the same spot to make a shadow," he wisecracked.[8] He attended baseball games in Boston, and played for the Young Red Wings youth team in Taunton, which won the 1912 city championship. Squeaky, as he was called, played right field.[9] Reardon made up for his small size by being a solid, speedy fielder. He was not content playing in games with kids his own age, so he played on semipro teams when he was 15. Reardon's mother remarried and the family moved to Los Angeles when he was 16.[10] By the time he was 17, he had thrown his arm out, and from then on concentrated on being an umpire.[11]

"We lived in Boyle Heights, which was a pretty rough section of the city," Reardon said. "I went to work as a messenger boy, riding a bicycle. When I turned 18, I went to work as a boilermaker's apprentice in the Southern Pacific Railroad shops."[12] This neighborhood toughened Reardon even more for a future umpiring career. "It was on the East Side and there was a mixed population of Irish and Jews … and it was plenty tough. … You had to either fight or at least be willing to fight. If you didn't you'd just have to move, that's all."[13] He started umpiring games for his church team at St. Benedict's. Soon, he was umpiring in sandlots all over Los Angeles. He would umpire and play in the railroad league games held over the noon lunch break.[14] This was where he acquired his nickname of Beans.

"Whenever people asked me where I was from, I told them Boston because I figured nobody in California knew where Taunton was. So one day, when I came up to bat, Lee Allen, a fancy Pullman car painter, yelled, 'Come on, Baked Beans, old boy, hit one now!' The crowd picked it up, and from then on everybody called me Beans."[15]

Reardon was befriended by Harry Hammer, a blacksmith who was a catcher on a semipro team, and soon Reardon was traveling with the team, helping wherever needed. One Sunday in Pasadena, California, an umpire was needed. Hammer suggested Reardon, saying, "That kid can umpire." Reardon umpired the game, and then was offered a job umpiring every Sunday for $3 per game. Reardon demanded another quarter for carfare. "Every Sunday he'd put six half-dollars right in the middle of my locker, and I'd say, 'Another quarter,'" Reardon recalled. "I always had to battle him for the other quarter."[16]

Players often found Reardon jobs in the semipro leagues, saying, "Take care of the kid; the little SOB can umpire."[17] Eventually, he was making more money as an umpire than as a boilermaker. During World War I, Reardon went to the San Pedro shipyards as a boilermaker's apprentice, and also umpired games there. In 1918 he umpired in the War Service League for $7.50 per game, with an $11 outfit, his first umpire uniform.[18]

Reardon moved to Bisbee, Arizona, in 1919, being promised he could find umpiring jobs while working a "soft" job in the copper mines. "Soft job, hell!" he recalled. "They put me to work 'mucking' on a 'slope' 1,400 feet underground. We'd dig out the ore with a pickaxe and shovel it into a big shaft close by. The boss told us to be careful not to step in that hole because it was 200 feet deep. It was damned hard work. … Had to string our lunches over a beam in the shaft to keep the rats from eating them. The rats were big as tomcats. … After three or four days I wondered what the hell I was doing there."[19] *The Sporting News* mentions Reardon umpiring in Bisbee for a weekend old-timers' league.[20] Reardon returned to Los Angeles shortly thereafter.

Reardon was umpiring a game in Pasadena involving the Los Angeles Angels of the Pacific Coast League. Angels manager Wade "Red" Killefer encouraged him to think about a career in umpiring. "You've got the ability and if you've got the courage, you don't need anything else," Killefer said.[21] They contacted Sammy Beer, a former Angels pitcher who was in Saskatoon, Saskatchewan. Beer found Reardon an umpiring job in the Class-B Western Canada League, making $250 a month plus expenses. "But that was better than swinging a 16-pound sledgehammer in the boiler shop 54 hours a week for 25 cents an hour."[22] Reardon was 22, and now a professional umpire. Reardon was extremely frugal, and saved $750 out of his total $1,000 salary for the four months. The league president asked him what he had been living on. Reardon winked and said, "On my good looks."[23]

Reardon's Calgary days were tough, with few amenities. "You had to dress in the groundkeeper's shack, where he kept his equipment," he recalled. "There was no shower, either. You just put your good clothes on over the dirt and sweat till you got back to the hotel. … In my day, you got no cab money. You had to wrestle your bag on a streetcar, dress in a shack that looked like an outhouse, umpire yourself with probably only a six-inch flag as a foul marker 450 feet from the plate."[24] There was also the rowdiness of the fans who "would follow you down the street and yell at you. … I had several street fights because I couldn't tolerate the names they were calling me."[25]

"You didn't have enough money for food, so you just hustled, that's all," Reardon said. "I stayed in a place in Moose Jaw across the street from the railroad station; had to run down the hallway to the bathroom. Umpires didn't get enough money in those leagues to rent a place with a toilet in your room. ... You had to be tough to survive."[26] Because many umpires quit after just a few games, Reardon's fare home was guaranteed only if he lasted the entire season. After one game, policemen offered to escort him through a back way in the park to avoid the ferocious fans waiting for him at the gate. Reardon rejected the offer, saying, "I didn't sneak in, and I won't sneak out."[27] "I came in the front gate and that's the way I'm going out, and if one of those fresh thugs makes a move at me, I'll flatten him. If you want to come with me, all right. But I don't need you," Reardon told the gendarmes.[28]

Umpire Beans Reardon may be seen in one baseball film (The Kid From Left Field) *and two non-sports features* (Internes Can't Take Money, Klondike Annie).

Reardon never backed down from a fight. Back in California, he umpired a Winter League game on November 21, 1920, between the Los Angeles White Sox and an all-star team. "Umpire Beans Reardon put down a slight demonstration of Bolshevism in the first of the sixth inning, when he called Boeckel out at the plate on Moore's throw to Ray," the *Los Angeles Times* reported. "Irish Meusel dissented, whereupon Beans pulled off his mask and chest protector and did a Jack Dempsey that made Irish wince with envy. About 25 cops intervened and pressed all the bellicose disposition out of both Meusel and Reardon and the game went merrily on."[29]

Reardon returned to Canada in 1921, and met New York Yankees scout Bob Connery, who was traveling through Canada looking for prospects. Connery recommended Reardon to PCL President William H. McCarthy, who hired him in 1922, telling him, "Now, I'm going to tell you something, Beans. We want umpires in this league, we don't want fighters."[30] Reardon did have a fistfight in San Francisco with player Paddy Siglin,[31] and newspapers carried pictures of the encounter. He also fought with manager Charlie Pick of Sacramento, who, after Reardon had thrown a player out, "came charging out of the dugout after me," Reardon recalled. "He threw a punch at me, but I was ready for him and we tangled. ... It was a better fight than many a one I've paid money to see since. We both got in some pretty good licks."[32] "Yes, I had a reputation as a fighter. But I really wasn't a fighter. I had some fights, but I didn't enjoy them. They just couldn't be avoided."[33]

In Portland, Oregon, fans would regularly throw seat cushions at Reardon at the end of the game. When asked if they ever threw the cushions before the game, Reardon joked, "Naw. Those fans up there wouldn't throw away a cushion they paid a nickel for until they had gotten their money's worth out of it."[34]

Reardon befriended major-league umpire Hank O'Day, and they would travel to the racetrack in Tijuana, Mexico, on Sundays in Reardon's Hudson Speedster. O'Day recommended Reardon to National League President John Heydler, and Beans was hired in November of 1925, after four years in the

PCL.[35] Heydler warned him to never be in any fights. Reardon objected, saying that being about 5-feet-6 and 130 pounds, you have to be prepared. Heydler responded, "Okay, but promise me you won't throw the first punch."[36]

At the train station on April 9, 1926, Reardon waved to the crowd that came to see him off. "I'll sure do my darnedest to make good back there," he yelled. The train was heading to St. Louis, and Reardon's major-league umpiring career had begun.[37]

"Reardon has curly brown hair, blue eyes, and a square cut chin. He speaks with a nasal twang, which is his birthright. He comes from Massachusetts — from Taunton," wrote Damon Runyon.[38] Reardon's career could have ended early when a play in Pittsburgh led to Brooklyn's Chick Fewster having some unkind words for him. The umpire spun him around and would have hit him if Rabbit Maranville hadn't grabbed his arm. "Rab probably saved my job," Reardon gratefully acknowledged.[39] On a return trip to Boston, a delegation from Taunton came to Braves Field to welcome "Squeaky" home, including Mayor Andrew J. McGraw, Police Chief John P. Duffy, and former teammates from the Young Red Wings, who made a presentation on "Reardon Day."[40]

One memorable game in Reardon's rookie year occurred on August 15, 1926. Brooklyn loaded the bases when Babe Herman hit a fly ball off the fence in right field. One run scored, but runners Dazzy Vance, Chick Fewster, and Herman all wound up on third base. "Damn it, wait a minute. I got to figure this out," Reardon yelled. He awarded the base to Vance and called Fewster and Herman out. "That's it. The side's out. Let's play ball, fellas." Herman doubled into a double play.[41]

Reardon never got along with Bill Klem, chief of the National League umpires. He disregarded Klem's order for NL umpires to wear a chest protector under their coat. Reardon wore the outside inflated protector used by American League umpires. Reardon said he promised his mother he would never get hurt or suffer an injury due to a lack of protection.[42] National League umpires were also asked to wear a four-in-hand tie, but Reardon wore a blue and white polka-dot bow tie for his entire career.[43]

In 1927 Reardon had a cameo in the MGM silent film *Slide, Kelly, Slide*, along with players Bob Meusel and Tony Lazzeri.[44] In 1928 he was cast as an umpire in the Richard Dix film *Warming Up*, which included several major leaguers. *Warming Up* was Paramount's first film with sound. In the transition between silent films and talkies, production companies were experimenting with synchronizing sound into the film. While there was no dialogue in the film, post-production editing added the crack of the bat and the roar of the crowd to the action on the field.[45] This film is in the category of "goat-gland films."[46] No copy of the film is known to exist.

In August 1929 Reardon had surgery for appendicitis. Under spinal anesthesia, he was able to watch the operation as it took place. Before it concluded, Reardon wisecracked, "Doc, you'd better take a good look around in there and if you see anything else I don't need, take it out, too."[47] Reardon missed the rest of the season and a chance to umpire in the 1929 World Series.[48] He recovered, and got married in Los Angeles on November 23, 1929, to Marie Lillian Schofield.[49] The couple settled in Los Angeles.[50]

Reardon umpired in the 1930 World Series, and considered it his biggest thrill in baseball. It was the first World Series he had ever seen, and he wore the commemorative ring for the rest of his life.[51] He joined a group of major leaguers in a tour of Japan in October of 1931.[52] "No Japanese player ever talks back, none ever disputes a decision and not even the spectators razz the umpire," he said.[53] Reardon lost 10 pounds, however, not stomaching the raw fish and eels.[54]

Reardon umpired the 1934 World Series as "a man with the poise of a Supreme Court judge. ... He will jerk his thumb with the austere finality of a Nero."[55] He felt anxiety before a World Series game. "I don't say I never called a wrong one — maybe plenty of 'em wrong. But I'd hate to call one in the Series when so much is riding on every pitch and every slide. ... The night before the big game always gives me the jitters."[56] Reardon was umpiring first base in

Game Seven when Ducky Medwick's hard slide into Marv Owen at third base led to a brawl and fans throwing debris on the field. Commissioner Kenesaw Mountain Landis removed Medwick from the game.

Reardon was also remembered for his wit and humor. Philadelphia Phillies manager Jimmie Wilson argued with him on a caught-stealing call, yelling, "You know something, Beans. There are fifty thousand people in the ballpark and you're the only SOB who thinks he's out." Reardon replied, "Yes, but I'm the only SOB who counts." Wilson returned to the dugout laughing.[57] A disgusted Hack Wilson once threw his bat up into the air after striking out. "If that bat comes down, Hack, you're outta the game," Reardon bellowed.[58] National League players often referred to Reardon as having "rabbit ears," claiming that you could whisper something at the Polo Grounds in New York and he would hear it while working a game in Boston.[59] Casey Stengel was managing in Boston and took exception to Reardon's ball-and-strike calls. Making his way up two of the three dugout steps, Stengel debated whether to come out and argue. Reardon warned him to stay right where he was. Finally, Stengel remarked, "I quit. You're the only bloke I've ever seen who can umpire and argue at the same time."[60]

Reardon was being accosted by a loudmouth fan one day, and looked into the crowd to identify him. As fate would have it, the fan was Reardon's waiter at a restaurant that night. He sheepishly took his order, and was extremely courteous to the umpire. Reardon asked the man why he, a total stranger, had been called such terrible names. "Well," the fan muttered, "I am an old man and I have slaved all my life. My bunions burn my feet. I am browbeat 12 hours a day. The chef curses me at one end; the customers throw scorched eggs in my face at the other. I go crazy. My only relief is to go to the ballpark and holler at you."[61]

Reardon's reputation for a no-nonsense, profanity-laced style became legendary. A player once asked NL President Ford Frick, "Mr. Frick, a ballplayer gets fined $50 for swearing at an umpire, right?" Ford concurred, and when the player said Reardon had sworn at *him*, Frick remarked, "Don't be mad. Consider it a compliment. That's like having anyone else say 'hello' to you."[62]

Reardon enjoyed the conflicts. "I never liked to toss 'em out of the game. If I had, there wouldn't have been anybody left to cuss at."[63] "If a player swore at me, I'd swear back at him. It was either that or chase him out of the game. And if I did that, I had to make out a report, and I'd rather leave him in."[64] Bob Broeg wrote in *The Sporting News* that Reardon would "rather exchange sulphuric insults than pull his rank. Reardon's four-letter forensics were never more eloquent than when he and Frank Frisch were raising their penetrating pipes in cheek-to-jowl arguments which were classical."[65] Frisch was once ejected by Reardon and fined $50. Later that night, Frisch phoned Reardon and invited him to the bar. Reardon recalled, "It not only cost him $50 and five rounds of beer, but I borrowed his car for the evening and then told him to phone the garage and tell 'em to fill 'er up."[66]

Reardon appeared in the 1935 Mae West film *Goin' to Town*,[67] and also received $50 a day "as technical advisor when they were shooting baseball films."[68]

Fans in Cincinnati showered Reardon with pop bottles after he made a call against the home team on July 17, 1935. "The shower of glassware from the right field pavillion furnished the most exciting interlude in the long game which was marked by much bickering on both sides. The missiles were aimed at Umpire Beans Reardon because of his ruling in the seventh inning…" wrote the Associated Press.[69] NL President Ford Frick fined umpires Reardon and John "Ziggy" Sears for inciting the crowd.[70]

Still, Reardon was grateful he hadn't been working in the copper mines all those years. "Pretty soft job you have at that, Beans," someone yelled to him on the New York subway. "Yeah!" Reardon hollered back. "Let 'em yell at me for two hours every day, and I have the rest of the time to myself."[71]

Reardon was behind the plate for Babe Ruth's "last hurrah" on May 25, 1935, when the Bambino, now with the Boston Braves, hit his final three home runs in a game at Pittsburgh. He also ejected Ruth in 1938, when he was coaching at first base for Brooklyn.[72]

Reardon would attend horse-racing events at Santa Anita, California, with celebrity friend Al Jolson, who could rarely match Reardon's knack for betting on the photo-finish winner. "I love to bet on what the photo will show on a photo-finish horse race," Reardon boasted. "I'll give any odds to any takers. But I don't get many takers. Guess people know I spent a lot of years calling quick decisions on fast action. … I can pick the winner by a whisker!"[73] However, Commissioner Kenesaw Mountain Landis prohibited Reardon from gambling.

Reardon stayed busy in the 1935 offseason. "Now I had two weeks' work with Mae West on that new one that's coming out, *Klondike Lou*, or something like that. I had another two weeks in that grand opera thing with Gladys Swarthout and Jan Kiepura, acting like a stagehand or an electrician. It was easy for me."[74] The Mae West feature was eventually titled *Klondike Annie*, and also included an appearance by Jim Thorpe.[75]

"You would have been a fine asset to baseball if you had stayed in the movies," Brooklyn manager Casey Stengel remarked to Reardon in 1936.[76]

Reardon suffered two sunstrokes during the 1936 season, and was ordered by doctors to take the rest of the year off. "I wasn't feeling very good about it," he remembered, "until I saw the paper the next day. There I read that the same day I collapsed a camel of Barnum and Bailey's circus passed out while they were taking it to a train. … It died two days later. I knew then that if the heat killed off a camel, maybe I could take it better than I thought."[77]

Reardon appeared in the 1937 film *Internes Can't Take Money*, starring Barbara Stanwyck and Joel McCrea.[78]

Apparently Reardon was also a landlord in the Los Angeles area; *The Sporting News* wrote that tenants of his apartment building were suffering from the unusually cold winter and "have demanded that Beans install bathtubs before another winter rolls around. They say they have no place to store their coal."[79]

Reardon umpired in the 1943 World Series. On a train trip from New York to St. Louis, a thief reached under the pillow on his Pullman berth and swiped his wallet, containing $300. Reardon saw the intruder slipping away and cornered him, leading to a scuffle in which he sprained his finger, but got his wallet back. The man locked himself into a lavatory, and then jumped out a window while the train sped along. "I had a heck of a time," Reardon recalled. "I was trying to get my money back and hold up my pajamas at the same time."[80]

In late 1944 Reardon joined a USO baseball tour to the South Pacific to entertain servicemen in World War II. "We'd put in 16 hours a day talking baseball to servicemen and answering questions. They just couldn't get enough," Reardon said. He stole the show with his tales of umpiring.[81] He returned in January of 1945 and traveled to Chicago to speak to owners of major war plants in the city.[82] "Before I started on the trip (to the Pacific) I thought I was tough," Reardon told his audience. "Now I know I'm not tough at all. How anybody can think he is tough, after seeing what those kids in the South Pacific are going through every day, stops me. I have seen kids without eyes, without arms, without legs—and without life. Just looking in on their courage makes me blush that I ever thought I was tough, but mighty proud that I was born in the same country from which they sprang."[83]

Reardon was an alternate umpire for the 1946 World Series, which paid him $750 plus expenses. He arrived mere moments before Game Six in St. Louis as his train was either delayed or broke down (according to two different reports) and he took a 100-mile cab ride from Effingham, Illinois, which cost him $25.[84]

Reardon loved to have a good beer, and would walk out of a bar if they didn't have Budweiser. His brand loyalty led to a second career for him. Budweiser offered him a job making advertisements and sharing his baseball stories in talks. In 1946, Reardon bought the Budweiser distributorship in Long Beach, California.[85]

On July 20, 1947, at Ebbets Field in Brooklyn, St. Louis led Brooklyn 2-0 entering the ninth inning. Ron Northey of the Cardinals hit a long fly ball to center field that hit the top of the wall. As Northey approached third base, Reardon signaled home run, which slowed Northey's pace and led to his being thrown out at the plate. The Cardinals protested the game, claiming deception by Reardon.[86] Brooklyn scored three in the bottom of the ninth to win the game, 3-2, but NL President Frick ruled the game a tie, despite the fact there was only one out recorded in the bottom of the ninth, "in the name of common sense and sportsmanship." Brooklyn won the makeup game on August 18.[87]

A fight broke out on Opening Day in Cincinnati, April 19, 1948, after a play at second base. A fan tussled with Reardon, while fellow umpire Jocko Conlan wrestled with a photographer.[88] In October of 1948, Reardon's souvenir warehouse was robbed—the burglar stealing five autographed baseballs. "The only baseballs they didn't take were the ones with my autograph," he reported.[89]

Also in 1948 a photographer appeared at Ebbets Field and took pictures of Reardon and fellow umpires Larry Goetz and Lou Jorda, as well as Brooklyn coach Clyde Sukeforth and Pittsburgh manager Bill Meyer. These were reference photographs Norman Rockwell would use to paint the cover of the *Saturday Evening Post* for April 23, 1949.[90] The painting, named *Tough Call, Game Called Because of Rain*, or *Bottom of the Sixth Inning*, depicts three umpires eyeing the rainfall. Lauren Applebaum writes, "Rockwell pays tribute to baseball's uncelebrated heroes, the umpires, who dwarf the ballplayers during a game. ..."[91] Reardon stands in the center, holding his chest protector and mask in one hand, and holding his other hand palm-up, catching raindrops.

In July of 1949, Marie Reardon was robbed in their home in Long Beach, California. She was bound and gagged in a closet while the robbers made off with $4,200 in jewelry. She was able to keep her wedding band when she pleaded, "It has never been off my finger."[92]

The 1949 season was Reardon's last as an umpire and he would now devote himself totally to his beer distributorship. "I'm getting out of umpiring. ... Umpiring is a good job and I'd do it again if I had my life to live over. I have to get up at 7 A.M. to take care of my business here. When I'm umpiring, I get out of bed at 10 A.M. and work a couple of hours a day. You can't beat those hours. And my salary comes in five figures."[93] Reardon retired after the 1949 World Series, but umpired at the Latin Olympics in Guatemala in late 1949 and some spring training games in the spring of 1950.[94]

Reardon appeared on NBC Radio in an episode of Ralph Edwards' *This Is Your Life* on April 19, 1950.[95] In his post-umpiring years he also wrote a column called "The Umpire" for the Newspaper Enterprise Association, which was carried in newspapers across the country. The Q&A style included random baseball trivia and umpiring questions sent in by readers.[96]

Marie Reardon died of a heart attack on March 9, 1953, at the age of 57. The couple had no children, but Marie had a grown son, Stanley Schofield, from a previous marriage.[97] Reardon continued to run his beer-distribution business, which was reported to be profiting $2 million yearly in 1953.[98] On July 31, 1953, Twentieth Century-Fox released the motion picture *The Kid From Left Field*," starring Dan Dailey and Anne Bancroft. Reardon portrayed an umpire.[99]

On June 28, 1954, Reardon married Nell Eugenia Schooler, who owned an aluminum-window business that provided windows for the United Nations building. She was an avid painter who had studied art in the Netherlands, and she painted a portrait of Nancy Reagan that hung in the White House.[100] Along with her paintings, the Reardons' den included Beans' whiskbroom, polka-dot bow ties, the Rockwell painting, and pictures with Gary Cooper and other movie stars. There was also a large picture of a nude Mae West. "She always sent him a copy of that picture every Christmas," Eugenia said. "No, I was never jealous."[101]

Reardon appeared on the November 14, 1954, episode of *The Jack Benny Show* entitled "The Giant Mutiny." The episode was a spoof on *The Caine Mutiny* and also included baseball managers Leo Durocher, Fred Haney, and Chuck Dressen, and pitcher Bob Lemon.[102] Reardon sponsored a youth baseball team in the Long Beach Police League called the "Little Beans."[103] He sold the Budweiser distributorship in 1967 to Frank Sinatra for around $1 million but continued to work for Budweiser, making speaking appearances around the country. "Everyplace I go I run into someone I've known in baseball," Reardon said.[104]

One of his stories involved the time he called baserunner Granny Hamner safe, but inadvertently gave the out sign. He asked Hamner if he had heard him call safe, and Hamner said yes. "I know," Reardon told him, "but only you and the second baseman heard it and 8,000 people saw me call you out. Granny, it's 8,000 to 3, and you're out." Another favorite story included a baserunning blunder by Tommy Henrich, who was tagged out. Henrich asked Reardon to let him stand there pointing his finger at the ump for a couple of minutes so fans would boo Reardon and forget Henrich's boneheaded play.[105]

Eugenia Reardon traveled with her husband, calling on customers at the local taverns. "The people loved to see Beans," she recalled. "He never tired of going out. He loved to talk. He was very witty about this funny business called baseball."[106] Beans and Eugenia frequently attended Dodgers and Angels home games. The Reardons loved art, and would often visit Paris, Eugenia's birthplace, and she would point out historic buildings to him. The very vocal Reardon would be humbled watching his favorite artist. "He'd come out and sit three or four hours in the studio and watch me paint. He never talked at all, just watched me," Eugenia fondly remembered.[107]

In 1970 Reardon was presented the Bill Klem Award for meritorious service to baseball. In response he said, "I'm very glad to receive the Klem Award, but I'll tell you the truth. Klem hated my guts and I hated his."[108] Reardon also sent a get-well card to old nemesis Frankie Frisch, who was hospitalized after a car accident. "When you get prayers from the bottom of the cold heart of an umpire, you should have quick results and a speedy recovery," Reardon wrote.[109]

Reardon died on July 31, 1984, at the age of 86, at his home in Long Beach, after suffering from arteriosclerosis and two strokes. He is buried with his first wife, Marie, at Calvary Cemetery in Los Angeles.

While he has never been inducted into the Baseball Hall of Fame, there is a part of him there. "I loved my little blue and white polka-dot bow tie," Reardon said. "That tie is more famous than I am; it's in the Hall of Fame."[110]

That tie could tell a lot of stories, too.

SOURCES

Besides the references cited in the Notes, the author consulted the following sources:

Ancestry.com

Beans Reardon file at the Baseball Hall of Fame, Cooperstown, New York.

Familysearch.org

Gerlach, Larry R. "Reardon, John Edward 'Jack,' 'Beans,'" in David L. Porter, ed., *Biographical Dictionary of American Sports: Q-Z* (Westport, Connecticut: Greenwood Press, 2000), 1257-1258.

NOTES

1. Harry A. Williams, "Bengals Belt Bees Blithely," *Los Angeles Times*, September 25, 1921: 19.

2. J.G. Taylor Spink, "Beans Calls Himself Out as Umpire," *The Sporting News*, October 12, 1949: 8.

3. Frank Graham, "Beans—the Vet Bluecoat Who Never Grew Up," *The Sporting News*, December 20, 1945: 2.

4. Tom Wall, *Augusta Chronicle*, May 16, 1941, notes that this information was contained in a Cincinnati baseball publication.

5. Larry R. Gerlach, *The Men in Blue: Conversations With Umpires* (New York: Viking Press, 1980), 4.

6. Ibid.

7. Gerlach, 23. The Reed & Barton silversmith shop began in Taunton in 1824. Taunton was nicknamed the Silver City because of its many silver-industry businesses. Reed & Barton, the last remaining silversmith company in Taunton, filed for Chapter 11 Bankruptcy in February of 2015. Charles Winokoor, "Silver City No More? Taunton's Reed & Barton Files for Bankruptcy," *Taunton Gazette*, February 19, 2015, tauntongazette.com/article/20150219/NEWS/150216074/13406/NEWS/?Start=1. Retrieved April 1, 2015.

8. Gerlach, 5.

9. Kerry Keene, "Taunton Native Donned Ump's Mask in Majors for 24 Years," *Taunton Gazette*, May 21, 1994: 7.

10. Some accounts say age 14 or 15. Reardon stated 16.

11. Graham.

12. Gerlach, 5.

13 Jack Diamond, "Play 'Em Safe, Call 'Em Safe, Says 'Beans,'" *San Francisco Chronicle*, January 14, 1936: 21.

14 Ibid.

15 Gerlach, 5.

16 Gerlach, 6.

17 Ibid.

18 Ralph S. Davis, "Reardon Became Ump, Without Being Player," article of unknown origin dated April 21, 1932, in Reardon's Hall of Fame file; "Beans' First Job Behind Plate Paid Him Just $3," *The Sporting News*, October 12, 1949: 8.

19 Gerlach, 6.

20 Edgar Munzel, "25 Years Lower Beans' Boiling Point," *The Sporting News*, August 31, 1944: 7.

21 Gerlach, 6-7.

22 Gerlach, 7.

23 Spink.

24 Munzel.

25 Ibid.

26 Gerlach, 7.

27 Gerlach, 8.

28 Graham,

29 Ed O'Malley, "Walter Mails Gets Jarring," *Los Angeles Times*, November 22, 1920: 119.

30 Gerlach, 8.

31 "Paddy Siglin Loses to 'Beans' Reardon," *Los Angeles Times*, August 19, 1922: 112.

32 Munzel.

33 Gerlach, 9.

34 "Baseball Pick-Ups Gathered From Hither and Thither," *Los Angeles Times*, November 30, 1924: A6.

35 "'Beans' Reardon Goes to National League," *Los Angeles Times*, November 6, 1925: B1.

36 Gerlach, 9. Reardon's *Sporting News* umpire card on the Retrosheet website lists him as 5-feet-9 and 190 pounds. Other sources, including Baseball-Reference.com, and the Internet Movie Database list him as 6 feet tall.

37 "Gene Tunney Arrives; Dempsey's Challenger Blows in as Kearns, Dorval, and 'Beans' Reardon Pull Out for East," *Los Angeles Times*, April 10, 1926: 11.

38 Damon Runyon, "Runyon Says," International Feature Service, in the *Harrisburg Evening News*, April 29, 1926: 19.

39 Gerlach, 9.

40 "Taunton Fans Coming Tomorrow to Do Honor to Reardon, Umpire in National League," article of unknown origin dated May 26 in Reardon's Hall of Fame file. The Braves hosted the Giants on May 28, 1926, in Reardon's first year, and he is listed in the box scores as umpiring that series.

41 Gerlach, 21; "Three Men on Third," research.sabr.org/journals/online/39-brj-1977/197-three-men-on-third.

42 Michael Gavin, "Wind Bags Again Vogue With NL Umps," *Boston Record American*, August 31, 1952, 18.

43 Associated Press, "Reardon to Retire as Umpire," *The Advocate* (Baton Rouge, Louisiana), October 4, 1949: 14.

44 Dan Thomas, "Big League Players in Hollywood," *Springfield* (Missouri) *Leader*, January 30, 1927: 28.

45 "Paramount's First Sound Film: A Newspaper Picture," *New York Times*, July 22, 1928: 93. Richard Dix, the male lead, portrayed Bert Tulliver, a baseball pitcher who tries out for the Yankees. He doesn't win a job in spring training, and endures the wrath of the team's star hitter and villain. He works at a carnival and draws the attention of Mary Post, daughter of the Yankees' owner, portrayed by Jean Arthur. She gets him another tryout with the Yankees, and he winds up in the "world's series." When the Yankees' starting pitcher is injured, Tulliver comes on to pitch, predictably with the bases loaded and no outs. Tulliver is also distressed in believing Mary will wed someone else. But then Mary nods to Tulliver that she will marry him, which is all the motivation he needs to strike out the side, the last of which was the villain who was now playing for Pittsburgh. Tulliver was the hero and Reardon was the home-plate umpire who called the villain out on strikes. The reviewer for the *New York Times*, however, was not impressed. "Paramount's first synchronized picture—'Warming Up'—appears to have been done in a little too much of a hurry. The synchronization is faulty in spots, the acting is not particularly good, and the plot reads like a success story from one of the lesser magazines." Another review from the *New York Times* concluded, "The synchronizing is such, however, that the smack of a ball against a bat is heard some time before Lucas (the pitcher) has finished winding up. … There is plenty of noise in the exciting parts, and music when it isn't so exciting." ("The Screen: The Great American Game," *New York Times*, July 16, 1928: 27).

46 Goat-gland films were attempts to add sound to already completed silent films. The term came from a surgical technique developed by John R. Brinkley in which he transplanted testicles from male goats into men suffering from low libido. Movie critics used the term for describing desperate attempts to bring new life into dead films. Despite the poor review, *Warming Up* was popular with the public, and New York's Paramount Theater broke existing house records. See "Grift, Goats, and Gonads: Historians Ponder the Colorful Career of John Brinkley, American Quack," *The Chronicle of Higher Education* No. 16 (2002), accessed March 13, 2015; Debra Ann Pawlak, *Bringing Up Oscar: The Story of the Men and Women Who Founded the Academy* (New York: Pegasus Books), 2011, Anthony Slide, *Silent Topics: Essays on Undocumented Areas of Silent Film* (Lanham, Maryland: Scarecrow Press (2005), 79.

47 From an article of unknown origin in Reardon's Hall of Fame file.

48 "Umpire 'Beans' Reardon Must Go Under Knife," *Boston Herald*, August 11, 1929: 13; "Augie Walsh Sold to Chicago," *Los Angeles Times*, September 14, 1929: 9.

49 "Did You Know That," *State Times Advocate* (Baton Rouge, Louisiana), December 7, 1929: 10.

50 "Umpire Reardon Weds Coast Girl," article of unknown origin in Reardon's Hall of Fame file.

51 Keene.

52 "1931 Tour of Japan," vintageball.com/1931Tour.html, retrieved April 12, 2015.

53 Japan Umpire's Eden, Says 'Beans' Reardon," *Evening Tribune*, San Diego, January 6, 1932: 16.

54 L.H. Gregory, "Gregory's Sports Gossip," *The Oregonian* (Portland, Oregon), January 6, 1932: 18.

55 Henry McLemore, United Press, "Night Before the Series Plain Hell on the Umps," *Omaha World Herald*, October 3, 1934: 18.

56 McLemore, 19.

57 Gerlach, 17.

58 Bob Broeg, "Beans Reardon Makes Himself Heard," *The Sporting News*, February 17, 1973: 40.

59 *Boston Herald*, May 21, 1931: 29.

60 Newspaper Enterprise Association, "Interference of Owners Blamed for Poor Umpiring," *Daily Illinois State Journal* (Springfield, Illinois), October 4, 1953: 21.

61 Jimmy Powers, "Rassle Riots Beneficial," *Omaha World Herald*, October 17, 1934: 13.

62 Newspaper Enterprise Association, "Reardon Still the Ump," *State Times Advocate* (Baton Rouge, Louisiana), May 18, 1967: 39.

63 Newspaper Enterprise Association, "Interference of Owners Blamed for Poor Umpiring," *Daily Illinois State Journal* (Springfield, Illinois), October 4, 1953: 21.

64 Jeane Hoffman, "Reardon Was Cussinest Ump in National Loop," *Los Angeles Times*, May 3, 1957: C3.

65 Broeg, "Beans Reardon Makes Himself Heard," 40.

66 Ibid.

67 "'Beans' in West Film," *San Diego Union*, January 20, 1935: 32.

68 "Umps Reardon in Movies," *Richmond Times Dispatch*, May 26, 1935: 22.

69 "Fans Throw Pop Bottles as Giants Defeat Redlegs: Umpire Angers Paying Guests," *Lexington* (Kentucky) *Herald*, July 18, 1935: 6.

70 "Umpires Given Fines by League President for Cincinnati Row," *Greensboro* (North Carolina) *Daily News*, August 24, 1935: 10; Wilbur Fogleman, "On the Rebound," *Riverside* (California) *Daily Press*, July 30, 1935: 11. Reardon challenged "the grandstand, bleachers and box-seat holders to come out collectively or in a single line of march to face him following that pop bottle shower…"

71 Harold Parrott, "Beans on the Pan!" *Brooklyn Daily Eagle*, April 25, 1935.

72 "Ruth and Grimes Put Out of Game," *Greensboro* (North Carolina) *Daily News*, August 8, 1938: 6.

73 Tex McCrary and Jinx Falkenburg, "It's Toughest Behind the Plate, Says Beans Reardon, on Last Job," *Boston Globe*, October 8, 1949: 13.

74 Jack Diamond.

75 "Mae West as 'Klondike Annie' at Roosevelt," *Seattle Daily Times*, May 18, 1936, 4; "Klondike Annie," Turner Classic Movies. tcm.com/tcmdb/title/80451/Klondike-Annie. Also in the film were boxers Ellsworth "Hank" Hankinson and Billy McGowan, as well as football player Dink Templeton.

76 Eddie Brietz, Associated Press, "Stengel and Ump Swap Fire Throughout Series," *Washington Evening Star*, April 17, 1936: 49.

77 Munzel.

78 imdb.com/title/tt0029050/?ref_=ttfc_fc_tt, retrieved April 12, 2015.

79 J.G. Taylor Spink, "Three and One," *The Sporting News*, April 29, 1937: 4.

80 Associated Press, "Beans Reardon 'Pins' Thief, Sprains Finger, but Gets $300 Back," *Boston Globe*, October 9, 1943: 5.

81 Charles C. Spink, "Beans Steals the Show at Base in New Guinea," *The Sporting News*, January 11, 1945: 4.

82 "Servicemen Want Major Baseball," *Rockford* (Illinois) *Morning Star*, January 13, 1945: 6; Walter Byers, "Aid of Sports is Sought to Speed Up War Production," *Daily Illinois State Journal* (Springfield, Illinois), January 19, 1945: 10.

83 Ed Burns, "Umpire Stirs Workers with Tearful Profanity," *The Sporting News*, February 8, 1945.

84 Will Cloney, "Sox 'Baby' Set for Big Test," *Boston Herald*, October 15, 1946: 17; "World Series Notes," *Rockford* (Illinois) *Morning Star*, October 15, 1946: 12. Reardon was seated next to NL President Ford Frick in the stadium for Game Seven in St. Louis. As Enos Slaughter scampered home from first base on a single in the eighth inning, sealing the championship for the Cardinals, Reardon began yelling, "Stop! Stop! Stop!" He later explained, "I didn't think he had a chance to score." Daniel W. Scism, "Sew It Seems," *Evansville* (Indiana) *Courier and Press*, October 17, 1946: 14.

85 L.H. Gregory, "Greg's Gossip," *The Oregonian* (Portland, Oregon), December 9, 1946: 2. Some even claimed Reardon told Northey to slow down, to which he responded "I was umpiring on third and when Northey thought it had gone into the stands for a home run … I was waving my arms in a circle,

85 signaling a home run. However, I did not speak to Northey. … I want to get one thing clear and that is I didn't tell him to slow down."

86 Some even claimed Reardon told Northey to slow down, to which he responded "I was waving my arms in a circle, signaling a home run. However, I did not speak to Northey…I want to get one thing clear and that is I didn't tell him to slow down." Associated Press, Reardon Denies 'Slow Down,' Yell," *Evansville* (Indiana) *Courier and Press,* July 27, 1947: 20.

87 Associated Press, "Frick Orders Replay of Card-Dodger Game," *Dallas Morning News,* July 26, 1947: 10. See also David W. Smith, "The Protested Game of July 20, 1947," in Lyle Spatz, ed., *The Team That Forever Changed Baseball and America: the 1947 Brooklyn Dodgers* (Lincoln: University of Nebraska Press, 2012), 201-202.

88 Associated Press, "Scuffle Spices Reds' Win," *Boston Herald,* April 20, 1948: 18. Later in the season, the umpiring crew of Conlan and Reardon had to be broken up due to the two arbiters not getting along with each other, "Umpires Troubles Increase," *Daily Illinois State Journal* (Springfield, Illinois), July 11, 1948: 18.

89 International News Service, "Nobody Wants His Autograph," *The Oregonian* (Portland, Oregon), October 16, 1948: 16.

90 "Game Called Because of Rain," Rockwell Center for American Visual Studies. rockwell-center.org/exploring-illustration/game-called-because-of-rain/. Retrieved April 4, 2015.

91 Lauren Applebaum, "Rockwell, Norman (1894-1978)," in Murray R. Nelson, ed., *American Sports: A History of Icons, Idols, and Ideas* (Santa Barbara, California: Greenwood, 2013), 1093-1094. Applebaum writes, "(W)hile the scenario depicted in *Tough Call* is just a game, the uncertainty of the outcome between these opponents relates to more serious political and economic uncertainties in America at the dawn of the Cold War. As weather is an uncontrollable force that can determine the future of the game, the image is juxtaposed with a headline on the magazine cover, which reads, 'What of Our Future?' by American financier and political consultant Bernard Baruch. … Thus, baseball performs in a covert fashion the conflicts of our world, providing an outlet to collectively confront tension under the guise of participating in an American tradition."

92 Associated Press, "Mrs. Beans Reardon Robbed of $4200," *Boston Traveler,* July 18, 1949: 21.

93 United Press, "Reardon Undecided Whether to Quit," *Riverside* (California) *Daily Press,* February 11, 1949: 12.

94 "Reardon, Although Retired, Goes on Emergency Duty," *The Sporting News,* March 29, 1950: 9.

95 UCLA Film & Television Archive—Ralph Edwards Collection. cinema.ucla.edu/sites/default/files/REmasterlist.pdf. Retrieved March 29, 2015.

96 For instance, in one such column Reardon answered questions on how many at-bats a batting champion needs to have, how an earned run is determined, and what constitutes a wild pitch and sacrifice hit. *Canton* (Ohio) *Repository,* July 12, 1952: 7.

97 Associated Press, "Umpire's Wife Dies," *San Diego Union,* March 11, 1953: 16; "Beans Reardon's Wife Dies in Long Beach," *Fresno Bee,* March 11, 1953: 7C.

98 Newspaper Enterprise Association, "Interference of Owners Blamed for Poor Umpiring," *Daily Illinois State Journal* (Springfield, Illinois), October 4, 1953: 21.

99 "The Kid From Left Field" overview. tcm.com/tcmdb/title/80194/The-Kid-from-Left-Field/. Retrieved March 30, 2015.

100 Dick Wagner, "Umpire's Wife Lives With Memories of Beans and Baseball," *Los Angeles Times,* January 14, 1988: SE10.

101 Wagner.

102 Jack Benny Program Season Five, Episode Four. tv.com/shows/the-jack-benny-program/the-giant-mutiny-126554. Retrieved March 30, 2015. William Buchanan of the *Boston Herald* was less than awed by the episode, writing, "Benny, Durocher, and Umpire Beans Reardon hit singles, but not enough runs were scored to call this show a real winner." William Buchanan, "Benny Scores Too Few Runs," *Boston Herald,* November 15, 1954: 27. Benny enjoyed the episode and praised the performances of Durocher and Reardon, saying that "Beans Reardon is another good one who would make a good actor." Wayne Oliver, Associated Press, "Benny Enthuses Over Durocher's TV Skit," *Aberdeen* (South Dakota) *Daily News,* November 19, 1954: 9.

103 Bob Van Scotter, " 'Miss Game?' 'No,' Answers Former Ump," *Rockford Morning Star* (Rockford, Illinois), April 15, 1959: C1.

104 Earl Gustkey, "Beans Reardon Still Calls 'Em as He Sees 'Em," *Los Angeles Times,* August 3, 1973: D14. Reardon claimed the $1 million selling price, although other accounts vary. Gerlach, 23.

105 Lynn Mucken, "Beans' Story String Relates Funny Side of Gentlemen in Blue," *The Oregonian* (Portland, Oregon), July 26, 1972: 6.

106 Wagner.

107 Wagner.

108 Chauncey Durden, "Sportview," *Richmond Times Dispatch,* February 18, 1970: 24; Sports *Illustrated,* November 15, 1989. si.com/vault/1989/11/15/121035/1970. Retrieved February 25, 2015.

109 Bob Broeg, "An Old Friend's Letter to Frisch," *The Sporting News,* March 31, 1973: 34.

110 Gerlach, 13.

BABE RUTH

BY ALLAN WOOD

DURING HIS FIVE FULL seasons with the Boston Red Sox, Babe Ruth established himself as one of the premier left-handed pitchers in the game, began his historic transformation from moundsman to slugging outfielder, and was part of three World Series championship teams. After he was sold to the New York Yankees in December 1919, his eye-popping batting performances over the next few seasons helped usher in a new era of long-distance hitting and high scoring, effectively bringing down the curtain on the Deadball Era.

George Herman Ruth was born to George Ruth and Catherine Schamberger on February 6, 1895, in his mother's parents' house at 216 Emory Street, in Baltimore, Maryland. With his father working long hours in his saloon and his mother often in poor health, Little George (as he was known) spent his days unsupervised on the waterfront streets and docks, committing petty theft and vandalism. Hanging out in his father's bar, he stole money from the till, drained the last drops from old beer glasses, and developed a taste for chewing tobacco. He was only six years old.

Shortly after his seventh birthday, the Ruths petitioned the Baltimore courts to declare Little George "incorrigible" and sent him to live at St. Mary's Industrial School, on the outskirts of the city. The boy's initial stay at St. Mary's lasted only four weeks before his parents brought him home for the first of several attempted reconciliations; his long-term residence at St. Mary's actually began in 1904. But it was during that first stay that George met Brother Matthias.

"He taught me to read and write and he taught me the difference between right and wrong," Ruth said of the Canadian-born priest. "He was the father I needed and the greatest man I've ever known."[1] Brother Matthias also spent many afternoons tossing a worn-out baseball in the air and swatting it out to the boys. Little George watched, bug-eyed. "I had never seen anything like that in my life," he recalled. "I think I was born as a hitter the first day I ever saw him hit a baseball."[2] The impressionable youngster imitated Matthias's hitting style—gripping the bat tightly down at the knobbed end, taking a big swing at the ball—as well as his way of running with quick, tiny steps.

When asked in 1918 about playing baseball at St. Mary's, Ruth said he had little difficulty anywhere on the field. "Sometimes I pitched. Sometimes I caught, and frequently I played the outfield and infield. It was all the same to me. All I wanted was to play. I didn't care much where."[3] In one St. Mary's game in 1913, Ruth, then 18 years old, caught, played third base (even though he threw left-handed), and pitched, striking out six men, and collecting a double, a triple, and a home run. That summer, he was allowed to pitch with local amateur and semipro teams on weekends. Impressed with his performances, Jack Dunn signed Ruth to his minor-league Baltimore Orioles club the following February.

Although he was a bumpkin with minimal social skills, at camp in South Carolina Ruth quickly distinguished himself on the diamond. That spring, the Orioles played several major league teams. In two outings against the Phillies, Ruth faced 29 batters and allowed only six hits and two unearned runs. The next week, he threw a complete game victory over the Philadelphia Athletics, winners of three of the last four World Series. Short on cash that summer, Dunn sold Ruth to the Boston Red Sox.

On July 11, 1914, less than five months after leaving St. Mary's, Babe made his debut at Fenway Park: he pitched seven innings against Cleveland and received credit for a 4-3 win. After being hit hard by Detroit in his second outing, Ruth rode the bench until he was demoted to the minor leagues in mid-August, where he helped the Providence Grays capture the International League pennant. Ruth returned to Boston for the final week of the 1914 season. On October 2, he pitched a complete game victory over the Yankees and doubled for his first major-league hit.

Babe spent the winter in Baltimore with his new wife, Boston waitress Helen Woodford, and in 1915, he stuck with the big club. Ruth slumped early in the season, in part because of excessive carousing with fellow pitcher Dutch Leonard, and a broken toe—sustained by kicking the bench in frustration after being intentionally walked—kept him out of the rotation for two weeks. But when he returned, he shined, winning three complete games in a span of nine days in June. Between June 1 and September 2, Ruth was 13-1 and ended the season 18-8.

In 1916, Ruth won 23 games and posted a league-leading 1.75 ERA. He also threw nine shutouts—an American League record for left-handed pitchers that still stands (it was tied in 1978 by the Yankees' Ron Guidry). In Game Two of the World Series, Ruth pitched all 14 innings, beating the Brooklyn Dodgers, 2-1. Boston topped Brooklyn in the series four games to one.

Ruth's success went straight to his head in 1917, and he began arguing with umpires about their strike zone judgment. Facing Washington on June 23, Ruth walked the first Senators batter on four pitches. Feeling squeezed by home plate umpire Brick Owens, Ruth stormed off the mound and punched Owens in the head. After Ruth was ejected, Ernie Shore came in to relieve. The baserunner was thrown out trying to steal and Shore retired the next 26 batters. Ruth got off lightly with a 10-day suspension and a $100 fine. He ended the year with a 24-13 record, completing 35 of his 38 starts, with six shutouts and an ERA of 2.01.

Although Ruth didn't play every day until May 1918, the idea of putting him in the regular lineup was first mentioned in the press during his rookie season. Calling Babe "one of the best natural sluggers ever in the game," Washington sportswriter Paul Eaton thought Ruth "might even be more valuable in some regular position than he is on the slab—a free suggestion for Manager [Bill] Carrigan."[4] The *Boston Post* reported that summer that Babe "cherishes the hope that he may someday be the leading slugger of the country."[5]

In 1915, Ruth batted .315 and topped the Red Sox with four home runs. Braggo Roth led the AL with seven homers, but he had 384 at-bats compared to Babe's 92. Ruth didn't have enough at-bats to qualify, but his .576 slugging percentage was higher than the official leaders in the American League (Jack Fournier .491), the National League (Gavvy Cravath .510), and the Federal League (Benny Kauff .509).

With the Red Sox offense sputtering after the sale of Tris Speaker in 1916, the suggestion to play Ruth every day was renewed when he tied a record with a home run in three consecutive games. Ruth hated the helpless feeling of sitting on the bench between pitching assignments, and believed he could be a better hitter if given more opportunity. In mid-season, with all three Boston outfielders in slumps, Carrigan was reportedly ready to give Babe a shot, but it never happened.[6] Ruth finished the 1917 season at .325, easily the highest average on the team. Left fielder Duffy Lewis topped the regulars at .302; no one else hit above .265. Giving Ruth an everyday job remained nothing more than an entertaining game of "what if"—until 1918.

The previous summer, the United States had entered the Great War; many players had enlisted or accepted war-related jobs before the season began. Trying to strengthen the Red Sox offense, about two weeks into the season, manager Ed Barrow, after discussions with right fielder and team captain Harry Hooper, penciled Ruth into the lineup. The move came only a few days after a Boston paper reported that team owner Harry Frazee had refused an offer of $100,000 for Ruth. "It is ridiculous to talk about it," Frazee said. "Ruth is our Big Ace. He's the most talked of, most sought for, most colorful ball player in the game."[7] Later reports revealed that the offer had come from the Yankees.[8]

On May 6, 1918, in the Polo Grounds against the Yankees, Ruth played first base and batted sixth. It was the first time he had appeared in a game other than as a pitcher or pinch-hitter and the first time he batted in any spot other than ninth. Ruth went 2-for-4, including a two-run home run. At that point, five of Ruth's 11 career home runs had come in New York. The *Boston Post*'s Paul Shannon began his game story, "Babe Ruth still remains the hitting idol of the Polo Grounds."[9]

The next day, against the Senators, Ruth was bumped up to fourth in the lineup—and he hit another home run—where he stayed for most of the season. Barrow also wanted Ruth to continue pitching, but Babe, enjoying the notoriety his hitting was generating, often feigned exhaustion or a sore arm to avoid the mound.[10] The two men argued about Ruth's playing time for several weeks. Finally, after one heated exchange in early July, Ruth quit the team. He returned a few days later and, after renegotiating his contract with Frazee to include some hitting-related bonuses, patched up his disagreements with Barrow.

"I don't think a man can pitch in his regular turn, and play every other game at some other position, and keep that pace year after year," Ruth said. "I can do it this season all right, and not feel it, for I am young and strong and don't mind the work. But I wouldn't guarantee to do it for many seasons."[11] Ruth then began what is likely the greatest nine- or ten-week stretch of play in baseball history. From mid-July to early September 1918, Ruth pitched every fourth day, and played either left field, center field, or first base on the other days. Ruth's double duty was not unique during the Deadball Era—a handful of players had done both—but his level of success was (and remains) unprecedented.[12] In one 10-game stretch at Fenway, Ruth hit .469 (15-for-32) and slugged .969 with four singles, six doubles, and five triples. He was remarkably adept at first base, his favorite position. On the mound, he allowed more than two runs only once in his last ten starts. The Colossus, as Babe was known in Boston, maintained his status as a top pitcher while simultaneously becoming the game's greatest hitter.

Ruth's performance led the Red Sox to the American League pennant, in a season cut short by the owners, partially because of dwindling attendance.

All draft-age men were under government order to either enlist or take war-related employment—in shipyards or munitions factories, for example—which led to paltry turnouts of less than 1,000 for many afternoon games that summer.

Ruth opened the World Series on September 5 against the Chicago Cubs with a 1-0 shutout. He pitched well in Game Four, despite having bruised his left hand during some horseplay on the train back to Boston, and his double drove in what turned out to be the winning runs. Those performances, together with his extra-inning outing in 1916, gave Ruth a record of 29 2/3 consecutive scoreless World Series innings, one of the records Ruth always said he was most proud of.[13] His streak was finally broken by Whitey Ford of the Yankees in the 1960s.

While with the Red Sox, Ruth often arranged for busloads of orphans to visit his farm in Sudbury for a day-long picnic and ball game, making sure each kid left with a glove and autographed baseball. When the

Red Sox were at home, Ruth would arrive at Fenway Park early on Saturday mornings to help the vendors—mostly boys in their early teens—bag peanuts for the upcoming week's games.

"He'd race with us to see who could bag the most," recalled Tom Foley, who was 14 years old in 1918. (Ruth was barely out of his teens himself.) "He'd talk a blue streak the whole time, telling us to be good boys and play baseball, because there was good money in it. He thought that if we worked hard enough, we could be as good as he was. But we knew better than that. He'd stay about an hour. When we finished, he'd pull out a $20 bill and throw it on the table and say 'Have a good time, kids.' We'd split it up, and each go home with an extra half-dollar or dollar depending on how many of us were there. Babe Ruth was an angel to us."[14]

To management, however, Ruth was a headache. His continued inability—or outright refusal—to adhere to the team's curfew earned him several suspensions and his non-stop salary demands infuriated Frazee. The Red Sox owner had spoken publicly about possibly trading Ruth before the 1919 season, when Babe was holding out for double his existing salary and threatening to become a boxer. However, Ruth and Frazee came to terms and the Babe's hitting made headlines across the country all season long. He played 110 games in left field, belted a record 29 home runs, and led the major leagues in slugging percentage (.657), on-base percentage (.456), runs scored (103), RBIs (113), and total bases (284). He also drove in or scored one-third of Boston's runs. But while Ruth also won nine games on the mound, the rest of the staff fell victim to injuries and the defending champs finished in the second division with a 66-71 record.

The sale of Ruth to the Yankees was announced after New Year's 1920 and although it was big news, public opinion in Boston was divided. Many fans were aghast that such a talent would be cast off, while others, including many former players, insisted that a cohesive team (as opposed to one egomaniac plus everyone else) was the key to success.[15]

"While Ruth, without question, is the greatest hitter that the game has ever seen, he is likewise one of the most selfish and inconsiderate men that ever wore a baseball uniform," Frazee explained. "Had he possessed the right disposition, had he been willing to take orders and work for the good of the club like the other men on the team, I would never have dared let him go."[16] And despite Ruth's record-setting (and attention-grabbing) 29 home runs, the Red Sox had finished in sixth place. Frazee considered the long balls "more spectacular than useful."[17]

He also intimated that the Yankees were taking a gamble on Ruth. It was a statement he would be later ridiculed for, but at the time the Yankees felt the same way. The amount paid ($125,000) was astronomical, Ruth ate and drank excessively, frequented prostitutes, and had been involved in several car accidents. It would have surprised no one if, for whatever reason, Ruth was out of baseball in a year or two.

Amidst this speculation over his future, on February 28, 1920, Babe Ruth left Boston and boarded a train for New York, on his way to spring training in Florida. He was still just 25 years old.

***

Babe Ruth arrived in New York City at the best possible time for his outsized hitting and hedonistic lifestyle. It was the Roaring Twenties, the Jazz Age, a time of individualism, more progressive social and sexual attitudes, and a greater emphasis on the pursuit of pleasure. (Prohibition, instituted in 1920, had no effect whatsoever.) Sportswriter Westbrook Pegler called it "the Era of Wonderful Nonsense."[18]

It was also a time when "trick pitches"—the emeryball, the spitter, and various ways of scuffing the ball—were outlawed. Both leagues began using a better quality (i.e., livelier) baseball. Ruth thrived—and over time, so did the players in both leagues.

The Babe got off to a slow start in 1920. He was in spring training for nearly three weeks before he crushed his first home run. Ruth also jumped into the stands to fight a fan who had called him "a big piece of cheese" (probably not a direct quote).[19] While tracking a fly ball during an exhibition game in Miami, Ruth ran into a palm tree in center field and was knocked unconscious.

After a disappointing April, in which he missed time due to a strained right knee, Ruth began May with home runs in consecutive games against the Red Sox. He went on to set a major league record for the month with 11 homers. That record lasted less than 30 days, when he smacked 13 long balls in June. He tied his own single-season record of 29 home runs—set the previous year with Boston—on July 16. Two weeks later, he had 37.

He finished the year with the unfathomable total of 54 home runs. He outhomered 14 of the other 15 major league teams. The AL runner-up was George Sisler, with 19; Cy Williams needed only 15 to top the National League. Ruth hit 14.6% of the American League's 369 home runs. For Barry Bonds to outdistance his peers in 2001 (when he set a new single-season mark of 73 home runs) as Ruth did in 1920, Bonds would have needed to hit 431 homers. In addition to this stunning display of power, Ruth was fourth in batting average at .376. His slugging percentage of .847 stood for more than 80 years—until Bonds reached .863 in 2001.

Ruth's arrival in New York began a stretch of offensive dominance the game will likely never see again. In the 12 seasons between 1920 and 1931, Ruth led the AL in slugging 11 times, home runs 10 times, walks nine times, on-base percentage eight times, and runs scored seven times. His batting average topped .350 eight times. In exactly half of those 12 seasons, he batted over .370. (Ruth once said that if he shortened his swing and tried to hit singles, he'd hit .600.[20])

Ruth's effect on the national game was nothing short of revolutionary. Leigh Montville, author of *The Big Bam*, wrote that Ruth's teammates reacted with the same sense of wonder as everyone else in America. "They never had seen anything like it. The game they had learned was being changed in front of their faces."[21]

Ruth also starred in a feature film entitled *Headin' Home*, which was filmed in Fort Lee, New Jersey. The plot, such as it was, starred Babe as a country bumpkin who makes good in big league ball—not exactly playing against type. According to *Variety*, "It couldn't hold the interest of anyone for five seconds if it were not for the presence of Ruth."[22] Babe often returned to the Polo Grounds after a morning of filming still wearing his movie makeup and mascara, much to the annoyance of manager Miller Huggins.[23]

During his final season in Boston, Ruth played most of his games in left field. When he joined the Yankees, and began playing his home games at the Polo Grounds, he played all three outfield positions. In 1920, Ruth started 84 games in right, 31 in left, and 25 in center. The following season, he was almost exclusively used in left, starting 132 of 150 games; he didn't play even one inning in right field. Once the Yankees moved into their own stadium in the Bronx, Ruth generally played right field at home and left field on the road. Although the Babe is remembered as mainly a right fielder, he started nearly as many games in left (1,040) during his career as he did in right (1,122).[24]

Ruth quickly became one of the most famous people in the country. On Yankees road trips, people with no interest in baseball traveled hundreds of miles to get a glimpse of the Babe. He was cheered wildly in every park—for rival fans, if Ruth smacked one out of the park, it hardly seemed to matter what the final score was.

Sunday baseball became legal in New York in 1919 and the fan base changed forever. Women and children came out regularly to the park. One of Ruth's most enduring nicknames—the Bambino—came from the Italian fans in the upper Manhattan neighborhood around the Polo Grounds.

Everyone wanted to know as much about Ruth as possible. The New York papers (more than 15 English-language dailies) began devoting more and more space to the Babe's exploits. Nothing was too trivial. According to sportswriter Tom Meany, if Ruth was seen "taking an aspirin, it was practically a scoop for the writer who saw him reach for the sedative."[25] Marshall Hunt was hired by the *Daily News* to write about the Babe—and only the Babe—365 days a year.[26]

"There was no such thing as no news with the Babe.... The Speed Graphic, the newspaper photographer's camera of choice, loved his broad face with its flat nose and tiny eyes, loved his absolutely unique look, features put together in a hurry, an out-of-focus bulldog, no veneer or sanding involved. This was a face that soon was instantly recognizable, seen again and again... The Babe was an incorrigible, wondrous part of everyone's family.... He was the life of everybody's party.... Laughing but earnest men in fedoras and off-the-rack suits, sportswriters, watched the sun rise and fall on his big head and were moved to grand statements. They typed the legend into place, adding layer upon layer of adjectives until often the man in the middle couldn't even be seen."[27]

In the 1920s, these giddy sportswriters were coming up with nicknames for Ruth nearly every day. His Boston nickname—the Colossus—morphed into the Colossus of Clout. From there, a seemingly endless—and often silly—list emerged: the Wizard of Wham, the Maharajah of Mash, the Rajah of Rap, the Caliph of Clout, the Sultan of Swat, the Behemoth of Bash, the Bazoo of Bang, the Potentate of Pow, the Wali of Wallop, the Prince of Pounders, and on and on.

His own name became a nickname, bestowed on someone who was the best in his or her field: the Babe Ruth of Surfing, the Babe Ruth of Bowling, the Babe Ruth of Poker. His last name became an adjective: "Ruthian," defined as "colossal, dramatic, prodigious, magnificent; with great power."[28] His teammates usually called him "Jidge" (for George).

The Yankees finished the 1920 season in third place with a 95-59 record, only three games behind Cleveland. It was their best showing in 10 years. They followed that up in 1921 by winning 98 games and their first-ever pennant. And somehow Ruth may have actually had a better year at the plate than he did in 1920. His batting average improved slightly (.376 to .378), and while his OBP (.532 to .512) and slugging (.847 to .846) dipped slightly, he drove in 168 runs and hit a career-high 16 triples. (According to manager Huggins, Ruth was the second-fastest player on the team.[29]) He also broke his own single-season home run record—for the third consecutive year—with 59. On July 18, Ruth became the game's career home run leader, hitting his 139th homer, passing Roger Connor. Ruth also set new season records for runs scored (177), extra base hits (119), and total bases (457)—three achievements that no player has yet matched.

Ruth also pitched in two games. On June 13, he allowed four runs in five innings. He also hit two home runs that day and finished the game in center field as the Yankees won, 13-8.

In September 1921, Ruth underwent three hours of tests at Columbia University to determine his athletic and psychological capabilities. Sportswriter Hugh Fullerton wrote up the findings for *Popular Science Monthly*:

> "The tests revealed the fact that Ruth is 90 per cent efficient compared with a human average of 60 per cent. That his eyes are about 12 per cent faster than those of the average human being. That his ears function at least

The one-and-only Babe Ruth, whose films include Headin' Home, Babe Comes Home, Speedy, *and* The Pride of the Yankees.

10 per cent faster than those of the ordinary man. That his nerves are steadier than those of 499 out of 500 persons. That in attention and quickness of perception he rated one and a half times above the human average. That in intelligence, as demonstrated by the quickness and accuracy of understanding, he is approximately 10 per cent above normal."[30]

The psychologists also discovered that Ruth did not breathe during his entire swing. They stated that if he kept breathing while swinging, he could generate even more power.

The Yankees faced their co-tenants in the Polo Grounds, the New York Giants, in the 1921 World Series. Ruth cut his left arm (which then became infected) during a slide in the second game and wrenched his knee in the fifth game. Babe made only one pinch-hitting appearance in the final three contests. The Yankees won the first two games, but the Giants took the best-of-nine series, five games to three.

After the World Series, Ruth and some other Yankees went on a barnstorming tour to earn extra money. This was in violation of the National Commission's 1911 edict that players on the two pennant-winning teams could not barnstorm after the World Series—enacted, perhaps, to preserve the integrity of the World Series or to limit the players' total income. Kenesaw Mountain Landis, newly installed as the game's first commissioner, suspended Ruth and fellow outfielder Bob Meusel for the first six weeks of the season, and fined them each $3,362—the amount of their 1921 World Series share.

When Ruth returned to the lineup on May 20, he was also named as the team's captain, succeeding Hal Chase (1912) and Roger Peckinpaugh (1914-21). The honor lasted less than one week. Ruth was again slow to get his bat started and after five games, he was hitting .095 and being booed.

On May 25, he was thrown out trying to stretch a single into a double and, furious at the call, threw dirt in umpire George Hildebrand's face. On his way towards the dugout, he spied a heckler and jumped into the stands, ready to fight. The fan ran away and Ruth ended up standing on the dugout roof, screaming, "Come on down and fight! Anyone who wants to fight, come down on the field!"[31] Ruth was fined $200 and was replaced as captain by shortstop Everett Scott.

Babe was also suspended for three days in mid-June for his part in an obscenity-laced tirade against umpire Bill Dinneen. When Ruth got the news the following day, he challenged Dinneen to a fist fight—and the suspension was increased to five days.[32] In the wake of the suspensions, Ruth made an effort to check his temper. On June 26, as some of his teammates argued with Dinneen, Babe merely sat down in the outfield grass and watched.[33]

Ruth played in only 110 games in 1922. His batting average dropped to .315, but he led the league with a .672 slugging percentage and his OBP of .434 was fourth-best.

The Yankees and the Giants met in the World Series for the second straight year. After a three-year experiment as a best-of-nine, the series was back to being a best-of-seven, where it has remained to the present day. The Giants swept the Yankees in five games (Game Two ended in a tie due to darkness). Ruth went 2-for-17.

The Yankees left the Polo Grounds and began 1923 in their own ballpark, directly across the Harlem River in the borough of the Bronx. Yankee Stadium was dubbed the House that Ruth Built, but with its short right-field porch, a more appropriate title might be the House Built for Ruth. Babe returned to his battering ways with a vengeance. He hit .393—if only four of his 317 outs had fallen for hits, he would have batted .400—and hit 41 home runs. Harry Heilmann of the Tigers led the AL with a .403 average.

The Yankees won their third straight pennant, finishing 16 games ahead of the Tigers. And for the third straight year, the World Series was an all-New York affair. This time, it was the Yankees, after losing two of the first three games, who prevailed. Ruth went 7-for-19 in the Series, with three home runs. However, all three came at the Polo Grounds. Giants' outfielder Casey Stengel hit the first World Series home run at Yankee Stadium.

Ruth won his only batting title in 1924, easily topping the AL at .378—almost 20 points higher than Charlie Jamieson's .359. Babe hit 46 home runs and tied for second with 124 RBIs. His .739 slugging percentage was more than 200 points higher than runner-ups Harry Heilmann and Ken Williams (both at .533). However, the Yankees finished in second place, two games behind the Washington Senators.

In 1925, the Yankees fell all the way to seventh, 69-85, 28 1/2 games out of first place. It was a bad year from the start. Ruth showed up for spring training at 256 pounds and went on to have the worst year of his career. He hit .290/.393/.543 (batting/on-base/slugging), with 25 home runs and a paltry 67 RBIs. This was also the year Ruth suffered what W.O. McGeehan of the *New York Tribune* famously called "The Bellyache Heard 'Round the World."[34] Ruth fell ill during the team's spring training exhibition tour. The initial story was that Ruth had eaten too many hot dogs, and the *New York Evening Journal* ran a photo of Ruth with 12 numbered franks superimposed on his stomach.[35]

However, it was clearly more serious than indigestion or a matter of Ruth being "run down and [having] low blood pressure," as the Yankees' team doctor claimed.[36] On April 17, Ruth had minor surgery for what doctors termed an "intestinal abscess"[37] and he did not return to the Yankees lineup until June. Several teammates hinted it might have been a sexually-transmitted disease; one teammate said it wasn't a bellyache, "it was something a bit lower."[38]

Whatever it was, it didn't cramp Ruth's style. Babe was staying out all night more often than not and by the end of the season, he was a physical wreck. In mid-December, Ruth realized if he wanted to continue playing ball into his thirties, he needed to do something different. He showed up at Artie McGovern's gymnasium on East 42nd Street in Manhattan, a well-known gym used by New York's rich and famous.[39]

Ruth committed himself to McGovern's strict regimen of exercise, diet, and rest. Six weeks later, by the time he was ready to head south for spring training, Ruth had lost 44 pounds and shed almost nine inches from his waistline.[40]

The Babe still had plenty of fun, obviously, but he never let himself get seriously out of shape again. As Robert Creamer wrote in *Babe: The Legend Comes to Life*, "From 1926 through 1931, as he aged from thirty-two to thirty-seven, Ruth put on the finest sustained display of hitting that baseball has ever seen. During those six seasons, he averaged 50 home runs a year, 155 runs batted in and 147 runs scored; he batted .354. ... From the ashes of 1925, Babe Ruth rose like a rocket."[41]

As Ruth rose, so did the Yankees. The Bombers went from seventh place to first, winning 91 games and the 1926 pennant. Ruth batted .372/.516/.737, with 47 home runs (runner-up Al Simmons had 19), and drove in 153 (36 more than his nearest challenger). The Yankees were also boosted by the great play of two rookie infielders: second baseman Tony Lazzeri and shortstop Mark Koenig. First baseman Lou Gehrig, in his second full season at age 22, led the league with 20 triples and 83 extra-base hits—one more than Ruth.

In Game Four of the World Series against the St. Louis Cardinals, Ruth belted three home runs. It was the first time he had ever hit three in one game—and it was the first time that had been done in a World Series game. This was also the game before which Ruth allegedly promised to hit a home run for 11-year-old hospital patient Johnny Sylvester.

The 1926 Series came down to a deciding seventh game at Yankee Stadium. New York trailed 3-2 in the bottom of the ninth inning, when Ruth walked with two outs. Bob Meusel was facing Grover Cleveland Alexander when Ruth took off for second. He was thrown out trying to steal—ending the game and the World Series.

The 1927 Yankees are often talked about as the greatest team in baseball history. New York finished with a 110-44 record, winning the league by a whopping 19 games and sweeping the Pittsburgh Pirates in the World Series. They scored 976 runs, 131 more than second-best Detroit.

Ruth's fabled 60 home runs—which he had become obsessed with since hitting 59 six years earlier—captured the headlines, but Gehrig, at age 24, had a better season. He outhit Ruth (.373 to .356) and nearly matched him in on-base percentage (.474 to .486), and slugging (.765 to .772). Gehrig had more extra base hits (117 to 97), total bases (447 to 417), and RBIs (173 to 165). He led the major leagues in doubles, RBIs, and total bases and was second in the American League in triples, home runs, hits, and batting average.

The Yankees won nine fewer games in 1928, but their 101-53 record was still good enough for a third straight pennant. Ruth batted only .323, but his 54 home runs helped him lead the major leagues in slugging at .709. The Yankees used only three pitchers as they swept the Cardinals in the World Series. Ruth batted .625 (10-for-16), with three doubles, three home runs, and a 1.375 slugging percentage. Gehrig hit .545 (6-for-11) and slugged 1.727.

In January 1929, Babe's first wife, Helen, died in a house fire in Watertown, Massachusetts. At the time, Helen was living with Edward Kinder, a dentist, and while the deed on the house listed Helen and Kinder as husband and wife, they were not, in fact, married. (Babe and Helen had never officially divorced.) Ruth was devastated by the news. At the funeral, he wept uncontrollably.[42]

Babe married Claire Hodgson on April 17. The following day, the Yankees—with numbers on the back of their uniforms for the first time—opened the season against the Red Sox. Babe, wearing his new #3, whacked a first-inning home run to left field and doffed his cap to Claire as he rounded the bases.

On August 11 in Cleveland, Ruth hit the 500th home run of his career. The *New York World* called it "a symbol of American greatness."[43] The man who retrieved the homer got two signed baseballs and, after posing for a photo with Ruth, the Babe slipped him a $20 bill.[44]

Miller Huggins passed away suddenly near the end of the 1929 season—and Babe lobbied for the manager's job for 1930. (Ruth would drop hints about wanting to manage for the next four years, but the Yankees never seriously considered it.) Ruth also asked for his salary to be increased to $100,000—this coming a few months after Black Tuesday and the start of what became the Great Depression. He ended up signing a two-year deal for $80,000 per season. With exhibition game receipts, movie shorts, personal appearances, and endorsements, Ruth probably earned close to $200,000 in 1930.

By the end of June 1930, Ruth was ahead of his 60-homer pace of 1927, but injuries slowed him down and he finished with 49.

The Yankees were an offensive juggernaut. In both 1930 and 1931, they scored more than 1,000 runs—an average of nearly seven runs per game. But it was the Philadelphia Athletics who won the pennant in 1929, 1930, and 1931 behind the big bats of Jimmie Foxx and Al Simmons and the pitching of Lefty Grove.

Babe Ruth, newly-minted New York Yankee, around the time he starred onscreen in Headin' Home.

In 1931, at age 36, Ruth had one of his finest seasons. He hit .373/.495/.700, with 46 home runs, 162 RBIs, 128 walks and 149 runs scored.

Ruth made his final trip to the World Series in 1932. Amazingly, in the seven-year reign of Ruth and Gehrig from 1929-1935, the Yankees won only one pennant. Gehrig (.349/.451/.621, 34 HR, 151 RBIs) and Ruth (.341/.489/.661, 41 HR, 137 RBIs) were ably assisted by Lazzeri, Bill Dickey, Ben Chapman and Earle Combs. However, it was Jimmie Foxx of the A's who led the league in home runs (58).

The Yankees swept the Chicago Cubs in the 1932 World Series, giving them wins in 12 straight World Series games. It was during the third game—October 1 at Wrigley Field—that Ruth added to his legend. The game was tied 4-4 when Ruth stepped in against Cubs starter Charlie Root with one out in the fifth inning. Ruth had already hit a three-run homer and flied to deep right, and the Cubs' bench-jockeying was at a fever pitch.

Everyone agrees that as Root threw two called strikes to Ruth, the Babe held up one and two fingers. What exactly happened before Root threw his 2-2 pitch will never be definitively known. The legend says Ruth pointed towards the center field bleachers, indicating that was where he was going to hit the next pitch. Or he may have been saying "I've still got one strike left." Or he was jawing with the hecklers in the Cubs' dugout.

Either way, Ruth swung and belted the ball to deep center field—one of the longest home runs seen at Wrigley—for his second home run of the afternoon. He laughed as he jogged around the bases, pointing and jeering at the Cubs dugout.

Of the many game stories written that afternoon, only one (Westbrook Pegler) mentioned Ruth "calling his shot."[45] Within two or three days, however, writers who had initially made no reference to Ruth's theatrics—and even a few who had not been in attendance at the park—were offering their own recollections. And thus a legend was born.[46] A 16mm home movie of the at-bat surfaced in 1999. The grainy film does show Ruth pointing his arm, but it's impossible to determine exactly what he is doing.

Root maintained that Ruth "did not point at the fence before he swung. If he had made a gesture like that, well, anybody who knows me knows that Ruth would have ended up on his ass."[47] As for the Babe, when asked whether he had really pointed to the bleachers, he smiled and said, "It's in the papers, isn't it?"[48]

It was Ruth's last trip to the World Series. He played on seven World Series champions: four with the Yankees (1923, 1927, 1928, 1932), and three with the Red Sox (1915, 1916, 1918). He was also on the losing side of three World Series teams with New York (1921, 1922, 1926).

1933 was Ruth's 20th season in major league baseball. He batted only .301 with 34 home runs, though he still led both leagues in walks. One of the season's highlights was the inaugural All-Star Game, played at Comiskey Field in Chicago. Ruth hit the game's first home run. He also robbed Chick Hafey of a home run in the eighth inning, to preserve the AL's 4-2 win.

The Yankees finished seven games behind the Senators and, in an effort to boost attendance for the last home game of the year, announced that Ruth would pitch against the Red Sox. The 39-year-old outfielder held the Red Sox without a run for five innings. With a 6-0 lead, he stumbled in the sixth, allowing a walk, five singles, and four runs. The Yankees held on to win, 6-5. Although Ruth prepared for the start by throwing batting practice for weeks, the complete game took its toll. He couldn't so much as comb his hair with his left arm for about a week.[49]

Ruth took a $17,000 pay cut in 1934. His $35,000 contract was still the highest in the game, but it was his lowest salary since 1921. On July 13, in Detroit, Babe hit his 700th career home run. (At that point, only two players had hit even 300 home runs: Lou Gehrig (314) and Rogers Hornsby (301).) Four days later, Ruth drew his 2,000th walk.

In August, during the Yankees' final trip to Fenway, a record crowd of 48,000 turned out on a Sunday afternoon, assuming it would be Ruth's last appearance in Boston. The fans cheered everything Ruth did. When he grounded out in his final at-bat, he was given a long, standing ovation. "Do you know that some of them cried when I left the field?" Ruth said afterwards. "And if you wanna know the truth, I cried too."[50]

On the other hand, on September 24, for what was rumored to be his final home game in a Yankees uniform, only 2,000 fans showed up. Babe played only one inning, being replaced by a pinch-runner after drawing a walk. He ended the year with a .288 batting average.

During the off-season, Ruth agreed to travel with an all-star team to Japan. In arranging for a passport, he discovered that his date of birth was February 6, 1895. He had always believed he was born on February 7, 1894.[51] He was actually a year younger than he had thought.

Yankees owner Jacob Ruppert, not wanting Ruth to return in any capacity in 1935, worked out a secret deal with Boston Braves owner Emil Fuchs. Fuchs would offer Ruth a contract that included the titles of "assistant manager" and "vice president."[52] Ruth loved the idea and when he informed Ruppert, the Yankee owner said he wouldn't stand in Ruth's way. At spring training in 1935, Ruth learned that the Yankees had already assigned his #3 to George Selkirk. They were also using his locker to store firewood.[53]

Ruth ended up playing in 28 games for the Braves, batting .181. The one bright spot came on May 25 in Pittsburgh. Ruth belted the final three home runs of his career, and drove in six runs. Career home run #714 disappeared over the right field roof—the longest home run ever hit at Forbes Field.

Many of the hitting records Ruth once held have been broken, but what cements Babe's status as the best to ever play the game is the combination of hitting for average, hitting with power, and his work on the mound. In addition to his batting exploits, Ruth also pitched in 163 games, with a record of 94-46 and a career ERA of 2.28 (12th-best in the modern era, since 1900). For 71 years, he was also the unlikely answer to a great trivia question: Who is the only major leaguer to pitch in at least 10 seasons and have a winning record in all of them? Ruth had winning records in 10 seasons: 1914-1921, 1930 and 1933. Andy Pettitte now holds the record at 13 seasons (1995-2007).

Ruth retired to a life of golf, fishing, bowling, and public appearances. In November 1946, he checked into French Hospital on 29th Street in Manhattan, complaining of headaches and pain above his left eye. It was cancer, though the newspapers never printed the word.

Babe Ruth Day was held at Yankee Stadium (and every other major league park) the following April. A crowd of 58,339 was there and many of them, players as well as fans, were shocked at how frail and shrunken the mighty Babe had become.

Ruth was in and out of the hospital for the next year. He returned to the Bronx one more time, on June 13, 1948, a rainy, cold day. Yankee Stadium was celebrating its 25th anniversary and Babe's #3 was being retired. Ruth was back in the hospital 11 days later. The cancer had spread to his liver, lungs, and kidneys. He knew he was dying.

Babe Ruth died at 8:01 p.m. on August 16, 1948. He was 53 years old. He is buried at the Gate of Heaven Cemetery in Valhalla, New York, next to his second wife Claire, who died in 1976.

Leigh Montville, author of *The Big Bam*, called Ruth "the patron saint of American possibility … The fascination with his career and life continues. He is a bombastic, sloppy hero from our bombastic sloppy history, origins undetermined, a folk tale of American success."[54]

The New York Times began its obituary: "Probably nowhere in all the imaginative field of fiction could one find a career more dramatic and bizarre than that portrayed in real life by George Herman Ruth."[55]

SOURCES

In addition to the sources cited in the Notes, the author also consulted Baseball-Reference.com.

NOTES

1 Allan Wood, *Babe Ruth and the 1918 Red Sox* (San Jose, California: Writers Club Press, 2001), 55.

2 Ibid.

FROM SPRING TRAINING TO SCREEN TEST

3 George Herman Ruth, *Babe Ruth's Own Book of Baseball* (New York: G.P. Putnam's Sons, 1928; Lincoln: University of Nebraska Press, Bison Books, 1992), 5-6.

4 Paul W. Eaton, *Sporting Life*, August 7, 1915.

5 "Talking It Over In The Dugout At Fenway Park," *Boston Post*, August 15, 1915.

6 The *Boston Globe* of June 12, 1916 reported: "Some one of these days Babe Ruth may become an outfielder. [Manager Bill] Carrigan, [pitcher Vean] Gregg and others think that with the proper training, the Baltimore slugger should make a whale of a player for the outer garden." The next day, the *Boston American* reported, "Babe is such a great hitter that Bill wants to have him in the lineup daily if possible. So fans at home don't be a bit surprised if Ruth soon becomes one of the Red Sox outfielders." Paul Shannon wrote in the *Boston Herald*, "[If] the batting of certain parties does not improve, big Babe Ruth may soon be a fixture in the Boston outfield." As quoted in Kerry Keene, Raymond Sinibaldi and David Hickey. *The Babe in Red Stockings: An In-Depth Chronicle of Babe Ruth with the Boston Red Sox 1914-1919* (Champaign, Illinois: Sagamore Publishing, 1997), 81.

7 Burt Whitman, "Frazee Rejects $100,000 Offer For Pitcher Ruth," *Boston Herald and Journal*, April 30, 1918.

8 "Frazee States Col. Ruppert Offered $150,000 For Ruth," *Boston Herald and Journal*, May 29, 1918. Frazee: "I think the New York man showed good judgment in making such a big offer. Ruth already is mighty popular in New York, and just think what he would mean to the Yankees if he were playing for them every day and hitting those long ones at the left field bleachers and the right field grandstand!"

9 Glenn Stout, *The Selling of the Babe: The Deal That Changed Baseball and Created a Legend* (New York: Thomas Dunne Books, 2016), 52.

10 Wood, 144, 146-147.

11 F.C. Lane, "The Season's Sensation," *Baseball Magazine*, October 1918: 472.

12 Wood, 204-206. Several players had both pitched and played in the field before Ruth, but none of them were as talented or successful. Guy Hecker pitched, played the outfield, and spent time at first base from 1882-90. In 1884, he won 52 games for the Louisville Colonels (American Association) and had a 1.80 ERA. Hecker was rarely among the league's top hitters, but his .341 average in 1886 won the batting title. Washington Senators pitcher Al Orth pulled double duty for several seasons, but when he led the American League in wins and complete games in 1906, he played only one game in the outfield. Doc White of the Chicago White Sox led the American League in 1907 with 27 wins, but appeared on the mound in all but two of his 48 games. In 1909, when he truly divided his time, he batted only .234 (although his on-base average was .347) and was 11-9 with a 1.72 ERA. Doc Crandall played second base and pitched for the St. Louis Terriers of the Federal League in 1914, leading his team in batting average (.309) and tying for the lead in wins (13). The following year, as a pitcher and pinch-hitter, Crandall won 21 games and batted .284.

13 Robert W. Creamer, *Babe: The Legend Comes To Life* (New York: Simon and Schuster, 1974), 177.

14 Interviews with Allan Wood, July 22, 1995, October 30, 1995, and January 5, 1997. Allan Wood, "Someone Can Recall Red Sox Title," *Baseball America*, March 6, 1997.

15 Fred Tenney and Hugh Duffy, former members of the Boston Beaneaters (National League), supported the deal. Tenney: "I agree with Frazee for he knows his business best. ... No ball player is indispensable to a team." Duffy: "Star players do not make a winning team. Players of ordinary ability working for the interest of the club are greater factors in the winning machine than the individual." Johnny Keenan, leader of Boston's Royal Rooters: "It will be impossible to replace the strength Ruth gave to the Red Sox. The Batterer is a wonderful player and the fact that he loves the game and plays with his all to win makes him a tremendous asset to a club." (*New York Times*, January 7, 1920: 22.) Orville Dennison, a fan living in Cambridge, wrote to the *Boston Globe*: "Many sane followers of baseball claim that there is no player in the game who is worth paying $100,000 for, and that if the Boston club obtained such a sum, it is the gainer." (Wood, 352.) Frazee: "[B]aseball fans pay to see games won and championships achieved. They soon tire of circus attractions. And this is just what Ruth has become." (Stout, 190.) Ed Cunningham of the *Boston Herald* noted that while Ruth "is of a class of ball players that flashes across the firmament once in a great while ... Stars generally are temperamental. This goes for baseball and the stage. They often have to be handled with kid gloves. Frazee has carefully considered the Ruth angle ... Boston fans undoubtedly will be up in arms but they should reserve judgment until they see how it works out." Ed Cunningham, "Red Sox Sell Babe Ruth to Yanks for More than $100,000," *Boston Herald*, January 6, 1920: 18.

16 "Babe Ruth Accepts Terms Of Yankees," *New York Times*, January 7, 1920: 22.

17 Wood, 352.

18 Kal Wagenheim, *Babe Ruth: His Life and Legend* (New York: Praeger Publishers, 1974), 62.

19 Leigh Montville, *The Big Bam: The Life and Times of Babe Ruth* (New York: Doubleday, 2006), 111.

20 . During the 1946 World Series, Ruth watched the St. Louis Cardinals employ a drastic shift against Ted Williams of the Boston Red Sox. Ruth told sportswriter Frank Graham: "They did that to me in the American League one year. I could have hit .600 that year slicing singles to left." Mark Gallagher, *The Yankee Encyclopedia* (6th Edition) (Champaign, Illinois: Sports Publishing LLC, 2003), 206.

21 Montville, 114.

22 *Variety*, September 24, 1920.

23 Marshall Smelser, *The Life That Ruth Built* (New York: Random House, 1975), 201.

24 Ruth's fielding statistics can be found at Baseball Reference (https://www.baseball-reference.com/players/r/ruthba01.shtml#all_standard_fielding).

25 Tom Meany, *Babe Ruth: The Big Moments of the Big Fellow* (New York: A.S. Barnes and Company, 1947), 84.

26 Montville, 167-71.

27 Montville, 159-60.

28 Paul Dickson, *The New Dickson Baseball Dictionary* (New York: Harcourt Brace & Company, 1999), 424.

29 Glenn Stout and Richard A. Johnson. *Yankees Century: 100 Years of New York Yankees Baseball* (Boston: Houghton Mifflin Company, 2002), 99.

30 Hugh Fullerton, "Why Babe Ruth is Greatest Home Run Hitter," *Popular Science Monthly*, October 1921. (The magazine's cover promised: "Babe Ruth's Home Run Secrets Solved by Science.")

31 Creamer, 258.

32 Creamer, 261.

33 Creamer, 262.

34 Montville, 203.

35 Wagenheim, 140. The caption read: "Notice how snugly they nestle in the vast cavern of his interior."

36 Montville, 203.

37 Stout and Johnson, 112.

38 Wagenheim, 140.

39 Montville, 216-18.

40 Montville, 218-21.

41 Creamer, 301.

42 Montville, 282-84.

43 Wagenheim, 196.

44 Montville, 293.

45 Creamer, 364, 367-68.

46 Stout and Johnson, 153.

47 Creamer, 366-67.

48 Creamer, 368. In *The Big Bam*, Leigh Montville writes: "He called shots all the time. He loved to create situations. It was for other people to determine what they meant. ... He challenged his entire environment. Whipped up all parties, then made them shut up. The specifics might be hazy, but the general story was not wrong." (312) The next day, Cubs starter Guy Bush, facing Ruth in the top of first inning, with men on first and second and no outs, drilled the Babe with a first-pitch fastball. Montville adds: "*Something* out of the ordinary [had] happened." (313)

49 Montville, 322.

50 Montville, 327.

51 Ibid.

52 Montville, 337-38.

53 Montville, 339.

54 Montville, 13.

55 Murray Schumach, "Babe Ruth, Baseball's Greatest Star and Idol of Children, Had a Career Both Dramatic and Bizarre," *New York Times*, August 17, 1948: 14. "A creation of the times, he seemed to embody all the qualities that a sport-loving nation demanded of its outstanding hero. ... Ruth [was] a figure unprecedented in American life. A born showman off the field and a marvelous performer on it, he had an amazing flair for doing the spectacular at the most dramatic moment."

BRET SABERHAGEN

BY ALAN COHEN

"Times of adversity make you stronger. And sometimes those times make you so tired that when your son says to you, 'Dad, I want to be there at the last game you pitch,' you tell him, 'Kid, you might have been there already.'"[1]

- Bret Saberhagen — August 8, 2001, one day after his last major-league game.

SUCCESS CAME EARLY FOR Bret Saberhagen. In only his second major-league season, 1985, the 21-year-old won the Cy Young Award with a 20-6 record and was named the Most Valuable Player in the World Series. With his Kansas City team winless in its first two games against St. Louis, he pitched the Royals to a 6-1 win in Game Three and, with everything on the line, pitched an 11-0 shutout in Game Seven to give Kansas City its first World Championship in baseball. For his efforts in 1985, he had been paid $150,000. At season's end, he was eligible for arbitration and won a third award, as the arbiter's decision yielded him $925,000 for the 1986 season.

He was on top of the world and was rated by writer Thomas Boswell as one of the three top pitchers in baseball (along with Dwight Gooden and John Tudor) going into the 1986 season. Saberhagen was heard to say, "I'm just going to do everything the same as last year. Take it one step at a time. Can't do too much too fast. I just have a feeling of confidence. Every time you go out there you have to think you're going to win or you won't. If I give the best Bret Saberhagen can give, then I'll be happy with it."[2]

However, in what was to become a pattern, the Saberhagen of the even-numbered years did not match up with the Saberhagen of the odd-numbered years.

He was born on April 11, 1964 in Chicago Heights, Illinois, but his formative years were spent in California. Bret is an only child. His parents Bob and Linda divorced when he was only 9 years old and, by then, the Saberhagens had relocated to the West Coast. Linda took a position in the accounting department of a retail store. Bob remained in his son's life, relocating to Chatsworth, California, and taking a position with a computer leasing firm in Encino, California.[3] Bret starred as a sophomore at Grover Cleveland High School in Reseda, California, and was selected the MVP of the West Valley League in 1980. However, he had an off-year the following season, although he also played a good shortstop and was one of his team's leading batters with a .333 average. In his senior year, when the basketball season extended into early spring, he rushed himself into shape, developing tendonitis in his shoulder. Just after Easter, he resumed pitching and put together a 6-0 record in his team's regular season. On the eve of the high school playoffs, the major-league draft was held. At this point, most scouts felt that his velocity was still suspect and this reduced his chances at being a high draft pick. But Royals scout Guy Hanson had seen Bret as he was rounding into form and Kansas City used its 19th round pick in the 1982 draft to select Saberhagen.[4]

Bret then went on to go 3-0 in the playoffs. His second playoff win came in the semifinals when he relieved in the first inning with none out and his team behind by five runs. Over the course of the remaining innings, he struck out 12 as his Cavaliers team came from behind to win, 7-6.[5] In the championship game, won by Cleveland 13-0, he pitched a no-hitter at Dodger Stadium to bring his overall high school record to 24-2, under the tutelage of coach Leo Castro. Were it not for a first-inning error by the Cleveland second baseman, Saberhagen, who struck out eight and retired the final 20 batters in a row, would have had a perfect game. After the game, he commented, "I didn't start thinking of it (the no-hitter) until the fifth inning (of the seven-inning contest). When I went out in the last inning, I was going for it."[6] His no-hitter was the first ever in the 44-year history of the city championship, and the last inning had its challenges. The first two of the final inning outs came on outstanding fielding plays by the first baseman and right fielder, respectively. After the final out, on a failed bunt attempt, Saberhagen said, "This is the best feeling I've ever had in my life. The rest of the team helped out and were with me all the way."[7]

Shortly thereafter, he was named City Player of the Year, and he signed with the Royals. Bret married his high school sweetheart, Janeane Inglett, in 1984. Their first child, Drew William Saberhagen, was born on October 26, 1985, eight hours before the start of Game Six of the 1985 World Series, and Saberhagen celebrated with a 2-0 win in Game Seven. They had two more children, daughter Brittany Nicole and son Daulton, before separating in 1992. Their divorce became final in 1994.

Saberhagen's minor-league career was brief. His first exposure to professional baseball was in the Florida Instructional League in the fall of 1982, where he pitched to a 7-2 record with a 2.36 ERA. He began the 1983 season with Fort Myers in the Class-A Florida State League, going 10-5 with a 2.30 ERA. He was named to the Southern Division team for the league's All-Star game. He was promoted before the end of the season to Class-AA Jacksonville in the Southern League where he won six of eight decisions and lowered his ERA to 2.91. In the Florida Instructional League that fall, he allowed only one earned run and walked only three batters in 47 innings.

He made it to the majors in 1984, becoming the youngest Royal ever, and got off to one of the rockier starts in major-league history. In his first appearances, he was called in from the bullpen to replace Paul Splittorff, who had been ineffective. The score was 4-2 in favor of the Yankees, and Burch Wynegar was standing on first base with only one out. Manager Dick Howser said, "Don't worry about the runner on first. He's not very fast and I don't think he'll be stealing. Just concentrate on the batter." To Saberhagen's surprise, catcher Don Slaught then called for a pitchout. However, Saberhagen was focused on the batter and threw a curve that crossed up his catcher and rolled to the back stop. The wild pitch advanced the runner to second base.[8] Saberhagen regained his composure and registered the next two outs. He went on to pitch 4 2/3 innings of scoreless ball that day, scattering three hits.

His first start came on April 19 against the Tigers, and resulted in his first career win. He went six innings, allowing only one run as the Royals defeated the Tigers 5-2, snapping a season opening nine-game winning streak by Detroit. He made a positive impression on Detroit pitching coach Roger Craig who said, "He's one of the best looking young pitchers I've seen. He's got as much poise as any young pitcher I've seen. I've seen guys with better stuff, but not many with as much poise."[9] In his first season, he went 10-11 with a 3.48 ERA.

In 1985, en route to a 20-6 record, becoming the fifth-youngest pitcher in major-league history to win 20 games, Saberhagen had a 2.87 ERA, third best in the league. He pitched with exceptional control and led the league with a 4.16 strikeout to walk ratio. He would go on to lead his league in that statistic two other times during his career, and his career ratio of 3.641 puts him at 18th place on the all-time list. He had gotten off to a slow start that year, but after May 12, he was 18-3 with a 2.54 ERA. His 20th win on September 30 put the Royals into a first-place tie with the Angels with six games left in the season. Five days later, they clinched the division and advanced to the League Championship Series. In the LCS, Saberhagen started Game Three but was knocked out of the box in the fifth inning. However, the Royals came back to win that game and Saberhagen was back on the mound in Game Seven. He bruised his thumb in the first inning and came out after three scoreless innings with the Royals leading 2-0. They went on to win the game and advanced to the World Series.

Bret Saberhagen appears as himself in The Scout *and* The Open Road.

1986 was a disaster. As Peter Gammons wrote in *Sports Illustrated*, he went from "Cy Young to Die Young."[10] The season started out well for him. His second start and first decision of the season was at Fenway Park on the afternoon of April 16. It was not a typical Fenway game. Only 11,164 fans were in attendance, and if one dallied too long at the concession stand, he would miss an inning or two, as the game took only two hours and five minutes to complete. Steve Balboni gave Saberhagen all the support he would need, leading off the second inning with a home run. Although the Royals could only muster five hits off Red Sox pitcher Al Nipper, Saberhagen, working quickly, limited the Red Sox singles by Tony Armas and Don Baylor in the early innings. He retired the last 15 batters in succession for a 1-0 shutout win.

After that, things did not pan out well for Saberhagen. His overindulgence on the banquet circuit after winning the Cy Young Award caught up with him. He lost his next two starts in April before hurling his second and last shutout of the season, defeating Baltimore 5-0 at Kansas City on May 2. It was his only win of the month, and at the end of May, his record stood at 2-5. The season wore on and the losses continued to outnumber the wins. Arm troubles were such that he was on the shelf from August 10 through September 5, and his record for the season was 7-12 with an ERA of 4.15. Looking back on the season during a winter when the phone stopped ringing with invites, Saberhagen said, "I still don't have any answers. If I could figure out what I did wrong, I'd do something about it. It's tough to pinpoint. The big thing was the injuries. That didn't help for sure. I did so many different things (to improve); it's hard to say what went wrong. Who knows? I just know I was expected to win at least 20 last year and I was very, very upset at the year I had."[11]

His salary was cut to $740,000, but he went to spring training in 1987 determined to turn things around. After his first spring start he said, "I've been thing about this (his first spring start) for a long time, especially the last week. I was concerned because of what happened last year. But I know that if I can get through the spring like I did today, I should have nothing less than 17 wins this season."[12] But he came back with a good season in 1987 and was named the comeback-player-of-the year. He won each of his first six starts including a shutout of Cleveland on May 9 that brought his ERA down to 1.59. His 4-0 record in April garnered him Player of the Month honors. Over the course of the season, he won 18 games, losing only 10. He was second in the league in both shutouts (four) and complete games (15), and his ERA was 3.36. He was named to his first All-Star team, and started the game on July 14 in Oakland, pitching three shutout innings marred only by a double off the bat of Andre Dawson. The Royals in a hotly contested West Division race (10 games separated the seven clubs) finished in second place, two games behind the Detroit Tigers.

At the beginning of the 1988 season Saberhagen had signed a lucrative three-year deal with the Royals. At the conclusion of the negotiations he said, "It turned out excellent for both sides. Now I don't have to keep going through this every year. It was driving me crazy."[13] He received $1.1 million in 1988, $1.25 million in 1989, and $1.375 million in 1990.

He was healthy in 1988, but his record fell to 14-16 with high numbers in all the wrong places. He led the league giving up hits (271) and allowed 110 earned runs as his ERA rose to 3.80. The only injury he sustained that year was when he tripped in his hotel room in New York in May and required 16 stitches to close the gash on his forehead and another five to sew up the laceration beneath his one of his eyes. More embarrassed than bruised, he did not miss a start.[14] It was a year of streaks for Saberhagen. In June, he was 4-1 with a 2.68 ERA, and at the end of June his record for the season stood at 10-6. After that, he was winless in his next five starts, in which he was charged with four losses. Over the last three months of the season was 4-10 with an ERA of 4.27. Even if Saberhagen had had a good season, the Royals would not have improved much on their third-place finish as the Athletics romped to the AL West title leading the pack by 13 games.

Saberhagen's second Cy Young Award season followed in 1989 when he went 23-6 with a league-leading ERA of 2.16. The durable Saberhagen pitched in at least 250 innings for the third year in a row, hurling a league high 262 1/3 innings. His first start of the season on April 10 was a harbinger of things to come. During the course of the season, he only lost successive games on one occasion, and that was in April. After April, he was 21-4 with a 1.93 ERA. He was left off the All-Star team, although his record at the All-Star break was 8-4. After the All-Star break his record bordered on the sensational, as he was 15-2 with a 1.74 ERA. His control during the season was exceptional as he walked only 43 batters while striking out 193. Although he committed a career high four errors during the season, he was awarded the only Golden Glove of his career. The Royals were in contention for most of the season, and on September first were 1 1/2 games out of first place. They finished at 92-70, but the Oakland A's distanced themselves from the pack in the late going. The Royals finished in second place, seven games behind the division champions.

By now you have guessed it - 1990 was a disaster. However, largely due to his record in the prior season when he had been snubbed, he was chosen to pitch in the All-Star Game on July 10. He pitched scoreless ball in the fifth and six innings, retiring each of the six batters he faced, and was awarded the win when the American League broke a scoreless tie in the top of the seventh inning and went on to win 2-0. His record was 5-7 when he had surgery in late July to have two loose bone chip fragments removed from his right elbow. He returned to the lineup later in the season and his record for the season was 5-9 with a 3.27 ERA. Not only was the season a disaster for Saberhagen, but the Royals hit the skids as well finishing in sixth place. At the end of the season, general manager John Schuerholz resigned. He had assumed the role after the 1981 season and was at the helm during Kansas City's first World Championship in 1985.

Would Saberhagen return to his normal odd-year form in 1991? Not right away. He lost three of his first four decisions and after righting the ship winning each of his five decisions in May, his rollercoaster ride with the disabled list continued when he was placed on the D. L. in June due to tendonitis in his shoulder. He returned from the DL on July 13 and his record stood at 9-6 with a 3.10 ERA after he defeated the Yankees at Kansas City on August 21. He had recorded his first shutout of the season on August 2, defeating Cleveland 4-0.

Six weeks after coming off the DL he pitched the game of his career. On August 26, 1991, he pitched the first no-hitter of his major-league career, defeating the Chicago White Sox, 7-0. He received help from official scorer Del Black. Black had initially rule a line drive by Chicago's Dan Pasqua a double, much to the chagrin of the 25,164 fans in attendance. However, after viewing several replays, he ruled that left fielder Kirk Gibson had misplaced the fifth-inning line drive. When the H changed to E on the scoreboard, the crowd erupted and Saberhagen, who was looking towards home plate at the time, knew that his ho-hitter was still intact. "You can pretty well tell by the crowd's reaction. I heard the crowd and figured what happened." He settled down, got out of the inning and when Frank Thomas grounded to second base with two outs in the ninth inning, Saberhagen had the fourth no-hitter in Royals history. Reflecting on his achievement, he said, "This is terrific, but there will never be anything better than the (1985) World Series."[15]

For the season, his record was 13-8, and his record during eight seasons with the Royals was 110-78. He had been paid $2.95 million in 1991 and would be going into the second year of an expensive longterm contract with a "small-market" team. He was "on the block," and after the 1991 season, he was traded to the Mets along with Keith Miller and Bill Pecota for Kevin McReynolds and Gregg Jefferies.

His first two seasons in New York were disappointing. Not only was his record disappointing but there were once again health issues. His first two starts in 1992 were a collective nightmare. In neither game did he make it past the fifth inning, and he allowed seven earned runs in each of those games. He was 0-2 and his ERA was 18.00. In his third start, he allowed five runs in the third inning against the Expos and then turned things around. The Mets came from behind and take him off the hook as he pitched three innings of scoreless ball before leaving the game in the for a pinch-hitter in the seventh inning.

He then became the Saberhagen the Mets were expecting. On April 23, he pitched nine shutout innings in a game that the Mets went on to win in the 13th inning, and on April 29 he spun a three-hit shutout as the Mets defeated Houston 1-0. His streak of consecutive scoreless innings ended at 26 in his next start when the Astros tallied a single run in the sixth inning. By then the Mets had a 5-0 lead and they went on to win 5-1, evening Saberhagen's record at 2-2.

However, he would only win one more game in 1992. In his first season with the Mets, he was only 3-5 as tendonitis, this time in his right index finger, resulted in his being on the shelf from May 16 through July 20 and starting only 15 games over the course of the season, the lowest number in his career to date.

In his new baseball home, he found new love after the breakup of his marriage to Janeane. They separated at the end of 1992, and he soon met his second wife, Lynn Critelli, who he married in 1996. They subsequently divorced.

After the 1992 season, he was awarded a three-year contract extension by the Mets, estimated at $15.4 million, but 1993 turned into a year of frustration. The Mets of 1993 were most definitely not the Mets of 1986, and by season's end their record was an unenviable 59-103. Frank Cashen and Davey Johnson were gone and the new regime of General Manager Joe McIlvane and manager Dallas Green were not receptive when it came to Saberhagen's clubhouse pranks. Two pranks during July 1993, one involving setting off a firecracker near reporters and another, involving spraying bleach, got him in trouble with management and in August a tirade in the clubhouse made headlines. Eventually he was suspended for the bleach spraying incident, and he missed time at the beginning of the 1994 season. He also was fined $15,384, a day's pay, which was contributed to the Eye Research Foundation of Central New York. For the season, Saberhagen was 7-7 with an ERA of 3.29 in 19 starts.

That season was abbreviated when he underwent surgery on August 3 for a tear in the medial collateral ligament in his right knee. The knee injury was sustained when he inadvertently stepped on a ball when he was jogging in the outfield. In September, he once again had elbow surgery.

In 1994, there were many changes. The National League went from two divisions to three and the Mets found themselves in a restructured Eastern Division with the Phillies, Expos, Braves, and Marlins. And the biggest change was Bret Saberhagen who reverted to his former self. He was still the prankster, but his actions showed a newfound maturity. "I've tried to change my habits around the clubhouse, not screw around so much. That's tough for me to do, because

I've always been a practical joker. But now before I do something, I think of the ramifications."[16] In the early part of the season, Saberhagen was receiving good run support and through June 25, his record was 7-4 with a 3.58 ERA. After that, it was lights out. He won each of his seven decisions and registered a 1.51 ERA in his final nine starts. During this time, he walked only five batters in 71 2/3 innings, and his strikeout to walk ratio was an eye-popping 11.00. For the season, which ended for him and everyone else in August, he was 14-4 with a 2.74 ERA with only 13 walks in 177 1/3 innings. He was third in the Cy Young Award voting and was named to his third All-Star team. This time around, he did not pitch as the game went into extra innings. He and José Rijo were the only pitchers left in the National League bullpen when the NL pushed across a run to win the game in the 10th inning. Oddly enough he was not named to the All-Star team in either of his Cy Young Award seasons.

In 1994, he also appeared in a movie. *The Scout* featured Brendan Fraser and Albert Brooks. Brooks, the scout, hired Saberhagen, playing himself, to throw pitches to Fraser, who played a baseball prospect in the film.

The 1995 Mets went from bad to worse and by August of that year, Saberhagen was 5-5 on a team that was going nowhere. He and his big money contract were gone from New York on August 1 as he was traded along with Dave Swanson to the Colorado Rockies for Arnie Gooch and Juan Acevedo. With Colorado, he was 2-1 in nine starts and spent two weeks on the shelf from August 27 through September 9.

He missed the entire 1996 season, undergoing surgery on May 28 that involved a titanium anchor being drilled into the bone of his right shoulder to hold together his rotator cuff. He signed a minor-league contract with the Boston Red Sox for the 1997 season. He pitched his way back to the majors and was 0-1 with a 6.58 ERA in 26 innings at the end of the 1997 season. He returned to the Red Sox in 1998.

And return he did. However, the durability wouldn't be there. The man who had hurled 76 complete games in his first 12 major-league seasons would go no further than the seventh inning in any of his 31 starts. He put together a 15-8 record with a 3.96 ERA. The Red Sox finished in second place with a 92-70 record, and advanced to the Division Series against the Cleveland Indians.

Saberhagen pitched the third game of the series and allowed three runs on only four hits in his seven innings of work, walking one and striking out seven. He took a no-hitter into the fifth inning when Jim Thome led off the inning with a homer for Cleveland's first run of the game. It tied the score at 1-1. The next two Cleveland hits were also solo home runs — a sixth-inning blast by Kenny Lofton and a seventh-inning shot by Manny Ramirez. The Red Sox were unable to come from behind, losing 4-3, and Saberhagen was tagged with the loss. It was Saberhagen's last appearance in 1998. Cleveland won the best-of-five series in four games.

His success in 1998 led to his being awarded the Tony Conigliaro Award by the Boston chapter of the Baseball Writers' Association of America for overcoming adversity.

In 1999, Saberhagen was unable to duplicate the success of the prior season, but he wasn't far off, going 10-6 and cutting his ERA to 2.95. He only started 22 games and paid three visits to the disabled list. The Red Sox once again finished second in the AL East and advanced to postseason play. Saberhagen started the second game of the Division Series against the Indians and had a rare bad day. His undoing came in the third inning and was initiated when Saberhagen's control abandoned him. He walked two batters and, with one out, gave up a triple to Omar Vizquel and a double to Roberto Alomar. Harold Baines, the eighth batter of the inning, came up with two on and two out and his three-run homer knocked Saberhagen out of the game. Cleveland won the game to take a 2-0 lead in the series, but the booming Boston bats won the next two games to force Game Five.

Saberhagen, given a chance to redeem himself, was once again ineffective. Given a two-run lead, he gave up three runs in the first inning and before an out was recorded in the second inning yielded two more. The knockout blow was a home run off the bat of Travis

Fryman. But the booming Boston bats, which had generated 32 runs in Games Three and Four, were not about to be silenced. The Sox came back to win Game Five, 12-8, and it was on to the League Championship Series against the Yankees. The Yankees won two of the first three games and in Game Four, Saberhagen took the mound against Andy Pettitte. Saberhagen was effective in his six innings, allowing three runs, only one of which (a Darryl Strawberry homer) was earned. However, he left the game on the wrong end of a 3-2 score. The Yankees broke the game open with six ninth-inning runs to take a commanding 3-1 lead in the series. The Red Sox were eliminated in five games.

But by 2000 Saberhagen was 36 years old and the pain had returned to his shoulder, causing him to miss the entire 2000 major-league season. He rehabbed that year, appearing in seven minor-league games, and also rehabbed in five games in 2001, returning to the mound at Fenway on July 27, 2001. He pitched six innings in a 9-5 defeat of the White Sox. It was his last major-league win. He followed up this outing with two losses and was placed on the disabled list one last time. He announced his retirement at the end of the 2001 season.

After baseball, Saberhagen retired to California, where he coached son Drew at Calabasas High School. He also did some film work. With Kevin Costner and former players Johnny Bench and George Brett, he appeared in the documentary *Field of Dreams Roundtable* in 2004, and he appeared as himself in the 2009 film *The Open Road*, with Justin Timberlake and Ted Danson.

In 2004, he established the Bret Saberhagen Make a Difference Foundation to help children fighting diabetes and other illnesses. In 2005, he was inducted into the Kansas City Royals Hall of Fame.

SOURCES

In addition to the sources listed in the Notes, Baseball-Reference.com and the articles listed below were used by the author.

Antonen, Mel, "Unique Surgery Saves Saberhagen's Shoulder, Career," *USA Today*, April 29, 1998: 1C.

Attner, Paul. "Common Work Habits Mark Return to Royalty: Saberhagen Has His head, Body Back into the Game," *The Sporting News*, May 25, 1987: 4.

Durso, Joseph, "Saberhagen is Near Perfect in Cy Young Voting," *New York Times*, November 16, 1989.

Frey, Jennifer, "Saberhagen Sounds Off at Mets' Management," *New York Times* June 22, 1994.

Frey, Jennifer, "The Joke's Up for Bret Saberhagen," *New York Times* February 27, 1994.

Kravitz, Bob, "Saberhagen Decision Offers No Guarantees," *Rocky Mountain News*, January 18, 1996: 2B.

Martinez, Michael, "Saberhagen Still the Same Old Kid: '85 Success Has Not Led to '86 Excess," *New York Times* News Service, February 23, 1986.

Moran, Malcolm, "On a Rainy Day, Saberhagen Throws a Tantrum," *New York Times*, August 7, 1993: 31.

Nightengale, Bob, "Saberhagen Signs for 3 Years, Riches," *The Sporting News*, February 22, 1988.

Nightingale, Dave, "Even in Odd Year, Saberhagen's No. 1," *The Sporting News*, July 9, 1990: 8.

Ocker, Sheldon, "Royals Get Breaks to Slip by Indians and Post 5-4 Win," *Akron Beacon-Journal*, May 4, 1987: D4.

NOTES

1. Gordon Edes, "Towel May End Up as His Next Throw," *Boston Globe*, August 9, 2001
2. Thomas Boswell. *The Heart of the Order* (New York, Doubleday, 1989), 278.
3. Lorenzo Benet. "Bret's Team—From the time he was 7, Baseball was Bret Saberhagen's Dream—His Parents helped make it Come True," *Daily News* (Los Angeles, California), November 6, 1985.
4. Vincent Bonsignore, *Daily News* (Los Angeles, California), May 7, 2002.
5. Joe Koenig, "Palisades Reaches the City Final Against Cleveland," *Los Angeles Times*, June 11, 1982: E15.
6. Randy Sparage, "Saberhagen's No Hitter Decides It," *Los Angeles Times*, June 15, 1982: D4.
7. Paul Vercammen, "Cavaliers Cradle City Baseball Crown After Hoping for a Lot Less," *Los Angeles Times*, June 17, 1982: V4
8. Bruce Nash and Allan Zullo, *The Baseball Hall of Shame 4* (New York, Simon and Schuster, 1990), 76-77.
9. "K. C. Rookie 1st to Tame Tigers," *Chicago Tribune*, April 20, 1984: C5
10. Peter Gammons, "Return of the Royal Nonesuch," *Sports Illustrated*, June 8, 1987.

11 Bob Nightengale, "Homework by Saberhagen gives him new Hope for 1987," *Kansas City Times*, January 14, 1987: 1-B.

12 Bob Nightengale, "Saberhagen Blots Out Past, Follows Plan in Spring Debut," *Kansas City Times*, March 11, 1987: E-1.

13 Bob Nightengale. *The Sporting News*, February 22, 1988.

14 *The Sporting News*, May 9, 1988: 17.

15 *The Pentagraph* (Bloomington, Illinois), August 27, 1991: B1.

16 *New York Post*, May 13, 1994.

ZIGGY SEARS

BY BRUCE BUMBALOUGH

JOHN WILLIAM "ZIGGY" SEARS was a minor-league outfielder from 1912 to 1928, a Texas League umpire from 1929 to 1934, a National League umpire from 1934 to 1945, a Pacific Coast League umpire in 1946, a scout for the Pittsburgh Pirates in 1947, a Texas League umpire from 1948 to 1951, and an actor in two baseball movies in 1948 and 1949.

Sears was born in Central City, Kentucky, to George T. and Mattie Sears on January 10, 1892. His father was a coal miner, a trade Ziggy Sears practiced briefly before attending college and then becoming a professional baseball player. He attended Western Kentucky State Normal School from 1910 to 1911. The college later became Western Kentucky University.[1]

Sears' baseball career began in 1912 when he played for the Winchester Hustlers/Nicholasville Orphans/Mount Sterling Orphans in the Class-D Blue Grass League. In 1913 and 1914, Sears played for Owensboro in the Class-D Kentucky-Illinois-Tennessee (Kitty) League, for Marshalltown in the Class-D Central Association, and for Streator in the Class-D Illinois-Missouri League. Sears married Hazel Phillips on February 2, 1915. That year, the 5-foot-11, 198-pound outfielder was with Streator and Marshalltown.

In 1916, while playing for Clinton in the Central Association, Sears was almost called up by the Detroit Tigers. Detroit purchased his contract, but a leg injury prevented him from joining the team. He stayed with Clinton and also played for the Central Association's Dubuque/Charles City franchise in 1917, the year his son Kenneth was born.

Sears' rise to fame began in 1918 when he began playing for stellar manager Jake Atz and the Fort Worth Panthers of the then Class-B Texas League. Atz was one of the best minor-league managers ever. The teams he managed in the Texas League won 1,566 games and lost 1,221. Both are the top marks for any manager in the league. His teams won six consecutive Texas League championships from 1920 to 1925 and five of six Dixie Series championships in those years. The Panthers finished second to Dallas in 1917 and 1918. They compiled the best record in the league in 1919 but lost to Shreveport in the playoffs.[2]

Atz gave Sears his nickname when Sears reported to the Panthers. Sears announced his name as John, but Atz decried there would be no "Johns" on his team. Atz's given name was John Jacob. Recalling a pitcher named Ziggy Shears, who had tried out for the Panthers the previous season, Atz gave Sears the moniker and forever branded Sears as Ziggy.[3]

Sears, a left-handed-hitting outfielder with good speed, most often played left field. From 1918 to 1926, he hit .290 with 277 doubles, 31 triples, and 87 home runs. He played in 1,256 games for the Panthers in those years. He also played for Fort Worth in 1927, but that data is not available. Sears' best season was 1925 when he hit .321 with 35 doubles, 2 triples, and 23 home runs. In a game against San Antonio in May 1925 he drove in 11 runs. Panthers team secretary Paul LaGrave valued Sears so highly that in 1926 he arranged for the outfield sod at old Panther Park to be moved to the new Panther Park, being built a few blocks east of the old park.[4] He sought to protect Sears' fragile ankles with the move.[5]

Sears played for Waco, Shreveport, and San Antonio in his final two seasons. At the end of the 1928 season, he asked Texas League President J. Doak Roberts for a job as an umpire, and Roberts accommodated him. Sears umpired in the Texas League until July of 1934, when he was hired by the National League.[6]

Sears was selected to work the 1935 All-Star Game after less than one full season in the National League. He also umpired in the 1938 and 1944 World Series. Illness prevented him from working the 1943 World Series. He stayed in the National League until the end of the 1945 season when he suffered a broken foot in the final game of the year.

In the book *Nice Guys Finish Last*, Leo Durocher related a story in which he got an ejection by Sears overturned. On August 16, 1945, Sears booted Durocher, then the Brooklyn Dodgers manager, for arguing balls and strikes. Durocher claimed he wasn't arguing Sears' call, but rather seeking clarification on it. On an appeal by Durocher, National League President Ford Frick overturned the ejection and Durocher said that Frick levied a fine on Sears. A few months later the league released Sears.[7]

Sears and Durocher had a rocky relationship. Sears ejected Durocher eight times between 1938 and 1945, including twice in the final months of the 1945 season. Sears led the league in ejections that year with eight.

The events that led to Sears' departure from the National League are unknown. Did he quit or was he fired? Did the number of ejections he made in his final season cause too much trouble for Ford Frick and the National League powers? Was the foot injury enough to bring the then 53-year-old Sears to thoughts of retirement? Did the hearing and fine combine with the injury and the exhaustion of an umpire at the end of a long season enough to bring Sears to seek his release?

Regardless, Ziggy Sears returned to baseball the following season. He worked in 1946 as an umpire in the Pacific Coast League, and then scouted for the Pirates in 1947 before returning to the Texas League as an umpire from 1948 to 1951.[8]

Sears appeared briefly in two baseball films in 1948 and 1949. The first was *The Babe Ruth Story*, starring William Bendix as Ruth. The film credits listed Sears as an umpire. Film critics generally regarded the movie as one of the worst baseball films ever produced. Leonard Maltin called it "perfectly dreadful."[9] Bosley Crowther, longtime film critic for the *New York Times*, said it was "a wallow in sloppy sentiment."[10]

As Crowther noted, the film presents Ruth as a naïve, lovable man-child prone to acting on impulse, often to his detriment. It is a sanitized and

Umpire Ziggy Sears standing up to Frankie Frisch; Sears's two film appearances are in The Babe Ruth Story *and* The Stratton Story.

heavy-handed version of Ruth's life and career. Bendix was right-handed and had no athletic ability. His efforts at baseball were comically amateurish. Ruth was, of course, left-handed and a great athlete. The picture of Ruth as the hard-drinking, womanizing, shrewd businessman was almost totally absent from the film.[11]

Sears also appeared, this time uncredited, in *The Stratton Story*. James Stewart played Monty Stratton. June Allyson played Stratton's wife, Ethel. Monty Stratton was a White Sox pitcher who came up in 1934 and established himself as a rising star. He had a career record of 36-23 with an ERA of 3.71 at the end of the 1938 season. Stratton accidentally shot himself while hunting in Texas in November of 1938. Doctors amputated his leg and provided him with a wooden prosthesis. After fighting through a bout of self-pity, Stratton learned to walk with the artificial leg and then to pitch. He eventually returned to the low minor leagues in Texas, where he pitched for seven seasons. Bill Dickey and Jimmy Dykes appeared in the film as themselves and Cleveland Indians pitching star Gene Bearden appeared as a pitcher for an All-Star minor-league team. Douglas Morrow, co-author of the screenplay, won an Oscar for the Best Writing, Motion Picture Story for his work on the film.[12]

In 1951 Sears suffered vision damage when he was hit by a thrown ball while working an exhibition game between the Dallas Eagles of the Texas League and the Milwaukee Brewers of the American Association. He retired from the game at the end of the season. He lived out his life in Houston and died there of a heart attack on December 16, 1956. His remains rest in Forest Park Cemetery in Houston.

Ken "Little Ziggy" Sears followed his father into baseball. He was a mascot for the Fort Worth Panthers as a child and attended the University of Alabama from 1936 to 1938. He signed with the St. Louis Cardinals as a catcher. By 1943 he was in the New York Yankees organization. Debuting in the major leagues on May 2, 1943, Sears played in 60 games, batting .278 with two home runs and 22 RBIs. Sears was in the US Navy in 1944 and 1945.[13] He played in seven games for the St. Louis Browns in 1946, hitting .333 with no home runs and one RBI. He finished his baseball career with Little Rock (Southern Association) and San Antonio (Texas League) in 1947 and Borger (West Texas-New Mexico League) in 1949.

After retiring from baseball, Ken Sears became a train engineer for the Rock Island Railroad.

He died in Bridgeport, Texas, on July 17, 1968.[14] He is buried in Greenwood Memorial Park, Fort Worth.[15]

SOURCES

In addition to the sources cited in the Notes, the author also consulted Retrosheet and Baseball-Reference.com.

NOTES

1. 1900 US Federal census for Muhlenberg County, Kentucky; 1910 US Federal census for Muhlenberg County, Kentucky; The History of WKU (wku.edu/wkuhistory), accessed June 23, 2016.
2. *2016 Texas League Media Guide and Record Book*. The Dixie Series was a postseason playoff between the champions of the Texas League and the Southern Association. It was played from 1920 to 1958.
3. John Sears file, Giamatti Research Center, National Baseball Hall of Fame, Cooperstown, New York.
4. A team secretary in those days was equivalent to a general manager today.
5. John Sears file, Giamatti Research Center.
6. John Sears file, Giamatti Research Center.
7. Leo Durocher and Ed Linn, *Nice Guys Finish Last* (New York: Simon and Schuster, 1975), 197-198.
8. John Sears file, Giamatti Research Center.
9. Leonard Maltin, *Leonard Maltin's Movie and Video Guide 2004* (New York: Plume, 2003).
10. *New York Times*, August 1, 1948.
11. *The Babe Ruth Story*, Internet Movie Database (imdb.com), accessed June 23, 2016.
12. *The Stratton Story*, Internet Movie Database (imdb.com), accessed June 23, 2016.
13. *The Sporting News*, January 13, 1944.
14. *Fort Worth Press*, July 18, 1968.
15. Ken Sears Memorial, Findagrave (findagrave.com), accessed June 23, 2016.

SAMMY SOSA

BY ERIC HANAUER

WHO IS THE REAL SAMMY Sosa? Is he the charismatic slugger whose home-run race with Mark McGwire brought baseball's fandom back from the ruins of the 1994 strike? Is he the Dominican shoeshine boy from a poverty-stricken family who became a hero in his country and the United States? Is he a steroid cheater who has never confessed? Is he the egotistical clubhouse cancer who walked out on his team during the last game of the 2004 season? This complex man was one of the most popular and controversial players of his time.

Nobody else has hit 60 home runs in three different seasons. Yet he didn't lead the league in any one of them. In the five-year period from 1998 through 2002 he hit 292 home runs, an average of 58 a year. Nobody has even come close, either clean or chemically assisted. He had seasons of 158 and 160 RBIs, and 10.3 WAR. He was an All-Star seven times and an MVP. His 609 home runs are the eighth highest of all time. Yet he's never been selected on more than 12.5 percent of Hall of Fame ballots. He barely remains on the list with only 8.6 percent in his fifth year of eligibility.

Samuel Peralta Sosa was born on November 12, 1968, in Consuelo, Dominican Republic, one of seven children. His father, Juan Bautista Montero, drove a tractor clearing sugar-cane fields. He died of a cerebral hemorrhage when Sammy was 6 years old. After Juan's death, his mother, Mireya, reverted to her maiden name, Sosa. She had dropped out of school in her teens and worked as a maid and a cook. Sammy and his brothers washed cars and shined shoes to bring in pesos for the family. All of them slept in a single room in the barrio.[1]

When Sammy was 13, Mireya moved to San Pedro de Macoris, where she married Carlos Maria Peralta. Conditions improved a bit, but Sammy, who was called Mikey by family and friends, prioritized work over school. He and older brother Luis established a business shining shoes for middle-class businessmen. One of them was Bill Chase, an American who was opening a shoe factory. He hired Sammy and became a surrogate father. He bought Sammy his first bicycle, and his first baseball glove.[2]

Although baseball is the national passion in the Dominican Republic, Sammy wanted to be a boxer. He trained seriously, but when Mireya found out, she made him promise to give it up. That's when he turned his focus to baseball.[3] At 14, he attracted the attention of a *buscone*, or informal agent, quit school, and joined a traveling team with real uniforms. At 15 he signed with the Phillies, but the contract was voided because he was underage. The following year was a parade of tryouts and rejections from other teams. Finally Omar Minaya and Amado Dinzey of the Texas Rangers signed him for $3,500.

Sosa made his official pro debut in 1986 at the age of 17, with the Gulf League Rangers in Sarasota, Florida. At the time he was lean and lithe, about 165 pounds, with speed rather than power his greatest asset. In 61 games he hit .275 with 4 home runs and 11 stolen bases. One of his teammates and best friends on the team was Juan Gonzalez.

The following year they moved up together to Class-A Gastonia, North Carolina. Sosa hit .279 with 11 home runs and 59 RBIs. He was also learning English, primarily by hanging with his American teammates.[4] By the end of the season, Sosa and Gonzalez were ranked one and two in the Rangers' farm system.

The next step was Charlotte in the High-A Florida State League. At 19, Sammy was one of the youngest players, hit only .229 and struck out 106 times. Yet he stole 42 bases and drove in 51 runs. At times his behavior roused the ire of some coaches, who were not used to dealing with Latin players, but Minaya protected him.[5] A strong season in Dominican winter ball brought an invitation to major-league spring training in 1989.

At this time, the Rangers were heavily invested in Latin players. Among them were Rafael Palmeiro, Ivan Rodriguez, Julio Franco, and Ruben Sierra. Sosa and Gonzalez were sent to Tulsa in the Double-A Texas League to start the season. By June, Sammy was hitting .297 with seven home runs, and made the All-Star team. On the parent club, Pete Incaviglia was placed on the disabled list with a sore neck, and Sosa was called up to replace him. He was 20 years old, and had been playing baseball for six years. He flew first class to New York, and on June 16, 1989, hit leadoff in Yankee Stadium, where he singled against Andy Hawkins in his first major-league at-bat. In the sixth inning he doubled off Hawkins and scored his first run.

The next stop for the Rangers was Fenway Park, with Roger Clemens on the mound. He struck out Sosa in the first inning, but in the fifth, Sammy hit one of Clemens's offerings over the Green Monster for his first major-league home run. After a hot start, Sosa started seeing more breaking balls, and his average plummeted to .238. The Rangers sent him to Triple-A Oklahoma City, where he moped a bit and wasn't hitting. However Larry Himes, then general manager of the White Sox, saw something he liked. He projected Sosa as a Minnie Minoso-type player, with speed and a strong outfield arm. So Himes traded aging Harold Baines and Fred Manrique to the Rangers for Sosa, Wilson Alvarez, and Scott Fletcher.

Sammy was sent to Triple-A Vancouver, where he hit .367 in 13 games. The White Sox called him up and he joined the team in Minnesota. In his White Sox debut, Sosa walked twice and went 3-for-3 with a two-run homer as Chicago won, 10-2. In 33 games he hit .273 with an OPS of .765. The first thing he did when he returned home was to buy a house for his mother, partly with a loan from Bill Chase, his businessman friend.

In 1990, the 21-year-old outfielder displayed both his raw talent and inexperience. He hit .233 made 13 errors, and struck out 150 times. Yet he hit 15 home runs, stole 32 bases, and drove in 70 runs. Walt Hriniak, the White Sox hitting coach, had some rigid ideas that conflicted with Sammy's free-swinging approach. It worked for some, but totally frustrated Sosa.[6] Although the team had a good year, Himes was fired at the end of the season because of conflicts with owner Jerry Reinsdorf. A year later, he would be the GM of the Cubs and trade for Sosa again.

Sammy married an American woman in 1990. It lasted only eight months before ending in divorce. By spring training 1991 he was still sorting through the resulting legal mess, his stepfather died, and the conflicts with Hriniak continued. Though he hit two homers on Opening Day, the White Sox platooned him with Cory Snyder. By July 19, he was hitting .200 and was demoted to Triple A. Recalled in August, he hit only .203 in 116 major-league games. About the only redeeming aspect of that lost season was meeting Sonia Rodriguez. They married the following year, and as of 2018 had six children.

Sosa went to spring training with the White Sox in 1992 amid trade rumors and reports that he was uncoachable. On March 30, Himes pulled the trigger on the best trade of his checkered Cubs tenure. He sent George Bell and $400,000 cash to the White Sox for Sosa and pitcher Ken Patterson. (A year later he made his worst transaction, by failing to meet Greg Maddux's reasonable demands and letting him sign with the Braves.) Sammy was ecstatic. On his way out, he told his White Sox teammates, "Okay boys. I'm out of here. You guys will see me again. I'm going to be the best player in this game."[7]

At age 23, Sosa was listed at 6 feet tall and a lithe 185 pounds. The Cubs played him in center field, because Andre Dawson was established in right, and hit him at the top two slots in the order because he was the fastest runner on the team. That didn't fit with Sammy's free-swinging style, and when he slumped, manager Jim Lefebvre moved him down in the lineup. He began to hit with power. On June 10 in St. Louis he hit two home runs, for the first time since Opening Day 1991. But a few days later a Dennis Martinez fastball broke a bone in Sosa's right wrist. That put him on the disabled list for six weeks.

He returned on July 27 and hit a home run in his first at-bat. The Cubs swept a three-game series against the Pirates at Wrigley Field. Sammy played a key role with clutch hits. In the final game, his 11th-inning home run won it, and for the first time the chant, "Sam-my, Sam-my" rang down from the stands. In nine games coming off the DL, he hit .385 with three home runs. But the next day fate struck again. He fouled off a pitch that broke a bone in his ankle. Sosa's season was finished. He had only 262 at-bats, hit .260 with 8 home runs and 15 stolen bases. But his hustle, speed, youth, and potential had made him a favorite with Cubs fans.

The next season, 1993, was Sosa's breakout year. Hitting coach Billy Williams and Lefebvre adopted a hands-off approach, encouraging him to just be himself. With Dawson gone, he returned to his natural position, right field. Sosa responded with 33 home runs, 93 RBIs, and 36 stolen bases, the first Cub to make the 30-30 club. At the time, only nine other players had achieved it. The highlight of the season came in Denver on the Fourth of July weekend. He went 6-for-6, giving him nine hits in a row, one short of the National League record. At the end of the season the Cubs signed Sosa to a new contract, for $2,950,000. He bought his mother another new house, and one for himself and Sonia in Santo Domingo.

In 1994 Tom Trebelhorn replaced Lefebvre as Cubs manager. He couldn't have got off to a worse start, losing 12 straight home games. By early May, the Cubs were 6-18. A toxic aura in the clubhouse labeled Sosa as a selfish player. He didn't help matters by sporting a gaudy gold necklace with a 30-30 pendant.[8] On the field he led the Cubs in nearly every offensive category. When the season was cut short in August by the players strike and the owners lockout, the Cubs were in last place. Sosa hit .300 with 25 homers, 70 RBIs, and 22 stolen bases in 105 games.

Before the strike was finally settled, there was some confusion about Sosa's free-agent status. His agent, Adam Katz, was in serious discussions with the Red Sox, but in the end Sosa remained a Cub. Himes and Trebelhorn were gone, replaced by Ed Lynch and Jim Riggleman. The Cubs were in the playoff race for a while. Sosa played in the All-Star Game for the first time, won a Silver Slugger Award, and finished eighth in the MVP balloting. He hit .268 with 36 homers, 119 RBIs, and 34 stolen bases.

On the eve of free agency in January 1996, the Cubs signed Sammy to a three-year, $16 million contract. He had bulked up to a listed 200 pounds, and was swinging for the fences. The fans in the right-field bleachers responded to his daily sprint and wave, but the reputation as a selfish player continued. At the All-Star break he was leading the league in home runs, but was not selected on the team. That stung, but Sosa continued to mash. On August 20 he led the league with 40 home runs and had 100 RBIs. But that day he was hit on the right hand by pitcher Mark Hutton of the Florida Marlins. His pisiform bone was broken, and surgery was required. Sosa's season was over. Despite missing the last six weeks, he finished fifth in the NL in home runs.

The Cubs' 1997 season was over by the third week. They lost their first 14 games, a club record. Sammy's contract status was in limbo, as his opt-out clause was being negotiated. Finally, on June 27, he signed a four-year, $42 million contract, making him the third-highest-paid player in baseball. The Cubs limped home with 94 losses, tied for the worst in the National League. Sosa's year yielded 36 home runs, 119 RBIs, and a .251 batting average with a league-leading 174 strikeouts. In and outside the clubhouse, he was labeled as a flop. Jeff Pentland was the new Cubs hitting coach in 1997. He spent that year getting to know Sosa, studying his approach, and formulating a plan. That plan came to fruition in 1998.

Pentland convinced Sammy that he didn't have to swing so hard to hit home runs. He also lowered Sammy's hands and introduced a foot tap as a timing device. Sosa was coached to become more selective, take walks, and hit to right field when that was all the pitcher gave him. Sosa wrote, "Of all the coaches I've had in my life, he is the one who has gotten the most out of me...."[9]

Sammy started the 1998 season slowly. By May 22 he had only eight home runs. The drought was

Sammy Sosa, who is seen onscreen in Hardball, On the Line, *and* Kissing a Fool.

broken with a 440-foot shot to center field off Maddux. By the end of the month he had 13, still 14 behind McGwire and trailing several others. In June, Sosa made history with 20 home runs, breaking Rudy York's 1937 major-league record of 18 in one month. At month's end the gap with McGwire was down to four, and the national media began to notice. Sammy's homer hop, heart tap, and kisses blown to his mother from the dugout, became staples on ESPN's *SportsCenter* and *Baseball Tonight*. On July 27 at Phoenix he hit the first grand slam of his career, driving in all the Cubs runs with two homers in a 6-2 win. It was the 247th of his career, which broke Bob Horner's record (207) for the most home runs before the first grand slam. Making up for lost time, Sosa hit another the next day. On August 19 he hit homer number 48 against the Cardinals to take the lead for the first time. It didn't last long, as Big Mac hit two in the same game. Later in the game, after Sosa walked, McGwire turned to him and said, "Hey, I think we're going to do it."[10]

As the pressure built, McGwire seemed to feel it more. Sosa embraced it, maintaining a happy face with the press and the fans, who in turn embraced him. When a bottle of Androstenedione was spotted in McGwire's locker, Sosa attributed his own physique to Flintstones Vitamins. Number 57 broke the Cubs' single-season record set by Hack Wilson in 1930. When Big Mac hit number 62 against the Cubs, Sosa ran in from right field and hugged him. In a dramatic September series at home against the Brewers, Sammy hit numbers 59 to 62 to tie McGwire. Number 63 in San Diego tied the race again. The overflow crowd gave Sammy a standing ovation on each trip to the plate. In the eighth inning the Padres were ahead, 3-2. The bases were loaded, Sammy got another standing O, then hit one into the upper deck for a 6-3 win. He took a curtain call as the San Diego management set off fireworks. Padres players later complained. On September 25, Sosa hit number 66 to take the lead for the final time. That lasted about a half-hour as Mac connected against Montreal. McGwire hit four the last two games of the season to finish with 70. Sosa hit .308 with 66 home runs, a league-leading 158 RBIs, 134 runs scored, 416 total bases, and 171 strikeouts. With the Cubs making the playoffs (and quickly eliminated by the Braves) Sammy was the winner of the MVP Award. He and McGwire were selected co-Sportsmen of the Year by *Sports Illustrated*. The Cubs had a day for Sosa in September and gave him a purple Plymouth Prowler. McGwire received a classic red 1962 Corvette from the Cardinals on his day.

The offseason brought more recognition and honors. President Leonel Fernandez of the Dominican Republic made Sammy an ambassador. When a hurricane hit his country, Sosa sparked humanitarian aid with money, publicity, and personally distributed food, water, and medicine. At the State of the Union address, President Bill Clinton introduced him and acknowledged his accomplishments. Endorsements and offers flooded his agent.

Sosa and McGwire repeated their race in 1999, but this time a jaded public wasn't nearly as excited. Rumors about performance enhancing drugs were swirling not only around them, but about the entire generation of sluggers that suddenly made 30 to 50 home runs commonplace. Sosa briefly addressed PEDs in his autobiography: "I have never used Andro, nor do I plan to. ... While it's true that I tried the food supplement Creatine once or twice, I never saw it have any particular impact on my body or development. ... I attribute my physical development to many years of strict weight training and proper nutrition. ..."[11]

The Cubs crashed in 1999, beset with injuries and bad vibes, losing 95 games and finishing last in their division. Some players resented Sosa's ego, his entourage, and his loud salsa music in the tiny clubhouse. Regardless, he had another banner year. On September 18 he became the first player to hit 60 home runs in more than one season. McGwire quickly caught up and finished with 65 to Sosa's 63. Sammy hit .288 and drove in 141 runs. He led the league in games played, 162, total bases, 397, and strikeouts, 171. Riggleman was fired and replaced by Don Baylor.

Sosa hit only 50 home runs in 2000, but led the league for the first time. He became more selective at the plate, hitting .320 with a higher OBP, .406, and OPS, 1.040, than in his 60-home-run years. He also won the Home Run Derby at the All-Star Game. The Cubs limped home in last place again.

In many ways, Sosa's 2001 season was better than his MVP year. He hit a career-high .328, led the league with 146 runs, 160 RBIs, 37 intentional walks, and 425 total bases. With 64 home runs, he became the only player in history to hit 60 three times. He finished strong, hitting .377 in his final 57 games. He was 10-for-15 with the bases loaded, including two grand slams, totaling seven for his career. In MVP voting he finished second behind Barry Bonds, who hit 73 homers in his monster year.

Sammy made cameo appearances in two movies that year: *Hardball* and *On the Line*. In 1997 he had appeared in *Kissing a Fool*. Each had low ratings on the Rotten Tomatoes website.[12]

Sosa won his second home run crown in 2002, with 49. On August 10 he hit three three-run homers in consecutive innings. It was the sixth three-homer game of his career, tying Johnny Mize's major-league record. Sosa's 122 runs scored led the league for the third time, to go along with a .288 average and .399 OBP. Sosa made his fourth All-Star Game start and won his sixth Silver Slugger. By now, rumors of steroid use and clubhouse dissension were rampant. But throughout the losing years, Cubs management promoted and indulged Sosa, as he kept putting people in the seats.

Dusty Baker took over as manager in 2003. The Cubs won the Central Division, and advanced to the League Championship Series, eventually blowing a three-games-to-one lead to the Florida Marlins. Sammy pitched in with 40 homers and 103 RBIs. At age 34, his bat was slowing down but he kept achieving milestones. On April 4 he became the 18th player to hit 500 home runs, and the first NL player with six consecutive 40-home-run seasons. In the playoffs that year, Sosa hit his first two postseason home runs. One came in the ninth inning of the first NLCS game against the Marlins, sending it into extra innings.

Two incidents that year may have contributed to Sosa's decline. On April 20, he was hit in the head by a Salomon Torres fastball that smashed his helmet. Concussion protocols weren't in place then, and Sammy played the next game. But he hit only one home run in his next 98 plate appearances. Then on June 3, his bat broke on a swing against the Tampa Bay Rays. Home-plate umpire Tim McClelland found cork in the center of the shattered club. Sosa was kicked out of the game, and eventually suspended for seven games. Sammy claimed it was a batting practice bat that he accidentally picked up. Sosa's other bats were X-rayed with no evidence of cork. But his credibility took a major hit. Whether the bats, or the concussion, or age, or backing off PEDs contributed to Sammy's decline is still a subject for debate.[13] During that season, random anonymous drug tests were administered to major-league players. In 2009 a list of players who failed was leaked to the *New York Times*. Sosa's name was on that list. A summary article was published in July.[14]

The 2004 season marked the closing of Sosa's era with the Cubs. He passed Ernie Banks for the team's career home-run record with 545. Other than that, it wasn't pretty. He went on the disabled list when a violent sneeze caused back spasms. He hit only .253 with 35 homers and 80 RBIs. During the final week of the season, the Cubs blew a wild-card lead and missed the playoffs. On the final day, Sammy asked Dusty Baker not to play him. He disappeared from the bench, and security cameras showed him driving away shortly after the game started. When his teammates found out, they vented their anger on his boombox. When Cubs management released the security tape to the press, it became evident that he couldn't return.

Trading from a position of disadvantage, the Cubs didn't get much. The Baltimore Orioles sent them Mike Fontenot, Jerry Hairston, and Mike Crothers for Sosa and cash. Sammy played in only 102 games in 2005, hitting .221 with 14 homers and 45 RBIs. His biggest headline came when he testified before a congressional committee in the PED investigations. Speaking in Spanish with a translator, he denied ever using steroids. Sosa and McGwire were excoriated for their testimony. To this day, the only actual link of Sosa with PEDs is that leaked report of a failed test in 2003.

Only one team offered Sammy a contract in 2006, and he didn't like the terms, so he sat out that year. Still, there was one more milestone to pursue. So he signed with the Texas Rangers in 2007 for the major-league minimum salary and a spring training invitation. On June 20, he hit his 600th career home run, off Cubs pitcher Jason Marquis. Ironically, Marquis was wearing Sammy's old number, 21. At age 38, Sosa hit .252 with 21 homers and 92 RBIs. It was a far more fitting finish than the down year with Baltimore.

With nothing left to prove, Sammy told his agent not to seek another contract. Since then, Sosa has mostly stayed out of the limelight. Occasionally there are reports of extravagant overseas birthday celebrations.[15] He has invested in and lent his name to several business ventures. His net worth is estimated at $70 million. That's a long way from shining shoes on the streets of San Pedro de Macoris.

The remaining loose thread is Sosa's relationship with the Cubs. He hasn't been invited to Cubs Conventions or historic Wrigley Field celebrations, or had his number 21 retired, although ownership and management from his playing days is gone. Other sluggers of the steroid era like Barry Bonds, Mark McGwire, and Manny Ramirez have been welcomed back like prodigal sons. Sosa hasn't. History is a major element of the Cubs' appeal. With the passing of Ernie Banks and Ron Santo, they are running low on iconic figures. Occasional rumors surface of contact between representatives, a need for apologies, and statements from bloggers and fans.[16] But as of 2018 Sosa remained in limbo with the organization where he spent the best years of a historic career.

SOURCES

In addition to the sources cited in the Notes, the author also consulted the following:

Baseball-Reference.com.

Chicago Tribune. Sammy's Season (Chicago: Contemporary Books, 1998).

Chicago Cubs Information Guides, 1993 and 2004.

Davis, Ryan. "Despite Cloud of Suspicion, Sammy Sosa's Career Is Still Hall-Worthy," January 7, 2015, cubsinsider.com/despite-cloud-suspicion-sammy-sosas-career-still-hall-worthy/.

Bernard, Zach Bernard. "Redefining Sammy Sosa's Baseball Legacy," January 4, 2016, baseballessential.com/news/2016/01/04/redefining-sammy-sosas-baseball-legacy/.

NOTES

1. Sammy Sosa with Marcus Breton, *Sosa, an Autobiography* (New York: Warner Books Inc. 2000), 24-25.
2. Sosa with Breton, 31-32.
3. Sosa with Breton, 41-42.
4. Sosa with Breton, 74.
5. Sosa with Breton, 86.
6. Sosa with Breton, 118.
7. Sosa with Breton, 126.

8   Joseph A. Reaves, "What Makes Sammy a Star?" *Chicago Tribune*, June 16, 1995.
9   Sosa with Breton, 183.
10 Sosa with Breton, 190.
11 Sosa with Breton, 191.
12 rottentomatoes.com/celebrity/sammy_sosa/.
13 Bradley Woodrum, "The Three Declines of Sammy Sosa," January 29, 2015, hardballtimes.com/the-three-declines-of-sammy-sosa/.
14 Michael S. Schmidt, "Sosa Is Said to Have Tested Positive in 2003," *New York Times*, June 16, 2006.
15 si.com/extra-mustard/2015/11/17/sammy-sosa-birthday-party-dubai.
16 Scott Miller, "Sammy Sosa in Exile: There's Silence Rather Than Apology From Former Cubs Star," February 25, 2015. bleacherreport.com/articles/2368638-sammy-sosa-in-exile-theres-silence-rather-than-apology-from-former-cubs-star.

MONTY STRATTON

BY GARY SARNOFF

IN THE LATE 1930'S, MONTY Stratton of the Chicago White Sox was one of the best and most praised pitchers in major-league baseball and was about to enter the prime of his career. "Monty Stratton looks as if he is going to furnish many a page in baseball history before he gives up," Philadelphia sportswriter James Isaminger wrote about the affable 6-foot-6 pitcher.[1] "He is the nearest thing to Grover Cleveland Alexander," said Cubs manager Charlie Grimm. "The same control, the same 'dip' on every pitch, the same smooth, confident motion."[2] But then came a dark November day in 1938 that would change the course of Stratton's life.

Monty Franklin Stratton was born on May 21, 1912, on his family's farm in Wagner, Texas. He was the sixth of nine children born to Lee Davis and Minnie Aster Corine Stratton. While growing up on the farm, Stratton was too occupied with school and working the family farm to dream about becoming a major leaguer, although he did find some time to occasionally play ball with the other kids. "I played wherever they wanted me to," he once said, which was usually first base or one of the outfield positions, but never pitcher.[3] In 1930 Monty's father, Lee Davis Stratton, died, leaving his widow the proprietor of the farm, thus forcing Monty to spend more time working the farm with less time for school and baseball. His heavy workload included attending to the livestock and working the cotton fields.

Stratton's journey through life changed on a spring day in 1931, when a group representing the Wagner High School student body paid a visit to the Stratton farm before an important game against a rival high school. The Wagner team was in dire need of a pitcher for the big game, and the students were confident that Shorty,[4] as the tall, lanky Stratton was called during his school days, was the one who could do the job. "I can't pitch," Stratton told them. "Never have pitched. You all is just plain screwy if you think I can pitch."[5]

"Even if you can't pitch, maybe you can scare 'em with your size," one of the students said. "And you can throw a baseball mighty fast."[6]

And so Shorty grabbed his mitt and tagged along with his classmates to the local field—and hurled a 2-0 shutout. His impressive performance created an opportunity for him to pitch for local semipro teams for as much as $2 a game.

In 1934, Stratton was pitching for manager Bill Webb's Galveston Buccaneers of the Texas League, a team boasting a working agreement with the White Sox. "He had grand control from the beginning," Webb would later say about his reason for signing Stratton.[7] At Galveston, Stratton pitched well enough to convince Webb that he was ready for the big leagues. The White Sox sent the husband-and-wife scouting team of Roy and Bessie Largent to check him out. One practice session was all it took for the two scouts to agree with Webb, and the White Sox paid $1,200 for Stratton.[8]

After joining the White Sox in late May, Stratton was tutored by manager Jimmy Dykes and coach Muddy Ruel on how to study batters. Ruel also taught him how include a mix of overhand pitches to go along with his side-arm stuff and how to throw a sinker. Chicago second baseman Jackie Hayes tagged the rookie pitcher with the nickname Gander, which would stick with him throughout his major-league career.[9]

On June 2, with the White Sox trailing the Tigers 10-0 in the sixth inning, Dykes believed the time was right for Stratton to pitch in his first major-league game. The scribes in the press box immediately commented on his height. "Monty Stratton, who appears eight feet tall, but is only six feet six, pitched the last three innings and held the enemy to two runs, principally because his mates executed a couple of sterling double plays," wrote the *Chicago Tribune's* Edward Burns.[10] One week later, feeling more seasoning was necessary, the White Sox sent Stratton to Omaha of the Western League.

At Omaha, Stratton became an immediate hit with the fans, for his size and his pitching; the local press referred to him as "that long lean fellow from the South with the amazing curve ball."[11] Handicapped by a lack of hitting and fielding support, he still managed to win eight of his 18 decisions and struck out 11 or more batters three times. Also while in Omaha, he met a local resident named Ethel Milberger, an "attractive brunette."[12] The two began a courtship that would lead to marriage in January of 1936.

In 1935 Stratton reported to the White Sox spring training camp with his heart set on pitching the entire season in Chicago. A leg injury, however, limited his playing time, and before the season began he was assigned to the St. Paul Saints of the American Association. "The boy is fast, but he's more than that," said Saints catcher Tony Giuliani after a warm-up session with the new pitcher. "He has a sinker which is really deceptive. And his control is very surprising."[13] Stratton won his first four games, and by mid-July he was 14-5, which earned him a spot on the league's All-Star team, where he continued to impress. "Stratton was far and away the outstanding performer on the field. He held the opposition hitless for three innings he worked, blazing his fastball by hitters and fooling them on his accurately breaking curve," wrote Gordon Gilmore of the *St. Paul Press*.[14] On August 29 the White Sox recalled Stratton, and a week later he pitched well in his first starting assignment, against the New York Yankees. "However, he had the misfortune to draw Charley Ruffing as an opponent. His season debut was impressive despite the score [Yankees 5, White Sox 4]," opined Edward Burns.[15]

Two weeks later Stratton faced another challenge when he was selected to start against the Cleveland Indians, who were riding an eight-game winning streak. "Stratton got off to an inauspicious start by allowing two first inning runs, but then held the Indians scoreless the rest of the way in a 9-2 Chicago win for his first major league win," said the *Chicago Tribune*.[16] He registered one more decision before the end of the season, a loss to the pennant-bound Tigers, to finish his 1935 major-league season at 1-2.

Tabbed a "prize rookie"[17] and predicted to "cast terror through the American League this season"[18] by sportswriter Irving Vaughn, Stratton was inserted into the White Sox starting rotation in 1936. In his first start of the season he beat the St. Louis Browns. He lost five of his next six starts, but according to Burns he was standing up well under the circumstances, and those setbacks were mostly due to "poor fielding techniques of (shortstop) Lou 'Butterfingers' Appling and lack of hitting support."[19] On May 25 it was reported that Stratton was suffering from a sore throat, while a further examination revealed a case of tonsillitis. Before a decision could be made about surgery, his appendix began to ache and would have to definitely be removed. As he recovered from surgery, another operation was performed to remove his tonsils. The two operations made Stratton inactive until late August. He did return to action and pitched three more wins to finish the season at 5-7.

Stratton's 1937 season began with a 5-1 win over the Browns. "Stratton operated in such talented fashion that most of the afternoon wore away before the enemy located second base," wrote Vaughn.[20] One week later he became the first American League pitcher of the season to record a shutout. By the time the All-Star break arrived, Stratton had 10 wins to earn a spot on the American League's All-Star roster. However, a wrist injury sustained while sliding into second base at St. Louis on July Fourth canceled his trip to the midsummer classic in Washington.

Stratton's injured wrist didn't cause him to miss any starts, and on July 31 he blanked the A's for his fifth shutout of the season. On August 5 he was pitching at Yankee Stadium in search of his 15th win when, in the bottom of the fifth, with Chicago ahead, 3-1, as Stratton threw to Yankees third baseman Red Rolfe, he felt a sharp pain in his throwing arm, forcing him to leave the game. Feeling he could work out the soreness, he continued to throw in the bullpen during the days that followed, but when that proved ineffective he submitted to an examination, which disclosed a tear in his right bicep. When he felt well enough to pitch, he returned to the rotation on August 29 against the Philadelphia Athletics, and was knocked out of the box by an avalanche of hits before the first inning was over. He took more time to heal and returned to pitch the final game of the season, during which he was said to "look fair" but not sensational in gaining his 15th win.[21] He finished his season with a 15-5 record, a 2.40 ERA and walked just 37 in 164⅔ innings pitched.

Before heading home to Texas for the winter, Stratton said he expected to win 20 to 25 games in 1938. On November 28 his wife gave birth to the couple's first child, a boy, Monty Jr.

Could Monty Stratton repeat his 1937 performance of 15 victories? He looked good in his first two spring-training outings. In his next game, against the Chicago Cubs, he burned a strike past Billy Herman, then turned to the dugout to call for manager Jimmy Dykes. He felt a sharp pain his arm and asked to be taken out.

After spending the night with his arm packed in ice, and reading reports in the newspapers the next morning that his career might be over, Stratton paid a visit to Dr. Charles Spencer, a bone and muscle expert who specialized in treating athletes. The doctor's diagnosis was that Stratton had sustained two tears in his right biceps, but predicted that he would be throwing again in 10 to 14 days. A few weeks later Stratton said his arm felt fine but he'd not been throwing. He said he planned to "cut loose" in a few days.[22] It was not until May 13, however, that he made his season debut. He pitched one inning. Edward Burns wrote that Stratton was not "a sensational success, but the fact that he was back in there" was a good sign.[23] Eleven days later he made his first start of the season and went the distance for the win, which, according to Burns, convinced observers that he would be as good as he was the previous season. Two weeks later, Stratton was said to be in "superb form" as he hurled another victory.[24] At the All-Star break, although not selected to the All-Star team, Stratton was 6-3, a great record considering that the White Sox were decimated by injuries. After the All-Star break, Stratton defeated the Yankees at Yankee Stadium, and came back to beat them again later in the season. He finished the 1938 season with 15 wins, "an impressive total for a man who missed seven weeks of the race," noted Vaughn.[25] He lost nine games, walked just 56 batters in 186⅓ innings, and posted a 4.01 ERA.

Once again Stratton headed back to Texas for the winter. During Thanksgiving weekend he drove his wife and child to spend the holiday with his family on his mother's farm, "where we were all born," said his brother Hardin.[26] It was a big weekend for Monty and Ethel, as Monty Jr. would be one year old on November 28. On the 27th, Stratton decided to take a stroll by himself near the farm and hunt rabbits with a .22 caliber pistol he had purchased the previous summer in Chicago. While he wandered along a path a half-mile from the house, he spotted a rabbit just ahead. He took out the gun, fired, and then, "Monty stuck the gun in his holster and thought he had it on 'safety,' but it wasn't," according to Hardin Stratton.[27] The gun fired and a bullet entered Stratton's right thigh and settled behind the knee. He fell to the ground in pain. Unable to walk, he yelled for help, but he was too far for anyone to hear. "That was 12:30 Sunday afternoon. Monty started crawling to the house, but it wasn't until a half-hour later that Leslie (another brother) heard him," recalled Hardin.[28] Ethel also heard him, and saw him frantically wave.[29] "Then we took him (by car) to the hospital in Greenville, 10 miles away".[30]

The small Greenville hospital's resources were limited and the bullet could not be located. "We rushed him 52 miles to Dallas," said Hardin."[31] At 6:30 that evening, the Strattons arrived at St. Paul Hospital in Dallas. Dr. Arthur Thomasson and his staff immediately went to work. The medical staff located the bullet and removed it. They tied the artery and began blood transfusions. "There was a complete severance of the popliteal artery behind the right knee, cutting off all blood supply to the lower leg," said Dr. Thomasson, who knew that collateral circulation was needed in order to prevent gangrene from setting in.[32]

The news of Stratton's accident quickly spread on the news wires and reached the White Sox. "We are communicating with our scout, Bob Tarlton, who is in Dallas," said White Sox secretary Harry Grabiner. "It is unfortunate, for Monty was one of the best pitchers in the American League. But baseball is secondary now. Our concern is about his health. We are hoping nothing more serious develops."[33]

The news the next morning was not good. "Collateral circulation failed to set up and gangrene set in," Dr. Thomasson said. "The leg turned black this morning, making the operation (amputation) imperative."[34] At 4:10 P.M. Stratton was placed under anesthetic, then went into surgery under the guidance of Thomasson and three other doctors. Seventy minutes later, the operation was over. When asked how he was doing, a nurse replied, "As well as expected."[35]

Four days later, an unidentified newsman was admitted to Stratton's hospital room, where he found the pitcher smoking a cigarette and reading a newspaper. Stratton told him he was "feeling normal again," and that he had shaved earlier that day for the first time since the accident. "It's been tough lying here, knowing that my baseball career is over," he said. "But I am alive and have my wife and youngster and friends. What more could a man want?" He also said he was amazed about the overwhelming support he was getting in the form of letters and telegrams. "I never knew I had so many friends. Fans, teammates and fellows I played against all wrote me. It's great to have friends."[36]

One week later the White Sox announced that Stratton would have a job with their team. "Monty has a job with us as long as he wants," said team owner Lou Comiskey.[37] "The White Sox are happy to do anything possible for a member of the organization struck down in his prime."[38] It was assumed that Stratton would work in the team's front office, but the indefatigable Stratton had other ideas about his future, and what he wanted was to return to the diamond. "If it can be done, I'll do it," he said.[39]

As Stratton recovered at the hospital, support continued to pour in. "I received about 15,000 letters from men, women, and children in every state of the Union. On Christmas Day I had 815 pieces of mail. It made me feel great. There was never a time when I was completely down in spirits."[40] He was fitted with an artificial leg made of wood, and with the help of a cane, he checked out of the hospital. Two weeks later, Stratton threw away the cane. He traveled with his wife and child to visit his in-laws in Omaha. While in Nebraska, he said he hoped to pitch for the White Sox in a scheduled exhibition game in April against the Cubs. He said he was playing catch with his wife, but was just lobbing the ball. He mentioned that he hoped to cut loose when the weather got warmer. When asked about his handicap to field his position, Stratton said he believed he could hold his own. He mentioned that his biggest problem would be running to first base.[41]

When the 1939 season began, Stratton was on the job, but not as a front-office employee. He'd become a member of the White Sox coaching staff and was

Monty Stratton, whose life story is charted in The Stratton Story, *starring Jimmy Stewart.*

serving as the team's batting-practice pitcher. To reporters he expressed his dream of returning to the game as a pitcher. "It will take time," he said. "By the end of the season, I will know for sure."[42] He was unable to pitch in the Cubs-White Sox exhibition as he hoped. As a nice gesture, the Cubs and White Sox agreed to give Stratton the game's gate receipts, plus the totals from concessions and parking, which combined with the gate receipts, totaled $29,845.25.[43]

Stratton kept his heart set on being able to pitch in a game during the season. Manager Jimmy Dykes heard his repeated request but feared that opposing teams would, "bunt him brutally."[44] Dykes promised Stratton that he could pitch on the last day of the season if the White Sox had third place clinched, but when that time came the White Sox were in fourth place, not third, and Stratton never got his chance.

After the 1940 season, Ethel gave birth to another boy, Dennis. At this point, after two seasons as a coach, Stratton returned to the farming life in Texas, but did not lose sight of returning to the pitcher's mound. "After I left the White Sox, I still wanted to pitch," he said. "My wife kept saying, 'if only we could find someone who will give you a chance. I just know you could win a lot of games.'"[45] Stratton stayed in shape by pitching to his wife, throwing against the barn and practicing coordination in his living room.

When the United States entered World War II in December 1941, Stratton attempted to enlist in the Army, but was rejected. A few weeks later, the offer he and his wife had hoped for arrived when the Lubbock (Texas) Hubbers of the West Texas-New Mexico League contacted him about pitching and managing the team in what was termed as an experiment. "I was mighty nervous," Stratton admitted about his first game managing Lubbock, "but the first inning wasn't so bad as I thought would be."[46] The league suspended its season in July, but Stratton was still determined to pitch. In order to continue, "our town got up a team. With all the able bodied fellows off to war, we didn't have much to choose from," said Stratton.[47]

After the 1942 season, Stratton was idle from baseball until he received an invitation three years later. "There was a semipro tournament goin' on in Houston and a writer was lookin' for a pitcher who could win one game for his team. He wanted to know if I could recommend somebody. I showed the letter to my wife and all day while I was workin' (on the farm) I was tryin' to think of someone. Well, I got home that night, and my wife told me she'd suggested me. 'Honey, you know that they don't want me,' I said. But they did, and I went down there and was lucky enough to pitch a two-hitter and at the same time make a hit against the other team that drove in the only two runs of the game."[48]

In 1946 the Class-C East Texas League resumed operations after the end of the war, and started looking for players. Stratton wrote to the Sherman team, and Guy Sturdy, the manager, invited him for a tryout. After watching the veteran pitcher throw a few, the manager not only signed Stratton, he predicted that he would win 25 games. In his first game the delighted Stratton hurled a 6-4 win before 2,000 fans who marveled at his ability to field. He had three assists and a putout and participated in a double play, while striking out 11. He also got a clean hit to center field, but as he limped his way to first base, his leg buckled. He tried to crawl to first base, but was thrown out by a few feet. After that the league inserted a courtesy-runner rule for Stratton for anytime he got on base.[49]

In Stratton's next game he fanned nine batters, allowed no walks, and pitched six perfect innings before allowing a hit in the seventh inning in a 6-1 win. By the season's halfway point he had 11 wins, and he went on to win 18 in all. The Philadelphia Sportswriters Association named him the recipient of the 1946 Most Courageous Athlete Award

"Monty, now all you need to make your life complete is have Hollywood make a picture about you," Ethel told him.[50] Others were thinking along the same line. "I was wondering the other day why a picture hadn't been done about the one-legged pitcher, Monty Stratton," wrote syndicated gossip columnist Hedda Hopper.[51]

In 1947 Stratton moved up a level to Class B at Waco, Texas, of the Big State League, where he posted a 7-7 record. A year later, the Strattons went to Hollywood to watch the making of the movie about his life, *The Stratton Story* (1949), directed by Sam Wood and starring Jimmy Stewart and June Allyson. While serving as an adviser on the set, Stratton also received $100,000 for his story.[52]

Stratton loved his time in Hollywood but admitted that he missed Texas and the farming life. He intended to retire from baseball, but his love for the game kept him active for a few more seasons. "Spring comes around and the grass gets green and baseball gets into your blood, I guess," said Stratton.[53] Another reason for his decision to continue to pitch was that the movie was a box-office hit and made him something of a celebrity. "A lot of people wanted to see me (pitch)," Stratton said.[54] He pitched in 14 games over the course of the next five seasons for various minor-league teams in Texas before packing it in as a professional.

Stratton continued to work on his farm with the same dexterity that he displayed during his remarkable pitching comeback. He drove a car and occasionally played catch with Ethel. He said he was never bothered by the loss of his major-league career or the artificial leg. "It now feels as if I was born with it," he said.[55] In 1961 Stratton was inducted into the Texas Sports Hall of Fame. A few years later he endured another tragedy when his son Dennis was found dead from a self-inflicted gunshot wound.

In 1980 Stratton received one more honor when he was inducted into the Texas Baseball Hall of Fame. A year later he was diagnosed with cancer, and he knew the end was near. "I was with my father the last week of his life," said Monty Jr., who worked several years for McDonnell Douglas Corporation in St. Louis. "He knew what was going on. He had no fear. One night he said he hoped that in lieu of flowers or some other remembrance, perhaps some memorial could be enshrined, maybe at a children's hospital. He thought it might serve as an inspiration to some youngster fearing a dismal future because of a loss of an arm or leg."[56]

Monty Stratton died on September 29, 1982, at the age of 70. He was buried at Memoryland Memorial Park in Greenville, Texas.

NOTES

1. *Philadelphia Inquirer*, August 1, 1937.
2. *Chicago Daily News*, November 30, 1938.
3. Ibid.
4. Unidentified newspaper article found in the Monty Stratton player file at the National Baseball Hall of Fame's Giamatti Research Center, Cooperstown, New York.
5. Unidentified newspaper press release, January 16, 1938, in Stratton file.
6. Unidentified newspaper clipping dated August 22, 1935, in Stratton file.
7. John Carmichael, "The Barber," 1937 article in Stratton file.
8. *Chicago Daily News*, November 30, 1938.
9. Unidentified newspaper in Stratton file.
10. *Chicago Tribune*, June 3, 1934. It was 3⅓ innings, to be more precise.
11. *Omaha World-Herald*, August 5, 1934.
12. *New York Times*, April 24, 1949.
13. *St. Paul Press*, April 9, 1935.
14. *St. Paul Press*, July 31, 1935.
15. *Chicago Tribune*, September 8, 1935.
16. *Chicago Tribune*, September 23, 1935.
17. *Chicago Tribune*, April 3, 1936.
18. *Chicago Tribune*, April 11, 1936.
19. *Chicago Tribune*, May 8, 1936.
20. *Chicago Tribune*, April 23, 1937.
21. *Chicago Tribune*, October 4, 1937.
22. *Chicago Tribune*, April 7, 1938.
23. *Chicago Tribune*, May 14, 1938.
24. *Chicago Tribune*, June 3, 1938.
25. *Chicago Tribune*, September 21, 1938.
26. Harold Sheldon, "Finishing the Stratton Story," *Baseball Digest*, September 1949.
27. Ibid.
28. Ibid.
29. Undated *Chicago Daily News* article in Stratton file.
30. Sheldon.
31. Ibid.

32. Ibid.
33. *Chicago Tribune*, November 28, 1938.
34. *Chicago Tribune*, November 29, 1938.
35. Ibid.
36. *Chicago Tribune*, December 23, 1938.
37. *Brooklyn Eagle*, December 11, 1938
38. *Chicago Tribune*, December 11, 1938.
39. *Chicago Tribune*, April 7, 1939.
40. Unidentified newspaper article dated April 20, 1939, in Stratton file.
41. *Chicago Tribune*, April 7, 1939.
42. Unidentified newspaper article dated April 20, 1939, in Stratton file.
43. *Chicago Tribune*, May 2, 1939.
44. Sheldon.
45. *Philadelphia Inquirer*, January 30, 1947.
46. L.H. Addington, "Monty Stratton's Courageous Comeback," June 1947 article, soiurce unidentified, in the Stratton file.
47. *Philadelphia Inquirer*, January 30, 1947.
48. Ibid.
49. Addington.
50. *New York Times*, April 24, 1949.
51. *Chicago Tribune*, December 23, 1946
52. *Washington Post*, September 7, 1947.
53. *Los Angeles Times*, June 19, 1950.
54. Unidentified newspaper article, July 14, 1974, in Stratton file. For more detailed information on the making of *The Stratton Story:* Rob Edelman, "Of Black Sox, Ball Yards, and Monty Stratton: Chicago Baseball Movies," in *North Side, South Side, All Around the Town: Baseball in Chicago* (*The National Pastime*, SABR, 2015).
55. *New York Times*, April 24, 1949.
56. *St. Louis Globe-Democrat*, October 28, 1982.

LOU STRINGER

BY BILL NOWLIN

A BALLPLAYER TURNED Hollywood actor and a car dealer who once sold a Corvette to Elvis Presley. Lou Stringer was all three.

Louis Bernard Stringer was born in Grand Rapids, Michigan, on May 18, 1917. When Lou was three years old, his father moved the family to East Los Angeles. Robert Stringer had been a wood mechanic, working with buzz saws, band saws, and other equipment that gave him some respiratory problems.[1] He developed a bad cough and was forced to retire, but with a large family (seven boys and one girl), others in the family began to pick up work so he didn't have to. Lou's mother, Josephine, never worked outside the home.

Most of Lou's brothers worked as mechanics. One ran an upholstery business. Lou's brother Al, five years younger, had worked out with the Cubs as early as 1941 but signed as a shortstop in the Yankees system. He played for three or four clubs in the American Association, but never made the majors.

Lou first started playing ball with the St. Bridget's grade school team in Los Angeles, competed in the local C.Y.O. league, and later attended Washington High School where he played shortstop on the high school team, a contemporary of Jerry Priddy. Six players in his high school club made it all the way to big league baseball: Stringer, Priddy, Cliff Dapper, Al Lyons, Roy Partee, and Eddie Morris. Lou played some semipro ball on city sandlots, often coached by a man named Mike Catron, before signing with the Cubs' organization. Credited with the signing were Jigger Statz and Pants Rowland, but Lou recalls, "Pants Rowland, he wasn't no scout. He was the manager for the club."[2]

After signing his contract, Lou was told to report to Ponca City, Oklahoma, the Cubs' affiliate in the Western Association. He played second base for Ponca City, appearing in 138 games both in 1937 and in 1938. He hit .263 the first year, and .286 the second, improving across the board in his power numbers at the same time. Stringer ranked second or third in the league in several offensive categories, and Ponca City won the pennant that year. The 19-year-old was earmarked for a year in Tulsa but got an invite to spring training when another player failed to show. Instead, he played in the Pacific Coast League for the Los Angeles Angels (alongside Statz) for both the 1939 and 1940 seasons. He hit .272 the first year, but cooled off just a bit to .263 the second, playing in 172 games during the 1940 campaign. He more than doubled his Western Association home run totals. However, Edward Burns, writing in the *Chicago Tribune*, noted, "It's Stringer's defensive skill that has the Cub management a-twitter with excitement."[3]

During the offseason, Stringer worked hard—one article reported 12 hours a day, seven days a week—at the North American Aviation Company plant.[4]

In 1941, Stringer had a very successful spring and Cubs manager Jimmy Wilson termed him "the best rookie I ever saw in spring training."[5] Needless to say, Lou made the Cubs, debuting on Opening Day, April 15, 1941. Batting seventh and playing short, Stringer had a 2-for-3 day, with a two-base hit and two runs scored. He also made four errors. The leftfielder was Lou Novikoff, whose career had paralleled Stringer's, all the way from Ponca City to Los Angeles to Chicago. Both had their Los Angeles contracts purchased by the Cubs on the same day in August 1940 and, training on Catalina Island in 1941, both made the club. There had been a little controversy beforehand. Both Stringer and Novikoff held out—unusual for minor leaguers who'd never had a taste of major league ball—but Commissioner Kenesaw Mountain Landis intervened and the two players more or less capitulated. "It was stupid. We didn't get anything out of it. I got $5,000 and that was what I got," Stringer said later.

Lou Stringer in his Red Sox days, with manager Joe McCarthy; Stringer appeared in a number of Hollywood films during the late-1940s/early-1950s.

Stringer had played only second base, but Billy Herman was a fixture at the keystone, so Stringer filled in at shortstop. On May 6, though, Herman was traded to the Brooklyn Dodgers. Stringer had effectively beaten out Herman for the job, but it was the Dodgers who went all the way to the World Series while the Cubs finished 30 games behind. Not surprisingly, though, Stringer very much liked skipper Jimmy Wilson. "I liked Jimmy. He was fine. Good dad, good husband. He was a good manager."

Playing in 145 games, Stringer hit .246, very good figures for a shortstop in that era. He was the first one of the Chicago Cubs to sign his 1942 contract, signing in October 1941. He played out the 1942 season, getting into 121 games and hitting .236, playing some at second base and some at third. With the war under way, he enlisted as a private in the Army Air Corps. He graduated from Air Force Mechanics School at Williams Field Advance Flying School in Chandler, Arizona in January 1943. "I went in as a mechanic and I come out as a (physical training) instructor," he recalled. "I handled all the PT for all the cadets who were there. There were three or four hundred cadets there and I had three or four classes every day for them and I headed up their PT. Williams Field, Arizona. That was an air base." He was sent to the Army's Physical Training Instructors School at Miami Beach. He graduated in November.

News reports indicate that Stringer did well in the service. A May 1943 story in the *Los Angeles Times* said that soldiering was his "greatest thrill" and he was named Soldier of the Month at Williams Field.[6] At the time of the story, Lou had a .425 average playing for the Williams Field Fliers.

Back from the war, Stringer played second, short, and third for the Cubs in 1946, but got only 209 at-bats, hitting .244. Cubs manager Charlie Grimm "never liked me," he said. Stringer was released to the Angels in January 1947 and the team won the Pacific Coast League pennant. Lou batted .293, driving in 72 runs. In February 1948, the Cubs sold him for the $10,000 waiver price to the New York Giants, who assigned his contract to the Hollywood Stars, also in the Coast League. The club played just 15 minutes from his house. It was another season he very much enjoyed, this time hitting an even .333 and leading the league with 50 doubles, while driving in 99 runs. At season's end, he was named both the team's MVP and the "most popular player." Manager Jimmy Dykes quit on August 28 and Stringer took over as player-manager. But right after Hollywood finished its season, the Red Sox purchased his contract, and he wasted no time getting to Boston. He'd finished up playing a doubleheader against Sacramento on September 19, took a plane that night, and found himself in a ball game in Detroit the evening of September 20. The *Los Angeles Times* story said that the Stars manager had been "fired" but he was fired "upward, like a space rocket. The Boston Red Sox bought him to help in their frantic fight for the American League pennant."[7]

He got into four games, and only had one hit in 11 times at the plate, but it was a home run. The Sox had another second baseman, named Bobby Doerr, and Stringer found himself in a utility role behind Doerr, Vern Stephens, and Johnny Pesky.

He really liked Pesky: "I got along real good with him. I happened to be Catholic and he was Catholic, and we got along real good. Go to church on Sunday and stuff. Dom DiMaggio, he was Catholic. We had quite a few Catholics on the club."

In 1949, Stringer stayed with the Sox and got into 35 games, but mostly defensively (he only had 41 at-bats, batting .268 during his limited opportunities.) Back for another full year in 1950, Lou had even less work, just 17 at-bats in 24 games. He hit .294. In his two-plus seasons with Boston, he only drove in nine runs.

During the off-seasons, starting right after the war, Stringer worked in the automobile business, selling cars in the Los Angeles area for Harry Mann Chevrolet. Mann later became, Stringer says, "the world's largest Corvette dealer."

The Red Sox let him go and he signed on with Hollywood for 1951, playing a full year and hitting .284. He wasn't entirely unhappy to be playing near home once more. "It's great, of course, to be in the majors," he told Al Wolf of the *Los Angeles Times*. "That's the goal of every ballplayer. And coming down again kinda hurts. But I'd rather play every day in the minors—especially here in my home town—than just sit on the bench in the big time. You go nuts doing nothing."[8] He had no gripes about Boston managers Joe McCarthy and Steve O'Neill, recognizing that the talent on those ballclubs was just so deep he wasn't truly needed. "I just couldn't seem to get a chance to show what I could do."[9] He also had a sense of humor. At one point, he explained why he never worried about slumps: "I've been in a slump all my life."[10] That's a little self-effacing for a

Lou Stringer as a "Chicago White Sox player," with Jimmy Stewart in The Stratton Story.

reserve middle infielder of the era with a fine .242 batting average.

After the season, he enjoyed a seven-week tour of Japan with Joe DiMaggio and a number of other players. "We played to over a million people. It was a great, great outing. Joe, Dom, and Vince DiMaggio there in the outfield, and I played third. I think we lost one game, and the only reason we lost that was a couple of the guys got so drunk they couldn't play."

He began 1952 with Hollywood, but then moved on to San Diego in May. The combined stats for the year show him hitting a solid .275 with 85 RBIs. The next year began with San Diego, but he moved to San Francisco and became player-manager there. The following four seasons saw Stringer move to a new city, as a player-manager each year. He managed and played for Yakima (1954), Boise (1955), Pocatello (1956), and Des Moines (1957). The final season started with the Des Moines Demons, where he lasted but 47 games. "Charley Grimm. He's the one that pushed me there. He was the big shot, a manager in the big leagues. He knew somebody there and that's the reason I went to Des Moines. I didn't know anybody there at all. I was lost when I went there. And we didn't win…so I just stopped and left after the middle of the season. I came back to L.A." A month later, the Hollywood Stars offered him a contract and he played in an even dozen games for Hollywood and San Francisco, but his pro ball career was really done.

Stringer spent a good deal of time appearing in a number of Hollywood films, particularly those with baseball themes such as *The Jackie Robinson Story* and *The Stratton Story*. He did a fair amount of acting work but became tired of all the downtime—standing around on movie sets—and went back to selling cars.

"I came back and went back to the automobile business. I was there for years. I made more money there than I ever did in baseball." Selling the Corvette to Elvis wasn't a hard sell, Stringer told Steve Buckley. "He called and ordered it over the phone. He wanted me to drive it out to this place he was staying at in Hollywood and drop it off….When we got there, he gave me a check, and that was pretty much it. Turns out he bought the car so he could give it to some girl. He was nice, but I don't think he said 20 words while I was there."[11]

Sounds a little reminiscent of Lou's teammate Ted Williams. "Ted was a loner. We'd all go out and eat dinner, except Ted. He mostly kept to himself, or he went fishing somewhere." Lou shared an early Ted Williams memory with Buckley, of a time that he was coming out of the batting cage and passed Williams. "He didn't know me very well yet, and he said, 'Hey, you, who's the best hitter in baseball?' And I said, 'You are.' And he said, 'You're goddamn right I am' as he walked away."

Lou married twice. His first wife, Helen, the mother of his two children, died in 1993. They had one daughter, Linda, and one son, Tom. "My son never played ball. He's a college graduate. He runs this place we're living right now." Stringer lived with his second wife Wilma in a retirement community near San Diego owned by his son and four partners.

On October 19, 2008, he died at Freedom Village at Lake Forest, California. He was survived by Wilma, his daughter Lynda and son Tom, as well as four grandchildren and three great-grandchildren.[12]

Note: An earlier version of this biography originally appeared in the book *Spahn, Sain, and Teddy Ballgame: Boston's (almost) Perfect Baseball Summer of 1948*, edited by Bill Nowlin and published by Rounder Books in 2008.

SOURCES

Thanks to Tom Stringer for assistance in preparing this biography.

NOTES

1. Much of the family information derives from an interview with Lou Stringer done on March 3, 2006 by Bill Nowlin.
2. All direct quotations by Lou Stringer come from the March 3, 2006 interview, unless otherwise noted.
3. Edward Burns, "Cubs Buy Novikoff, Stringer from Angels; Report on '41," *Chicago Tribune*, August 31, 1940: 17.
4. For an article on Stringer prior to induction, see Braven Dyer, "Lou Stringer Slated to Be Drafted Soon," *Los Angeles Times*, November 11, 1941: 19.
5. "Wilson Labels Stringer Best Rookie He Ever Saw in Training," *Los Angeles Times*, April 1, 1941: A9.

6 "Soldiering Top Thrill, Claims Lou Stringer," *Los Angeles Times*, May 28, 1943: A12.

7 Al Wolf, "Lou Stringer 'Fired'—Up to Boston Red Sox," *Los Angeles Times*, September 20, 1948: C1.

8 Al Wolf, "Stringer Says He Wants Action," *Los Angeles Times*, January 26, 1951: C2.

9 Ibid.

10 Harold Kaese, "The Slump—It Eludes None," *Boston Globe*, June 8, 1969: 96.

11 Steve Buckley, *Boston Red Sox: Where Have You Gone?* (Champaign, Illinois: Sports Publishing, 2005), 72.

12 "Lou Stringer," obituary, *Orange County Register*, October 23, 2008.

TONY TARASCO

BY WILL OSGOOD

"IN RIGHT FIELD, TARASCO going back to the track, to the wall ... and what happens here? He contends that a fan reaches up and touches it, but Richie Garcia says, 'No!' it's a home run," Bob Costas shouted through the broadcast microphone over a raucous Yankee Stadium crowd.

The moment: Game One of the 1996 American League Championship Series, bottom of the eighth inning, Yankees trailing their AL East rivals, the Baltimore Orioles, 4-3, with rookie phenom shortstop Derek Jeter at the plate.

Because of this one moment, Jeter and journeyman outfielder Tony Tarasco will always be linked in baseball history. The reality, though, is that Jeter would enjoy a long career with many more postseason triumphs, more than all but a handful of players who have ever lived. Tarasco had only two postseason at-bats, and struck out in both of them, once for the Braves in 1993 and once for the Orioles in 1996.

The real link, however, is between Tarasco and 12-year-old Jeffrey Maier, the boy who reached over the right-field wall at Yankee Stadium on that memorable October evening to take away what likely would have been a key second out for Orioles reliever Armando Benitez. Benitez, it should be noted, sprinted out to the right-field fence as fast as he could to get in his two cents with Garcia, the right-field umpire.

This was the beginning of another Yankees dynasty, and of Jeter taking the reigns as "Mr. October" from former Yankees great Reggie Jackson. It is fun to speculate on how history may have turned out differently had Maier kept his glove to himself and allowed Tarasco to catch the ball.

Whether Tarasco would have caught the ball is another question. It took multiple replays for the three-man NBC crew of Costas, Joe Morgan, and Bob Uecker to recognize that the ball was clearly in the field of play when Maier fished it out of the air. It took a few more replays and arguments for the three to agree Tarasco, though he did not leap as high as he could to attempt to make a catch, would have likely caught the ball if not for the *uncalled* fan interference.

The result was 15 minutes of fame for Maier, a tie ballgame the Yankees would go on to win, and the pinnacle moment of Tarasco's eight-year big-league career. To say, though, that it was the only notable moment of Tarasco's career, and especially of his life, would be to sell Tarasco short as a player and man.

Of all the men who have played major-league baseball, few have had as compelling a story as Tarasco's.

After being born on December 9, 1970, in New York City, and raised for the first nine years of his life in the Washington Heights neighborhood of Upper Manhattan, Tony spent the rest of his childhood on the other coast in Santa Monica, California, not far from South Central Los Angeles. He was an older cousin to 17-year major-league shortstop Jimmy Rollins.

Tony's father, Giacinto, moved the family to the opposite coast because Tony was often getting into trouble. Being mere miles from South Central and Tony becoming a part of the world-famous Santa Monica Graveyard Crips was not exactly the answer to keeping his son out of trouble.

Tony became friends with members of the Crips and joined their gang. Tarasco once reminisced about his time in Santa Monica, "A lot of what I was doing in the early part of the '80s was no different from what you would see in *West Side Story*, a lot of street gangs and fighting and stuff. As I got into high school, it started to get a little rougher. It was a lot more violent. There was more shooting and stuff."[1]

"I was never a soldier in the gang," Tarasco told Jack Curry of the *New York Times*. "Soldiers do everything. I was into the hustle so I could make a few bucks and dress nice for the girls. I was never into the raw dog, dirty stuff." Tarasco said that six of his friends had been killed on the streets—he bore a tattoo honoring one of them—and, Curry added, "he once missed a drive-by shooting at a fast-food restaurant because he was in the bathroom."[2]

Yet Tarasco was mostly able to avoid the lure of the streets. He reported engaging in some of the activities of his gang, but said he only took part because he wanted to have nice clothes in order to impress girls at school. For him, the gang was the group of friends he spent time with when he was not busy playing ball.

And for Tarasco they proved to be not what they were often portrayed as: violent hotheads. They understood he had unusual ability. His bat, his legs, his arm; all were gifts he received. He did not have the option to waste them. For this reason, his friends in the gang pushed him away from the gang life. They knew he had the chance to do what every kid who comes from such an environment dreams of doing. He had the chance to get out and make something of his life.

To that end, Tarasco did not merely survive the streets. He got out. And he was able to do so because he was one of the best baseball players to ever play at Santa Monica High School, the academy better known for producing acting talents like Emilio Estevez and brother Charlie Sheen, Rob Lowe, and Sean Penn.

The most notable athlete from Santa Monica High of recent times is Baron Davis, a point guard who starred at UCLA for two years before enjoying a long, star-studded career in the NBA with the Charlotte and New Orleans Hornets, Golden State Warriors, and Los Angeles Clippers.

Not surprisingly, Davis, before, during, and after his basketball career, pursued acting, directing, and producing, in addition to music endeavors. It is simply what kids from Santa Monica do.

Perhaps, then, it is no surprise that Tarasco, too, tried his hand at acting, though his roles were far from the starring variety. They barely even qualified as cameo roles. Like Davis, Tarasco first pursued entertainment opportunities prior to reaching stardom as an athlete. And like Davis, he continued after his playing career was completed.

His first role came in 1991, when Tarasco was toiling through the minor leagues in the Atlanta Braves farm system. His role: "baseball player," in the 1991 film, *Talent for the Game*. When the film was released, Tarasco was a 21-year-old outfielder on the rise in the Braves organization, which itself was on the rise.

In the film Tarasco, however, was a member of the Kansas City Royals, a bit ironic given that he would wear a Royals uniform in the twilight of his playing career, though never in a regular-season contest. Tarasco was one of a number of big leaguers past, present, and future in the cast. Among them were Bobby Tolan, Derrel Thomas, Lenny Randle, Rudy Law, Phil Lombardi, and Steve Ontiveros. The reality is that Tarasco's role in the film was about as memorable as the bulk of his playing career in the big leagues, other than the episode already highlighted in the 1996 ALCS.

But that, too, is probably short-changing Tarasco's accomplishments as major-league baseball player. For the career, the numbers do not appear terribly impressive: .240 batting average, 34 home runs, 118 runs batted in, and 151 runs scored.

For some players, that is a season. Then again, Tarasco was not a power-hitting slugger. His game was speed, especially in the outfield, which enabled him to become one of the better defensive outfielders of his generation.

In eight seasons, Tarasco made just seven errors defensively. The seven errors covered 522 chances as a defender. That is good for a career .987 fielding percentage. Using more advanced methods of evaluating defensive performance, Tarasco routinely saved his team runs. By 1994, his second year in the big leagues, Tarasco was good for negative runs as a defender.

By prorating his totals to a full 162-game season, Tarasco saved his Braves 15 runs as a left fielder. By the time he got to the Orioles in 1996, he was good for 30 saved runs over the course of a season, now as a right fielder. His best defensive season, by this measure, came in 1997, when he was good for 36 runs saved over a full season, while playing left field.³

Much of these numbers, which are still in their relative infancy in baseball parlance, came about because of Tarasco's incredible speed and instincts. He would routinely catch a ball that off the bat seemed destined to fall in for a hit. It took baserunners time to learn Tarasco caught almost everything.

In 1995 alone, Tarasco turned three double plays as an outfielder, an unusually high number for someone who played in only 126 games, 114 of which he began in the starting lineup. Tarasco, however, was not only a defensive wizard in that first full season after major-league baseball's last major player strike. Despite playing in only 126 games, his three double plays were one less than outfielders Bernard Gilkey and Sammy Sosa, the league leaders in the category, had.

In his only season with the Montreal Expos, 1995, Tarasco was a dynamic playmaker. He had by far his most plate appearances in a season, 495. Tarasco hit .249 but was on base at a .329 clip thanks to 51 walks, 12 of which were intentional. Those 12 free passes show opponents' respect for the 25-year-old outfielder. In his lone season north of the border, he also hit a career-high 14 home runs with 40 RBIs.

The speed that made him such a slick defender was ever present on the basepaths as well. The 15th-round draft pick out of high school stole 24 bases in 27 attempts. He never stole more than five in a season again. With the Expos he set a personal high with 64 runs scored. His next best season was 1997, when he scored 26 times.

The 6-foot, 185-pound outfielder was one of three Braves traded in an April 6, 1995, deal when he went from Atlanta to Montreal. The deal included outfielder Marquis Grissom. Tarasco was probably the least notable name involved in the deal.

Just one year later, after a solid 1995 campaign, Tarasco was dealt in a look-to-the-future cost-cutting move for Baltimore's Sherman Obando, like him an outfielder and pinch-hitter.

The 1996 season, his first foray into the American League, was a less-than-smooth ordeal for Tarasco. He played in only 31 games for the Orioles and had just 84 at-bats. He hit .238 with a .297 on-base percentage and slugged only .310. After May 11 he was shipped to the minors.

His minor-league campaign in that season was only minimally better: 41 games for three different teams, 146 at-bats, .260 batting average, .360 on-base percentage, and a .390 slugging percentage.⁴ The 1996 season was a struggle through and through for Tarasco, making it improbable that the moment he is most known for would even occur. Then again, his defense alone was deemed worth a postseason roster spot.

Tarasco's postseason career was not one to write home about. He had one at-bat in Game One of the 1993 NLCS, in the top of the 10th in a tie game against the Phillies. There were runners on second and third with two outs, but Mitch Williams struck him out. The Phillies won in the bottom of the 10th. His only other at-bat was for the Orioles in 1996, and he struck out then as well. He was used defensively in one other game in each series. It may be less of a

Tony Tarasco, forever linked to Jeffrey Maier, played "Pablo" in The Helix...Loaded *and a mere baseball player in* Talent for the Game.

surprise that Tarasco would end up as a glorified extra in multiple film projects. Born to a Sicilian father and a mother from Trinidad, Anthony Giacinto Tarasco, especially in his playing days, had the kind of looks that would attract Hollywood. The film *Talent for the Game* was not the only time he struck a pose for the camera.

He also played Pablo in the 2005 feature, *The Helix … Loaded*. As was true before, Tarasco's role was not a large one. This time around Tarasco should feel fortunate he was not a featured star. The 97-minute action comedy barely earned two stars on the IMDB movie page.[5] Another movie critic site, rottentomatoes.com, gave it a 14 percent audience score.[6] The film, which featured Scott Levy and Vanilla Ice, was an epic flop.

It did little to bring Tarasco additional notoriety, following his last few mostly forgettable years in the big leagues. His most memorable moment in the big leagues (in a negative way) was followed by his next busiest offensive season, once again with the Orioles.

In late March 1998, Tarasco was selected off waivers by the Cincinnati Reds; he played just 15 games with Cincinnati. He spent most of the season in Triple-A Indianapolis, where he hit .313 in 90 games. A year later, he signed as a free agent with the New York Yankees, but played just 14 games for the pinstripers. He hit .295 in 95 games for their Triple-A Columbus Clippers. The calendar passed by Y2K, plus a couple more years, before Tarasco would see time in the big leagues again. In 2000, he had played in Japan's Central League for the Hanshin Tigers. He signed with the New York Mets for 2001, and spent most of the time in Triple A again, with the International League's Norfolk Tides. He hit. 292, with a .371 on-base percentage.

While Tarasco's playing career didn't quite turn out as hoped for, and his acting career was essentially a big flop, it cannot be said his career was uneventful or even undistinguished.

To speak to the former, Tarasco was involved in three other controversial New York City baseball stories during the late 1990s and early 2000s.

But during Tarasco's brief stint as a Yankee in 1999, the reserve outfielder caused a stir by walking up to the plate to a profanity-laced "Tommy's Theme" from the well-known New York City hip-hop trio The Lox. Tarasco pleaded innocence, despite his penchant for living life on the edge, at least in comparison to the average Yankee, claiming he had asked for the edited version to be played as his walk-up song. Whether true or not, the Yankees fired the scoreboard operator in charge of playing the song. Once again Tarasco was able to get out of responsibility for a major glitch at Yankee Stadium involving him.[7]

The last of the three moments was the most egregious and ultimately one Tarasco couldn't escape blame over. After a 6-3 Mets home loss to the division rival Atlanta Braves on June 26, 2002, Tarasco and relief pitcher Mark Corey smoked a joint of marijuana somewhere just outside Shea Stadium.[8]

The 27-year-old Corey burst into convulsions. Once it was learned that he was okay, and that personal issues in his life were to blame for his taking part in this illegal act, eyes began to shift toward Tarasco. What role did he play in this episode beyond taking part?

Given his youthful inclusion in an LA gang, and a continued "rough" exterior, Tarasco seemed to be a possible perpetrator of wrongdoing against his teammate. Media members wondered whether Tarasco had laced the marijuana with something stronger, thereby making it more potent and more likely to throw a well-conditioned athlete like Corey into the multiple episodes.[9]

Earlier in that year Tarasco was investigated by Major League Baseball for a nightclub incident involving a woman who began experiencing seizures after sipping a drink.[10] Thus there was precedent for asking the question of whether Tarasco was a serial drug lacer. In neither case was he found guilty, and he went on to have a better career as a coach than as a player. But no matter what else happened in his baseball career, it would always be the evening of October 9, 1996, he was best known for.

As a coach Tarasco worked his way through the Washington Nationals' minor-league system, helping to develop young players most specifically in the two areas in which he particularly excelled as a pro:

baserunning and his work in the outfield. He played a large role in overseeing the development of future superstar outfielder Bryce Harper, whom the organization took with the number-1 overall pick in 2010 as a high-school catcher from Las Vegas. By his age 24 season Harper became a better-than-average defensive outfielder, in addition to being one of the most dangerous hitters in the game, and an aggressive and effective baserunner.

The experienced coach was integral to the success of developing the Nationals' deep bench as well, and the development of lesser known prospects into big-time contributors at the big-league level. Case in point: Michael Taylor, a shortstop with little upward trajectory in the organization had he remained at that position. But then the front office decided to make him an outfielder and turn him over to Tarasco.

"I remember the first day he went out to play. We worked out for a couple days, took him through his foundation and just talked to him about a few things," Tarasco said. "He went gap to gap, from one side of the gap to the other side of the gap on the wall and made a play. At that moment, you just knew that (vice president of player development) Doug Harris and (general manager) Mike Rizzo had made the right decision in moving him over to center field."[11]

Taylor went on to make a splash at the big-league level, right about the same time Tarasco found himself wearing a Nationals uniform and manning the first-base coaching box under manager Matt Williams. He coached first base for the Nationals from 2013 through 2015. Unfortunately for all involved, including Tarasco, the Nationals underachieved with Williams at the helm, costing not only him but his entire coaching their jobs.[12]

Tarasco quickly landed another job, this time in the San Diego Padres organization as the minor-league roving outfield and baserunning coordinator — essentially his job in the Nationals' organization prior to his promotion to the major-league club.[13]

Would Tarasco have had so many opportunities in baseball or outside of it if not for his role that fateful October evening in 1996? It's almost impossible to say for sure. But it is clear that he and Jeffrey Maier gained notoriety they may not have otherwise.

The two would meet again five years later at a youth baseball camp in Demarest, New Jersey. Maier, as a 17-year-old, was a coach. Tarasco was brought in as a guest speaker. As told by a camper who was there, the two shook hands and talked. As Tarasco addressed the young baseball hopefuls, one asked if there was anyone there he would like to fight?[14]

By all accounts, Tarasco downplayed the question and did not address the elephant in the room. His critics might point to that moment as one of his most mature as a big leaguer. Others might say it's just how you would expect him to handle it. Either way, their meeting was a reminder that both gained their notoriety primarily from one very memorable moment. Tarasco's story, though, is about much more than having a home run taken from his grasp.

Instead, it's about a kid who overcame great odds to carve out a long career in baseball.

NOTES

1. Norm Wood, "A Touch of Tarasco Sauce," articles.dailypress.com/2001-07-05/sports/0107050009_1_santa-monica-high-to-ny-tarasco-rich-kids, July 5, 2001, accessed March 10, 2017.
2. Jack Curry, "Tarasco's Agenda: Gang Life to Yanks," *New York Times*, May 16, 1999.
3. baseball-reference.com/players/t/tarasto01-field.shtml, accessed June 16, 2017.
4. m.mlb.com/player/123094/tony-tarasco?year=2002&stats=career-r-hitting-minors, accessed June 16, 2017.
5. imdb.com/title/tt0401462/, accessed June 16, 2017.
6. rottentomatoes.com/m/the_helix_loaded, accessed June 16, 2017.
7. Peter Botte, "A.J. Burnett and Curtis Granderson Get Changeup on Yankees Scoreboard's Closed-Captioning," nydailynews.com/sports/baseball/yankees/burnett-curtis-granderson-changeup-yankees-stadium-scoreboard-closed-captioning-article-1.166812. April 15, 2010, accessed September 22, 2017.
8. "Two Mets players caught smoking marijuana," foxnews.com/story/2002/06/29/two-met-players-caught-smoking-marijuana.html, September 22, 2017.
9. Michael Morrissey, "Drug Talk Sends Mets Into Shell," nypost.com/2002/06/29/drug-talk-sends-mets-into-shell/, October 9, 2017.

10 "Two Mets Players Caught Smoking Marijuana," foxnews.com/story/2002/06/29/two-met-players-caught-smoking-marijuana.html, September 22, 2017.

11 Bryan Kerr, "Tony Tarasco on Outfielder Michael Taylor: 'The kid's a specimen,'" masnsports.com/byron-kerr/2014/07/tony-tarasco-on-outfielder-michael-taylor-the-kids-a-specimen.html. July 3, 2014, accessed September 30, 2016.

12 Chelsea Janes, "For Some Nationals Coaches, End Evokes Memories of the Beginning," https://www.washingtonpost.com/sports/nationals/for-some-fired-nationals-coaches-end-evokes-memories-of-the-beginning/2015/10/05/57587f42-6ba0-11e5-aa5b-f78a98956699_story.html?utm_term=.12145e81834b, October 5, 2015, accessed September 22, 2017.

13 Dennis Lin, "Padres Announce Minor League Staffs for 2016," sandiegouniontribune.com/sports/padres/sdut-padres-announce-minor-league-staffs-for-2016-2016jan14-story.html, January 14, 2016, accessed September 22, 2016.

14 Contillo, "The Second Time They Met, Jeffrey Maier Didn't Dare Mess With Tony Tarasco," deadspin.com/5922164/the-second-time-they-met-jeffrey-maier-didnt-dare-mess-with-tony-tarasco, July 2, 2012, accessed September 22, 2017.

JIM THORPE

BY DON JENSEN

JIM THORPE WAS THE GREATEST all-around athlete of the Deadball Era. In addition to playing major-league baseball for six seasons, the 6-foor-1, 185-pound Thorpe was an Olympic champion in the pentathlon and decathlon and at one point the greatest American football player in history, according to a 1977 *Sport* magazine poll. One sportswriter called him the "most marvelous creation fashioned in human likeness that has ever inhabited the earth,"[1] but others described him as simple-minded, lazy, averse to training, and unable to hold his liquor. Thorpe's disappointing baseball career –he played in 289 National League games and hit only .252 with seven home runs and 29 stolen bases—demonstrated what multi-sport athletes like Michael Jordan have since discovered: that mere possession of superb natural tools doesn't guarantee success on the diamond. "I can't seem to hit curves," Jim admitted. "I believe I could hit .300 otherwise."[2]

Grandson of the famed Chippewa warrior Black Hawk, James Francis Thorpe was born on May 28, 1887, on the Sac and Fox Indian reservation near Prague, in the Oklahoma Territory. His father, Hiram, was a blacksmith who married at least five Native American women and fathered more than 20 children. Because of his early athletic prowess, Jim received the Indian name Wa-tho-huck ("Path Lit by Lightning") from his mother, Charlotte. He became a disciplinary problem after his twin brother, Charles, died at age 9. Jim's truancy finally angered his father so much that he sent Jim to the Carlisle Indian School in Pennsylvania in 1904. A vocational institution operated by the federal government to teach Indians industrial skills and integrate them into society, Carlisle was, according to one of its former athletes, "nothing but an eighth-grade school, but they called us a college."[3]

In the fall of 1907, legendary Carlisle coach Glenn "Pop" Warner convinced Thorpe to try out for the football team. Jim excelled as a halfback, punter, and kicker, but in 1909 he withdrew from Carlisle (one of several times he left the institution) and worked on a farm in North Carolina. During the summers of 1910-11 he accepted $60 per month to play baseball for Rocky Mount and Fayetteville of the Eastern Carolina League. Encouraged by Warner—and with an eye toward the 1912 Olympics—Thorpe returned to Carlisle in 1911-12. He was sensational on the gridiron against major collegiate foes, and Walter Camp selected him for the All-America football team in both years.

With his triumphs at the Stockholm Olympics in 1912, Jim Thorpe's fame spread worldwide. "Sir, you are the greatest athlete in the world," declared Sweden's King Gustav.[4] After the Games, however, Thorpe was forced to return his medals and trophies when the Amateur Athletic Union discovered that he had played minor-league baseball. It was a crushing blow that Jim never overcame. "I did not play for money," he wrote in a letter to the AAU president. "I was not very wise in the ways of the world and did not realize this was wrong. I hope I will be partly excused by the fact that I was simply an Indian School Boy and did not know that I was doing wrong because I was doing what many other college men had done, except they did not use their own names."[5]

Stripped of his amateur status, Thorpe signed a three-year contract in February 1913 for the staggering sum of $6,000 per season to play baseball for the New York Giants, who beat out five other clubs in signing the "red-skinned marvel."[6] It was the most ever paid to a major-league rookie. The agreement included a $500 signing bonus, and Warner received $2,500 for steering Jim to the Giants. "There can be no denying that he is a great prospect," wrote one observer, "and many critics would not be surprised if, under [John]

McGraw's careful tutelage, he developed into another Ty Cobb."[7] At the signing ceremony, however, the Giants manager admitted that he had never seen Thorpe in action; he didn't know what position he played or even whether he hit right- or left-handed (Thorpe was right-handed).

At spring training in Marlin Springs, Texas, Thorpe got off to a rocky start by showing up late for an exhibition game. He received time at first base and the outfield, and it soon became evident that he had difficulty with breaking pitches. During the 1913 season Thorpe was used primarily as a pinch hitter and pinch runner, compiling only 35 at-bats in 19 games and hitting .143 with two stolen bases. "I felt like a sitting hen, not a ballplayer," he said.[8] It wasn't a happy time. His roommate, Chief Meyers, remembered a night when Jim came in late and woke him up. "He was crying, and tears were rolling down his cheeks," Meyers recalled. "'You know, Chief,' he said, 'the King of Sweden gave me those trophies, he gave them to me. But they took them away from me, even though the guy who finished second refused to take them.'"[9]

On the 1913-14 World Tour, Thorpe brought along his first wife (he eventually had three), but McGraw viewed his behavior as inappropriate for a married man and lectured him on the dangers of drinking and playing cards. After playing most of the 1914 season in the American Association with Milwaukee, he spent most of 1915 in the Eastern League, hitting a combined .303 with 22 steals for Harrisburg and Jersey City. While with the latter club Thorpe was sued for his involvement in a saloon brawl, but the former club released him because he had a "disturbing influence on the team."[10]

In 1914, he had appeared in 30 games for the Giants, batting .194. In 1915, he only got into 17 Giants games, but hit slightly better — .231. Over his

Between 1931 and 1950, all-around athlete Jim Thorpe had roles in dozens of films, from Hollywood classics to B-Westerns.

first three seasons, his major-league stats saw him produce only five RBIs in 66 games and 102 plate appearances.

Thorpe was back in Milwaukee in 1916. In the press McGraw insisted that although Jim was still raw, he was a fast learner with excellent instincts and would eventually become a star. Privately, however, the Giants manager was beginning to have his doubts.

After playing in four mid-April games at the start of the 1917 season, Thorpe was loaned by McGraw to the Cincinnati Reds, then managed by Christy Mathewson. "Jim would take only two strides to my three," said teammate Edd Roush. "I'd run just as hard as I could, and he'd keep up with me just trotting along."[11] Recalled from the Reds on August 1, Thorpe appeared in 26 more games for the Giants and ended the only big-league season in which he appeared in over 100 games with a composite average of .237.

The Giants won the pennant. Thorpe's only postseason appearance was an odd one. He was in the batting order for Game Five of the 1917 World Series, played at Comiskey Park on October 13. He was in the starting lineup, to bat sixth in the order against southpaw Reb Russell. The Giants scored one run and had baserunners on first and second with two outs. McGraw wanted to get another run home and had the left-handed hitting Dave Robertson pinch-hit for Thorpe against right-handed White Sox reliever Eddie Cicotte. Robertson singled in the second run, and replaced Thorpe in right field. Thus, Thorpe had not played a moment in the game. Ring Lardner wrote, "Jim stayed in the batting order until it was his turn to bat. Then he put his ugly brown sweater back on and resumed his habitual seat in the wigwam."[12]

In 1918 he appeared in only 58 games all year, batting .248 with 11 RBIs. and the following season he had appeared in just two as of May 21. After Jim complained about his lack of playing time, the Giants traded him to the Boston Braves for washed-up pitcher Pat Ragan. Thorpe hit .327 in 60 games for the Braves, by far his best major-league performance, but 1919 proved to be his last season in the majors.

In each of his six seasons in the major leagues, his batting average improved over the prior year.

All told, Thorpe appeared in 289 major-league games, with a career batting average of .252. He did not draw that many bases on balls (27); his career on-base percentage was .286. He struck out 122 times in 698 at-bats. Thorpe homered seven times, four of them while on load to the Reds, and drove in 82 runs. He scored 91. As a fielder, his career fielding percentage was .951. He primarily played left field (89 games), right field (72), and center (38), with two games (13 innings total) at first base.

Over the next three years Jim Thorpe played baseball for several minor-league clubs, putting up respectable statistics but focusing most of his energies on professional football, which he had been playing during the offseason since he founded the famous Canton Bulldogs in 1915.

Thorpe had trouble adjusting to life after his career in professional sports. In 1928 he was playing semipro baseball at his home reservation in Oklahoma when he unsuccessfully sought a job with Waterbury of the Eastern League. Two years later, he traveled to Southern California as master of ceremonies for C. C. Pyle's cross-country marathon. He settled there, working as a ditch digger on a WPA project and as an extra and bit player in motion pictures. Though past the age of enlistment, Thorpe joined the merchant marine in 1945 and served on an ammunition ship.

Between 1931 and 1950, Thorpe appeared in 70 films, a number of which are classics or well-remembered titles. He was a New York theatergoer in the original *King Kong* (1933); a pirate in Michael Curtiz's *Captain Blood* (1935); a "John Doe applicant" in Frank Capra's *Meet John Doe* (1941); an Indian in Raoul Walsh's *They Died With Their Boots On* (1941); a ship's passenger in the Bob Hope-Bing Crosby comedy *Road to Utopia* (1945); a convict in Walsh's *White Heat* (1949); and another Indian in John Ford's *Wagon Master* (1950). He wore baseball uniforms in Joe E. Brown's *Alibi Ike* (1935) and the Buster Keaton short *One Run Elmer* (1935), and he even appeared as a Carlisle football player in *Fighting Youth* (1935), a curio involving communist agitators who infiltrate a college campus. Primarily, however, Thorpe played a range of roles in such B-Westerns as *Moonlight on the Prairie* (1935), *Treachery Rides the Range* (1936), *Cattle Raiders* (1938), *Frontier Scout* (1938), *Arizona Frontier* (1940), and *Beyond the Pecos* (1945).

Burt Lancaster played Thorpe in the 1951 biopic *Jim Thorpe, All-American*. The film depicts his being stripped of his medals for playing minor-league ball. Warner Bros., the studio that produced the film, paid Thorpe $15,000 for his services as technical advisor. Additionally, Mort Blumenstock, the studio's head of publicity, donated $2,500 toward an annuity fund for Thorpe.[13] It was around this time that he also tried to develop a nightclub act. However, after Thorpe underwent an operation for lip cancer in November 1951, newspapers reported that he was penniless.

Jim Thorpe was 65 years old when he died of a heart attack in his trailer home in Lomita, California, on March 28, 1953. Though he'd been operating a nearby bar, his death certificate listed his occupation simply as "Athlete." Jim's third wife had his body interred in Shawnee, Oklahoma, before she moved it to Tulsa. In 1957 the body was transferred once again, to Mauch Chunk and East Mauch Chunk, Pennsylvania—a place Thorpe had never been. Hoping to transform themselves into a tourist center, the towns merged and renamed themselves Jim Thorpe in his honor. His surviving sons tried to use the courts to have his body returned to Sac and Fox land in Oklahoma. The Third U.S. Circuit Court of Appeals, however, ruled in 2014 that Thorpe's remains should stay where they were. Son Bill Thorpe, though disappointed with the

*When not swinging a bat, Jim Thorpe appeared onscreen as a New York theatergoer (*King Kong*), a pirate (*Captain Blood*), a convict (*White Heat*), and-- of course-- an Indian (*They Died With Their Boots On, Wagon Master*).*

decision, said, "It's been a good place. They've taken good care of him and continued the name."[14]

In 1953 the Associated Press selected Thorpe as the greatest American athlete of the first half of the 20th century. He is a member of the Pro Football, College Football, and National Track and Field Halls of Fame. After a long campaign led by Thorpe's daughter Grace, the International Olympic Committee reversed its 1912 decision on Thorpe's eligibility in 1983, reissuing his gold medals and adding his name to its list of Olympic champions.

Note: An earlier version of this biography appeared in Tom Simon, ed., *Deadball Stars of the National League* (Washington, D.C.: Brassey's, Inc., 2004).

SOURCES

For this biography, the author used a number of contemporary sources, especially those found in the subject's file at the National Baseball Hall of Fame Library.

NOTES

1 "Greatest Living Athlete," *Omaha World-Herald*, July 28, 1912: 18. Kate Buford attributes the original quotation to the *Philadelphia Inquirer* in her book *Native American Son: The Life and Sporting Legend of Jim Thorpe* (New York: Knopf, 2010).

2 Bob Hersom, "Thorpe Remembered for Baseball Prowess," *The Oklahoman*, June 3, 2006.

3 Joe Guyon, quoted in Dave Anderson, "Jim Thorpe's Medals," *New York Times*, June 22, 1975: 199.

4 Associated Press, "Great Jim Thorpe Wants Sons to Follow Diamond, Not Gridiron," *Hartford Courant*, April 6, 1940: 11.

5 Robert W. Wheeler, *Jim Thorpe, World's Greatest Athlete* (Norman: University of Oklahoma Press, 1981), 145.

6 *Des Moines Register*, January 9, 1926: 8.

7 Hersom.

8 Ray Robinson, *Matty: An American Hero* (New York: Oxford University Press, 1993), 153.

9 William A. Cook, *Jim Thorpe: A Biography* (Jefferson, North Carolina: McFarland, 2011), 88.

10 Ibid., 138.

11 Charles Einstein, *The Fireside Book of Baseball* (New York: Simon & Schuster, 1987), 322.

12 Ring W. Lardner, "In the Wake of the News," *Chicago Tribune*, October 14, 1917: A1. The White Sox won the game in the end, 8-5. They won Game Six as well, winning the World Series, four games to two.

13 Kate Buford, *Native Son: The Life and Sporting Legend of Jim Thorpe* (New York, Alfred A. Knopf, 2010).

14 Associated Press, "Pennsylvania Town Named For Jim Thorpe Can Keep Athlete's Body," CBS News, October 23, 2014. http://www.cbsnews.com/news/pennsylvania-town-named-for-jim-thorpe-can-keep-athletes-body/

BOB UECKER

BY ERIC ARON

WHEN BOB UECKER WAS sent down to the minor leagues in 1961 after breaking camp with the Milwaukee Braves, manager Charlie Dressen told him, "There is no room in baseball for a clown." [1] Dressen could not have been more wrong. While no one would dispute that professional baseball is a business, Bob Uecker has spent more than a half-century in the game reminding us that the national pastime should also be about fun. "Mr. Baseball," as he is known to both casual and diehard baseball fans alike, has been a player, broadcaster, coach, actor, all-around ambassador for the game, and, yes, comedian. Beloved for his self-deprecating humor, he would be the first person to make fun of his rather unremarkable playing career, particularly his offensive statistics. "Uke," *Sports Illustrated*'s William Taaffe once said, "is the man who made mediocrity famous". [2]

In six seasons (1962-67) as a major-league catcher (almost all of it as a backup), Uecker batted exactly .200. In 297 games (217 starts) he got 146 hits, hit 14 home runs, and drove in 74 runs. "Anybody with ability can play in the big leagues. ... But to be able to trick people year in and year out the way I did, I think that was a much greater feat," he once said.[3] In truth, he was a solid defensive catcher, with a career fielding percentage of .981. He played for the Milwaukee/Atlanta Braves, St. Louis Cardinals, and Philadelphia Phillies. In the Cardinals' world-championship season of 1964, he was the backup to Tim McCarver. He did not play in the World Series. In 2003 he was honored by the Baseball Hall of Fame with the Ford C. Frick Award, presented annually to a broadcaster.

The first Milwaukee native to be both signed and traded by the Braves, Uecker joked that the highlight of his major-league career was when he "walked with the bases loaded to drive in the winning run in an intersquad game in spring training." [4] Another time he said of his career highlights, "I had two. I got an intentional walk from Sandy Koufax (He also hit a home run; both came on July 24, 1965, at Dodger Stadium), and I got out of a rundown against the Mets." [5] On being intentionally walked by Koufax, he joked, "I was pretty proud of that until I heard that the commissioner wrote Koufax a letter telling him the next time something like that happened, he'd be fined for damaging the image of the game." [6]

Robert George Uecker was born on January 26, 1935, in Milwaukee, Wisconsin, although he jokes to the contrary: "My mother and father were on an oleo margarine run to Chicago back in 1934, because we couldn't get colored margarine in Milwaukee. On the way home, my mother was with child. Me. And the pains started, and my dad pulled off into an exit area, and that's where the event took place. ... There were three truck drivers there. One guy was carrying butter, one guy had frankfurters, and the other guy was a retired baseball scout who told my folks that I probably had a chance to play somewhere down the line." [7]

Parents Gus and Sue Uecker were Swiss immigrants who came to Wisconsin in the 1920s. Gus was a tool and die maker. He played soccer in his native Switzerland. "That's where I got my talent," Uecker said. [8] Even during the Great Depression, Gus was able to support his wife, son, and two daughters, earning $3 to $4 a day working on cars.[9] Uecker called his father a great family man who never let him down. He said, "In the minors, when I was making $250 a month and the money ran out, he was there."[10] Gus had a circulation problem in his legs. The conditioned worsened over the years, and by the end of the 1962 season, his legs had to be amputated. He died a few years later.

Uecker attended a technical high school in Milwaukee, where he played baseball and basketball. He would ride his bike eight blocks to Borchert Field, home of the minor-league Milwaukee Brewers, where he would see his idols Alvin Dark, Johnny Logan, Heinz Becker, and Danny Murtaugh play. He made his baseball team as a pitcher after a scout saw how hard he could throw. The story goes that at the age of 18, he became a catcher when a teammate handed over his gear to him, asking if he could do any better.[11] In his joking fashion he gave a different version of his switch: "My first game, my parents and everybody was there, my friends, and the manager came out to take me out of the game. I didn't want to come out because I was embarrassed. I said, 'Let me face this guy one more time, because I struck him out the first time I faced him.' He said, 'I know, but it's the same inning. I've got to get you out of here.' And that was my move to catching."[12]

Uecker didn't finish high school and in 1954, at the age of 20, he enlisted in the Army. He hoped to avoid going overseas by playing military baseball with soldiers who had played in the minors or in college. At the time he had done neither, so he made up a college and lied. He claimed he had played at Marquette, given that it was a college in his native Milwaukee. "Marquette didn't have a team, but they never checked," he said.[13] He played at Fort Leonard Wood in Missouri, and later at Fort Belvoir, Virginia, where he teamed with shortstop and future Cardinals teammate Dick Groat.

Coming out of the service, he signed with his hometown Braves in 1956 for $3,000. "I could have signed with the Phillies or the Pirates. The Yankees were also interested at that time."[14] He bounced around the minors for six years, playing for Braves affiliates at all levels and showing decent batting ability and some power. In 1956, his first year, he played for two teams in Class C, Eau Claire (Northern League) and Boise (Pioneer League). Between the two clubs he hit 19 home runs. Appearing in 53 games for Boise, he also had a .312 average. With Eau Claire, Evansville and Wichita in 1957 he hit 15 homers. He kept moving up the ladder, and with Boise and Atlanta (Southern Association) in 1958, he hit 22 home runs. In 1959 he played for Jacksonville and Wichita, and in 1960 he was with Triple-A Louisville and Indianapolis. He spent 1961 with just one team, Louisville, where

he hit .309 with 14 home runs, and began the next season with the Brewers.

Uecker made his major-league debut on April 13, 1962, grounding out as a pinch-hitter against the Los Angeles Dodgers' Don Drysdale at Dodger Stadium. His hometown debut came on April 19 at Milwaukee's County Stadium. Facing the San Francisco Giants and Juan Marichal, he was the starting catcher, going 0-3 with two strikeouts and a walk. His first major-league hit came on May 3 at Connie Mack Stadium in Philadelphia. He replaced Joe Torre and singled to left off Art Mahaffey.

After a season of backing up Torre and Del Crandall, Uecker finished the 1962 season on a high note. On September 29 he caught Warren Spahn in the left-hander's 327th victory, which broke Eddie Plank's record for the most victories by a left-hander. Uecker went 3-for-4 with three singles, driving in

Despite his Mendoza Line–like career batting average, Bob Uecker earned great acclaim as a broadcaster, movie and television actor, and comedian.

two runs in the 7-3 triumph over the Pittsburgh Pirates in Milwaukee. The next day was the last day of the season. Uecker caught again, and his hit first major-league home run, off Pittsburgh's Diomedes Olivo. Uecker got into 33 games that season and hit .250. He started the 1963 season with the Brewers but got into only nine games as the third-string catcher before being sent down in June to Triple-A Denver, where he batted .283 in 52 games.

While Milwaukee manager Bobby Bragan always liked Uecker defensively, catchers Joe Torre and Ed Bailey made him expendable, and on April 9, 1964, he was traded to the St. Louis Cardinals for two minor leaguers, catcher Jimmie Coker and outfielder Gary Kolb. During his two years in St. Louis, Uecker was used sparingly. Neither manager Johnny Keane nor his successor, Red Schoendienst, stuck with him very long. He was pulled if he wasn't hitting well and generally played only when another catcher was injured or a late-game substitution was made. The primary receiver Uecker backed up during those years was Tim McCarver. Uecker had just 106 at-bats and hit .198 in the World Series season, but McCarver (who also made a successful second career as a broadcaster) praised him for helping to keep the World Series team loose. He said, "If Bob Uecker had not been on the Cardinals, then it's questionable whether we could have beaten the Yankees."[15]

The 1964 National League pennant race was one of the closest and most exciting of all time. After going 21-8 in September, the 93-69 Cardinals finished just one game ahead of both the Phillies and Reds, who along with the Giants were all alive going into the season's final weekend. Gene Mauch's Philadelphia team had a 6½-game lead with 12 games remaining, but blew the pennant by losing 10 straight. As for the NL champs, Uecker called them "the loosiest, goosiest team ever to come from ten games behind to reach the World Series"[16]

McCarver played every inning of the World Series, hitting .478. "Sat my way through it," Uecker wrote. "Called it from the bullpen. Yankee fans threw garbage at us, and I picked it up and threw it back."[17] Bob did however contribute in his own way, through his usual antics. During pregame ceremonies before Game One in St. Louis, he found a neglected marching band tuba in the outfield. He picked it up and started shagging fly balls with pitcher Roger Craig.

McCarver broke his finger early in the 1965 exhibition season and Uecker was the Opening Day receiver, catching ace Bob Gibson against the Chicago Cubs. The game was the kind of contest Uecker would joke about while doing his post-career shtick. It was a 10-10 tie at Wrigley Field, which didn't have lights yet, and was called by the umpires after 11 innings on account of darkness. Uecker was injured in the sixth inning after slamming into a wall while attempting to catch a foul ball. He had been picked off trying to steal home the previous inning, apparently crossed up on coaching signs. Gibson had one of the worst outings of his career, going only 3⅓ innings and giving up five runs on six hits. (Future Hall of Famer Steve Carlton made his major-league debut in the game, walking the only batter he faced.)

Uecker hit .228 in 53 games and after the season he was traded to the Phillies with shortstop Groat and first baseman Bill White for catcher Pat Corrales, outfielder Alex Johnson, and pitcher Art Mahaffey. The 1966 season was the closest he came to being a primary catcher. He had 237 plate appearances, platooning with Clay Dalrymple, who had 404 plate appearances. Always quick to discuss his own futility, Uecker summed up his experiences as a hitter for the Phillies: "With Philadelphia, I'd be sitting on the bench and (manager) Gene Mauch would holler down "grab a bat, Bob, and stop this rally."[18]

Uecker's favorite line about his time in Philadelphia was when he was once fined by a police officer for being intoxicated on the street. "They fined me $50 for being intoxicated and $400 for being on the Phillies."[19] "My managers didn't want me in the game. Heck, they didn't want me on the bench. Kids ask which club I played for. Nobody, but I sat for a lot."[20] Ironically, his best offensive season was in 1966. As a Phillie, he hit seven of his 14 career home runs while establishing a career high in hits with 43.

On June 6, 1967, Uecker was traded by the Philadelphia Phillies to the Atlanta Braves for utilityman Gene Oliver. The Braves wanted Uecker specifically to catch Phil Niekro's knuckleball. "I had caught (knuckleballers) Bob Tiefenauer in Milwaukee and Barney Schultz in St. Louis, so I had a basic idea of how to survive back behind the plate."[21] In 59 games he caught for the Phillies he had 25 passed balls, and led the National League with 27 overall. Two weeks after the trade he hit his only major-league grand slam, off Ron Herbel of San Francisco.

During 1968 spring training, Uecker and his Atlanta teammates Deron Johnson and Clete Boyer were involved in a nightclub fight in West Palm Beach, Florida, on March 21, 1968, at the Cock 'n Bull Restaurant. Uecker was struck on the head with a beer bottle and required 48 stitches to close the wound. On the field he re-aggravated an injury suffered in a motorcycle accident. He was released as a player and coach on April 2. His final major-league game had been on September 29, 1967.

Capitalizing on his gift as a storyteller, Uecker became a public-relations ambassador for the Braves. "I did stand-up, weird and ignorant stuff about my career—anything for a laugh," he said.[22] In 1969 Uecker's broadcasting career began with WSB-TV, on which he did television work with Ernie Johnson and Milo Hamilton. His career as a personality in television and movies took off after he did an opening act for Don Rickles at jazzman Al Hirt's Atlanta nightclub.[23] Beginning in 1970 Uecker made close to 100 appearances on Johnny Carson's *Tonight Show*, doing three to five shows a year.[24]

He said Carson was the first to refer to him as "Mr. Baseball." Carson "didn't know that much about baseball but as we went along he let me do whatever I wanted," Uecker recalled. "As a matter of fact, when I started doing the shows in New York, you get a script to follow and promote whatever you want to talk about. After about the tenth time I did the show Johnny said, 'Do you need this stuff?' and I said, 'No, I thought you did.' So from then on we pretty much just ad-libbed and went along and whatever he said I just jumped in and went along with it."[25] His on-air relationship with Carson concluded with Carson's retirement from late-night television in 1992.

As he continued his entertainment career, Uecker was lured back to his native Milwaukee by Brewers owner Bud Selig. The 1970 Brewers were in their inaugural season, a franchise purchased by Selig after the Seattle Pilots went bankrupt after their first season. Uecker initially signed with the Brewers as a scout before becoming the club's radio voice. "Worst scout I ever had," Selig said. "We sent him up to the Northern League, and the next thing I know (general manager) Frank Lane comes raging into my office asking what kind of scout I hired. The report was smeared with gravy and mashed potatoes."[26] "Yeah, I did scouting, if you could call it that," Uecker said. "For every guy, I wrote, 'Fringe major leaguer,' so in case he made it nobody could say, 'How'd you miss that guy?'"[27]

Clearly his talent lay behind the microphone, and on September 4, 1971, the Brewers announced that Uecker would broadcast games on TV and radio. "I've never signed a contract with the Brewers since I've been broadcasting and I never will," he said in 1999. "Whatever we agree on, we have a talk and a handshake, and I don't even think that I have had a handshake the last ten years."[28] On radio station WTMJ he first partnered with friend and colleague Merle Harmon. Tom Collins filled in as well. "Merle Harmon helped me from the start," Uecker wrote. "I'd never done (radio) baseball when I joined him in the booth, not unless you count my play-by-play into beer cups in the bullpen. Beer cups don't criticize, [but] people do. ... Merle and Tom Collins let me do color, then play-by-play, and saved me if I screwed up."[29]

While achieving quick fame as a buffoon on TV, Uecker slowly grew as a play-by-play announcer on radio. "It's amazing to think of now, given his ability, but Bob's problem then was in finding stuff to ad-lib," recalled Tom Collins. "He'd constantly repeat the count and the score, and swing his legs like a pendulum, and smoke cigarette after cigarette."[30] Uecker honed his craft with hard work. "I had everything to learn and I spent ten years learning it. ... I didn't try to wisecrack my way through it."[31] In a rare moments of seriousness, he said he never spoke badly of or criticized a player on the air, reasoning, "I know how hard this game is to play."[32] Uecker, who became the main play-by-play man in 1980, said he preferred radio over television: "You paint a picture in the mind. It's a kick to make baseball come alive to a guy hundreds of miles away who's never seen your home park."[33]

Uecker was serious behind the mike. The only time he let loose in the booth is in a blowout at Miller Park, said former broadcast partner Jim Powell (1996-2008). "It's a 9-1 game, that's when the buttons at home get pushed [off]. That's when everyone tunes in. ... When it's 9-1, Bob becomes Uke. It's a lopsided game where he really gets going."[34]

While continuing his radio work with the Brewers in the '70s, Uecker went national and helped telecast play-by-play for ABC *Monday Night Baseball* from 1976 to 1982. During his tenure there, which included All-Star Games, League Championship Series, and World Series games, he teamed up in the booth with an initial crew of Bob Prince, Warner Wolf, and Howard Cosell. Cosell in particular had great chemistry with Uecker, playing the straight man while Bob was his comedic foil. Cosell once teased him on the air, saying that he didn't know what the word "truculent" meant. "Sure I do," Bob said one night in Minneapolis, "If you had a truck and I borrowed it, that would be a truck-u-lent." Cosell paused and said to the national audience, "Need I say any more?"[35]

Uecker co-hosted a variety of television shows in the 1970s and '80s, among them ABC's *The Superstars, Battle of the Network Stars,* and *Bob Uecker's Wacky World of Sports*. He also appeared in a number of commercials. The ones he is best remembered for were for Miller Beer, both starring himself and as part of the ex-jock Miller Lite All-Stars. In his first ad he appeared outside a tavern only to be locked out because a fan asks him if he is Bob Uecker. In a sequel, he gets into the bar by claiming that he is actually Yankees pitching legend Whitey Ford. "So I lied," he says as he looks into the camera.[36] A popular Ueckerism was born in another Miller ad when he thinks that management has given him the best seats in the ballpark. Ready to sit down close to behind home plate, he is escorted elsewhere by an usher while bragging, "I must be in the front rooow."[37] He has in fact been placed way up in the nosebleed seats, as animated and excited as ever.

While his career as the radio voice of the Brewers continued, Mr. Baseball landed his first major acting gig in 1985. It was a new ABC sitcom about a family in suburban Pittsburgh. *Mr. Belvedere* was based on a 1949 Gwen Davenport novel, *Belvedere*, which first was made into films starring Clifton Webb. The small-screen version was similar in story to the Hollywood films. Christopher Hewitt played Lynn Belvedere, who was hired as a nursemaid for the family's three children. Uecker was the patriarch of the family, a sportswriter named George Owens. "A lot of his character was picked up from my own," Uecker said.[38] To do the show, the Brewers granted him permission to shoot episodes in Hollywood in the late summer and early fall. He continued to make Miller Lite commercials and make appearances on the *Tonight Show*. He even hosted *Saturday Night Live* once, on October 13, 1984. *Mr. Belvedere* was by all accounts a successful show, running for six seasons from 1985 to 1990.

In 1989 Uecker's acting career reached new heights when he appeared in the comedy movie *Major League*, starring Tom Berenger, Wesley Snipes, and Charlie Sheen, with a plot about a woman who inherits the Cleveland Indians from her late husband. She wants to move the team to a warmer climate, yet the only way she can get out of a contract is by fielding a bad team with low attendance. The players foil her plans by making the playoffs. Uecker played the gregarious yet often inebriated team broadcaster Harry Doyle. Many of the film's scenes were shot in Milwaukee's County Stadium.

With the release of the film, Uecker made himself a household name while introducing him to a new generation of fans. The Harry Doyle line of "Juuuuuust a bit outside," which described a wild pitch, became a piece of baseball popular culture. It has become an oft-quoted phrase like "There's no crying in baseball" (*A League of Their Own*), or "Chicks dig the long ball" (a late 1990s Nike commercial with pitchers Tom Glavine and Greg Maddux). Uecker reprised his role as Harry Doyle in two sequels. He enjoyed making the first two movies, but as for *Major League 3: Back in the Minors*, he said, "Three stunk. ... It was on airplanes the day after we finished it."[39] Upon the first *Major League*'s 20th anniversary in 2009, Uecker said, "It seems to be playing more now than when it originally came out. ... Every day I run into someone at the ballpark or on the street and they say, 'Hey, I saw you in that movie ... it was on again today.' I mean, I go into clubhouses all the time and these players today are playing it in clubhouses before the game."[40]

At one point Uecker considered leaving broadcasting to concentrate full time on acting, doing commercials, making movies, and appearing on television. It was not helping that Milwaukee was fielding some consistently bad teams. Such an example was the 1984 Brewers, who finished last in the American League East, 36½ games behind the World Series champion Detroit Tigers. In the end he decided to stay put, declaring, "I could have left there a long time ago, but no matter what I do, I'm staying. All the television stuff, the movies, the sitcoms, the commercials, that's all fun. All I wanted to do is come back to Milwaukee every spring to do baseball."[41]

Over the years Uecker has called some of the biggest games in Brewers history. He was behind the mike on July 20, 1976, when former teammate Hank Aaron hit his 755th and final home run. He was there when the "Harvey's Wallbangers" Brewers clinched their first and only American League pennant in 1982 (The team switched to the National League's Central Division in 1998), and he called Juan Nieves' April 15, 1987, no-hitter, as of 2011 the only one in franchise history, and Robin Yount's 3,000th hit, on September 9, 1992.

In the 1990s, Uecker helped call the 1995 and 1997 World Series on NBC-TV alongside Bob Costas and Joe Morgan. In 2003 he received the prestigious Ford C. Frick Award for Broadcasters, denoted by a plaque at the Hall of Fame. Even in accepting the award he couldn't resist a few jokes. He thanked all the people he worked with in the booth over the years: "I remember working first with Milo Hamilton and Ernie Johnson. And I was all fired up about that, too, until I found out that my portion of the broadcast was being used to jam Radio Free Europe. And I picked up a microphone one day and it had no cord on it, so I was talking to nobody."[42]

He also didn't forget to thank his family for sticking with him over the years: "My family is here today (Uecker has been married and divorced twice with two daughters, Leann and Sue Ann, and two sons, Bobby Jr. and Steve).[43] My kids used to do things that aggravate me, too. I'd take them to the game and they'd want to come home with a different player. "But my two boys are just like me. In their championship Little League game, one of them struck out three times and the other one had an error allowing the winning run to score. They lost the championship, and I couldn't have been more proud. I remember the people as we walked through the parking lot throwing eggs and rotten stuff at our car. What a beautiful day."

In addition to winning the Ford Frick Award, Uecker has been named Wisconsin Sportscaster of the Year five times by the National Sportscasters and Sportswriters Association. He was named to the Wisconsin Performing Artists Hall of Fame in 1993 and inducted into the Wisconsin Athletic Hall of Fame in 1998. He was elected into the National Radio Hall of Fame in 2001.

In 2006 Uecker's 50th year in professional baseball, the Brewers placed a number 50 in their "Ring of Honor," near the retired numbers of Hall of Famers Robin Yount and Paul Molitor. Three years later, on May 12, 2009, Uecker's name was also added to the Braves Wall of Honor inside Miller Park. In March 2010, in an honor likely no other major-league baseball player will ever claim, Uecker was inducted into the WWE Wrestling Federation's Hall of Fame for participating in *Wrestlemania III* and *IV* in the 1980s.

Finally, the words of his famous home-run call "Get up! Get up! Get outta here! Gone!'" were inscribed in the lights above Miller Park. Perhaps more fittingly, there are 106 obstructed-view seats in the upper terrace level above home plate that cost only $1 in honor of Uecker's Miller Lite "Front Row" commercial. As of 2011 he could still be heard calling Brewers games on WTMJ-AM radio with partner Cory Provus. "It's been great," he said in a 2005 ceremony marking 50 years in baseball, "I'd like to do this again 50 years from now when I get to 100. Wherever I am, dig me up. Bring me back here. A couple times around the warning track and take me back to the hole where you picked me up."[44]

SOURCES

Statistics and game information found through http://www.baseball-reference.com and retrosheet.org.

NOTES

1. Bob Uecker and Mickey Herskowitz, *Catcher in the Wry: Outrageous but True Stories of Baseball* (New York: Jove Books, 1982), 25.
2. Curt Smith, *Voices of Summer: Ranking Baseball's 101 All-Time Best Announcers* (New York: Carroll and Graff Publishers, 2005), 269.
3. Uecker, op. cit., 4.
4. Curt Smith, *Voices of the Game: The Acclaimed Chronicle of Baseball Radio & Television Broadcasting From 1921-Present.* (New York: Simon & Schuster, 1992), 420.
5. Larry Stewart, "Just a Bit Outside the Bounds of Reality," The Inside Track Morning Briefing, *Los Angeles Times*, May 23, 2006.
6. "A Life Of Detours: Confessions of a Feather-Hitter," *Christian Science Monitor*, July 24, 1961.
7. Uecker, op. cit.: Introduction.
8. Smith, *Voices of Summer:* 266.
9. Uecker, *Catcher in the Wry*, 12.
10. Ibid.
11. Michael Hiestand, "Broadcaster spin years: Punchless former catcher casts out baseball's best punchlines," *USA Today*, October 14, 1997.
12. Adam McCalvy, "Brewers celebrate native son Uecker; 'Mr. Baseball' honored as Milwaukee's first home-grown player," MLB.com, May 12, 2009
(http://mlb.mlb.com/news/article.jspymd=20090512&content_id=4686608&vkey=news_mlb&fext=.jsp&c_id=mlb&partnerId=rss_mlb)
13. Hiestand, "Broadcaster spin years."
14. Chuck Greenwood, "As Voice of the Brewers, Uecker 'Just Started Talking,'" *Sports Collectors Digest*, February 5, 1999.
15. Andrew Milner, *The St. James Encyclopedia of Popular Culture*, 2000.
16. Uecker, *Catcher in the Wry*, 31.
17. Richard Sandomir, "World Series, as told by Bob Uecker," *New York Times*, October 15, 1995.
18. "A Life of Detours," *Christian Science Monitor*.
19. Smith, *Voices of Summer*, 267.
20. Ibid.
21. Greenwood, "As Voice of the Brewers."
22. Peter Carlson, "They Locked Bob Uecker Out of the Bar, but they can't keep him out of the announcer's booth," *People*, September 18, 1983.
23. Smith, *Voices of Summer*, 411.
24. Greenwood, "As Voice of the Brewers."
25. Bob Costas Interview with Bob Uecker, MLB Network, September 28, 2010.
26. Richard Sandomir, "Bob Uecker Returns to the Booth." *New York Times*, August 13, 2010.
27. Ibid.
28. Greenwood, "As Voice of the Brewers."
29. Dan O'Donnell and Jay Sorgi, "Remembering Merle Harmon," NBC Milwaukee, May 18, 2009. http://www.todaystmj4.com/news/local/45359962.html
30. Smith, *Voices of the Game*, 412.
31. "They Locked Bob Uecker Out of the Bar," *People*. September 19, 1983.
32. Bob Costas Interview with Bob Uecker, MLB Network, September 28, 2010.
33. Curt Smith, *The Storytellers. From Mel Allen to Bob Costas: Sixty Years of Baseball Tales from the Broadcast Booth.* (New York: Macmillan, 1995), 267.
34. Shannon Ryan, "Finally, the Front Row: Baseball's Funnyman Gets a Seat in the Hall," *Philadelphia Inquirer*, July 23, 2003.
35. Uecker, *Catcher in the Wry*, 113.
36. Bob Uecker Miller Lite commercial, 1984. (http://www.youtube.com/watch?v=_Ql7m9LQULM&feature=related)
37. Smith, *Voices of Summer*, 269.
38. Lauren Simon, "Uecker To Star in new TV sit-com," *USA Today*, March 6, 1985.
39. Bob Costas Interview with Bob Uecker, MLB Network, September 28, 2010.
40. Ben Platt. "Popularity of 'Major League' remains: Classic Baseball Comedy Celebrates its 20th Anniversary." MLB.com, April 7, 2009. (http://mlb.mlb.com/news/article_entertainment.jsp?ymd=20090407&content_id=4147526&vkey=entertainment&fext=.jsp)

41 Michael Hunt, "Uecker Heading For Hall," *Milwaukee Journal-Sentinel*, March 14, 2003.

42 Bob Uecker Ford Frick Award presentation Speech, National Baseball Hall of Fame, July 27, 2003.

43 Ibid.

44 Drew Olson, "Uecker Celebrates Golden Anniversary," *Milwaukee Journal-Sentinel*, August 27, 2007.

PETE VUCKOVICH

BY RORY COSTELLO

Pete Vuckovich was a menacing figure. He was big: 6-feet-4 and 220 pounds (or more). He glowered over a Fu Manchu mustache and often had a few days' growth elsewhere to go with his long, unkempt hair. While pitching, he had "a streak of calculated weirdness."[1] Rasputin comparisons arose, and he encouraged them, applauding the Mad Monk's "extreme mental energy and intense concentration."[2] To those who knew him, Vuckovich was funny and friendly—but his on-field demeanor was just right for his small yet memorable role as the unpleasant, tobacco-spitting "Clu Haywood" in the 1989 cult classic *Major League*.

As a player, the combative Vuckovich combined mound psychology with a very wide repertoire. It made the righty effective for several years in the late 1970s and early '80s. With the Milwaukee Brewers, he led the American League in winning percentage in both 1981 and 1982. He won the AL Cy Young Award in 1982, helping the Brewers to the pennant.

Arm problems then curtailed Vuckovich's career. He pitched in just three games in 1983 and missed all of '84. He retired as a player after spring training 1987. Vuckovich soon came back to baseball, though, as a color commentator for Brewers telecasts. He went on to serve the Pittsburgh Pirates, Seattle Mariners, and Arizona Diamondbacks in various capacities for more than 20 years.

Peter Dennis Vuckovich was born on October 27, 1952, in Johnstown, Pennsylvania. "Having a life at all was his biggest victory—actually a series of victories," said St. Louis sportswriter Mike Eisenbath. "He had many brushes with death. Vuke was born with the umbilical cord wrapped around his neck; he suffered undiagnosed appendicitis that led to peritonitis when he was 1½; he had a benign tumor removed from his head a year later."[3]

The close calls didn't end there. As a high-school sophomore, complications from his appendicitis episode led to emergency surgery. "I almost cashed it in right there," he said in 1982. At age 21, he drove over an 80-foot embankment at 105 miles per hour. The car rolled over several times, yet somehow he walked out of it. After that he was installing a 15,000-volt reactor, which shorted. "Six more inches and I'd have been fried like a piece of bacon."[4]

Vuckovich's parents were both of Serbian descent. His father was Lazo Vuckovich, a steel-mill worker. His mother, Bosiljka (née Gjurich), was a homemaker known for her baked goods, especially orehnjača, or Serbian nut roll. They were fondly known as "Laze" and "Bossie" or "Bosa"—but they also went by the Americanized names Louis and Betty. Pete was the only boy among five children. His sisters were named Dianne, Karyn, Melanie, and Maryann.[5]

Vuckovich's childhood baseball heroes were Roberto Clemente, Bob Gibson, and Juan Marichal.[6] He was later compared to "The Dominican Dandy" for using varied arm angles. Pete knew he wanted to be a pitcher when he was 8 years old.[7] He inherited some ability from his father, a noted pitcher in fast softball circles around Johnstown. He was largely a self-made player, though, because "Dad was too busy earning a living in the steel mills."[8]

At Conemaugh Valley High School in Johnstown, Vuckovich stood out in three sports, also including football (as a receiver) and basketball (as a forward).[9] The school's baseball field was later named in his honor.

After graduating in 1970, Vuckovich turned down football scholarships from Navy, Pitt, Michigan State, and other major schools. Instead, he attended Clarion State College in northwestern Pennsylvania—mainly because his wife-to-be, Anna Kuzak, was going there.[10]

Staying in school also kept Vuckovich out of the Vietnam War. Of this, he later remarked, "I've taken a lot of guff along the way but that's politics and I don't want to get into politics."[11] He aimed to become a schoolteacher.[12]

Though Vuckovich had mainly been a pitcher in high school, he had filled in across the infield, so he told Clarion baseball coach Joe Knowles that he could play anywhere but catcher. "Maybe I shouldn't have said that," Vuckovich recalled, "but I was cocky back then. Coach Knowles said I'd play second base—the position I had probably the least experience with." However, he proved more valuable as a pitcher.[13] He was All-Conference in the Pennsylvania State Athletics Conference from 1972 through 1974 and an NAIA All-American in 1974.[14]

While in high school and college, Vuckovich also played with the All American Amateur Baseball Association. Johnstown has hosted the AAABA's annual tournament since 1945. Vuckovich became the first player from his hometown to appear in that tourney for four consecutive years (1969-72).

On the recommendation of scout Fred Shaffer, the Chicago White Sox selected Vuckovich in the third round of the June 1974 amateur draft.[15] He split that summer between Appleton (Class-A Midwest League) and Knoxville (Double-A Southern League).

Vuckovich then jumped to Triple A in 1975. With Denver of the American Association, he went 11-4 with a 4.34 ERA in 19 games. That May he thanked White Sox pitching coach Johnny Sain, saying, "He taught me all my breaking pitches in spring training—I mean everything—curve, slider, how to make the fastball sink, how to throw a changeup."[16]

Vuckovich got his first call to the majors that August, appearing twice before going back to Denver as Terry Forster came off the disabled list. As he later told it, Chicago manager Chuck Tanner had scouted him, liked what he'd seen, and said, "You're coming with me." To Tanner's great surprise, Vuckovich said that he didn't want to go, but explained that he wanted to be with Denver because he thought the Bears could win the Triple-A championship. Tanner agreed to send Vuckovich back for the league playoffs, which Denver lost in six games.[17] Vuckovich returned to the big club in September and got into two more games. He would not hurl again in the minors until 1986.

Also in 1975, Vuckovich married Anna. They had three sons: Lazo (like his grandfather, also known as Louis), Peter, and Damian.[18] Pete Jr. was also drafted by the White Sox out of Clarion (48th round, 2004) but injury cut his career short. In 2017, he became a scout for the Brewers.[19]

Vuckovich pitched in Puerto Rico for the Ponce Leones during the winter of 1975-76 and "showed well."[20] His manager was Ken Boyer, later his skipper with St. Louis. "Ken's the man who got me thinking like a big leaguer," Vuckovich later remarked. "He said to give it my best and not to let the little things bother me. He taught me the importance of concentration."[21]

For the White Sox in 1976, Vuckovich started seven times in 33 appearances, posting marks of 7-4, 4.65. He later took a swipe at manager Paul Richards (who'd succeeded Tanner) about how he was used. "I'll tell you what [Richards] knew about pitching. He made me a reliever, and he made Goose Gossage a starter."[22]

The AL added two new franchises—Seattle and the Toronto Blue Jays—for the 1977 season. In November 1976, the Blue Jays took Vuckovich as the 19th pick in the expansion draft. "To be truthful," he said the next year, "I didn't think that much about whether or not I would be protected. If I got drafted, I figured it was because somebody wanted me and I'd still be in the big leagues."[23]

Five years later, though, he thought differently. "It was a stupid decision for the White Sox to make. I had a pretty good idea even at 23, and I cared a lot. But I suppose it was all business for them. Maybe they spent $50,000 developing me, and they got $150,000 for me in the draft [actually $175,000]. So, they made $100,000 off the whole thing."[24] The team did run on a shoestring budget under Bill Veeck's ownership then.

Vuckovich was the first player to report to spring training for the Blue Jays. Manager Roy Hartsfield promptly told him, "We will not have any long hair or beards. Mustaches on the upper lip are OK, but that's all." Vuckovich, who said he'd had a mustache since he was 17, was already sporting his Fu Manchu.[25]

Vuckovich remained a swingman for Toronto, going 7-7, starting eight times in 53 games with a team-leading 3.47 ERA. He recorded the franchise's first save (on the frigid Opening Day at Exhibition Stadium) and its first shutout (as he outdueled Jim Palmer in Baltimore on June 26). However, that was his only season with the Jays. In December, he and a player to be named later (John Scott) went to the St. Louis Cardinals for Victor Cruz and Tom Underwood. Two days later, the Cardinals dealt away another pitcher known for his Fu Manchu and ferocity: Al Hrabosky. Earlier in 1977, "The Mad Hungarian" had clashed with manager Vern Rapp and owner Gussie Busch over Rapp's ban on facial hair.

St. Louis beat writer Neal Russo called Vuckovich a good prospect after the trade.[26] He was right. During his first season with the Cardinals, Vuckovich posted a 12-12 record, but his ERA was a career-best 2.54, third in the National League behind Craig Swan and Steve Rogers. He was a reliever to begin the year, but Ken Boyer—who'd replaced Rapp as manager in April—put him in the rotation in early June.

Vuckovich blossomed immediately as a starter. In late July, Cardinals pitching coach Claude Osteen—who'd helped Vuke as a teammate in 1975—said, "He's a master at changing speeds, and he does it with total command of three or four basic pitches, with quite a few variations of each kind of pitch. He's deceptive, too."[27]

On August 8, after a complete-game win over the Philadelphia Phillies, Vuckovich credited much of his success to his ability to remain calm and collected under pressure. That game report noted the "sometimes strange behavior" that inspired another nickname—"Vuke the Spook"—and that he worked more quickly than most pitchers.[28] A few weeks later, the great Bob Gibson—also noted for his brisk pace—said, "I've watched him on television and like his tenacity and the rapidity with which he works. He's already found that the quicker you pitch, the

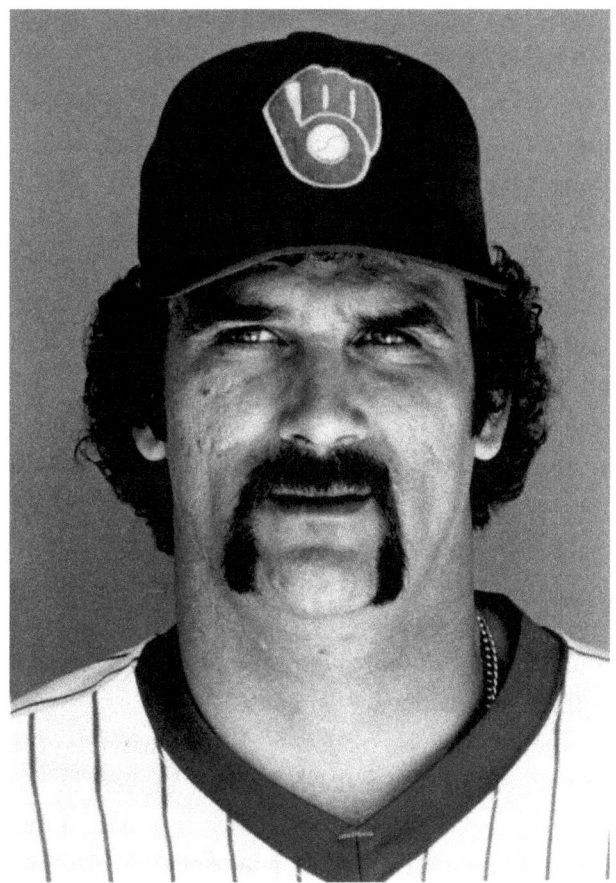

Pete Vuckovich, perfectly cast-- and a memorable presence-- in Major League.

more your defense is likely to be on its toes to make the good plays behind you."[29]

Vuckovich remained a capable starter for the Cardinals in 1979-80, winning 27, losing 19, and posting a 3.50 ERA. Mike Eisenbath cited Vuckovich's variety of pitches and arm slots—and, in particular, his fiercely competitive nature. Vuke later said, "I really hate hitters. They're goofy. They're trying to get me, to ruin my career, so I hate them. That's the way it has to be—them or me. I want it to be me."[30] Yet his free spirit was also visible as he belly-flopped through puddles in the outfield and hung an "out to lunch" sign over his locker.[31]

On December 12, 1980, St. Louis and Milwaukee—who would face each other in the 1982 World Series—swung a seven-player deal. The Cardinals traded Rollie Fingers, Ted Simmons, and Vuckovich for pitchers Dave LaPoint and Lary Sorensen, outfielder Sixto Lezcano, and another outfielder, touted prospect David Green. It started off in October with an even-up swap proposal from St. Louis: Vuckovich for Sorensen.³² But it developed into a blockbuster, with many moving parts before everything fell into place. In the final analysis, both sides benefited.³³

Vuckovich could be droll. When asked why he thought Cardinals manager/general manager Whitey Herzog traded him, he replied, "Whitey wanted to build a team on speed and I never really ran that well."³⁴

In Milwaukee, Vuckovich struggled early in 1981 but turned his season around after coach Cal McLish suggested using a no-windup delivery even with no one on base.³⁵ Vuke went on to lead the AL with 14 wins during the strike-interrupted season; he lost just four. He came in fourth in the AL Cy Young Award voting—the winner was Fingers.

The Brewers also made it to the postseason for the first time. They faced the New York Yankees in the AL Division Series, and Vuckovich appeared in two games. He started and won Game Four, allowing one unearned run in five innings. In Game Five at Yankee Stadium, he faced the Yankees' final batter; New York eventually won the pennant.

The 1982 Brewers were called "Harvey's Wallbangers" because manager Harvey Kuenn had such a potent batting order. Yet they wouldn't have won the AL pennant without respectable pitching. The team ERA of 3.98 was sixth in the AL, but not far behind the league-best 3.80. There were no dominant starters—but they got the job done.

Vuckovich led the staff with 18 wins against 6 losses. He was in hot water often—his WHIP in 1982 was 1.5. Yet more often than not, he got himself out of the jams; his ERA was just 3.34. "He gets further behind, works deeper in counts, throws more pitches and generally contradicts more canons of pitching with more success than anybody else in baseball," said sportswriter Tom Boswell.³⁶

Interesting observations of Vuckovich in '82 come from Daniel Okrent's book *Nine Innings*, which focused on a game between the Brewers and Baltimore Orioles on June 10 of that season. For example, "If considered looniness won ball games, the eccentric Vuckovich would forever be a success." Okrent also noted the hurler's habits of crossing his eyes as he stared in for the sign and (while holding runners on) "twitching his head rapidly ... again and again, as if he had a violent tic." Catcher Simmons, Vuckovich's closest friend on the team, thought it helped the pitcher as much as his strange delivery did.³⁷

Center fielder Gorman Thomas (who looked like a brother to Vuke) expanded. "You could look past the goofy hair and the growth on the face. He'd go out there and pitch with two different brands of shoes on. He'd have Puma on one foot and Adidas on the other. It was almost like he was semi-clownish. Yet he knew what he was doing and he'd get other people to focus more on his mannerisms than on what they're supposed to be doing."³⁸

Beneath the quirky trappings, though, Vuckovich's intensity was unrivaled. Thomas added, "I don't think I ever saw anybody who would be so competitive when it was time to pitch. It's hard to stay 100 percent, 100 miles per hour, 24 hours a day. But when it was Pete's day to pitch, it was more than tunnel vision. It was straw vision. That's how finely tuned he was. He was that way every time I saw him pitch."³⁹

Vuckovich started twice in the 1982 ALCS against the California Angels. In Game Two, he gave up four runs in an eight-inning complete game, losing to Bruce Kison, who went all the way. In Game Five, he allowed three runs in 6⅓ innings and left the game as the pitcher of record on the losing side. But the Brewers took the lead with two in the seventh and held on to win the pennant.

Vuckovich also started twice in the World Series. In Game Three, he allowed six runs (four earned) in 8⅔ innings and took the loss. In Game Seven, he took a 3-1 lead into the sixth inning but put the tying runs on base and was pulled. The bullpen couldn't hold the lead, and though Vuckovich got no decision, the Cardinals won the championship.

Vuke had been pitching while hurt.⁴⁰ As Roger Angell later wrote, he was "in great pain during the final stages of the pennant race.... In late September, two days after receiving a cortisone shot in his shoulder, he somehow went 11 full innings against the Red Sox, throwing 173 pitches, and won the game."[41] After his first outing against St. Louis, Vuckovich was stoic: "I get paid to take the ball when they give it to me, and I get paid to give it back when they ask for it."[42] When he retired, he said that he carried on because the pennant race would have been a bad time to "walk."[43]

A few weeks later, the Cy Young Award was announced. Five pitchers got first-place votes, but Vuckovich got 14 of the 28 and outdistanced runner-up Jim Palmer. "I feel great about it, but I can't take full credit for it," he said. "I just happen to be lucky enough to be out there on the days the team's playing well enough to be a winner."[44]

Indeed, "He Doesn't Look Pretty, but He Wins," proclaimed *Baseball Digest*'s cover story in May 1983. By the time it appeared, though, Vuckovich was on the disabled list. In March, an arthrogram revealed a tear in his rotator cuff. He put the downtime to good use, though, gaining his first experience as a cable TV commentator for the Brewers. He also filled in for Bob Uecker on the radio when Ueck was calling games for ABC-TV.[45]

Vuckovich started throwing gingerly on the sidelines in May.[46] His progress continued, and he made it back at the end of August. He pitched well in his first two starts, going five innings in each and surprising Simmons with his velocity. In the third, however, he was hit hard and pulled a hamstring. The Brewers kept him sidelined after that for fear that he might reinjure his arm.[47]

Before the 1984 season, Vuckovich was cautiously optimistic after a busy offseason continuing his exercise program. However, he wasn't ready for Opening Day because of pain from a bone spur in his right shoulder.[48] The resulting surgery included muscle repair as well as removal of the spur. It kept him out for the whole season. Yet again, he wasn't idle — he charted pitches, worked the radar gun, and studied hitters' tendencies. This too laid the foundation for his future career.[49]

Vuckovich was back in action in 1985 but was largely ineffective in 22 starts (6-10, 5.51). A shoulder strain landed him on the DL in May and June, and he underwent surgery for a large calcium deposit and another small bone spur in mid-September. That November, he became a free agent after refusing a minor-league assignment.[50]

Milwaukee invited Vuckovich to spring training in 1986 as a nonroster player. At the end of camp, he announced his retirement and went to work for the Brewers as a scout and minor-league instructor. In August, however, he wanted to see if he could still pitch. He joined Milwaukee's Triple-A club in Vancouver.[51] He did well (2-1, 1.26 in six games) and got back to the majors in September, going 2-4, 3.06 in six starts.

Vuckovich was a nonroster invitee again in 1987, but he retired for good on April 1, saying, "I'm a realist. I have an awareness of myself."[52] He finished with a lifetime record in the majors of 93-69 and an ERA of 3.66. Charlie O'Brien, who caught Vuckovich during that last spring training, summed up his career nicely. "He had a great feel for pitching. ... [T]he word that comes to mind is guile. ... He marched to his own drummer. ... He liked a cold beer and a good time, and he liked to play baseball. He was willing to do whatever it took to win."[53]

Vuckovich, who then lived in the Milwaukee suburb of Hales Corners, tended bar at "Stormin' and Vuke's," the joint he co-owned with Gorman Thomas.[54] He was also involved in local civic affairs. At the opening of the Samson Jewish Community Center in Whitefish Bay in September 1987, he helped teach youngsters how to play baseball along with Sal Bando and Bill Castro.[55]

Major League was filmed at Milwaukee's County Stadium in the summer of 1988. The project — like many Hollywood movie properties — had been in gestation for years. But when it finally got the green light, the cast included many inspired choices, and Vuckovich was one of them. Originally he was to play opposing closer Duke Simpson, but writer/director David S. Ward liked Vuckovich's look so much that he was given a slightly bigger role. Vuke then brought in his old Brewers teammate Willie Mueller to take over as Simpson.[56]

The new part was well suited to Vuckovich's image. In April 1989, shortly after the film was released, *Sports Illustrated* wrote, "Former Brewers pitcher and dirtball Pete Vuckovich plays Yankee slugger and dirtball Clu Haywood." The article quoted Bob Uecker's line as announcer Harry Doyle: "He [Haywood] leads the majors in most offensive categories, including nose hair."[57] A 2016 article described the character as "awesomely gross," noting that his "favorite pastime, apart from hitting dingers, is to call rookies Hayes and Vaughn 'meat' whenever he gets the chance."[58]

Vuckovich made another juicy little contribution to the film. In one scene, Haywood approaches the plate and says to catcher Jake Taylor (played by Tom Berenger): 'How's your wife and my kids?' The line wasn't in Ward's script; he told Vuckovich to improvise something that major-leaguers would say. What's more, "Stormin' and Vuke's" was a regular off-hours hangout for the cast and crew while they were on location in Milwaukee.[59]

Vuckovich was an analyst on Brewers telecasts from 1989 through 1991. Then Ted Simmons, whom the Pirates had hired as GM in February 1992, invited his old friend and batterymate to join the Pittsburgh organization. It was ideal because no big-league franchise was closer to family in Johnstown. Vuke stayed with the Bucs for 20 seasons, through 2011. He was first a roving pitching instructor (1992-93) and then special assistant to GM Cam Bonifay (1994-95). In 1996 he was promoted to assistant GM/director of player personnel.[60]

Shortly after the '96 season ended, the Pirates made Vuckovich the big club's pitching coach, a longstanding goal of his. He replaced Ray Miller because "the club didn't feel Miller's methods were resulting in progress. Vuckovich will coach attitude and mental approach as much as mechanics." A subsequent report noted that he would "spend a lot of time getting to know young players, trying to determine the best way to tap their talents."[61]

Vuckovich held that position for four seasons (1997-2000). When the Pirates hired Lloyd McClendon as manager, he and Bonifay turned over the coaching staff.[62] As a result, bullpen coach Spin Williams moved up and Vuke returned to the front office. He continued to work as special assistant to Bonifay, and later to David Littlefield, then Neal Huntington.

Vuckovich joined the Mariners as a special assistant to GM Jack Zduriencik before the 2012 season. His job included much travel, scouting amateurs and pros, as well as visiting with minor-league teams. Zduriencik, who'd been scouting director for the Pirates from 1991 through 1993, respected his old colleague's baseball mind. In November 2013, Vuckovich was a candidate for pitching coach with the Phillies, but he removed his name from consideration.[63] The job went to his former Milwaukee teammate Bob McClure.

Seattle fired Zduriencik in August 2015, and that October Vuckovich was part of the ensuing organizational purge.[64] A few months later, he became a roving scout for the Diamondbacks. When asked what brings a scout the most satisfaction, Vuckovich said, "Being right on a player. ... That's what you strive to do."[65]

In late 2017, Pete and Annie Vuckovich still called Johnstown home. "It's where I grew up, and where my wife and I met. Even when I was playing, in the off-season we always came home to Johnstown," he said just before taking the Diamondbacks job. Vuckovich is a member of the Sports Halls of Fame of Cambria County, Clarion University, the AAABA, Western Pennsylvania, and Pennsylvania. He remained happy and confident at work. "Baseball has been my whole life. It's what I know, and I know it better than most."[66]

SOURCES

Internet resources

Cambria County Sports Hall of Fame (ccshof.org/member/pete-vuckovich/).

Official website of the AAABA Tournament (aaabajohnstown.org/).

Findagrave.com.

Betty Vuckovich funeral announcement (hindmanfuneralhomes.com/obituary/betty-bosa-j-vuckovich/).

newspapers.com.

NOTES

1 Daniel Okrent, *Nine Innings* (Boston: Houghton Mifflin Company, 1985), 237.

2 Neal Russo, "Vuckovich: Unusual Man With Some Evil Pitches," *St. Louis Post-Dispatch*, July 25, 1978: 36.

3 Mike Eisenbath, *The Cardinals Encyclopedia* (Philadelphia: Temple University Press, 1999), 300.

4 Bob Verdi, "Close Calls All Go Vuckovich's Way," *Chicago Tribune*, March 18, 1982. Tom Boswell, "Brewers' Vuckovich Becomes Off-the-Wall Force on the Mound," *Washington Post*, October 13, 1982.

5 David L. Porter, editor, *Biographical Dictionary of American Sports*, Volume 2, Q-Z (Westport, Connecticut: Greenwood Press, 2000), 1607. The Vuckovich parents' Serbian nicknames are visible on the pictures of their shared grave marker at find-agrave.com. There are various references to Lazo Vuckovich as "Louis," including his 2005 obituary in the *Johnstown Tribune-Democrat*. The *Biographical Dictionary of Sports* entry gives Bossie's Americanized name as "Betty Jane." See also Betty Vuckovich funeral announcement.

6 "Life Inside the Diamond," Clarion University website, January 4, 2016.

7 Rick Hummel, "Birds V-Sign Stands for Vuke and Victory," *The Sporting News*, May 3, 1980: 13.

8 Neal Russo, "'Gimme the Ball, Often,' Vuckovich Tells Cards," *The Sporting News*, February 25, 1978: 54.

9 "Mariners Name Pete Vuckovich Special Assistant to the General Manager," MLB.com, September 16, 2011. Football position comes from *Indiana* (Pennsylvania) *Gazette*, accessed via newspapers.com. Basketball position comes from email to Rory Costello from Mike Mastovich of the *Johnstown Tribune-Democrat*, October 5, 2017.

10 Bob Broeg, "McBride Deal Wins Belated OK," *St. Louis Post-Dispatch*, September 3, 1978: 76.

11 Hummel, "Birds V-Sign Stands for Vuke and Victory."

12 Verdi, "Close Calls All Go Vuckovich's Way."

13 "Life Inside the Diamond."

14 "Mariners Name Pete Vuckovich Special Assistant to the General Manager."

15 Russo, "'Gimme the Ball, Often,' Vuckovich Tells Cards."

16 "Pitcher Credits Sain," *The Sporting News*, May 17, 1975: 38.

17 "Life Inside the Diamond."

18 Porter, op. cit., 1608. Front-office biographies, Pittsburgh Pirates, MLB.com. Date unknown, but could range from 2008 to 2011.

19 Pete Vuckovich Jr. profile on LinkedIn.com.

20 Jerome Holtzman, "Dent, Downing Only Chisox Certain of Regular Berths," *The Sporting News*, March 6, 1976: 11.

21 Russo, "'Gimme the Ball, Often,' Vuckovich Tells Cards."

22 Okrent, *Nine Innings*, 207. The original source of this quote is uncertain.

23 Neil MacCarl, "Shear Locks, Jays Order Vuckovich," *The Sporting News*, March 12, 1977: 43.

24 Verdi, "Close Calls All Go Vuckovich's Way."

25 MacCarl, "Shear Locks, Jays Order Vuckovich," 46.

26 Neal Russo, "Devine Gives Royal Look to New Card Hand," *The Sporting News*, December 24, 1977: 59.

27 Neal Russo, "Brother Vuckovich a Wheelhorse for Cards," *The Sporting News*, August 5, 1978: 20.

28 "Cards Spook Phillies," *Pittsburgh Press*, August 9, 1978: 56.

29 Broeg, "McBride Deal Wins Belated OK."

30 Eisenbath, op. cit., loc. cit. Original source of quote: "The Pete Vuckovich Story Is Filed Under 'Sci-Fi,'" *St. Louis Post-Dispatch*, February 8, 1983: 30.

31 Hummel, "Birds V-Sign Stands for Vuke and Victory."

32 Okrent, *Nine Innings*, 206.

33 Dave Anderson, "Trade That Brewed the 6-Pack Series," *New York Times*, October 12, 1982.

34 Boswell, "Brewers' Vuckovich Becomes Off-the-Wall Force on the Mound."

35 Tom Flaherty, "Vuckovich Brewers' Big Bargain," *The Sporting News*, June 27, 1981: 25.

36 Boswell, "Brewers' Vuckovich Becomes Off-the-Wall Force on the Mound."

37 Okrent, *Nine Innings*, 71, 237.

38 Mike Mastovich, "From AAABA to Cy Young, Vuckovich Made His Pitch," *Johnstown Tribune-Democrat*, August 5, 2007.

39 Mike Mastovich, "Competitiveness, Talent Took Vuckovich to the Top of Baseball," *Johnstown Tribune-Democrat*, October 8, 2016.

40 Tom Flaherty, "Vuke Shares Credit With Teammates," *The Sporting News*, November 15, 1982: 53.

41 Roger Angell, "The Arms Talks," *The New Yorker*, May 4, 1987.

42 Stan Hochman, "Life in the Fast Lane Doesn't Faze Vuckovich," *Philadelphia Daily News*, October 15, 1982.

43 Mike Mastovich, "Vuckovich Honored: Area Ex-Big-Leaguer to Take Spot With Pennsylvania's Best," *Johnstown Tribune-Democrat*, October 23, 2008.

44 "Vuckovich Says He's Happy," Associated Press, November 4, 1982.

45 Peter Gammons, "Brewers' First Three Rank with Best," *The Sporting News*, May 2, 1983: 14.

46 Tom Flaherty, "Outlook Bleak for Vuckovich," *The Sporting News*, March 28, 1983: 42. Flaherty, "Simmons Hits .300 Jackpot," *The Sporting News*, May 23, 1983: 22.

47 Tom Flaherty, "Vuckovich's Return Impresses Brewers," *The Sporting News*, September 19, 1983: 14; Flaherty, "Job in Jeopardy, but Kuenn's Secure," *The Sporting News*, October 3, 1983: 17.

48 Tom Flaherty, "Vuckovich Is Cautiously Optimistic," *The Sporting News*, February 27, 1984: 36. Flaherty, "Hurts Hamper Molitor, Vucko," *The Sporting News*, April 9, 1984: 15.

49 Mastovich, "Vuckovich honored: Area Ex-Big-Leaguer to Take Spot With Pennsylvania's Best."

50 Tom Flaherty, "As Vuckovich Exits, Porter Returns," *The Sporting News*, September 23, 1985: 20; Flaherty, "Yount Will Return to Center Field," *The Sporting News*, December 2, 1985: 48.

51 "A.L. Notebook: Brewers," *The Sporting News*, August 11, 1986: 17.

52 Tom Flaherty, "Facing the Inevitable," *The Sporting News*, April 13, 1987: 16.

53 Charlie O'Brien and Doug Wedge, *The Cy Young Catcher* (College Station, Texas: Texas A&M University Press: 2015), 18-19.

54 "Brewers' First Loss of Season Fails to Dampen Fan Enthusiasm," United Press International, April 22, 1987.

55 "Thousands Celebrate Opening of Sampson [sic] JCC," *Wisconsin Jewish Chronicle*, September 25, 1987: 3.

56 Jonathan Knight, *The Making of "Major League,"* (Cleveland: Gray & Company, 2015), exact page number unavailable online.

57 Steve Wulf, "Too Bush for the Bigs," *Sports Illustrated*, April 17, 1989. This article spelled the character's first name as "Klu," as have other sources over the years.

58 Danny Kelly, "'Major League' Is Baseball," *The Ringer*, July 22, 2016.

59 Knight, op. cit. Mike Oz, "'Major League' Turns 25—Here Are 15 Things You Didn't Know About the Movie," Yahoo! Sports, April 7, 2014. Chris Nashawaty, "A League of Its Own," *Sports Illustrated*, July 4, 2011.

60 "Mariners Name Pete Vuckovich Special Assistant to the General Manager." Mike Mastovich, "Johnstown native Pete Vuckovich Starts New Baseball Chapter as Diamondbacks Scout," *Johnstown Tribune-Democrat*, January 6, 2016.

61 John Mehno, "Pittsburgh Pirates," *The Sporting News*, October 21, 1996, 20. Mehno, "Pittsburgh Pirates," *The Sporting News*, November 11, 1996: 37.

62 John Mehno, "Pittsburgh," *The Sporting News*, November 6, 2000.

63 Jim Salisbury, "Phils Feel Rejection in Pitching Coach Search," NBC Sports Philadelphia, November 11, 2013.

64 "Sources: Mariners' Front Office Overhaul Begins With Four Changes," Foxsports.com, October 5, 2015.

65 Mastovich, "Johnstown Native Pete Vuckovich Starts New Baseball Chapter As Diamondbacks Scout."

66 "Life Inside the Diamond."

RUBE WADDELL

BY DAN O'BRIEN

HE ENTERED THIS WORLD on Friday the 13th and exited on April Fools Day. In the 37 intervening years, Rube Waddell struck out more batters, frustrated more managers, and attracted more fans than any pitcher of his era. An imposing physical specimen for his day, the 6-foot-1, 196-pound Waddell possessed the intellectual and emotional maturity of a child—although a very precocious and engaging one at that. "There was delicious humor in many of his vagaries, a vagabond impudence and ingenuousness that made them attractive to the public," wrote the *Columbus Dispatch*.[1] Waddell's on- and off-field exploits became instant legends.

Known to occasionally miss a scheduled start because he was off fishing or playing marbles with street urchins, Waddell might disappear for days during spring training, only to be found leading a parade down the main street of Jacksonville, Florida, or wrestling an alligator in a nearby lagoon. Despite these and other curious distractions, Waddell's immense physical ability was undeniable. He complemented a blazing fastball with a wicked curve and demonstrated excellent control with both. His strikeout-to-walk ratio was nearly 3-to-1 for his career (almost 4-to-1 in his record-setting season of 1904.)

Connie Mack, who managed Waddell for six seasons in Philadelphia, believed that Waddell had "the best combination of speed and curves" of any pitcher who played the game.[2] Without Mack's patience and guidance, though, Rube Waddell might be nothing more than a humorous footnote in baseball history. Mack was the only manager able to tolerate Rube for any extended period, and that was only six seasons. But Waddell always remained a Connie Mack favorite. "Dad always had a gleam in his eye when he told stories about Rube Waddell," said Connie's daughter, Ruth Mack Clark. "Dad really loved the Rube."[3]

Waddell's antics have become the stuff of legend, occasionally embroidered to make this larger-than-life character appear even more preposterous. No, Waddell didn't regularly bolt from the mound to chase a passing fire wagon. But his fascination with fires was genuine. He regularly assisted firefighters, from a bucket brigade in Pewaukee, Wisconsin to large metropolitan departments in Philadelphia, Cleveland, Detroit, or Washington. Yes, on occasion Waddell did direct his infielders to the sidelines and strike out the side in the final inning—but only in exhibitions, never in a regular-season game.

One of the great myths concerns Waddell's background, which helped perpetuate the "rube" or hayseed image that adorned his career. Contrary to popular presumption, his father was not a farmer. John Waddell, a native Scotsman, labored in the Pennsylvania oil fields as an employee of the National Transit Company, a division of Standard Oil. While living in Bradford, Pennsylvania—at one time the center of the world oil production—John's wife, Mary Forbes Waddell, gave birth to their sixth child on October 13, 1876. Christened "George Edward," the future "Rube" Waddell was also known as "Ed" or "Eddie" in family circles.

In the early 1890s the Waddells relocated to Butler County, Pennsylvania and settled in the town of Prospect. In Butler County and the surrounding area, the reputation of a burgeoning pitching talent began to grow. Teenager Ed Waddell swiftly advanced from the sandlots to play for a number of semipro baseball teams in the region. In August 1896, newspapers in Titusville and Oil City made passing mentions of an Oil City pitcher named "Rube" Waddell, the first known references to his famous nickname.

In August of 1897, without so much as an inning in minor-league baseball, Waddell's reputation earned him a tryout with the National League's Pittsburgh Pirates. His seating assignment at a team meal earned

Colorful, wacky, ill-fated Rube Waddell was a big draw on the theater circuit; he also appeared in two early documentaries, Game of Base Ball *and* Rube Waddell and the Champions Playing Ball with the Boston Team.

him a release before he ever appeared in a game. "Rube sat beside Manager (Patsy) Donovan," the *Louisville Courier-Journal* reported. "Patsy heard him talk and released him as soon as breakfast was over."[4]

The visiting Louisville Colonels saw promise in the young left-hander and signed him. Rube made his major-league debut on September 8, 1897, a 5-1 loss to Baltimore, the defending league champion. A week later, he relieved in a lost cause against Pittsburg.

Louisville management believed Waddell needed more seasoning before testing the majors for a full season. Accordingly, he began the 1898 campaign with Detroit of the Western League. The relationship didn't last long. Waddell pitched in nine games for Detroit before he left the team after a squabble over a fine. He pitched briefly in Chatham, Ontario and finished the year in Homestead, Pennsylvania. Waddell returned to the Western League in 1899 with Columbus, Ohio, where he enjoyed his first successful season in organized baseball, as he notched a 26-8 record for Columbus and Grand Rapids before rejoining Louisville in the final month of the season and winning seven of nine decisions.

Following the 1899 season, Rube made a brief return to Columbus, where he married Florence Dunning, the first of his three wives. To no one's surprise, Florence received a divorce from Rube in 1901 on the grounds of "gross neglect of duty."[5]

Prior to the start of the 1900 season, the Louisville franchise was contracted from the National League, but Colonels owner Barney Dreyfuss purchased a half-interest in the Pirates and arranged for the "trade" of 10 of his players to Pittsburg, including Waddell. Pitching for Pittsburg, Waddell paced National League pitchers in 1900 in ERA (2.37) and was second in strikeouts (130), but also finished with a losing record (8-13) and missed nearly two months of the season.

Fred Clarke, the Pirates' player-manager, was a strict disciplinarian and had little use for Waddell's irresponsible nature. In early July, Clarke suspended Waddell, who then hooked up with a number of semipro teams in western Pennsylvania, finally landing in Punxsutawney. Connie Mack, then manager of Milwaukee's American League team, was in need of pitching. He received permission from Pittsburg to sign Waddell, with the stipulation that Waddell would return to the Pirates if they so desired. Mack convinced Waddell to leave "Punxy" and the southpaw became an immediate sensation in Milwaukee. He won 10 games in a little more than a month, including both halves of a 22-inning doubleheader at Chicago. Impressed by Waddell's work with the Brewers, the Pirates asked for his return.

Clarke and Rube survived the remainder of the 1900 season without major eruptions but more problems arose the following season. In May 1901 Waddell's contract was sold to the Chicago Orphans. After winning 14 games (in 28 decisions) for the struggling Chicago team, Rube jumped ship again and landed with a number of semipro teams in Wisconsin. In November Rube hooked on with a barnstorming team for a tour of California. Extremely popular with the West Coast fans, Rube signed with the California League's Los Angeles Looloos for the 1902 season.

Waddell stayed in Los Angeles for only a few months before Mack, now managing the Philadelphia Athletics, enticed him to leave California to bolster the A's depleted pitching staff. Waddell agreed, and Mack sent a pair of Pinkerton escorts to ensure Waddell made it east.

Only 87 games remained on the A's schedule when Waddell pitched his first game on June 26, yet the left-hander finished the season with a 24-7 record. Rube also led the league with 210 strikeouts, 50 more than runner-up Cy Young, who pitched 108 1/3 more innings. The Athletics, only two games above .500 when Rube entered the fray, finished 30 games above the break-even mark and won their first American League pennant.

In little more than half a season Waddell had established himself as one of the game's premier pitchers and Philadelphia's most bankable star. The Athletics' attendance doubled from the previous year to a league-leading 420,000. Cigars, soap, and liquor were among the products named after Waddell. The 1902 season also saw the emergence of Osee Schrecongost as Rube's favorite catcher. Waddell and Schreck (as his name was often truncated) soon became known as baseball's wackiest battery mates, as famous for their off-the-field frolics as their on-field production.

The 1903 season was the most tumultuous in the erratic career of Rube Waddell. In June he was married for the second time, this time to a Massachusetts girl named May Wynne Skinner whom he had met three days earlier. It was the beginning of a very stormy relationship. The marriage lasted nearly seven years but the couple only infrequently lived together and Mrs. Waddell often had her husband jailed for non-support. In July, American League president Ban Johnson suspended Waddell for five days after he climbed into the stands to beat up a spectator, a known gambler who had baited the pitcher.[6] Despite starting the season 13-3, Waddell limped home to a 21-16 record. Still, he struck out a record 302 batters, even though his season ended prematurely on August 25 when he failed to appear for his scheduled start in Cleveland. Mack, weary of Rube's frequent unexcused absences, suspended him for the remainder of the season. A week later, Waddell patched up his differences with Mack, signed a contract for the following season with which he agreed to "live up to the regular rules," with "no favors allowed."[7]

From September to December Waddell toured with a theater company, performing as himself in a melodrama entitled *The Stain of Guilt*. Baseball's matinee idol was a big draw at the theaters as well. Critics, though, were largely unimpressed with Waddell's acting skills. "He is let out only two minutes in each scene," wrote the *Chicago Journal*, "and the ensuing repair bills are pretty bulky for even those few minutes."[8]

After numerous disagreements over advance pay, the company jettisoned Rube during its run in Philadelphia, unceremoniously dumping his bags in the alley.[9] He immediately began tending bar in nearby Camden, New Jersey. His 1904 campaign progressed without serious incident. Waddell won 25 games and registered a 1.62 ERA, the second-best of his career. He also extended his post-1900 single season strikeout record to 349, a major-league total unsurpassed until Sandy Koufax whiffed 382 in 1965.

The Rube also demonstrated his more compassionate side when Athletics' center fielder Danny Hoffman was knocked unconscious by a fastball to the temple. "Someone went for an ambulance, and the players crowded around in aimless bewilderment," wrote Connie Mack. "Somebody said that Danny might not live until the doctor got there. Then the man they had called the playboy and clown went into action. Pushing everybody to one side, he gently placed Danny over his shoulder and actually ran across the field." Rube flagged down a carriage, which carted the pair to the nearest hospital. Rube, still in uniform, sat at Hoffman's bedside for most of the night, and held ice to Hoffman's head.[10]

The 1905 season was even better for Waddell, at least statistically. He led the AL in strikeouts (287) games pitched (46), ERA (1.48) and wins (27). His most spectacular victory was a 20-inning contest against Boston's Cy Young on July 4, 1905. Both future Hall of Famers went the distance and Rube performed cartwheels off the mound once the A's secured the 4-2 victory. According to legend, Rube bartered free drinks with the ball he used to defeat Young in the game. Before long, dozens of bartenders had this "genuine" souvenir in their possession.

Despite this success, the 1905 season ended on a sour note for Waddell. Again, he missed most of the season's final month. After another Waddell victory over Young at Boston on September 8, the A's headed back home to Philadelphia. While changing trains in Providence, Waddell and teammate Andy Coakley engaged in a friendly scuffle over a straw hat. Rube fell and injured his shoulder.[11] His season was over, with the exception of two ineffective appearances in the last two days of the regular season, and he did not appear in the Athletics' five-game defeat to the New York Giants in that year's World Series. Not everybody believed the straw hat tale, however. Rumors were rampant that gamblers had paid Waddell to sit out the series.

Mack believed Waddell was never quite the same after the straw hat incident. In 1906 Waddell's ledger sagged to 15-17. Despite his losing record, Waddell ranked among the league leaders with eight shutouts, including a one-hitter over the Detroit Tigers. Waddell's drinking problem escalated during the season, and a rift developed between Waddell and Schrecongost, who had sworn off the bottle. In 1907, Rube improved his record to 19-13 but he was ineffective down the stretch as the A's fought tooth-and-nail with Detroit for the AL pennant. In a key game against the Tigers on September 30, Waddell came on in relief of Jimmy Dygert and failed to hold a three-run lead. Although the game ended in a 17-inning deadlock, the Athletics' collapse was a crushing blow to their pennant hopes and proved to be Waddell's death knell in Philadelphia. In the "interest of team harmony," Mack sold Waddell to the St. Louis Browns on February 7, 1908—a week after Waddell's wife sued him for divorce. Shortly afterward, Waddell was accused of assault and battery on both his parents-in-law.[12] The resulting legal difficulties prevented him from pitching in Massachusetts, where a warrant for his arrest awaited, during the 1908 and 1909 seasons.

Waddell responded with another 19-win season in 1908, helping the much-improved Browns to stay in the pennant race, though the club faded to fourth place by season's end. Not quite the dominant force he once was, Rube was still a box office bonanza. "He paid for himself in three games after he was bought," wrote *St. Louis Post Dispatch* columnist John L. Wray. "He had added many thousands to the exchecquer [sic] since that time—paid admissions that would never have arrived at the gate but for the fact that Rube was scheduled to work."[13] The Browns enjoyed a 48 percent boost in home attendance to more than 618,000, second in the American League, while the Athletics' attendance dropped by nearly 30 percent. On July 29, Rube enjoyed a measure of revenge against his old mates when he struck out 16 Athletics, tying the American League single-game record.

In 1909, Waddell's record slipped to 11-14 with only 141 strikeouts, as his skills began to show obvious decline. His 2.37 ERA was barely better than the league average. On April 4, 1910, after his ugly divorce from wife no. 2 was finalized, Rube married wife no. 3, 19-year-old Madge Maguire. Another tempestuous marriage followed. Rube's major-league days were also numbered. He appeared in only 10 games, all but two in relief. The Browns released him in August, leaving him to finish out the year with Newark in the Eastern League.

In 1911, Waddell won 20 games for Joe Cantillon's Minneapolis Millers, helping the Millers to another American Association championship. The following winter, Waddell lived with Cantillon at the manager's farm in Hickman, Kentucky, a small village situated on a bend of the Mississippi River. When flood waters threatened to swallow the town, Rube stood in icy water for hours helping stack sandbags for the levee. As a result, he contracted a severe case of pneumonia. His system weakened, Waddell soon became a victim of tuberculosis. He pitched one more season for Minneapolis and a part of another with two teams in the Northern League but by November of 1913 his health had reached the critical stage.

Cantillon paid Waddell's way to a sanitarium in San Antonio to be close to his parents, who had moved in with Rube's younger sister in nearby Boerne, Texas. Connie Mack and Athletics' partner Ben Shibe paid for Waddell's medical care, with orders that "Waddell should have the best of medical attention and nursing, and that no expenses should be spared to either help the once mighty Rube regain his health, or to ease his sufferings if his battle is to be a losing one."[14]

The once powerful Waddell, now down to 130 pounds, passed away on April 1, 1914, a few months shy of his 38th birthday. "He was the greatest pitcher in the game, and although widely known for his eccentricities, was more sinned against than sinner," said Mack. "He may have failed us at times but to him, I and the other owners of the Athletics ball club, owe much."[15] He was laid to rest in Mission Burial Park South, in San Antonio.

Note: An earlier version of this biography originally appeared in David Jones, ed., *Deadball Stars of the American League* (Washington, D.C.: Potomac Books, Inc., 2006).

SOURCES

In addition to the sources cited in the Notes, the author also consulted several dozen newspapers and other publications, and the following books:

Honig, Donald. *Baseball America* (New York: Touchstone, 2001)
Mack, Connie. *My 66 Years in the Big Leagues* (Philadelphia: John Winston Co., 1950)
McGraw, John. *My Thirty Years in Baseball* (New York: Boni & Liveright, 1923)
Okkonen, Mark. *Baseball Memories, 1900-1909* (New York; Sterling, 1992)
Ritter, Lawrence S. *The Glory of Their Times* (New York: Harper Perennial, 2010)
Spink, Alfred H.. *The National Game* (Carbondale, Illinois: Southern Illinois University Press, 2000)
The Sporting News, *Cooperstown, Where the Legends Live Forever* (New York: Random House, 1988)

Interview Bill Waddell, great-nephew of Rube Waddell, ca. 2005-06.

NOTES

1. *Columbus (Ohio) Sunday Dispatch*, April 5, 1914:14. Repeated in *The Literary Digest*, April 18, 1914.
2. Grantland Rice, "Sportlight," *Indianapolis Star*, October 18, 1944: 15.
3. Personal conversation with Ruth Mack Clark, ca. 2005-06.
4. *Louisville Courier-Journal*, September 16, 1897: 6.
5. "Rube Waddell's Wife Obtains A Divorce," *Springfield* (Ohio) *Sun*, April 6, 1902.
6. *Washington Post*, July 19, 1903: H10.
7. *Philadelphia Evening Bulletin*, September 1, 1903: 11.
8. *Chicago Journal*, October 12, 1903.
9. F. C. Richter, "PHILADELPHIA NEWS/The Erratic Waddell's Theatrical Career End," *Sporting Life*, December 26, 1903: 5.
10. Connie Mack, "The One and Only Rube," *Saturday Evening Post*, March 14, 1936, Vol. 208 Issue 37: 12-110.
11. J. G. Taylor Spink, ed., "Rube Waddell/His Life, Laughs and Laurels," *Baseball Register*, St. Louis: The Sporting News, 1944), 16.
12. *Lynn* (Massachusetts) *Daily Item*, February 9, 1905: 1.
13. John L. Wray, "Wray's Column," *St. Louis Post Dispatch*, August 15, 1909: 29.
14. "Shibe And Mack Will Look After Rube Waddell," *San Antonio Express*, February 20, 1914.
15. *Philadelphia North American*, April 2, 1944.

LEON WAGNER

BY JAY BERMAN

MAYBE IT WAS LEON Wagner's bad luck to have been born too soon. A major-league outfielder for 12 years, Wagner was a two-time All-Star who averaged 29 home runs and 87 RBIs from 1961 through 1966. Still, because of fielding deficiencies that were either imagined (his opinion) or real (his managers' views), he always seemed to be fighting for playing time. His final season in the majors was 1969, just four years before the advent of the designated hitter, a spot that would seem to have been a perfect fit for him.

Leon Lamar Wagner was born on May 13, 1934, in Chattanooga, Tennessee. He and his parents, Eugene and Hattie Lee Wagner, moved to the Detroit area when Leon was an infant, when his father was hired by a foundry. In 1952 Wagner graduated from Inkster High School—Inkster is now a town of 30,000 about 20 miles west of Detroit. He was a three-sport athlete for Inkster's Vikings, starring in baseball, basketball, and football. Wagner next enrolled at Tuskegee University—then known as Tuskegee Institute—in Alabama, on a football scholarship. He was there for three semesters before returning to Michigan, where he found a job in the auto industry.

Before the 1954 season, New York Giants scout Ray Lucas signed Wagner, who was playing for a sandlot team called the Inkster Panthers. Wagner was sent to the Danville (Illinois) Dans of the Class-D Mississippi-Ohio Valley League that spring. He played in 125 games for Danville and led the league with 160 hits. He had 24 home runs and 115 RBIs, that latter figure still a Danville team record, and hit .332. In a sign of things to come, Wagner also led the league's outfielders with 14 errors.

The offensive numbers persuaded the Giants to move Wagner up a step to the Class-C Northern League in 1955. Playing for the St. Cloud (Minnesota) Rox, he led the league with 29 home runs and 127 RBIs and hit .313. Once again, he committed 14 errors in the outfield. The next year with Danville (Virginia) of the Carolina League, he batted .330 and led the league with 51 homers and 166 RBIs. With Danville he played with three other future major-league stars—shortstop Jose Pagan, third baseman Tony Taylor, and first baseman Willie McCovey.

After the 1956 season Wagner was drafted into the US Army, with whom he spent 14 months at Fort Carson, Colorado, driving a Jeep. After the year off from baseball, the Giants advanced him to Phoenix in 1958 to join their new Pacific Coast League team. The New York Giants had moved to San Francisco, and their top farm club was now in Phoenix. Wagner's stay was brief. After 65 games in the PCL, in which he hit .318 with 17 home runs and 58 RBIs, he was recalled by the Giants and made his big-league debut on June 22, 1958.

Taking over left field, Wagner appeared in 74 games and hit 13 home runs in his rookie year with 35 RBIs and a .317 average. Garry Schumacher, a Giants public-relations executive, told *San Francisco Examiner* sports editor Curley Grieve shortly after Wagner was called up that Wagner reminded him of a "left-handed Hank Aaron" the way "he crushes that ball."[1] Jack Schwarz, a Giants farm system executive, recalled that Wagner had not been impressive when signed and was about to be released, but pleaded for another chance. "Anybody who loves baseball that much deserves another chance," Schwarz told reporters.[2]

Even early in his big-league career, Wagner faced questions about his outfield play. Grieve, in an August 23, 1958, column, wrote: "Unfortunately, Wagner can't field like he can hit," but he quoted Wagner as claiming that he was "not a bad outfielder."[3]

That was as close as Wagner would ever get to full-time status in San Francisco. Manager Bill Rigney had expressed reservations about his defense, telling a writer from *Newsday* years later that Wagner "didn't even care about fielding" when he was with the Giants.[4] Wagner made five errors in that first half-season, and Rigney opted to use Jackie Brandt in left field for most of the 1959 season. Brandt appeared in 137 games while Wagner was in 87, recording only 5 home runs and 22 RBIs while his average slumped to .225. It was the first time at any level that Wagner had ever failed to hit .300. On December 15, 1959, the Giants traded Wagner and third baseman Daryl Spencer to the St. Louis Cardinals for second baseman Don Blasingame. Within days, some Bay Area writers speculated that the team had given up too much for the light-hitting Blasingame, a defensive specialist.[5]

Wagner said after the trade that he "was never given any encouragement in San Francisco," and that Rigney and coach Salty Parker "would give me the hard look" if he misplayed a ball in the outfield.[6] He denied being a poor outfielder but acknowledged that alongside Willie Mays, Brandt, and Felipe Alou, "I had to look bad by comparison."[7]

Wagner had few opportunities to play regularly for the 1960 Cardinals, who had Stan Musial, Curt Flood, and Joe Cunningham as regulars. He spent extra time during spring training working on his defense with manager Solly Hemus and coach Harry Walker. Shortly before the season began, Hemus said Wagner was "at least average" defensively, and Walker—who had Wagner chasing fly balls hit to him by a modified pitching machine—said Wagner's ability to track fly balls and his throwing had improved.[8]

What didn't improve was his hitting. Playing sparingly and often only as a pinch-hitter, Wagner appeared in only 39 games for the Cardinals with 4 home runs and 11 RBIs. One of those home runs may have meant a bit more to him than the others. On April 12, in his first time back in San Francisco since being traded, Wagner hit the first-ever home run at Candlestick Park, the Giants' brand-new stadium. Wagner was hitting .214 on June 15 when the Cardinals optioned him to Rochester. Things improved somewhat in the International League, where

Leon Wagner, whose film credits include A Woman Under the Influence *and* The Bingo Long Traveling All-Stars & Motor Kings.

he hit 16 home runs and drove in 48 in 93 games, but his .265 average marked the first time he had been under .300 in the minors.

While Wagner was too early to take advantage of the DH, he was just in time for baseball's expansion. The American League had operated with eight teams since it was established in 1901, but two new clubs—the Los Angeles Angels and Washington Senators—had been created and would begin play in 1961.

Wagner was traded to the Angels in mid-April and almost immediately became a star. Playing as a regular for the first time at age 27, Wagner led the expansion club with 28 home runs, while his 79 RBIs were second on the team. He hit .280 and even led the team's outfielders with 12 assists. Wagner was reunited with manager Bill Rigney, who had held the same post in San Francisco. The day he was acquired,

Rigney told the Associated Press, "I like the way he swings the bat."[9]

In 1962, his second season in Los Angeles, the approachable Wagner became a favorite with sportswriters. He got off to a great start that year, hitting nine home runs in the team's first 18 games. He told *Los Angeles Times* writer Braven Dyer in early May that "I'm playing baseball with everything I have and that's the only way I know how to play it."[10]

The same writer asked Rigney how good he thought Wagner could be. "He can be one of the very best," Rigney said, "and he can hit 40 or so home runs. If he keeps away from bad pitches, he will become one of the American League's outstanding hitters."[11] Rigney was right. Wagner enjoyed the best year of his career in 1962, setting personal records for home runs (37), RBIs (107), doubles (21), triples (5), and base hits (164). He hit .268, and finished fourth in the MVP voting.

From 1959 through 1962, there were two All-Star Games each year. Wagner was MVP of the second 1962 game, at Chicago's Wrigley Field, with a two-run homer, two singles, and a key catch in the AL's 9-4 win. Of his catch, which took an extra-base hit away from George Altman, Wagner told writers: "A man don't have to be a bad fielder all his life. It isn't that hard to catch baseballs."[12] He called the All-Star Game performance "the biggest thrill of my life."[13] In large part as a result of Wagner's great year, the Angels finished third with an 86-76 record in only their second year of existence.

Wagner had another great start in 1963, contending for the league lead in home runs, batting, and RBIs until mid-July. He then cooled off, finishing at .291 with 26 home runs and 90 RBIs, but earned another All-Star Team selection.

Surprisingly, Wagner was traded to Cleveland on December 2, 1963, for pitcher Barry Latman and first baseman Joe Adcock. A few weeks later, Wagner was asked for his feelings about the trade. His response: "I don't see how anybody could be happy over leaving the Angels. I'm going to miss the players. I'll miss [Rigney] more than anything. He's the man who brought me back from the minors and I'll never forget it. … I'm trying to take the trade the way a ballplayer should. It's business."[14] One Los Angeles columnist wrote, "It is difficult to see how the trade can help Los Angeles."[15]

The deal turned out to be as one-sided as it had seemed it might be. Latman was 6-10 as a part-time starter and reliever in 1964, while Adcock hit 21 home runs for the Angels, but with only 64 RBIs. Wagner, on the other hand, enjoyed one of his best seasons in his first year in Cleveland. Playing in 163 games, he hit 31 home runs, drove in 100 runs, and even stole 14 bases, displaying a side of his game not seen before.

Wagner became as popular with Cleveland writers as he had been with those in Los Angeles. He never ducked the press and frequently had a humorous response for the mundane questions ballplayers often face. He often referred to himself as Daddy Wags. One columnist called him the Good Humor Man, after the popular brand of ice cream that was sold door-to-door from a truck. Another, writing of Wagner's easygoing attitude, quoted him as saying, "I don't dig people who put baseball in the same class with going to church. I don't kick water coolers or throw (batting) helmets. Maybe if other players watch me, they'll take a lesson from me and not be so grouchy."[16]

Wagner told another writer that when he was hitting well in 1964 and former teammate Mays was going through a slump in San Francisco, he called Mays and told him, "How'd you do today, Willie? Oh, not so good, huh? That's too bad. By the way, I hit another one today. It don't look so hot when a little old $30,000 ballplayer like me starts leaving $100,000 men in the dust."[17] Mays hit 47 home runs that year to Wagner's 31. Cleveland teammate Bob Chance said of Wagner, "Daddy Wags is a good storyteller. It's not that Daddy Wags don't tell the truth. It's just he embroiders it."[18]

Wagner apparently was a good fit with fans, as well. *Cleveland Press* reporter Regis McAuley wrote in June 1964, "On the public relations side of things, Daddy Wags is batting and fielding 1.000. He is in demand for speeches and appearances and he fractures his audiences. He is also very generous with his autographs, which makes him an idol of the kids who hang around the park."[19]

Wagner had another solid year in 1965, smacking 28 home runs, driving home 79 runs, and batting a career-high .294. After a game-winning July home run off Baltimore's Milt Pappas, he joked that he knew Pappas would throw him a fastball "because I was concentrating."[20] Pappas had retired him on similar pitches in the fourth and sixth innings and so when he came to bat in the eighth inning of a 2-2 game with Rocky Colavito on first base, he expected another fastball "because I'm a thinkin' ballplayer. It was my turn to hit one."[21]

Wagner was given to predicting great things for himself, most often in jest. He denied having said he would hit 65 home runs but then added, "I guess I am capable. If Roger Maris hit 61, I can hit 70." Still, when he signed his contract for 1966, he told reporters, "One of these years—this might be the one—I'm gonna hit 55 to 60 home runs."[22]

But 1966 turned out to be a year of mixed results for Wagner. His 23 home runs were his fewest as a starter, as were his 66 RBIs. He did hit a respectable .279 after lifting his average 25 points after the All-Star Game, and credited being in the lineup every day for the resurgence. "When I go to bed at night," he told sportswriter Russell Schneider, "I know I'll be in the game the next day. Before I go to sleep, I think about the pitcher I'll be facing. I concentrate on what he threw me last time, what kind of pitches he uses in this situation or that one, and things like that. When you don't know if you're playing the next day, you think—and worry—about other things."[23]

Shortly before spring training in 1967, Wagner revealed a serious side to his personality. He said he had spoken with Indians general manager Gabe Paul about a future in baseball after his playing career ended. "Mr. Paul has led me to believe that I might be the first (African-American) to get a good job in baseball when my playing days are through. Of course, that's a long way off, but I kinda think I could get a good scouting job ... a responsible job, you know ... one that has administrative duties."[24]

Wagner's numbers dropped again in 1967. Now 33, he had just 15 home runs and 54 RBIs while platooning with Colavito. Still, he went to spring training with the Indians in 1968 predicting he'd hit 40 home runs "if they'll let me play every day."[25] Alvin Dark, the new manager, reportedly had little confidence in Wagner's defensive skills, and played him sparingly at the start of the season.[26] On June 13, he was traded to the Chicago White Sox for Russ Snyder.

As Wagner's playing time diminished, he became a successful pinch-hitter, leading the league in 1968 with 46 appearances. But he only had 211 at-bats for the season and managed just one home run and 24 RBIs to go with an average of .261. He continued to fight platooning, telling the *Chicago Sun-Times'* Jerome Holtzman, "I don't need to be platooned. Against one or two of the tough left-handers, a right-handed hitter might have a better chance, but that doesn't always work. If I had played every day since I came up in 1958, I'd have 400 homers."[27]

Wagner's playing career was nearly at an end. After spending spring training in 1969 with the Cincinnati Reds, he was eventually signed to a minor-league contract by the Giants, who assigned him to Phoenix in May. He got into 78 games, hitting 6 home runs, driving in 41 runs, and batting .295. In June, he said he was pleased to be back in the minor leagues, free from pressure.[28] He hinted that he was considering an offer to play in Japan, but nothing came of it.

Teammates voted Wagner the club's Most Inspirational Player. He got a late-season call from the Giants, appeared in 11 games and had 4 hits in 12 at-bats. He played his final game in the major leagues on October 2, 1969. He was released six days later. Wagner returned to Phoenix for 45 games in 1970 but hit only .189.

Wagner gave baseball one last try in 1971, signing with the Pacific Coast League's Hawaii Islanders as a coach and player. He was a full-time coach for a month, but hit a two-run home run in his first at-bat in more than a month. He also was married in Honolulu that year. In 75 games, Wagner had 9 home runs, 33 RBIs, and a .252 average. The San Diego Padres' farm team had several other former major-league players, including Clete Boyer, Lee Maye, and George Brunet.

In those pre-free-agency days, most players had to work winter jobs to augment their baseball salaries. While with the Angels, Wagner was partner in a men's clothing store that used the slogan "Buy your rags from Daddy Wags." He also was a partner in a record store and worked briefly as a Los Angeles County youth counselor.

Wagner's post-baseball life was nothing like what he had envisioned after that conversation with Gabe Paul back in 1967. He tried acting, appearing in John Cassavetes' 1974 film *A Woman Under the Influence*, and as a member of a 1930s barnstorming team in *The Bingo Long Traveling All-Stars & Motor Kings*, two years later.

He sold cars for three years in Honolulu after his playing career ended and held a similar job after moving to Los Angeles. He did public-relations work for a Los Angeles-area racetrack. He and his wife were in the news briefly early in 1972 when he was beaten and she received minor gunshot wounds when gunmen confronted them near the Wagners' Los Angeles apartment in an apparent robbery.

But mostly, Wagner disappeared from view until he was found dead on January 3, 2004, inside a converted closet behind a Los Angeles video store. He was 69. Friends told *Los Angeles Times* columnist Bill Plaschke he had been using drugs for years and had never forgiven the Angels for trading him. "I don't think he ever got over being traded," Mudcat Grant, a teammate in Cleveland, said.[29]

Lou Johnson, an outfielder for whom Wagner was traded when he joined the Angels in 1961, and a member of the board of directors of the Baseball Assistance Team, a group that helps former players in need, analyzed Wagner's death in a conversation with Plaschke this way: "Remember the first time they sent astronauts into space, and they weren't afraid until they landed in the ocean? That's what happens to some old ballplayers, particularly from our era, particularly African American. When we retire, it's like landing in the middle of the ocean without a rowboat."[30]

Johnson said that Wagner's son, Leon Jr., and daughter, Lei Juana Wagner, repeatedly tried to help their father in his later years but were rebuffed. Wagner was married to Sherry Stewart in 1959, to Doris Jean Hudson in 1965, and to Phyllis Crawford in 1971. All three marriages ended in divorce.

Cleveland columnist Bob Dolgan remembered two of Wagner's quips in a story a few days after the outfielder's death. "When a … writer saw him in the whirlpool and asked, 'Is your arm sore?' Wagner replied, 'No. There's nothing wrong with my arm. It's the elbow.' And a magazine quoted him as saying he caught the ball with one hand because "when you use two hands, the other one just gets in the way."[31]

Hal Lebovitz, who covered baseball in Cleveland for more than 60 years, remembered Wagner in a column a few days after his death in this way: "Leon Wagner was one of the most pleasant, friendliest players I ever knew. Always had that incandescent smile. Yet he appears to have died … without friends or family to claim his body. … I can shut my eyes and still see his smile. But what happened along the way that caused him to leave alone?"[32]

SOURCES

In addition to the sources cited in the Notes, the author consulted numerous other sources including:

Daniel, Dan. "Do Giants Rue Trade of Spencer to Cards?" *New York World Telegram*, March 31, 1964.

Dolgan, Bob. "A Perfect Blend of Homers and Humor," *Cleveland Plain Dealer*, January 9, 2004.

Dyer, Braven. "Cheerful Cheeky—He's Bad Joke to Chuckers," *Los Angeles Times*, April 6, 1963.

Dyer, Braven. "Wagner's Wails Rankle Angels, Bring Hot Reply," *Los Angeles Times*, March 21, 1964.

Jacobson, Steve. "Leon's New Image: Leather Craftsman," *Newsday*, July 31, 1962.

Lustig, Dennis. "Whatever Happened to Leon Wagner," *Cleveland Plain Dealer*, exact date unknown, 1980.

"Wagner Is Real Good Hitter," *San Francisco Examiner*, July 13, 1958.

United Press International, April 1, 1969.

NOTES

1. Curley Grieve, "Giants' Top Brass Tabs Wagner One of Coming Greats in Batting," *San Francisco Examiner*, August 23, 1958.
2. Curley Grieve, "Despite Slump, Mays Still Greater Than Anyone Else; Does Everything," *San Francisco Examiner*, July 13, 1958: 10.
3. Grieve, "Giants' Top Brass Tabs Wagner One of Coming Greats in Batting."
4. Joe Donnelly, "Players in the Corner," *Newsday*, August 11, 1964.
5. Dan Daniel, "Do Giants Rue Trade of Spencer to Cards?" March 31, 1960. Unidentified publication in Wagner's Hall of Fame file.
6. Stan Isaacs, "Life With the Giants Too 'Salty' for Leon," *Newsday*, March 15, 1960, in Wagner's Hall of Fame file.
7. Ibid.
8. Ibid.
9. Associated Press, "Wagner, ex-Card, to Angels," April 14, 1961.
10. Braven Dyer, "Angels' Wagner Believes He's Capable of 61 homers," *Los Angeles Times*, May 6, 1962.
11. Ibid.
12. Dan Daniel, "All-Star Win First Since '59," *New York World Telegram*, July 31, 1962.
13. Ibid.
14. Braven Dyer, "Daddy Wags Demolished Tribe Hurlers," *Los Angeles Times*, December 21, 1963.
15. Ibid.
16. Regis McAuley, "Daddy Wags Beats War Drums, Injuns Awaiting Game Hum," *Cleveland Press*, June 13, 1964.
17. Donnelly.
18. Regis McAuley, "Daddy Wags Beats War Drums, Injuns Awaiting Game Hum," *Cleveland Press*, June 13, 1964.
19. Ibid.
20. Russell Schneider, "Leon Wagner," *Cleveland Plain Dealer*, July 17, 1965.
21. Ibid.
22. Hal Lebovitz, "Wags Hits Clean-up on Young Toughies," *Cleveland Plain Dealer*, March 20, 1965.
23. Russell Schneider, "Daddy Wags, Playing Regularly, Puts Pep Into Sputtering Indians," *Cleveland Plain Dealer*, August 20, 1966.
24. Russell Schneider, "Daddy Wags Eyes Buckpasser Role," *Cleveland Plain Dealer*, February 18, 1967.
25. Russell Schneider, "Daddy Wags Promises 40 HRs 'If They Let Me Play,'" *Cleveland Plain Dealer*, March 16, 1968.
26. Russell Schneider, "Indians Obtain Hall and Snyder to Buttress Flychasing Brigade," *Cleveland Plain Dealer*, June 29, 1968.
27. Jerome Holtzman, "'Intelligent'—That's Wags' Word for White Sox," *Chicago Sun-Times*, July 6, 1968.
28. Regis McAuley, "Daddy Wags Enjoys Minors—Less Pressure, More Laughs," *Cleveland Press*, June 21, 1969.
29. Bill Plaschke, "Bitter Ending," *Los Angeles Times*, January 25, 2004.
30. Ibid.
31. Hal Lebovitz, "Sad Ending," *Lorain* (Ohio) *Morning Journal*, January 11, 2004.
32. Ibid.

EDGAR "BLUE" WASHINGTON

BY MARK V. PERKINS

THE MERE MENTION OF EDGAR "Blue" Washington evokes thought and a curious smile, as he is undoubtedly one of the rarest of all Negro League treasures. During the early part of the twentieth century, Edgar flaunted his athleticism as a gallant young prizefighter in open-air boxing arenas in Southern California and on weekend afternoons could be found toeing the rubber for the semiprofessional Los Angeles White Sox, where his moundsmanship landed him a slot in the starting rotation of Rube Foster's famed Chicago American Giants baseball club. After a few years in the sandlots, he held down first base for a fledgling Kansas City Monarchs franchise before hanging up his spikes to forge a career as a motion picture film actor. Edgar Washington, a brave African-American man, earning a scattered living in an unyielding world: boxer, ballplayer, actor — a true pioneer.

Washington was a ruggedly charismatic character, whether knocking heads, bruising baseballs or performing his own movie stunts as a close family friend, Woody Strode, marveled in his autobiography, *Goal Dust: The Warm and Candid Memoirs of a Pioneer Black Athlete and Actor*: "Athletically, Blue had the ability to do just about any damn thing he wanted. He was a hell of a baseball player, a big powerful man; he went about six-feet-five and weighed well over 200 pounds."[1] Washington's unshakable image followed him like a star throughout his life: boisterous, entertaining and forever a rolling stone. Strode explained: "Blue was a playboy, for want of a better name. He liked the girls, bright lights, and so forth and he really put his heart and soul into it.... Blue could have been a star. At one point they gave him his own dressing room.... Blue was making seventy-five dollars a day when guys were making ten, fifteen dollars a week. He'd get four or five days in, have $300 in his pocket and nobody would see him again until the money was gone. The Washington family was constantly looking for Blue because some director was holding up a production until he could be found."[2]

Edgar Hughes Washington was born on February 26, 1898, in Los Angeles, and was raised along with five siblings.[3] His mother ran a nursery at the local grammar school and took additional work that included anything from janitorial work to sewing in order to raise her family.[4] Edgar was a rambunctious kid with an appetite to go along with his larger-than-life stature. His family called him "Biscuits," for he would often devour an entire pan of baked delights before his brothers and sister arrived home from school.[5] The nickname that eventually stuck was "Blue," and it came from none other than Frank Capra, one of his best pals in the ethnically diverse surroundings of Lincoln Heights, East Los Angeles, and later one of the most powerful film directors in Hollywood during the 1930s and '40s.[6]

Boxer Kid Blue

Rather than follow in the footsteps of his older brothers as laborers at the local brickyard, the 14-year-old, nearly 6-foot, 170-pounder began boxing professionally as "Kid" Blue (after fudging his age). In a time when Jack Johnson reigned as the first African-American world heavyweight champion, Blue fought gamely against well-seasoned opponents 10 years his senior, enduring relentless hecklings in the largest arenas the area had to offer. He fought a four-round exhibition match against 6-foot-2-inch Harry Wills, then holder of the World Colored Heavyweight Championship. A *Los Angeles Times* newspaper article published on November 23, 1914, described the previous afternoon's bout: "Gosh! Harry Wills floors Blue.... The Children's Hospital got $323.96, Kid Blue got a sore jaw.... Wills took himself thoroughly in earnest, wading into Kid Blue in the second round of their argument and precipitating him upon his posterior organism. Four rounds with Blue, two with Jimmy Carter and four with Bob Summerville constituted a day's work for the tall guy."[7]

Washington's professional boxing career is chronicled in Kevin R. Smith's *The Sundowners: The History of the Black Prizefighter 1870-1930, Volume II, Part One.* As Kid Blue, he fought a half-dozen times without defeat in three years, debuting with an August 23, 1912, first-round knockout of Jim Newton and concluding his career with a September 21, 1915, six-round draw against Arthur Collins.[8]

Remaining true to Blue's character, a retrospective article titled "Graveyards Close When He Quits" in the *Times* on August 19, 1920, reads: "One of Harold Lloyd's supporting cast is an old-time colored heavyweight boxer named 'Kid' Blue, who never loses an opportunity of telling how 'bad' he used to be. 'On the level, now,' said Lloyd. 'Were you a tough man in the ring—just how tough were you?' 'Draw yo' own conclusions, Mistah Lloyd,' answered the solemn veteran, 'when Ah stopped fightin' they closed up the graveyards.'"[9] Acclaimed boxing historian Smith followed with "Edgar was well-liked in Hollywood. He had a friendly manner, was intelligent and always ready to make people laugh. In his early career he worked a great deal with Harold Lloyd, the silent film comedian who was a master of physical stunts. Lloyd was close enough with Blue that the former rented the ex-fighter one of his bungalows in Los Angeles. Lloyd found Blue to be amusing and often times retold stories to the press of Edgar's musings."[10]

To those who knew him, Blue was considered to be a "bad boy," an attitude molded from the rough-and-tumble neighborhood in which he grew.[11] Between stints in the ring, trouble reluctantly found young Washington when on December 8, 1914, a *Los Angeles Times* article noted that "two young colored men awaited trial on charges of auto machine thefts" and that one of these youths, Edgar Washington, would come up for trial in the juvenile court.[12] The results of which are irrelevant as Washington sidestepped the chain gang, donned vertical stripes and went on to compete with the finest players on two of the greatest baseball teams in Negro League history.

Pitcher Ed Washington

While pitching for Lonnie Goodwin's Los Angeles White Sox, Rube Foster—the Father of Black Baseball—discovered Edgar during the Chicago American Giants' 1916 West Coast spring-training schedule. Washington was invited to travel along and pitch for the legendary team, one comparable to the fabled New York Yankees' Murderers' Row, at a time when Babe Ruth was still polishing his pitching skills as a member of the Boston Red Sox. This Giants team produced three National Baseball Hall of Famers: Pete Hill, Pop Lloyd, and of course Foster.

During Washington's brief tenure with the American Giants, he pitched in seven games, recording three victories against one loss versus white aggregations of the Pacific Coast and Northwestern Leagues.[13] "Ed Washington," as the sportswriters initially referred to him, ruled the mound with an unorthodox pitching style. Of his first appearance, a March 31, 1916, contest against the Portland Beavers in Sacramento, the *Chicago Defender* on April 8, reported the action:

"Inability to hit the offerings of Ed Washington, 18-year-old pitching phenom picked up in Los Angeles by 'Rube' Foster and the poor fielding of Shortstop Ward were two things that beat Portland again Friday, the American Giants walking off with the second game by a 5 to 2 score. With a deceiving underhanded delivery and some shoots a sight more deceiving than his delivery, Washington tolled on the mound to good effect. Inning after inning Mack [Walter "Judge" McCredie] sent his heavy hitters to the plate, only to have the majority of them return to their starting point. Portland's two runs were not primarily the fault of the youthful black hurler. They were both made after Second Baseman Bauchman had allowed two men on bases by boots on easy chances. ... Although Portland got men on in the second and third, they were unable to get around, due to the effective pitching of Washington."[14]

The *Portland Oregonian* on April 1, 1916, carried another account of Washington's near-shutout pitching performance headlined, "Colored Giants With

Edgar "Blue" Washington and young John Wayne in Haunted Gold. *Courtesy Kysa Lenán Washington.*

Gem'm'm Known as Washington in Box Wallop Beavers":

"The Chicago Colored Giants gave his Coast League hopes another severe lacing today—the second straight. This time the score was 5 to 2. ... The colored gentleman plunked the boys for some 13 safety big swats. ... Washington was having the time of his life out there in the box for the Negroes. ... He allowed only five hits and would have pitched a shutout except for a couple of boots by Bauchman in the seventh inning."[15]

As good fortune would have it, Washington's string of stellar pitching performances seemed to all but guarantee him a spot on the Giants' Opening Day roster. On April 29 the *Chicago Defender* printed an enthusiastic article with the lead "American Giants open to-day, big crowd see opener, eighteen-year-old Washington may pitch":

"The Chicago American Giants left Chicago October 15, and when they return they will have been gone just six months and fifteen days. They won the Winter League pennant in California, jumped from Los Angeles to Havana, Cuba, a distance of 4,700 miles, to play in the Cuban Winter League, winning seven and losing eight games. Then they jumped to Sacramento, keeping their spring schedule intact. They have won 57 games and lost 15 up to date. When the Giants hit Chicago they will have traveled over 20,000 miles. ... Rube picked up a youngster from Los Angeles named Washington and he is a comer, a cool clever pitcher with a curve ball and plenty of nerve to use it. ... Mr. Foster has plenty up his sleeve.

Come out and welcome the boys and see a real ball game."[16]

However, unbeknownst to the local Chicagoans, Washington's string of remarkable pitching performances had begun to unravel. In a rocky start on April 16, 1916, he hit a batter, walked four, and allowed five runs to score in one inning. Catching up with the game on the 29th, the *Defender* headlined its story "American Giants Win Uphill Game 10-8, Rube Sends Washington to the Showers When He Blows."[17]

Back then, word traveled slowly to the Eastern periodicals, and it wasn't until the May 6 *Defender* hit the streets that the tale unfolded: "Woods and Washington given walking papers, failure to keep in condition costs Los Angeles boy his place. ... The boys were all well, but the two new faces we expected to see were missing. Woods had been handed his release because his arm went back on him and Washington, the kid pitcher of Los Angeles, who was the most promising in years, was found with a couple questionable characters (white, at that), and too much King Alcohol under his belt. No place on a ball team for those who want to get soused, and the little blue slip was handed Washington, to his dismay. Any manager is forced to have discipline. So be it with Foster."[18]

Down the coast, the *California Eagle* picked up the story on April 29 and offered another twist, as sportswriter Hilbert L. Rozier questioned in his column: "We never had any reason to believe 'Rube' Foster doesn't know much about ball players until he sent Washington and Woods home. Woods says that Rube told them their arms needed rest but we are inclined to believe he was a little bit out of form when he said this. When 'Blue' Washington was pitching at Seal Garden last Sunday he crossed Baker, his catcher up. Baker side-stepped and the ball went all the way to the grandstand before striking the ground. The grandstand is 90 feet back of the home plate. Does not look much like a sore arm, does it?"[19]

With a giant opportunity spoiled, Blue returned home, hooked on with his former White Sox teammates and seamlessly assumed his pitching duties. Washington also earned his keep as the team's hard-hitting shortstop and put together a banner 1916-17 season.[20] At one point during the season, the White Sox strolled along undefeated as described in

The only known photograph of Edgar "Blue" Washington's pitching days with the 1916 Chicago American Giants. Pictured left to right are: Pete Hill; Harry Bauchman; Steve Dixon; Tom Johnson; Judy Gans; Bruce Petway; Rube Foster; Leroy Grant; Washington; unknown #1 (possibly C. Bernice Wood); John Henry "Pop" Lloyd; unknown #2 (possibly Clarkson Brazelton); and Frank Duncan. This panoramic photo was taken by Stuart Thomson in mid-April 1916 inside Athletic Park, Vancouver, British Columbia. It was auctioned in the spring of 2012 by Robert Edward Auctions and sold for an astounding $38,513.00. (Positive player identifications by Gary Ashwill and Mark V. Perkins)

a *San Diego Tribune* article dated October 19, 1916: "The White Sox claim to have passed through the present season without suffering the sting of defeat, and are most hopeful of burying the most bragged of San Diegans along with the rest they have laid on the wayside. ... Goodwin has a staff of three pitchers and two catchers, but will likely employ his star battery Edgar Washington and Tommy Shores. Washington is said to possess a tremendous amount of steam."[21]

The September 22, 1916, *Chicago Defender* boasted, "Far Western Champions Los Angeles White Sox; Managed by Lonnie Goodwin, recognized as the best baseball man in the west. He was one of the best pitchers in baseball, being the official scout of the American Giants. It was from his club that the American Giants were able to use Woods and Washington, two of his star pitchers, on their recent trip on the coast; both are highly spoken of by Rube Foster. In the past four years the American Giants was the only club that has bested them in a series of games. Out of thirty-six games they have played this season they have returned victorious in thirty. They will play in the Winter league this fall in California, having been voted the franchise of the American Giants, who will play the winter in Palm Beach, Florida."[22]

On September 12, 1918, Washington honored his country and registered for the World War I draft, though he was not selected for service.[23] Prior to enlistment, he married 16-year-old Marion Lenán, from Kingston, Jamaica, who gave birth to their son, Kenneth Stanley Washington, on August 31, 1918.[24] Kenny Washington eventually became a football legend, the first African-American to play baseball at UCLA, the first Bruin player to be named an All-American and to have his number retired.[25] His teammate, Jackie Robinson, described him as the greatest football player he had ever seen, adding that Kenny "had everything needed for greatness — size, speed, tremendous strength, and was probably the greatest long passer ever."[26] Kenny was the first black to reintegrate the National Football League, signing a contract to play professional football for the Los Angeles Rams in 1946. Had Kenny been allowed to come directly into the league at his prime, when he was the number-one player in the nation in 1940, he could have been one of the greatest players in NFL history.[27]

Indeed, the Washingtons were a family of firsts. Edgar's younger brother Roscoe "Rocky" Washington holds the distinction of being the first black lieutenant on the Los Angeles Police Department.[28] Rocky's wife, Hazel, a socialite who became a business partner with actress Rosalind Russell, earned her star as one of Hollywood's first black licensed hairdressers. It's important to note that Uncle Rocky and Aunt Hazel are credited for raising the young Kenny Washington and setting the standard that carried him into the prestigious UCLA.[29] Grandson Kenny Washington Jr. was a baseball star at the University of Southern California, as were great-grandsons Kraig and Kirk Washington, both of whom were drafted by the Chicago Cubs and played minor-league baseball.[30]

Ballplayer-actor Edgar "Blue" Washington and his Chicago American Giants teammates.

Slugger Blue Washington

While Blue eked out a living playing semipro ball, he hankered for the bright lights of Hollywood and stumbled onto the silver screen with his comedic silent film debut in *Rowdy Ann* (1919), with moderate success.[31] By the spring of 1920, however, Washington was invited to join his former Los Angeles White Sox teammates George "Tank" Carr and John Wesley Donaldson as members of J.L. Wilkinson's newly formed Kansas City Monarchs.[32] After his debut with the club, the *Kansas City Star* wrote on April 19, "The batting of Edgar Washington was a feature. He got four hits out of as many trips to the plate. Two of the wallops were 3-baggers, one coming with the bases loaded and the other with two teammates on."[33] The *Kansas City Sun* hopped on the Blue bandwagon with a May 1 article touting, "On first base is Big Blue Washington, a new man from Los Angeles, Mendez says he has a find, a hard hitter and a player with lots of pep."[34]

Washington was the starting first baseman for the Monarchs and dotted sports pages with outstanding play as noted by the *Chicago Defender* during a May 9, 1920, league game that spoiled the debut of the St. Louis Giants: "There were no thrill producing stunts on either side until the sixth, when with two outs, Washington, the movie star from the coast, now playing first base for the Monarchs, slammed one out in right field for two sacks; Donaldson followed with a two out station blow to left field, the movie star scoring."[35]

Blue furthered his batting exploits on May 22 as a *Muncie* (Indiana) *Morning Star* article described the action: "The K.C. squad batted around and Washington had the unique distinction to make a double and triple in one inning. ... Triples by Lightner, Washington and Shively went to the fence."[36] Word galloped around baseball circles, for both his baseball prowess and big-screen success as a May 22 spread offered by the *Chicago Defender* noted: "Blue Washington, who has been featured recently in the motion picture, 'Haunted Spooks,' is playing first base for the K.C.'s and he is not only a grand fielder, but he is one of the heaviest batters in the game today."[37]

After a few months of arduous barnstorming, Washington made history when he played in the Monarchs' very first Negro National League game at Association Park in Kansas City on May 29, 1920.[38] He played his final game on June 15, appearing as a pitcher, and was unceremoniously knocked out of the box in the first inning after allowing five runs.[39] In 24 official league games, the 6-foot-2 slugger batted .275 with 16 RBIs for a heralded Monarchs team that boasted future Hall of Famers José Méndez and Bullet Rogan.[40] Why did his promising baseball career end so abruptly? Perhaps one could venture a guess that all the ballyhooed press had gone to his head. One thing for sure, and not so surprisingly for athletes from any era, he would again rejoin the Los Angeles White Sox for few games in December 1920 and was believed to have played a number of California Winter League independent play games with Alexander's Giants.[41]

Actor Blue Washington

While using the screen name "Edgar Blue," Washington became one the earliest African-American actors in the silent-film era, having been selected for some of the finest comedic and dramatic roles of his time. As Blue Washington, he holds the distinction of being one of only two black cowboy sidekicks ever featured in B-westerns, appearing opposite John Wayne in *Haunted Gold* (1932).[42] Blue acted in some of Hollywood's classics: *The Birth of a Nation* (1915),[43] the first ever epic and highest-grossing silent film of its era; *Beggars of Life* (1928); the original *King Kong* (1933); and *Gone With the Wind* (1939).[44] He acted alongside Richard Arlen, Lex Barker, Charlie Bowers, Warner Baxter, Wallace Beery, Louise Brooks, Bing Crosby, Mildred Davis, Bob Hope, Dorothy Lamour, Vivien Leigh, Harold Lloyd, Ken Maynard, and Fay Tincher.

On July 24, 1927, *Los Angeles Times* film columnist Norbert Lusk described Washington's on-screen performance: "'Blood Ship' Hailed as Best Picture of Week in Gotham. ... Blue Washington, a colored actor, has been singled out for honorable mention on the score of vivid and spontaneous acting."[45] In a film review published in the *Afro-American* on May 4, 1929, Blue's acting abilities were given quite a boost with his portrayal of "Big Mose" in Paramount Pictures' first sound film with dialogue: "In 'Beggars of Life' Edgar Blue Washington, race star, was signed by Paramount for what is regarded as the most important Negro screen role of the year."[46]

Author Thomas Cripps noted Washington's on-screen abilities in *Slow Fade to Black: The Negro in American Film 1900-1942*: "After years of conversation movies began to catch up with social change by creating some Negro roles that were far more assimilationist than would have been possible in the actual life of the twenties. In one of his first pictures, *Beggars of Life*, William Wellman adapted Jim Tully's picaresque tale of hobo life to the screen. Louise Brooks played a young girl who accidentally kills her brutal foster father. Richard Arlen's hobo helps her escape to the dangers of hobo jungles and the brutality of 'Oklahoma Red' (Wallace Beery). Along the way Edgar 'Blue' Washington, a sometime Los Angeles policeman, appears as Mose, a black wanderer who joins the pair in their struggle. Throughout their brief alliance he is their equal and their champion. When Red and Arkansas Snake fight over the girl, it is Mose who knocks a knife from the Snake's hand. He is the train-wise hobo who can elude the railroad police and miraculously forage for food. … In their final moments together Mose and Red dress a corpse in the girl's clothes and set it afire in a boxcar

Edgar "Blue" Washington (as the Butler, gazing from the foot of the staircase) is one of the title apparitions taunting Harold Lloyd in Haunted Spooks

in order to let the girl escape to Canada. Mose covers the escape by elaborately 'tomming' the police. Even so, despite Washington's central role, *Variety* took no notice of his presence."[47]

Cripps followed with a similar critique in a subsequent film: "Rare was a role like Blue Washington's tribal chief who kills a Boer in *Passion Song* (1928). Generally blacks remained exotic atmosphere for white plots even though the bulk of racial ambiguity peered through."[48] Although Washington's landmark role in *Haunted Gold* stands as his most visible, he is thought to have appeared in close to 100 films. Vintage Hollywood movie posters, lobby cards and glossies featuring Washington's image have fetched a premium in the collectible markets.

The spotlight on Washington's acting career dimmed with stereotypical roles in movies such as *Law of the Jungle* (1942), *Tales of Manhattan* (1942), and *Tarzan's Magic Fountain* (1949), after which he faded into obscurity with brief, uncredited screen performances in *Stars and Stripes Forever* (1952), *The Wings of Eagles* (1957),[49] and *The Horse Soldiers* (1959).[50] Author and Negro Leagues baseball researcher Gary Ashwill noted: "According to some accounts Blue had to endure hazing and practical jokes from white co-workers, and often appeared in the credits as 'handyman' instead of actor."[51]

The recollections are varied, but none encapsulates his personality more than in Woody Strode's memoir: "Blue could have been a star. At one point they gave him his own dressing room. They made a picture in which he was the star but they never did release it because towards the end Blue screwed up and disappeared. It was called *Ormsby the Faithful Servant*. Blue played Ormsby. They shot the last scenes out on the Santa Cruz Island and Blue never showed up. They spent a lot of money on that picture; Blue alone was getting $750 a week. I've never forgotten that; that was a fortune. And it was that production that pretty much ended his career in the movies."[52]

As far as the historical marker left from his extensive acting career goes, the closing sentiment should suffice; Edgar "Blue" Washington, a film pioneer and for such trailblazing efforts, for which a host of African-American successors are unwittingly grateful.

Edgar Hughes "Blue" Washington, died on September 15, 1970, at Mira Loma Hospital in Lancaster, California. He was laid to rest on September 18 at Evergreen Memorial Park, the oldest existing cemetery in Los Angeles.[53] A single burial in a double-grave plot became his eternal resting place. Beside him lies son Kenny, who died less than a year later, on June 24, 1971.[54]

Acknowledgments: I would like to thank Gary Ashwill and Peter Gorton, who both contributed mightily. John Klima, who urged me as "Blue's champion" to fight the good fight, and Jeremy Krock, with the *Negro Leagues Grave Marker Project*, honoring those forgotten baseball stars, like Blue Washington, with proper visual remembrances.

NOTES

1 Woody Strode and Sam Young, *Goal Dust: The Warm and Candid Memoirs of a Pioneer Black Athlete and Actor* (Aurora, Ontario: Madison Books, 1984), 53.

2 Ibid.

3 Author Mark V. Perkins has chosen February 26 as Edgar Washington's birthday, although February 6 is listed in the Social Security index and February 12 is listed on his death certificate (and thus canonized as the official date), since the February 26 date is written on the earliest document known to be signed by Washington himself, his World War I draft registration card.

4 Donald Bogle, *The Story of Black Hollywood: Bright Boulevards, Bold Dreams* (New York: Ballantine Books, 2005), 142.

5 Woody Strode and Sam Young, 53.

6 Joseph McBride, *Frank Capra: The Catastrophe of Success* (Jackson, Mississippi: University Press of Mississippi, 1992), 35.

7 "Gosh! Harry Wills Floors Blue," *Los Angeles Times*, November 23, 1914.

8 Kevin R. Smith, *The Sundowners: The History of the Black Prizefighter 1870-1930, Volume II Part One* (New York: CCK Publications, 2006), 94.

9 "Graveyards Close When He Quits," *Los Angeles Times*, August 19, 1920.

10 Kevin R. Smith, 93.

11 Donald Bogle, 142.

12 "Comb City for Auto Thieves," *Los Angeles Times*, December 8, 1914.

13 Email correspondence with Gary Ashwill, 2012.

14. "Beaver Veteran Hurler Looks Same to Giants," *Chicago Defender*, April 8, 1916.

15. Roscoe Fawcett, "Hig And Sothoron Lose To Tune of 5-2," *Portland Oregonian*, April 1, 1916.

16. "American Giants Open To-Day," *Chicago Defender*, April 29, 1916.

17. "American Giants Win Uphill Game 10-8," *Chicago Defender*, April 29, 1916.

18. Home Run, "E. Pluvius Is King," *Chicago Defender*, May 6, 1916.

19. Hilbert L. Rozier, "Our Athletics," *California Eagle*, April 29, 1916.

20. William F. McNeil, *The California Winter League: America's First Integrated Professional Baseball League* (Jefferson, North Carolina: McFarland & Company, 2002), 60. See also email correspondence with Peter Gorton, 2012, The John Wesley Donaldson Network, "Teams," johndonaldson.bravehost.com/t.html and "Calendars 1917-1919" johndonaldson.bravehost.com/ds.html, accessed January 1, 2013.

21. "White Sox Proud Record," *San Diego Tribune*, October 19, 1916.

22. "Brilliant Pitchers' Battle to Sox, 4-3," *Chicago Defender*, September 22, 1916.

23. National Archives, Atlanta. William F. McNeil, 61. See also Agate Type, "George Carr, Movie Actor, August 12, 2007." agatetype.typepad.com/agate_type/george-carr/, accessed January 1, 2013.

24. Woody Strode and Sam Young, 52. Personal and telephone interviews with Kysa Lenán Washington, 2012.

25. Woody Strode and Sam Young, 59; Donald Bogle, 143; Baseball Reference, BR Bullpen, "Kenny Washington" baseball-reference.com/bullpen/Kenny_Washington, accessed January 1, 2013.

26. Thomas G. Smith, "Outside the Pale: The Exclusion of Blacks From the National Football League, 1934-1936," *Journal of Sports History*, Vol. 15, No. 3 (Winter 1988): 266, aafla.org/SportsLibrary/JSH/JSH1988/JSH1503/jsh1503d.pdf, accessed January 1, 2013.

27. "Lost History: The NFL's Jackie Robinson," *Sports Illustrated*, October 12, 2009. Kenny Washington Stadium Foundation, "Kenny," kwsfoundation.org/kenny/, accessed January 1, 2013. Personal, telephone, email correspondence with Stephen Lampson, 2012. Additionally, Kenny Washington appeared in a number of films, from *While Thousands Cheer* (1940), an all-black-cast sports drama, to *The Jackie Robinson Story* (1950), in which he is credited as the "Tigers Manager."

28. US Census Bureau, 1930 US Census; Agate Type, "Forgotten Negro Leaguers, Ajay Deforest Johnson, Part II," July 4, 2008, posted by Gary Ashwill, agatetype.typepad.com/agate_type/forgotten_negro_leaguers/, accessed January 1, 2013; Association Of Black Law Enforcement Executives, A History Of Honorable Service Since 1886, "Lieutenant Roscoe "Rocky" Washington," ablelapd.com/article__rockywashington_pg2.html, accessed January 1, 2013.

29. Donald Bogle, 141.

30. Black College Nines, Black Pioneers of College Baseball, "Kenny Washington (UCLA)," February 16, 2010, blackcollegenines.com/?p=790, accessed January 10, 2013. Personal interview, telephone interview, email correspondence with Kirk Washington, 2012, and personal interview with Kraig Washington, 2012.

31. Internet Movie Database IMDb, "Blue Washington," imdb.com/name/nm0913405/, accessed January 1, 2013.

32. Email correspondence with Peter Gorton, 2012. The John Wesley Donaldson Network, "Teams" johndonaldson.bravehost.com/t.html, and The John Wesley Donaldson Network, "Calendars 1917-1919" and "Calendars 1920-1922," johndonaldson.bravehost.com/ds.html, accessed January 1, 2013. See also Agate Type, "George Carr, Movie Actor," August 12, 2007. Posted by Gary Ashwill, agatetype.typepad.com/agate_type/george-carr/, accessed January 1, 2013. "The Monarchs Play Today," *Kansas City Star*, April 18, 1920.

33. "An Easy Win for the Monarchs," *Kansas City Times*, April 19, 1920.

34. "Sports," *Kansas City Sun*, May 1, 1920.

35. Dave Wyatt, "K.C. Monarchs Trim the St. Louis Giants," *Chicago Defender*, May 15, 1920.

36. "Slugfest Held at Walnut Park," Muncie (Indiana) *Morning Star*, May 23, 1920.

37. "K.C. Monarchs Here Sunday," *Chicago Defender*, May 22, 1920.

38. "The Monarchs Play Today," *Kansas City Star*, May 29, 1920.

39. Email correspondence with Peter Gorton, 2012. See also The John Wesley Donaldson Network, "Teams" and "Calendars 1920-1922." "A Late Rally Beat Monarchs," *Kansas City Times*, June 16, 1920.

40. Seamheads, "Edgar Washington," seamheads.com/NegroLgs/player.php?ID=811, accessed January 1, 2013.

41. William F. McNeil, 74, 78.

42. Boyd Magers, "The Westerns Of John Wayne," westernclippings.com/westernsof/johnwayne_westernsof.shtml, accessed January 1, 2013.

43. Joseph McBride, 63. Internet Movie Database IMDb, "Blue Washington," imdb.com/name/nm0913405/, accessed January 1, 2013.

44. American Film Institute Catalogue of Feature Films AFI, "Blue Washington," afi.com/members/catalog/SearchResult.aspx?s=&retailCheck=&Type=PN&CatID=DATABIN_CAST&ID.=22331&AN_ID=16710&searchedFor=Blue_Washington, accessed January 1, 2013.

45 Norbert Lusk, "Columbia Produces Success," *Los Angeles Times*, July 24, 1927.

46 "Wings, Beggars of Life, Sawdust Paradise," *The Afro-American*, May 4, 1929.

47 Thomas Cripps, *Slow Fade to Black: The Negro in American Film 1900-1942* (New York: Oxford University Press, 1977), 154, 165.

48 Ibid.

49 Internet Movie Database IMDb, "Blue Washington," imdb.com/name/nm0913405/, accessed January 1, 2013.

50 Author Mark V. Perkins' positive identification of Edgar "Blue" Washington appearing as "Himself-Blue," servant at Newton Station Hotel, a previously undocumented credit in John Ford's thunderous motion-picture spectacle *The Horse Soldiers* (1959), starring John Wayne and William Holden.

51 Email correspondence with Gary Ashwill, 2012.

52 Woody Strode and Sam Young, 53.

53 Personal and telephone interviews with Marvel Washington, 2012.

54 Evergreen Memorial Park, Los Angeles.

BERNIE WILLIAMS

BY ROB EDELMAN

CENTER FIELD AT YANKEE Stadium is hallowed ground. Once upon a time, Joe DiMaggio and Mickey Mantle patrolled this section of the House That Ruth Built. Now, granted, Bernie Williams — whose 16-season New York Yankees career lasted from 1991 to 2006 — may at best be a borderline Cooperstown inductee, but he is a more-than-worthy successor to Joe D. and The Mick as a center fielder par excellence. Plus, as was the case with his two predecessors, the Bronx Bombers were his only major-league team. It is understandable, then, that "Bern Baby Bern" predates "Feel the Bern" as a catchphrase among fans of another celebrated Bernie: Senator Bernie Sanders, the 2016 presidential hopeful.

Actually, Bernie Williams's given name is Bernabé (rather than Bernard). He was born Bernabé Williams Figueroa Jr. on September 13, 1968, in San Juan, Puerto Rico. His father, Bernabé Sr., was a merchant seaman and his mother, Rufina, was a high-school teacher-principal and college professor. The family resided in the Bronx during the year after Williams's birth but then settled in Vega Alta, a town around 45 minutes outside San Juan. As a youngster, Williams played Little League and Babe Ruth League baseball; among his opponents were future major leaguers Ivan Rodriguez and Juan Gonzalez. He also regularly attended winter-league games, but baseball was not his sole sport. At age 15, he won four gold medals and a silver medal at the 1984 Central American and Caribbean Junior Championships in Athletics, an international track meet held in San Juan, and was acknowledged as one of the world's fastest 400-meter runners in his age group.[1] (Ironically, during his major-league career, Williams never became a feared basestealer, swiping only 147 bases and adding eight more during the postseason.)

Williams grew to be a 6-foot-2, 205-pounder. He was just 16 when, in 1985, New York Yankees scout Roberto Rivera noticed him and wished to sign him. The youngster was dispatched to a baseball training camp in Connecticut, and was inked by the team on his 17th birthday. As he began his minor-league career, he attended the University of Puerto Rico; at this juncture his intention was to earn a degree in biology and, perhaps, also take pre-med classes. But he decided to focus on baseball, realizing that his studies could impede his rise within the Yankees system.

Williams's first minor-league season came in 1986, when he was assigned to the Gulf Coast League Yankees, the team's Rookie League affiliate; he appeared in 61 games, hit a respectable .270 with 2 home runs and 25 RBIs, and was selected to the league's All-Star team. At the time he was strictly a right-handed hitter and speed still was a part of his game, as he pilfered 33 bases. Then in 1987, Williams split the season between Fort Lauderdale in the Class-A Florida State League (where he hit .155 in 25 games) and Short Season-A Oneonta in the New York-Penn League (where he improved to .344, also in 25 games). On November 8 he was added to the Yankees' 40-man roster.

Williams's true breakout minor-league season came in 1988, when he hit a robust .335 (with 7 home runs and 45 RBIs) in 92 games for Prince William in the Class-A Carolina League. He won the league's batting title, but also was sidelined for the season after fracturing the right navicular bone in his wrist while crashing into the outfield wall in a July 14 game against Hagerstown. The following year, Williams arrived at Yankees spring training as a much-heralded prospect. "He is their phenom this spring, their kid with unlimited talent and untapped potential," wrote Michael Martinez in the *New York Times*. "He is only 20 years old, but the coaches who work with him daily say he has the skills of a big leaguer. The people in the front office speak of his intellectual and his physical growth. They all say he simply can't miss." Added Frank Howard, the Yankees' hitting coach, "He's a quality-looking athlete. He has fantastic bat speed, he can sting the ball and he has great reflexes."[2]

But Williams still was a work-in-progress. He was promoted to the Columbus Clippers of the Triple-A International League at the start of the 1989 campaign, but after hitting just .216 in 50 game, he was demoted to the Double-A Eastern League Albany-Colonie Yankees, where he improved to .252 in 91 games. On February 23, 1990, he married the former Waleska Ortega; they have three children (Bernie Jr., Beatriz, and Bianca). Initially, the family resided in northern New Jersey, with Waleska and the youngsters spending the school year in Puerto Rico. Then in 1999, they purchased a home in Armonk, New York. "Once we had an opportunity to settle in, we fell in love with the area," Williams declared in 2003. "It's very quiet. It feels like the countryside. It looks a little like the part of Puerto Rico where I grew up."[3]

The budding big leaguer spent the entire 1990 season at Albany-Colonie, where he made it into 134 games and hit .281 with 8 home runs and 54 RBIs while leading the league with 98 walks and 39 stolen bases. His prospect status was on the rise: He was named an Eastern League and *Baseball America* Double-A All-Star and was cited by *Baseball America* as the second-best Eastern League prospect. Also, while in the minors, he began using both hands while playing Wiffle ball with a sibling. In so doing, he realized that he could effectively hit left-handed; he queried Buck Showalter, his manager at both Fort Lauderdale and Albany-Colonie, to win the okay to practice switch hitting—and so he began coming to bat for the first time from the left side of the plate.

During the following two campaigns, Williams further established himself at Columbus, respectively hitting .294 in 78 games and .306 in 95 games. Baseball-Reference.com lists conflicting figures for his career minor-league batting average, home-run total, and total number of games; representative numbers are .285, 48, and 660. Nonetheless, two months into the 1991 season, he was primed for his

Bernie Williams, center fielder extraordinaire and acclaimed guitarist.

big-league bow. "Clearly, there are (Clippers) players ready for promotion," wrote the *New York Times'* Michael Martinez on June 11. One of them was Bernie Williams. "He's got all the tools," observed Clete Boyer, a Columbus coach. "When he gets up there, he should stay."[4] What surely was the season's highlight for Williams was his major-league debut, which came on July 7 against the Baltimore Orioles. Replacing the injured Roberto Kelly, he was the starting center fielder, batting eighth and going 1-for-3 with a sacrifice fly and two RBIs in a 5-3 loss. "It's very different," Williams declared of playing before 43,505 fans in the Bronx ballyard. "I've been dreaming of this since I signed six years ago." He said he "was nervous out there at first. I didn't expect this many fans."[5] Williams's first big-league hit was a ninth-inning single off Greg Olson, and his initial home run came seven days later against California's Chuck Finley. Prior to his call-up, Williams had been named to the Triple-A All-Star team, but his promotion prevented him from appearing. He was the Bronx Bombers' starting center fielder for the remainder of the season, playing in 85 games and batting .238 with 3 home runs and 34 RBIs. His big-league high point was a five-hit game against the Cleveland Indians on October 5.

Across the decades, rookies in all sports have been subjected to hazing by their veteran peers. Bernie Williams was no different. However, his mild manner made him a special target for Mel Hall, a Yankee flychaser. As reported in a 2014 *SB Nation* article penned by Greg Hanlon, "With Williams, Hall took rookie hazing to abusive extremes. … He called Williams 'Bambi,' mocking his large doe eyes, which were magnified by his bulky glasses. Alternately, he called him 'Mr. Zero,' Hall's assessment of Williams' value. He once taped a sign on Williams' locker saying 'Mr. Zero,' and would say, 'Shut up, Zero,' whenever Williams tried to speak, something that reportedly once nearly brought Williams to tears. Things got so vicious that management interceded on Williams' behalf. 'Mel was basically bullying Bernie and we put an end to it,' responded Buck Showalter … who was then a Yankee coach. …"[6]

In 1992 Williams was back in Columbus but he also spent part of the season with the Yankees. He started off in the Bronx but was returned to the Clippers on April 15 after appearing in two games. Clearly, he was not destined to remain at Triple A as he was fourth in the International League in slugging percentage, fifth in on-base percentage, and fifth in the batting race, making it into 95 games and hitting .306. His nine triples were tied for the league lead; he was the Yankees' minor-league player of the month in June and an International League midseason and postseason All-Star. Most impressive of all, *Baseball America* rated him the fourth-best International League prospect. After his recall to the Bronx on July 31, he appeared in 60 games and hit .281 with 5 home runs and 26 RBIs. Williams played left field in four games and right field in another four, but was shifted to center field on August 7. From then on, he appeared in every game and played every inning for the rest of the season, and also was the Yankees' leadoff hitter. His 1992 highlights included a 10-game hitting streak (September 2 through 13) and a four-hit game on September 12. After the season, he briefly played for Arecibo in the Puerto Rican winter league before sustaining ligament damage in his left knee and undergoing arthroscopic surgery on December 19.[7]

The 1993 campaign was extra-special for Williams: His minor-league apprenticeship was completed, and he spent the entire season with the Yankees as the starting center fielder. However, a slow start resulted in George Steinbrenner, the easily exasperated Yankees owner, putting pressure on general manager Gene Michael to trade Williams. Rumor had it that he would be swapped for Larry Walker of the Montreal Expos, but the deal was not consummated.[8] For the season, Williams appeared in 139 games — a muscle strain in his rib cage sidelined him for 23 games between May 13 and June 7 — and he hit a respectable if unspectacular .268, with 12 home runs and 68 RBIs. He was the team's leadoff hitter through the All-Star break; from then on, he mostly batted sixth. His season high points included his smashing his first grand slam on June 14 off the Boston Red Sox' Danny Darwin — the Yankees won the game 4-0 — and hitting in 21 straight games between August 1 and August 23.

The following season, Williams' batting average improved to .289 (with 12 home runs and 57 RBIs) in 108 games. He returned to the leadoff spot for 28 games, during which he hit .362, but also batted sixth, seventh, and eighth. This success may be contrasted to his .178 average for the month of April. His top performances that year included hitting homers in three consecutive games between June 6 and June 8; on June 6, he enjoyed his initial two-homer game (against the Texas Rangers), in which he drove in seven runs. On that occasion, he joined Mickey Mantle, Roy White, Tom Tresh, and Roy Smalley as the fifth Yankee to homer from both sides of the plate in the same game.

Then in 1995, Williams established himself as an upper-echelon big leaguer, appearing in 144 games and hitting .307 (with 18 home runs and 82 RBIs). Yet again, he started off slowly; for the first two months of the season, he hit .204 with 4 homers and 14 RBIs, but hit .333 for the rest of the season (and .354 during the month of August). While he stole eight bases—he and Pat Kelly trailed only Luis Polonia, who pilfered 10—by now it was clear that he was no big-league basestealer. However, while the Yankees were shut down by the Seattle Mariners in the American League Division Series, Williams's postseason debut was a stellar one; in five games he hit .429 with two homers and five RBIs.

Still, George Steinbrenner kept insisting that Williams be traded. For one thing, he was not easy to categorize. Despite his speed, he was no basestealer. Despite his ability to run down fly balls, his throwing arm was less than powerful. While a steady hitter, he was no slugger. That season the Yankees owner even wished to swap him to the San Francisco Giants for Darren Lewis, a fellow center fielder. Such a deal was never consummated. Williams also was displeased when the team renewed his contract for what in baseball terms was a paltry $400,000. He was eligible for arbitration the following season and asked for $3 million; the team countered with $2.555 million, which the ballplayer did not accept. He ended up being awarded $2.6 million in arbitration.[9]

In 1996 Williams proved that the numbers he compiled during the previous campaign were no aberration. He played in 143 games, hitting .305 and establishing what then were career zeniths with 29 home runs and 102 RBIs. His accomplishments that season included three two-home-run games and eight RBIs in a 12-3 triumph against the Detroit Tigers on September 12. He improved on his 1995 postseason performance, hitting .471 with 5 home runs and 11 RBIs in the ALDS and American League Championship Series. While he was the ALCS MVP, his numbers sank in the World Series against the Atlanta Braves; he hit just .167 with a single home run and four RBIs. But no other Yankee matched his RBI total and his home run in the eighth inning of Game Three helped win the game—and allow the Yankees their first world championship since 1978.

Starting in 1997, Williams not only entered his major-league prime but further solidified his status as an elite player and top-of-the-list Yankee. In 129 games he hit .328 (coming in fourth in the American League batting race) with 21 home runs and 100 RBIs, and also earned his initial Gold Glove award. He was seventh in the league in on-base percentage (.408) and eighth in runs scored (107); he was named to his initial All-Star team and in August was the American League Player of the Month, hitting .395 with 8 home runs and 23 RBIs. On the downside, he had two stints on the disabled list, both for strained left hamstrings, and hit just .118 in the five-game ALDS against the Cleveland Indians. And after the campaign, he yet again found himself the subject of trade rumors. One report had him going to the Detroit Tigers for a bevy of young pitchers.[10] Another possible trade involved swapping Williams to the Chicago Cubs for center fielder Lance Johnson.[11]

It was the Yankees' good fortune that Williams was not dealt, as he became the 1998 American League batting champion. In 128 games, he hit .339, homering 26 times and driving in 97 runs. He was his league's Player of the Month in May, when he hit .402 with seven home runs and 27 RBIs. He won another Gold Glove, earned a spot on the All-Star squad, was second in his league in on-base percentage (.422), and finished seventh in the MVP voting. The Yankees' 114-48 campaign was an American League record—and Williams became the first-ever player to win the batting title, a Gold Glove, and a world championship during the same season. While that summer was far from perfect—on June 11, he began a 31-game stint on the disabled list because of a strained right knee, and he hit just .188 during the postseason—he did enter the upper stratosphere of baseball salaries, signing a seven-year, $87.5 million contract on November 25. Also included was an eighth-season $15 million club option. The negotiating with the team was lengthy and contentious; the Yankees were hoping to sign Albert Belle, who instead inked with the Baltimore Orioles. Additionally, the Yankees were involved in a bidding war with the Boston Red Sox for Williams's services.[12]

Williams' all-time best season came in 1999, when he hit .342 in 158 games—third in the AL batting race—while belting 25 home runs and driving in 115 runs. His 202 hits then were a career high, as were his number of games played and RBI total along with his 116 runs and 100 walks. His seven four-hit games were tops in the majors, with two coming against Tampa Bay on June 22 and June 23; yet again, he made his league's All-Star team, and his status as a feared hitter was demonstrated by his being intentionally walked three times in a game against Tampa Bay on September 26. In the postseason, he hit .273 with two home runs and eight RBIs; in the first ALDS game against Texas, he went 3-for-5 with six RBIs. However, most impressive of all, Williams's elite Yankee status was illustrated by his joining Lou Gehrig, Babe Ruth, Joe DiMaggio, and Mickey Mantle as the only Bronx Bombers to drive in at least 100 RBIs and score at least 100 runs in three separate seasons. He and Derek Jeter became the first Yankees with at least 200 hits in the same season since Gehrig and DiMaggio in 1937.

Williams followed up in 2000 by hitting .307 in 141 games and setting career zeniths with 30 home runs and 121 RBIs. He earned the most All-Star Game votes of any American League flychaser; perhaps his best games of the season came on April 23, when he went 3-for-4 with two homers (one lefty and one righty) and five RBIs, and June 17, when he was 4-for-4 with seven RBIs. However, he sat out seven games, starting on August 19, with a right rib cage strain. In the three postseason series, against Oakland, Seattle, and the Mets, Williams hit a respectable .279 with two home runs and five RBIs.

Williams maintained his solid play in 2001, appearing in 146 games and hitting .307 with 26 home runs and 94 RBIs. His 38 doubles were a career high, and he was an American League All-Star for the fifth straight season; among the three hits he collected on June 2 against Cleveland were the 1,500th of his career. Even though he hit only .220 during the postseason, his 11 RBIs were tops for the Yankees—and he was the first player to hit homers in three consecutive ALCS games. But his season's low point had nothing to do with baseball. On April 9 he missed 10 games upon returning to Puerto Rico to be with his father, who was afflicted with pulmonary fibrosis; then in mid-May, he went home again upon the passing of Bernabé Sr., missing a three-game series against Oakland.[13]

Then in 2002, Williams appeared in 154 games and finished third in the AL batting race with a .333 average. He hit 19 home runs and drove in 102 runs; his 204 hits were a career high, and he was 5-for-15 in four postseason games. But this was his final season as a .300 hitter. His average sank to .263 in 2003; he appeared in 119 games, hitting 15 home runs and driving in 64 runs. Still, his name was increasingly appearing on team career stat lists. His 1,950 total hits ranked eighth all-time in Yankees annals; his 241 homers were seventh; his 1,062 RBIs ranked ninth; his 372 doubles ranked fifth. He got his 1,000th RBI on April 2, doubling against the Blue Jays. There were downs in 2003: On May 23 he landed on the 15-day disabled list with a torn medial meniscus in his left knee, for which he underwent arthroscopic surgery. But there were ups: He hit .318 in 17 postseason games; his 19th postseason home run, belted in Game Three of the World Series, was the all-time major-league high, exceeding Reggie Jackson and Mickey Mantle; and his 66 postseason RBIs broke the record of 63 held by David Justice.

The 2004 campaign had Williams hitting .262 in 148 games, with 22 home runs and 70 RBIs. His injuries and illnesses were mounting; he failed to accompany the team to its opening series in Japan, as he was felled by appendicitis. However, on June 10, he became the seventh Yankee to reach the 2,000-hit plateau when he singled against Colorado. Six days later he hit his 250th career home run. And on August 6, he doubled for the 390th time in his career, besting Joe DiMaggio's 389 and taking over fourth place on the all-time Yankee list. Two days later he smashed his 10th grand slam, topping the nine hit by Mickey Mantle and Yogi Berra. He now ranked fourth among all Yankees in this category, behind only Lou Gehrig (with 23 grand slams), DiMaggio (13), and Babe Ruth (12). And he enjoyed a solid postseason, hitting .296 with 3 home runs and 13 RBIs.

Then, in 2005—the final year of his eight-year contract—Williams's batting average sank to .249. In 141 games, he hit 12 home runs and drove in 64 runs. But he was just the 10th Yankee to don pinstripes for 15 seasons; in a game against Baltimore on September 27, his 2,215th hit bested DiMaggio's total and elevated him to fourth place on the team's all-time list. Notwithstanding, the Yankees announced on August 2 that they would not pick up Williams's option for the following season, preferring a $3.5 million buyout. "It's a formality," Williams declared at the time. "I don't think it means I'm going to be a Yankee or not going to be a Yankee. They can still talk to me when the end of the year comes."[14] That December Brian Cashman, the team's general manager, re-signed Williams to a one-season, $1.5 million contract. He put up respectable numbers in 2006, playing in 131 games and hitting .281 with 12 home runs and 61 RBIs. On July 26 his career hit total reached 2,300; on August 16 his 443rd double ranked him second on the all-time team list. That year he also played for his Puerto Rican homeland in the World Baseball Classic. But 2006 was Williams's final major-league season. He wished to return in 2007 and even was willing to be a backup outfielder and occasional pinch-hitter, but he was offered only a minor-league contract with the opportunity to come to spring training and compete for a roster spot. He refused the invitation.

In his career, Williams appeared in 2,076 games. He had 2,336 hits in 7,869 at-bats, of which 449 were doubles, 55 were triples, and 287 were home runs. He drove in 1,257 runs while scoring 1,366. His lifetime batting average was a more-than-respectable .297. He also played in every postseason from 1995 to 2006. In 121 total games, he came to bat 465 times with 128 hits, 29 doubles, and 22 home runs. He drove in 80 runs while scoring 83; his postseason batting average was .275; and his number of game appearances and home-run and RBI totals were tops in major-league history. He was on every American League All-Star team from 1997 through 2001; he won four Gold Gloves (1997, 1998, 1999, and 2000); and he was an American League Silver Slugger in 2002. He was second in the American League in on-base percentage in 1998 (.422) and fourth in 1999 (.435). He was third in on-base plus slugging in 1998 (.997). Williams was a part of four Yankees world championships (1996, 1998, 1999, and 2000).[15]

Even though Williams was unwilling to sign with another major-league team for 2007, the 38-year-old ballplayer refused to officially retire. The following year, he played for Gigantes de Carolina in the Puerto Rico Baseball League, hoping that this would lead to a roster spot on the team that would represent his country in the 2009 World Baseball Classic. "I have as good a chance as anybody to make that team," he declared. "A lot of good players out there, so it's gonna be hard to try and make that team. But I like my chances. They're probably as good as anybody else's."[16] And so he arrived at the Yankees' 2009 spring-training camp to work out, eager to play in the Classic—and perhaps be one of the 25 Bronx Bombers to head north at the start of the season. "After doing this for 16 or 17 years, you get some of that baseball thing back in your system," he noted. "It's like, 'Whoa, maybe I can do this for a couple more years.' I guess that's part of the fantasy that I try not to allow myself to live."[17] But of course, his big-league career was finished.

Despite this, Williams was winning accolades as an all-time-great Yankee. He received a thunderous, 102-second standing ovation upon his first appearance at Yankee Stadium since 2006. The date was September 21, 2008; it was the final game at the "old" ballyard, and he was the final "old-timer" introduced. The following year, he played for his country in the World Baseball Classic, walking twice but getting no hits in five at-bats. Then in 2012, Williams debuted on the Hall of Fame ballot, receiving 55 votes (or 9.6 percent of the balloting). That number fell to 19 in 2013; the 3.3 percent total eliminated him from Cooperstown consideration. But in May 2014 the Yankees announced that he would be honored with a plaque in the Stadium's hallowed Monument Park; on February 16, 2015, the team revealed that his number 51 would be retired. Both occurred in a ceremony on May 24. Williams began his speech by declaring, "This is unbelievable. Never in my wildest dreams I would have thought that a skinny little ... kid from Puerto Rico could be here this day, and (for) this celebration." He observed, "I am so proud to represent Puerto Rico." He thanked Gene Michael for not trading him, Roy White for working on his left-handed swing, Willie Randolph for giving him sage advice—and suggesting that he embrace his success—Joe Torre for "being there for me," and his teammates for "letting me be a part of some of the greatest years of my life." While he wished he could still play, he declared, "You don't want the 2015 version of Bernie Williams. This one is more suited for a guitar than for a bat."[18] As he was so honored, sportswriter Ian O'Connor, who covered Williams for years, observed that he "forever (carried) himself in pinstripes with dignity and grace. He didn't measure up to DiMaggio and Mantle as a player, but go ahead and read the accounts of life with the late Yankee greats and decide if they measured up to Williams as role models and men."[19]

As an ex-big leaguer, Bernie Williams has not rested on his on-field accomplishments. Early on, his talents as a classical guitarist rivaled his athletic ability. At age 8, he became enamored of the flamenco guitar music his father played for him. Five years later he began attending San Juan's Escuela Libre de Musica high school, a private performing-arts institution. Even after signing his pro contract, he regularly played his guitar as a form of relaxation, often in his team's clubhouse.

Never was Bernie Williams ever the stereotypical jock. According to longtime New York sportswriter Joel Sherman, he "was quiet, shy, and predisposed to internalize life. He was nice but not overly friendly. He was bright yet often projected flightiness. He seemed almost to travel in a dream state." Sherman added, "Sitting off alone in a corner, strumming his guitar, was heaven for Williams." In this regard, as Williams explained to Sherman, "I always had to prove I could play. They all saw me and always thought I was too mild, that I wasn't tough enough, that I didn't care, that my mind was not into baseball. But none of that was true."[20]

Williams of course *was* into baseball, but he evolved across time into an acclaimed guitarist. He was inspired by a range of musical styles (including jazz, classical, pop, Brazilian, and Latin), and became adept at both acoustic and electric guitar. His debut album, the jazz-rock-tropical music-influenced *The Journey Within*, was released in 2003. On it, he plays lead and rhythm guitar and also penned seven of the album's 12 numbers; among them are "La Salsa En Mi" and "Desvelado," which link his affection for jazz and his Puerto Rican roots. He is joined here by a first-rate group of musicians, including Béla Fleck, Kenny Aronoff, Shawn Pelton, Luis Conte, Leland Sklar, Tim Pierce, and David Sancious. *The Journey Within* made it to number 3 on *Billboard's* Contemporary Jazz Chart. Then in 2009 came a second album, *Moving Forward*, which debuted at number 2 on the Contemporary Jazz Chart, and for which he earned a Grammy nomination. Here, his collaborators include Bruce Springsteen, Jon Secada, Dave Koz, and Patty Scialfa. Two years later, he co-authored the appropriately titled book *Rhythms of the Game: The Link Between Music and Athletic Performance*. He has over the years performed on countless occasions in numerous venues. One example: In 2014, he played "Take Me Out to the Ball Game" on the field in Fenway Park in a pregame ceremony before Derek Jeter's final big-league appearance.

Williams's charitable enterprises include his involvement with Little Kids Rock, an organization that stresses the importance of music education for disadvantaged youth. However, his connection to popular culture is not limited to his musicianship. In "The Abstinence," a 1996 episode of *Seinfeld*, George Costanza (Jason Alexander)—who refers to himself as "assistant to the (Yankees) traveling secretary"—offers batting tips to Williams and Derek Jeter. Bernie's one line, to George: "Are you the guy who put us in that Ramada in Milwaukee?"[21] He also has participated in a pair of films with baseball connections. *Henry & Me* (2014) is the animated tale of a cancer-stricken boy who is guided by his guardian angel on a journey in which he meets past and present Yankee greats. Williams does his own voice, as do other Bronx Bombers from Yogi Berra to Reggie Jackson to Hideki Matsui; Luis Guzmán, Chazz Palminteri, Paul Simon, David Mantle, and Hank Steinbrenner respectively voice Lefty Gomez, Babe Ruth, Thurman Munson, Mickey Mantle, and George Steinbrenner. (Alex Rodriguez's presence and voice were deleted in the wake of his 162-game suspension for the 2014 season.) Then in *Straight Outta Tompkins* (2015), the tale of a troubled teen and budding baseball player who is abandoned by his businessman father and ends up immersed in New York's drug culture, Williams acts the role of a "college baseball scout."

But Bernie Williams's true passion is his music. In May 2016 he earned a bachelor's degree in jazz composition from the Manhattan School of Music, where he had studied for the previous four years. "I think anybody could go out there and play some chords and be very passionate about it and break some guitars, put them on fire, whatever, to get the people's attention," he told *New York Post* columnist Ken Davidoff. "And that could be a certain part of success. But I think to me, it's just trying to be the best musician that I can and having the respect of the music industry and the people that are really playing."[22]

While attending the school, Williams blended in with his fellow students, many of whom were a quarter-century his junior. "Once I finally started talking to him and getting to know him, it was clear right away that he didn't want anybody to give him special treatment or act like he was more than just a fellow student," explained Ryan DeWeese, 21. "He is such a genuine guy who really cares about his music, education, and his peers, even if they are a bit younger than he is." Williams himself added, "I will eventually begin working on an album and would like to tour around the world with my band. I'm very excited about the next chapter in my life."[23]

NOTES

1. Mitchell Stephens, "Bernie Williams: On Westchester, His Music and, Oh Yeah, the Yankees," *Westchester Magazine*, July 2003.
2. Michael Martinez. "Spring Phenom a Yankee Perennial," *New York Times*, February 26, 1989: S3.
3. Stephens.
4. Michael Martinez, "Looking Up While Down on Yanks' Farm," *New York Times*, June 11, 1991: B11.
5. Filip Bondy, "Another in Columbus Crew Gets to Discover Stadium," *New York Times*, July 8, 1991: C6.
6. sbnation.com/2014/7/15/5883593/the-many-crimes-of-mel-hall.
7. m.mlb.com/player/124288/bernie-williams.
8. espn.go.com/mlb/story/_/id/12926321/new-york-yankees-bernie-williams-uncommon-dignity-grace.
9. Joel Sherman, *Birth of a Dynasty: Behind the Pinstripes With the 1996 Yankees* (Emmaus, Pennsylvania: Rodale Inc., 2006), 242-243.
10. Murray Chass, "Baseball; Williams, Nearly a Tiger, Is Still a Yankee for Now," *New York Times*, November 20, 1997: C3.
11. George King, "Survivor in Pinstripes: Yanks Were Smart Not Trading Bernie Williams," *New York Post*, February 24, 2002: 92.
12. Buster Olney, "Yankees Capitulate, Keeping Williams in $87.5 Million Pact," *New York Times*, November 26, 1998: A1.
13. Jack Curry, "Williams's Father Dies of a Heart Attack," *New York Times*, May 15, 2001: D4.
14. "The Yankees Decline an Option on Williams," *New York Times*, August 3, 2005: D3.
15. m.mlb.com/player/124288/bernie-williams.
16. Christian Red, "Former Yankee Bernie Williams Burns for One More Shot at Plate, While Adding to His Musical Legacy," *New York Daily News*, January 18, 2009.
17. Jack Curry, "Williams Casts Look Toward the Majors," *New York Times*, March 4, 2009: B14.
18. youtube.com/watch?v=OHODIrkfZiI.
19. espn.go.com/mlb/story/_/id/12926321/new-york-yankees-bernie-williams-uncommon-dignity-grace.
20. Joel Sherman, 242, 244.
21. seinfeldscripts.com/TheAbstinence.htm.
22. Ken Davidoff, "How Bernie Williams Blended in for 4 Years of Music School," *New York Post*, May 12, 2016.
23. Evan Grossman, "Bernie Williams Hits the Right Notes With Classmates as former Yankees Star Nears Graduation From Manhattan School of Music," *New York Daily News*, May 12, 2016.

TODD ZEILE

BY JON SPRINGER

IN A 16-YEAR CAREER MARKED by steady production, Todd Zeile was literally all over the place. He was traded five times, released once, and signed five separate free-agent contracts, toiling for 11 different organizations: Cardinals, Cubs, Phillies, Orioles, Dodgers, Marlins, Rangers, Mets, Rockies, Yankees, Expos, and Mets again.

Ironically it was Zeile's very dependability—production that was always pretty good if rarely at the level of superstar peers, along with a practical and professional on-field demeanor hardened by his firsthand experience of baseball as a business—that turned him into the peripatetic icon of his era: You always knew what you were getting with Todd Zeile. When it was all over in 2004, he'd crafted an odd legacy: Of the 97 players in the All-Star Game era to have amassed both 2,000 hits and 250 home runs, Zeile was the only of them never to have been named to an All-Star team.[1]

His frequent travels, Zeile once said, left him with "one degree of separation from everybody,"[2] including contacts in Hollywood that helped him launch a post-career endeavor as an entertainment magnate and a baseball broadcaster, among other efforts in business. His itinerant baseball career and the highlights he witnessed along the way led Joe Torre to describe Zeile as "the Forrest Gump of baseball,"[3] though a movie about his career might be titled *Have Bat, Will Travel*.

Todd Edward Zeile was born in Van Nuys, California, on September 9, 1965. For his father, Frank Todd Zeile, who also went by the name Todd, it must have a doubly joyous occasion. That night, 17 miles away in Dodger Stadium, Sandy Koufax threw a perfect game to defeat the Chicago Cubs, 1-0.

F. Todd Zeile was a big Dodgers fan who professed to have been in attendance at the first game at Dodger Stadium in 1962,[4] and had been an accomplished semipro pitcher and infielder playing around the San Fernando Valley in the late 1950s and early 1960s. He had overcome what his son later called "a difficult childhood"[5] which had included a stint living in his car. He was a high-school dropout who nevertheless rose to head an aeronautics company that developed flight systems, and was an "inspiration" to his son.[6]

Todd's mother, Sammee (Spooner) Zeile, was an editor at a local newspaper. Todd was their second and youngest child; a brother, Michael, had been born 14 months earlier, in July of 1964.

The Zeile brothers were both good athletes who were baseball teammates at Hart High in Santa Clarita, California. With Mike in the outfield and Todd behind the plate, the Indians advanced to the final game of the 1982 California Interscholastic Federation Class 2-A playoffs, but lost 1-0 to Norwalk High. A teammate, Mike Halcovich, said Hart would have won the game were it played anywhere else but at Dodger Stadium, where dimensions were just large enough to contain a long drive by Todd Zeile, who was a junior that year.[7]

The following year, Zeile batted .520 for Hart and was a first team all-CIF selection. The Kansas City Royals selected him in the 13th round of the June draft that summer, but he chose to attend UCLA on a baseball scholarship.

The Bruins went 39-21 and won the Pacific 10 Southern Division title in 1986 behind a hard-hitting team that included future big leaguers Zeile, Jeff Conine, Torey Lovullo, and Tony Scruggs. Zeile, then a junior at UCLA, was the first of nine players from that squad selected in the June amateur draft, picked by the St. Louis Cardinals 55th overall, a second-round supplemental pick for having lost free agent Ivan DeJesus. Zeile was signed by scout Marty Keough, and began his pro career that summer for the Erie Cardinals of the short-season New York-

Penn League, for whom he hit 14 home runs and drove in 63 runs, both club highs.

A steady ascent continued in 1987 with Springfield of the Class-A Midwest League, where Zeile hit .292 with 25 home runs and 106 RBIs, earning the league's co-MVP honors with Greg Vaughn of the Beloit Brewers. Zeile also blasted two home runs in the circuit's all-star game, marking him for future stardom.

"We've had some great catchers through the years but I think Zeile is going to make you forget all of them," Cardinals director of player development Lee Thomas said that summer.[8]

Exploits as a minor-league slugger were one thing; Zeile's star was also rising by association. He'd met the noted US Olympic gymnast Julianne McNamara when they were classmates at UCLA. They married in 1989, months before Zeile would make his big-league debut.

A broken thumb suffered playing winter ball in the Dominican Republic delayed Zeile's start to the 1988 season but once healed he hit 19 home runs for Double-A Arkansas. He hit another 19 for Triple-A Louisville in 1989 when he was called up to the major leagues for the first time on August 16, swapping teams with reserve infielder Jim Lindeman.

Zeile's major-league debut came during a doubleheader at Cincinnati's Riverfront Stadium on August 18. He pinch-hit for Dan Quisenberry in the eighth inning of the first game and grounded out against the Reds' Tom Browning. He started the second game behind the plate for the Cardinals, collecting his first and second major-league hits. Before the Cardinals left Cincinnati, Zeile had connected for his first big-league home run, a solo line shot to left off the Reds' Tim Leary on August 20.

A right-handed batter and thrower, Zeile was listed at a solid 6-feet-1 and 190 pounds. He stood upright, still, and relaxed in the batter's box—a style he said he patterned after his boyhood idol, Steve Garvey of the Dodgers.[9] Unlike Garvey, Zeile tended to step toward third base when he swung, opening up and facing the pitcher directly upon contact. He maintained a grip on the bat with both hands all the way around his left shoulder and back down again, providing a hacking lift on balls he frequently drove to left and left-center.

Veteran Tony Peña, a 1989 All-Star, was the Cardinals' regular catcher when Zeile arrived, backed up by a young defensive specialist, Tom Pagnozzi. The Cardinals let Peña go over the offseason with the idea of giving the catching job to Zeile full-time in 1990. He was also looked at as a major means of improving a St. Louis offense that was near the bottom in runs scored in '89. The team made no major personnel moves that offseason. "Zeile's RBI potential is a soothing tonic to the Cards' fruitless offseason efforts to put more meat in the bat rack," Dan O'Neill of the *St. Louis Post-Dispatch* wrote prior to the season.[10]

Cardinals fans of 1990 were, however, left asking, "Where's the beef?" Zeile hit 15 home runs as a rookie—but that total led the team as it sputtered to a 70-92 season and last place, 25 games behind the NL East-winning Pirates. Manager Whitey Herzog, in his 11th season in St. Louis, resigned in disgust in early July, with Red Schoendienst serving briefly as interim manager and Joe Torre arriving in August.

The pairing of Torre and Zeile was a fateful one. Torre in his playing days was a one-time Cardinals catcher who turned into a star after becoming a third baseman, and he proposed the same transition for Zeile. Pagnozzi was the Cards' starting catcher and Zeile the regular third baseman, beginning in 1991.

The transition wasn't easy for Zeile, who would lead National League third basemen with 25 errors in 1991, while teammate Pagnozzi won a Gold Glove. Moreover, Zeile was still adjusting to big-league pitching and the prospect of being a power hitter in spacious Busch Stadium. But it wasn't a bad year overall. Honing a line-drive approach, Zeile upped his batting average from .244 to .280 in '91, though he hit just 11 home runs—again enough to lead a power-starved club, which in the first full season under Torre rebounded to an 81-81 record.

The Cardinals moved the fences in at Busch Stadium for the 1992 season but the change didn't help Zeile, who suffered through a disappointing campaign (.257, 7 home runs, 48 RBIs in 548 plate appearances) that included a short hospitalization for taking a bad hop off his face and a demotion to Louisville in August. "Our priority is really to salvage the end of this year for him," Torre said. "I told him he needs to get away from the fishbowl."[11] In the meantime, hitting coach Don Baylor criticized Zeile for a seeming indifference to the situation: Despite his struggles, Baylor said, Zeile never asked for help.[12]

When he got off to a slow start again in 1993, talk had begun about sitting Zeile in favor of reserve Stan Royer,[13] but Zeile caught fire just in time, hitting 14 of his 17 home runs after the All-Star break and finishing with a .277 batting average and a career-high 103 RBIs. It was the Cardinals' first 100-RBI season by a third baseman since Torre drove in 137 in 1971.

Zeile was careful not to take a victory lap, professing a pride in keeping emotions in check whether he was succeeding or struggling—a stance that occasionally would be interpreted as aloofness. His clean-shaven fastidiousness made him something of an oddball amid the prevailing dirtbag culture of his era. "He's a good kid, he really is," Herzog told the *Los Angeles Times* in 1997. "But he's so damn laid back. We used to try to get him more fiery. We wanted him to throw helmets, cuss after he struck out, pump his fist, damn near anything to show emotion. But I'll tell you what, he wouldn't change.... You aren't going to change Todd Zeile."[14]

Zeile had a stressful 1994 on and off the field. In January, the Northridge earthquake badly damaged Todd and Julianne's home in Valencia, forcing them and 6-week-old son Garrett to move in with Julianne's parents. "Basically, the epicenter was right in our backyard," he said.[15] Young Garrett was then hospitalized for a week with a serious respiratory illness.[16]

In February, Zeile lost a salary arbitration hearing with the Cardinals in which he said the club made its case behind his defensive struggles at third base. For Zeile, it was hard not to be sore: feeling as though he reluctantly made the move to third base for the good of the team, only to be punished for it personally. "When I was at the arbitration hearing," he recalled, "I listened to them rag me about my defense up hill and down dale."[17]

On the field, Zeile set a career high with 19 home runs that would have been more were it not for the strike beginning in August that wound up ending the season prematurely. As the Cardinals' player representative, Zeile helped to make that tough call. "I was a little leaguer. I wanted to see baseball too," Zeile said in a message of sympathy to young fans when the strike hit. "But baseball is a business based on confrontations."[18]

Zeile's aloofness was likely on general manager Walt Jocketty's mind when Zeile was abruptly traded to the Chicago Cubs on June 17, 1995—hours before Jocketty also fired Torre in an extraordinary midseason reset. The Cardinals don't often trade their favorite sons to the rival Cubs, but Zeile's contention that St. Louis had withdrawn a contract extension offer after he'd injured a thumb in spring training—a matter of dispute with the front office—seemed to invite such a response.

"We're not happy with the chemistry and focus of this team," Jocketty said at the time. "If you saw Todd Zeile play, you could see he's not a real aggressive person in his approach to the game. He was kind of at one gait.

Todd Zeile, former major leaguer and future entertainment industry magnate.

"Todd Zeile was not happy here," he added. "We didn't want someone here who wasn't happy."[19]

The trade—Zeile for veteran starter Mike Morgan, plus minor leaguers Francisco Morales and Paul Torres—was hardly consequential for either side. Zeile, who struggled with recurring hand injuries that year, hit just .227 with a paltry .271 on-base percentage over 325 plate appearances with Chicago. The Cubs failed to offer Zeile a 1996 contract, making him a free agent. Morgan, who was also a free-agent-to-be, was re-signed by St. Louis, but released midway through a mediocre '96 campaign.

Lee Thomas, who as a Cardinals executive had raved about Zeile as a youngster, was quick to scoop him up again, this time as the general manager of the rebuilding Philadelphia Phillies. Playing with a $2.5 million, one-year contract, Zeile banged out 25 home runs and drove in 99 runs that season, although it didn't all come for Philadelphia: With the Phillies hopelessly out of the race and Baltimore pushing for the postseason, Zeile and fellow veteran Pete Incaviglia were dealt to the Orioles in late August for fringe pitchers Garrett Stephenson and Calvin Maduro.

The trade allowed Zeile to log a major-league best 163 regular-season games that year—plus nine additional games during his first trip to the postseason, as the Orioles (88-74) won the American League wild-card slot and knocked off the Central Division-winning Cleveland Indians, three games to one, in the Division Series. In a hard-fought ALCS vs. the New York Yankees, Zeile hit .364 with three home runs, but the Orioles fell to the eventual World Series-winning Yankees, four games to one.

The '96 ALCS marked the first of four postseason series vs. the late '90s Yankees juggernaut in which Zeile was a losing combatant: His clubs (the 1998 and 1999 Texas Rangers and the 2000 New York Mets) also met their ends at the hands of the Yankees in the postseason. The Yankees were world champions in each of those years.

Success on a one-year deal in 1996 did what it was supposed to and gave Zeile new possibilities as 1997 approached. Ultimately, he got that and more: a chance to return home to Los Angeles and play for his boyhood rooting interest, the Dodgers. The deal was for three years and $10 million—figures Zeile later described as a hometown discount.

"Honestly, if you go back in the 100-year history of the Dodgers, there was a revolving door at third base," Fred Claire, Dodgers executive vice president, said. "Hopefully now we have the guy to stop that traffic."[20]

That of course turned out to be wishful thinking. After a productive 1997—cracking a career-best 31 home runs, and knocking in 90 runs for a Dodger teams that would fall short by two games to the worst-to-first Giants in the NL West—Zeile in 1998 found himself repeating his 1995 scenario all over again: traded in midseason amid an unresolved contract dispute. Only this time, the contract in question wasn't his.

The Mike Piazza trade shook baseball, up to and including Todd Zeile. Unhappy that the homegrown future Hall of Famer—who could become a free agent after the '97 season—had spurned the club's offer of a contract extension and was thought to be holding out for a $100 million deal, the Dodgers under President Bob Graziano initiated trade talks with the Florida Marlins, which then were in the midst of a massive teardown. The deal—then the most expensive in terms of swapped contracts in baseball history—sent Piazza and Zeile to Florida in exchange for Gary Sheffield, Bobby Bonilla, Charles Johnson, Jim Eisenreich, and Manuel Barrios.

The trade came with implicit understanding that Florida would make subsequent deals for its new arrivals.

Naturally, Zeile had just put down roots, moving his young family—which by this time included wife Julianne and two young children—to a new home in Westlake Village.[21] He didn't shop for real estate in South Beach, but Zeile hit well in Florida—.291/.374/.427 over 270 plate appearances and was on the move again at the July trade deadline, swapped to the Texas Rangers for minor leaguers Dan DeYoung and Jose Santos, neither of whom ever reached the big leagues.

The trade not only elevated Zeile 32 games in the standings, it averted a promise to his Marlins teammates that he'd dye his hair blond if he were still in Miami after the trade deadline.[22] The Rangers made room for Zeile by dispatching their current third baseman, Fernando Tatis, in a separate trade the same day to St. Louis for Royce Clayton and Todd Stottlemyre. All three new additions contributed as Texas prevailed in a season-long wrestling match for the AL West title with the Angels, who stood pat at the deadline.

Zeile made it through the entire 1999 season with the Rangers—a 95-win season marking their second consecutive division crown—playing 156 games, with 41 doubles, 24 home runs, 98 RBIs, and a career-best .293 batting average. But Texas scored just one run over the course of a three-game sweep at the hands of the Yankees in the Division Series. (Zeile's one-time trade counterpart, Mike Morgan, now playing with his seventh club, was a Rangers teammate that year. Morgan eventually became the first player ever to toil for 12 different teams, briefly holding the all-time record now belonging to Octavio Dotel, who had 13 different employers.)

Once again a free agent, Zeile said he hoped for a return to Los Angeles but wound up choosing between offers from Texas and the New York Mets. The Mets' winning offer of three years and $18 million came with the understanding that Zeile would have to move across the diamond to first base, where the Mets were seeking a successor to departed free agent John Olerud. Zeile through that point in his career had appeared at first base 76 times.

Zeile lacked the sex appeal New Yorkers like in their free agents and was replacing a wildly popular and productive figure in Olerud, but he ultimately proved up to the task. He was not only adequate defensively but turned in Zeile-like offensive numbers (.268/.356/.467, 22 home runs, 79 RBIs, in 153 games) that helped the Mets (94-68) earn the NL wild card, then march into the World Series, Zeile's first and only fall classic as player.

Zeile had an outstanding postseason for the 2000 Mets. He drove in eight runs in the club's five-game victory over his former St. Louis club in the NLCS, and was the Mets' most productive hitter in the Subway Series, but was also an unlucky participant in what many observers consider to be the Series' pivotal play. In the sixth inning of a scoreless Game One, with two out and Timo Perez on first, Zeile blasted a long drive off Yankees starter Andy Pettitte. The ball bounced off the padding at the very top of Yankee Stadium's left-field wall and back onto the field of play.

Evidently convinced the drive would clear the fence, Perez had slowed his pace between first and second base and briefly raised a fist in celebration before realizing the ball would stay in play. That momentary hesitation was just enough: left fielder Dave Justice fired in to shortstop Derek Jeter, who made an acrobatic and accurate throw from the foul line behind third base in time to catch a sliding Perez at home, turning what at best looked to be a two-run homer, or at worst an RBI double, into an inning-ending, rally-killing play. The Mets lost the game in 12 innings and a golden opportunity to gain momentum in a Series in which all five games were decided by two runs or less. Had Todd Zeile done one more push-up, Mets fans lamented, anything could have happened.

By this point in his career, Zeile appeared to have accepted his fate as a baseball wanderer. Determined to make the most of New York, he rented an apartment in Greenwich Village, made a point to see the city's cultural attractions and often rode the 7 train to games in Flushing. "I enjoy the city. I enjoy the theater. I enjoy the museums. I enjoy the cultural diversity. It's exactly what I hoped for."[23]

The Big Apple was fun while it lasted. Battling elbow woes, Zeile saw his power numbers take a dip in 2001, and the Mets (82-80) slipped along with him to a disappointing third-place finish. In a strenuous offseason remake, New York shipped Zeile and $3 million of his $6.4 million salary to the Colorado Rockies as part of a three-team, 11-player deal that also involved the Milwaukee Brewers. Seeking more offense, the Mets weeks before had worked a trade with the Anaheim Angels for their first baseman, Mo Vaughn.

Going back across the diamond to third base, Zeile had a bit of a rebound year in Colorado, producing 18 home runs and 87 RBIs. He also made his first appearance on the mound while Colorado absorbed a 16-3 beating at the hands of the Dodgers. Throwing mostly knuckleballs, Zeile gave up a leadoff single to Cesar Izturis but induced Chad Kreuter to ground into a double play and then struck out Wilkin Ruan. (Zeile put his career 0.00 ERA on the line two years later as a member of the Mets but coughed up five runs on four hits and two walks in a 19-10 Mets loss in Montreal.)

In 2003, Zeile joined the ranks of his postseason nemesis and former manager Joe Torre as a member of Yankees, but at age 37, didn't take well to the reserve role he was offered. Platooning at first base, third base, and designated hitter with his 2000 Mets teammate, Robin Ventura, Zeile was hitting only .210 when he asked for his release in August. He was subsequently signed by the Montreal Expos, his 11th team, days later and logged his 2,000th major-league game for them while providing right-handed reserve strength.

The Mets re-signed Zeile for what turned out to be his final season in 2004. Mostly in a reserve role for a team that finished a disappointing 20 games under .500, Zeile managed to reach, then surpass, milestones of 250 home runs and 2,000 hits that year. He had already announced he would retire prior to the final game of the season, on October 3. That game was also the last in history for the Montreal Expos, who would relocate to Washington in 2005, and the final game in the Mets' managerial career of Art Howe, who already had been informed his contract wouldn't be renewed. But the day belonged to Zeile.

In the bottom of the sixth inning, Zeile reached for a high delivery from Claudio Vargas and lined it over the fence in left for a three-run homer in what would turn out to be his final big-league at-bat. Zeile at his own request had started the game behind the plate—his first stint catching since 1990, going out as he went in.

During a road trip in Los Angeles during that 2004 season, the normally clean-shaven Zeile sported the beginnings of hefty beard. That's because he used the visit to Hollywood to shoot scenes in a movie in which he made an appearance as a drifter. The film, titled *Dirty Deeds* and released in 2005, was the debut production of Zeile's Green Diamond Entertainment, which counted among its investors Zeile's former teammates Jason Giambi, Mike Piazza, Tom Glavine, Al Leiter, and Cliff Floyd.[24]

The R-rated teen comedy was savaged by critics and Zeile reportedly lost millions in the endeavor. "It was a great education but a costly one," he said. "I lost more than I would have paid in tuition if I'd gone to film school for 10 years."[25]

In Hollywood, as in baseball, Zeile's slumps didn't last forever. He'd struck up a friendship with actor Charlie Sheen—they'd met in Dodger Stadium in 1997—and Zeile had considerably better success producing Sheen's comedy television series *Anger Management*.

Anger Management grew out of Zeile's pitch to Sheen to make a show about a baseball player adjusting to a post-baseball life—although Sheen played the lead role of Charlie Goodson against Zeile's type—beset by a bad temper.

Zeile maintained a close friendship with Sheen even as the actor endured a turbulent personal life that spilled into the public arena, resulting in Sheen's high-profile termination from the hit television program *Two and a Half Men*. One way they connected, Zeile said, was through baseball.

"I was kind of in the eye of the storm and try [sic] to be a stable force in Charlie's life that was going like a tornado around us," Zeile told the *New York Post*. "I would try and clear his mind by taking him to batting practice and going to big-league parks. It was an outlet for him. He's a baseball fanatic and a very knowledgeable baseball fan."[26]

Zeile said he had maintained an interest in movies and entertainment since childhood—his favorite baseball movie is *The Natural*—and launched his production career with the help of Bill Civitella, a Hollywood talent manager who was also Zeile's neighbor in Westlake Village.²⁷

In addition to *Dirty Deeds*, Zeile produced or co-produced *I Am*, a movie about the Ten Commandments released to video in 2010, as well as the *Comedy Central Roast of Charlie Sheen*; three seasons of *Anger Management*, which aired on FX from 2012-2014; a comedy video called *Lip Service*; and *The Miracle of San Quentin*, a movie in production as of 2017. Zeile's acting credits include two appearances on the TV comedy *The King of Queens*, and he was one of several major leaguers to play themselves in a 1997 *Saturday Night Live* sketch.²⁸

Zeile, whose marriage to Julianne McNamara ended in divorce in 2015, retained an entertainment connection as a recurring analyst on SNY, the Mets' television network, as well as the MLB Network. The father of four can also watch his daughter Hannah perform as Kate Pearson on the NBC series *This Is Us* (in its second season in 2017), his son Garrett on stage as a musician, and his nephew Shane Zeile, his brother Mike's son, play outfield in the Detroit Tigers organization, which drafted Shane out of UCLA in 2014. Zeile's other ventures include investments in a charter-jet business aimed at athletes, a role as chief business development officer at a sports video game firm called Bit Fry Game Studios, and work on the board of the Juvenile Diabetes Association.

NOTES

1. Christina Kahrl, "The All-Star Game's Uninvited," ESPN.com, July 5, 2011. espn.com/blog/sweetspot/post/_/id/13274/the-uninvited.
2. "Exclusive Interview: Todd Zeile," Bleeding Yankee Blue, September 19, 2011. bleedingyankeeblue.blogspot.com/2011/09/exclusive-interview-todd-zeile.html.
3. Albert Chen, "How Baseball Vet Todd Zeile Went From Run Producer to Movie Producer," *Sports Illustrated*, July 1, 2015. si.com/mlb/2015/07/01/todd-zeile-hollywood-producer-charlie-sheen-profiles.
4. Bob Nightengale, "Zeile Slides Home," *Los Angeles Times*, April 8, 1997: B-12.
5. Lisa Olson "Showing Zeile for the Game, and Life," *New York Daily News*, March 6, 2001. nydailynews.com/archives/sports/showing-zeile-game-life-article-1.915650
6. Ibid.
7. Author interview with Mike Halcovich, September 19, 2017.
8. "NL East Notes," *The Sporting News*, November 16, 1987: 54.
9. Zach Schonbrun, "The Batter's Box Gets a Little Boring," *New York Times*, July 21, 2016. nytimes.com/2016/07/24/sports/baseball/the-batters-box-gets-a-little-boring.html.
10. Dan O'Neill, "Zeile (the Baseball Card) Is Batting a Ton," *St. Louis Post-Dispatch*, January 7, 1990: 6-F.
11. George Rorrer, "Zeile Trying to Recapture His Old Zeal With Birds," *Louisville Courier-Journal*, August 12, 1992: D-1.
12. Ibid.
13. Rick Hummel, "Zeile's Recent Efforts Leave Torre Hopeful," *St. Louis Post-Dispatch*, June 20, 1993: 3-F.
14. Bob Nightengale, "Steal of a Zeile," *Los Angeles Times*, February 26, 1997: C-1.
15. Dan O'Neill, "Shaken Lives: Zeiles Regroup, *St. Louis Post Dispatch*, January 28, 1994: D-1.
16. Ibid.
17. Rick Hummel, "Phillies Counterpunch, Sign Jefferies," *St. Louis Post-Dispatch*, December 15, 1994: D-1.
18. Mike Eisenbath, "Baseball Takes a Walk," *St. Louis Post-Dispatch*, August 13, 1994: C-1.
19. Rick Hummel, "Cards Swing 2-Edged Sword," *St. Louis Post-Dispatch*, June 17, 1995: C-1.
20. Nightengale, "Zeile Slides Home."
21. Steve Springer, "After a Year and a Half, Zeile's Dream Is Over," *Los Angeles Times*, May 16, 1998: S-3.
22. Mike Berardino, "Zeile, Johnson Move On," *South Florida Sun Sentinel*, August 1, 1998: C-1.
23. Joe LaPointe, "For Zeile, a Dream Takes on Reality," *New York Times*, October 17, 2000. nytimes.com/2000/10/17/sports/baseball-2000-playoffs-for-zeile-a-dream-takes-on-reality.html
24. Larry Carrol, "Major Leaguers Hoping for a Home Run with 'Dirty Deeds,'" MTV.com, August 25, 2005. mtv.com/news/1508378/major-leaguers-hoping-for-a-home-run-with-dirty-deeds/.
25. Chen, "How Baseball Vet Todd Zeile Went From Run Producer to Movie Producer."
26. Justin Terranova, "Todd Zeile Went From Charlie Sheen Wingman to SNY Analyst," *New York Post*, April 20, 2017 nypost.com/2017/04/20/todd-zeile-went-from-charlie-sheen-wingman-to-sny-analyst/.
27. Patrick Goldstein, "Exit Stadium, Enter Studio," *Los Angeles Times*, June 8, 2004: E-1.
28. Internet Movie Database, imdb.com/name/nm1156788/.

GENE AUTRY

BY WARREN CORBETT

GENE AUTRY WAS THE KIND of man who paid the bills for old friends in their old age, rode in the front seat beside his chauffeur, and showed up in the bar of his resort hotel to lead guests in a sing-along. During his heyday as a singing cowboy, his fans ranged from the obvious—Johnny Cash and Willie Nelson—to the improbable—Franklin D. Roosevelt and Ringo Starr. Thirty years after he quit performing, his theme song, "Back in the Saddle Again," returned to the pop charts on the movie soundtrack for *Sleepless in Seattle*.

He once described himself as "a frustrated ballplayer," and delighted in his second career as a baseball owner.[1] The Angels were his passion for the last four decades of his life. A portly, perpetually smiling man decked out in a western suit and a big Stetson—white, of course—Autry often traveled with his team and spent lavishly on free agents in futile pursuit of a championship. The Angels retired number 26 in honor of their 26th man.

Autry never was a cowboy, but he played one on TV and radio and in movies. "I was the first of the singing cowboys," he said. "I'm not sure I was the best. But when you're first it doesn't matter. No one can ever be first again."[2]

He introduced two of the most popular Christmas songs, and invested his Hollywood earnings to build a fortune that landed him on *Forbes* magazine's list of the 400 richest Americans for 10 years. His television sidekick, Pat Buttram, said, "Gene Autry used to ride off into the sunset. Now he owns it."[3]

Orvon Grover Autry was born in Tioga, Texas, on September 29, 1907, the first child of Delbert Autry and the former Elnora Ozment. He seldom spoke of his childhood because he wanted to forget most of it. His father was generally worthless, absent more often than present, and his mother and her four children had to depend on the charity of relatives in Texas and Oklahoma. Orvon dropped out of high school to help support the family as a railroad telegrapher.[4]

When he was 12, he had saved $8 from farm chores to buy a guitar out of the Sears Roebuck catalog. He liked to tell of the night that the world's most famous Oklahoma native, Will Rogers, walked into a railroad depot, heard him picking and singing, and encouraged his dream of a music career. The tale may be a press agent's invention; its first documented appearance didn't come until after Rogers' death.

At 20, Orvon traveled to New York in search of a recording contract, but was turned away. He came home with a new name, Gene Autry, probably borrowed from a popular crooner, Gene Austin, whom he met on the trip.

In his first radio gig, at KVOO in Tulsa, he was billed as Oklahoma's Yodeling Cowboy and imitated country star Jimmie Rodgers. His first hit record, "That Silver-Haired Daddy of Mine," propelled him to the big time on Chicago's *WLS Barn Dance*, the model for Nashville's enduring *Grand Ole Opry*.

During a trip home to Oklahoma, Autry met Ina Mae Spivey and married her four months later, on April 1, 1932. The wedding was so sudden that some friends thought it was an April Fool's prank, but the marriage lasted 48 years. After Gene's mother died that spring, his two sisters and brother moved in with the newlyweds. Ina, just 21, became their surrogate mother. The Autrys never had children.

On July 4, 1934, he, Ina, and his comic sidekick, Smiley Burnette, left Chicago for Hollywood in Gene's Buick. He thought movies would help sell his records. His debut was a singing cameo in *In Old Santa Fe*, starring a leading cowboy actor, Ken Maynard. The greenhorn appeared stiff and awkward on screen. Embarrassed, he decided to go back to radio. But Maynard was supportive and gave him a small part in a serial, *Mystery Mountain*. Autry was more singer than cowboy; a stunt man had to step in when he couldn't handle a galloping horse.

Autry's big break came when Maynard was fired for his drunken tantrums. The newcomer took over the lead role in a bizarre 12-part serial, *The Phantom Empire*, where he played a singing cowboy battling robots and mad scientists. (Years later, when Maynard was living in a trailer park, Autry sent him monthly checks. He made donations to several other early benefactors who were needy in their declining years.)

Three years after Autry arrived in Hollywood, a trade publication named him the #1 star of action melodramas in 1937. His movies for Republic Pictures followed a simple formula for wholesome, if bland, family entertainment: Good guy defeats bad guy, but never shoots first and never kills anybody. Hero gets girl, but never kisses her. Kissing was allowed in the early films, but the clinches disappeared when the studio realized that Autry's core audience was pre-teen boys, who didn't go for that mushy stuff. They preferred to see him with his horse, Champion.

While Autry made action movies, they were unconventional westerns. Before signing him to his first contract, a studio executive had complained that he lacked "virility."[5] At 5-feet-9, he was not tall, muscular, or imposing. *New York Times* critic Bosley Crowther described him as a "medium-height, sandy-haired, pink-cheeked, blue-eyed, baby-faced fellow."[6] Nor was he an acrobatic horseman like Maynard and the king of silent-screen cowboys, Tom Mix. Songs took on a larger role in Autry films than gunplay or fistfights.

By 1937 he was making $6,000 per picture, equivalent to around $100,000 in 2017, but was still ridic-

Gene Autry, ex-singing cowboy and owner of the Los Angeles American League franchise.

ulously underpaid given his popularity.[7] He went on strike.

During his holdout, Republic brass created a replacement singing "cowboy" they named Roy Rogers. Born Leonard Slye in Cincinnati, he had had bit parts in several Autry films.[8] The two became rivals, but friendly ones.

From his earliest days, Autry used every avenue to turn his fame into money. The Sears catalog sold Gene Autry Roundup guitars, and he was said to be the first Hollywood star to put his name on comic books, school lunchboxes, jeans, and more than 100 other products, though he refused to endorse cigarettes.[9] With records, songbooks, and personal appearances, his outside income exceeded his film earnings.

Autry took his stage show to England and Ireland in 1939. It was a triumph; his biographer, Holly George-Warren, likened it to the Beatles' first American tour.[10] A reported 250,000 people jammed the streets of Dublin for a look at the cowboy. In the crowd was another American tourist, P.K. Wrigley, the owner of the chewing-gum company. When Wrigley returned home, he ordered his ad agency to sign Autry for a weekly CBS radio show sponsored by Doublemint gum. That added a new profit center to Autry's empire, giving him a foothold in all entertainment media.

His career reached its pinnacle when theater owners voted him the #4 male box-office attraction of 1940, behind Mickey Rooney, Clark Gable, and Spencer Tracy. It was a stunning achievement for a B-movie actor whose greatest appeal was in small towns rather than big-city film palaces. His income in 1941 approached half a million dollars.

Autry's reign as the #1 western star ended while he was serving in the Army Air Corps during World War II. When he sued Republic trying to get out of his contract, the studio retaliated by promoting Roy Rogers, who was found unfit for military service because of a bad back. In 1943 Rogers climbed to #1, a pedestal Autry never regained. *Life* magazine headlined a cover story on Rogers, "King of the Cowboys."[11]

Seeing harsh evidence that stardom was temporary, Autry turned his energy toward business after the war. He bought radio and television stations and hotels, and invested in oil wells and real estate. When the California Supreme Court finally freed him from his Republic contract, he formed his own production company to make movies in partnership with Columbia, one of the major studios. The arrangement gave him control of his work as well as a tax shelter.

He also resumed his radio show and personal appearance tours, and enjoyed six top-10 records in 1947. In the fall he released "Here Comes Santa Claus," a song he co-wrote after he heard a child's exuberant shout at a Christmas parade.[12] It became a holiday standard, but nothing compared to his next Christmas song.

"Rudolph the Red-Nosed Reindeer" carried Autry to the top of *Billboard*'s country and pop charts for the first time and sold two million copies in 1949, with millions more to follow. It is often said to be the second best-selling Christmas record in history, after Bing Crosby's "White Christmas," but the *Guinness Book of World Records* lists it in third place behind another Crosby hit, "Silent Night."

In 1950 Autry was the first major movie star to jump into television. William Boyd, whom he dismissed as a third-rate actor, had become a TV cowboy sensation by recycling cut-down versions of his old Hopalong Cassidy movies, igniting a children's craze for "Hoppy" merchandise.

Autry began starring in weekly original half-hour films on CBS-TV. His company produced three more western series for the network. One was *Annie Oakley*, the first TV western with a female star, his sometime girlfriend Gail Davis.

But Autry's career was sliding downhill, and so was he. His new records weren't selling. Television killed many of the small-town theaters that had showcased his movies. So-called adult westerns, such as *High Noon* and TV's *Gunsmoke*, made the singing cowboys seem campy. He released his last feature film in 1953.

His heavy drinking, which began during the war, was interfering with his work. After he missed a number of shows, his longtime sponsor, Wrigley, canceled his radio and TV series in 1956. His live performances became unreliable. Although his loyal staff tried to cover for him, fans saw him fall off his horse and appear too drunk to mount up.

As Autry's entertainment career fizzled out, his business portfolio continued to expand. One of his biggest money-makers was Los Angeles radio station KMPC. The station aired Dodgers games after the team moved west in 1958, but its signal was too weak to reach club owner Walter O'Malley's home at Lake Arrowhead. O'Malley moved the broadcasts to a more powerful outlet, one he could hear.

KMPC, billed as Southern California's sports station, needed a new anchor for its summer schedule. Autry thought he had found one when Hank Greenberg came calling in November 1960. The home run slugger turned baseball executive had secretly won the American League's blessing to put an expansion team in Los Angeles in 1961. Autry was negotiating for broadcast rights when Greenberg's plans blew up.

O'Malley didn't want to share the LA market. He leaned on Commissioner Ford Frick, and the commissioner decreed that O'Malley deserved compensation for allowing a competing team into "his" territory. Hearing that, Greenberg walked away, throwing the AL expansion blueprint into "frightful chaos," as the writer Frank Finch put it.[13] With a franchise already awarded to Washington, the league had to have a tenth club to balance the schedule, and time was slipping away.

The familiar story is that Autry went to the AL meeting hoping to secure radio rights for the new franchise, and wound up owning the team. In fact, published reports identified him as a bidder for the team before the meeting, and he said he became interested as soon as Greenberg dropped out: "I thought it was all Greenberg. When it appeared it wasn't, the thought occurred to me that I'd like that franchise."[14] When he went to the league meeting, Autry brought along his choice for general manager: Fred Haney, an LA resident who had managed the Milwaukee Braves to two pennants.

AL owners were facing ridicule over their bungled expansion when they met in St. Louis on December 5. Just as in the movies, the hero in the white hat came riding to the rescue. The league welcomed him as a savior, and why not? He was a famous, popular—and rich—man who wanted to own a ball club.

But O'Malley exacted a stiff price. The new team would have to pay him $350,000 for a ticket of admission to enter Los Angeles. Instead of sharing the 90,000-seat LA Coliseum with the Dodgers, the American League club would play its first season in the city's minor-league ballpark, Wrigley Field, with room for about 22,000. That ensured that the team would lose money. Beginning in 1962, it would be O'Malley's tenant in his new park, under construction at Chavez Ravine, paying a minimum $200,000 in rent, or 7.5 percent of gate receipts. O'Malley would keep all parking revenue and some of the take from concessions.

In addition, O'Malley didn't want competition from television. He televised only 11 Dodger games—those in San Francisco against the archrival Giants—and the new club was limited to the same number.

All told, Autry estimated the deal was worth $750,000 a year to the Dodgers. After a meeting with O'Malley that lasted nearly all night, he agreed to pay. It was the price of doing business.[15]

"For me, it's the realization of a lifetime dream," Autry said.[16] He had played semipro ball in his youth and claimed to have been invited to a Cardinals tryout camp. While filming his movies, he had organized pickup games during breaks, and had once owned a share of the Pacific Coast League's Hollywood Stars.

The new team adopted the name of LA's other PCL entry, the Angels. Casey Stengel, recently fired by the Yankees, turned down an offer to be the manager. Haney talked to Leo Durocher, but Durocher's price was apparently too high. The club hired Bill Rigney, who had succeeded Durocher as manager of the Giants.

Because of the delay in awarding the franchise, Haney had only a week to prepare for the player draft that would stock the Angels' roster. Stengel gave him a rundown on the available players, who were mostly benchwarmers and over-age veterans. AL teams were permitted to keep their front-line talent and top prospects.

Haney went for well-known names in the draft, hoping to convince LA fans that the castoffs were a real big-league team. But Ted Kluszewski, Eddie Yost, Ned Garver, and Bob Cerv had to look backward to see their 34th birthdays. Haney did grab a pair of young minor leaguers who became franchise cornerstones, shortstop Jim Fregosi and catcher Buck Rodgers. After the draft he acquired pitching prospect Dean Chance.

During spring training Autry put the players up at his hotel in Palm Springs, California, and mounted a bicycle to lead them in a parade to the ballpark.

The Angels opened their inaugural season with eight games on the road. They lost seven of them. The home opener produced defeat number 8 before an embarrassing turnout of just 11,931. The club rallied to a 70-91 record, still the most victories by a first-year expansion team, finishing eighth in the standings but ninth in attendance, drawing barely 600,000.

In their second season, the Angels startled the league by charging into the pennant race. They held first place on the Fourth of July and finished third, with 86 victories. Attendance nearly doubled in their first year in O'Malley's new ballpark. Its formal name was Dodger Stadium, but the Angels called it Chavez Ravine.

Autry soon began looking for a way to climb out of the ravine. He vented his complaints in unchar-

Gene Autry, in his singing cowboy days, chatting with U. S. Vice President John Nance Garner, center, and an unidentified third party.

acteristically blunt language: "Chavez Ravine is an expensive stadium to operate, Walter O'Malley is a difficult landlord, the Angels are treated as a stepchild by the Dodgers, ... we are playing in the shadow of the Dodgers and we must build our own fan following elsewhere."[17] On August 31, 1964, he broke ground for a new stadium in Anaheim, 30 miles south, to be paid for by the city.

Renamed the California Angels, the team moved into its new home in 1966. But attendance continued to lag far behind the Dodgers, who were setting records and piling up giant profits. The Angels were Southern California's stepchild team. They settled into mediocrity, usually in the bottom half of the standings.

Autry yearned for a championship, but he was a hands-off owner. "I've tried hard not to interfere with the men on the firing line," he said. "I have wondered often why a manager did this or that, but I have tried to restrain my second-guessing."[18] Some critics thought that was why the Angels didn't win: The owner didn't demand it. "Gene is a fan," a former general manager, Dick Walsh, said. "The team is a plaything, a fun thing."[19]

Instead of getting tough during losing seasons, Autry treated players and managers as friends. "He knew every player and knew everything about his players ... their kids' names, their wives' names," pitcher Clyde Wright said. Autry went along on many road trips and made the rounds in the clubhouse before home games asking, "Anything you need?"[20]

Fireballer Nolan Ryan was one of the team's few stars in the 1970s. He set the single-season strikeout record and pitched four of his seven no-hitters for the Angels. Ryan was as big a Gene Autry fan as any 9-year-old boy: "I can honestly say he is among the greatest men I have ever had the pleasure to know."[21]

When free agency arrived after the 1976 season, Autry saw a chance to lift his club out of mediocrity. All it took was money, and he and his minority partner, Signal Companies, had plenty. The Angels signed three of the top-ranked free agents — outfielders Joe Rudi and Don Baylor and second baseman Bobby Grich — to long-term contracts totaling $5.25 million, equivalent to $22 million in 2017.

That doesn't sound like much in the context of 21st century salaries, but in 1976 it was an unprecedented splurge that outraged many of Autry's fellow owners. "I still don't think all this is good for baseball," he said. "But this is the way it is now, and there are certain facts of life we're going to have to live with."[22]

While he was counting on the pricey players to win games, Autry was also counting on an axiom of the entertainment business: Stars sell tickets. Attendance more than doubled in the next three years. After adding seven-time batting champion Rod Carew to their collection of free agents, the Angels won their first American League West title in 1979, then won again in 1982 and 1986. Each time they lost the league championship series.

Ina Autry died of cancer in 1980. Although they were outwardly devoted, her husband had spent large chunks of their 48-year marriage on the road or on location for his films, and had affairs with several of his leading ladies and uncounted groupies. Friends said Ina shut her eyes to all that. Most important, she had nurtured him through periods of uncontrolled drinking and unsuccessful attempts to quit.

Autry's family life was always a pain. He supported his ex-convict father and his father's second family for decades. His brother, Dudley, was an unfortunate chip off the old block, a wastrel and an alcoholic who tried and failed to ride the family name to a singing career and often ended up on Gene's payroll. Dudley's ex-wife, a trick-rope artist, also exploited the Autry name to help her career.

Eighteen months after Ina's death, the 73-year-old Autry married Jacqueline Ellam, who was 34 years younger. A former bank executive, Jackie took over management of his businesses as he aged.

In his last years, Autry became a leading philanthropist in Southern California. He spent about $100 million to establish the Autry Museum of the American West, now known as the Autry National Center. (He had lost his first collection of western artifacts in a house fire in 1941.) He gave $5 million to build a wing of the Eisenhower Medical Center in Palm Springs, where he and Jackie had a home.

Autry spent more years of his life as a baseball owner than as a singing cowboy, but the World Series eluded him. "For sure, baseball has been the most exciting and frustrating experience of my life," he said. "In the movies, I never lost a fight. In baseball I hardly ever won one."[23]

He turned over control of the Angels to his wife in 1990. In May 1995 Autry announced an agreement in principle to sell operating control of the team to the Walt Disney Company. Soon afterward the Angels climbed into first place and adopted the rallying cry "Win one for the cowboy," but they blew an 11-game lead and lost the Western Division title to Seattle in a one-game playoff.

The Disney deal closed in early 1996, ending Autry's active involvement. The company acquired 25 percent of the franchise with an option to buy the rest after his death. Autry continued to attend Angels games when he was able. He contracted lymphoma and died at 91 on October 2, 1998. He was mourned as a good man, an American success story, and, for many, a reminder of happy childhood.

Autry called himself a personality, not a singer or actor. "When I started, they said I couldn't act," he once recalled. "Other people said I couldn't sing, but I sure as hell could count."[24]

Four years after Autry's death, the Angels won the 2002 pennant and defeated the Giants in the World Series to claim their first championship. In the joyful clubhouse after Game Seven, manager Mike Scioscia hoisted a bottle of champagne to toast the cowboy.

Acknowledgments

This biography was reviewed by Jan Finkel and fact-checked by Stephen Glotfelty.

NOTES

1. Myrna Oliver, "Gene Autry Dies," *Los Angeles Times*, October 3, 1998: 24.
2. Al Martinez, "2 Old-Time Cowboy Stars Reflect a Heroic Age," *Los Angeles Times*, February 27, 1977: II-6.
3. Bruce Fessier, "Autry was sunshine in lots of lives," *Desert Sun* (Palm Springs, California), October 3, 1998: 3.
4. If not otherwise credited, information about Autry's personal life and Hollywood career comes from Holly George-Warren, *Public Cowboy no. 1: The Life and Times of Gene Autry* (New York: Oxford University Press, 2007).
5. George-Warren, 138.
6. Bosley Crowther, "A Cowboy Without a Lament," *New York Times*, August 6, 1939: X3.
7. Inflation calculator at https://data.bls.gov/cgi-bin/cpicalc.pl.
8. The apartment building where Slye was born stood on the future site of Riverfront Stadium, home of the Big Red Machine. He liked to say he was born on second base. Laurence Zewisohn, "Happy Trails: The Life of Roy Rogers," http://www.royrogers.com/roy_rogers_bio.html, accessed May 19, 2017.
9. Some Gene Autry cowboy suits were made of flammable fabric. Two children died from fires and others were hurt. Autry was the target of several lawsuits over the product.
10. George-Warren, 182.
11. *Life*, July 12, 1943.
12. Autry is credited as co-writer on more than 300 songs, but many of those are "star credits." Singing stars often took writing credit on songs they popularized, and some songwriters didn't mind because the famous name made the song more salable.
13. Frank Finch, "Rumors have AL expanding," *Los Angeles Times*, December 4, 1960: H5.
14. Jeanne Hoffman, "Autry Set to Build Angels in 120 Days," *Los Angeles Times*, December 13, 1960: IV-5. The first mention of Autry as one of the bidders was before the AL meetings of November 22 and December 5: Paul Zimmerman, "Greenberg Out, L.A. Team Up for Bids" *Los Angeles Times*, November 18, 1960: II-1.
15. Finch, "It's Official! Angels to Play in 1961," *Los Angeles Times*, December 8, 1960: IV-1; Andy McCue, *Mover and Shaker: Walter O'Malley, the Dodgers, & Baseball's Westward Expansion* (Lincoln: University of Nebraska Press, 2014), 292-293.
16. Hoffman.
17. Al Carr, "When and Will Angels Move?" *Los Angeles Times*, February 9, 1964: 14
18. Ross Newhan, "No. 26 on the Wall, No. 1 in their Hearts," *Los Angeles Times*, October 3, 1998: C6.
19. Ron Rapaport, "Angels Haven't Had a Sweet 16," *Los Angeles Times*, October 12, 1976: III-1.
20. Tom Singer, "Tribute precedes Autry's induction to Hall," mlb.com, July 19, 2011, http://m.mlb.com/news/article/21960212//, accessed May 22, 2017.
21. Ibid.
22. Dick Miller, "Rudi, Baylor Give Angels Case of Flag Fever," *The Sporting News*, December 4, 1976: 65.
23. Oliver.
24. Richard Simon and Susan King, "Friends and fans recall an American icon," *Los Angeles Times*, October 3, 1998: 25.

RON SHELTON: ON COBB, BULL DURHAM, AND BASEBALL-ON-SCREEN

BY ROB EDELMAN

IN THE BASEBALL FANTASY *FIELD of Dreams*, the spirits of various diamond greats come to play ball on a field rising magically out of Midwestern corn stalks. "Ty Cobb wanted to play," chuckles Shoeless Joe Jackson. "But no one could stand the son-of-a-bitch when we were alive, so we told him to stick it."

In 1994, this "son-of-a-bitch" was the subject of a film all his own. It was *Cobb*, written and directed by Ron Shelton, minor-league journeyman turned major-league Hollywood player.

On the field Tyrus Raymond Cobb, the Georgia Peach, had an exemplary major-league career, lasting from 1905 through 1928. No other batter has matched his lifetime batting average of .366. Only Pete Rose has bested his total of 4,189 hits.

The story goes that, in 1958, Lefty O'Doul was questioned about how Cobb would fare against contemporary pitching. O'Doul responded that Cobb might hit .340. Why so low, he was asked? "You have to remember," he replied, "the man is 72 years old."[1]

Off the field, however, Ty Cobb was something else altogether. He was an unabashed racist who lamented the South's loss of the Civil War. He constantly carried a loaded gun. He was a vicious, foulmouthed brawler and tyrant. It is no surprise that he was so disliked by his fellow players.

"Cobb was the original trash talker," Shelton explained in an interview just after his film's release. "He was a Southern redneck who taunted everybody all the time, even his own teammates."[2] This is the Ty Cobb that Shelton depicts on screen.

But *Cobb* does not focus on the man in his playing days. It is set in the twilight of Cobb's life, and examines what Shelton described as the "curious relationship" between Cobb (played by Tommy Lee Jones) and sportswriter Al Stump (Robert Wuhl). In 1960 Stump was hired to ghostwrite the faded legend's whitewashed autobiography, *My Life in Baseball: The True Record*.

The two spent nearly a year together. A truer picture of the man emerged in Stump's 1994 book *Cobb: A Biography*, in which Cobb is portrayed as an argumentative, sickly, booze-soaked old man who was, as Stump writes, "contemptuous of any law other than his own."[3]

"He's in very poor health now," Shelton said of Stump, who passed away in December 1995, one year after the film's release. "But I got to know him very well before I began writing the film. For this reason it's filled with many anecdotes about Cobb that had never before been printed."

Shelton is one for making literary references, in both his films and his conversation. He contrasted the Cobb-Stump relationship to what might have been "if Samuel Johnson hired Boswell at gunpoint." In *Bull Durham*, his instant-classic baseball film, which came to theaters in 1988, one of his characters is noted for quoting Walt Whitman and William Blake.

But while the subject of *Cobb* is a Hall of Fame ballplayer, Shelton does not consider it a baseball movie. He sees no relation between *Cobb* and *Bull Durham*, which is as pure a baseball story as has ever been filmed.

"I am fascinated by people like Ty Cobb, who can be so sociopathic and dysfunctional outside their craft and so brilliant in it," he said. "Cobb was a fascinating set of contradictions. He was an uncommonly brilliant athlete who was equally uncommonly obsessed. You can only marvel at his numbers—and also at his abominable behavior."

He added that the film also "is about an old man who's been called immortal, and how he faces his mortality." In *Cobb*, Shelton asks questions that are well worth pondering, and which resonate today: Why do we in America make heroes out of people like Ty Cobb? Why do we forgive the abysmal behavior of a man whose main contribution to society is the ability to hit .366?

Not all less-than-saintly sports heroes—and they are endless, and have appeared on big-time rosters for decades—are as downright appalling as Cobb. Others simply are uncouth. "Deion Sanders, for instance, can get away with his outrageous behavior because he's so damn good," Shelton noted. "He can pull off all his jive. But if he wasn't Deion Sanders, he'd just be another boor."

Others, meanwhile, are more paradoxical. Shelton said his conception of Cobb was being contrasted to O.J. Simpson. It is a comparison he does not buy. "O.J. Simpson is a man with a public image and a private reality," he observed. "Ty Cobb was completely different. His antics were not hidden. All of them made the front page. But nobody cared. Because he hit .367, he was able to meet with presidents. If he had hit .267, he would have been in jail."[4]

The critical reaction to *Cobb* was what Shelton described as "most curious" and "schizophrenic." He explained, "I could show you 400 reviews. Two hundred of the critics loved the film; 200 hated it. There's been no middle ground."

Two examples: Peter Travers, in *Rolling Stone*, dubbed *Cobb* "the *Raging Bull* of baseball movies," adding that "Jones gives a landmark performance (and) Shelton's strong, stinging film (is) one of the year's best. ...";[5] the *San Francisco Chronicle's* Peter Stack described the film as a "histrionic portrait (that) comes across like a fly ball that thuds on the ground. ..." Stack labeled Jones's performance "tiresome," noting that the actor "succeeds only in running the awful and pathetic Cobb into the ground."[6]

The uneven nature of its critical reception plus the inability of Warner Bros., the film's distributor, to properly market *Cobb* resulted in a limited release for the film. On the other hand, *Bull Durham*, Shelton's first feature as director-writer, not only was a smash hit: It earned him the Writers Guild of America's Best Original Script award, the Best Script prize from the National Society of Film Critics (as well as kudos from critics' organizations in Boston, Los Angeles, and New York), and a Best Original Screenplay Academy Award nomination.

Indeed, *Bull Durham* is a film that Shelton was destined to make. He was born Ronald Wayne Shelton on September 15, 1945, in Whittier, California. A shortstop-second baseman, the 6-foot-1, 185-pounder was taken by the Baltimore Orioles in the 39th round of the 1966 major-league June Amateur Draft. From 1967 through 1971, he toiled in the bushes with the Stockton Ports, Bluefield Orioles, and Dallas-Fort Worth Spurs, topping out with the Triple-A Rochester Red Wings. His minor-league numbers were unspectacular: a .251 batting average in 479 games, with 425 hits in 1,691 at-bats.

As any baseball film aficionado knows, *Bull Durham* contrasts Crash Davis (Kevin Costner), an aging catcher for the minor-league Durham Bulls who during the course of the story breaks the bush-league record for career four-baggers, and Ebby Calvin "Nuke" LaLoosh (Tim Robbins), a raw rookie hurler famously described as possessing a "million-dollar arm, but a five-cent head."[7] The third major character—the one who cites Whitman and Blake—is Annie Savoy (Susan Sarandon), a sexy baseball groupie who each spring selects one Bull as a season-long lover.

Across the years all three have become iconic screen characters. In August 2015 Mike Hessman, a (mostly) career minor leaguer, belted his 433rd dinger, setting the all-time bush-league record. In report after report of the accomplishment, Hessman was referred to as the real-life Crash Davis, the modern-era Crash Davis. In fact, later that month, when his Toledo Mud Hens were playing the Durham Bulls, Hessman was presented with a framed Crash Davis jersey. "I don't mind," he declared. "I guess that's me. It's fun. It's cool. And I have the record. It's good to be known for something."[8]

As for "Nuke" LaLoosh, the story goes that the character was inspired by Steve Dalkowski, otherwise known as "The Fastest That Never Was." In the early 1960s Dalkowski pitched in the Baltimore Orioles farm system. Granted, he just may have been the hardest thrower ever, but he was unable to harness his control and never made it to "The Show"; the yarns Shelton heard about Dalkowski (whose career predated his) supposedly added to his creating the character.

However, in *Fastball*, the 2016 documentary written and directed by Jonathan Hock and narrated by Kevin Costner, it is noted that LaLoosh "was based in part on Dalkowski or Sidd Finch, George Plimpton's imaginary pitcher who threw 168 miles per hour."[9] Twenty-eight years earlier, upon the film's release, Shelton told the press, "All characters and fictional people are composites. Every team I played on had one or two wild young pitchers who could throw the ball through a brick wall, but never got the Zen aspects of the game together."[10]

At the time, Greg Arnold, a pitcher who played with Shelton before retiring at age 22 in 1971, claimed that he was Shelton's inspiration. "There was no other ('Nuke') LaLoosh," he stated. "He (Shelton) knows it and I know it, and that's all that really matters. He'll go to bed in September with $4 million or $5 million, and I'll go to bed knowing one thing—that I am the Nuke."[11] (In his career, Arnold appeared in 83 games, walking 315 batters and striking out 413 in 476 innings.)

Lastly, in one of the most oft-quoted passages from any baseball film, Annie Savoy professes her belief in "the Church of Baseball." "I've tried all the major religions, and most of the minor ones," she declares. "I've worshipped Buddha, Allah, Brahma, Vishnu, Siva, trees, mushrooms, and Isadora Duncan. I know things. For instance, there are 108 beads in a Catholic rosary and there are 108 stitches in a baseball. When I learned that, I gave Jesus a chance. But it just didn't work out between us. The Lord laid too much guilt on me.

"I prefer metaphysics to theology. You see, there's no guilt in baseball, and it's never boring, which makes it like sex. There's never been a ballplayer slept with me who didn't have the best year of his career."[12]

Annie Savoy and her super-fandom aside, in *Bull Durham* Shelton conjured up a knowing ode to minor-league baseball and baseball players, not to mention the pressures faced by wannabes who yearn for their shot in "The Show." The underlying point here is that, in the end, pro sports is a business. "It's about the players as people, the very real pressures they face," he noted. "For example, are they gonna get promoted? Are they gonna lose their jobs?"

Undeniably, the film's enduring popularity has reverberated across the decades. One of countless examples: On May 28, 2016, *New York Post* columnist

Ron Shelton, back in the day, as a Rochester Red Wing.

Kevin Kernan casually observed, "Earlier this year, Noah Syndergaard said his pitching world changed for the better over the past year when he finally learned how to loosen his grip on the baseball and hold it like an egg, as they explained in the movie *Bull Durham*."[13]

The film also has transcended the sports page, and has come to define Shelton's show-biz success. In 2010 TBS announced that he had signed to write and executive-produce the *Bull Durham*-esque *Hound Dogs*, an hourlong TV comedy pilot centering on the minor-league Nashville Hound Dogs. "As he did with *Bull Durham*, Shelton will draw from his own experiences as a minor leaguer," reported *Entertainment Weekly*.[14] But the show was not picked up, and *Hound Dogs* emerged as a 2011 made-for-television movie.

Then in 2013, the Topps Pro Debut baseball card set featured *Bull Durham* cut signature cards of Costner, Sarandon, Robbins, and Robert Wuhl (who plays Coach Larry Hockett); three years later, the Topps Archives set included seven *Bull Durham* insert cards along with autographed cards of Shelton and various cast members. The property also was transformed into a stage musical, which premiered in Atlanta in 2014. Shelton contributed the show's book; the essence of the story is summed up in the three-sentence description found on the show's website: "CRASH loves Annie. NUKE loves Annie. ANNIE loves Baseball."[15]

Then in 2016, he was co-executive producer (along with Eric Gagne and Ben Lyons) of *Spaceman*, a biopic directed by Brett Rapkin and starring Josh Duhamel as Bill "Spaceman" Lee.

Back in the 1990s, while researching the book *Great Baseball Films*, I queried real-life major leaguers on their feelings toward baseball-on-screen. Phil Rizzuto commented that those who truly know the game should be hired for their expertise. "They should have ex-ballplayers, groundskeepers (and) newspapermen to make (the films more) realistic," pronounced Scooter.[16]

Rizzuto easily might have cited Ron Shelton as the ideal baseball-movie architect. So it was not surprising that *Bull Durham* was lauded by baseball professionals. "I thought it was a great movie," Don Mattingly told me in a Yankee Stadium pregame conversation. "I played in the South Atlantic League, (and the film) was pretty close to capturing life in the minor leagues. It was pretty cool."[17] "When it came out," reported Shelton, "Will Clark (then of the San Francisco Giants) was passing out garter belts in the locker room. Apparently, the Giants really embraced the movie."

Even the comments that were more critical at least acknowledged the film's uniqueness. "The most true-to-life (baseball films) have been made in recent years," observed Joe L. Brown, the son of comic actor Joe E. Brown and the longtime Pittsburgh Pirates general manager, who was interviewed for *Great Baseball Films*. "*Bull Durham* was good, but I didn't like all the profanity. Some of the incidents in it seemed outlandish, but there was truth to it as it showed some of the experiences kids have in the lower minor leagues."[18]

Shelton's reason for making *Bull Durham*, he explained, was that he "felt no one had made a sports movie right." The majority of baseball films focus on the glory of the game, on-field drama, underdog heroes hitting game-winning home runs in the last of the ninth or striking out a fearsome opponent's heaviest hitter with the bases loaded. "I generally don't like them," he noted. "They're not relative to anything other than a publicist's idea of their subjects."

For example, Shelton cited two celluloid biographies of Babe Ruth: *The Babe Ruth Story*, a 1948 film starring William Bendix; and 1992's *The Babe*, with John Goodman. "Neither of them worked," he said. "The first in particular is nothing more than a campy exercise. How can you believe William Bendix, who looked to be about 45 when he made this film, in his scenes (playing Babe) as a 16-year-old orphan?"

He added that fans "don't understand that athletes don't hate other athletes. The Dodger players don't hate the Giant players. The fact of the matter is that they all hate management. They all have much in common with labor.

"My view of sports is from the field, the locker room, the team bus. I tend to tell stories from the

Ron Shelton, in the present-day, signing autographs at Frontier Field, the Rochester Red Wings ballpark; on July 7, 2017, he was inducted into the team's Hall of Fame.

field, not the 30th row of the bleachers." With this in mind, Shelton was ideally suited to direct *Jordan Rides the Bus* (2010), a 51-minute episode of *30 for 30*, the ESPN documentary series. There, he charts Michael Jordan's early 1990s foray into minor-league baseball.

Shelton's approach remains consistent in the non-baseball films he has directed and scripted: *White Men Can't Jump* (1992), the story of two urban basketball hustlers (Woody Harrelson and Wesley Snipes); *Tin Cup* (1996), about a self-destructive golfer (also played by Kevin Costner); and *Play It to the Bone* (1999), with Harrelson and Antonio Banderas as aging boxers and best pals who agree to face off in the ring. Sports also are present in films that Shelton only scripted or co-scripted: football (1986's *The Best of Times*); basketball (1994's *Blue Chips*); and boxing (1996's *The Great White Hype*).

However, even when baseball is not the focus of the story, Shelton manages to sneak references to the sport into his scenario. For instance, in *Tin Cup*, it is revealed near the finale that the hero, Roy "Tin Cup" McAvoy, won his nickname as a schoolboy baseball player. In one sequence, McAvoy even yells out "Louisville Slugger" as he belts a golf ball with a baseball bat.

In his earliest films, Shelton is credited only as screenwriter. He was inspired to work behind the camera because, as he explained, "I wanted to direct my own words. I didn't like the way they'd been interpreted on screen." One exception is *Under Fire*, whose script Shelton co-authored with Clayton Frohman: a 1983 drama set in Nicaragua just before the fall of dictator Anastasio Somoza to the revolutionary Sandinista forces. "I was pleased with the way that one was made," Shelton said.

One of the secondary characters in *Under Fire* is Pedro, a bomb-throwing Sandinista who greatly admires then-Baltimore Orioles pitcher Dennis Martinez. Pedro autographs a baseball and instructs an American reporter to give it to Martinez when she returns to the United States. With a grand gesture, he dons an Orioles cap and hurls a grenade with pinpoint accuracy, just as his idol would burn in fastballs.

"Kid's got a hell of an arm," observes a photojournalist. Pedro then declares, "Dennis Martinez, he is the best. He is from Nicaragua. He pitches major leagues. ... You see Dennis Martinez, you tell him that my curveball is better, that I have good scroogie. ..."[19] Seconds later, Pedro is felled by a bullet.

"I didn't want to make an ideological movie about the Nicaraguan revolution," explained Shelton. "I didn't want to make a movie for the already converted. But how could I make the Sandinista point of view understandable to audiences? I decided to do it through baseball, by having a young revolutionary infatuated with baseball." Pedro is a character who, as Shelton said, "is not gonna talk about Karl Marx. He's gonna talk about Earl Weaver."

In *Under Fire*, Shelton honors the type of little-known but devoted ballplayer with whom he feels an affinity by naming one of the characters, a political flack, after career minor-league pitcher-manager Hub Kittle. Kittle entered baseball as a player in 1937 and began managing in 1948, but kept returning to the mound for years after his final full season as a pitcher. In 1980, at age 63, he even hurled an inning for the Triple-A Springfield Redbirds. (Kittle finally debuted in the majors in 1971, as a Houston Astros coach.)

Hub Kittle may be a relatively obscure baseball professional. Ty Cobb may be one of the most famous names in baseball history. But which one would you rather have coaching your kid's Little League baseball team?

Still, *Bull Durham*—and not *Cobb* or any of his other films—remains Ron Shelton's masterpiece. Upon its release, I described it as "a tremendously entertaining film and arguably the most knowing of all baseball movies."[20] This was true in 1988, and it remains so in 2016.

The original version of this article was published in 1997 in Issue 17 of *The National Pastime*.

Special thanks to Rory Costello and John-William Greenbaum for their comments on the "origin" of "Nuke" LaLoosh.

NOTES

1. Earl Gustkey, "Ty Cobb: No Better Player Swung a Bat; No Worse a Person Played the Game," *Los Angeles Times*, September 12, 1985.
2. All remarks from Ron Shelton are from an interview conducted by the author in December 1994, unless otherwise indicated.
3. Al Stump, *Cobb: A Biography* (Chapel Hill, North Carolina: Algonquin Books of Chapel Hill, 1994), 6.
4. Research by Pete Palmer resulted in two base hits—which had been double-counted—being subtracted from Cobb's career batting average, edging it down from .367 to .366.
5. rollingstone.com/movies/reviews/cobb-19941202.
6. sfgate.com/movies/article/FILM-REVIEW-Tommy-Lee-Jones-Strikes-Out-as-3028597.php
7. Line from *Bull Durham* screenplay.
8. Johnette Howard, "Minor League HR King Mike Hessman—the Real-Life Crash Davis—Had Career Worth Celebrating," *ESPN.com*, December 14, 2015.
9. Line from *Fastball* narration.
10. Mark Hyman, "No Bull: Ex-Player Claims He Inspired 'Durham' Character," *Daytona Beach Sunday News-Journal*, July 3, 1988: 5D.
11. Ibid.
12. Lines from *Bull Durham* screenplay.
13. Kevin Kernan, "Get Michael Pineda Out of Yankees Rotation Right Now," *New York Post*, May 28, 2016.
14. Mandi Bierly, "Ron Shelton to Pen Minor League Baseball Comedy for TBS. Can We Call Up Costner (or Russell)?" *Entertainment Weekly*, October 21, 2010.
15. bulldurhammusical.com/.
16. Rob Edelman, *Great Baseball Films* (New York: Citadel Press, 1994), 16.
17. On-field pregame interview with author at Yankee Stadium, July 1994.
18. Edelman, 16.
19. Lines from *Under Fire* screenplay.
20. Rob Edelman, quoted in *New Haven Register*, 1988.

THOMAS TULL: ON DARK KNIGHTS, HANGOVERS, AND BASEBALL

BY ROB EDELMAN

How does a man of modest background become a billionaire Hollywood player?

For Thomas Tull, his status as a Tinseltown powerhouse is the result of a combination of fortuity, hard work, and relentless drive. It is the byproduct of his forming his own film company and producing or executive-producing such box-office blockbusters as *The Dark Knight* (2008) and *The Dark Knight Rises* (2012), and *The Hangover* (2009) and its two sequels (released in 2011 and 2013). Granted that in his heart of hearts he is a comic-book geek and a superhero fanboy, but he also is a baseball zealot who has made two highly regarded, high-profile sports films: *42* (2013), a biopic emphasizing the struggles of Jackie Robinson to play major-league baseball; and *Fastball* (2016), a documentary that offers a knowing overview of baseball in the twenty-first century.

If one wishes to "make it" in the movies, having a famous parent to place a phone call and request a favor opens doors that otherwise will be shut. But Tull has no such pedigree; his childhood was as far removed from Hollywood as Paris, Texas, is from Paris, France. He was born in 1970 and grew up in Endwell, New York, a hamlet west of Binghamton. His dental-hygienist mother was a single parent, and he helped support her and his two younger sisters by shoveling snow and mowing lawns. "Struggling as a family financially, I grew up within the confines of constantly worrying (whether) the light is going to get turned off," he recalled in 2016. "I think you can get drive from that."[1]

As a youngster, Tull played baseball and football and even earned a gridiron scholarship to Hamilton College, in Clinton, New York, from which he graduated in 1992. His initial intention was to become a lawyer but he entered the business world instead, first opening Smart Wash, a chain of laundromats, and eventually founding Tax Services of America, the owner-operator of Jackson-Hewitt tax-preparation franchises. He then became a venture capitalist. Most significantly, in 2001, he moved on to the Convex Group, an Atlanta-based private-equity firm, eventually becoming its president.

Tull then turned his interests westward, to Southern California and the movie industry. In 2003 he left Convex, raised between $500 million and $600 million to bankroll film projects, and co-founded Legendary Pictures, a production company. Two years later, Legendary linked up with Warner Bros. to co-finance and co-produce films. In 2009 Tull became Legendary's majority shareholder. In 2013 the company connected with Universal Pictures in a union that was similar to Tull's Warner Bros. hookup. Then in 2016, Legendary became a subsidiary of the Dalian Wanda Group, a Chinese conglomerate.

Tull's fascination with superheroes has greatly impacted his choice of projects. Many of his films are name brands: *Superman Returns* (2006); *Ninja Assassin* (2009); *Watchmen* (2009); *Clash of the Titans* (2010); *Jonah Hex* (2010); *Man of Steel* (2013); *Godzilla* (2014); *Dracula Untold* (2014); *Jurassic World* (2015) … These are the kinds of films that are box-office record-breakers. According to Hollywood.com, Legendary is "perhaps the most progressive and successful motion picture production company to be formed in the 2000s. ..."[2] In a 2013 *New York Times* profile, it was noted that Tull's "aggressiveness and aw-shucks charm made him one of the most successful walk-on players in movie history."[3]

His passion for baseball has resulted in the production of *42* and *Fastball*, films that never will rake in the box-office bucks of a *Dark Knight* or *Hangover*. This fervor is emphasized in the first line of the *Times* piece: "During the baseball strike of 1995, Thomas Tull, then a 24-year-old laundromat owner, was audacious enough to turn up at a training camp for the Atlanta Braves. They looked at his swing and sent him home."[4] If Tull was fated to never sign a pro contract, his accomplishments have allowed him a different kind of access to professional sports. In 2009 he became a part-owner of the Pittsburgh Steelers, a team he had been rooting for since he was 4 years old. Then in 2012, he tried but failed in a bid to purchase the San Diego Padres. The following year, he was elected to the board of directors of the National Baseball Hall of Fame and Museum.

Tull additionally produced *42*, which of course is not the first film to spotlight Jackie Robinson's integrating the major leagues. Back in 1950, three years after Robinson first played for the Brooklyn Dodgers, he starred as himself in *The Jackie Robinson Story*; other aspects of his life were examined in the made-for-TV movies *The Court-Martial of Jackie Robinson* (1990) and *Soul of the Game* (1996). Notwithstanding, given his importance not just in baseball history but in twentieth century American culture, a retelling of Robinson's story has never ceased appealing to filmmakers. Since the mid-1990s, Spike Lee had been attempting to mount a Robinson biopic, but the project did not materialize. Robert Redford also wished to produce one, in which he would play Branch Rickey.

Then in 2011, Tull and Legendary Pictures announced their plans to make the film with the assistance of Rachel Robinson, Jackie's widow. Chadwick Boseman, whose previous credits primarily were on TV series episodes, was cast as Robinson, with Harrison Ford playing The Mahatma, and rising film and television actor Nicole Beharie portraying Rachel. A who's who of baseball names appear in the scenario, with actors cast as Leo Durocher, Dixie Walker, Pee Wee Reese, Wendell Smith, Ben Chapman, Clyde Sukeforth, Burt Shotton, Clay Hopper, Bobby Bragan, Eddie Stanky, Red Barber, Ralph Branca, and Happy Chandler, among others.

Thomas Tull, producer of 42, *the Jackie Robinson biopic.*

C.J. Nitkowski, ex-major leaguer-turned writer/radio host/TV analyst, plays Dutch Leonard.

42 was released in April 2013. That July, Tull was honored by the National Baseball Hall of Fame and Museum, and I asked him if he was familiar with *The Jackie Robinson Story*. "I've seen clips, but I haven't seen the entire film," was his response. He added, "I talked about it with Rachel. But it was a different voice, and I didn't want it to influence *42*."[5] It is understandable that the creator of a new film would discourage comparisons with earlier, similar projects because of the desire to focus on its marketing. In this case, as Tull explained while addressing the crowd at Cooperstown's Doubleday Field, *42* is "the most important film I'll ever do." He recalled, "I had the privilege of bringing Hank (Aaron) to set. And I can assure you, even Harrison Ford was nervous that day." Finally, Tull observed, "After making *Batman*, *Superman*, and other superhero movies, the greatest 'superhero' movie that could be made is about Jackie Robinson."[6]

Fastball, Tull's baseball-centric follow-up, spotlights the heralded fastball pitchers, from Walter Johnson and Bob Feller to Sandy Koufax and Bob Gibson to Nolan Ryan and Aroldis Chapman. *Fastball* also offers a knowing overview of baseball in the twenty-first century as it stresses the phenomenon of pitcher after pitcher entering games for an inning and challenging hitters by throwing horsehides 95 or 100-plus miles per hour. And given Tull's profile within the film industry, it is no wonder that a gallery of baseball celebs were enlisted as interviewees, from current superstars—this list begins with Justin Verlander, David Price, Bryce Harper, Andrew McCutchen, and Derek Jeter—to such "old-timers" as Joe Morgan, Goose Gossage, Mike Schmidt, Al Kaline, Ernie Banks, and Hank Aaron. There is a direct connection between *Fastball* and *42* that transcends baseball; as Bob Gibson is interviewed, he cites the racism American-style that so defined the late 1950s and '60s, when he was establishing himself as a future Hall of Famer.

And speaking of Hall of Famers, a number of ballplayers who were present in Cooperstown in May 2016 for the Hall of Fame Classic were queried as to how they felt about the content of *Fastball*. What were their opinions on the demise of the complete game and the arrival of the speedballing specialists? Rollie Fingers, the mustachioed relief pitcher, declared, "It's probably the biggest change (in the sport). It's much more specialized, and it seems to be working." But he added, in relation to his own career, "I don't think *I* could do it." Noted then-borderline Hall of Famer Alan Trammell, "We all are used to the way the game was played during our era, but times change and we have to be open-minded." And he was quick to note that "the game today *is* very healthy." Hall of Famer Ryne Sandberg observed, "It's just different today. It's the nature of the game. There are very different arms in the bullpen, and you want to (use them). … It's a new piece to the puzzle."[7]

Given Tull's Cooperstown connection, it was no surprise that *Fastball* was the opening-night selection of the Hall's 10th Annual Baseball Film Festival, held in September 2015. And it was Tull who approached Jonathan Hock, an Emmy-nominated documentarian, to helm the film. "First, he wanted to create the film every parent, kid, and baseball fan in the world will want to put in the DVD player every March for the next 50 years to get psyched for the baseball season, and fall in love all over again with the game," Hock observed. "And second, he wanted to put a stake in the ground and do the impossible—to compare pitchers from different eras and figure out who threw the fastest ever."[8]

Several years earlier, Tull returned to his alma mater to address students on his "journey from Hamilton to Hollywood." "I never in a million years planned to be in the movie business," he noted, adding that the two questions any filmmaker should ask before embarking on a project are: "Is it a great story?" and "How are you going to market the film?" He added, "No matter how fascinating the techno toys are, if the story isn't there (people will walk out disappointed)."[9] Finally, in relation to his out-of-left-field success, Tull on another occasion observed, "If somebody came in and pitched me it as a script, I would say it's too far-fetched."[10]

NOTES

1. Natalie Robehmed. "Box Office Billionaire: How Legendary's Thomas Tull Used Comics, China and a Secret Formula to Remake Hollywood," *Forbes*, February 29, 2016.
2. hollywood.com/celebrities/thomas-tull-57636550/.
3. Brooks Barnes and Michael Cieply, "Film Financier Faces a Critical Juncture," *New York Times*, February 3, 2013.
4. Ibid.
5. wamc.org/post/rob-edelman-now#stream/0.
6. Ibid.
7. Interviews by the author conducted in Cooperstown on May 28, 2016.
8. m.mlb.com/news/article/118994038/fastball-dials-up-heat-on-the-big-screen.
9. hamilton.edu/news/story/thomas-tull-92-discusses-his-journey-from-hamilton-to-hollywood.
10. imdb.com/name/nm2100078/bio?ref_=nm_ov_bio_sm.

DE WOLF HOPPER, DIGBY BELL, AND THE FIVE A'S

BY ROB EDELMAN

ACROSS THE DECADES, PROfessional actors and athletes have shared a special camaraderie. Both are paid entertainers, performing for the pleasure of the masses. So not surprisingly, many thespians are vocal supporters of their favorite ball teams. Back in the day, for example, Tallulah Bankhead was a famed New York Giants fan-atic. ("There have been only two geniuses in the world, Willie Mays and Willie Shakespeare," she once observed.) Celebs from Pearl Bailey to Jerry Seinfeld have adored the New York Mets. Billy Crystal bleeds New York Yankees pinstripes. Bill Murray is a vocal Chicago Cubs rooter. Ben Affleck loves the Boston Red Sox. The list is endless.

This actor-baseball connection is no twentieth-century phenomenon. It dates from the last decades of the nineteenth century, prior to the dawn of the motion picture (not to mention the popularity of radio and television). Back then, the best-known American actors were New York-centric stage stars: They may have toured the provinces, but they always came home to Manhattan. And more than a few were fervent sports fans. "Many actors are fond of athletic enjoyments," observed the *New York Dramatic Mirror* in 1889. "The natural game has no stauncher worshippers than those of its devotees that are connected with the stage."[1]

Two such fan-atics were De Wolf Hopper and Digby Bell. Not only were they best pals and acclaimed entertainers: They also predated Tallulah Bankhead as fervent New York Giants devotees. The duo regularly attended Giants games; they and other late-nineteenth-century notables were members in good standing of "The High and Mighty Order of Baseball Cranks of Gotham," a group that inhabited their own section in the Polo Grounds grandstand. Indeed, in his 1927 memoir, Hopper noted that "Digby Bell had converted me to baseball. ... We were at the Polo Grounds every free afternoon."[2] They also followed the team on road trips and palled around with players. One of endless examples: On April 21, 1889, the *New York Times* reported that, on the previous day, Edward "Ned" Williamson, "the popular short stop of the Chicago Club," arrived in New York and was feted at a supper by restaurateur Nick Engel. Among those present were Hopper, Bell, and a blend of baseball folk, entertainers, and civic figures.[3]

Hopper and Bell also were acknowledged baseball experts. In a review of *A Ball Player's Career*, a reminiscence penned by Cap Anson in 1900, an unnamed writer began his critique by noting, "Joy untold will burst into the hearts of thousands of lovers of the National game when they learn that 'Pop' Anson has written a book. Who knows more about baseball than he? Why, not even Digby Bell or De Wolf Hopper."[4] Thirty-eight years later, *New York Times* columnist John Kieran dubbed the duo "as rabid a pair of fans as ever rooted home a run or roasted an umpire."[5]

Legend has it that Hopper and Bell were even partially responsible for dubbing the team the Giants. Some sources claim that the name caught on in June 1885 when Jim Mutrie, the team's manager, referred to his players as "My big fellows! My Giants!" after an extra-inning triumph over the Philadelphia Phillies. Others note that Mutrie might have employed the name earlier that season. However, in 1936, Horace C. Stoneham, the team's president, declared that the nickname was directly related to Hopper and Bell. An "editorial note" printed in the *New York Times* claimed that, upon arriving home from a successful road trip in 1883, the actors were among a group of fans who told Mutrie that the team had played "like giants."[6]

*   *   *

The lives of Digby Bell and De Wolf Hopper reflect on both the American theater and the baseball world during the last two decades of the nineteenth century. Bell was born in Milwaukee in 1849 and died in Miss Alston's Sanitarium on West 61st Street in Manhattan 68 years later. He won fame as an actor-comedian who, as noted in his *New York Times* obituary, was "one of the best known of American light opera singers. Some of his best known roles were in the operas of Gilbert and Sullivan."[7] But baseball was never far from his thoughts. On September 12, 1888, the *Times* reported that Bell was in excellent spirits. *Boccaccio*, an opera featuring the actor, had just opened at Wallack's Theatre and was a "pronounced success." The paper noted that Bell "was thinking how pleasant it was not to have anything new to study, no rehearsals, and nothing more serious to worry about than an occasional defeat of the Giants, for he is a baseball crank of the first magnitude. ..."[8]

The year before, Bell had traveled with the team to Boston. Upon returning, he observed, "I never saw the boys play better in my life. They hit the ball hard, ran the bases like sprinters, and their fielding—well, it was just superb." He added, "Don't I wish that De Wolf Hopper had been in Boston! Why, he would just go into ecstasies if he saw the manner in which the Giants handled [King] Kelly and his eight shadows." Bell then went on to offer a detailed description of the "unjust" decision-making on the part of "Umpire Sullivan."[9]

Hopper, who was born in New York City in 1858, was described in his 1935 *New York Times* obit as the "noted musical comedian, whose career on the stage extended into the youthful memories of the oldest theatregoers ..."[10] The fifth of his six wives was Hedda Hopper, the actress and gossip columnist of note; William Hopper, their offspring, was best known for playing private detective Paul Drake on the long-running *Perry Mason* TV series. But Hopper's lasting fame was linked to his countless renderings over a 45-year timespan of "Casey at the Bat," the Ernest Lawrence Thayer classic. He first performed "Casey" at Wallack's Theatre on August 14, 1888, less than a month before Bell's *Boccaccio* played that venue. The actor then was appearing with the McCaull Opera Company in *Prince Methusalem*—both he and Bell were McCaull regulars—and Hopper recited the poem during the second act to amuse the New York Giants and Chicago White Stockings players who were in attendance as guests of the management. (Coincidentally, one noteworthy winning streak ended just as Hopper debuted "Casey at the Bat." Earlier that day, the White Stockings bested Tim Keefe by a 4-2 score, thus handing the Giants star hurler his first loss after 19 straight victories.)

Hopper's "Casey" connection was not limited to the stage. In 1916 he starred onscreen in *Casey at the Bat*, a feature-length drama that is an extension of the poem. The actor plays Casey, a grocery clerk and "the baseball hero of Mudville," who is devoted to his niece (May Garcia). On the day of an important game against Frogtown, she injures herself while climbing a tree and he refuses to leave her side. The yells of the fans persuade Casey to come to the rescue of his team in the ninth inning, but he strikes out as he notices a messenger in the ballpark who he thinks has arrived with bad tidings about the child.[11]

Happily, there is a filmed record of Hopper actually reciting "Casey." In 1922 he did so in a DeForest Phonofilm, utilizing the sound-on-film technology developed by Theodore Case, and the result is a fascinating, unintentionally funny curio. Hopper, garbed in a tuxedo, a slightly askew bowtie, and the most obvious hairpiece, emerges from behind a curtain. "I am very glad that 'Casey at the Bat' has been asked for," he tells the camera, boastfully adding that if he "should forget a line or two here or there ... most anyone could prompt me." He then recites the poem, becoming so involved in its emotion that his eyes close and pop open at the appropriate dramatic moments. Hopper orates as if he is trying to reach the patron in the last row of a theater balcony; back in 1922, sound-on-film was revolutionary and actors knew nothing of playing down to the camera. But to say that Hopper chews the curtain behind him is no understatement. He trills his *r*'s and *wr*'s; at the finale, as he describes how there is no joy in Mudville, he is practically bawling. After completing the recitation, Hopper bows slightly, smiles, and disappears behind the curtain.[12]

But Hopper's love of baseball transcended his fame as the premier "Casey" interpreter. At his death, he was performing in Kansas City, Missouri, despite his failing health and, as reported in the *New York Times* on September 24, 1935, "A strange rounding out of fate appeared in the actor's last words, which referred to his interest in baseball. ... At 11 o'clock last night Mr. Hopper had insisted upon sitting up in bed to smoke a pipe while he looked over the sports pages of a newspaper. Physicians insisted that he needed a rest and tried to persuade him to go to sleep. But he waved them aside with a characteristic gesture. 'See you tomorrow, Doc,' he said. 'I never sleep until 3 A.M. anyway. Run along while I see what the (St. Louis) Cards did.'" The following morning, a nurse discovered that Hopper had died in his sleep.[13]

In an homage to Hopper published in the paper, it was noted that by 1888 the actor "had been a baseball fan for years, had spent every free afternoon at the game and had with Digby Bell put on an annual Sunday night benefit for the local team."[14] Certainly, the duo was not the first to entertain entire ballclubs. For example, on July 16, 1877, the Boston and Chicago nines were in the audience at Chicago's Adelphi Theatre. On May 5, 1884, the Grand Rapids team was on hand for a performance of *Iolanthe* in Grand Rapids; the following evening, they were joined by the Muskegon team for a performance of *Olivette* in Muskegon. But Hopper and Bell were the first to do so regularly.

In their presentations, they often concocted baseball-related entertainment. Such was the case when Hopper debuted his "Casey" recitation. Another example: On October 15, 1888, the *New York Times* reported that Hopper and Bell were among the organizers of a "roaring benefit" at the Star Theatre for the New York nine, which had just been crowned "League champions of 1888." "Enthusiastic patrons of the pastime willingly paid $5 and $10 for seats," the paper reported, adding, "It was estimated that the benefit would net the players between $4,000 and $5,000." Some of the era's top actors performed, and many of the numbers were baseball-related. "De Wolf Hopper and Harry Kernell entertained the audience in their own peculiar way for not less than half an hour," the *Times* observed, "and the former made some felicitous remarks about the national game." The finale, featuring Hopper, Bell, and British-American actress/contralto Laura Joyce Bell, Digby's second wife, was "a comic baseball scene. Digby Bell, wearing a bird cage for a mask, a washboard for a protector, and boxing gloves, stood behind a china plate, where Laura Joyce Bell gracefully wielded a bat and waited eagerly for Hopper, standing in a low-neck dry goods box, to pitch. The scene was irresistibly comic."[15]

And still another: On June 10, 1891, the *Times* reported, "Friday will be baseball night at Palmer's Theatre. Manager Mutrie of the Giants and Capt. Anson of the Chicago club have accepted an invitation from Manager Harry Askin of the 'Tar and Tartar' company and Digby Bell for that night." The paper added that "Mr. Sydney Rosenfeld and Digby Bell in collaboration have fixed up a lot of bright lines sparkling with diamond dust, so that the players will feel quite at home. Digby Bell will also recite his poem, 'The Boy on the Fence'..."[16] (Various sources list alternate titles for Bell's creation. Some call it "The Boy on the Left Field Fence." In 1909 Bell cut an Edison recording titled "The Tough Kid on the Right Field Fence." It was hyped in *The Edison Phonograph Monthly* for its "realistic baseball talk indulged in by the youngster from a 'deserved' seat on the right field fence. He tells the home team how to play the game and what he thinks of them when their playing isn't up to his standard. The Record ought to be a real treat to everyone who understands the language of our national game."[17] The following year, Bell recorded a second baseball ditty: "The Man Who Fanned Casey." And yet another was "A Baseball Monologue.")

Hopper and Bell were thrilled whenever their Giants copped what then was the equivalent of a World Series victory. In 1894 the Giants bested the Baltimore nine to win the Temple Cup, which was

Digby Bell, celebrated American actor and fervent New York Giants fan.

presented to the team in a ceremony at the Broadway Theatre. The venue was decorated with bunting, flags, pennants, and other baseball-linked items. The *New York Times* reported on October 11 that Hopper, Bell, and "a few other cranks have interested themselves sufficiently to undertake the distribution of seats and boxes for the occasion. Yesterday Messrs. Hopper and Bell astonished the members of the Stock Exchange by appearing in their midst. In the interest of the cause three choice boxes were sold for $100 each, and seats in the orchestra were readily bought, the brokers paying $5 each for them." The proceeds were divided among the Giants players.[18]

During this period, newspapers featured accounts of the efforts of Hopper, Bell, and others to organize baseball-related benefits for ailing colleagues. On May 25, 1886, two actor-nines—one consisting of comedians and the other of tragedians—battled each other in the Polo Grounds in what the *New York Times* described as "a match ... for the benefit of the family of the demented playwright, Bartley Campbell." Playing for the comedians were Hopper, Burr McIntosh ("a new and handsome leading man [with] a record as a heart wrecker"), Francis Wilson ("the funny man in 'Ermine'" and later the first president of Actors Equity), and Robert C. Hilliard ("the Adonis of Brooklyn society"); the tragedian nine consisted of dramatic actors and stage managers. McIntosh, a former Princeton University sprinter who a quarter-century later would play Squire Bartlett onscreen in D.W. Griffith's *Way Down East*, was described as "the best ball player in either of the teams, and he opened the scoring with a home run which gladdened the hearts of the ladies and which made the gentlemen envious." Additionally, three kegs of beer were placed near third base. All ballplayers who made it to third were encouraged to take a swig of the brew. The five-inning contest ended with the comedians on top, 19-7.[19]

Then, as reported in the *Times* on July 31, 1887, a "game of baseball has been arranged by members of the theatrical profession at present in the city, to take place at the Polo Grounds Thursday, Aug. 4, for the benefit of the popular soubrette, Miss Rachel Booth, whose illness during the past season has so seriously interfered with the fulfillment of her business engagements." The "nines, umpires, and scorers" were selected from a long list of "well-known actors," among them Hopper, Bell, Hilliard, William Hoey, umpire-turned-actor Frank Lane, and Maurice Barrymore, father of John, Lionel, and Ethel.[20] And then on September 7, 1888, Hopper and Bell participated in a Polo Grounds contest pitting actors and journalists, which the *Times* labeled "one of the funniest games of ball in the annals of American history." Hopper manned first base; his "long frame was attired in a loud red-and-yellow striped bathing suit, a life preserver, a pair of boxing gloves, and a straw bonnet, (which) would have made the veriest pessimist believe there was something worth laughing at in life after all." Bell, meanwhile, was garbed "in his 'Black Hussar' schoolboy suit" and "pitched in the

English bowling style." The game was a benefit for Carl Rankin, a well-known minstrel who was terminally ill; he passed away two months later.[21]

* * *

It was during this period that show folk were banding together to form organizations of various types and for various purposes. In 1874 a group of actors established the Lambs Club, a social club; Hopper served as its president from 1900 to 1902. In 1888 Edwin Booth founded The Players, for the purpose of "the promotion of social intercourse between the representative members of the dramatic profession and the kindred professions of literature, painting, sculpture and music, and the patrons of the arts."[22] Hopper and Bell were among those involved with the White Rats of America, a male-only labor union formed in 1900, which lobbied for actors rights and against the monopolistic practices of vaudeville theater owners.

Meanwhile, athletic clubs of all kinds were sprouting up. The April 5, 1890, edition of the *New York Clipper* included a lengthy list of scheduled events for dozens of these organizations, from the Canadian Amateur Athletic Association to the Scottish American Athletic Club, the Acorn Athletic Club, and the Lorillard Debating and Athletic Association.[23] Quite a few were baseball-oriented. The Amateur Baseball League, for example, comprised teams representing the New Jersey Athletic Club, Staten Island Cricket Club, Staten Island Athletic Club, and Englewood Field Club, with a championship series played each season.[24]

One such organization even linked actors with athletics. In 1889, Hopper, Bell, and other baseball-loving celebrities established the Actors' Amateur Athletic Association of America, otherwise known as the Five A's (or 5 A's). On the afternoon of April 25, its organizers convened at Manhattan's Bijou Opera House, where they adopted a constitution, agreed on the regulations that would govern the group, and elected officers. As reported in the *New York Times*, the constitution "provides that any gentleman who derives his living from the theatrical profession is eligible to [sic] membership if, of course, he is in good standing." The organization was described as "a representative social athletic club of theatrical men, and the athletic feature will be carried out as soon as practicable." Additionally, a "clubhouse will be secured, and will be fitted up with gymnasium, library, billiard and pool tables, bathing facilities, and other conveniences." Dues were $1 per month; those who joined were assessed an initiation fee of $5; those wishing a life membership were charged $50.[25]

Given his standing as a theatrical luminary and his fascination with baseball, it was not surprising that De Wolf Hopper became the Association's president. The first vice president was Burr McIntosh. William H. Crane, an actor-producer who enjoyed a 50-plus-year career primarily on the stage, was the second vice president. Not all the officers were performers. Two in fact were then affiliated with the Fourteenth Street Theatre. J. Wesley Rosenquest, its manager (and later owner), was the treasurer, while James T. Maguire, its business manager, was the secretary. Those on the governing committee were performers. The most prominent were Digby Bell and John Drew, described by critic-columnist-writer Ward Morehouse as the "leading light comedian of the era," who was the uncle of John, Lionel, and Ethel Barrymore.[26] Among the others on the committee: Robert Hilliard; Frank Lane; and Nat C. Goodwin, a comic actor best known for his mimicry.

The following month, the Association rented the clubhouse of the Land and Water Club, near Whitestone, Queens, but quickly realized that the cost would be prohibitive. So they sublet the property; for the time being, members could exercise on a track operated by the Manhattan Athletic Club. Almost immediately, they formed a "nine" and began scheduling ballgames. The May 10 *Brooklyn Daily Eagle* reported that "De Wolf Hopper and Bob Hilliard will be in their glory to-day. There is no matinee today and at the Manhattan Athletic Club's grounds … the actors' nines of the County Fair Club and the American Actors' Athletic Association will play a match at 4 P.M."[27] The following month, the group held its inaugural track-and-field meet. Members competed in foot races, high jumps, mile walks, and broad jumps, with baseball represented via "throwing the baseball" and "running bases" contests.[28] The *New York Herald* categorized the actor-athletes as "the heavy men, the juvenile men, the walking gentlemen and the deep, scowling villains of the stage," adding that the "elongated comedian De Wolf Hopper stood on the field as judge and frequently became very much excited. Digby Bell ... was also a judge and graced the meeting with his own peculiar smile. ..." Lastly, the "obstacle race" winner even came away with the "De Wolf Hopper Cup."[29]

Then in July, it was back to baseball as the Five A's traveled to Middletown, New York, to battle a squad from the New York State Homeopathic Asylum for the Insane. Here, the thespians were bested by the "insane young gentlemen,"[30] but this victory came with a bit of chicanery. As reported in the *New York Press*, an "elaborate spread was prepared for the Actors before the game, and to this the jolly Thespians afterward laid their defeat. While the overfed Actors were dozing in various parts of the field the erstwhile lunatics knocked out 20 runs. The actors scored but 8. Of course this was a tremendous victory for the Asylums, and their joy nearly sent the convalescent patients back to padded cells." On a second visit, "the wily Asylums again tried to steer the actors up against a sumptuous spread, but they were not to be taken in. ...The Asylums' pitcher went back to his pristine wildness ..." and he and his teammates lost to the Five A's, 17-2.[31]

It was at this time that the Association rented a property, at 43 West 28th Street, that would serve as its clubhouse and headquarters and be furnished in "a 'rich, not gaudy' manner." Amenities would include "a parlor gymnasium and a plunge bath."[32] By then, membership had topped 320. And the Five A's were not the only organization to settle into a new residence: For part of the 1889 season and all of 1890, the New York Giants played their home games in what would be the second of three different Polo Grounds. Upon seeing the spacious new ballyard, slugger Roger Connor predicted that no player ever would belt a ball over the center-field fence. Not surprisingly, however, Connor himself was the first to do so, and a policeman reportedly retrieved the horsehide and returned it to the ballplayer. As noted in the *New York Press*, "Connor presented it to De Wolf Hopper, who will have it gilded, appropriately inscribed and hung up in the (Five A's) club house. ..."[33]

Additionally, more ballgames featuring the Five A's were scheduled. On August 15 they took on a reporters' nine at the Polo Grounds. McIntosh was the Association's pitcher, while Hopper was an umpire; the final score was 13-12 in favor of the actors. More than 1,200 patrons paid 50 cents each to watch the contest, with the money split between the organizations.[34] And the following year, they even played exhibitions against two pro teams. One, appropriately, was the New York Giants. It was noted in the April 16, 1890, *New York Sun* that the Five A's "did not do themselves justice yesterday. ... For three innings they played fairly good ball, but one or two bad plays completely broke them up, and then it became simply a question as to how many runs the big fellows would make." (The final score of the nine-inning contest was 34-2 in favor of the Giants.)[35] The actors also suited up against Ward's Wonders, a Brooklyn club in the newly formed Players League.[36] The Wonders were captained and managed by John Montgomery Ward, who in 1885 established the Brotherhood of American Base Ball Players, a secret organization that supported players rights. The Players League, which ceased to exist after one season, was an offshoot of the Brotherhood.

The Five A's filed its certificate of incorporation in March 1890; its listed purpose was "to encourage all manly sports and to promote physical culture and social intercourse."[37] It also was announced that, on Decoration Day, an Association nine would trek to New Jersey to take on the Red Bank Athletic Club. The following month was a busy one for the group. On June 12, they sponsored a track-and-field event at the Manhattan Athletic Club grounds. The competition included races, dashes, walks, hurdles, high jumps, and a "throwing baseball for members" contest.[38] Then on June 25, they took on the Manhattan

Athletic Club's baseball team in a game that, as announced in the *New York Times*, "promises to be quite a notable one among amateur baseball people."[39]

Off the playing field, the Association sponsored benefits to raise money both for themselves and for charity. On June 10, 1889, the *New York Press* reported that Five A's members participated in a benefit at Palmer's Theatre to solicit funds for victims of the Johnstown Flood, which had occurred a week and a half earlier.[40] Five days later, the *National Police Gazette* noted that they "gave a matinee performance at the Metropolitan Opera House last week, in aid of the building fund. It was a big affair: The house was packed; the lobbies were full of girls selling flowers and fellows standing around and buying them. Our athletic actors got up a splendid programme." Some were baseball-related: Hopper and actor Wilton Lackaye, for example, appeared in a comic skit in which they respectively played Cleopatra and Mark Antony. In it, Antony "dresses himself in a baseball umpire's outfit and Cleopatra rushes around with a big lobster attached to her girdle."[41] Exactly one year later, a second benefit was organized at the same venue. The *National Police Gazette* described one of its highlights as a "monster minstrel exhibition" featuring more than 20 performers, among them Hopper and Bell.[42]

In January 1891 members served as ushers in a program at the Broadway Theatre. That May, the organization put together yet another entertainment at the Metropolitan Opera House, with the program including everything from the De Wolf Hopper Opera Company chorus backing up Della Fox as she performed her song "Columbia" to a scene from *Romeo and Juliet*. The finale featured the "Five A's Circus," spotlighting a hodgepodge of riders, acrobats, gymnasts, vaulters—and Hopper as the ringmaster.[43] In February 1893 the Association organized a benefit, held at the Star Theatre, with the *New York Times* reporting that the "house was crowded, and the audience appeared to greatly enjoy the efforts of a score of well-known performers. ..."[44] Then in May 1894 a Five A's benefit was held at Tony Pastor's Theatre. The *Times* noted, "Many of the leading vaudeville artists now in the city have volunteered for the occasion. ..."[45]

De Wolf Hopper, celebrated American actor, "Casey at the Bat" performer, and fervent New York Giants fan.

Not all those associated with the Five A's were acknowledged stars. One of the more notable was a future legend of the silent cinema who then was a 20-something struggling to establish himself on the stage. In 1892 the "Professional Cards" sections of quite a few issues of the *New York Dramatic Mirror* cited review quotes from various productions featuring William S. Hart ("Mr. W.S. Hart, [as] Phasarius, has the most difficult part in the play, but he renders it most acceptably," wrote the *Louisville Courier Journal*), and added that he may be contacted through the Five A's. The *Mirror* also ran the following: "W.S. Hart, Leading Support, MacLean-Prescott Company" and "W.S. Hart, Leading Man, Mlle. Rhea's Company, 1892-93." His address remained in "care (of) Five A's, 43 West 28th Street, New York."[46]

Nonetheless, all was not sunshine and smiles with the Five A's. In May 1893 the organization's hierarchy began publicly condemning what the *New York Times* described as the "financial forgetfulness" of many of its members. More than 100 of them reportedly were in arrears of their dues, not to mention the cost of beer and wine that had been imbibed in the clubhouse. That May each one received a letter, signed by "Alfred D. Lind, Attorney and Counsellor at Law," threatening legal proceedings if the funds remained unpaid. The club, noted Lind, "has a lot of dead timber on its hands and it wants to get rid of it. Many of its members think it is a big thing to belong to this great club of professionals, but they think it is too much for a good thing to pay for it."47 The following month, two of them were the first to be sued: Lee Harrison, an actor, who owed the Five A's $51.65; and Charles Davis, the business manager of Proctor's Theatre, who owed $17.90. "I've started the ball rolling with these two suits," declared Lind, "and others will follow."48

Then in January 1894, the Association nearly was evicted from its quarters. Its rent had not been paid for two months and it was reported in the *New York Sun* that the Five A's "has been in difficulties for some time. It recently tried to collect some $7,000 outstanding dues."49 *The New York World* noted that its members in good standing were "much depressed" over the eviction. While the crisis was averted when enough money was collected to meet the rent, it was announced that "the club is now looking for smaller quarters."50

Apparently, none were found and, within a couple of years, the Five A's quietly disappeared from the public record. No longer were there media accounts of their fundraisers and sporting contests, baseball and otherwise. A host of other businesses soon occupied their West 28th Street clubhouse, including music publishers, florists, and "dramatic agents"; one was the fledgling William Morris agency, which went into business at this address as "William Morris, Vaudeville Agent." Most interestingly, in 1896, Vitascope, an early film-production company, built an open-air studio on its roof. Two years later, in relation to the Five A's, the *New York Dramatic Mirror* quietly noted that "the society gave up its clubrooms several years ago."51

By then, the ballyhoo that accompanied the Five A's inception had dissipated—and De Wolf Hopper and Digby Bell were immersing themselves in other theatrical enterprises. When Bell died in June 1917, more than 500 Lambs Club members and an unspecified number of Players Club representatives attended his funeral. Hopper was one of the pallbearers.52 And when Hopper died, in September 1935, two of the subheads on the *New York Times* report of his funeral arrangements were: "Delegations from Players and Lambs to Attend Services" and "Every Branch of the Theatrical Profession to Be Represented Among Pallbearers."53

Of course, by that time, no pallbearer was aligned with the Actors' Amateur Athletic Association of America.

NOTES

1. "Athletic Actors," *New York Dramatic Mirror*, May 4, 1889: 6.
2. De Wolf Hopper and Wesley Winans Stout, *Once a Clown, Always a Clown* (Boston: Little Brown and Company, 1927), 76.
3. "Short Stops," *New York Times*, April 21, 1889: 3.
4. "Morality in Books," *New York Times*, June 2, 1900: BR12.
5. John Kieran. "Sports of the Times: Si Sets Things Right," *New York Times*, September 5, 1938: 21.
6. "Nickname of 'Giants,'" *New York Times*, February 22, 1936: 11.
7. "Digby Bell, Actor, Dies in 69th Year," *New York Times*, June 21, 1917: 13.
8. "A Cold Night for Digby Bell," *New York Times*, September 12, 1888: 8.
9. "Sullivan Has Friends Who Say Boston People Who Criticize Him Are Cranks," *New York Times*, August 18, 1887: 3.
10. "De Wolf Hopper, 77, Dies in Kansas City," *New York Times*, September 24, 1935: 23.
11. Rob Edelman, *Great Baseball Films* (New York: Citadel Press, 1994), 51.
12. Edelman, 51-52.
13. "De Wolf Hopper, 77, Dies in Kansas City."
14. "Hopper Idol of Playgoers for Half Century," *New York Times*, September 24, 1935: 23.
15. "The Pennant Is Theirs," *New York Times*, October 15, 1888: 5.
16. "Theatrical Gossip," *New York Times*, June 10, 1891: 8.
17. *The Edison Phonograph Monthly*, Vol. VII, No. 5, May 1909: 18.
18. "To Receive the Temple Cup," *New York Times*, October 11, 1894: 6.
19. "It Was a Comic Victory. Actors Make a Frantic Attempt to Play Ball," *New York Times*, May 26, 1886: 5.
20. "Actors To Play Baseball," *New York Times*, July 31, 1887: 12. Throughout her life, Ethel Barrymore—who was born in 1879 and debuted on Broadway in 1895—prided herself on her love of baseball. Barrymore family biographer Margot Peters noted that Ethel "knew the batting averages and pitching records of every player in the major leagues; during the World Series, she hung over her radio." In 1951, she cited her all-around major-league all-star team: Hal Chase [first base]; Charlie Gehringer [second base]; Pie Traynor [third base]; Honus Wagner [shortstop]; Babe Ruth [left field]; Tris Speaker [center field]; Ty Cobb [right field]; Mickey Cochrane [catcher]; and Walter Johnson, Christy Mathewson, and Carl Hubbell [pitchers]. Then on October 12, 1952, she was the mystery guest on *What's My Line?*, the TV game show. Given the time of year, it was not surprising that the first question panelist Dorothy Kilgallen asked her was, "May I assume that you are not in baseball?" After her identity was established, host John Daly observed, "I understand that you have a rather substantial interest in a thing called baseball." After she acknowledged this, Daly asked Barrymore if she was in town for the World Series. She responded that she had seen "all of them on television." Margot Peters reported that on June 17, 1959—the day before her death—Ethel "listened to a Dodgers-Milwaukee Braves doubleheader.")
21. "A Comedy of Errors: Yesterday's Benefit Ball Game Between Actors and Journalists," *New York Times*, September 8, 1888: 3.
22. theplayersnyc.org/history.
23. "Athletic. Coming Events," *New York Clipper*, April 5, 1890: 8.
24. *The Sun's Guide to New York* (New York: R. Wayne Wilson and Company, 1892), 88.
25. "Actors' Athletic Club," *New York Times*, April 26, 1889: 4.
26. Ward Morehouse, *Matinee Tomorrow: Fifty Years of Our Theater* (New York: Whittlesey House, 1949), 2.
27. "The Babies Win," *Brooklyn Daily Eagle*, May 10, 1889: 1.
28. *Outing: An Illustrated Monthly Magazine of Sport, Travel and Recreation,* The Outing Company Limited, April 1889-September 1889: 59-60.
29. "Thespian Athletes on the Field," *New York Herald*, June 13, 1890: 9.
30. *Documents of the Assembly of the State of New York* (Albany: James B. Lyon, State Printer, 1890), 93-94.
31. "Lunatics As Ball Tossers," *New York Press*, March 23, 1890: 19.
32. "Theatrical Gossip," *New York Times*, July 31, 1889: 8.
33. "Diamond Tips," *New York Press*, July 11, 1889: 4.
34. "A Plucky Rally," *Brooklyn Daily Eagle*, August 16, 1889: 1.
35. "Sport With the Base Ball," *New York Sun*, April 16, 1890: 4.
36. covehurst.net/ddyte/brooklyn/1890.html.
37. "General Metropolitan News," *Chicago Tribune*, March 20, 1890: 2.
38. "Actors as Athletes," *New York Times*, June 13, 1890: 2.
39. "A Great Baseball Day," *New York Times*, June 24, 1890: 3.
40. "Stars of Hope for Johnstown," *New York Press*, June 10, 1889: 2.
41. "Masks and Faces," *National Police Gazette*, June 15, 1889: 2.
42. "Masks and Faces," *National Police Gazette*, June 14, 1890: 2.
43. "Notes of the Stage," *New York Times*, May 24, 1891: 13.
44. "Degradation of Amusement," *New York Times*, February 27, 1893: 8.
45. "Theatrical Gossip," *New York Times*, May 3, 1894: 8.
46. "Professional Cards," *New York Dramatic Mirror*, February 6, 1892: 7; February 20, 1892: 7; April 23, 1892: 8; May 7, 1892: 14; September 17, 1892: 17; October 19, 1892: 17; November 5, 1892: 17; December 10, 1892: 17; etc.
47. "Five A's After Delinquents," *New York Times*, May 18, 1893: 8.

48 "Five A's Members Sued," *New York Herald*, June 15, 1893: 13.

49 "Five A's and No W's," *New York Sun*, January 16, 1894: 2.

50 "The '5 A's' Nearly Evicted," *New York World*, January 16, 1894: page number undecipherable.

51 "Questions Answered," *New York Dramatic Mirror*, October 8, 1898: 14.

52 "Digby Bell's Funeral," *Billboard*, June 30, 1917: 4.

53 "De Wolf Hopper Funeral Friday," *New York Times*, September 25, 1935: 23.

HBO MOVIE 61*

BY ANDY STRASBERG

AS A KID GROWING UP IN New York during the 1950s, I was obsessed with the game of baseball. My all-time favorite player became Roger Maris, just after he was acquired in 1960 by my favorite team, the New York Yankees, from the Kansas City Athletics.

As a 14-year-old kid, I became friends with Maris and caught his first National League home run at Forbes Field when I was 18. The story has appeared in a 1989 issue of *Sports Illustrated*, *The Wall Street Journal*, the book *Baseball Lives* by Mike Bryan, *Readers Digest*, in *Chicken Soup for the Baseball Fan's Soul*, etc. The friendship continued with his family after he died in 1985 and Roger's grandson is named after me and he is my godson.

Once I started working in the front office of the San Diego Padres in 1975, my Maris story circulated throughout the professional baseball Industry.

Over the years, the bond I had with Maris and his family has been documented in national publications, books, on radio, and on TV.

In 2000, four years after leaving the Padres organization, I returned to my office and listened to my voicemail messages.

One of the calls was from a person who identified himself as Ross Greenburg of HBO. The only message he left was to call him back. While I quickly recognized that the number had a New York City area code, I didn't know at the time that Ross was the president of HBO Sports.

When Ross answered the phone, he asked me if I had any idea why he had called me. Being a wise guy, I said, "Sure, Ross, I figure you're with HBO and you'd like me to try HBO for 30 days for free to see if I like it and would want to subscribe."

Fortunately for me, he laughed and then explained the reason for the call.

"Andy, we just hired Billy Crystal to direct a movie about Roger Maris and Mickey Mantle and that incredible 1961 Yankees season. We have spoken to representatives from the commissioner's office, the Yankees front office, and the Baseball Hall of Fame. Each group has recommended that you should be involved because of your knowledge of Maris and that 1961 team. HBO would like to hire you as a technical consultant for the movie."

I was floored and said that if the Maris family gave me their approval for my involvement, then I'd do it.

Lucky for me, Roger's widow, Pat, gave me her OK and I was now in the moviemaking business.

"The greatest summer of my life was 1961. The Yankees' Mantle and Maris provided the excitement and drama as they both attempted to break the single season home run record.

The second greatest summer of my life was the summer of 2000 when I was able to relive that 1961 summer."

—Billy Crystal, Director of *61**

I agree.

During the summer of 2000 I was given the opportunity to travel back in time and visit places and live experiences that had eluded me the first time 1961 happened. I was prepared. I knew what to look for, where to go, and whom I wanted to meet. I would get to be 13 years old again.

For me the process of making a movie was fascinating, interesting, and entertaining. The experiences I had on the HBO set of *61** were memorable. I met talented people and formed new friendships. It became apparent to me that the success this movie would enjoy was the result of a subject for which everyone has an insatiable appetite. It contained a heavy flavoring of realism and was spiced with de-

The Reel and the Real: the filming of 61*.

tails. It has a sprinkle of dreams and just a pinch of make-believe. America was hungry for this movie and HBO knew that. And there was only one chef, er, I mean director, who could carefully prepare it and serve it up just right …

The Director

Someone on the set told me that Billy Crystal had the movie recorded in his head. He knew what every scene looked like and how it should be shot. In order for Billy to bring that vision to life and make it into a reality, he hired a team that was unbeatable. The result produced a powerful, emotional, and dramatic film about two baseball legends.

I asked members of the crew if the 61* set was typical of other movie sets. The answer was always "no." The HBO 61* movie set's personality was a reflection of Billy Crystal. It was largely formed by the admiration of those people who hold Billy in such high esteem and wanted to be there for him.

Yes, Billy Crystal is the same sensitive, lovable, humorous, personable person off the screen as he is on the screen. And frankly I was amazed that he was taking into consideration that he had meetings before and after he stepped onto the set and worked 15 hours a day. Now add the fact that many days the temperature reached close to 100 degrees, and the humidity must have been in the 90s, plus there were three sets of kids under 4 years of age running around the set crying with planes flying overhead interrupting scenes. Billy patiently handled it all and was simply incredible.

Pop quiz time. It's a true-or-false test.

1. Is Billy Crystal a perfectionist?
2. Does Billy Crystal know baseball?
3. Was Billy Crystal obsessed with detail for the movie 61*?
4. Did everyone on the set believe that Billy was the perfect director for this movie?
Answers: 1. True. 2. True. 3. True. 4. Absolutely true!

During a break when a scene was being set up several members of the staff started talking about tennis. It was casual make-conversation talk. Billy heard the remarks and quickly pointed out that the only subject on the set to be discussed was baseball. He said it in a joking manner and got a laugh. I took it seriously and thought the same thing. In fact I would have taken it one step further. … My rule would have been that the only subject discussed *off* the set would be baseball.

The movie set's personality was a reflection of Billy Crystal, his love for Mantle, Maris, and baseball. How many directors during breaks would pick up a glove and have a catch with the players (actors), play pepper or talk baseball? I quickly realized that it was common knowledge that everyone who worked on this movie had the utmost respect and admiration for Billy. I observed Billy for a couple of months and agree that he is most deserving of those accolades.

The Script

The script was incredibly important, as I knew that this movie would be the legacy by which people would know my childhood hero Roger Maris. My biggest concern was that the Roger Maris I had followed as a kid could possibly be transformed and become unrecognizable as William Bendix's portrayal of Babe Ruth or Anthony Perkins's of Jimmy Piersall.

*61**'s screenwriter, Hank Steinberg, had managed to capture the essence of Roger Maris without making him into a "Hollywoodized" caricature of himself. Hank recognized that Roger was a family man who enjoyed playing baseball and was not interested in the bright lights and exposure that he received. Hank provided the lines for the principal actors to say that would bring out their personalities, attitudes, frustrations, and philosophies of life. I am amazed at Hank Steinberg's talent.

Equally important, Ross Greenburg of HBO and Billy Crystal approved the script and then brought it to life.

The Actors

I'm convinced that if Roger Maris had met Barry Pepper he would have been impressed with his athleticism, dedication to his craft, and his love of baseball. Roger might have also thought that he was looking in a mirror. I am convinced that Barry's acting abilities exceed his strong resemblance to Roger. And there were times that I thought Barry was Roger.

The very first thing Barry said to me was that he wanted to know everything about Roger. He wanted to know if Roger walked with his thumb in his pants pocket and his fingers hanging outside. Barry demonstrated daily his incredible dedication to his craft. In fact, one day Barry became ill due to the fact that he doesn't smoke, but for the film smoked unfiltered cigarettes as Roger did in 1961. I was amazed to watch Barry enjoying his time between takes with the actresses portraying 8-year-old Susan Maris rather than go back to his trailer. Barry was connecting with these young actresses in a very special way that has nothing to do with acting but has everything to do with who Barry Pepper was as a person.

Maybe an even better example of Barry's obsession with the role was the fact that after I told him about Roger's fascination with a board game called Labyrinth, Barry started using it when he wasn't shooting a scene or lifting weights.

Every time I turned around it seemed that Barry was pumping iron. Barry's workout did not have a schedule or a special location. He did it everywhere throughout the day to build up his arms so that they would resemble Roger's. Unbeknownst to the viewers, moments before he walked into the Raytown house for a scene, Barry did at least 20 curls. Talk about dedication.

Thomas Jane, who played Mickey Mantle, told former big leaguer Reggie Smith—the baseball coach for the movie—that he didn't have any bad habits when it came to playing baseball. He said that because he didn't play baseball! Thomas's transformation into the Mick as a ballplayer was nothing short of amazing.

I was very much impressed with both actors' ability to not only act, but also to personify the larger-than-life person they were portraying and at the same time swing a bat!

I enjoyed Chris Bauer's portrayal of Bob Cerv. Chris was the comic relief in the movie and played it perfectly. Bauer is a major-league rising star! I thought Bruce McGill's Ralph Houk was perfect. I especially liked his argument with the umps in right field after a fan had thrown a chair on the field at Roger. It looked so natural for Bruce to argue the way he did that I didn't think he was acting. It was then that I realized that's exactly what he wanted us to think. Anthony Michael Hall was a perfect Whitey Ford. He was Mick's buddy and a street-smart kid. A tough assignment had to be playing Yogi Berra. To begin with, I think Yogi in real life was a caricature of himself. Paul Borghese embraced the Berra role in a way that you would have thought Paul grew up in St. Louis with Joe Garagiola.

The Crew

There were leagues of unsung heroes behind the cameras.

The crew shared a common trait. They were tireless workers, striving for perfection, and always willing to please.

There were camera operators, sound technicians, makeup artists, grips, gaffers, production assistants, and production designers. Job responsibilities on a movie set are endless but I'm convinced that their work is critical to the movie's success.

Personally, I spent more time with a few select members of the crew in preproduction and immediately recognized their talents and dedication. C.J. MacGuire was in charge of props. One of many challenges C.J. ran into was finding the perfect baseball glove for Barry Pepper to use in the movie. Keep in mind that Roger's glove was a Spalding model and that Spalding hadn't made gloves for big leaguers in at least a couple of decades. But C.J. got it done, including the stamped Roger Maris name in the pocket of the glove.

Dan Moore was in charge of providing wardrobe for every human seen in the movie. I'm talking about every piece of clothing, shoes, and socks. The trailer that housed everything was practically the size of a hotel banquet room. Dan not only had to get the right look but the right fit for everyone. The ballplayers were Dan's responsibility too. I'm talking about sani's, stirrup socks, belts, fitted caps, and vintage baseball gloves, not to mention flannel baseball jerseys. I was amused at the solution Dan Moore came up with when he encountered a catcher who wore an XXL shirt for the Washington Senators. There was only one jersey that could solve the dilemma. So Dan took the WA off a WASHINGTON road jersey and transplanted it to the front of a BOSTON jersey that was big enough for the XXL catcher. Because the catcher's chest protector covered everything but the first two and last two letters, the problem was fixed.

Everyone who worked on this movie was an artist. Regardless of whether it was the guys who recreated the monuments in center field, built the Yankees' right-field fence, or, as Anne McCulley did, decorated each set. It was Anne's artistry and necessary excruciating attention to detail that provided placement of background objects and getting the right look for the right feel. I'm referring to the objects in the ballplayers' lockers to all the items in Claire Ruth's living room. There were times that when I first walked on a set that I felt that I was in a museum.

By no means am I slighting others who were equally dedicated to the effort, but these were the folks who I had the most contact with.

Secrets

Some things don't always appear to be what they appear to be. I found out the secret to shooting a scene with the crowd clapping/cheering when the actors have lines that need to be heard. The cheering part was obvious. Everyone was instructed to "act" like they were cheering without saying a word. The clapping part was little bit tricky. The common mistake I found out is when a person claps and their

*Author Andy Strasberg and Barry Pepper, playing Roger Maris in 61**

hands don't touch. This sometimes looks phony because the camera angle could pick up the fact that it's obvious. So the key to clapping without sound is having the heels of your hands touch but not your palm or fingers. Try it. No sound!

Many of the scenes took place in the Ambassador Hotel. This is the same hotel that at one time was the home of the famous Coconut Grove nightspot and the tragic site of the assassination of Robert F. Kennedy. It was explained to me at the time that the hotel was used for music videos and movies. Instead of building a set with four walls the production just moves into the hotel. So it was possible that you could walk down the hall and see Mickey's hospital room, Mickey's hotel suite, Claire Ruth's living room, and Toots Shor's restaurant.

Anthony Michael Hall is a natural righty and in order to make his Whitey Ford pitching scenes look authentic Dan Moore provided a uniform that was a mirror image of what it really was. In other words the Yankee "NY" was reversed as was the number "16." The result was that when Hall threw right-handed and the film was flopped he appeared as a lefty. This movie trick was used in the film classic *The Pride of The Yankees*. Gary Cooper played the role of Lou Gehrig. Cooper was a righty and instead of teaching him to become a lefty, the filmmakers used the same technique.

Pop quiz
1. Who is the only Yankee in the movie?

Answer: At one point the script had dialogue for a radio announcer from the Angels to call Roger's 50th homer. I saw this as an opportunity for my good friend, a former Yankees second baseman who was at the time a Padres broadcaster, to participate. I gave a recorded audition cassette to Billy, who must have liked what he heard. Jerry Coleman got the job!

The Sets

Upon entering the re-creation of the Yankees home clubhouse, I remarked to Billy that the only thing missing was the smell of sweat. "Don't worry," he replied, "we'll have that, too, in a couple of hours." This was a very special place for me because it was one of those places that I only dreamed about in 1961. The re-creation of the locker room was mind-boggling. Even the hanging lights and bubble gum were just right. I found myself hanging around Roger's locker even when they were done shooting a scene.

The Los Angeles Coliseum was transformed into Baltimore's 1961 Memorial Stadium. This is the same Coliseum that was the site of the 1984 Olympics and the home of the Los Angeles Dodgers in 1958. Everything was there. The scoreboard. The trees behind the fence, the dugouts, and the bullpen. And the most beautiful manicured baseball diamond. There was one shot that you can see over the Orioles pitcher's shoulder when Hurricane Esther was having an effect on the trees. Well, the real story of those shaking leaves took place when Billy realized that the wind machine he had brought in was not getting the desired effect. It was easily fixed when a bunch of guys (no, these are not the people Hollywood lists as grips in the credits) climbed into the trees and started shaking them on cue. It worked beautifully!

Tiger Stadium brought back many memories for me. It was the site of Roger's first homer in the majors when he was with Cleveland. But my fondest memory now is that it was transformed into my beloved Yankee Stadium of 1961. When I walked onto the field that first day of filming, I could not stop my goose bumps for almost 45 minutes. My allergies must have been affected by something in the air because when I went to right field and looked around and remembered, my eyes started tearing. This is where I had spent a good portion of my youth. Maybe too much time, according to my parents. Now I realized it wasn't Yankee Stadium but this was my time-travel voyage, and I enjoyed every second of it.

Special Effects

After the movie was completed it was time for the computer-generating artists to work their magic and complete the effect of 1961. The special effects used in this movie are so good that you don't realize that they're special effects. Some examples included the Yankee Stadium façade, the Bronx community in back of the Yankee Stadium bleachers, and making a crowd of 350 people look like thousands.

NOTES

- Every Maris child under 10 years old who appeared in the movie was a set of twins.
- The baby playing Randy Maris was a girl.
- The scene of Roger visiting a sick boy in Baltimore didn't make the final edit. Even though it happened it was thought to be too much of movie cliché and would undermine the integrity of the movie.
- The sleeves on Barry Pepper's Yankee uniform were cut short just the way Roger wore them throughout his career.
- Barry never buttoned his top uniform button similar to the way Roger wore his jersey.
- Before a scene was shot the player portraying right-handed Rocky Colavito wore his baseball glove on the wrong hand in the outfield. It was corrected moments before the camera started rolling. As it happens, the scene apparently ended up on the proverbial cutting-room floor.
- During the backyard-barbecue scene, there's a bag of Roger Maris "Fla –Vor– itt Hickory Chips," which was an actual product that Roger endorsed when he was with Kansas City.
- A 1961 Post Cereal box featuring Roger Maris on the front and baseball cards on the reverse can be seen briefly in Pat's kitchen in the Raytown, Missouri, home.
- Former major-league knuckleball pitcher Tom Candiotti was Hoyt Wilhelm in the movie. In order to accentuate the natural crook in Wilhelm's neck, Candiotti wore his Baltimore Orioles cap on a tilt.
- It took approximately four hours for a Jiffy Lube Station in LA to be transformed into a 1961 ESSO station for the Queens, New York, gas station scene.
- The actor Bobby Hosea, who portrayed Elston Howard, also played O.J. Simpson in a TV movie.
- Over 800 baseball players auditioned for roles as extras.
- The writers voted again for the 1960 American League MVP. For the movie the Baseball Writers Association of America had to approve the reproduction of the 1960 MVP award that Roger receives on Opening Day in 1961.
- Prior to a scene, Billy noticed a "fan extra" with a Fu Manchu mustache sitting over the dugout. He instructed someone to replace the mustached extra, as it didn't look appropriate for 1961. When the extra was informed and explained the reason for his removal he requested a razor and shaved off the mustache while sitting behind the Yankee dugout. The result was that he didn't lose his seat—just his mustache.
- The 1961 Tigers batboy had the role down pat. He was the real Tigers batboy from 1999.
- Every seat in Tiger Stadium had to be painted or covered in the 1961 Yankee Stadium teal blue.
- When Barry Pepper hit home run #61 for the movie, the ball traveled over 300 feet and the date was August 12, 2000.
- Barry posed in re-creations of Roger's baseball cards from 1957, 1960, and 1961 that were used as props in a number of scenes.

The End

My mother and father passed away years ago. I wish they could have seen this movie and how I was involved. While I was growing up, my parents had many concerns about my obsession toward baseball and in particular my idol Roger Maris. My parents always used to tell me they wished I knew my schoolwork as well as I knew baseball because, they explained to me, baseball would not help me later on in life. (Slow down the *61** movie credits to see who was right)

Everyone involved in this process treated me with compassion and kindness. HBO's Ross Greenburg and Billy Crystal understood what this movie meant to the memory of my childhood hero. We didn't talk about it. We just looked at each other and they knew. These are very special people who understand. I was extremely fortunate to have had a chance to meet them and experience the sense of traveling back in time.

When Roger hit his 61st homer I noticed that after he shook hands with Yogi Berra and the Yankees batboy but before he reached the dugout a fan jumped from the stands near the dugout to congratulate him with a pat on the back and a handshake. I was 13 at the time and wanted to be that fan, during the filming of *61** I was 52 and still wanted to be that fan ... thanks to Billy Crystal and Ross Greenburg, I finally got to be that fan.

BIG LEAGUER: A SMALL-TIME FILM WITH BIG-TIME PERSONALITIES

BY FREDERICK C. BUSH

MOST CASUAL BASEBALL fans are familiar with such well-known movies as the Lou Gehrig biopic *The Pride of the Yankees*, the myth-making twosome of *The Natural* and *Field of Dreams*, and the irreverent *Bull Durham*, but there are numerous films that have been largely forgotten even by diehard baseball and film aficionados. The 1953 Metro-Goldwyn-Mayer release *Big Leaguer* falls into the latter category of cinema which is, in all likelihood, due to the fact that the real-life stories of some individuals involved in the project are of more interest than the characters and events in the film itself.

Later in his career, director Robert Aldrich called *Big Leaguer* "a nineteen-day marvel," intended to be little more than theater-filler for MGM.[1] Aldrich went on to greater fame as director of movies like *The Dirty Dozen* (1967) and the football-themed *The Longest Yard* (1974), but *Big Leaguer* marked his theatrical-film debut. In addition to cutting his teeth in cinema on the set of this film, Aldrich had the opportunity to work with longtime Hollywood star Edward G. Robinson, who was best known for his gangster roles in such films as *Little Caesar* (1931) and *Key Largo* (1948).

In his heyday, Robinson would have had no part of such a low-budget effort, but this was the first major-studio film role he had been offered in three years due to the fact that he had run afoul of the House Un-American Activities Committee.[2] Robinson was twice called to testify before the HUAC, in 1950 and 1952. Though he sought to distance himself from his liberal political activities in the 1930s and 1940s, he was "effectively 'graylisted' from Hollywood," which resulted in film producers being hesitant to hire him.[3]

Robinson was also known to be a baseball fan, which likely helped him to embrace his role as Hans Lobert, a former Deadball Era infielder who was working as a scout and instructor for the New York Giants at the time the film was made. Though Robinson's name still gave clout to his film, Aldrich developed some doubts about the casting choice. He recalled, "Eddie Robinson was a marvelous actor and a brilliant man, but he was not physically coordinated. He would walk to first base and trip over home plate."[4]

Robinson's lack of agility stood in contrast to the real-life John "Hans" Lobert, whom he was portraying. Lobert was born on October 18, 1881, and began his major-league playing career with the Pittsburgh Pirates in 1903. The first Pirates player Lobert met was future Hall of Famer Honus Wagner, who dubbed the new rookie "Hans Number Two" because they shared the same first name.[5] Lobert played for five different teams over the course of a 14-year career in the majors; he batted .274 with 1,252 hits and 316 stolen bases.

Lobert went on to become a baseball lifer. After his playing career ended, he coached the West Point baseball team from 1918 to 1925 before returning to the New York Giants—the last team for which he had played—as a coach. In 1934 he became a coach with the Philadelphia Phillies, another of his former teams, and ended up as the team's manager for the 1942 season. The Phillies' 42-109 record that year was, according to Lobert, "enough to end a beautiful friendship."[6] After two years as a coach for the Cincinnati Reds, Lobert returned to the Giants in 1945 and worked for the franchise until his death on September 14, 1968, by which time his life in Organized Baseball had spanned a total of 66 years.

Edward G. Robinson as Hans Lobert, with actor Jeff Richards in Big Leaguer.

The real Hans Lobert, a mentor of ballplayers.

Although Hans Lobert was a real person who did indeed work for the New York Giants and the movie was filmed at the Giants' training complex in Melbourne, Florida, *Big Leaguer* is a fictional film that indulges in several of the clichés that abound in much of baseball cinema. Robinson's Hans Lobert character runs a training camp that allows him to scout and to train prospects for the New York Giants. The movie alternates between faux-documentary narration about the training camp and the true action involving the characters.

The clichés involve the conflicts surrounding the primary prospects in the camp. Adam Polachuk (Jeff Richards) is an immigrant's son whose father believes he is studying law while he is actually pursuing a baseball career. To complicate matters further, Polachuk falls in love with Lobert's niece, who is portrayed by Vera-Ellen in the only non-dancing role of her career. Tippy Mitchell (Bill Crandall) is the son of a former star first baseman and is unable to tell his father that he would rather be an architect than a ballplayer. Lastly, there is pitching prospect Bobby Bronson (Richard Jaeckel), who is rejected by the Giants and then is signed by the rival Brooklyn Dodgers. Lobert is worried that Bronson will come back to haunt him by fulfilling his potential with the Dodgers, and he becomes concerned that the Giants might dismiss him or end his training program altogether. As Hollywood would have it, however, all turns out well in the end.

Though the film's content is trite, considerable effort was expended to portray the baseball scenes as realistically as possible. For one thing, Lobert was retained as technical adviser to tell Aldrich and the actors how things should play out and so that Robinson could learn to mimic his mannerisms. Lobert was paid the grand sum of $2,000 for providing his expertise.[7] In addition to that, several former ballplayers had minor roles, including future Los Angeles Dodgers executive Al Campanis, Bob Trocolor, and Tony Ravish; Jeff Richards had also been a baseball prospect at one time, but an injury had derailed his shot at a professional career. Lobert recalled that the ballplayers received $10 per day for their roles and that another $10 was added if they actually had a speaking part in a particular shot.[8]

The most notable player to appear in *Big Leaguer* was Hall of Fame pitcher Carl Hubbell, who had won 253 games and the 1933 World Series with the Giants. According to Lobert, Hubbell received $5,000 for his cameo role as himself, a paycheck that was commensurate with his status in comparison to that of Lobert and the other ballplayers on the set.[9]

Big Leaguer received mixed reviews upon its release. One critic called it "nothing more than a double-bill entry," while *Variety* magazine wrote that Robinson was "good as the camp founder and believable in the hokum that has been mixed in with fact."[10] The Giants' training camps were certainly a fact, and Lobert continued to conduct them, even in as far away a locale as the Virgin Islands. In November 1958 the Giants sent Lobert to St. Thomas and St. Croix for two weeks to work with the Virgin Islands Baseball Clinic Committee to plan instructional classes.[11] Hollywood may not have ventured out on a limb with *Big Leaguer's* content, but the real Giants franchise showed that it was willing to go much farther than Melbourne, Florida, in search of new talent.

NOTES

1 Robert Bock, *The Edward G. Robinson Encyclopedia* (Jefferson, North Carolina: McFarland & Company, Inc., 2002), 43.

2 Hal Erickson, *The Baseball Filmography, 1915-2001*, 2nd edition (Jefferson, North Carolina: McFarland & Company, Inc., 2002), 92.

3 Ibid. According to Robert Aldrich, being "graylisted" was worse than being blacklisted: "Since Robinson was not overtly accused of anything, the HUAC would not give him a chance to publicly defend himself and thus encourage producers to hire him."

4 Bock, 44.

5 Lawrence S. Ritter, *The Glory of Their Times*, enlarged edition (New York: William Morrow, 1984), 189.

6 Ritter, 185.

7 Henry W. Thomas and Neal McCabe, eds., *The Glory of Their Times*, audiobook, by Lawrence S. Ritter (HighBridge Company, 1998), CD.

8 Ibid. It may be of some interest that Bing Russell, the father of actor Kurt Russell and grandfather of former major leaguer Matt Franco, appeared in an unbilled role. (See imdb.com/name/nm0751032/) Bing Russell later owned the Portland Mavericks, an independent minor-league baseball team, from 1973-77. The Mavericks lived up to their name and were featured in a 2014 documentary film, *The Battered Bastards of Baseball*.

9 Ibid.

10 Bock, 44.

11 "'Hans' Lobert of Giants to Hold Clinic," *Virgin Islands Daily News*, November 18, 1958.

BALL FOUR, THE TELEVISION SERIES: AHEAD OF ITS TIME?

BY RON BRILEY

IN THE FALL OF 1976, CBS Television premiered the television series *Ball Four*, based upon the 1970 book by former major-league pitcher Jim Bouton, a best-seller that took the form of a baseball diary of the 1969 season. That year Bouton pitched for the expansion Seattle Pilots before being traded to the Houston Astros, with whom he ended the season. Bouton was also a beneficiary of editorial guidance from sportswriter Leonard Schecter, and the influential *Ball Four* was selected by the New York Public Library as one of the hundred most important books of the twentieth century.[1] Bouton's book was reflective of the national mood in the late 1960s and early 1970s in which established institutions like major-league baseball were questioned by a new generation and rising counterculture. In *Ball Four*, Bouton departed from the hero-worshipping tradition of baseball and sport literature, presenting a more realistic depiction of athletes, among them Mickey Mantle of the New York Yankees, as men who struggled with issues of drinking and marital fidelity. In addition, Bouton exposed the degree of hypocrisy present in the national game at its highest level with evidence of sexism, racism, and drug abuse. The baseball establishment led by Commissioner Bowie Kuhn slammed the book, as did many of Bouton's former teammates. The general public, however, loved the book, which changed the nature of sport journalism.

Thus, it is not surprising that CBS was intrigued with the idea of a television series based on the book and developed by Bouton. Although he was a relatively inexperienced actor, CBS also decided that Bouton would play the lead as pitcher Jim Barton of the Washington Americans who was compiling a baseball diary for *Sports Illustrated*. It was difficult, however, for the television scripts to reflect the brutal honesty of Bouton's book because CBS scheduled the show for 8:30 P.M. Eastern Standard Time. This brought *Ball Four* into conflict with network censors as the show was broadcast during the Federal Communications Commission-mandated hour of early evening "family friendly" viewing. The more adult themes of the book were overshadowed by juvenile humor, and the television series failed to develop an audience. *Ball Four* was canceled after only five episodes. While some critics insist that the show failed to reach its promise due to censorship issues, Bouton concedes that he lacked television experience and there were quality issues with *Ball Four*. In addition, baseball-themed shows have not done well on the small screen, but Bouton speculates that in the less restrictive atmosphere of cable television *Ball Four* might work today.[2] Such discussion, however, tends to ignore the fact that the television series lacked the antiestablishment political punch that made Bouton's book so appealing.

Bouton's background offers little indication that he would emerge as an antiestablishment figure on the national baseball scene. He was born on March 8, 1939, in Newark, New Jersey, to a middle-class family. When Jim was 16, his business-executive father moved the family to Chicago Heights, Illinois, where Jim enjoyed some success as a high-school and American Legion pitcher. After earning a scholarship to Western Michigan University in 1958, Bouton was signed to a contract by the New York Yankees. After working his way through the minor-league chain, Bouton joined the Yankees for the 1962 season. The following year he became an All-Star, winning 21 games with a 2.53 earned-run average. A fierce competitor, Bouton threw so hard that he knocked off his cap with many deliveries. In 1964, Bouton enjoyed another excellent season with a record of 18 wins and 13 losses accompanied by a 3.02 earned-run average. In addition to his fine pitching, Bouton earned the reputation as a ballplayer who was willing to challenge Yankee management and speak his mind with the press.[3]

Bouton suffered from a sore arm in 1965, and he finished the season with a won-loss mark of 4-15, while the Yankees suffered through their first losing season since 1925. The right-handed pitcher bounced back the following season with a 2.69 earned-run average, but he managed to win only three games for the last-place Yankees. In 1967, both Bouton and the Yankees struggled, with the pitcher spending part of the season with the club's Triple-A affiliate in Syracuse. Bouton opened the 1968 season in New York, but his contract was sold to the Seattle Pilots, an American League expansion club that would begin play in 1969. Thus, Bouton spent the 1968 baseball campaign with the Triple-A Seattle Angels and experimented with throwing the difficult-to-control knuckleball. He also wrote a piece for *Sport* voicing his support for a boycott of the 1968 Mexico City Olympics if teams from apartheid South Africa were allowed to participate in the games.[4]

During the 1969 season, Bouton appeared in 73 games with the Pilots and Astros, winning two games with an earned-run average of 3.96. He was beginning to establish some mastery of the knuckleball, but the hoopla surrounding the publication of *Ball Four* derailed his career in Houston. After being demoted to Oklahoma City in the summer of 1970, Bouton announced his retirement from the game. However, the publicity surrounding the publication of *Ball Four* made Bouton a household name.

Jim Bouton (right) and John Thorn, Major League Baseball's Official Historian, sharing the stage at SABR's 47th annual convention in New York City.

Commissioner Bowie Kuhn was appalled by *Ball Four*, and he did not consider its publication to be in the best interests of baseball. He summoned Bouton to his office and was rather shocked when the pitcher arrived accompanied by Marvin Miller and Dick Moss from the players union. If Kuhn expected an apology from Bouton, the commissioner and baseball establishment certainly failed to receive one. Kuhn issued a statement asserting his displeasure with *Ball Four* but indicated that his office would not be taking any action against Bouton. In his memoir *Hardball*, Kuhn maintained that he confronted Bouton because he simply did not believe the stories put forth in the book, but in hindsight the commissioner regretted providing Bouton with the publicity to sell more books.[5]

Although earlier player memoirs such as Jim Brosnan's *The Long Season* and *Pennant Race* drew the ire of the baseball establishment and were denounced for violating the sanctity of the locker room, the reaction to Brosnan was less vitriolic as his approach was more intellectual and detached.[6] Bouton, on the other hand, described the sexual and drinking escapades of baseball icon Mickey Mantle, who claimed that he never read *Ball Four*. Mantle was championed by Yankee teammates such as Tony Kubek and Elston Howard, who was Bouton's catcher during the pitcher's tenure with the New York club. Howard described Bouton as "a very self-centered and selfish man" who was angry with the Yankees for trading him after the right-hander became a losing pitcher. Rather than being a heroic chronicler of the truth, Howard depicted Bouton as a loner who was selling out his former teammates for 30 pieces of silver.[7]

In response to such criticism, Bouton asserted, "I simply wanted to write what baseball was really like. I wasn't trying to prove anything, good or bad. I like quite a bit about the game, and I wanted to share the fun that I've had in the game with the fans, showing them what the game is really like, the good parts and the bad parts."[8] As for Howard, he never reconciled with Bouton, and his widow, Arlene, remained bitter toward Bouton in her 2001 memoir, arguing that the former Yankee took baseball publishing to a new low.

She maintained, "Today, I have nothing to do with the man. For whatever reason, he took a number of cheap shots at Elston, the man who was his catcher when he was a twenty-one game winner in 1963."[9] To the Howards loyalty mattered. Bouton was self-centered and failed to give Elston and the Yankees the credit they deserved for his success. On the other hand, Bouton was an antiestablishment type who perceived baseball ownership as a monopoly controlling player compensation and limiting freedom of movement through the reserve clause. He was an advocate for social justice in baseball as well as American society.

For many readers, Bouton was an intellectual athlete who could place baseball within the larger historical and cultural changes that were taking place in the United States and world during the late 1960s and early 1970s. For example, Bouton relates a trip that he and teammate Gary Bell took to Berkeley while the Seattle club was playing in Oakland. They encountered numerous student activists who were protesting the Vietnam War, racism, and poverty. Bouton concluded that perhaps the real problem in America was that there were too many people like himself and Bell when more advocates for social change were needed. Bouton wrote, "Gary and I are really the crazy ones. I mean, we're concerned about getting the Oakland Athletics out. We're concerned about making money in real estate, and about ourselves and our families. These kids, though, are genuinely concerned about what's going on around them. They're concerned about Vietnam, poor people, black people. They're concerned about the way things are and they're trying to change them."[10] Upon learning that a member of his fan club was dispatched to Vietnam, Bouton quipped, "It just doesn't seem right that a member of my fan club should be fighting in Vietnam. Or that anybody should."[11] And Bouton also believed that protest could bring about change. In *Ball Four*, he observed that tennis officials in South Africa were discussing the possibility of an integrated Davis Cup team; however, South African leaders were quick to assert that these conversations were not in response to planned protests and boycotts of the apartheid nation. Bouton retorted, "And the increase in the number of swimming pools in Harlem has nothing to do with the riots and the troops withdrawals have nothing to do with the protest movement and the baseball owners broadened our pension coverage not because of any strike but out of an innate sense of fair play. Yeah, surrre."[12]

Bouton was also critical of hypocrisy in American society as well as the baseball establishment. He commented upon baseball owners who espoused support for the free-enterprise system while exercising monopoly control over players through the reserve system. He poked fun at the anti-intellectualism and sexism of players and management who did not know how to respond to Bouton's Seattle teammate Steve "Orbit" Hovley, who grew his hair long and was an avid reader. Bouton also had little patience for those who attributed their on-the-field success to God as if the Deity was a baseball fan. The pitcher confessed, "I've been tempted sometimes to say into a microphone that I feel I won tonight because I don't believe in God. I mean, just for the sake of balance, to let the kids know that a belief in a deity or 'Pitching for the Master' is not one of the criteria for major-league success. But I guess I never will." The iconoclast, however, did criticize evangelist Billy Graham for seeking to discount racial urban unrest by suggesting that communists were behind the civil-rights movement. Speaking of Graham, Bouton wrote, "When a man of his power, a man with such a following makes a statement like that, he is diverting attention from the real causes of riots in the ghettoes. As a result he delays solutions to those real problems, and this is dangerous. My heavens, you'd think I had insulted Ronald Reagan."[13] Bouton also disturbed more conservative parents by responding to a question about young men with long hair by asserting, "The thing that disturbs me about long hair is not the fact that suddenly a whole lot of kids in this country decided to let their hair grow, but that a whole nation of adults would let it disturb them to the point where they were ready to expel otherwise excellent students from school simply because of their long hair."[14] Bouton, however, adopted a less critical tone when in *Ball Four* he described the way many ballplayers with too much time on their hands objectified women and poked fun of gays.

But it was the sexual hijinks along with the stories of alcohol abuse and amphetamine use that most angered traditionalist sportswriters. Bouton had betrayed the sanctity of the locker room, and sportswriter Dick Young demanded that Commissioner Kuhn and the Players Association take action to censure Bouton. Joe Falls denounced Bouton for revealing privileged information, concluding, "This business of telling-it-like-it-is is strictly the bunk. It's a nice, catchy phrase that has a very idealistic sound to it, but nobody ever really tells it how it is, nor is anyone expected to." An even more strident tone was taken by Wells Twombly, who dismissed *Ball Four* as "an impudent betrayal of trust, good old rotten Hollywood-style keyhole reporting."[15]

Other reviews of *Ball Four* attempted to place Bouton's reporting within a broader cultural context. Writing for the *New York Times Book Review*, Rex Lardner acknowledged that for some traditionalists *Ball Four* was an anathema, but he concluded, "In an era of sophisticated reappraisal, it is a gem of honest, good-naturedly biased reporting." In a similar vein, Roger Angell argued that Bouton's book "never settles into the sportswriting clichés of debunking and anecdotage. What he has given us, rather, is a rare view of a highly complex public profession seen from the innermost inside view of an ironic and courageous mind." In *Christian Century*, George G. Hill encouraged readers to carefully examine *Ball Four* as it constituted "a positive contribution to the needed moral reordering of America." Striking a more literary note, Cleveland Amory observed that *Ball Four* was no mere baseball book, "any more than Mark Twain's *Life on the Mississippi* is about riverboats." Picking up on these literary themes, David Halberstam observed that both Bouton and his critics agreed that baseball was "the great American game, a reflection of what we are and who we are." But rather than the virtuous institution described by many establishment sportswriters, Bouton found baseball to be a manifestation of American culture that was "more often than not run by selfish, stupid owners, men who deal with their ballplayers in a somewhat sophisticated form of slavery, that despite the reputation of a melting pot, baseball dugouts reek of the same racial and social tensions and decisions that scar the rest of the country, that the underlying social common denominator is fairly crude and reminiscent of nothing so much as one's high-school locker room."[16]

While *Ball Four* was praised by literary critics and resonated with the growing antiestablishment views of many American readers whose faith in American institutions was soon to be further tested with the Watergate scandal, the baseball establishment had little use for Bouton. Increasingly unable to control his knuckleball, Bouton was out of baseball before the conclusion of the 1970 season. With strong earnings from *Ball Four*, Bouton decided that he wanted to spend more time with his family, accepting a position as an evening sports reporter with an ABC Television New York City affiliate. Continuing to march to his own drummer, Bouton reported primarily upon high-school and local sports rather than the major-league New York City franchises. He also broadened the exposure of his audience by participating in such activities as roller derby. Baseball historian Mark Armour concludes, "Bouton's broadcasts were popular with the public, though the local professional teams were unhappy that he had no interest in simply promoting their business as television had been doing for years." In response to his many baseball critics such as Pete Rose who limited his literary review of *Ball Four* to "Fuck you, Shakespeare," Bouton and his editor Schecter penned *I'm Glad You Didn't Take It Personally*."[17]

Meanwhile, Bouton had not succeeded in getting baseball out of his system as he suggested in his final line from *Ball Four*, "You see, you spend a good piece of your life gripping a baseball and in the end it turns out that it was the other way around all the time."[18] He continued to play baseball with amateur clubs in suburban New Jersey. In addition, he spent a few weeks in 1975 with the Single-A Portland (Oregon) Mavericks of the Northwest League. He had regained control of his knuckleball and pitched well in five games with Portland, winning four games while posting an impressive 2.20 earned-run average. Any thoughts of a baseball comeback, however, were placed on hold when an opportunity arose to produce a television series based upon *Ball Four*. According to Bouton, the series was an outgrowth of ideas generated at the Lion's Head Bar in Greenwich Village while drinking with his friends *Newsday* television critic Marvin Kitman and *New York Post* sportswriter Vic Ziegel. Bouton described the show's creation as somewhat of a lark, commenting, "We just thought it might be a good thing to do. It certainly was fun to listen to all these characters. So why couldn't a sitcom be just as funny as the real players, the real guys." After submitting the project to CBS Television, Bouton asserts, he and his friends were rather surprised when the network gave a green light to the series with the proviso that the creators remain as the chief writers for the program. The network hoped that *Ball Four* might resonate with audiences that made such ensemble situation comedies as *Barney Miller*, *Welcome Back Kotter*, and *M*A*S*H* major hits during the 1970s.[19]

Bouton did not find the television creative process as satisfying as he originally anticipated, observing, "Our plan was sit around and write in the daytime, but since it took so long to come up with anything, we'd still be writing stuff at two in the morning."[20] The slow pace of the writing worried CBS executives who often visited the writers to make suggestions, but Bouton and his friends were often contemptuous of the television people who demonstrated little understanding of baseball and its culture. After all, it was under the ownership of CBS from 1964 to 1973 that the New York Yankees struggled at the box office and in the field, finishing last in 1966 and drawing below one million fans in 1973.[21]

But most of the conflict between the show's creators and CBS executives was over the show's unfortunate scheduling during the Federal Communications Commission-mandated family hour programing. Part of the appeal of Bouton's book was colorful and profane language employed by such baseball characters as Seattle Pilots manager Joe Schultz. There was no way in 1976 that viewers on network television were going to hear Schultz's exclamation of "shitfuck." Bouton, however, was frustrated that considerable time was wasted with rather arbitrary decisions such as approving "horse-crock" rather than "horseshit." CBS censors had a reputation for closely monitoring the content of its programming as was evident during the late 1960s with the controversy arising from network executives attempting to censor the popular *Smothers Brothers Comedy Hour*. Thus, the CBS Standards and Practices Department nixed "any spitting, burping, chewing of tobacco, popping of 'greenies,' or any other potential offensive behavior from the show's characters." Apparently this directive also included any affirmation that rookie pitcher Bell Westlake (David James Carroll) was gay, but it was all right to make fun of his feminine characteristics. Westlake was one of the first gay characters on network television, but CBS was not prepared to acknowledge this. And perhaps American audiences in 1976 were no more ready than baseball locker rooms for an openly gay character. Today television viewers are more open, but Major League Baseball still often struggles with the acceptance of gay athletes. Summing up his arguments with the censors, Bouton lamented, "We were not allowed to put any of the grittiness of life in the majors on the screen."[22]

In addition, the show included little baseball action. Most of *Ball Four*'s scenes were staged in the locker room or hotel rooms of the players rather than on the baseball diamond. Thus, most of the show was filmed on stage in New York City before a live television audience. *Ball Four* seemed artificial, and Bouton assigned the censors primary responsibility for its failure, leading some to conclude that the *Ball Four* television series was ahead of its time. However, baseball in general has not fared well on television. Even shows based on popular films such as *A League of Their Own* and *The Bad News Bears* failed to resonate with television viewers, and Steven Bochco, who created such police drama hits as *Hill Street Blues* and *NYPD Blue*, could not entice an audience for his baseball production *Bay City Blues*. An exception to this history of baseball on the small screen is *Eastbound & Down*, which aired from 2009 to 2013 on HBO. Cable television provided greater freedom for the show's creators and focused upon a politically incorrect former major-league pitcher, perhaps based on the exploits of John Rocker, who returns to his hometown and becomes a substitute teacher. Thus, Bouton acknowledges that perhaps his television series was ahead of its time and might fare much better today with the more permissive environment of cable television.[23]

Another problem for the series was the decision to cast Bouton in the lead as journal-writing pitcher Jim Barton. Bouton had some acting experience, having portrayed villain Terry Lennox in the 1973 Robert Altman production of *The Long Goodbye* featuring Elliott Gould as private detective Philip Marlowe. However, he had no experience with comedy, which most performers acknowledge as being more difficult than drama. While Bouton quipped that CBS signed him for the lead because he was willing to work cheap, baseball historian Peter Golenbock was quite critical of the network for overextending Bouton. Golenbock observed, "I think too much of it was placed on Jim's shoulders. He was a ballplayer, and he was an author, and he was a fabulous sportscaster, but he didn't have a great deal of experience in show business. And my sense was that he didn't get the help that he could have had, either as a TV writer or an actor. But I give the guy a tremendous amount of credit for having the balls to go out there and be the lead in a TV show. A lot of people would have said, 'I can't do this.'"[24]

While the ensemble cast also included black and Latino players, Bouton's character Barton bonded primarily with his catcher Rhino Rhinelander, played by former professional football player Ben Davidson. Best known for his All-Star play with the Oakland Raiders, the 6-foot-8-inch defensive end also played with the Green Bay Packers and Washington Redskins. After retiring from football, Davidson tried his hand at acting, appearing in such films as *M*A*S*H* and *Conan the Barbarian* in addition to *Ball Four*. However, perhaps Davidson was best known by television viewers for his Miller Lite commercials. Bouton loved working with Davidson, whose physical improvisations, such as hanging one of the actors from a clubhouse clothes hook by the back of his shirt, were not appreciated by CBS executives. The rapport between Bouton and Davidson, nevertheless, tended to make the show a white buddy project quite a bit different from the more multicultural themes of the book.[25]

Reviews and rating for *Ball Four* were poor. *Sports Illustrated* was disappointed by the show's "mediocrity," while the series faced strong network completion in its time slot from *The Bionic Woman* on ABC and *Little House on the Prairie* on NBC. *Ball Four* was sandwiched between the two popular CBS situation comedies *Good Times* and *All in the Family*, and when ratings indicated that *Ball Four* was having a negative impact on viewership for these two programs, the baseball series was canceled after airing only five episodes. Rather than expressing anger over the rapid cancellation of the program, Bouton seemed to be more relieved, commenting, "Ohhh, thank you! Now we can live our lives—we can sleep, we can have weekends, we can have friends over. We can be real people again! God, please don't let me write any more scripts."[26] Pulling the plug on *Ball Four* also allowed Bouton, at age 38, to pursue his dream of returning to major-league baseball. In September 1978 he was called up by the Atlanta Braves after pitching well for the team's Savannah farm club in the Southern League. Bouton appeared in five games with the Braves while compiling a record of 1-3 and a 4.97 earned-run average. Having achieved his goal, Bouton retired from the game he loved, although with his writing and activism such as preserving Wahconah Park in Pittsfield, Massachusetts, he hardly faded from the public eye.[27]

In retrospect, Bouton has few regrets regarding his brief career in television programing. He did not bemoan the fact that *Ball Four* was canceled so quickly by CBS, which demonstrated little faith in the project and gave the series precious little time to foster a following. Employing hindsight, Bouton recognizes the failures of the show and expresses relief that *Ball Four*'s episodes are unavailable today with the exception of the show's opening credits featuring a theme song from popular folk/rock artist Harry Chapin. Of his *Ball Four* television experience, Bouton concludes, "I never think about it as a negative in my life. It's not like, 'Oh boy, we really screwed that up,' or, 'That was terrible!' It was so much fun just to sit there and fail at a very high level."

Yet, Bouton offers little insight into the actual content of the show and how *Ball Four* may have contributed to its own demise. An important aspect of Bouton's book is the author's commentary on the larger culture and the changes taking place within American society. Thus, Bouton's observations on topics such as the Vietnam War, race relations, youth culture, campus protest, and fashion such as long hair for males are essential elements of the book's appeal to many younger baseball fans. In a similar fashion, the commercial success of *The Bad News Bears* as a film in 1976 was due to how the picture reflected changing views of American society and sport. According to historian David Zang, *The Bad News Bears* was "the most subversive sports film ever made" as it challenged the traditional interpretation of sport as building character. Instead, Zang argues, "From their beer-guzzling coach to their foulmouthed shortstop to their juvenile delinquent hitting star, the Bears were heroes that only a society that had lost its sense of moral infallibility could love."[28] A female pitching star along with Latino and African-American players also made the Bears representative of a more inclusive society. And Bouton's book seemed to capture this sense of cultural change. Peter Golenbock insists that *Ball Four* "absolutely changed sportswriting. When I started writing, the idea was that I wanted to write books with the same honesty as *Ball Four*." Accordingly, Golenbock asserts that he would not have been able to write *The Bronx Zoo*, an account of the Yankees and George Steinbrenner in the late 1970s, without Bouton's example and courage in taking on the baseball establishment.[29]

Bouton initially seemed to recognize that his television project required the same broad cultural focus as his book. He hoped that the show would antagonize Commissioner Kuhn and provide an antidote for the *Game of the Week*, but Bouton recognized that the series would need to attract a wide range of viewers, especially women. Bouton insisted, "The book had appeal to women because it told them interesting things about people. The reason women are turned off by sports on television is the way it is presented. It comes from a statistical point of view and that's boring. Women's participation is healthier than men's. Men may appreciate statistics—not women." The series, accordingly, would not concentrate exclusively on baseball. Bouton concluded, "Most of the story lines will be about ordinary people, facing ordinary people, facing ordinary situations—love, life, overweight problems, politics."[30]

There is little indication that Bouton followed his own advice in developing the television series. From reviews and the opening credits of the show Ball Four appears primarily focused upon the sexual escapades and locker-room antics of its protagonists. For example, the opening credits feature the players leaning out of a hotel-room window and employing binoculars to leer at women, while there are no major female characters in the production. There is some effort to create diversity with black and Latino teammates, as well as a gay player, but the emphasis is upon the antics of pitcher Barton (Bouton) and catcher Rhinelander (Davidson), making the show more of a traditional white buddy story. In summarizing the series for the 20th anniversary edition of Ball Four, Bouton emphasized the male comradery of the locker room while eschewing the political commentary that characterized the book and its cultural impact. Bouton wrote, "A locker room is a freewheeling place where anything goes, offering more flexibility than a living room or a classroom. It's like an army barracks where people expect put-down humor, ethnic jokes, gross sarcasm, and insults. The partial nudity with male cheesecake potential should attract a large female audience. Players from every ethnic group, economic level, and educational background are thrown together naturally in an occupation which causes constant tension. And, the best part of all, if an actor demands a bigger contract, he can simply be traded."[31] These limitations were also noted by Melissa Ludtke in her review of Ball Four for Sports Illustrated. Ludtke argued, "The mediocrity of the opening show is particularly unfortunate because Bouton had hoped to give a true portrayal of his baseball experience in the series. Pill-popping, religion and women sports-writers in the locker room and homosexuality are some of the issues that he would like to cover. With fewer than one-third of this season's new prime-time shows likely to survive until spring, the odds seem slim that 'Ball Four' will last long enough to fully explore baseball's other side."[32]

The book also included male bonding and the objectification of women, but the fact that such sexual escapades by well-known athletes could be publicly acknowledged provided an opportunity to question the larger society that was seemingly missing from the television series. Bouton's Ball Four shocked many in the baseball establishment by speaking openly of sexual liaisons between players and baseball groupies or Annies. Similar tales were told regarding Babe Ruth and so-called baseball Daisies in the 1920s, but post-World War II baseball endeavored to produce a sanitized version of the game and its heroes. Bouton's exposé blew the lid off baseball's ostensible allegiance to family and consensus values. In an essay on gender and baseball, historian David Voigt found positive possibilities in baseball's shift from paternal to maternal values, arguing, "It is fair to say that Bouton learned that freedom to talk about sex is directly related to freedom to criticize other institutions. Which is after all the essence of the matrist trend—that matrism is laden with opportunities for expanded personal freedom provided that enough Americans are willing to exercise the right."[33] Nevertheless, the freedom celebrated by Bouton often provided opportunities for men to sexually exploit women in the gendered renditions of "studs" and "sluts" rather that offering a sexually egalitarian playing field.

Female baseball fans in the 1970s, however, refused to accept male-defined roles. During the decade, women moved beyond the role of the "other"; filing lawsuits to open up the baseball training ground of Little League to girls and lobbying for passage of Title IX, which sought to provide equality of opportunity for women in the nation's schools and universities.

Tilla Vahanian, a New York City psychiatrist, told the *New York Times* that competitive play enhanced the self-esteem of women. According to Vahanian, "The old stereotype was that sport was a purely masculine endeavor, and women did not attend sports events for fear of losing their femininity. But now we find that a great comradeship exists between men and women when they can share roles." Another woman told *TV Guide*, "Guys have this obsession that girls who like baseball are groupies. I mean, if a guy likes one of the Pittsburgh Pirates does that mean he is after him sexually."[34] This kind of commentary challenging the male hegemony in baseball is what Voigt had in mind when he suggested that sexual freedom could bring greater equality to American society as well as the sport of baseball. Thus, perhaps one of the major reasons for the failure of *Ball Four* as a television series is not that Bouton's project was ahead of its time, but rather that in regard to gender roles it was behind the changing times.

NOTES

1. Jim Bouton with Leonard Schecter, *Ball Four: Twentieth Anniversary Edition* (New York: Wiley Publishing, 1990; originally published 1970); and *The New York Public Library's Books of the Century* (New York: Oxford University Press, 1996).

2. Dan Epstein, "*Ball Four*, You're Out: How a Classic Baseball Book Became a Failed Baseball Sitcom," Vice Sports, September 22, 2016 <sportsvice.com/en_us/article/ball-four-book-became-a-failed-baseball-sitcom> (accessed March 1, 2017).

3. For background information on Jim Bouton see Mark Armour, "Jim Bouton," SABR BioProject, <bioproj.sabr.org/bioproj.cfm?a=1234&pid=1366> (accessed July 5, 2016); and Leonard Schecter, "Jim Bouton—Everything in Its Place," *Sport* (March 1964): 71-73.

4. Jim Bouton, "A Mission to Mexico City," *Sport* (August 1969): 30.

5. For the meeting between Bouton and Kuhn see Jim Bouton with Leonard Schecter, *I'm Glad You Didn't Take It Personally* (New York: William Morrow & Company, 1971), 68-79; Lowell Reidenbaugh, "Author Bouton Hits Jackpot—With Bowie's Assist," *The Sporting News*, August 8, 1970; and Bowie Kuhn, *Hardball: The Education of a Baseball Commissioner* (New York: Basic Books, 1987): 72-73.

6. Jim Brosnan, *The Long Season: An Inside Chronicle of the Baseball Year as Seen by a Major League Pitcher* (New York: Harper & Row, 1960); and Brosnan, *Pennant Race: The Classic Game-by-Game Account of a Championship Season, 1961* (New York: Harper Paperbacks, 2017; originally published 1962).

7. Joseph Durso, "Elston Howard Replies," *New York Times*, August 8, 1970.

8. Reidenbaugh, "Author Bouton Hits Jackpot."

9. Arlene Howard with Ralph Wimbish, *Elston and Me: The Story of the First Black Yankee* (Columbia: University of Missouri Press, 2001), 164-165.

10. Bouton, *Ball Four*, 145.

11. Ibid., 119.

12. Ibid., 194.

13. Ibid., 168-169 and 214.

14. Ibid., 215.

15. Dick Young, "Young Ideas," *The Sporting News*, June 8, 1970; Joe Falls, "A Blast at Bouton Brand of Realism," *The Sporting News*, June 20, 1970; Wells Twombly, "Beware of Snoopy Colleagues," *The Sporting News*, June 20, 1970.

16. Rex Lardner, "The Oddball With a Knuckleball," *New York Times Book Review*, July 26, 1970; Roger Angell, "Ball Four," *New Yorker*, 46 (July 25, 1970): 79; George G. Hill, "Down in the Dugout," *Christian Century*, 87 (September 23, 1970); 1126; Cleveland Amory, "Trade Winds," *Saturday Review*, 53 (August 1, 1970): 10-11; and David Halberstam, "Baseball and the National Mythology," *Harper's Magazine*, 241 (September 1970): 22-25.

17. Armour, SABR BioProject, and Bouton, *I'm Glad You Didn't Take It Personally*.

18. Bouton, *Ball Four*, 398.

19. Epstein, "*Ball Four*," Vice Sports.

20. Ibid.

21. Marty Appel, *Pinstripe Empire: The New York Yankees From Before the Babe to After the Boss* (New York: Bloomsbury, 2012).

22. Epstein, "*Ball Four*," Vice Sports; David Biancalli, *Dangerously Funny: The Uncensored Story of the "Smothers Brothers Comedy Hour"* (New York: Touchstone, 2010); Billy Bean with Chris Bull, *Going the Other Way: An Intimate Memoir of Life In and Out of Major League Baseball* (New York: Marlowe & Company, 2005); and Glenn Burke with Erik Sherman, *Out at Home: The True Story of Glenn Burke, Baseball's First Openly Gay Player* (New York: Berkley Books, 2015).

23. John Fester, "Baseball-themed TV Series Have Been Few and Short Lived," *Sporting News*, September 21, 2016 <sportingnews.com/mlb/news> (accessed February 15, 2017).

24. Rob Neyer, "*Ball Four* Changed Sports and Books," ESPN, June 15, 2000. <espn.go.com/mlb/ballfour/neyer.html> (accessed May 9, 2004).

25 Lisa Dillman, "Ben Davidson Dies at 72; Oakland Raider, Fixture in Beer Commercials," *Los Angeles Times*, July 4, 2012.

26 Epstein, "*Ball Four*," Vice Sports; and Melissa Ludtke, "Two Strikes on 'Ball Four,'" *Sports Illustrated*, September 27, 1976: 38.

27 See the book Jim Bouton, *Foul Ball* (North Egremont, Massachusetts: Bulldog Publishing, 2010).

28 David W. Zang, *Sports Wars: Athletes in the Age of Aquarius* (Fayetteville: University of Arkansas Press, 2001), 141-142.

29 Peter Golenbock quoted in Neyer, "*Ball Four* Changed Sports and Books"; and Sparky Lyle with Peter Golenbock, *The Bronx Zoo: The Astonishing Inside Story of the 1978 World Champion New York Yankees* (New York: Crown, 1979).

30 Jay Sharbutt, "Bouton Stars in Series Created From His Book," *Sarasota Journal*, September 22, 1976.

31 Bouton, *Ball Four*, 419.

32 Ludtke, "Two Strikes on 'Ball Four,'" 38.

33 David Voigt, "Sex in Baseball: Reflections of Changing Taboos," *Journal of Popular Culture*, 12:3 (December 1978): 402.

34 Gerald Eskenazi, "In the Stands, Many Cheers Have a Higher Pitch," *New York Times*, June 6, 1977; and Grace Lichtenstein, "They'd Rather Break a Date Than Miss a Game; Women Sports Fans Are Coming Out of the Closet," *TV Guide* (March 6, 1976), 8-11.

BASEBALL AND COCA-COLA: A MATCH MADE IN AMERICA

BY ROB EDELMAN

IF THE MOST ICONIC SPORTS-related Coca-Cola television ad features a child offering a Coke to an injured football star—Mean Joe Greene, the Pittsburgh Steelers Hall of Famer—countless hurlers and hitters have hawked the product across the decades. The Greene spot first aired in 1979; however, starting in the early 1950s, the Coca-Cola Company has produced scores of TV ads employing baseball imagery.

Brooks Robinson is the star of a 1964 Coca-Cola spot, filmed in glorious black-and-white. He is shown hitting an inside-the-park home run. Then, he drinks a Coke while talking about the hit and revealing his thought processes while rounding the bases. A 1966 ad includes a montage of split-second views of sports stars in action. One of them is Willie Mays. Variations exist of a second 1966 Mays spot featuring the Say Hey Kid in the outfield, racing after a ball just as it is hit and making a running onehanded catch. Then he is shown in the dugout and locker room— and in close-up, drinking a Coke. A 1987 ad, designed for the Spanish-speaking market, spotlights Fernando Valenzuela, then coming off his lone 20-win season. El Toro is shown at a Little League game and in the stands, wearing a baseball cap with a Coke logo. A 1984 Diet Coke spot features a montage of celebrities, including Chuck Yeager, Christie Brinkley, and forever-dieting Tommy Lasorda.

Some Coke ads were produced for local markets. In 1966, the Milwaukee Braves relocated to Atlanta, the corporate headquarters of Coca-Cola. Bobby Bragan, the team's manager, starred in a spot titled "Stadium Tour." The ad includes vintage black-and-white images of the interiors and exteriors of Atlanta Stadium, the team's home through 1996. (In the mid-1970s, Atlanta Stadium became known as Atlanta-Fulton County Stadium.) Bragan is the narrator, and he emphasizes that Coke will be available in the newly-christened big league ball yard. Other Coca-Cola ads have been linked to local teams and regions. A series of 1989 spots, collectively titled "Under the Sun," feature brief clips of Houston Astros, Texas Rangers, and Los Angeles Dodgers batters at home plate.

Some ads feature actors playing athletes or fans. A 1952 ad, titled "Baseball Boy," depicts an adolescent who is obsessed with the game. A girl he apparently likes is unimpressed with his pitching motion. The ad jumps ahead in time, with the boy now a college player. The girl has altered her view of his athletic abilities, and the two savor a Coke. "The Big Pitch," a 1958 ad, features a hurler throwing a game's first pitch. Afterward, he enjoys a Coke. A 1967 ad, titled "Baseball," consists of photos of ballplayers in competition, edited together to simulate movement. A batter stands at the plate. A pitcher hurls the ball. The batter hits the ball, and slides into a base. A 1985 ad, titled "Fly Ball," features an outfielder running backwards and making a leaping catch, with his glove right in front of a boy in the stands. The ballplayer then tosses the ball to the youngster. Other ads mirror changes in American society. In "The Curve Ball," a 1991 ad, a young black man demonstrates his ability to throw a curveball while his white friend tosses a fastball. The two men share a camaraderie, and drink Coke. One hardly can imagine this ad airing on television in the 1950s.

During the late 1960s, the modern-era feminist revolution was making its first rumblings. However, one forward-thinking Coke ad, which aired back in 1962, features a female pitcher playing softball. She pitches—and drinks Coke. The point of the ad is that the product gives you "Zing!" The Establishment conservatism in the face of feminism is reflected in one 1968 spot featuring a little girl attempting to pitch in a game in which her teammates and opponents are boys. A batter hits a ball right into her glove, but she does not know what to do with it—much to the annoyance of her teammates. Her cap falls off her head. She picks up the cap, instead of throwing the ball. Predictably, she is chastised because she "plays like a girl."

As equal opportunity for women became more generally accepted within the American mainstream, the tone of ads featuring girl ballplayers also changed. Several variations exist of a 1976 spot featuring a baseball coach talking about his team and explaining how he serves them Coke— particularly from new, two-liter plastic bottles. The ad's "punchline" is that his players are girls, and he is depicted as being proud of them and happy to be their coach. A 1980 ad for Sprite, a Coca-Cola Company product, begins with a girl swinging at a pitch and missing. She perseveres and, at the end, swings her bat and hits the ball.

In all these ads, an attempt is made to visually and verbally link Coca-Cola with youth, vitality, and good feelings, to make the product synonymous with all that is upbeat about America. It is no surprise, then, that baseball has been so much a part of Coca-Cola advertising.

BASEBALL PLAYERS TURNED ACTORS

Note: Both of the ads described here were viewed compliments of The Coca-Cola Archives. For further information, go to: http://memory.loc.gov/ammem/ccmphtml/colahome.html

BASEBALL AND CLASSIC TELEVISION: A BRIEF OVERVIEW

BY ROB EDELMAN

ONE COULD PEN A BOOK OR perhaps even an encyclopedia on the manner in which baseball and television have merged across the decades. Such a volume not only would explore the manner in which ballgames have been broadcast on TV both locally and nationally and the celebrated sportscasters who announce them. It would feature everything from the history of baseball stars hawking products or appearing as guests on talk shows or quiz shows to the presence of the sport and its players on TV series.

For indeed, baseball on the small screen transcends game broadcasts and recaps on the evening news. Take, for example, ballplayers appearing in commercials. Back in the 1950s and '60s, the inimitable Yogi Berra peddled the Yoo-Hoo chocolate drink ("Who says Yoo-Hoo's just for kids?"); more recently before his death, he advertised AFLAC, the supplemental insurance provider. ("And they give you cash, which is just as good as money.") Ballplayers have been associated with a rainbow of products, from Mr. Coffee (Joe DiMaggio) to Advil (Nolan Ryan) to Nike (Greg Maddux, Tom Glavine, Ken Griffey Jr., Don Mattingly, Bo Jackson ...). An iconic but long-retired athlete even can win new fame among the emerging generations by appearing in a popular television ad. Such is the case with Joe D. He first became the Mr. Coffee spokesperson in 1974, 23 years after ending his playing career and six years after Simon and Garfunkel asked, in the lyrics of the chart-topping song "Mrs. Robinson," "Where have you gone, Joe DiMaggio?" To many of those growing up in the 1970s, Joltin' Joe was more identified as the pitchman for Mr. Coffee than as the New York Yankees Hall of Famer who fashioned a 56-game hitting streak, or even as Marilyn Monroe's ex-husband.

The list of ballplayers hawking products on TV is endless. In one comical ad, bonnet-clad, corn-chomping Mickey Mantle and Willie Mays harmonize the lyrics "Everything's better with Blue Bonnet on it." In another, Billy Martin and George Steinbrenner argue the merits of Lite Beer from Miller, with the manager claiming that the product is "less filling" and the owner overriding him with the opinion that it "tastes great." In one ad, Don Drysdale hypes a series of baseball cards, found on Post cereal boxes, which feature the likenesses of 200 star players; in another, he shells for Poolsaver, a motorized swimming-pool cover. A veritable all-star team covering the generations—CC Sabathia, Evan Longoria, Jim Thome, Carlton Fisk, Lou Piniella, Rickey Henderson, Rollie Fingers, Randy Johnson, Ozzie Smith—join up for a *Field of Dreams*-inspired Pepsi ad. And so on ...

In recent decades, the latest World Series hero or MLB icon will strut across a stage and heartily grasp hands with a late-night TV host. One of countless examples: In a piece penned in 2014, when David Letterman announced his retirement from late-night television, ESPN's Jim Caple surveyed his baseball connection. Back in 1986, Letterman spent an entire show paying homage to Harmon Killebrew. Ted Williams was a guest in 1993; Hank Aaron appeared on several occasions; Derek Jeter, Jorge Posada, and Andy Pettitte celebrated their World Series triumph in 2009; and Bud Selig and David Ortiz were on the show in 2013. Various Letterman "Top 10 Lists" highlighted the sport. In one, Curt Schilling recited the "Top 10 Secrets Behind the Red Sox 2004 Comeback"; topping the list was "We got Babe Ruth's ghost a hooker and now everything's cool." Regarding the "Top 10 Good Things About a Possible Baseball Strike," Letterman quipped, "Fun to think with each passing day Alex Rodriguez is out another 85 grand";

one of the "Top 10 Things Going Through A-Rod's Mind" after he was hit by a 3-and-0 pitch in his left bicep was, "Hey, that's my injection arm." But the host not only spotlighted baseball celebs. On one 1985 show, he referred to Terry Forster as a "fat tub of goo"—and the chunky relief pitcher eventually came on the show. He arrived onstage chomping on a "David Letterman sandwich," which he described as a delicacy with "a lot of tongue on it." Forster admitted that while in the bullpen he would exchange autographed baseballs for hot dogs with fans; his favorite ballyard was "Houston," where "big tubs of beer" could be purchased for "a buck seventy-five."[1]

These days, the home-run derby has become a staple of the All Star Game TV lineup; back in 1960, *Home Run Derby* was a TV series that featured sluggers from Hank Aaron and Bob Allison to Wally Post and Willie Mays battling each other in home run-hitting contests filmed at Los Angeles' Wrigley Field, a conveniently located venue employed in endless baseball films and TV shows. Conversely, in the medium's earliest years, so many shows were broadcast live from New York City-based studios—and quite a few New York Yankees, New York Giants, and Brooklyn Dodgers made appearances. One even was the first-ever "mystery guest" on *What's My Line?* (1950-1967), the popular prime-time CBS game show. He was Phil Rizzuto, the beloved Bronx Bomber "Scooter," and the date was February 2, 1950. Years before he morphed into an aging self-caricature on Yankees broadcasts whose "holy cannoli" banter was at once cherished and lampooned, Rizzuto was quiet and serious-minded in this and his other *What's My Line?* appearances. And he was far from the lone big leaguer to be seen on the show; before the end of 1950, on June 21 and August 16, Dizzy Dean and Jackie Robinson were "mystery guests." During the show's early years, a lengthy roster of the ballplayers guesting on *What's My Line?* were affiliated with the New York nines. If non-New York players appeared—on June 24, 1956, 11 Cincinnati Reds comprised the "mystery guest"—it was because they were passing through town. On that date, the Reds had battled the Dodgers in an Ebbets Field twin bill.[2]

Since the medium's earliest years, baseball has had a presence in a range of TV series episodes. Some showcase top Tinseltown talent. In 1956—almost two decades before its screen version—"Bang the Drum Slowly" was presented "live from New York" as a segment of *The United States Steel Hour* (1953-1963). Paul Newman, then a budding Hollywood superstar, plays Henry Wiggen, "left-hand pitcher for the New York Mammoths" who won 26 games in '52, while Albert Salmi and George Peppard are cast as Bruce Pearson and Piney Woods.[3] The year before, the legendary John Ford helmed "Rookie of the Year," broadcast on *Screen Directors Playhouse* (1955-1956); the teleplay involves Mike Cronin (John Wayne), a cynical small-town sportswriter who determines that a hot young New York Yankee rookie is the son of an ex-star who was thrown out of baseball for taking a bribe.[4] Then in 1962, Ford directed "Flashing Spikes," an episode of *Alcoa Premiere* (1961-1963), which features James Stewart as Slim Conway, an ex-big leaguer wrongly banned from baseball for taking a bribe and accused of corrupting a young phenom. The program is "Presented by Fred Astaire," who also narrates. Joining Stewart in the cast are Don Drysdale, playing a pitcher named Gomer—rest assured that his surname is not Pyle; Vin Scully as "The Announcer"; Art Passarella as "The Series Umpire"; Vern Stephens as "The 1st Baseball Player"; John Wayne's son, Pat; and The Duke himself, billed as "Michael Morrison" and cast as "The Marine Sergeant." (Wayne's birthname was Marion Morrison.)[5]

Sandy Koufax with Alan Young, the star of TV's Mr. Ed, *and Mister Ed himself.*

The Dodgers Go Hollywood: Sandy Koufax shows off his no-hit baseballs to Milton Berle.

"Flashing Spikes" is not the only teleplay in which real-life baseball personalities mix with actors. One example is "High Pitch," an original mini-musical a là *Damn Yankees* that was broadcast in 1955 on *Shower of Stars* (1954-1958). *I Love Lucy*'s William Frawley, himself a famed baseball fan-atic, plays Gabby Mullins, manager of the Brooklyn Hooligans, a perennial last-place nine. Vivian Vance, who was Ethel to Frawley's Fred Mertz, is Mullins's wife. In the opening scene, a ballgame is being broadcast on television. Mel Allen, the show's "special guest," is the announcer. Coming to the plate is Ted Warren (Tony Martin), described by Allen as "the big slugger of the Spartans who once played for the Hooligans." Warren promptly homers, and Mel promptly interviews Mullins.[6]

(Frawley brings his love of the sport to Fred Mertz, his *I Love Lucy* character. In "Lucy Is Enceinte," the classic 1952 episode in which Lucy tells Ricky she is pregnant, Fred enters with a ball, bat, glove, and New York Yankees cap. He hands the latter three to Lucy, "for my godson." Regarding the baseball, he adds: "And wait'll you see the name on this. That's the name of the best ballplayer the Yankees ever had." "Uh, Spalding," Lucy blurts out, after glancing at it. "C'mon, honey, turn it around," Fred instructs. "Oh, Joe DiMaggio," Lucy declares. "You betcha," Fred responds, taking a mock batting stance. "Ol' Joltin' Joe himself." Indeed, Frawley might have suggested this dialogue, as he and the Yankee Clipper were close friends.)[7]

The Pride of the Yankees (1942), starring Gary Cooper as Lou Gehrig, is perhaps the most beloved baseball film of its era. But it is not the lone Hollywood property to spotlight Gehrig, his wife, Eleanor, and the disease that doomed him. Over two decades before *A Love Affair: The Eleanor and Lou Gehrig Story* (1977), a made-for-TV movie, another Gehrig teleplay—"The Lou Gehrig Story"—was an episode of *Climax!* (1954-1958). The program, which dates from 1956, bookends footage of the real Gehrig on July 4, 1939, the day in which he was honored at Yankee Stadium, with images of him at bat and in the field. Wendell Corey plays Gehrig, Jean Hagen is Eleanor, and the story spotlights their deep affection. "I just can't hit anymore," the perplexed Yankee tells his worried wife. "If I can't play ball anymore ... I'll learn to do something else." Ellie tells him, "You're it. You're the works...," adding that it "hasn't got anything to do with your batting average. ..." But Lou is obsessed with breaking out of his slump and endlessly watches footage of him homering off Dizzy Dean. A hardnosed—and fictional—young Yankee named Rusty (Russell Johnson) lambastes him for his play, insisting that "the great Gehrig" be benched, while Bill Dickey (Harry Carey Jr.), his best friend and teammate, steadfastly supports him. However, after not feeling pain after accidentally pouring hot coffee over his hand and then tripping and falling, it is clear that Gehrig is battling more than a batting slump.[8]

One of the more intriguing early baseball episodes—this one featuring no ballplaying celebrity guests—is "The Mighty Casey," a 1960 segment of *The Twilight Zone* (1959-1964). "The Mighty Casey" is the story of the lowly Hoboken Zephyrs, a once-upon-a-time major-league nine whose ballyard, as host-narrator Rod Serling explains, has become a "mausoleum of memories." "We're back in time now," he adds, and the setting is tryout day in Hoboken, New Jersey, where one of the wannabes is Casey, a left-handed hurler. What makes Casey special is that he is not human; he is a robot who, as his creator notes, has "only been in existence three weeks." Casey is signed by the Zephyrs and promptly fans 18 batters and pitches a three-hit shutout. But upon his being beaned, a doctor determines that he has no heart. In order to qualify as a pro, Casey is operated on and given one. But with a heart, he no longer is mighty: He is just another ordinary athlete who has difficulty fanning opposing hitters. Despite its fantasy element, "The Mighty Casey" features references to real baseball stars. Casey is not intimidated by Joe DiMaggio because he has never heard of Joe D. The robot is described as having the talent of "three Bob Fellers." The baseball commissioner declares that Zephyrs opponents will be angered by Casey's origin, noting that "the other clubs 'er gonna scream bloody murder. I could just hear Durocher now."[9]

The episode was tinged by tragedy. Paul Douglas originally played "Mouth" McGarry, the Zephyrs skipper who is described by his general manager as possessing the "widest mouth in either league." Elements of "The Mighty Casey" are reminiscent of Douglas's two baseball films: *It Happens Every Spring* (1949), involving a college professor-turned pitcher (played by Ray Milland) whose Casey-like hurling wins ballgames; and the original *Angels in the Outfield* (1951), in which Douglas plays a McGarry-like manager. However, right after filming the show, Douglas died of a heart attack. He looked perpetually haggard in his scenes and, as Serling stated, "We were watching him literally die in front of us." So the episode was reshot, with Jack Warden replacing Douglas.[10]

A couple of years before the filming of "The Mighty Casey," the Brooklyn Dodgers had relocated to Los Angeles—and the team now was a stone's throw from California's then-burgeoning television production. Granted, non-Dodger names kept popping up on TV shows: Mickey Mantle, for example, appeared as himself in "Second Base Steele," a 1984 episode of *Remington Steele* (1982-1987), and "The Field," a 1989 episode of the Bob Uecker sitcom *Mr. Belvedere* (1985-1990); and in 1971 even guested on *Hee Haw* (1969-1997), the country-oriented comedy-variety show. And Jason Giambi played a New York cabdriver in *The Bronx Is Burning* (2007), an eight-episode ESPN miniseries depicting the 1977 New York Yankees season. But given the opening of the West to big-league baseball, a host of Los Angeles Dodgers began popping up on TV series. (Dodgers players en masse are seen in a number of films, including 1958's *The Geisha Boy*, a Jerry Lewis comedy, and 1962's *Experiment in Terror*, a thriller. *The Geisha Boy* features an exhibition game between the Dodgers and a Japanese nine, with Pee Wee Reese, Charlie Neal, Jim Gilliam, Gil Hodges, Gino Cimoli, Carl Furillo, Duke Snider, Carl Erskine, and Johnny Roseboro appearing in brief color clips. The finale of *Experiment in Terror* is set in Candlestick Park, where the Dodgers are battling the San Francisco Giants. During the game there are expressive close-ups of Don Drysdale taking signs from his catcher, nodding, winding up, and pitching. Giant Harvey Kuenn is seen cracking a double; he is followed to the plate by Felipe Alou. Dodger Wally Moon appears in close-up as he clutches a bat. He beats out an infield hit to shortstop Jose Pagan and Vin Scully describes the ensuring rhubarb, whose participants include Giants Mike McCormick, Ed Bailey, Willie McCovey, and Joe Amalfitano.)

Among the biggest Dodgers names to appear on the small screen is the aforementioned Don Drysdale. Not all his TV appearances were in acting roles. He and his then-bride Ginger (whom he divorced in 1982) are seen in a February 26, 1959, episode of *You Bet Your Life* (1950-1961). "In case there may be some isolated listener who has never heard of Don Drysdale, he just happens to be one of the greatest pitchers in the world today and he happens to be playing for the Los Angeles Dodgers" was how George Fenneman, the show's announcer, introduced the 22-year-old pitcher to host Groucho Marx. As the newlyweds kibitz with Groucho, Ginger recalls first meeting Don and how they were engaged 17 days later.[11]

That November Drysdale and two "impostors" were guests on *To Tell the Truth* (1956-1968). "One of these men is a pitcher for the world champion Los Angeles Dodgers," an announcer informs the audience; in this pre-mass-media era, it was logical that none but the most diehard baseball fan would immediately recognize the ballplayer. But Don Ameche, one of the four panelists, did, and disqualified himself. The others—Monique Van Vooren, Kitty Carlisle, and Tom Poston—all correctly selected the real Drysdale, with Carlisle (who admitted that she never had seen a baseball game) explaining her pick by declaring that he somehow "has that baseball look."[12]

On occasion Drysdale was joined by Dodgers teammates. Five of them—Ron Perranoski, Tommy Davis, Willie Davis, Frank Howard, and Moose Skowron—appeared with him in a 1964 broadcast of *The Joey Bishop Show* (1961-1965). The ballplayers harmonize as they perform a Sammy Cahn-written parody of Cahn and Jimmy Van Heusen's "High Hopes," with Drysdale singing lead. He begins, "When they all said that the Dodgers was dead, that's when we came to life…" And the words "high hopes" are replaced first by "Koufax" and then by "Drysdale."[13] (The previous year Drysdale even recorded a pair of ballads for Reprise records. Their titles were "Give Her Love" and "One Love.")

Indeed, in the early 1960s, Drysdale was being primed for show-biz stardom. He was good-looking, with a fine screen presence. At the time, Eddie Cantor was featured on a radio program, appropriately titled, *Ask Eddie Cantor*, in which he answered questions submitted by listeners. One of them, on the June 14, 1961, broadcast, was: "Is Don Drysdale the best-looking Dodger?"[14] The pitcher began appearing on TV series, particularly in such westerns as *Lawman* (1958-1962), in a 1960 episode titled "The Hardcase"; *The Rifleman* (1958-1963), which starred ex-ballplayer-turned actor Chuck Connors, in "Skull," a 1962 episode; and *Cowboy in Africa* (1967-1968), also featuring Connors, in a 1968 episode titled "Search and Destroy." In "Millionaire Larry Maxwell," a 1960 episode of *The Millionaire* (1955-1960), Drysdale's character is named Eddie Cano; in "The Spitball Kid," a baseball-related 1969 episode of *Then Came Bronson* (1969-1970), he is Art Gilroy, a scout; in "The Big Game," a 1969 episode of *The Flying Nun* (1967-1970) that involved a convent baseball team, Drysdale is billed as "The Umpire" while Willie Davis is "The Manager."

Most prominently, Drysdale guest-starred as himself in a host of baseball-linked scenarios, from "Who's on First," a 1963 episode of *Our Man Higgins* (1962-1963), to "The Two-Hundred-Mile-an-Hour Fast Ball," a 1981 episode of *The Greatest American Hero* (1981-1983). Between 1962 and 1964, he made four appearances on *The Donna Reed Show* (1958-1966), with three featuring baseball-themed titles: "The Man in the Mask"; "My Son the Catcher" (with Willie Mays); and "Play Ball"; the fourth is titled "All These Dreams." "Play Ball," which also features Mays and Leo Durocher, involves autographed baseballs to be sold for charity and a ballgame between hospital personnel and a college freshman nine. Along the way, Durocher gets to comically trash umpires. Beyond its nostalgia quotient, "Play Ball" is a mirror of its era. Here, adult males—even doctors—are collectively out of shape; exercise and ballplaying only are reserved for the young. Meanwhile, women are collectively baseball-illiterate.[15]

In a *Leave It to Beaver* (1957-1963) episode from 1962 titled "Long Distance Call," the *Mayfield Press* headline is "Don Drysdale's Homer Beats Giants"; this inspires The Beaver (Jerry Mathers) and a couple of his pals to place—what else? –a long-distance phone call to Drysdale, "their favorite baseball player," at Dodger Stadium. They pool their pocket change, and are convinced that the cost only will be a dollar, but a mini-crisis results as the total mounts. But The Beaver does get to ask Drysdale to autograph his glove. It's a Warren Spahn model, but the ever-amenable Dodger tells him, "Well, I'll autograph it anyway."[16] Then in "The Dropout," a 1970 episode of *The Brady Bunch* (1969-1974), Mike Brady (Robert Reed) is designing Drysdale's new house. "You know, baseball's been real good to me," the pitcher observes. Mike invites the ballplayer home to meet his boys, resulting in son Greg (Barry Williams) becoming convinced that his future is as a big-league hurler.[17]

Coming in a strong second to Drysdale as a TV guest star is Leo Durocher, who coached the Dodgers between 1961 and 1964. In "The Clampetts and the

Mickey Mantle and Willie Mays switch from baseball caps to bonnets and munch on corn in a 1980 Blue Bonnet Margarine ad.

Dodgers," a 1963 episode of *The Beverly Hillbillies* (1962-1971), bank president Milburn Drysdale—who is no relation to Don, but the name of one of the show's supporting characters—sets up a golf game in which Jed (Buddy Ebsen) and Jethro (Max Baer Jr.) will play with Durocher (whose surname the Clampetts constantly pronounce as "Doooorocher"). But of course, the boys think they are going hunting, where they will be "shooting golfs" and "dodging golfs." Jethro declares, of Durocher, "Miss Jane says he's a famous dodger." Adds Elly May (Donna Douglas), "He's so good, he coaches all other dodgers." Leo then is seen at Dodger Stadium mentoring real ballplayers during batting practice, and a pitching prospect confuses bank president Drysdale with pitching star Drysdale. Eventually Jed and Jethro meet Durocher at the Wilshire Country Club, where they are mistaken for caddies. But Jethro's talent for tossing a baseball (which he thinks is "another one of them big eggs") convinces Leo that he has stumbled upon a legitimate prospect, whom he describes as "a one-man pitching staff" who possesses "the greatest arm since Satchel Paige." Actor Wally Cassell appears as Dodgers general manager Buzzy Bavasi; when Jethro declares that he wants no money for throwing baseballs, the GM responds, "O'Malley will love you." But Jethro never will make the majors: In order to throw a baseball at a lightning-fast speed, he must smear his hand with possum fat.[18]

"Leo Durocher Meets Mister Ed," a 1963 episode of *Mister Ed* (1958-1966), opens with the title character, a talking horse, wearing a Los Angeles Dodgers cap; plus, his stable is crammed with team memorabilia. A Dodgers game, announced by Vin Scully, is on television, and the nine is in a terrible slump. "Those bums should have stayed in Brooklyn," a flustered Mister Ed declares. Wilbur (Alan Young), Mister Ed's owner, is convinced that Leo the Lip is "going to want some tips on how to help his players," and the horse is all too willing to offer them. How did Mister Ed come to be such an expert? Well, it is revealed that, once upon a time, he "played in the Pony League." Wilbur and Mister Ed end up at Dodger Stadium, where they meet Willie Davis, John Roseboro, Moose Skowron, and "the old strikeout king, Sandy Koufax." And of course, there is Leo Durocher. Upon being introduced to the horse, Leo quips, "For a minute, I thought it was Casey Stengel." Sandy then pitches batting practice to Davis and Roseboro, with Mister Ed offering his expertise. Plus, with bat in mouth, the horse hits against Koufax and, via some crafty editing, smashes a homer. Mister Ed asks Wilbur if the Dodgers might sign him as a player. "A horse on the Dodgers!" is his incredulous response. "Well, why not," Mister Ed quips. "They already got a Moose."[19]

Then in "Herman the Rookie," a 1965 episode of *The Munsters* (1964-1966), Herman Munster (Fred Gwynne) hits fungoes in a park while mentoring Eddie, his young son. One travels eight blocks and lands on the head of Durocher just after he observes, "If we can come up with a power hitter, I mean a guy (who) can hit the long ball, I think my old club is a cinch to win the pennant." Durocher seeks out Herman, who excitedly shows up for a Dodgers tryout. The balls he belts are lightning-fast and lightning-far and, in a then-topical reference, Durocher notes, "I don't know whether to sign him with the Dodgers or send him to Vietnam." However, while in the field, Herman crashes through a fence and throws a ball so hard that it explodes — and he is not signed because, as he explains, "Mr. O'Malley said it would cost him $75,000 to put the Dodger Stadium back in shape every time I played. ... And they said the insurance companies wouldn't allow the players on the same field with me."[20]

Featured in "Herman the Rookie" is a reference to the Dodgers' former home city. Upon entering the Munsters' creepy abode, Durocher quips, "I've never seen a place like this in my whole life. Not even in Brooklyn."[21] Briefly appearing as a catcher is Ken Hunt, the stepfather of series regular Butch Patrick, who plays Eddie. Between 1959 and 1964, Hunt appeared in 310 major-league games with the Yankees, Angels, and Senators. None were with the Dodgers.

As the decades passed, the Drysdales and Durochers of the sport need not have guested on a sitcom for there to be a baseball motif. In "Bang the Drum, Stanley," a 1988 episode of *The Golden Girls* (1985-1992), Dorothy Zbornak (Beatrice Arthur) is visited by Stanley (Herb Edelman), her lying, cheating ex-husband. "I was out taking a drive listening to the Dodgers on the radio and I got a sudden urge to see a ballgame," he tells Dorothy. And he adds, "Dorothy, I was thinking about us. Good old days back in Brooklyn. Ebbets Field. Those long summer nights sitting in the bleachers eating hot dogs, rooting for the Dodgers and kissing passionately between innings." But Dorothy reminds Stanley that they never were together at Ebbets Field. Stanley's faux reminiscing is a plot to sweet-talk Dorothy into lending him some money.[22]

Then in "Where's Charlie," a 1991 episode, bawdy Blanche Devereaux (Rue McClanahan) begins dating — and coaching — Stevie (Tim Thomerson), a professional ballplayer. "Oh, you got Blanche's number from the wall in the dugout," quips Sophia (Estelle Getty), who is Dorothy's mother and queen of the one-liners. Blanche then equates baseball with sex. "Now look, you have to discover the sensuality of baseball," she tells Stevie. "(There are) many, many, many similarities between baseball and making love. The mental preparation. The rush of adrenaline. The unspecified duration of the game." Sophia chimes in, "And you should hear the cheers coming from Blanche's room on Old Timers Day!" This is followed by a *Bull Durham* reference.[23]

Across the decades, the central characters on hit TV series have been lawyers, doctors, cops ... rarely have they been ballplayers. And when baseball has been featured, the shows usually are flops. *The Bad News Bears* and *A League of Their Own*, both hit movies, were short-lived TV series (in 1979-1980 and 1993 respectively). The one-episode presence of

Johnny Bench in *Bears* and Doug Harvey and Ken Brett in *League* had no impact on the ratings.

How many viewers remember *Hardball* (1994), spotlighting the Pioneers, an inept ballclub? A cameo appearance by Barry Bonds couldn't save this one. Or *A Whole New Ballgame* (1995), with Corbin Bernsen as a ballplayer-turned-sportscaster? Or *Clubhouse* (2004-2005), about a 16-year-old New York Empires batboy? Ron Darling's one-episode presence as an announcer was no ratings boost. More successful was HBO's *Eastbound & Dawn* (2009-2013), featuring Danny McBride as Kenny Powers, a burned-out ex-big leaguer-turned physical-education teacher. One promising entry is *Pitch*, which premiered in 2016 and spotlights Genevieve "Ginny" Baker (Kylie Bunbury), the first woman to make the majors, hurling for the San Diego Padres. However, two failed shows that remain worthy of scrutiny are *Ball Four* (1976), inspired by Jim Bouton's landmark book, with Bouton himself starring as Jim Barton, ballplayer-turned-*Sports Illustrated* writer; and *Bay City Blues* (1983), centering on the Bluebirds, a fictional minor-league nine from Bay City, California, that was created by Steven Bochko and Jeffrey Lewis, of *Hill Street Blues* fame.

Nonetheless, baseball-on-the-small-screen occasionally has resonated with viewers. One obvious example is *Cheers* (1982-1993), the iconic sitcom featuring Ted Danson as Sam Malone, ex-Red Sox reliever whose career was wrecked by drink. The sitcom primarily is set not in the Fenway environs but in the Boston bar that Sam had purchased; Ernie Pantusso (Nicholas Colasanto), Malone's bartender, was his former coach. Still, baseball sporadically made its way into *Cheers* storylines. In "Breaking In Is Hard to Do," from 1990, arbiter Doug Aducci (Clive Rosengren) enters Cheers. Sam calls him "one of the best damn umpires in the American League," but the two immediately immerse themselves in an on-field-style brawl as the ex-hurler recalls a game between the Red Sox and Yankees. It is the ninth inning. The Sox are down by a run. Malone is on the mound, and he angrily declares that Aducci "calls ball four on Munson. Next guy up is Chambliss, knocks one right out of the park."[24] And in "Pitch It Again, Sam," a 1991 episode, New York Yankee Dutch Kincaid (Michael Fairman) beseeches Sam to pitch to him on the team's "Dutch Kincaid Day." His reasoning: He belted a homer on practically every occasion in which he faced Sam, and he was hoping for a repeat performance.[25]

On occasion real Massachusetts celebrities appear on *Cheers* as themselves, from John Kerry and Michael Dukakis to Kevin McHale. Two are Boston Red Sox. In 1983's "Now Pitching, Sam Malone"—a title with a double meaning—Luis Tiant is seen in a TV ad hawking a beer but flubs the tagline "You don't feel full with Fields, you just feel fine."[26] Then in "Bar Wars," from 1988, Wade Boggs walks into Cheers and introduces himself. "Yeah, pal, and I'm Babe Ruth," responds disbelieving bar regular Norm (George Wendt). "And I'm Dizzy Dean," quips Cliff (John Ratzenberger). But the punchline belongs to Woody (Woody Harrelson), the ever-clueless bartender, when he chimes in, "I'm Woody Boyd."[27]

The Simpsons (1989-) occasionally has spotlighted the sport. In "Homer at the Bat," broadcast in 1992, Homer leads the Springfield Nuclear Power Plant softball nine into the league finals. Mr. Burns, a Steinbrenner-like tyrant, rids the team of its employee-players; his ringer-substitutes, who all recorded their own voices, are Darryl Strawberry, Roger Clemens, Don Mattingly, Ozzie Smith, Wade Boggs, Ken Griffey Jr., Jose Canseco, Steve Sax, and Mike Scioscia.[28]

Another sitcom with knowing baseball references is *Seinfeld* (1989-1998), in which George Costanza (Jason Alexander) spends several seasons as a Yankees employee and comically tussles with "Big Stein," otherwise known as George Steinbrenner (voiced by Larry David). In "The Opposite," a 1994 episode, job applicant Costanza first mixes with potential employer Steinbrenner and The Boss politely declares, "Nice to meet you." Costanza tells him, with the Yankee Stadium field seen through a window, "Well, I wish I could say the same, but I must say, with all due respect, I find it very hard to see the logic behind some of the moves you have made with this fine organization. In the past 20 years, you have caused myself and the city of New York a good deal of distress as we have watched you take our beloved Yankees and reduced them to a laughingstock, all for the glorification of your massive ego." To which Steinbrenner responds, "Hire this man!"[29]

Jerry Seinfeld is a noted New York Mets fan; in "The New Friend," a two-part episode also called "The Boyfriend, Part 1" and "The Boyfriend, Part 2" that aired in 1992, his character meets and befriends Keith Hernandez, the ex-Met first sacker. Jerry and his pals are in awe of Keith, but complications arise when Hernandez begins dating Elaine (Julia Louis-Dreyfus). She tells Jerry, "I've never seen you jealous before." And Jerry responds, "Well, you're not even a fan. I was at Game Six—you didn't even watch it."[30]

An alleged "spitting incident" also plays a role in the scenario. The date was June 14, 1987, and Newman (Wayne Knight) recalls that he and Kramer (Michael Richards) were "enjoying a beautiful afternoon in the right-field stands when a crucial Hernandez error (led) to a five-run Phillies ninth. Cost the Mets the game." Kramer chimes in, "Our day was ruined. There was a lot of people, you know, they were waiting by the players' parking lot. Now we're coming down the ramp. ... Newman was in front of me. Keith was coming toward us (and) as he passes Newman turns and says, 'Nice game pretty boy.' Keith continued past us up the ramp." And Newman continues, "A second later, something happened that changed us in a deep and profound way from that day forward." "What was it?" Elaine wonders. Kramer answers her: "He spit on us ... and I screamed out, 'I'm hit!'" Newman adds, "Then I turned and the spit (ricocheted off) him and it hit me." But Jerry is a nonbeliever, explaining that "the immutable laws of physics contradict the whole premise of your account." Eventually, it is revealed that Mets reliever Roger McDowell was the culprit.[31] Hernandez and George Steinbrenner also reappear in the show's final episode; they attend the trial of Jerry, Costanza, Kramer, and Elaine, who are accused of cracking jokes about and filming an overweight robbery victim. The "baseball insider" references continue, as Frank Costanza (Jerry Stiller),

George's father, asks Steinbrenner, "How could you give $12 million to Hideki Irabu?"[32]

In terms of popularity, *The Dick Van Dyke Show* (1961-1966) is the *Seinfeld* of its era. Dick Van Dyke, Mary Tyler Moore, Rose Marie, Morey Amsterdam, and Larry Mathews play Rob and Laura Petrie, Sally Rogers, Buddy Sorrell, and Ritchie Petrie. Carl Reiner, the show's creator, occasionally appears as Alan Brady, the egomaniacal TV star who employs Rob, Sally, and Buddy as comedy writers. However, the show's unsold 1959 pilot, titled *Head of the Family*, features a completely different cast. Reiner himself is Rob (whose surname is pronounced "Peetrie"); Barbara Britton, Sylvia Miles, Morty Gunty, and Gary Morgan play Laura, Sally, Buddy, and Ritchie, while the Brady character is named "Alan Sturdy." And the storyline is New York baseball-centric. There are casual references to Casey Stengel and Hank Bauer, and the plot centers on 6-year-old Ritchie's complaining to Laura that "daddy never plays baseball with me..." He follows up with a question: "Why couldn't you marry Mickey Mantle? ... Well, I love Mickey. Don't you love Mickey?" (Toronto fans might chuckle over the name of the street on which the Petries' suburban abode is located. It is neither Lou Gehrig Lane nor Bronx Bomber Byway but Blue Jay Blvd.!) [33]

And finally, a show that is not baseball-centric still might offer a knowing peek into the pressures and realities of ballplayers, not to mention the essence of the sport. In an episode on *Lou Grant* (1977-1982) titled "Catch"—surely, a name with a double meaning—*Los Angeles Tribune* reporter Billie Newman (Linda Kelsey) meets and falls for Ted McCovey (Cliff Potts), who is introduced as a Los Angeles Dodgers "catcher who was third-string until they traded him to the Bay Area last winter." Ted also has been playing for "14 years, 10 in the majors." Not surprisingly, the first time he is mentioned, he is mistaken for Willie McCovey. Soon enough, Ted is put on irrevocable waivers by the Giants. "Kid they called up to replace me was battin' .385 in Triple A," he explains, adding, "You know what baseball done for me? Treated me like a kid the past 14 years and now suddenly they're tellin' me I'm an old man." But there is a happy ending here, as Ted takes a job as a Dodgers scout.[34]

"Catch" and "Wedding," its follow-up episode, both aired in 1981 — and both feature references that place the storyline in the proper timeframe. In "Wedding," Ted is about to propose to an unsuspecting Billie. Before he can do so, she asks him, "Does it have something to do with baseball? Did you find another Valenzuela?" Billie also thinks that ERA stands for "Equal Rights Amendment," which she hopes will pass, and not "Earned Run Average." Both episodes are peppered with baseball links. Ted is convinced that marriage to Billie will be fruitful because of his "catcher's instinct." And the preacher who marries them is an ex-ballplayer who traded "the horsehide for the cloth."[35]

The "Catch" teleplay also offers a potent explanation of why baseball matters. As they spend time together, Billie — who is no baseball fan — complains that the game is "so slow." "It's like saying your life is slow," Ted responds. "What does that mean? There's so much going on (in baseball). Every pitch is another decision. Where to play the hitter. What to throw him. (What happens) if the runner goes on the pitch. Who's on deck? You take a chance (or) you play the percentages. There's a thousand decisions in a game. … Probabilities. Statistics. … The mutations are infinite. A game could go on forever. … I've played 5,500 games, give or take, since Little League. I've watched a couple thousand more. Never played the same game twice. And every one, a situation comes up (that) I'd ever seen before."[36]

NOTES

1. espn.go.com/mlb/story/_/id/10731028/mlb-baseball-miss-david-letterman.
2. Rob Edelman. "What's My Line? and Baseball," *The Baseball Research Journal*, Fall 2014: 36.
3. youtube.com/watch?v=rPc9keZ1clo.
4. free-classic-tv-shows.com/Drama/Screen-Directors-Playhouse/1955-12-07-s1-ep10-Rookie-of-the-Year/index.php.
5. youtube.com/watch?v=Xmzknb3hWAQ.
6. Rob Edelman and Audrey Kupferberg, *Meet the Mertzes* (Los Angeles: Renaissance Books, 1999), 149, 153.
7. Edelman and Kupferberg, 173.
8. youtube.com/watch?v=fsuwx8xVpuU.
9. youtube.com/watch?v=N1Qs24BfR5I.
10. twilightzonevortex.blogspot.com/2012/07/mighty-casey.html.
11. youtube.com/watch?v=qzhVOKqlIDc.
12. youtube.com/watch?v=rKld2Z_X-Co.
13. youtube.com/watch?v=8nwCYqk0DeM.
14. youtube.com/watch?v=iApcQ2zerc4.
15. youtube.com/watch?v=YaDLOtLoFuc.
16. youtube.com/watch?v=srLiKccFFRw.
17. hulu.com/watch/633526.
18. youtube.com/watch?v=-288A4pp6VI.
19. youtube.com/watch?v=uAY58hsMVnI.
20. youtube.com/watch?v=cR9HDJW9Jmk.
21. Ibid.
22. youtube.com/watch?v=Uy-AkWsUqVw.
23. youtube.com/watch?v=YMBgWl1rgY8.
24. youtube.com/watch?v=idBHtrs-Xy4.
25. imdb.com/title/tt0539831/.
26. avclub.com/tvclub/cheers-now-pitching-sam-malonelet-me-count-the-way-67192.
27. youtube.com/watch?v=979ArlkjFck.
28. See the SABR book *Nuclear-Powered Baseball* (Phoenix: SABR, 2016).
29. youtube.com/watch?v=vWCGs27_xPI.
30. seinfeldscripts.com/TheBoyfriend1.htm.
31. Marissa Payne, "And the Best Sports of All Time on 'Seinfeld' Was…," *Washington Post*, July 3, 2014.
32. youtube.com/watch?v=dzeuvZc1KI8.
33. youtube.com/watch?v=Ll22fkwOhH4; youtube.com/watch?v=wvdzwsTj9_4.
34. youtube.com/watch?v=ozeeyoJyOmo.
35. youtube.com/watch?v=CoZC5rvqHRc.
36. youtube.com/watch?v=ozeeyoJyOmo.

CONTRIBUTORS

AUDREY LEVI APFEL is a Managing VP and research analyst for Gartner, Inc., advising organizations worldwide and publishing research on technology trends and projects. Her contribution to this book is part of her lifelong passion and interest in all things baseball - particularly New York baseball. She was raised in Queens, in the shadow of Shea Stadium. Audrey resides in the strong baseball outpost of Stamford, Connecticut - where Bobby Valentine and Brian Cashman have been known to rappel off of a 22-story building together at Christmastime dressed as elves.

ERIC ARON has contributed a number of bios for the BioProject website and book projects. Originally hailing from Rye, New York, he now lives in Boston. Currently, he is an exhibit interpreter and guide at the Edward M. Kennedy Institute for The United States Senate.

LAWRENCE BALDASSARO, Professor Emeritus of Italian at the University of Wisconsin-Milwaukee, is the author of *Beyond DiMaggio: Italian Americans in Baseball*, editor of *Ted Williams: Reflections on a Splendid Life*, and co-editor of *The American Game: Baseball and Ethnicity*. He has published articles in numerous sports encyclopedias and journals, has been a contributing writer for the Milwaukee Brewers magazine since 1990, and wrote the chapter on sports for *The Routledge History of Italian Americans*.

RUSSELL A. BERGTOLD grew up on the southside of Chicago. His passion for baseball began in 1969 as he unwittingly rooted for the crosstown Cubs. Although that season ended in heartache for Cub fans, a lifelong loyalty was forged as he continually waited for "next year." Russ worked on the grounds crew at Wrigley Field from 1992-1994 before joining the International Brotherhood of Electrical Workers in 1995 where he currently serves as a Journeyman Wireman. He recently earned a Master's Degree in Communication from Governors State University in Illinois. Still relatively new to SABR, this is his second contribution.

JAY BERMAN is a retired professor of journalism who joined SABR in 1982 and currently lives in Manhattan Beach, California.

MICHAEL BETZOLD wrote *Queen of Diamonds: the Tiger Stadium Story* with Ethan Casey and is a Detroit freelance writer and former reporter and baseball columnist for the *Detroit Free Press*.

CHARLIE BEVIS is the author of seven books on baseball history, most recently *Red Sox vs. Braves in Boston: The Battle for Fans' Hearts, 1901–1952*. A member of SABR since 1984, he has contributed more than four dozen biographies to the SABR BioProject as well as several to SABR books, including *The 1967 Impossible Dream Red Sox*. He is an adjunct professor of English at Rivier University in Nashua, New Hampshire, and lives in Chelmsford, Massachusetts.

After pursuing undergraduate and graduate degrees in history from West Texas State University and the University of New Mexico, **RON BRILEY** taught history and film studies for thirty-eight years at Sandia Prep School in Albuquerque, New Mexico, where he also served as assistant head of school and is now faculty emeritus. Briley has also served on numerous committees for the Organization of American Historians and American Historical Association. A Distinguished Lecturer for the Organization of American Historians, he is the author of six books and numerous scholarly articles and encyclopedia entries on the history of sport, music, and film.

BRUCE BUMBALOUGH first went to a Detroit Tigers game with his mother and brother in 1952. He has loved the Tigers since that game. Bruce was born in Detroit and holds a Master of Library Science degree from the University of Mississippi. He did extensive graduate study in history at the University of North Texas. Bruce lives in the Fort Worth, Texas, area with his wife Shirley and is a retired librarian. He is currently working on a book about the Dixie Series and has written on LaGrave Field and minor-league baseball in the Dallas-Fort Worth Metroplex.

FREDERICK C. BUSH and former big-leaguer Hans Lobert, who is featured in his article, have much in common: 1) They both lived in Pittsburgh, PA for parts of their lives; 2) Lobert played briefly for the Pirates, and Bush later cheered for the same franchise; 3) Lobert is featured in Lawrence Ritter's *The Glory of Their Times*, and Bush has read Ritter's book; 4) Lobert coached the baseball team at the US Military Academy (Army) at West Point for eight years, and Bush grew up as the son of a career US Army soldier. Add in the fact that both men hail from German ancestry, and it becomes obvious that Bush is practically a latter-day Lobert, who was fated to write about his predecessor for this book.

ALAN COHEN has cried through *Pride of the Yankees* and cheered through *The Jackie Robinson Story*. He has been a SABR member since 2011, serves as Vice President-Treasurer of the Connecticut Smoky Joe Wood Chapter, and is the datacaster (stringer) for the Hartford Yard Goats. He has written more than 35 biographies for SABR's bio-project. He has expanded his research into the Hearst Sandlot Classic (1946-1965), an annual youth All-Star game which launched the careers of 88 major-league players, as well as a player who appeared in *The French Connection*. He has four children and six grandchildren and resides in West Hartford, Connecticut with his wife Frances, one cat (Morty) and two dogs (Sam and Sheba).

WARREN CORBETT of Bethesda, Maryland, is the author of *The Wizard of Waxahachie: Paul Richards and the End of Baseball As We Knew It*, and a contributor to SABR's BioProject.

RORY COSTELLO is co-chair and chief editor of the BioProject Committee. He has contributed to a variety of SABR bio books. The first baseball movie that made an impression on him was *Bang the Drum Slowly*. Rory lives in Brooklyn with his wife Noriko and son Kai.

ROB EDELMAN is the author of *Great Baseball Films* and *Baseball on the Web* (which Amazon.com cited as a Top 10 Internet book), and is a frequent contributor to *Base Ball: A Journal of the Early Game*. He offers film commentary on WAMC Northeast Public Radio and is a longtime Contributing Editor of *Leonard Maltin's Movie Guide* and other Maltin publications. With his wife, Audrey Kupferberg, he has coauthored *Meet the Mertzes*, a double biography of Vivian Vance and super-baseball fan William Frawley, and *Matthau: A Life*. His byline has appeared in *Total Baseball, The Total Baseball Catalog, Baseball and American Culture: Across the Diamond, NINE: A Journal of Baseball History and Culture, The National Pastime: A Review of Baseball History, The Baseball Research Journal*, and histories of the 1918 Boston Red Sox, 1947 Brooklyn Dodgers, 1947 New York Yankees, and 1960 Pittsburgh Pirates. He is the author of a baseball film essay for the Kino International DVD *Reel Baseball: Baseball Films from the Silent Era, 1899-1926*; is an interviewee on several documentaries on the director's cut DVD of *The Natural*; was the keynote speaker at the 23rd Annual NINE Spring Training Conference; and teaches film history courses at the University at Albany (SUNY).

GREG ERION is retired from the railroad industry and currently teaches history part time at Skyline Community College in San Bruno, California. He has written several biographies for SABR's BioProject and was very active in helping the Games Project. He and his wife Barbara lived in South San Francisco, California. Greg died shortly before this book was published.

In the summer of 1984 **EDDIE FRIERSON** began his research on the life and career of one of baseball's greatest pitchers, Christy Mathewson. As a young native of Nashville, Tennessee, he and his sisters sang with the famed gospel Bill Gaither Trio. Eddie helped pitch his Hillwood High School baseball team to a State Championship in 1977. While at UCLA it became clear that this right-hander "wasn't going to make the bigs" so he made the most of his time in Westwood and obtained his degree in Theatre Arts. With his one-man play, *Matty*, Frierson combines the best of both worlds and has gone farther in baseball through the stage than he ever would have on the field (including celebrating the 75th Anniversary of the Hall of Fame's Inaugural Class with the families of Babe Ruth, Ty Cobb, Honus Wagner and Walter Johnson.)

Eddie has performed on both coasts in dozens of theatrical productions. He has received numerous awards and was heard all over the country as the voice of PETCO Pet Stores. He has also been featured in hundreds of television shows, cartoons and many feature films. Listen carefully in the movie *The Rookie* while Dennis Quaid loosens up in the pen in Durham as you'll hear Eddie announce, "Your attention please ... now batting for the Bulls, number 38, Eddie Frierson!"

JOHN GABCIK was born and raised in Chicago, and has been following the White Sox since 1952. He writes biographies and game stories for SABR, concentrating on under-appreciated White Sox pitchers and other personalities. He also helps Retrosheet develop game play-by-play recreations. He is retired, and lives in Brevard, North Carolina.

ERIC HANAUER is a widely published writer and underwater photographer, with nearly 1,000 magazine articles and four books. His scuba diving adventures have taken him to some 50 countries around the world. For 35 years his day job was Associate Professor of Kinesiology at California State University Fullerton, where he also coached swimming and water polo, and founded the scuba diving program. His main claim to fame was developing the grab start. He owes all this to lack of baseball skill as a youth, which led him into the water as a second choice. Hanauer is a lifelong Cubs fan, ever since his first Wrigley Field game at the age of nine. For more, see his website, www.ehanauer.com.

BILL HICKMAN was the long-serving Chair of SABR's Pictorial History Committee. He currently maintains the "near major leaguers" data base on the SABR website. Having grown up in Chicago, he is happy to call the Cubs the World Series Champions of 2016. Now living in Maryland, he has served in a leadership capacity for years with the Bethesda Big Train summer collegiate league baseball team. During his college years, he worked in a box office for a summer stock theater, where movie stars of yesteryear entertained the audiences, so his interest in movie personalities was stimulated at an early age.

PAUL HOFMANN is the Associate Vice President for International Programs at Sacramento State University. He is a native of Detroit, Michigan and lifelong Detroit sports fan. His research interests include 19th century and pre-World War II Japanese baseball. He is also an avid baseball card collector. Paul currently resides in Folsom, California.

JAY HURD, a longtime member of SABR, contributes to the SABR BioProject, and studies the Negro Leagues, women in baseball, and the literature of baseball. He retired from Harvard University, in 2008, where he served as the Preservation Review Librarian for Widener Library. Now a resident of Bristol, Rhode Island, he is a regular attendee of the Southern New England Lajoie-Start Chapter of SABR. He supports and collaborates research with local libraries, historical societies, and museums. Jay is a fan of the Boston Red Sox.

DON JENSEN is editor of *Base Ball: A Journal of the Early Game,* and a longtime member of the SABR Nineteenth Century and Deadball Committees. He has written extensively on the game before 1920, especially its role in the Sporting Life of the Gilded Age. Jensen received the SABR Nineteenth Committee President's Award for research in 2015. He is currently a Senior Fellow at the Center for Transatlantic Relations, Johns Hopkins School of

Advanced International Studies and the Center for European Policy Analysis, both in Washington, DC.

MAXWELL KATES is a chartered accountant who lives and works in midtown Toronto. A SABR member since 2001, he considers *City Slickers* to be his favourite baseball movie. Although perhaps not baseball in the traditional sense, the film does contain enough references to Willie Mays, Mickey Mantle, Hank Aaron, Roberto Clemente, and that third baseman for Pittsburgh in 1960 - "Don Hoak!"

SEAMUS KEARNEY has loved baseball movies since his childhood. He still remembers the plot of *Rhubarb*. He believes today's high-five-after-a-dinger is in the original *The Babe Ruth Story* (William Bendix—ugh). And he's a big fan of *Trouble with the Curve* for the clogging and "I heard it."

ADAM KLINKER is a Pushcart Prize-nominated writer living in Omaha, Nebraska, with his wife and three young children. He is a graduate of the University of Nebraska-Lincoln, and holds a master's degree in English from the University of Kansas. Spring and summer cramp his movie-watching style, given nightly followings of the Pittsburgh Pirates and Kansas City Royals. But come the end of the baseball season, he will indulge in a film or two. His favorite baseball movie is *The Natural*, though he longs for a remake that hews closer to Malamud's novel — bitter, no-lights-exploding ending and all.

TED LEAVENGOOD is a SABR member and the author of three books, including *Ted Williams and the Washington Senators*, and *Clark Griffith, the Old Fox of Washington Baseball*. He is managing editor and regular contributor to the historical baseball site, Seamheads.com, and has been a frequent contributor elsewhere, including MASN Sports. Before retirement, he worked as an urban planner for the U.S. Department of Housing and Urban Development, Fairfax County, Virginia, and the City of Atlanta. He lives in Chevy Chase, Maryland, with his wife.

BOB LEMOINE lives in New Hampshire, where he works as a high school librarian and adjunct professor. A SABR member since 2013, he has contributed to several SABR projects, including being a co-editor with Bill Nowlin on 2016's *Boston's First Nine: the 1871-75 Boston Red Stockings*. He does occasionally see a movie or two when not researching baseball.

LEN LEVIN is a retired newspaper editor. Nowadays, when there isn't a good baseball movie to see, he copyedits SABR articles and edits the decisions of the Rhode Island Supreme Court.

BILL NOWLIN has been an extra in three baseball films—alas, never on camera—*Eight Men Out*, *Field of Dreams*, and *Fever Pitch*. He even had to get a period haircut for *Eight Men Out*. In his time off-set, he has authored or edited something like 60 baseball books. It's not the Oscars, but Rounder Records (which he co-founded) have won something like 50 Grammy Awards. In 2016, he and his partners were inducted into the International Bluegrass Music Hall of Fame.

Co-editor Bill Nowlin, center, as an extra in the John Sayles film, Eight Men Out.

A new contributor to SABR, **EMMET NOWLIN** currently resides in Cambridge, Massachusetts. Although somewhat interested in managing the first space hotel, he does not intend to pursue the venture, or ever travel to space.

DAN O'BRIEN is an American journalist, author and screenwriter with an emphasis in sports, having written books, television sports stories, magazine articles and a screenplay. A graduate of the University of Missouri's School of Broadcast Journalism, O'Brien is a former television anchor, reporter and producer, including stints with network affiliates in six states and Washington DC. He is co-author of the books *Mark May's Tales from the Washington Redskins* and *MizzouRah! Memorable Moments in Missouri Tiger Football History*.

His documentaries and special programming earned an Emmy Award for his series on women's athletics at the University of Miami. *Speed, Crash, Rescue*, about safety issues in the Indy Car Racing League, received worldwide distribution.

O'Brien was a script consultant for two films by director Ryan Little, *Outlaw Trail: The Treasure of Butch Cassidy* and *Forever Strong*. He has written a screenplay based on the life of Hall of Famer George (Rube) Waddell, titled *Rube*.

WILL OSGOOD is a former sports journalist who wrote for *Bleacher Report*, *FanSided*, and *Cover 32*. He graduated from San Diego State University in 2010 with a degree in Communication while minoring in Religious Studies. He is currently pursuing his Master of Divinity degree from Reformed Theological Seminary in Jackson, Mississippi. Will is a die-hard Cubs fan who cannot make up his mind on whether he loves the City of Chicago or New Orleans more.

MARK V. PERKINS, a talented artist, born August 1, 1960 in Auburn, California, became enamored with the Baltimore Orioles while witnessing the team's crushing defeat in the 1969 Fall Classic. At a time when ballgames were decided in afternoon sunlight, Mark sketched portraits of his favorite baseball stars; the finest of which were mailed with a s.a.s.e. to the players' respective ballclubs with the hope that he would receive their coveted autographs! These school-penciled likenesses ran the gamut from Henry Aaron to Earl Weaver, a personal response from "Cool Papa" Bell, a rubber-stamped signature from 95-year-old Joe Wood and dozens in between. In 1986, then-editor Cliff Kachline bestowed an honor for Mark to prepare cover portraits for SABR's *Fifteen Annual Baseball Research Journal* to coincide with the featured article. Nearly three decades later – spurned on by bouts as an author – Mark lobbied SABR's Baseball Biography Project Committee and was chosen to write Edgar "Blue" Washington's official bio, a piece which garnered multiple citations in several major publications and Internet resources.

RICHARD J. PUERZER is an associate professor and chairperson of the Department of Engineering at Hofstra University. He has contributed to a number of SABR Books, including *Mustaches and Mayhem: The Oakland Athletics: 1972-1974* (2015) and *The 1986 New York Mets: There Was More Than Game Six* (2016). His writings on baseball have also appeared in: *NINE: A Journal of Baseball History and Culture*, *Black Ball*, *The National Pastime*, *The Cooperstown Symposium on Baseball and American Culture* proceedings, and *Spitball*.

GARY A. SARNOFF is an active member of SABR and PFRA (Professional Football Research Association). He writes for SABR's Bioproject and is the chairman of the Ron Gabriel Award Committee, which honors the author(s) best research work pertaining to the Brooklyn Dodgers on a yearly basis. In addition, he writes for *Nats News*, *Base Ball: A Journal of the Early Game* and is the author of two books (*The Wrecking Crew of '33* and *The Yankees First Dynasty*). He resides in Alexandria, Virginia.

MARK SOUDER is from Fort Wayne, Indiana which he represented in the United States Congress for 16 years. Officially retired, he still does some political commentary in Indiana and has been working on a multi-year project about the history of baseball and politics. It was prompted by his participation as a lead questioner in the Congressional Steroid Hearings. His SABR writings have included articles in the 2015 Chicago and 2017 New York editions of *The National Pastime*, several presentations at the Nineteenth Century Baseball Conference (FRED) n Cooperstown, and articles in the books *Boston's First Nine* and *Puerto Rico and Baseball*.

JON SPRINGER (@Springer66) is the founder of the *Mets by the Numbers* project and author of the book by the same name. A SABR member since 1993, he is currently at work on a book about the 1884 Wilmington Quicksteps. Jon is a business writer and resides in Brooklyn with his family.

ANDY STRASBERG, a native New Yorker, realized a lifelong dream of working in Major League Baseball, when he began a career that lasted 22 years with the San Diego Padres in 1975.

Andy served as a technical consultant and made his acting debut for the HBO movie *61** directed by Billy Crystal. In 2008 Strasberg co-authored the book *Baseball's Greatest Hit: The Story of Take Me Out to the Ball Game* and was responsible for the USPS to issue a stamp commemorating the 100th anniversary of the song "Take Me Out to the Ball Game."

Currently Strasberg continues to work on an ambitious baseball project—Baseball Fantography (www.Fantography.com) and released the first *Baseball Fantography* book (Abrams Images) in April 2012. The objective is to collect snapshots taken by fans who are amateur photographers of their experience as it relates to Major League Baseball other than game action over the last 100 years.

CLAYTON TRUTOR teaches U.S. History at Northeastern University's College of Professional Studies. He has contributed to the SABR Biography Project for the past four years. He also covers college football for SB Nation. You can follow him on Twitter: @ClaytonTrutor

JOSEPH WANCHO has been a SABR member since 2005. He currently serves as the chair of the Minor League Research Committee. He is the author of *So You Think You're A Cleveland Indians Fan?* (Sports Publishing, 2018).

PHIL WILLIAMS lives in Oreland, Pennsylvania, and has been a SABR member since 2007. He has contributed numerous articles to SABR's BioProject on Deadball Era figures, with a soft spot for Athletics and Phillies who were cheered (or jeered) by his Philadelphia baseball ancestors.

GREGORY H. WOLF was born in Pittsburgh, but now resides in the Chicagoland area with his wife, Margaret, and daughter, Gabriela. A professor of German studies and holder of the Dennis and Jean Bauman Endowed Chair in the Humanities at North Central College in Naperville, Illinois, he has edited six SABR books, most recently *When Pops Led the Family. The 1979 Pittsburgh Pirates* (with Bill Nowlin, 2016) and *Dome Sweet Dome. History and Highlights From 35 Years of the Houston Astros* (2017). He is currently working on projects about Sportsman's Park in St. Louis and Crosley Field in Cincinnati. Since January 2017, he has served as co-director of SABR's BioProject.

Andy Strasberg on the set of 61*

ALLAN WOOD has written about sports, music, and politics for numerous newspapers and magazines since 1980. He is the author of *Babe Ruth and the 1918 Red Sox* and the co-author of *Don't Let Us Win Tonight: An Oral History of the 2004 Boston Red Sox's Impossible Playoff Run*. He has contributed to five books published by the Society for American Baseball Research as both a writer and editor. He also has written "The Joy of Sox" blog since 2003. He was born and raised in Vermont and now lives in Ontario, Canada.

THANKS AND ACKNOWLEDGEMENTS

Mark Armour

Ryan Brecker

Sarah Coffin, Boston Red Sox

Bob Cullum, Leslie Jones Photography

Audrey Kupferberg

Sean Lahman

Mitch Nathanson

Ted Ryan, of The Coca-Cola Company

Aaron Schmidt, Boston Public Library

Tom Stringer

SABR BioProject Team Books

In 2002, the Society for American Baseball Research launched an effort to write and publish biographies of every player, manager, and individual who has made a contribution to baseball. Over the past decade, the BioProject Committee has produced over 6,000 biographical articles. Many have been part of efforts to create theme- or team-oriented books, spearheaded by chapters or other committees of SABR.

THE 1986 BOSTON RED SOX:
THERE WAS MORE THAN GAME SIX
One of a two-book series on the rivals that met in the 1986 World Series, the Boston Red Sox and the New York Mets, including biographies of every player, coach, broadcaster, and other important figures in the top organizations in baseball that year. .
Edited by Leslie Heaphy and Bill Nowlin
$19.95 paperback (ISBN 978-1-943816-19-4)
$9.99 ebook (ISBN 978-1-943816-18-7)
8.5"X11", 420 pages, over 200 photos

THE 1986 NEW YORK METS:
THERE WAS MORE THAN GAME SIX
The other book in the "rivalry" set from the 1986 World Series. This book re-tells the story of that year's classic World Series and this is the story of each of the players, coaches, managers, and broadcasters, their lives in baseball and the way the 1986 season fit into their lives.
Edited by Leslie Heaphy and Bill Nowlin
$19.95 paperback (ISBN 978-1-943816-13-2)
$9.99 ebook (ISBN 978-1-943816-12-5)
8.5"X11", 392 pages, over 100 photos

SCANDAL ON THE SOUTH SIDE:
THE 1919 CHICAGO WHITE SOX
The Black Sox Scandal isn't the only story worth telling about the 1919 Chicago White Sox. The team roster included three future Hall of Famers, a 20-year-old spitballer who would win 300 games in the minors, and even a batboy who later became a celebrity with the "Murderers' Row" New York Yankees. All of their stories are included in Scandal on the South Side with a timeline of the 1919 season.
Edited by Jacob Pomrenke
$19.95 paperback (ISBN 978-1-933599-95-3)
$9.99 ebook (ISBN 978-1-933599-94-6)
8.5"x11", 324 pages, 55 historic photos

WINNING ON THE NORTH SIDE
THE 1929 CHICAGO CUBS
Celebrate the 1929 Chicago Cubs, one of the most exciting teams in baseball history. Future Hall of Famers Hack Wilson, '29 NL MVP Rogers Hornsby, and Kiki Cuyler, along with Riggs Stephenson formed one of the most potent quartets in baseball history. The magical season came to an ignominious end in the World Series and helped craft the future "lovable loser" image of the team.
Edited by Gregory H. Wolf
$19.95 paperback (ISBN 978-1-933599-89-2)
$9.99 ebook (ISBN 978-1-933599-88-5)
8.5"x11", 314 pages, 59 photos

DETROIT THE UNCONQUERABLE:
THE 1935 WORLD CHAMPION TIGERS
Biographies of every player, coach, and broadcaster involved with the 1935 World Champion Detroit Tigers baseball team, written by members of the Society for American Baseball Research. Also includes a season in review and other articles about the 1935 team. Hank Greenberg, Mickey Cochrane, Charlie Gehringer, Schoolboy Rowe, and more.
Edited by Scott Ferkovich
$19.95 paperback (ISBN 9978-1-933599-78-6)
$9.99 ebook (ISBN 978-1-933599-79-3)
8.5"X11", 230 pages, 52 photos

THE TEAM THAT TIME WON'T FORGET:
THE 1951 NEW YORK GIANTS
Because of Bobby Thomson's dramatic "Shot Heard 'Round the World" in the bottom of the ninth of the decisive playoff game against the Brooklyn Dodgers, the team will forever be in baseball public's consciousness. Includes a foreword by Giants outfielder Monte Irvin.
Edited by Bill Nowlin and C. Paul Rogers III
$19.95 paperback (ISBN 978-1-933599-99-1)
$9.99 ebook (ISBN 978-1-933599-98-4)
8.5"X11", 282 pages, 47 photos

A PENNANT FOR THE TWIN CITIES:
THE 1965 MINNESOTA TWINS
This volume celebrates the 1965 Minnesota Twins, who captured the American League pennant in just their fifth season in the Twin Cities. Led by an All-Star cast, from Harmon Killebrew, Tony Oliva, Zoilo Versalles, and Mudcat Grant to Bob Allison, Jim Kaat, Earl Battey, and Jim Perry, the Twins won 102 games, but bowed to the Los Angeles Dodgers and Sandy Koufax in Game Seven
Edited by Gregory H. Wolf
$19.95 paperback (ISBN 978-1-943816-09-5)
$9.99 ebook (ISBN 978-1-943816-08-8)
8.5"X11", 405 pages, over 80 photos

MUSTACHES AND MAYHEM: CHARLIE O'S THREE TIME CHAMPIONS:
THE OAKLAND ATHLETICS: 1972-74
The Oakland Athletics captured major league baseball's crown each year from 1972 through 1974. Led by future Hall of Famers Reggie Jackson, Catfish Hunter and Rollie Fingers, the Athletics were a largely homegrown group who came of age together. Biographies of every player, coach, manager, and broadcaster (and mascot) from 1972 through 1974 are included, along with season recaps.
Edited by Chip Greene
$29.95 paperback (ISBN 978-1-943816-07-1)
$9.99 ebook (ISBN 978-1-943816-06-4)
8.5"X11", 600 pages, almost 100 photos

SABR Members can purchase each book at a significant discount (often 50% off) and receive the ebook edtions free as a member benefit. Each book is available in a trade paperback edition as well as ebooks suitable for reading on a home computer or Nook, Kindle, or iPad/tablet.
To learn more about becoming a member of SABR, visit the website: sabr.org/join

The SABR Digital Library

The Society for American Baseball Research, the top baseball research organization in the world, disseminates some of the best in baseball history, analysis, and biography through our publishing programs. The SABR Digital Library contains a mix of books old and new, and focuses on a tandem program of paperback and ebook publication, making these materials widely available for both on digital devices and as traditional printed books.

Greatest Games Books

TIGERS BY THE TALE:
GREAT GAMES AT MICHIGAN AND TRUMBULL
For over 100 years, Michigan and Trumbull was the scene of some of the most exciting baseball ever. This book portrays 50 classic games at the corner, spanning the earliest days of Bennett Park until Tiger Stadium's final closing act. From Ty Cobb to Mickey Cochrane, Hank Greenberg to Al Kaline, and Willie Horton to Alan Trammell.
Edited by Scott Ferkovich
$12.95 paperback (ISBN 978-1-943816-21-7)
$6.99 ebook (ISBN 978-1-943816-20-0)
8.5"x11", 160 pages, 22 photos

FROM THE BRAVES TO THE BREWERS: GREAT GAMES AND HISTORY AT MILWAUKEE'S COUNTY STADIUM
The National Pastime provides in-depth articles focused on the geographic region where the national SABR convention is taking place annually. The SABR 45 convention took place in Chicago, and here are 45 articles on baseball in and around the bat-and-ball crazed Windy City: 25 that appeared in the souvenir book of the convention plus another 20 articles available in ebook only.
Edited by Gregory H. Wolf
$19.95 paperback (ISBN 978-1-943816-23-1)
$9.99 ebook (ISBN 978-1-943816-22-4)
8.5"X11", 290 pages, 58 photos

BRAVES FIELD:
MEMORABLE MOMENTS AT BOSTON'S LOST DIAMOND
From its opening on August 18, 1915, to the sudden departure of the Boston Braves to Milwaukee before the 1953 baseball season, Braves Field was home to Boston's National League baseball club and also hosted many other events: from NFL football to championship boxing. The most memorable moments to occur in Braves Field history are portrayed here.
Edited by Bill Nowlin and Bob Brady
$19.95 paperback (ISBN 978-1-933599-93-9)
$9.99 ebook (ISBN 978-1-933599-92-2)
8.5"X11", 282 pages, 182 photos

AU JEU/PLAY BALL: THE 50 GREATEST GAMES IN THE HISTORY OF THE MONTREAL EXPOS
The 50 greatest games in Montreal Expos history. The games described here recount the exploits of the many great players who wore Expos uniforms over the years—Bill Stoneman, Gary Carter, Andre Dawson, Steve Rogers, Pedro Martinez, from the earliest days of the franchise, to the glory years of 1979-1981, the what-might-have-been years of the early 1990s, and the sad, final days.and others.
Edited by Norm King
$12.95 paperback (ISBN 978-1-943816-15-6)
$5.99 ebook (ISBN978-1-943816-14-9)
8.5"x11", 162 pages, 50 photos

Original SABR Research

CALLING THE GAME:
BASEBALL BROADCASTING FROM 1920 TO THE PRESENT
An exhaustive, meticulously researched history of bringing the national pastime out of the ballparks and into living rooms via the airwaves. Every play-by-play announcer, color commentator, and ex-ballplayer, every broadcast deal, radio station, and TV network. Plus a foreword by "Voice of the Chicago Cubs" Pat Hughes, and an afterword by Jacques Doucet, the "Voice of the Montreal Expos" 1972-2004.
by Stuart Shea
$24.95 paperback (ISBN 978-1-933599-40-3)
$9.99 ebook (ISBN 978-1-933599-41-0)
7"X10", 712 pages, 40 photos

BioProject Books

WHO'S ON FIRST:
REPLACEMENT PLAYERS IN WORLD WAR II
During World War II, 533 players made the major league debuts. More than 60% of the players in the 1941 Opening Day lineups departed for the service and were replaced by first-times and oldsters. Hod Lisenbee was 46. POW Bert Shepard had an artificial leg, and Pete Gray had only one arm. The 1944 St. Louis Browns had 13 players classified 4-F. These are their stories.
Edited by Marc Z Aaron and Bill Nowlin
$19.95 paperback (ISBN 978-1-933599-91-5)
$9.99 ebook (ISBN 978-1-933599-90-8)
8.5"X11", 422 pages, 67 photos

VAN LINGLE MUNGO:
THE MAN, THE SONG, THE PLAYERS
40 baseball players with intriguing names have been named in renditions of Dave Frishberg's classic 1969 song, Van Lingle Mungo. This book presents biographies of all 40 players and additional information about one of the greatest baseball novelty songs of all time.
Edited by Bill Nowlin
$19.95 paperback (ISBN 978-1-933599-76-2)
$9.99 ebook (ISBN 978-1-933599-77-9)
8.5"X11", 278 pages, 46 photos

NUCLEAR POWERED BASEBALL
Nuclear Powered Baseball tells the stories of each player—past and present—featured in the classic Simpsons episode "Homer at the Bat." Wade Boggs, Ken Griffey Jr., Ozzie Smith, Nap Lajoie, Don Mattingly, and many more. We've also included a few very entertaining takes on the now-famous episode from prominent baseball writers Jonah Keri, Joe Posnanski, Erik Malinowski, and Bradley Woodrum.
Edited by Emily Hawks and Bill Nowlin
$19.95 paperback (ISBN 978-1-943816-11-8)
$9.99 ebook (ISBN 978-1-943816-10-1)
8.5"X11", 250 pages

SABR Members can purchase each book at a significant discount (often 50% off) and receive the ebook edtions free as a member benefit. Each book is available in a trade paperback edition as well as ebooks suitable for reading on a home computer or Nook, Kindle, or iPad/tablet.
To learn more about becoming a member of SABR, visit the website: sabr.org/join

SABR BioProject Books

In 2002, the Society for American Baseball Research launched an effort to write and publish biographies of every player, manager, and individual who has made a contribution to baseball. Over the past decade, the BioProject Committee has produced over 2,200 biographical articles. Many have been part of efforts to create theme- or team-oriented books, spearheaded by chapters or other committees of SABR.

THE YEAR OF THE BLUE SNOW:
THE 1964 PHILADELPHIA PHILLIES
Catcher Gus Triandos dubbed the Philadelphia Phillies' 1964 season "the year of the blue snow," a rare thing that happens once in a great while. This book sheds light on lingering questions about the 1964 season—but any book about a team is really about the players. This work offers life stories of all the players and others (managers, coaches, owners, and broadcasters) associated with this star-crossed team, as well as essays of analysis and history.
Edited by Mel Marmer and Bill Nowlin
$19.95 paperback (ISBN 978-1-933599-51-9)
$9.99 ebook (ISBN 978-1-933599-52-6)
8.5"X11", 356 PAGES, over 70 photos

THE MIRACLE BRAVES OF 1914
BOSTON'S ORIGINAL WORST-TO-FIRST CHAMPIONS
Long before the Red Sox "Impossible Dream" season, Boston's now nearly forgotten "other" team, the 1914 Boston Braves, performed a baseball "miracle" that resounds to this very day. The "Miracle Braves" were Boston's first "worst-to-first" winners of the World Series. Refusing to throw in the towel at the midseason mark, George Stallings engineered a remarkable second-half climb in the standings all the way to first place.
Edited by Bill Nowlin
$19.95 paperback (ISBN 978-1-933599-69-4)
$9.99 ebook (ISBN 978-1-933599-70-0)
8.5"X11", 392 PAGES, over 100 photos

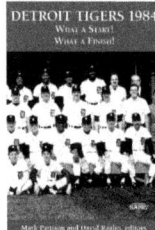

DETROIT TIGERS 1984:
WHAT A START! WHAT A FINISH!
The 1984 Detroit tigers roared out of the gate, winning their first nine games of the season and compiling an eye-popping 35-5 record after the campaign's first 40 games—still the best start ever for any team in major league history. This book brings together biographical profiles of every Tiger from that magical season, plus those of field management, top executives, the broadcasters—even venerable Tiger Stadium and the city itself.
Edited by Mark Pattison and David Raglin
$19.95 paperback (ISBN 978-1-933599-44-1)
$9.99 ebook (ISBN 978-1-933599-45-8)
8.5"x11", 250 pages (Over 230,000 words!)

THAR'S JOY IN BRAVELAND!
THE 1957 MILWAUKEE BRAVES
Few teams in baseball history have captured the hearts of their fans like the Milwaukee Braves of the 1950s. During the Braves' 13-year tenure in Milwaukee (1953-1965), they had a winning record every season, won two consecutive NL pennants (1957 and 1958), lost two more in the final week of the season (1956 and 1959), and set big-league attendance records along the way.
Edited by Gregory H. Wolf
$19.95 paperback (ISBN 978-1-933599-71-7)
$9.99 ebook (ISBN 978-1-933599-72-4)
8.5"x11", 330 pages, over 60 photos

SWEET '60: THE 1960 PITTSBURGH PIRATES
A portrait of the 1960 team which pulled off one of the biggest upsets of the last 60 years. When Bill Mazeroski's home run left the park to win in Game Seven of the World Series, beating the New York Yankees, David had toppled Goliath. It was a blow that awakened a generation, one that millions of people saw on television, one of TV's first iconic World Series moments.
Edited by Clifton Blue Parker and Bill Nowlin
$19.95 paperback (ISBN 978-1-933599-48-9)
$9.99 ebook (ISBN 978-1-933599-49-6)
8.5"X11", 340 pages, 75 photos

NEW CENTURY, NEW TEAM:
THE 1901 BOSTON AMERICANS
The team now known as the Boston Red Sox played its first season in 1901. Boston had a well-established National League team, but the American League went head-to-head with the N.L. in Chicago, Philadelphia, and Boston. Chicago won the American League pennant and Boston finished second, only four games behind.
Edited by Bill Nowlin
$19.95 paperback (ISBN 978-1-933599-58-8)
$9.99 ebook (ISBN 978-1-933599-59-5)
8.5"X11", 268 pages, over 125 photos

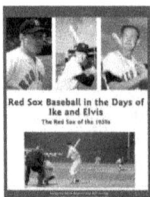

RED SOX BASEBALL IN THE DAYS OF IKE AND ELVIS: THE RED SOX OF THE 1950S
Although the Red Sox spent most of the 1950s far out of contention, the team was filled with fascinating players who captured the heart of their fans. In Red Sox Baseball, members of SABR present 46 biographies on players such as Ted Williams and Pumpsie Green as well as season-by-season recaps.
Edited by Mark Armour and Bill Nowlin
$19.95 paperback (ISBN 978-1-933599-24-3)
$9.99 ebook (ISBN 978-1-933599-34-2)
8.5"X11", 372 PAGES, over 100 photos

CAN HE PLAY?
A LOOK AT BASEBALL SCOUTS AND THEIR PROFESSION
They dig through tons of coal to find a single diamond. Here in the world of scouts, we meet the "King of Weeds," a Ph.D. we call "Baseball's Renaissance Man," a husband-and-wife team, pioneering Latin scouts, and a Japanese-American interned during World War II who became a successful scout—and many, many more.
Edited by Jim Sandoval and Bill Nowlin
$19.95 paperback (ISBN 978-1-933599-23-6)
$9.99 ebook (ISBN 978-1-933599-25-0)
8.5"X11", 200 PAGES, over 100 photos

SABR Members can purchase each book at a significant discount (often 50% off) and receive the ebook editions free as a member benefit. Each book is available in a trade paperback edition as well as ebooks suitable for reading on a home computer or Nook, Kindle, or iPad/tablet.
To learn more about becoming a member of SABR, visit the website: sabr.org/join

The SABR Digital Library

The Society for American Baseball Research, the top baseball research organization in the world, disseminates some of the best in baseball history, analysis, and biography through our publishing programs. The SABR Digital Library contains a mix of books old and new, and focuses on a tandem program of paperback and ebook publication, making these materials widely available for both on digital devices and as traditional printed books.

Classic Reprints

BASE-BALL: HOW TO BECOME A PLAYER
by John Montgomery Ward
John Montgomery Ward (1860-1925) tossed the second perfect game in major league history and later became the game's best shortstop and a great, inventive manager. His classic handbook on baseball skills and strategy was published in 1888. Illustrated with woodcuts, the book is divided into chapters for each position on the field as well as chapters on the origin of the game, theory and strategy, training, base-running, and batting.
$4.99 ebook (ISBN 978-1-933599-47-2)
$9.95 paperback (ISBN 978-0910137539)
156 PAGES, 4.5"X7" replica edition

BATTING by F. C. Lane
First published in 1925, *Batting* collects the wisdom and insights of over 250 hitters and baseball figures. Lane interviewed extensively and compiled tips and advice on everything from batting stances to beanballs. Legendary baseball figures such as Ty Cobb, Casey Stengel, Cy Young, Walter Johnson, Rogers Hornsby, and Babe Ruth reveal the secrets of such integral and interesting parts of the game as how to choose a bat, the ways to beat a slump, and how to outguess the pitcher.
$14.95 paperback (ISBN 978-0-910137-86-7)
$7.99 ebook (ISBN 978-1-933599-46-5)
240 PAGES, 5"X7"

RUN, RABBIT, RUN
by Walter "Rabbit" Maranville
"Rabbit" Maranville was the Joe Garagiola of Grandpa's day, the baseball comedian of the times. In a twenty-four-year career that began in 1912, Rabbit found a lot of funny situations to laugh at, and no wonder: he caused most of them! The book also includes an introduction by the late Harold Seymour and a historical account of Maranville's life and Hall-of-Fame career by Bob Carroll.
$9.95 paperback (ISBN 978-1-933599-26-7)
$5.99 ebook (ISBN 978-1-933599-27-4)
100 PAGES, 5.5"X8.5", 15 rare photos

MEMORIES OF A BALLPLAYER
by Bill Werber and C. Paul Rogers III
Bill Werber's claim to fame is unique: he was the last living person to have a direct connection to the 1927 Yankees, "Murderers' Row," a team hailed by many as the best of all time. Rich in anecdotes and humor, Memories of a Ballplayer is a clear-eyed memoir of the world of big-league baseball in the 1930s. Werber played with or against some of the most productive hitters of all time, including Babe Ruth, Ted Williams, Lou Gehrig, and Joe DiMaggio.
$14.95 paperback (ISNB 978-0-910137-84-3)
$6.99 ebook (ISBN 978-1-933599-47-2)
250 PAGES, 6"X9"

Original SABR Research

INVENTING BASEBALL: THE 100 GREATEST GAMES OF THE NINETEENTH CENTURY
SABR's Nineteenth Century Committee brings to life the greatest games from the game's early years. From the "prisoner of war" game that took place among captive Union soldiers during the Civil War (immortalized in a famous lithograph), to the first intercollegiate game (Amherst versus Williams), to the first professional no-hitter, the games in this volume span 1833–1900 and detail the athletic exploits of such players as Cap Anson, Moses "Fleetwood" Walker, Charlie Comiskey, and Mike "King" Kelly.
Edited by Bill Felber
$19.95 paperback (ISBN 978-1-933599-42-7)
$9.99 ebook (ISBN 978-1-933599-43-4)
302 PAGES, 8"x10", 200 photos

NINETEENTH CENTURY STARS: 2012 EDITION
First published in 1989, *Nineteenth Century Stars* was SABR's initial attempt to capture the stories of baseball players from before 1900. With a collection of 136 fascinating biographies, SABR has re-released *Nineteenth Century Stars* for 2012 with revised statistics and new form. The 2012 version also includes a preface by **John Thorn**.
Edited by Robert L. Tiemann and Mark Rucker
$19.95 paperback (ISBN 978-1-933599-28-1)
$9.99 ebook (ISBN 978-1-933599-29-8)
300 PAGES, 6"X9"

GREAT HITTING PITCHERS
Published in 1979, *Great Hitting Pitchers* was one of SABR's early publications. Edited by SABR founder Bob Davids, the book compiles stories and records about pitchers excelling in the batter's box. Newly updated in 2012 by Mike Cook, *Great Hitting Pitchers* contain tables including data from 1979-2011, corrections to reflect recent records, and a new chapter on recent new members in the club of "great hitting pitchers" like Tom Glavine and Mike Hampton.
Edited by L. Robert Davids
$9.95 paperback (ISBN 978-1-933599-30-4)
$5.99 ebook (ISBN 978-1-933599-31-1)
102 PAGES, 5.5"x8.5"

THE FENWAY PROJECT
Sixty-four SABR members—avid fans, historians, statisticians, and game enthusiasts—recorded their experiences of a single game. Some wrote from inside the Green Monster's manual scoreboard, the Braves clubhouse, or the broadcast booth, while others took in the essence of Fenway from the grandstand or bleachers. The result is a fascinating look at the charms and challenges of Fenway Park, and the allure of being a baseball fan.
Edited by Bill Nowlin and Cecilia Tan
$9.99 ebook (ISBN 978-1-933599-50-2)
175 pages, 100 photos

SABR Members can purchase each book at a significant discount (often 50% off) and receive the ebook editions free as a member benefit. Each book is available in a trade paperback edition as well as ebooks suitable for reading on a home computer or Nook, Kindle, or iPad/tablet.
To learn more about becoming a member of SABR, visit the website: sabr.org/join

Society for American Baseball Research
Cronkite School at ASU
555 N. Central Ave. #416, Phoenix, AZ 85004
602.496.1460 (phone)
SABR.org

Become a SABR member today!

If you're interested in baseball — writing about it, reading about it, talking about it — there's a place for you in the Society for American Baseball Research. Our members include everyone from academics to professional sportswriters to amateur historians and statisticians to students and casual fans who enjoy reading about baseball and occasionally gathering with other members to talk baseball. What unites all SABR members is an interest in the game and joy in learning more about it.

SABR membership is open to any baseball fan; we offer 1-year and 3-year memberships. Here's a list of some of the key benefits you'll receive as a SABR member:

- Receive two editions (spring and fall) of the *Baseball Research Journal*, our flagship publication
- Receive expanded e-book edition of *The National Pastime*, our annual convention journal
- 8-10 new e-books published by the SABR Digital Library, all FREE to members
- "This Week in SABR" e-newsletter, sent to members every Friday
- Join dozens of research committees, from Statistical Analysis to Women in Baseball.
- Join one of 70 regional chapters in the U.S., Canada, Latin America, and abroad
- Participate in online discussion groups
- Ask and answer baseball research questions on the SABR-L e-mail listserv
- Complete archives of *The Sporting News* dating back to 1886 and other research resources
- Promote your research in "This Week in SABR"
- Diamond Dollars Case Competition
- Yoseloff Scholarships

- Discounts on SABR national conferences, including the SABR National Convention, the SABR Analytics Conference, Jerry Malloy Negro League Conference, Frederick Ivor-Campbell 19th Century Conference, and the Arizona Fall League Experience
- Publish your research in peer-reviewed SABR journals
- Collaborate with SABR researchers and experts
- Contribute to Baseball Biography Project or the SABR Games Project
- List your new book in the SABR Bookshelf
- Lead a SABR research committee or chapter
- Networking opportunities at SABR Analytics Conference
- Meet baseball authors and historians at SABR events and chapter meetings
- 50% discounts on paperback versions of SABR e-books
- Discounts with other partners in the baseball community
- SABR research awards

We hope you'll join the most passionate international community of baseball fans at SABR! Check us out online at SABR.org/join.

--- ✂ --------------------------------------

SABR MEMBERSHIP FORM

	Annual	3-year	Senior	3-yr Sr.	Under 30
Standard:	❏ $65	❏ $175	❏ $45	❏ $129	❏ $45
Canada/Mexico:	❏ $75	❏ $205	❏ $55	❏ $159	❏ $55
Overseas:	❏ $84	❏ $232	❏ $64	❏ $186	❏ $55

(*International members wishing to be mailed the Baseball Research Journal should add $10/yr for Canada/Mexico or $19/yr for overseas locations.*)
Senior = 65 or older before Dec. 31 of the current year

Participate in Our Donor Program!
Support the preservation of baseball research. Designate your gift toward:
❏ General Fund   ❏ Endowment Fund   ❏ Research Resources   ❏ _____
❏ I want to maximize the impact of my gift; do not send any donor premiums
❏ I would like this gift to remain anonymous.

Note: Any donation not designated will be placed in the General Fund.
SABR is a 501 (c) (3) not-for-profit organization & donations are tax-deductible to the extent allowed by law.

Name _____

E-mail* _____

Address _____

City _____ ST _____ ZIP _____

Phone _____ Birthday _____

Dues $_____
Donation $_____
Amount Enclosed $_____

Do you work for a matching grant corporation? Call (602) 496-1460 for details.

If you wish to pay by credit card, please contact the SABR office at (602) 496-1460 or visit the SABR Store online at SABR.org/join. We accept Visa, Mastercard & Discover.

Do you wish to receive the *Baseball Research Journal* electronically? ❏ Yes ❏ No

* Your e-mail address on file ensures you will receive the most recent SABR news.   Our e-books are available in PDF, Kindle, or EPUB (iBooks, iPad, Nook) formats.

Mail to: SABR, Cronkite School at ASU, 555 N. Central Ave. #416, Phoenix, AZ 85004